THE

D1180948

BY THE SAME AUTHOR

Passages from Antiquity to Feudalism

Lineages of the Absolutist State

Considerations on Western Marxism

Arguments within English Marxism

In the Tracks of Historical Materialism

A Zone of Engagement

English Questions

The Origins of Postmodernity

Spectrum

THE NEW OLD WORLD

PERRY ANDERSON

VERSO

London • New York

This paperback edition published by Verso 2011
First published by Verso 2009
© Perry Anderson 2009
All rights reserved

The moral rights of the author have been asserted

1 3 5 7 9 10 8 6 4 2

Verso
UK: 6 Meard Street, London W1F 0EG
US: 20 Jay Street, Suite 1010, Brooklyn, NY 11201
www.versobooks.com

Verso is the imprint of New Left Books

ISBN-13: 978-1-84467-721-4

British Library Cataloguing in Publication Data
A catalogue record for this book is available from the British Library

Library of Congress Cataloging-in-Publication Data
A catalog record for this book is available from the Library of Congress

Typeset by Hewer Text UK Ltd, Edinburgh
Printed in Sweden by ScandBook AB

For Alan Milward

CONTENTS

ACKNOWLEDGMENTS

The first versions of the following essays were published in the *London Review of Books*: 'Origins', 4 January and 26 January 1996; 'Outcomes', 20 September 2007; 'France (I)', 2 September and 23 September 2004; 'Germany (I)', 7 January 1999; 'Italy (I)', 21 March 2002; 'Italy (II)', 26 February and 12 March 2009; 'Cyprus', 24 April 2008; 'Turkey', 11 September and 25 September 2008. 'Germany' (II) was published in *New Left Review* No. 57, May–June 2009. An earlier version of 'Theories' was given as a Max Weber Lecture at the European University Institute in 2007.

I owe many debts in the writing of this book. I would like to thank, for their criticism or advice, my editors at the *LRB* and *NLR*, Mary-Kay Wilmers and Susan Watkins; and my friends Sebastian Budgen, Carlo Ginzburg, Serge Halimi, Çağlar Keyder, Peter Loizos, Franco Moretti, Gabriel Piterberg, Nicholas Spice, Alain Supiot, Cihan Tuğal; and in particular Zeynep Turkyilmaz, without whom I could not have written adequately on Turkey.

Unable, by reason of circumstance, to contribute to a volume in honour of Alan Milward, I have dedicated this book to him, though it is so unlike his work. It was his writing, of which I express my admiration in these pages, that first made me want to say something about Europe.

FOREWORD

Europe, as it has become more integrated, has also become more difficult to write about. The Union that now stretches from Limerick to Nicosia has given the continent an encompassing institutional framework of famous complexity, over-arching the nations that compose it, that sets this part of the world off from any other. This structure is so novel, and in many respects so imposing, that the term 'Europe', as currently used, now often refers simply to the EU, as if the two were interchangeable. But, of course, they are not. The difference has less to do with the scattered pockets of the continent that have yet to join the Union than with the intractable sovereignty and diversity of the nation-states that have done so. The tension between the two planes of Europe, national and supranational, creates a peculiar analytic dilemma for any attempt to reconstruct the recent history of the region. The reason can be put like this. However unprecedented it may be historically, the EU is unquestionably a polity, with more or less uniform effects throughout its jurisdiction. Yet in the life of the states that belong to it, politics—at an incomparably higher level of intensity—continues to be overwhelmingly internal. To hold both levels steady within a single focus is a task that has so far defied all comers. Europe, in that sense, seems an impossible object. It is no surprise that the literature on it tends to divide into three disconnected kinds: specialized studies of the complex of institutions that comprise the EU; broad-brush histories or sociologies of the continent since the Second World War, in which the Union features at best sporadically, if at all; and—still much the largest output—national monographs of one kind or another.

In due course, no doubt, the difficulty will be overcome. But for the moment, only makeshifts seem within reach. The solution attempted here is discontinuous. Composed of successive essays, the first part of this book looks at the past and present of the

Union, as it was conceived by its founders, and modified by their successors; how it came to acquire the forms it possesses today, and what kinds of public self-consciousness and patterns of scholarship—the two are quite distinct—have developed around them. European integration is taken throughout as a project whose economic purposes and practices—which form the overwhelming bulk of its activities—have always, in differing directions, been the pursuit of politics by other means. Despite many disclaimers, this remains as true today as at the time of the Schuman Plan.

The second part of the book moves to the national level. It looks at the three principal countries of the original six that signed the Treaty of Rome, comprising 75 per cent of the population of the European Economic Community it brought into being: France, Germany and Italy. Historically, these can be considered the core lands of the integration process. France and Germany were from the start, as they have continued to be, its two most powerful drivers and monitors. Italy played a less significant role than Belgium or the Netherlands in the creation of the Common Market, and its early years, but in due course was more critical for the direction taken by an expanded Community. Not only the largest economies and most populous states of continental Europe, France, Germany and Italy also enjoy, by common consent, the richest cultural and intellectual history. The structure of politics within each is inseparable from that history, and in considering its development I have tried to give a sense of the cultural setting in which events have unfolded in the past twenty years or more. Without some attempt at this, there is little hope of capturing in any country the textures of national life, that necessarily escape the bureaucratic integument of the Union. Each of the three surveyed in these pages has been the theatre of a major drama in recent years, each distinct, and all disjunct from the evolution of the EU. Germany has been transformed by unification. Italy has seen the collapse of one Republic and the rapid involution of another. France has suffered its first crisis of confidence since it was recast by De Gaulle. Such changes allow of no uniform treatment, and the approach of the chapters devoted to each varies accordingly.

Although Paris, Berlin and Rome loom largest in the conference-room—the only continental states in the G-7 of the time—they are far, of course, from representing, even by proxy, Western Europe since the end of the Cold War as a whole. I do not regret the omission of Britain, whose history since the fall of Thatcher has been of little moment. But I would have liked to have written of Spain, whose modernization, though relatively placid, has been a significant feature of the period. The smaller countries of the region are another occasion for regret, since I have never believed that modesty of size means paucity of interest, and miss any treatment of Ireland, where I largely grew up. If space—to some extent, also time—has dictated these limitations, knowledge is naturally the larger barrier to moving in any way comprehensively below the level of the Union. Who could hope to write competently or evenly about its twenty-seven states? The intractability of this problem is posed even more sharply in Eastern Europe, whose languages are less widely read and affairs often less documented, and whose states are bunched closer together in magnitude, making selection between them potentially more arbitrary. This has not meant any general neglect of attention to them. Their release from Communism has, on the contrary, attracted a large literature, as has their—still ongoing—inclusion within the EU, justifiably regarded as one of the Union's major achievements.

This ground is now so well trodden that it seemed better to look further east, to the outermost limit of the existing Union, and its prospective further extension into Asia. Accordingly, the third part of this book looks at Cyprus, which joined the EU in 2004, and at Turkey, accepted as a candidate for entry two years earlier. Here extreme opposites of size have been closely entangled: one country of less than a million, another of over seventy million, that will soon overtake Germany to become larger than any current member of the Union. If the relationship between the two poses the most explosive immediate item on the agenda of EU enlargement, the candidature of Turkey confronts 'Europe', understood as the Union, with far its biggest future challenge. The scale of that challenge is of another order from that involved in the absorption of the former Comecon region. But its exact nature is much less ventilated. The reason is not hard to see. Integration of the former Communist zone disturbed no reigning ideas in Western Europe; indeed, on the whole, truths could be told that comforted them. The fate of Cyprus and the pull of Turkey, by contrast, pose awkward questions for the good conscience of Europe, which polite—official and media—opinion have repressed. Just how awkward will be seen below. The light the new Eastern Question shines on the self-image of the Union can be compared, historically speaking, to that shed by the old on the Concert of Powers.

In considering it, I have adopted a longer time-span than in the second part of the book, and concentrated more strictly on the political history of the two societies concerned. The general background to the recent period in the trio of big West European states can largely be taken for granted, as so many familiar chapters in the record of the twentieth century. This is not the case in either Cyprus or Turkey, requiring a more extended reconstruction of the ways in which each has reached its present condition. That is no surprise, and calls for little comment. More questionable is the combination of a narrower time-span with a broader focus in treatments of France, Germany and Italy. All contemporary history is less than true history, given lack of records and foreshortened perspective. Any attempt to capture a modern society across a couple of decades, at point-blank range, is inevitably precarious. The dangers of what a French tradition condemns as a *coupe d'essence* are plain, and I am conscious of having run them. The simplifications or errors they imply, as well as those of more ordinary ignorance or misjudgement, will be corrected by others in due course. Although composed over a decade, the essays that make up successive chapters were written at different conjuctures within it, and bear their mark. I have reworked them relatively little, preferring to let them stand as testimonies of the time, as well as reflections on it. Each is dated at its head.

The unity of the period under question, which sets the parameters of the book, is that of the neo-liberal ascendancy. Historically, this was defined by two great changes of regime. The first came at the turn of the eighties, with the arrival of the Thatcher and Reagan governments, the international deregulation of financial markets and the privatization of industries and services that followed it in the West. The second, at the turn of the nineties, saw the collapse of Communism in the Soviet bloc, followed by the extension eastwards of the first in its wake. In this double vortex, the shape of the European Union altered and every country within it was bent in new directions. How these pressures worked themselves out, at supranational and at national level, and what external as well as internal policies were driven by them, is one of the book's recurrent themes. Today the neo-liberal system is in crisis. The general view, even of many of its one-time champions, is that its time has passed, as the world sinks into the recession that began in the last quarter of 2008. How far that system will have been modified, if and when the current crisis recedes, or what will replace it, remains to be seen. All these pages, save the second part of the chapter on France, were written before the collapse of financial markets in the United States. Other than noting the onset of the crisis, I have not altered them to cover its effects so far or to come, but consider these in the reflections that conclude the book, which review more generally ideas of Europe, past and present.

England has, from the beginning, produced more Eurosceptics than any other country that has joined the EU. Although critical of the Union, this is not an outlook I share. In 1972 *New Left Review*, of which I was then editor, published a book-length essay by Tom Nairn, 'The Left against Europe?', as a special issue.[1] At the time, not only the Labour Party in Britain, but the overwhelming majority of socialists to the left of it, were opposed to the UK's entry into the EEC, which had just been voted through Parliament by a Conservative government. Nairn's essay not only broke with this massed consensus, but remains even today, a quarter of a century later, the most powerful single argument ever made for support to European integration from the left—nothing comparable has ever emerged from the ranks of its official parties, Social-Democratic, Post-Communist, or Green, that now wrap themselves in the blue banner with gold stars. The Union of the early twenty-first century is not the Community of the fifties or sixties, but my admiration for its original architects remains undiminished. Their enterprise had no historical precedent, and its grandeur continues to haunt what it has since become.

The European ideology that has grown up, around a changed reality, is another matter. The self-satisfaction of Europe's elites, and their publicists, has become such that the Union is now widely presented as a paragon for the rest of the world, even as it becomes steadily less capable of winning the confidence of its citizens, and more and more openly flouts the popular will. How far this drift is irreversible no one can tell. For it to be checked, a number of illusions will have to be abandoned. Among them is the belief, on which much of the current ideology is founded, that within the Atlantic ecumene Europe embodies a higher set of values than the United States, and plays a more inspiring role in the world. This doctrine can be rejected, to the advantage of America, by dwelling on how much that is admirable they share,

---

1. *New Left Review* I/75, September–October 1972, pp. 5–120, which subsequently appeared as a book under the same title (Harmondsworth 1973).

or to the detriment of Europe, how much that is objectionable. For Europeans, the second criticism is the more needed.[2] Not only their difference, but their autonomy, from America is less than they imagine. Nowhere are current relations between them illustrated so vividly as in the field of EU studies itself, to which the third essay here on the Union is devoted.

By and large, this field forms a closed universe of often highly technical literature, with few outlets to any wider public sphere. In Europe, it has generated a vast industry of professional articles, research papers and consultancies, much of it financed by Brussels, which if it does not command the heights of the terrain, occupies an ever extending plain below them. The density of pan-European exchanges across it is without precedent, and these exchanges along with innumerable others—conferences, workshops, colloquia, lectures in adjacent disciplines, from history and economics to law and sociology—have created what should comprise the bases of an intellectual community capable of lively debate across national borders. Yet in practice, there is still remarkably little of that. In part, this has to do with the characteristic tares of the academy, when scholarship turns inwards only to a profession rather than also outwards to a broader culture. In larger measure, however, it is a reflection of the lack of any animating political divisions in this—in principle—eminently political field, occupied chiefly by political scientists. To speak of a *pensée unique* would be unfair: it is more like a *pensée ouate*, which hangs like a pall over too much of it. The media offer little, if any, counterbalance, columns and editorials hewing in general to a Euro-conformism more pronounced than that of chairs or think-tanks.

One effect of such unanimism is to undermine the emergence of any real public sphere in Europe. Once all agree in advance on what is desirable and what is not—*vide* successive referenda— no impulse to curiosity about the life and thought of other

---

2. For the former, see the statistical fireworks of Peter Baldwin, *The Narcissism of Minor Differences: Why America and Europe are Alike*, New York 2009, which sets out to confound anti-American prejudice across the Atlantic, by showing—with brio—that if West European societies are taken as a set, by most indicators American society falls at various points within the same range, and not infrequently outperforms its smugger counterparts. Such comparisons, of course, bypass the enormous difference between the American state and its European opposites—the US dwarfing any European country in military, political and ideological power, not to speak of an EU that lacks the attributes of a nation-state, let alone one the size of a continent.

nations is left. Why take any interest in what is said or written elsewhere, if it merely repeats, in all essentials, what is already available here? In this sense, it might well be thought that the echo-chambers of today's Union are less genuinely European than much of the cultural life of the inter-war, or even pre–First World War period. There are not many equivalents today of the correspondence between Sorel and Croce, the collaboration between Larbaud and Joyce, the debate among Eliot, Curtius and Mannheim, the arguments of Ortega with Husserl; not to speak of the polemics within the Second and early Third Internationals. Intellectuals formed a much smaller, less institutionalized group in those days, with deeper roots in a common humanist culture. Democratization has dispersed this, while releasing a vastly larger number of talents into the arena. However, whatever its fruits elsewhere—they obviously are many—it has not so far led to much of a republic of letters in the European Union. The hope of this book is to contribute towards one.

I. THE UNION

ORIGINS

1995

Mathematically, the European Union today represents the largest single unit in the world economy. It has a nominal GNP of about $6 trillion, compared with $5 trillion for the US and $3 trillion for Japan. Its total population, now over 360 million, approaches that of the United States and Japan combined. Yet in political terms such magnitudes continue to be virtual reality. Beside Washington or Tokyo, Brussels remains a cipher. The Union is no equivalent to either the United States or Japan, since it is not a sovereign state. But what kind of formation is it? Most Europeans themselves are at a loss for an answer. The Union remains a more or less unfathomable mystery to all but a handful of those who, to their bemusement, have recently become its citizens. Well-nigh entirely arcane to ordinary voters, a film of mist obscures it even in the mirror of scholars.

I

The nature of the European Union must have some relation to the origins of the Community which it now subsumes— although, in a typically alembicated juridical twist, does not supersede. Some political clarity about the genesis of its structure seems desirable as a starting-point for considering its future. This is a topic on which there is still no uncontroversial ground. The historical literature has from the outset tended to be unusually theoretical in bent—a clear sign that few familiar assumptions can be taken for granted. The dominant early scholarship held to the view that the forces underlying the post-war integration of Western Europe should be sought in the growth of objective—not only economic, but also social and cultural—interdependencies between the states that made up the initial Coal and Steel Community and its sequels. The tenor of this first wave of interpretation was neo-functionalist, stressing the additive logic of institutional development: that is, the way modest functional changes tended to lead to complementary alterations along an extending path of often involuntary integration. Cross-national convergence of economic transactions, social exchanges and cultural practices had laid the basis for gradual advance towards a new political ideal—a supranational union of states. Ernst Haas, who thought the beginnings of this process relatively contingent, but its subsequent development path-determined, produced in the late fifties what is still perhaps the best theorization of this position in his *Uniting of Europe*.

The second wave of interpretations, by contrast, has stressed the structural resilience of the nation-state, and seen the post-war integration of Western Europe not as a glide-path towards any supranational sovereignty, but on the contrary as the means of reinvigorating effective national power. This neo-realist theme comes in a number of different versions, not all of them concordant. Far the most powerful and distinctive is the work of Alan Milward. There is some irony in the fact that the country which has contributed least to European integration should have produced the historian who has illuminated it most. No other scholar within the Union approaches the combination of archival mastery and intellectual passion that Milward has brought to the question of its origins.

His starting-point was at a productive tangent to it. Why, he asked, did economic recovery in Europe after the Second World War not repeat the pattern that occurred after the First—an initial spurt due to physical restocking, followed by erratic fits and starts of growth and recession? In *The Reconstruction of Western Europe 1945–51* (1984), he set aside conventional explanations—the arrival of Keynesianism; repair of war damage; larger public sector; high defence spending; technological innovation—and suggested that the basis of the completely unprecedented boom, which started as early as 1945 and lasted till at least 1967, lay rather in the steady rise of popular earnings of this period, against a background of long-pent-up unsatisfied demand. This model of growth, in turn, was sustained by new arrangements between states, whose 'pursuit of narrow self-interest'[1] led to both trade liberalization and the first limited measures of integration in the Schuman Plan.

It is on the way these arrangements developed into the European Economic Community that Milward's subsequent work has focussed, with a mass of empirical findings and increasingly sharp theoretical thrust. Both his great study *The European Rescue of the Nation-State*, and its coda in *The Frontiers of National Sovereignty*, are sustained polemics against neo-functionalist overestimation of the importance of federalist conceptions of any kind—dismissed as a pack of pieties in a caustic chapter on 'The Lives and Teachings of the European Saints'. Milward's central argument is that the origins of the Community have little or nothing to do with either the technical imperatives of interdependence—which may even have been less significant at mid-century than fifty years earlier—or the ethereal visions of a handful of federalist worthies. They were rather a product of the common disaster of the Second World War, when every nation-state between the Pyrenees and the North Sea was shattered by defeat and occupation.

From the depths of impotence and discredit into which pre-war institutions had fallen, a quite new kind of structure had to be built up after peace returned. The post-war states of Western Europe were laid, Milward contends, on a much wider social basis than their narrow and brittle predecessors, for the first time integrating farmers, workers and petty-bourgeois fully into the political nation with a set of measures for growth, employment and welfare. It was the unexpected success of these policies within each country that prompted a second kind of broadening, of cooperation between countries. Morally rehabilitated within their own borders, six nation-states on the continent found they could strengthen themselves yet further by sharing to common advantage certain elements of sovereignty. At the core of this process was the magnetic pull of the German market from an early date on the export sectors of the other five economies—complemented by the attractions for German industry of easier access to French and Italian markets, and eventual gains for particular interests like Belgian coal and Dutch agriculture. The European Economic Community, in Milward's vision, was born essentially from the

---

1. Alan Milward, *The Reconstruction of Western Europe 1945–51*, London 1984, p. 492.

autonomous calculations of national states that the prosperity on which their domestic legitimacy rested would be enhanced by a customs union.

The strategic need to contain Germany as a power also played a role. But Milward argues that it was an essentially secondary one, which could have been met by other means. If the driving force behind integration was indeed pursuit of security, the kind of security that really mattered to the peoples of Western Europe in the fifties was social and economic: the assurance that there would no return to the hunger, unemployment and dislocations of the thirties. In the age of Schuman, Adenauer and De Gasperi, the desire for political security—that is, reinsurance against German militarism and Soviet expansionism, and even the wish for 'spiritual' security afforded by Catholic solidarity—was so to speak an extension of the same basic quest. The foundation of the EEC lay in the 'similarity and reconcilability'[2] of the socio-economic interests of the six renascent states, set by the political consensus of the post-war democratic order in each country. In Milward's view, this original matrix has held fast down to the present, unaltered by the enlargement of the Community or the elaboration of its machinery.

The one significant further advance in European integration, the Single Market Act of the mid-eighties, reveals the same pattern. By then, under the pressure of global economic crisis and mounting competition from the US and Japan, the political consensus had shifted, as electorates became resigned to the return of unemployment and converted to the imperatives of sound money and social deregulation. Milward does not conceal his dislike for the 'managerial clap-trap and narrow authoritarian deductions from abstract economic principles'[3] which orchestrated this change of outlook. But it was the general turn to neo-liberalism, sealed by Mitterrand's abandonment of his initial Keynesian programme in 1983, that made possible the convergence of all member states, including the UK in Thatcher's heyday, on the completion of the internal market—each calculating, as in the fifties, the particular commercial benefits it would reap from further liberalization

---

2. Alan Milward and Vibeke Sorensen, 'Interdependence or Integration: A National Choice', in Alan Milward, Frances Lynch, Ruggiero Ranieri, Federico Romero, Vibeke Sorensen, *The Frontiers of National Sovereignty: History and Theory 1945–1992*, London 1993, p. 20.

3. *The European Rescue of the Nation-State*, London 1992, p. xi.

within the Community. Once again the nation-state remained
master of the process, yielding certain of its juridical prerogatives
only to enhance the sum of its material capacities to satisfy the
domestic expectations of its citizenry.

The cumulative power of Milward's account of European
integration, hammered home in one case-study after another,
each delivered with tremendous drive—institutional detail
and theoretical attack racing imperiously across the keyboard,
individual portraits pedalled sardonically below—has no equal.
But its very force raises a number of questions. Milward's
construction as a whole rests on four assumptions, which can
perhaps be formulated without too much simplification as follows.

The first, and most explicit, is that the traditional objectives of
international diplomacy—the rivalrous struggle for power in an
inter-state system: 'world politics' as Max Weber understood it—
were always of secondary weight in the options that led to post-
war European integration. Milward argues that this truth is as
valid today as it ever was. Whether the states of the Community
proceed with further integration, he writes in his conclusion,
'depends *absolutely* on the nature of domestic policy choices' (my
italics).[4] Inverting the classical Prussian axiom, Milward postulates
a virtually unconditional *Primat der Innenpolitik*. Foreign policy,
as once conceived, is not dismissed: but it is taken to be ancillary
to the socio-economic priorities of the nation-state.

The second assumption—logically distinct from the first—is
that where external political or military calculations entered the
balance of policy-making, they did so as extensions of the internal
pursuit of popular prosperity: security in a complementary
register. Diplomatic objectives are germane, but only in continuity,
rather than conflict, with the concerns of a domestic consensus.
The latter in turn—here we reach a third assumption—reflects the
popular will as expressed in the ballot-box. 'The preponderant
influence on the formulation of national policy and the national
interest was always a response to demands from electors', and
'it is by their votes . . . that citizens will continue to exercise the
preponderant influence in defining the national interest'.[5] It was

---

4. *The European Rescue of the Nation-State*, p. 447.

5. 'Conclusions: The Value of History', in *The Frontiers of National Sovereignty*,
pp. 194, 201.

because the democratic consensus, in which the voices of workers, clerks and farmers could at last be properly heard, was so similar across Western Europe that nation-states inspired by the new aims of social security could take the first momentous steps of integration. Here—least prominently, yet still discernible—is a final suggestion: that where it really mattered, there was an ultimate symmetry in the participation of the states that formed the original customs union, and completed the internal market.

Primacy of domestic objectives, and continuity of foreign goals with them; democracy of policy formation, and symmetry of national public opinions. An element of caricature is inseparable from all compression, and Milward's work is subtle and complex enough to contain a number of counter-indications, some of them quite striking. But roughly speaking, these four claims convey the main emphasis of his work. How robust are they? One way of approaching the question is to notice how Milward treats his starting-point. The absolute origin of movement towards European integration is located in the Second World War. Few would dissent. But the experience of the war itself is viewed in a quite particular light, as a cataclysm in which the general brittleness of pre-war political structures—lacking any broad democratic base—was suddenly revealed, as one nation-state after another crumpled in the furnace of conflict.

This is one legitimate and productive way of looking at the Second World War, which does set the stage for the story of post-war reconstruction leading to integration that Milward tells. Yet, of course, the war was not just a common ordeal in which all continental states were tested and found wanting. It was also a life-or-death battle between Great Powers, with an asymmetric outcome. Germany, which set off the struggle, never actually collapsed as a nation-state—and least of all because of any narrowness of popular support. Its soldiers and civilians resisted the Allies unflinchingly, to the end.

It was the memory of this incommensurable experience during the war—of the scale of German military supremacy, and its consequences—that shaped European integration quite as much as the commensurate tasks of rebuilding nation-states on a more prosperous and democratic basis after the war, on which Milward concentrates. The country centrally concerned was inevitably France. It is no accident that the French contribution to the construction of common European institutions has been out of all proportion to the weight of France within the overall economy

of Western Europe. The political and military containment of
Germany was a strategic priority for France from the outset, well
before there was any consensus in Paris on the commercial benefits
of integration among the Six. Once Anglo-American opposition
ruled out any re-run of Clemenceau's attempt to hold Germany
down by main force, the only coherent alternative was to bind it
into the closest of alliances, with a construction more enduring
than the temporary shelters of traditional diplomacy.

At the centre of the process of European integration, therefore,
has always lain a specifically bi-national compact between
the two leading states of the continent, France and Germany.
The rationale for the successive arrangements between them,
principally economic in form, was consistently strategic in
background. Decisive for the evolution of common European
institutions were four major bargains between Paris and Bonn.
The first of these was, of course, the Schuman Plan of 1950,
which created the original Coal and Steel Community in 1951.
If the local problems of French siderurgy, dependent on Rhenish
coal for its supply of coke, were one element in the inception
of the Plan, its intention was far broader. Of the two countries,
Germany possessed much the larger heavy industrial base. France
feared its potential for rearmament. On the other hand, Germany
feared continued international military control of the Ruhr. The
pooling of sovereignty over their joint resources gave France
safeguards against the risk of renascent German militarism, and
freed Germany from Allied economic tutelage.

A second milestone was the understanding between Adenauer
and Mollet that made possible the Treaty of Rome in 1957.
Overriding reservations from the Finance Ministry in Bonn and
the Foreign Ministry in Paris, the two governments reached an
accord that secured German and French goods industries free
entry into each other's markets, on which each was already highly
dependent for its prosperity, while holding out the prospect
of increased imports by the Federal Republic of French farm
produce. Adenauer's *placet* for this deal, in the face of fierce
liberal opposition from Erhard—who feared higher French social
costs might spread to Germany—was unambiguously political
in inspiration. He wanted West European unity as a bulwark
against Communism, and a guarantee that eventual German
reunification would be respected by France. In Paris, on the other
hand, economic counsels remained divided over the project of a
Common Market until rival proposals from London for a free

trade area looked as if they might be more attractive to Bonn, threatening the primacy of Franco-German commercial ties. But it was not the technical opinion of *hauts fonctionnaires* that decided the issue,[6] nor the personal preference of Mollet himself—who had always favoured European integration but been quite unable to carry his party two years earlier, when the EDC was killed off by SFIO votes. What swung the balance was the political shock of the Suez crisis.

Mollet headed a government far more preoccupied with prosecution of the Algerian War, and preparations for a strike against Egypt, than with trade negotiations of any sort. Anglophile by background, he was committed to an understanding with Britain for joint operations in the Eastern Mediterranean. On 1 November 1956 the Suez expedition was launched. Five days later, as French paras were pawing the ground outside Ismailia, Adenauer arrived in Paris for confidential talks on the Common Market. He was in the middle of discussions with Mollet and Pineau, when Eden suddenly rang from London to announce that Britain had unilaterally called off the expedition, under pressure from the US Treasury. In the stunned silence, Adenauer tactfully implied the moral to his hosts.[7] The French cabinet drew the lesson. America had reversed its stance since Indochina. Britain was a broken reed. For the last governments of the Fourth Republic, still committed to the French empire in Africa and planning for a French bomb, European unity alone could furnish the necessary counterweight to Washington. Six months later, the Treaty of Rome was signed by Pineau; and in the National Assembly it was the strategic argument—the need for a Europe independent of both America and Russia—that secured ratification.

The third critical episode came with the advent of De Gaulle. The first really strong regime in France since the war inevitably altered the terms of the bargain. After clinching a Common Agricultural Policy to the advantage of French farmers in early 1962, but failing to create an inter-governmental directorate among the Six, De Gaulle initiated talks for a formal diplomatic axis with Bonn in

---

6. For the extent of the hostility to integration in the administrative elite, see Gérard Bossuat, 'Les hauts fonctionnaires français et le processus d'unité en Europe occidentale d'Alger à Rome (1943–1958)', *Journal of European Integration History*, No. 1, Vol. 1, 1995, pp. 87–109.

7. Christian Pineau, *Le grand pari: L'aventure du traité de Rome*, Paris 1991, pp. 221–23.

the autumn. France was by now a nuclear power. In January 1963 he vetoed British entry into the Community. In February Adenauer signed the Franco-German Treaty. Once this diplomatic alliance was in place, De Gaulle—notoriously hostile to the Commission headed by Hallstein in Brussels—could check further integration of the EC so long as he was in power. The institutional expression of the new balance became the Luxembourg compromise of 1966, blocking majority voting in the Council of Ministers, which set the legislative parameters for the Community for the next two decades.

Finally, during a period of relative institutional standstill, in 1978 Giscard and Schmidt together created the European Monetary System to counteract the destabilizing effects of the collapse of the Bretton Woods order, when fixed exchange rates disintegrated amid the first deep post-war recession. Created outside the framework of the Community, the EMS was imposed by France and Germany against resistance even within the Commission, as the first attempt to control the volatility of financial markets, and prepare the ground for a single currency within the space of the Six.

For the first three decades after the war, then, the pattern was quite consistent. The two strongest continental powers, adjacent former enemies, led European institutional development, in pursuit of distinct but convergent interests. France, which retained military and diplomatic superiority throughout, was determined to attach Germany to a common economic order, capable of ensuring its own prosperity and security, and allowing Western Europe to escape from subservience to the United States. Germany, which enjoyed economic superiority already by the mid-fifties, needed not only Community-wide markets for its industries, but French support for its full reintegration into the Atlantic bloc and eventual reunification with the zone—still officially *Mitteldeutschland*—under the control of the Soviet Union. The dominant partner in this period was always France, whose functionaries conceived the original Coal and Steel Community and designed most of the institutional machinery of the Common Market. It was not until the deutschmark became the anchor of the European monetary zone for the first time that the balance between Paris and Bonn started to change.

The high politics of the Franco-German axis tell a story older than that of voters in pursuit of consumer durables and welfare payments. But if it suggests neither a new primacy of domestic concerns nor, inevitably, symmetry of national publics—the other member-states scarcely match the significance of these two—it does appear to confirm the overwhelming importance Milward gives to purely inter-governmental relations in the history of European integration. Yet if we look at the institutions of the Community that emerged from it, there is a shortfall. A customs union, even equipped with an agrarian fund, did not require a supranational commission armed with powers of executive direction, a high court capable of striking down national legislation, a parliament with nominal rights of amendment or revocation. The limited domestic goals Milward sees as the driving-force behind integration could have been realized inside a much plainer framework—the kind that would have been more agreeable to De Gaulle, had he come to power a year earlier, and that can be found today in the Americas, North and South. The actual machinery of the Community is inexplicable without another force.

That, of course, was the federalist vision of a supranational Europe developed above all by Monnet and his circle, the small group of technocrats who conceived the original ECSC, and drafted much of the detail of the EEC. Few modern political figures have remained more elusive than Monnet, as Milward observes in the couple of wary pages he accords him. Since he wrote, however, there has appeared François Duchêne's excellent biography, which brings him into much clearer focus. In an acute and graceful work that does not minimize the anomalies of Monnet's career, Duchêne draws an arresting portrait of the 'Father of Europe'.

The provincial reserve and propriety that surrounded his person were misleading. Monnet is a figure more out of the world of André Malraux than of Georges Duhamel. The small, dapper Charentais was an international adventurer on a grand scale, juggling finance and politics in a series of spectacular gambles that started with operations in war procurements and bank mergers, and ended with schemes for continental unity and dreams of a global directorate. From cornering Canadian brandy markets to organizing Allied wheat supplies; floating bond issues in Warsaw and Bucharest to fighting proxy battles with Giannini in San Francisco; liquidating Kreuger's empire in Sweden to arranging railroad loans for T.V. Soong in Shanghai; working with Dulles to set up American Motors in Detroit and dealing with Flick to sell off chemical concerns in Nazi Germany—such were the staging-posts to the post-war *Commissariat au Plan* and the presidency of the High Authority, to the Companion of Honour and the first Citizen of Europe.

Monnet's marriage gives perhaps the best glimpse of his life, still only visible in part, between the wars. In 1929 he was floating a municipal bond in Milan, at the behest of John McCloy, when he fell in love with the newly wed wife of one of his Italian employees. There was no divorce under Mussolini, and a child was born to the married couple two years later. Attempts to get the union annulled were resisted by the husband and father, and refused by the Vatican. By 1934 Monnet's headquarters were in Shanghai. There one day he headed for the Trans-Siberian to meet his lover in Moscow, where she arrived from Switzerland, acquired Soviet citizenship overnight, dissolved her marriage, and wed him under the banns of the USSR. His bride, a devout Catholic, preferred these unusual arrangements—Monnet explained—to the demeaning offices of Reno. Why Stalin's government allowed them, he could never understand. It was a tense time for a wedding: Kirov was assassinated a fortnight later. Subsequently, when her repudiated Italian spouse attempted to recover his four-year-old daughter in Shanghai, Madame Monnet found refuge from the kidnapper in the Soviet consulate—an establishment of some fame in the history of the Comintern. By the end of 1935, still holding a Soviet passport, she obtained residence in the US, when Monnet relocated to New York, on a Turkish quota. We are in the corridors of *Stamboul Train* or *Shanghai Express*.

Cosmopolitan as only an international financier could be, Monnet remained a French patriot, and from the eve to the end of the Second World War worked with untiring distinction for the victory of his country and the Allies, in Paris, London, Washington, Algiers. In 1945, appointed by De Gaulle to head France's new planning commission, Monnet was a logical choice. The organizer of the Plan for Modernization and Equipment is with reason described by Milward as 'a most effective begetter of the French nation-state's post-war resurgence'.[8] Here, however, he was in a substantial company. What made Monnet different was the speed and boldness with which he slipped this leash when the occasion arose. His opportunity came when in late 1949 Acheson demanded of Schuman a coherent French policy towards Germany, for which the Quai d'Orsay had no answer. It was Monnet's solution—the offer of a supranational pooling of

8. *The European Rescue of the Nation-State*, p. 334.

steel and coal resources— that set the ball of European integration rolling. The larger part of the institutional model of the EEC eight years later descended directly from the ECSC Monnet's circle designed in 1950.

There is no doubt that, as Milward suggests, Monnet's initiatives in these years owed much to American encouragement. His decisive advantage, as a political operator across national boundaries in Europe, was the closeness of his association with the US political elite—not only the Dulles brothers, but Acheson, Harriman, McCloy, Ball, Bruce and others—formed during his years in New York and Washington, abundantly documented by Duchêne. Monnet's intimacy with the highest levels of power in the hegemonic state of the hour was unique. He was to become widely distrusted in his own country because of it. How much of his European zeal, both compatriots at the time and historians since have asked, was prompted by his American patrons, within the strategic framework of the Marshall Plan?

The structural interconnexion was indeed very close. It is possible that Monnet was first set thinking about post-war integration by discussions in the US, and certain that his subsequent achievements depended critically on US support. But his political inspiration was nevertheless quite different. American policy was driven by the relentless pursuit of Cold War objectives. A strong Western Europe was needed as a bulwark against Soviet aggression, on the central front of a world-wide battle against Communist subversion, whose outlying zones were to be found in Asia, from Korea in the north to Indochina and Malaya in the south, where the line was being held by France and Britain.

Monnet was strangely unmoved by all this. In France itself he got on well with CGT leaders after the liberation. He considered the colonial war in Indochina, financed by Washington, 'absurd and dangerous'; feared the Korean War would escalate American pressure for German rearmament to a point where French public opinion would reject the sharing of sovereignty envisaged in the Schuman Plan; thought Western fixation with the Soviet menace a distraction. As late as June 1950 he told the editor of the *Economist* that the underlying purpose of the ECSC was 'the setting up of a neutralized group in Europe—if France need not fear Germany, she need have no other fears, i.e. Russia'.[9] The

---

9. François Duchêne, *Jean Monnet: The First Statesman of Interdependence*, New York 1994, pp. 226–8, 198.

important task was to build a modern and united Europe, capable
in the long run of an independent partnership with the United
States. 'We would transform our archaic social conditions', he
wrote in 1952, 'and come to laugh at our present fear of Russia'.[10]
American power set the limits of all political action in Europe,
and Monnet knew better than anyone how to work within them.
But he had an original agenda of his own, which was diagonal to
US intentions.

Where did it come from? Monnet had lived through two
devastating European conflicts, and his over-riding goal was to bar
the road to another one. But this was a common preoccupation of
his generation, without inspiring any general vision of federalism.
Part of the reason was that the passions of the Cold War so
quickly succeeded the lessons of the World War, displacing or
surcharging it in another set of priorities for the political elites
of Western Europe. Monnet was detached from these. His career
as a deracinated financial projector, adrift from any stable social
forces or national frontiers, left him at a psychological angle to
the conventional outlook of his class. As Duchêne points out,
people thought Monnet 'lacked political values', because he did
not care very much about the 'struggles over economic equality
springing from the French and Russian Revolutions'.[11] It was this
relative indifference—not exactly the same as insensibility—that
freed him to act so inventively beyond the assumptions of the
inter-state system in which these struggles were fought out.

Although he was proud of his country, Monnet was not
committed to the framework of the nation-state. He opposed the
French nuclear deterrent and tried to dissuade Adenauer from
signing the Franco-German Treaty. From the conception of the
ECSC onwards, he worked consistently for supranational goals
in Europe. He was initially cool towards the idea of the EEC,
which he did not originate, thinking the Common Market to be a
'rather vague' scheme—he was anyway not particularly impressed
with doctrines of free trade. Milward makes much of his
paradoxical underestimation of the potential of a customs union
for integration, but the question Monnet put as early as 1955—
'Is it possible to have a Common Market without federal social,

---

10. Duchêne, *Jean Monnet*, p. 228.
11. *Jean Monnet*, p. 364.

monetary and macro-economic policies?'[12]—is still the central
issue before the European Union forty years later. The order of the
phrasing is significant. A banker by profession, Monnet was not
economically conservative. He always sought trade-union support
for his schemes, and late in life even expressed sympathy with
the student movement of 1968, whose warning of social injustice
stood for 'the cause of humanity'.[13]

On the other hand, Monnet was a stranger to the democratic
process, as conventionally understood. He never faced a crowd
or ran for office. Shunning any direct contact with electorates,
he worked among elites only. From Milward's standpoint, in
which European integration flowed from the popular consensus
inside each nation-state, as expressed at the polls, this was in itself
enough to condemn him to the irrelevance that affected federalism
more largely. It is more plausible, however, to draw the opposite
lesson. Monnet's career was emblematic, in a particularly pure
way, of the predominant character of the process that has led to the
Union we have today. At no point until—ostensibly—the British
referendum of 1976 was there any real popular participation in
the movement towards European unity.

Parliamentary majorities, of course, had to be stitched together,
and corporate interests squared: there was room for alert lobbies
or cross-grained deputies to put in their word. But the electorates
themselves were never consulted. Europe was scarcely mentioned
at the polls that in January 1956 brought the Republican Front to
office in France—they were fought over the Algerian conflict and
the appeal of Poujade. But the critical point on which the fate of
the EEC finally turned was the switch of a few dozen SFIO votes
in the National Assembly that had blocked the EDC, in response
to the climate after Suez. The weakest performer in Milward's
theoretical quartet is here. The democratic foundations he
ascribes to the whole process of integration were quite notional.
There was an absence of popular opposition to plans designed
and debated on high, which received mere negative assent
below. In his most recent writing, Milward himself comes close
to conceding as much. The reality is the one Duchêne describes:
'The situation was not revolutionary, and voters were neither a
motor nor a brake'.[14]

---

12. *Jean Monnet*, p. 270.
13. Jean Monnet, *Mémoires*, Paris 1976, p. 577.
14. *Jean Monnet*, p. 357.

But if this is so, what enabled Monnet and his associates to play the role they did in the bargaining between chancelleries? If we ask why the outcome of European integration was *not* as lopsidedly inter-governmental as a neo-realist logic would appear to imply—was not, in other words, something closer to the kind of framework that, let us say, Mendès-France or De Gaulle (or later Thatcher or Major) would have approved—the answer is two-fold. Firstly, among the Six the smaller nations were predisposed to federalist solutions. The Benelux countries, whose own customs union was adumbrated in exile as early as 1943, were states whose only prospect of significant influence in Europe lay in some kind of supranational framework. It was two foreign ministers from the Low Countries—Beyen in the Netherlands and Spaak in Belgium—who originated the key moves that led to the eventual brokerage of the Treaty of Rome. Beyen, who first actually proposed the Common Market, was not an elected politician, but a former executive for Philips and director of Unilever parachuted straight from the IMF into the Dutch cabinet. Milward, forgetting his strictures on Monnet, rightly salutes him.

There was, however, a second and much heavier weight that descended on the federalist side of the scales. That was, of course, the United States. Monnet's strength as an architect of integration did not lie in any particular leverage with European cabinets—even if he eventually came to enjoy the confidence of Adenauer—but in his direct line to Washington. American pressure, in the epoch of Acheson and Dulles, was crucial in putting real—not merely ideal—force behind the conception of 'ever greater union' that came to be enshrined in the Treaty of Rome. In so far as it tends to underplay this role, Milward's account can be taxed not with excess but insufficiency of realism.

At the same time US policy throws into sharp relief the last of Milward's postulates. For consistent American patronage, at critical moments pressure, for far-reaching European integration did not correspond to the interests or demands of any important domestic constituency. In the decisions reached, US voters counted for nothing. More significantly, when the potential for economic competition from a more unified Western Europe, equipped with a common external tariff, was registered by the Treasury, the Department of Agriculture and the Federal Reserve, they were firmly overridden by the White House and the State Department. American politico-military imperatives, in the global conflict with Communism, trumped commercial calculation without the slightest difficulty. Eisenhower informed Pineau that the realization of the Treaty of Rome would be 'one of the finest days in the history of the free world, perhaps even more so than winning the war'.[15] Pregnant words, from the Supreme Allied Commander.

Milward is entirely clear about US priorities, which he describes with his customary trenchancy. But he does not pursue the theoretical issue they pose for his interpretive scheme. In America, at least, continuity between domestic agendas and foreign objectives did not obtain. There was a clear-cut conflict between them. Was this just an American exception, without echo in Europe? Milward himself provides the evidence that it was not. For there was, after all, one major country of Western Europe which did not take the path of integration.

Why did the United Kingdom, under both Labour and Conservative rule, reject the logic of the Six? Surely the domestic consensus behind rising popular standards, based on the maintenance of full employment and the welfare state, was even more complete in Britain than in France or Italy, with their still intransigent mass Communist parties, or Germany with its doughty champions of economic liberalism? On the chequerboard of major political forces, there were no English counterparts of Marty or Erhard; and in the vocabulary of continental Europe no equivalents to Butskellism. If the predominant impetus to integration was a popular quest for socio-economic security codified in a strong national consensus, should Britain in the age of Attlee or Macmillan not have been foremost in it?

Although he points out the elements of an economic configuration that set the UK somewhat apart from the Six— the structure of agricultural subventions, the role of sterling, the salience of Commonwealth markets—Milward does not argue that it therefore made sense for Britain to stay out of Europe. On the contrary, he judges that 'failure to sign the Treaties of Rome was a serious mistake'.[16] His explanation for the error is that the British political establishment, arrogant and provincial, clung to the belief that the UK was 'still in some sense a great power whose foreign policy should reflect that position'. Its ignorance of the nearby world was richly distilled by Harold Macmillan's remark to his intimates that it was 'the Jews, the Planners and the old

---

15. *The European Rescue of the Nation-State*, p. 375.
16. *The European Rescue of the Nation-State*, p. 433.

cosmopolitan element' who were to blame for the supranational tendencies of the European Commission.[17]

What the detail of Milward's account suggests is that for fifteen years after the war British policy towards European integration was essentially settled by rulers who put calculations— or miscalculations—of political power and prestige before estimates of economic performance. The misfit between this pattern and the overall framework of *The European Rescue of the Nation-State* is too plain to escape his notice. On a more tentative note than usual, he offers the ingenious suggestion that because the crisis of the British state in the inter-war and war-time years was less acute than on the continent, 'so the search for a new consensus after 1945 was more limited', and— despite appearances—the result 'perhaps weaker'. He goes on to remark: 'The prosperity it brought was also more limited and the United Kingdom was eventually to lead the attack on the post-war consensus of which it had only been one of the lesser beneficiaries'.[18]

The possibility of a provocative revision of Paul Addison's *Road to 1945* can be glimpsed here. The assumption remains, however, that it was the degree of social consensus which governed the pace of economic growth and the fate of European policy. But 'consensus' is an evasive term, notoriously close to euphemism, that parades rather than defines a democratic will. Its usage is best confined to the elites that like to talk of it. In this sense, there was indeed a consensus in Britain, and—*pace* Milward—a singularly strong one: but it had little or nothing to do with elections.

The over-statement in Milward's argument comes from an attractive political impulse. A radical and humane attachment to the achievements of the post-war welfare state—the material improvements in the lives of ordinary people it brought—is the underlying motif of his work. If these were the products of democratic choices within the nation-state, can the same pressures not be given credit for the new forms of cooperation between states? The temptation of this move leads to a quizzical heuristic hybrid—what might be called, stressing the oxymoron, a diplomatic populism. But if Milward yields to this out of one side of his radical temper, the other side—a robust impatience with sanctimonies of any kind—repeatedly checks him.

---

17. *The European Rescue of the Nation-State*, pp. 395, 432.
18. *The European Rescue of the Nation-State*, p. 433.

So his recent writing strikes a more ambivalent note. 'Votes and voters', he now concedes, 'are less important than our original hypothesis suggested'.[19] Instead of relying on the claims of consensus, Milward now proposes the notion of allegiance—'all those elements which induce citizens to give loyalty to institutions of governance'—as the key to understanding European integration.[20] The substitution is salutary. Compared with consensus, a democratic emulsion, allegiance is an older and stiffer physic. The feudal cast of the term Milward now recommends as capable of integrating the different strands involved in the emergence of the Community is more appropriate. It bespeaks not civic participation, but customary adhesion: obedience in exchange for benefits—Hobbes rather than Rousseau. This is certainly closer to Western realities.

'The only defence for national government since 1945 we have offered', Milward writes, 'is that it has better represented popular will than in the past, even if still only partially and imperfectly. That is, for us, the historical reason why it has survived'—a survival, however, that he judges to have been 'finely balanced'.[21] Has reinforcement by European integration put it beyond danger? By no means. The rescue may prove only a temporary reprieve. After the promise of its title, Milward's major book closes with what seems like a retraction: 'the strength of the European Community' lies after all 'in the weakness of the nation-state'.[22]

If these contrary notes do not reach harmony, the historical richness of Milward's work exceeding its theoretical scheme, this is also partly because his later work—unlike his earlier— proceeds by topical selection rather systematic narration. Without simultaneous tracking of the different forces which he in principle admits were at work, the relative contribution of each to the process of integration cannot be adjudicated on equal terms. Such a narrative waits on a fuller opening of the archives. In its absence, what provisional conclusions are reasonable?

There were at least four principal forces behind the process of integration. Although these overlapped, their core concerns were quite distinct. The central aim of the federalist circle round

---

19. *The Frontiers of National Sovereignty*, p. 195.
20. 'Allegiance: The Past and the Future', *Journal of European Integration*, 1995, No. 1, Vol. 1, p. 14.
21. *The European Rescue of the Nation-State*, p. 186.
22. *The European Rescue of the Nation-State*, pp. 446–7.

Monnet was to create a European order that would be immune to the catastrophic nationalist wars that had twice devastated the continent, in 1914–18 and 1939–45. The basic objective of the United States was to create a strong West European bulwark against the Soviet Union, as a means to victory in the Cold War. The key French goal was to tie Germany down in a strategic compact leaving Paris *primus inter pares* west of the Elbe. The major German concern was to return to the rank of an established power and keep open the prospect of reunification. What held these different programmes together was—here Milward is, of course, entirely right—the common interest of all parties in securing the economic stability and prosperity of Western Europe, as a condition of achieving each of these goals.

This constellation held good till the end of the sixties. In the course of the next decade, two significant shifts occurred. The first was an exchange of Anglo-Saxon roles. The belated entry of the UK brought another state into the Community of nominally comparable weight to France and West Germany; while on the other hand, the US withdrew to a more watchful stance as Nixon and Kissinger started to perceive the potential for a rival great power in Western Europe. The second change was more fundamental. The economic and social policies that had united the original Six during the post-war boom disintegrated with the onset of global recession. The result was a sea-change in official attitudes to public finance and levels of employment, social security and rules for competition, that set the barometer for the eighties.

Thus the last effective step of integration to date, the Single European Act of 1986, exhibits a somewhat different pattern from its predecessors, although not a discontinuous one. The initiative behind the completion of the internal market came from Delors, a convinced federalist recently appointed as French head of the Commission. At governmental level the critical change was, as Milward rightly stresses, the conversion of the Mitterrand regime at Delors's prompting to orthodox liberal discipline—soon after the turn to the right that brought Kohl to office in Germany. This time, however, a third power played a role of some significance— Thatcher collaborating in the interest of deregulating financial markets, in which British banks and insurance companies saw prospects of large gains; while Cockfield in Brussels gave the project its administrative thrust.

The higher profile of the Commission in this episode was testimony of a certain change in the balance of institutional forces within the Community, which the Act itself modified by the introduction (more properly reinstatement) of qualified majority voting inside the Council of Ministers. On the other hand, the French stamp on the proto-federal machinery in Brussels was never more pronounced than during the Delors presidency, while Paris and Bonn retained their traditional dominance within the web of inter-governmental relations. The result of thirty years of such integration is the strange institutional congeries of today's Union, composed of four disjointed parts.

Most visible to the public eye, the European Commission in Brussels acts as—so to speak—the 'executive' of the Community. A body composed of functionaries designated by member-governments, it is headed by a president enjoying a salary considerably higher than that of the occupant of the White House, but commanding a bureaucracy smaller than that of many a municipality, and a budget of little more than 1 per cent of area GDP. These revenues, moreover, are collected not by the Commission, which has no direct powers of taxation itself, but by the member-governments. In a provision of which conservatives can still only dream in the US, the Treaty of Rome forbids the Commission to run any deficit. Its expenditures remain heavily concentrated on the Common Agricultural Policy, about which there is much cant both inside and outside Europe—US and Canadian farm support being not much lower than European, and Japanese much higher. A certain amount is also spent on 'Structural Funds' to aid poor or rust-belt regions. The Commission administers this budget; issues regulatory directives; and—possessing the sole right of initiating European legislation—proposes new enactments. Its proceedings are confidential.

Secondly, there is the Council of Ministers—the utterly misleading name for what is in fact a parallel series of inter-governmental meetings between departmental ministers of each member-state, covering different policy areas (about thirty in all). The Council's decisions are tantamount to the legislative function of the Community: a hydra-headed entity in virtually constant session at Brussels, whose deliberations are secret, most of whose decisions are sewn up at a bureaucratic level below the assembled ministers themselves, and whose outcomes are binding on national parliaments. Capping this structure, since 1974, has been the so-called European Council composed of the heads of government of each member-state, which meets at least two times a year and sets broad policy for the Council of Ministers.

Thirdly, there is the European Court of Justice in Luxembourg, composed of judges appointed by the member-states, who pronounce on the legality or otherwise of the directives of the Commission, and on conflict between Union and national law, and have over time come to treat the Treaty of Rome as if it were something like a European Constitution. Unlike the Supreme Court in the US, no votes are recorded in the European Court, and no dissent is ever set out in a judgement. The views of individual judges remain unfathomable.

Finally there is the European Parliament, formally the 'popular element' in this institutional complex, as its only elective body. However, in defiance of the Treaty of Rome, it possesses no common electoral system: no permanent home—wandering like a vagabond between Strasbourg, Luxembourg and Brussels; no power of taxation; no control over the purse—being confined to simple yes/no votes on the Community budget as a whole; no say over executive appointments, other than a threat in extremis to reject the whole Commission; no right to initiate legislation, merely the ability to amend or veto it. In all these respects, it functions less like a legislative than a ceremonial apparatus of government, providing a symbolic facade not altogether unlike, say, the monarchy in Britain.

The institutional upshot of European integration is thus a customs union with a quasi-executive of supranational cast, without any machinery to enforce its decisions; a quasi-legislature of inter-governmental ministerial sessions, shielded from any national oversight, operating as a kind of upper chamber; a quasi-supreme court that acts as it were the guardian of a constitution which does not exist; and a pseudo-legislative lower chamber, in the form of a largely impotent parliament that is nevertheless the only elective body, theoretically accountable to the peoples of Europe. All of this superimposed on a set of nation-states, determining their own fiscal, social, military and foreign policies. Up to the end of the eighties the sum of these arrangements, born under the sign of the interim and the makeshift, had nevertheless acquired a respectable aura of inertia.

In the nineties, however, three momentous changes loom over the political landscape in which this complex is set. The disappearance of the Soviet bloc, the reunification of Germany and the Treaty of Maastricht have set processes in motion whose scale can only be compared to the end of the war. Together, they mean that the European Union is likely to be the theatre of an extraordinary conjunction of divergent processes in the coming years: the passage to a European monetary union; the return of Germany to continental hegemony; and the competition among ex-Communist countries for entry. Can any predictions be made about the outcomes that might emerge from a metabolism of this magnitude?

At this historical crossroads it is worth thinking back to the work of Monnet and his circle. Historically, state-construction has proceeded along three main lines. One is a gradual, unplanned, organic growth of governmental authority and territory, such as occurred in—let us say—late mediaeval France or early modern Austria, whose architects had little or no idea of long-term objectives at all. A second path is the conscious imitation of pre-existing models, of a kind that first really emerges in Europe in the eighteenth century, with the emulation of French Absolutism by its Prussian or Piedmontese counterparts. A third and historically still later path was deliberate revolutionary innovation—the creation of completely new state forms in a very compressed period of time, under the pressure either of popular upheavals like the American or Russian revolutions, or elite drives like the Meiji Restoration in Japan.

The process of statecraft set in train by the projectors—the term of Burkean alarm can be taken as homage—of a federal Europe departed from all these paths. It was without historical precedent. For its origins were very deliberately designed, but they were neither imitative of anything else, nor total in scope; while the goals at which it aimed were not proximate but very distant. This was an entirely novel combination: a style of political construction that was at once highly voluntarist, but pragmatically piecemeal— and yet vaultingly long-range. Relying on what he called a 'dynamic disequilibrium', Monnet's strategy was an incremental totalization, en route to a hitherto unexampled objective—a democratic supranational federation. The implications of his undertaking did not escape him. He wrote: 'We are starting a process of continuous reform which can shape tomorrow's world more lastingly than the principles of revolution so widespread outside the West'.[23] It is one of the great merits of Duchêne's biography that it seeks so intelligently to take the measure of this innovation, which he calls—by contrast with conquest, adjustment or upheaval—'that rarest of all phenomena in history, a studied

---

23. Duchêne, *Jean Monnet*, p. 390.

change of regime'.[24] This is a striking formula. Yet there is in it at once a certain over-statement, and under-statement. The changes were more improvised than studied; but at stake was more than a regime.

Looking back, who can deny the genius of this conception of political advance—as if the ambitions of Napoleon could be married to the methods of Taaffe? On the other hand, it exacted a characteristic price. If all historical undertakings are subject to the fatality of unintended consequences, the more deliberate they are the more pronounced the gap may become. The 'construction of Europe' set in train by Monnet and his circle was an enterprise of unrivalled scope and complexity, which yet nearly always relied on drab institutional steps and narrow social supports. Historically, it was bound to lead to what it did—that is, a persistent pattern of consequences that disconcerted and foiled the intentions of its architects.

The series of these bafflements has been continuous down to the present. In the fifties Monnet wanted Euratom and was landed with the Common Market; working for a supranational union, what he eventually got was an inter-governmental consortium dominated by the statesman most opposed to everything he stood for, De Gaulle. The General in turn thought his procedural fixture in the sixties would stymie the bureaucratic pretensions of the Commission—which in fact rebounded more strongly than ever out of them in the seventies. In the eighties, Mrs Thatcher believed the Single European Act would repeat and extend the deregulated internal market she championed in the UK—only to discover it leading towards the single currency she most detested. The hopes of Jacques Delors are still with us. Is it likely their fate will differ in the nineties?

2

On New Year's Day 1994, Europe—the metonym—changed names. The dozen nations of the Community took on the title of Union, though as in a Spanish wedding, the new appellation did not replace but encompassed the old. Was anything of substance altered? So far, very little. The member-states have risen to fifteen, with the entry of three former neutrals. Otherwise things are much as they were before. What is new, however, is that everyone

---

24. *Jean Monnet*, p. 20.

knows this is not going to last. For the first time since the war,
Europe is living in anticipation of large but still imponderable
changes to the part that has stood for the whole. Three dominate
the horizon.

The first is, of course, the Treaty of Maastricht. We can set aside
its various rhetorical provisions, for vague consultation of foreign
policy and defence, or ineffectual protection of social rights, and
even ignore its mild emendations of the institutional relations
within the Community. The core of the Treaty is the commitment
by the member-states, save England and Denmark, to introduce
a single currency, under the authority of a single central bank, by
1999. This step means an irreversible move of the EU towards real
federation. With it, national governments will lose the right either
to issue money or to alter exchange rates, and will only be able
to vary rates of interest and public borrowing within very narrow
limits, on pain of heavy fines from the Commission if they break
central bank directives. They may still tax at their discretion, but
capital mobility in the single market can be expected to ensure
increasingly common fiscal denominators. European monetary
union spells the end of the most important attributes of national
economic sovereignty.

Secondly, Germany is now reunited. The original Common
Market was built on a balance between the two largest countries
of the Six, France and Germany—the latter with greater economic
weight and slightly larger population, the former with superior
military and diplomatic weight. Later, Italy and Britain provided
flanking states of roughly equivalent demographic and economic
size. This balance started to break down in the eighties, when the
EMS proved to be a zone pivoting on the deutschmark, the only
currency never to be devalued within it. A decade later, Germany's
position has been qualitatively transformed. With a population of
over eighty million, it is now much the largest state in the Union,
enjoying not only monetary but increasingly institutional and
diplomatic ascendancy. For the first time in its history, the process
of European integration is now potentially confronted with the
emergence of a hegemonic power, with a widely asymmetrical
capacity to affect all other member-states.

The third great change has followed from the end of Communism
in the countries of the former Warsaw Pact. The restoration of
capitalism east of the Elbe has further transformed the position of
Germany, both by reinstating it as the continental *Land der Mitte*
which its conservative theorists always—with reason—insisted it

would once again become, and—a less noticed development—by
reducing the significance of the nuclear weapons that France and
Britain possessed and it lacked. Yet more significant, however, is
the currently expressed desire of virtually all the East European
countries, and some of the former Soviet lands, to join the EU.
As things stand, the total population of these candidates is about
130 million. Their inclusion would make a Community of half
a billion people, nearly twice the size of the United States. More
pointedly still, it would approximately double the membership
of the European Union, from fifteen to some thirty states. A
completely new configuration would be at stake.

Historically, these three great changes have been interconnected.
In reverse order, it was the collapse of Communism that allowed
the reunification of Germany that precipitated the Treaty of
Maastricht. The shock-wave moved from the east to the centre
to the west of Europe. But causes and consequences remain
distinct. The outcomes of these processes obey no single logic.
More than this: to a greater extent than in any previous phase of
European integration, the impact of each is quite uncertain. We
confront a set of *ex ante* indeterminacies that, adopting a Kantian
turn of phrase, might be called the three amphibologies of post-
Maastricht politics. They pose much more dramatic dilemmas
than is generally imagined.

The Treaty itself offers the first. Its origins lie in the dynamism of
Delors's leadership of the Commission. After securing passage of
the Single European Act in 1986, Delors persuaded the European
Council two years later to set up a committee largely composed
of central bankers, but chaired by himself, to report on a single
currency. Its recommendations were formally accepted by the
Council in the spring of 1989. But it was the sudden tottering of
East Germany that spurred Mitterrand to conclude an agreement
with Kohl at the Strasbourg summit in the autumn, putting the
decisive weight of the Franco-German axis behind the project.
Thatcher, of course, was implacably opposed.

But she was comprehensively outmanoeuvred, not least by the
continental regime she most disliked, which sat in Rome. The
otherwise impregnable self-confidence of *The Downing Street
Years* falters disarmingly whenever its heroine comes to Europe.
The titles of the chapters speak for themselves. The ordinary
triumphal run—'Falklands: The Victory'—'Disarming the Left'—
'Hat Trick'—'Not So Much a Programme, More a Way of Life'—
'The World Turned Right Side Up'—is interrupted by a faintly

woeful note. We enter the world of 'Jeux Sans Frontières' and 'Babel Express', with its 'un-British combination of high-flown rhetoric and pork-barrel politics', where 'heads of government would be left discussing matters that would boggle the mind of the City's top accountants', and 'the intricacies of European Community policy really test one's intellectual ability and capacity for clear thinking'.[25]

The uncharacteristic hint of humility is well founded. Thatcher appears to have been somewhat out of her depth, as a persistent tone of rueful bewilderment suggests. The leitmotif is: 'Looking back, it is now possible to see'—but 'I can only say it did not seem like that at the time'.[26] Many are the occasions that inspire this mortified hindsight. Exemplary in its comedy is the Milan summit of the European Council in 1985, which ensured the inclusion of qualified majority voting in the Single European Act. 'Signor Craxi could not have been more sweetly reasonable'—'I came away thinking how easy it had been to get my points across' (sic). But lo and behold on the following day: 'To my astonishment and anger, Signor Craxi suddenly called a vote and by a majority the council resolved to establish an IGC'.[27] Five years later, the precedent set at Milan proved fatal at Rome. This time it was Andreotti who laid the ambush into which Thatcher fell head over heels, at the European summit of October 1990. 'As always with the Italians, it was difficult throughout to distinguish confusion from guile', she haplessly writes, 'But even I was unprepared for the way things went'.[28] Once more, a vote to convene an IGC was sprung on her at the last minute, this time on the even more provocative topic of political union. Her explosion at Andreotti's silken trap finished her. In London, Geoffrey Howe took a dim view of her reaction, and within a month she was ejected from office. No wonder she hated her Italian colleagues so cordially, to the point of saying: 'To put it more bluntly, if I were an Italian I might prefer rule from Brussels too'.[29]

Thatcher respected Delors ('manifest intelligence, ability and integrity'), liked Mitterrand ('I have a soft spot for French charm') and could put up with Kohl ('style of diplomacy even more direct

25. Margaret Thatcher, *The Downing Street Years*, London 1993, pp. 727, 729–730.
26. *The Downing Street Years*, p. 536.
27. *The Downing Street Years*, pp. 549–51.
28. *The Downing Street Years*, pp. 765–6.
29. *The Downing Street Years*, p. 742.

than mine'). But Andreotti she feared and detested from the start. At her very first G-7 summit, within a few months of coming to power, she found that

> he seemed to have positive aversion to principle, even a conviction that a man of principle was doomed to be a figure of fun. He saw politics as an eighteenth-century general saw war: a vast and elaborate set of parade-ground manoeuvres by armies that would never actually engage in conflict but instead declare victory, surrender or compromise as their apparent strength dictated in order to collaborate on the real business of sharing the spoils. A talent for striking political deals rather than a conviction of political truths might be required by Italy's political system and it was certainly regarded as *de rigueur* in the Community, but I could not help but find something distasteful about those who practised it.[30]

Andreotti's judgement of Thatcher was crisper. Emerging from one of the interminable European Council sessions devoted to the British rebate, he remarked that she reminded him of a landlady berating a tenant for her rent.

The increasing role of Italy as a critical third in the affairs of the Community was a significant feature of these years. The Report on Economic and Monetary Union of 1989 that laid the basis for Maastricht was drafted by an Italian, Tommaso Padoa-Schioppa, the most trenchant advocate of a single currency, and it was also the initiative of an Italian—Andreotti again—that at the last minute added an automatic deadline of 1999 into the Treaty, to the consternation of the British and of the Bundesbank. Nevertheless, the final shape of the bargain reached at Maastricht was essentially of French and German design. The central aim for Paris was a financial edifice capable of replacing the unilateral power of the Bundesbank as the *de facto* regulator of the fortunes of its neighbours, with a *de jure* central authority over the European monetary space in which German interests would no longer be privileged. In exchange Bonn received the security system of 'convergence criteria'—in effect draconian conditions for abandonment of the deutschmark, which Italian theorists of a single currency had always rejected—and the fixtures and fittings of 'political union'.

The diplomatic origins of the Treaty are one thing. Its economic effects, if implemented, are another. What is the social logic of the monetary union scheduled to come into force by the end of the decade? In a system of the kind envisaged at Maastricht, national

---

30. *The Downing Street Years*, pp. 70, 742, 736.

macro-economic policy becomes a thing of the past: all that
remains to member-states are distributive options on—necessarily
reduced—expenditures within balanced budgets, at competitive
levels of taxation. The historic commitments of both Social and
Christian Democracy to full employment and social services of
the traditional welfare state, already scaled down or cut back,
would cease to have any further institutional purchase. This is
a revolutionary prospect. The single obligation of the projected
European Central Bank, more restrictive even than the charter
of the Federal Reserve, is the maintenance of price stability. The
protective and regulative functions of existing national states will
be dismantled, leaving sound money as the sole regulator, as in
the classical liberal model of the epoch before Keynes.

The new element—namely, the supranational character of
the future monetary authority—would serve to reinforce such a
historical reversion: elevated higher above national electorates than
its predecessors, it will be more immune, and not only by statute,
from popular pressures. Put simply, a federal Europe in this sense
would not mean—as Conservatives in Britain fear—a super-state,
but *less* state. Hayek was the lucid prophet of this vision. In his
1939 essay 'The Economic Conditions of Interstate Federalism'
he set out the current logic of European monetary union with
inspired force and clarity. After arguing that states within such a
union could not pursue an independent monetary policy, he noted
that macro-economic interventions always require some common
agreement over values and objectives, and went on:

> It is clear that such agreement will be limited in inverse proportion to
> the homogeneity and the similarity of outlook and tradition possessed
> by the inhabitants of an area. Although, in the national state, the
> submission to the will of a majority will be facilitated by the myth of
> nationality, it must be clear that people will be reluctant to submit to
> any interference in their daily affairs when the majority which directs
> the government is composed of people of different nationalities and
> different traditions. It is, after all, only common sense that the central
> government in a federation composed of many different people will
> have to be restricted in scope if it is to avoid meeting an increasing
> resistance on the part of the various groups which it includes. But
> what could interfere more thoroughly with the intimate life of the
> people than the central direction of economic life, with its inevitable
> discrimination between groups? There seems to be little possible
> doubt that the scope for the regulation of economic life will be
> much narrower for the central government of a federation than for
> national states. And since, as we have seen, the power of the states
> which comprise the federation will be yet more limited, much of the

interference with economic life to which we have become accustomed
will be altogether impracticable under a federal organization.[31]

Maastricht, in this account, leads to an obliteration of what is
left of the Keynesian legacy that Hayek deplored, and most of
the distinctive gains of the West European labour movement
associated with it. Precisely the extremity of this prospect, however,
poses the question of whether in practice it might not unleash
the contrary logic. Confronted with the drastic consequences of
dismantling previous social controls over economic transactions
at the national level, would there not soon—or even beforehand—
be overwhelming pressure to reinstitute them at supranational
level, to avoid an otherwise seemingly inevitable polarization of
regions and classes within the Union? That is, to create a European
political authority capable of re-regulating what the single
currency and single-minded bank have deregulated? Could this
have been the hidden gamble of Jacques Delors, author of the Plan
for monetary union, yet a politician whose whole previous career
suggests commitment to a Catholic version of social-democratic
values, and suspicion of economic liberalism?

On this reading, Hayek's scenario could well reverse out into
its opposite—let us say, the prospect drawn by Wynne Godley. As
the Treaty neared ratification, he observed:

---

31. Friedrich Hayek, *Individualism and Economic Order*, Chicago 1948, pp.
264–5. Retrospectively, Hayek's clairvoyance is all the more striking for the distance
between the context in which he was writing and the arrival of European Monetary
Union. His essay published in September 1939, was a contribution to the debates
around differing conceptions and schemes of federal union in the leading forum
devoted to these, *The New Commonwealth Quarterly*. Its immediate background
was the sudden wave of enthusiasm in the wake of Munich for schemes of federal
union as a barrier against Nazi expansion, set off by the American publicist Clarence
Streit's call for the world's fifteen democracies to league together against the Axis
powers (see below p. 497). Intellectually, Hayek was inspired by the case made by
Lionel Robbins for the "deplanning" of the interventionism of the past half century'
(*Economic Planning and International Order*, London 1937, p. 248; *The History
of Freedom and Other Essays*, London 1907, p. 98), and by Acton's belief that 'of
all checks on democracy, federalism has been the most efficacious and the most
congenial'. Politically, he seems to have viewed Streit's proposal for a Democratic
Union stretching from the United States through Britain to Australia with
understandable scepticism, plumping instead, along with Robbins, for an Anglo-
French union once the war had broken out. By the time of *The Road to Serfdom*
(1944), he was commending Ivor Jenning's now forgotten treatise *A Federation for
Western Europe* (1940) for post-war consideration. But when European integration
eventually got under way with the Schuman Plan, the Coal and Steel Community
was too dirigiste to win his sympathy.

The incredible lacuna in the Maastricht programme is that while it contains a blueprint for the establishment and modus operandi of an independent central bank, there is no blueprint whatever of the analogue, in Community terms, of a central government. Yet there would simply *have* to be a system of institutions which fulfils all those functions at a Community level which are at present exercised by the central governments of the individual member countries.[32]

Perhaps because he feared just such arguments, Hayek himself had changed his mind by the seventies. Influenced by German fears of inflation if the D-mark was absorbed in a monetary union (by then he was based in Freiburg), he decided that a single European currency was not only a utopian but a dangerous prescription.[33] Certainly, it was more than ever necessary to take the control of money out of the hands of national governments subject to electoral pressures. But the remedy, he now saw, was not to move it upwards to a supranational public authority; rather, it was to displace it downwards to competing private banks, issuing rival currencies in the market-place.

Even on the principled right there have been few takers for this solution—which Padoa-Schioppa, perhaps with a grain of malice, commends as the only coherent alternative to his own.[34] But misgivings about what the kind of single currency envisaged by the Treaty of Maastricht might mean for socio-economic stability are widely shared, even among central bankers. With nearly twenty million people currently out of work in the Union, what is to prevent huge permanent pools of unemployment in depressed regions? It is the governor of the Bank of England who now warns that, once devaluations are ruled out, the only mechanisms of adjustment are sharp wage reductions or mass out-migration; while the head of the European Monetary Institute itself, the Belgian-Hungarian banker (and distinguished economist) Alexandre Lamfalussy, in charge of the technical preparations for the single currency, pointedly noted—in an appendix to the report of the Delors Committee, of which he was a member—that if 'the only global macroeconomic tool available within the EMU would be the common monetary policy implemented by the European central banking system',

---

32. Wynne Godley, 'Maastricht and All That', *London Review of Books*, 8 October 1992.

33. Friedrich Hayek, *Denationalisation of Money: The Argument Refined*, London 1978, pp. 19–20.

34. Tommaso Padoa-Schioppa, *L'Europa verso l'unione monetaria*, Turin 1992, pp. xii, 189.

the outcome 'would be an unappealing prospect'.[35] If monetary union was to work, he explained, a common fiscal policy was essential.

But since budgets remain the central battleground of domestic politics, how could there be fiscal coordination without electoral determination? The 'system of institutions' on whose necessity Godley insists is only conceivable on one foundation: it would perforce have to be based on a genuine supranational democracy at Union level, embodying for the first time a real popular sovereignty in a truly effective and accountable European Parliament. It is enough to spell out this condition to see how unprepared either official discourse or public opinion in the member-states are for the scale of the choices before them.

What, secondly, will be the position of Germany in the Europe envisaged at Maastricht? The accelerator towards monetary union was pressed not merely by the hopes or fears of bankers and economists. Ultimately more important was the political desire of the French government to fold the newly enlarged German state into a tighter European structure in which interest rates would no longer be regulated solely by the Bundesbank. In Paris the creation of a single currency under supranational control was conceived as a critical safeguard against the reemergence of German national hegemony in Europe. At the same time, even sections of the German political class and public opinion, somewhat in the spirit of Odysseus tying himself to the mast to protect himself from temptation, were inclined—at any rate declaratively—to share this view. On both sides, the assumption behind it was that a European monetary authority would mean a reduction in the power of the nation-state that was economically strongest, namely the Federal Republic.

No sooner was the Treaty signed, however, than exactly the opposite prognosis took shape, as German interest rates at levels not seen since the twenties inflicted a deep recession on neighbouring countries, and German diplomatic initiatives in the Balkans—once again, as in the early years of the century, shadowing Austrian manoeuvres—stirred uneasy memories. Conor Cruise O'Brien has expressed the alternative view most trenchantly. Commenting on the Yugoslav crisis, in which Bonn claimed to be moved only by the principle of national self-determination—not so applicable, of

---

35. 'Macro-coordination of fiscal policies in an economic and monetary union', *Report on Economic and Monetary Union in the European Community*, Luxembourg 1989, p. 101.

course, to lesser breeds: Chechens, Kurds or Macedonians—he wrote:

> Germany was in favour of the recognition of [Croatia and Slovenia]. The rest of the Community was against, and the United States strongly so. Faced with such an apparently powerful 'Western consensus', on any such matter, the old pre-1990 Bundesrepublik would have respectfully backed away. The new united Germany simply ignored the United States, and turned the Community around. Germany recognized the independence of Croatia and Slovenia, and the rest of the Community followed suit within a few days. The reversal of the Community position was particularly humbling for the French . . . The two new republics are now part of a vast German sphere of influence to the east . . . German economic hegemony in Europe is now a fact of life, to which the rest of us Europeans must adjust as best we can. To press ahead with federal union, under these conditions, would not 'rein in' the mighty power of united Germany. It would subject the rest of us to German hegemony in its plenitude.[36]

Just this fear, of course, was the mobilizing theme of the campaign against ratification of Maastricht in the French referendum a few months later. The French electorate split down the middle on the issue of whether a single currency would reduce or enhance the power of the strongest nation-state on the continent. The majority of the political elite, led by Mitterrand and Giscard, in effect argued that the only way to neutralize German predominance was monetary union. Their opponents, led by Séguin and De Villiers, retorted that this was the surest way to bring it about. The dispute was fought out against the background of the first monetary tempest set off by the raising of the German discount rate in June, which ejected the lira and the pound from the Exchange Rate Mechanism in the final week of the campaign. A year later it was the turn of the franc to capsize in waves of speculation whipped to storm-height by the line of the Bundesbank.

We now have a vivid inside account of these events in Bernard Connolly's book *The Rotten Heart of Europe*. The coarseness of its title and cover is misleading: a sign more of the self-conscious *encanaillement* of smart publishing than of authorial quality. The book suffers from an occasional lapse of taste, and liking for melodrama. But for the most part it is a highly literate and professional study. Indeed, piquantly so. A crypto-Thatcherite

---

36. Conor Cruise O'Brien, 'Pursuing a Chimera', *Times Literary Supplement*, 13 March 1992.

at the highest levels of the Community's financial apparatus in Brussels, Connolly is at the antipodes of Thatcher's bemusement in the field of European politics. His book displays an unrivalled mastery of the nexus between banking and balloting in virtually every member-state of the EC: not just France, Germany, Italy or the UK, but also Belgium, Denmark, Portugal and Ireland are covered with dash and detail. (The only significant exception is the Netherlands, whose ambivalence between liberal economics and federal politics is consigned to an exasperated footnote). Chauvinist convictions have produced a cosmopolitan *tour de force*.

Connolly's standpoint is based on a principled hostility, not merely to a single currency, but to fixed exchange rates between different currencies—in his eyes, a dangerous and futile attempt to bridle the operation of financial markets, which can only stifle the economic freedom on which the vitality of a disorderly economic system depends. 'Western capitalism contained is Western capitalism destroyed', as he pithily puts it.[37] Describing the dogfights of 1992–3 inside the ERM, his sympathies are with the most adamant German opponents of concessions to their neighbours' concerns over interest rates, above all the crusty figure of Helmut Schlesinger, then chairman of the Bundesbank. But the sympathy is strictly tactical—Schlesinger is applauded for an intransigence whose effect was to undermine any prospect of stability in the ERM, so exposing in advance the unviability of EMU. It involves no idealization of the Bundesbank, the myth of whose 'independence' of political influence Connolly punctures effectively—its policies corresponding with remarkable regularity to the needs of the CDU/CSU in the electoral arena.

Today the German political class, in which nationalist reflexes are no longer so dormant, is having second thoughts about monetary union, as the prospect of a single currency has come to look ambiguous on the other side of the Rhine too. Could it be that Germany received shadow rather than substance in the bargain at Maastricht? In chorus, Waigel for the ruling coalition and Tietmeyer for the central bank have been upping the ante for monetary union, with stentorian demands for 'strict compliance' with the convergence criteria appended to the Treaty (public debt no higher than 60 per cent and public deficit no more than 3 per cent of GDP, inflation within 1.5 and interest rates 2 per cent of the three best performers in the Union) and a 'Stability

---

37. Bernard Connolly, *The Rotten Heart of Europe*, London 1995, p. 64.

Pact' beyond them. This orchestrated clamour has no legal basis, since in the text signed at Maastricht the convergence criteria are not unconditional targets to be met, but 'reference values' to be moved towards; and whether or not sufficient movement has been achieved is for the Commission alone—not the Federal Republic or any other government—to decide. These provisions were the work of Philippe Maystadt, foreign minister of Belgium, a country with good reason to insist on flexibility, and certain memories. In its disregard for legal niceties, or small neighbours, the tone of current German diplomacy has become increasingly Wilhelmine.

Nevertheless, it is a striking fact that so far this 'Teutonic tirading', as Adorno once called it, has met no rebuff. Paris, far from reacting, has been eager to accommodate. For Connolly, this is only to be expected. Under Mitterrand, the attitude of the French elite has been a Vichy-like subservience to German economic power. In its pursuit of a *franc fort* requiring punitive interest rates to maintain alignment with the D-mark at the cost of massive unemployment, this establishment has committed treachery against the French people. Noting the widespread alienation from the political class evident in every recent poll, and recalling with relish the country's long traditions of popular unrest, Connolly—who describes himself as a Tory radical—looks forward with grim satisfaction to the explosion of another revolution in France, when the population becomes aware of the price it is paying for monetary union, and rises up to destroy the oligarchy that sought to impose it.[38]

Premonitions of this kind are no longer regarded as entirely far-fetched in France itself. For the moment the prospect is less dramatic, but still fraught enough. The Maastricht referendum revealed the depth of the division in French opinion over the likely consequences of a single currency—would it lead, in the stock question, to a Europeanized Germany or to a German Europe? The victory of Jacques Chirac in the subsequent presidential elections guarantees that the tension between antithetical calculations will continue to haunt the Elysée. For no French politician has so constantly oscillated from one position to the other, or so opportunely reflected the divided mind of the electorate itself. Clambering to power on a platform challenging the bipartisan consensus of the Rocard-Balladur years, *la pensée unique* that gave higher priority to a strong franc than to job creation, after a

---

38. *The Rotten Heart of Europe*, pp. 391–2.

few mis-starts Chirac in office has reverted frantically to financial orthodoxy again. The Juppé government is now administering even tougher doses of retrenchment to force the deficit down to Maastricht levels.

Yet even the tightest budgetary rectitude is no guarantee of a *franc fort*. The 'convergence criteria', as Connolly rightly insists, are completely unrealistic in their exclusion of growth and employment from the indices of a sound economy. Designed to reassure financial markets, they satisfy only central bankers. The markets themselves are not mocked, and will sooner or later mark down any currency where there is widespread unemployment and social tension, no matter how stable are prices or balanced are public accounts—as the French Treasury discovered in the summer of 1993. The current domestic course of the Chirac regime can only tighten already explosive pressures in the big cities at the cost of its electoral credibility, on which that of its exchange rate also depends. The massive street protests of late November could be a harbinger of worse trouble to come. The regime's slump in the opinion polls is without precedent in the Fifth Republic. An image of zealous compliance with directives from the Bundesbank involves high political risks.

Chirac's resumption of nuclear tests can be seen as a clumsy attempt to compensate for economic weakness by military display—demonstratively flexing the one strategic asset the French still possess that the Germans do not. The result has been merely to focus international opprobrium on France. Partial or hypocritical though much of this reaction has been (how many pasquinades have been written against the Israeli bomb?), Chirac's experiments remain pointless. Forcible-feeble in the style of the man, they can scarcely affect the political balance of Europe, where nuclear weapons are no longer of the same importance. At a moment when French diplomacy ought to have been engaged in winning allies to resist German attempts to harden the Treaty of Maastricht, for which France's immediate neighbours Italy, Belgium and Spain were more than ready, it was gratuitously incurring a hostile isolation. On present performance, Chirac could prove the most erratic and futile French politician since Boulanger.

Nevertheless, contrary to received opinion, in the end it will be France rather than Germany that decides the fate of monetary union. The self-confidence of the political class in the Federal Republic, although swelling, is still quite brittle. A cooler and tougher French regime, capable of public historical reminders, could prick its bluster without difficulty. Germany cannot back out of Maastricht, only try to bend it. France can. There will be no EMU if Paris does not exert itself to cut its deficit. The commitment to monetary union comes from the political calculations of the elite, and the world of classical state-craft—a foreign policy determined to check German and uphold French national power. The socio-economic costs of the *franc fort* have been borne by the population at large. Here, absolutely clear-cut, there is a conflict between external objectives and domestic aspirations of the kind Alan Milward would banish from the record of earlier integration. How much does it matter to ordinary French voters whether or not Germany is diplomatically master of the continent again—are not the creation of jobs and growth of incomes issues closer to home? In France the next years are likely to offer an interesting test of the relative weights of consumption and strategy in the process of European integration.

Meanwhile the pressures from below, already welling up in strikes and demonstrations, can only increase the quandaries above. On the surface, the French elite is now less divided over Maastricht than at the time of the referendum. But it is no surer that the single currency will deliver what it was intended to. Germany bound—or unbound? In the space of the new Europe, the equivocation of monetary union as an economic project is matched by the ambiguity of its political logic for the latent national rivalries within it.

Finally, what of the prospects for extending the European Union to the east? On the principle itself, it is a striking fact that there has been no dissent among the member-states. It might be added that there has also been no forethought. For the first time in the history of European integration, a crucial direction has been set, not by politicians or technocrats, but by public opinion. Voters were not involved; but before the consequences were given much consideration, editorialists and column-writers across the political spectrum pronounced with rare unanimity any other course unthinkable. Enlargement to the east was approved in something of the same spirit as the independence of former republics of Yugoslavia. This was not the hard-headed reckoning of costs and benefits on which historians of the early decades of European integration dwell: ideological good-will—essentially, the need to recompense those who suffered under communism—was all. Governments have essentially been towed in the wake of a media consensus. The principle was set by the press; politicians have been left to figure out its applications.

Here the three leading states of Western Europe have divided. From the outset Germany has given priority to the rapid inclusion of Poland, Hungary, the former Czechoslovakia and more recently Slovenia. Within this group, Poland remains the most important in German eyes. Bonn's conception is straightforward. These countries, already the privileged catchment for German investment, would form a security *glacis* of Catholic lands around Germany and Austria, with social and political regimes that could—with judicious backing for sympathetic parties—sit comfortably beside the CDU. France, more cautious about the tempo of widening and mindful of former ties to the countries of the Little Entente—Romania or Serbia—has been less inclined to pick regional favourites in this way. Its initial preference, articulated by Mitterrand in Prague, was for a generic association between Western and Eastern Europe as a whole, outside the framework of the Union.

Britain, on the other hand, has pressed not only for rapid integration of the Visegrád countries into the EU, but for the most extensive embrace beyond it. Alone of Western leaders, Major has envisaged the ultimate inclusion of Russia. The rationale for the British position is unconcealed: the wider the Union becomes, in this view, the shallower it must be—for the more national states it contains, the less viable becomes any real supranational authority over them. Once stretched to the Bug and beyond, the European Union will evolve in practice into the vast free-trade area which in the eyes of London it should always have been. Widening here means both institutional dilution and social deregulation: the prospect of including vast reserve armies of cheap labour in the East, exerting downward pressure on wage costs in the West, is a further bonus in this British scenario.

Which outcome is most likely? At the moment the German design has the most wind in its sails. In so far as the EU has sketched a policy at all, it goes in the CDU's direction. One of the reasons, of course, is the current convergence between German calculations and Polish, Czech and Hungarian aspirations. There is some historical irony here. Since the late eighties publicists and politicians in Hungary, the Czech lands, Poland and more recently Slovenia and even Croatia have set out to persuade the world that these countries belong to a Central Europe with a natural affinity to Western Europe, and that is quite distinct from Eastern Europe.

The geographical stretching involved in these definitions can be extreme. Vilnius is described by Czesław Miłosz, for example, as a Central European city.[39] But if Poland—let alone Lithuania—is really in the centre of Europe, what is the east? Logically, one would imagine, the answer must be Russia. But since many of the same writers—Milan Kundera is another example—deny that Russia has ever belonged to European civilization at all,[40] we are left with the conundrum of a space proclaiming itself centre and border at the same time.

Perhaps sensing such difficulties, an American sympathizer, the *Spectator*'s foreign editor Anne Applebaum, has tacitly upgraded Poland to full occidental status, entitling her—predictably disobliging—inspection of Lithuania, Belarus and Ukraine *Between East and West*.[41] Another way out of them is offered by Miklós Haraszti, who argues that while current usage of the idea of Central Europe may make little geographical sense, it does convey the political unity of those—Poles, Czechs, Magyars—who fought against Communism, as distinct from their neighbours who did not. More Romanians, of course, died in 1989 than in the resistance of all three countries combined for many years. Today, however, the point of the construct is not so much retrospective as stipulative: originally fashioned to repudiate any connexion with Russian experience during the Cold War, it now serves to demarcate superior from inferior—i.e., Romanian, Bulgarian, Albanian, etc.—candidates for entry into the EU.

But geopolitical concepts rarely escape their origins altogether. The idea of *Mitteleuropa* was a German invention, famously theorized by Max Weber's friend Friedrich Naumann during the First World War. Naumann's conception remains arrestingly topical. The Central Europe he envisaged was to be organized around a Germanic nucleus, combining Prussian industrial efficiency and Austrian cultural glamour, capable of attracting satellite nations to it in a vast customs community—*Zollgemeinschaft*—and military

---

39. Czesław Miłosz, 'Central European Attitudes', in George Schöpflin and Nancy Wood (eds), *In Search of Central Europe*, London 1989, p. 116.

40. Milan Kundera, 'The Tragedy of Central Europe', *New York Review of Books*, 26 April 1984; see also George Schöpflin, 'Central Europe: Definitions and Old and New', *In Search of Central Europe*, pp. 7–29.

41. London 1994. Like most writers in this genre, Applebaum is not always consistent—in the mediaeval period, Poland is accounted an 'average central European country': p. 48.

compact, extending 'from the Vistula to the Vosges'.[42] Such a unified *Mitteleuropa* would be what he called an *Oberstaat*, a 'super-state' able to rival the Anglo-American and Russian empires. A Lutheran pastor himself, he noted regretfully that it would be predominantly Catholic—a necessary price to pay—but a tolerant order, making room for Jews and minority nationalities. The Union it created would not be federal—Naumann was an early prophet of today's doctrine of subsidiarity too. All forms of sovereignty other than economic and military would be retained by member-states preserving their separate political identities, and there would be no one all-purpose capital, but rather different cities—Hamburg, Prague, Vienna—would be the seat of particular executive functions, rather like Strasbourg, Brussels and Frankfurt today.[43] Against the background of a blue-print like this, it is not difficult to see how the ideological demand for a vision of Central Europe in the Visegrád countries could find political supply in the Federal Republic.

But given that widening of some kind to the East is now enshrined as official—if still nebulous—policy in the Union, is it probable that the process *could* be limited to a select handful of former Communist states? Applications for admission are multiplying, and there is no obvious boundary at which they can be halted. Europe, as J.G.A. Pocock once forcibly observed, is not a continent, but an unenclosed sub-continent on a continuous land mass stretching to the Bering Strait. Its only natural frontier with Asia is a strip of water, at the Hellespont, once swum by Leander and Lord Byron. To the north, plain and steppe unroll without break into Turkestan. Cultural borders are no more clearly marked than geographical: Muslim Albania and Bosnia lie a thousand miles west of Christian Georgia and Armenia, where the ancients set the dividing-line between Europe and Asia. No wonder Herodotus himself, the first historian to discuss the question, remarked that 'the boundaries of Europe are quite unknown, and no man can say where they end . . . but it is certain that Europa [he is referring to the beauty borne away by Zeus] was an Asiatic, and never even set foot on the land the Greeks now call Europe, only sailing [on her bull] from Phoenicia to Crete'. The irony of Herodotus perhaps still retains a lesson for us. If Slovakia is a candidate for entry into today's Union, why not Romania? If Romania, why not Moldova? If Moldova, why not the Ukraine? If the Ukraine, why not Turkey?

42. Friedrich Naumann, *Mittleleuropa*, Berlin 1915, pp. 3, 129–31, 222ff, 254ff.
43. Naumann, *Mitteleuropa*, pp. 30, 67–71, 232–8, 242.

In a couple of years, Istanbul will overtake Paris to become the largest city in what—however you define it—no one will contest is Europe. As for Moscow, it is over two centuries since Catherine the Great declared in a famous *ukaz* that 'Russia is a European nation', and the history of European culture and politics from the time of Pushkin and Suvorov onwards has enforced her claim ever since. De Gaulle's vision of a Europe 'from the Atlantic to the Urals' will not lightly go away. All the stopping-places of current discussion about widening the EU are mere conveniences of the ring of states closest to it, or of the limits of bureaucratic imagination in Brussels. They will not resist the logic of expansion.

In 1991 J.G.A. Pocock remarked that

> 'Europe' . . . is once again an empire in the sense of a civilised and stabilised zone which must decide whether to extend or refuse its political power over violent cultures along its borders but not yet within its system: Serbs and Croats if one chances to be Austrian, Kurds and Iraqis if Turkey is admitted to be part of 'Europe'. These are not decisions to be taken by the market, but decisions of the state.[44]

But as Europe is not an empire in the more familiar sense of the term—a centralized imperial authority—but merely (as he put it) 'a composite of states', with no common view of their borderlands, it is not surprising that its *limes* has yet to be drawn by the various chancelleries. Since he wrote, however, there has been no shortage of expert opinion to fill the gap.

For example Timothy Garton Ash, one of the first and keenest advocates of a PCH fast track, has recently adjusted his sights. 'Having spent much of the past fifteen years trying to explain to Western readers that Prague, Budapest and Warsaw belong to Central and not to Eastern Europe, I am the last person to need reminding of the immense differences between Poland and Albania', he writes in the *Times Literary Supplement*. 'But to suggest that there is some absolutely clear historical dividing line between the Central European democracies in the so-called Visegrád group and, say, the Baltic states or Slovenia would be to service a new myth'.[45] Instead, the dividing-line must be drawn between a Second Europe numbering some twenty states which he

---

44. J.G.A. Pocock, 'Deconstructing Europe', *London Review of Books*, 19 December 1991; now in *The Discovery of Islands*, Cambridge 2005, p. 287.

45. Timothy Garton Ash, 'Catching the Wrong Bus?', *Times Literary Supplement*, 5 May 1995.

describes as 'set on a course' towards the EU; and a Third Europe that does not share this prospect, comprising Russia, Belarus, Ukraine and—a cartographical nicety—Serbia.

A dichotomy so visibly instrumental is unlikely to be more durable than the mythical distinction it has replaced. At the end of his *Orchestrating Europe*, a capacious and strangely zestful guide through the institutional maze and informal complications of the Union, Keith Middlemas looks out on a somewhat broader scene. Europe, he suggests, is surrounded by an arc of potential threat curving from Murmansk to Casablanca. To hold it at a distance, the Union needs a belt of insulation, comprising a 'second circle' of lands capable of integration into the Community, shielding it from the dangers of the 'third circle' beyond—that is, Russia, the Middle East and Black Africa. In this conception the respective buffer zones logically become Eastern Europe, Cyprus and Turkey in the Eastern Mediterranean, and the Maghreb. Middlemas, however, explains that while the first two are ultimately acceptable into the Union, the third remains inconceivable. For 'the countries of the Maghreb are irrelevant as a barrier to a sub-Saharan Africa, which presents no threat except via small numbers of illegal immigrants'. In fact, on the contrary, 'the *threat* comes from North Africa itself'.[46] If this is a more ecumenical approach than that of Garton Ash, who expressly excludes Turkey from Europe, it traces the same movement, common to all these tropes—a slide to aporia. Every attempt so far to delimit the future boundaries of the Union has deconstructed itself.

For the moment, it is enough to register that 'Europe Agreements', formally designated as antechambers to entry, have been signed by six countries: Poland, the Czech Republic, Hungary, Slovakia, Romania and Bulgaria; and that four more are impending (Slovenia and the Baltic states). It is only a matter of time before Croatia, Serbia, Macedonia, Albania and what is left of Bosnia join the queue. Does this prospect—we might call it an inverted domino effect, in which the pieces fall inwards rather than outwards—mean that the British scenario will come to pass? Harold Macmillan once spoke, with a homely national touch, of his hope that the Community, when exposed to the beneficent pressure of a vast free-trade area, would 'melt like a lump of sugar in a cup of tea'.[47] Such remains the preferred vision of his

---

46. Keith Middlemas, *Orchestrating Europe*, London 1995, pp. 664–5.
47. Duchêne, *Jean Monnet*, p. 320.

successors. Their calculation is that the more member-states there are, the less sovereignty can practically be pooled, and the greater is the chance that federal dreams will fold. How realistic is it?

There is no doubt that enlargement of the Union to some two dozen states would fundamentally alter its nature. If its existing arrangements were simply extended east, the cost of integrating the Visegrád quartet alone could mean an increase of 60 per cent in the Union budget. There is no chance of the existing member-states accepting such a burden, at a time when every domestic pressure is towards tax reduction. That leaves either reducing current support to farming communities and poorer regions in the west, composed of voters with the power to resist, or watering down the *acquis communautaire* to create a second-class membership for new entrants, without benefit of the transfers accorded to first-class members.

These are just the fiscal headaches attending rapid expansion. There are also the material consequences for the former Communist economies. If the effort of adhering to the convergence criteria for monetary union is already straining prosperous Western societies to breaking point, can impoverished Eastern ones be expected to sustain them? No previous candidates, however initially disadvantaged, had to scale such a macro-economic cliff. Contemplating the requirements of EMU, it is not suprising that enthusiasts for expansion are starting to call for the whole idea of a single currency to be dropped. For Garton Ash, the needs of Warsaw and Prague dovetail with what is anyway the wisdom of London. 'Europe could perhaps use a little more British thinking at the moment', he writes of monetary union, 'with "British" here meant in the deeper sense of our particular intellectual tradition: sceptical, empirical and pragmatic'.[48] The suspicion that EMU and Eastern enlargement might be incompatible is shared from the opposite standpoint by the unlikely figure of Jacques Attali, who regards the single currency as a valid but now lost cause, and enlargement as a German project that will lead away from a federal Europe, for which most of the national elites, mesmerized by American culture, anyway have no appetite. *L'Europe ne s'aime pas*, he glumly observed at the end of the Mitterrand experience.[49]

Maastricht is unlikely to evaporate so easily. But the hazards of enlargement do not just lie in the economic pitfalls it poses for

---

48. Garton Ash, 'Catching the Wrong Bus?'
49. Jacques Attali, *Europe(s)*, Paris 1994, pp. 15, 147–50, 181–99.

new or old members. Even if derogations of various kinds—from the Common Agricultural Policy, from the Structural Funds, from the single currency—were to be made for what were once the 'captive nations', a more fundamental difficulty would remain, of a purely political nature. To double its membership could cripple the existing institutions of the Union. Already the original balance of the Six or the Nine has been thrown out of kilter in the Council of Ministers. Today the five largest states—Germany, France, Italy, Britain and Spain—contain 80 per cent of the population of the Union, but command only just more than half of the votes in the Council. If the ten current ex-Communist applicants were members, the share of these states would fall even further, while the proportion of poor countries in the Union—those now entitled to substantial transfers—would rise from four out of fifteen to a majority of fourteen out of twenty-five.

Adjustment of voting weights could bring the *pays légal* some way back towards the *pays réel*. But it would not resolve potentially the most intractable problem posed by enlargement to the east, which lies in the logic of numbers. Ex-satellite Europe contains almost exactly as many states as continuously capitalist Europe (at the latest count, sixteen in the 'East' to seventeen in the 'West', if we include Switzerland), with a third of the population. Proliferation of partners on this scale, no matter how the inequalities between them were finessed, threatens institutional gridlock. *Rebus sic stantibus*, the size of the European Parliament would swell towards eight hundred deputies; the number of commissioners rise to forty; a ten-minute introductory speech by each minister attending a Council yield a meeting of five hours, before business even started. The legendary complexity of the already existing system, with its meticulous rotations of commissarial office, laborious inter-governmental bargains and assorted ministerial and parliamentary vetoes, would be overloaded to the point of paralysis.

In such conditions, would not widening inevitably mean loosening? This is the wager in London, expressed more or less openly according to venue, from the FCO to the *TLS*. In the long term, the official line of thinking goes, expansion must mean defederalization. Yet is this the only logical deduction? Here we encounter the final amphibology. For might not precisely the prospect of institutional deadlock impose as an absolute functional necessity a much more centralized supranational authority than exists today? Coordination of twelve to fifteen member states can just about operate, however cumbersomely, on a basis of consensus. Multiplication to thirty practically rules this out. The more states enter the Union, the greater the discrepancy between population and representation in the Council of Ministers will tend to be, as large countries are increasingly outnumbered by smaller ones, and the weaker overall decisional capacity would become. The result could paradoxically be the opposite of the British expectation—not a dilution, but a concentration of federal power in a new constitutional settlement, in which national voting weights are redistributed and majority decisions become normal. The problem of scale, in other words, might force just the cutting of the institutional knot the proponents of a loose free trade area seek to avoid. Widening could check or reverse deepening. It might also precipitate it.

Each of the three critical issues now facing the European Union— the single currency, the role of Germany, and the multiplication of member-states—thus presents a radical indeterminacy. In every case, the distinctive form of the amphibology is the same. One set of meanings is so drastic it appears subject to capsizal into its contrary, giving rise to a peculiar uncertainty. These are the political quicksands on which the Europe to come will be built.

OUTCOMES

2007

An epiphany is beguiling Europe. Far from dwindling in historical significance, the Old World is about to assume an importance for humanity it never, in all its days of dubious past glory, possessed. At the end of *Postwar*, his eight-hundred-page account of the continent since 1945, the historian Tony Judt exclaims at 'Europe's emergence in the dawn of the twenty-first century as a paragon of the international virtues: a community of values held up by Europeans and non-Europeans alike as an exemplar for all to emulate'. The reputation, he eagerly assures us, is 'well-earned'.[1] The same vision grips the seers of New Labour. *Why Europe Will Run the 21st Century* declaims the title of a manifesto by Mark Leonard, the party's foreign policy *Wunderkind*. 'Imagine a world of peace, prosperity and democracy', he enjoins the reader. 'What I am asking you to imagine is the "New European Century"'. How will this entrancing prospect come about? 'Europe represents a synthesis of the energy and freedom that come from liberalism with the stability and welfare that come from social democracy. As the world becomes richer and moves beyond satisfying basic needs such as hunger and health, the European way of life will become irresistible'.[2] Really? Absolutely. 'As India, Brazil, South Africa, and even China develop economically and express themselves politically, the European model will represent an irresistibly attractive way of enhancing their prosperity whilst protecting

---

1. *Postwar*, London 2005, p. 799.
2. Mark Leonard, *Why Europe Will Run the 21st Century*, London 2005, pp. 7, 85.

their security. They will join with the EU in building "a New European Century" '.[3]

Not to be outdone, the futurologist Jeremy Rifkin—American by birth, but by any standards an honorary European: indeed a personal adviser to Romano Prodi when he was president of the European Commission—has offered his guide to *The European Dream*. Seeking 'harmony, not hegemony', he tells us, the EU 'has all the right markings to claim the moral high ground on the journey toward a third stage of human consciousness. Europeans have laid out a visionary roadmap to a new promised land, one dedicated to re-affirming the life-instinct and the Earth's indivisibility'.[4] After a lyrical survey of this route—typical staging-posts: 'Governing without a Centre', 'Romancing the Civil Society', 'A Second Enlightenment'—Rifkin, warning us against cynicism, concludes: 'These are tumultuous times. Much of the world is going dark, leaving many human beings without clear direction. The European Dream is a beacon of light in a troubled world. It beckons us to a new age of inclusivity, diversity, quality of life, deep play, sustainability, universal human rights, the rights of nature, and peace on Earth'.[5]

These transports may seem peculiarly Anglo-Saxon, but there is no shortage of more prosaic equivalents on the continent. For Germany's leading philosopher, Jürgen Habermas, Europe has found 'exemplary solutions' for two great issues of the age, 'governance beyond the nation-state' and systems of welfare that 'serve as a model' to the world. So why not triumph in a third? 'If Europe has solved two problems of this magnitude, why shouldn't it issue a further challenge: to defend and promote a cosmopolitan order on the basis of international law?'[6]—or, as his compatriot the sociologist Ulrich Beck puts it, 'Europeanisation means creating a new politics. It means entering as a player into the meta-power game, into the struggle to form the rules of a new global order. The catchphrase for the future might be: Move over America—Europe is back'.[7] Over in France, Marcel Gauchet, theorist of democracy and an editor of the country's central journal of ideas, *Le Débat*, explains that 'we may be allowed to

---

3. *Why Europe Will Run the Twenty-First Century*, p. 4.

4. Jeremy Rifkin, *The European Dream: How Europe's Vision of the Future is Quietly Eclipsing the American Dream*, Cambridge 2004, p. 382.

5. *The European Dream*, p. 385.

6. Jürgen Habermas, *The Divided West*, Cambridge 2006, p. 43.

7. 'Ulrich Beck, Understanding the Real Europe', *Dissent*, Summer 2003.

think that the formula the Europeans have pioneered is destined eventually to serve as a model for the nations of the world. That lies in its genetic programme'.[8]

I

Self-satisfaction is, of course, scarcely unfamiliar in Europe. But the contemporary mood is something different: an apparently illimitable narcissism, in which the reflection in the water transfigures the future of the planet into the image of the beholder. What explains this degree of political vanity? Obviously, the landscape of the continent has altered in recent years, and its role in the world has grown. Real changes can give rise to surreal dreams, but they need to be calibrated properly, to see what the connexions or lack of them might be. A decade ago, three great imponderables lay ahead: the advent of monetary union, as designed at Maastricht; the return of Germany to regional preponderance, with reunification; and the expansion of the EU into Eastern Europe. The outcome of each remained *ex ante* indeterminate. How far have they been clarified since?

Of its nature, the introduction of a single currency, adopted simultaneously by eleven out of fifteen member-states of the EU on the first day of 1999, marked the most punctual and systematic transformation of the three. It was always reasonable to suppose its effects would be the soonest visible, and most clear-cut. Yet this has proved so only in the most limited technical sense, that the substitution of a dozen monies by one (Greece joined in 2002) was handled extremely smoothly, without glitch or mishap: an administrative *tour de force*. Otherwise, contrary to general expectations, the net upshot of the monetary union that came into force in the Eurozone eight years ago remains inconclusive. The stated purpose of the single currency was to lower transaction costs and increase predictability of returns for business, so unleashing higher investment and faster growth of productivity and output.

But to date the causes have failed to generate the results. The dynamic effects of SEA, the 'single market act' of 1986, held by most orthodox economists to be an initiative of greater significance than EMU, had already been wildly oversold—the official Cecchini Report estimated it would add between 4.3 and

---

8. 'Le problème européen', *Le Débat*, No. 129, March–April 2004, p. 66.

6.4 percent to the GDP of the Community whereas in reality it yielded gains of little over 1 per cent. So far, the pay-off for EMU has been even more disappointing. Far from picking up, growth in the Eurozone initially slowed down, from an average of 2.4 per cent in the five years before monetary union, to 2.1 in the first five years after it. Even with the modest acceleration of 2004–7, it remains below the level of the eighties. In 2000, on the heels of the single currency, the Lisbon summit promised to create within ten years 'the most competitive and dynamic knowledge-based economy in the world'. In the event, the EU has so far recorded a growth rate well below that of the US, and lagged far behind China. Caught between the scientific and technological magnetism of America, where two-fifths of all scientists—some 400,000—are now EU-born, and the cheap labour of the PRC, where average wages are twenty times lower, Europe has not had much to show for its bombast.

Not only has the performance of the single-currency bloc been well below the American. More pointedly, the Eurozone has been outstripped by those countries within the EU which declined to scrap their own currencies—Sweden, Britain, and Denmark all posting higher rates of growth over the same period. Casting a further shadow over the legacy of Maastricht, the Stability Pact, which was supposed to ensure that fiscal indiscipline at national level would not undermine monetary rigour at supranational level, has been breached repeatedly and with impunity by both Germany and France, the two leading economies of the Eurozone. Had its deflationary impact been enforced, as it was on a weaker Portugal, in less position to resist, overall growth would have been yet lower.

Still, it would be premature to think that any unequivocal verdict on monetary union was yet in. Its advocates point to Ireland and Spain as success stories within the Eurozone, and look to the general economic upturn of the past year, led by Germany, as a sign that EMU may at length now be coming into its own. Above all, they can vaunt the strength of the euro itself. Not only are long-term interest rates in the Eurozone below those in the US. More strikingly, the euro has overtaken the dollar as the world's premier currency in the international bond market. One result has been to power a wave of cross-border mergers and acquisitions in Euroland itself, evidence of the kind of capital deepening the architects of monetary union envisaged. Given the notorious volatility of relative regional and national standings in the world economy—Japan's is only the most spectacular reversal of fortune since the eighties—might not the Eurozone, after somewhat more than seven lean years, now be poised for their biblical opposite?

Here, clearly, much depends on the degree of European interconnexion with, or insulation from, the US economy which dominates global demand. The mediocrity of Eurozone performance since 1999, attributable in the eyes of economic liberals to statist inertias and labour-market rigidities which it has taken time to overcome, but that are now giving way, has unfolded against the background of a global conjuncture, driven principally by American consumption, that for the last five years has been highly favourable—world economic growth averaging over 4.5 per cent, a rate not seen since the sixties. A large part of this boom has come from rocketing house prices, above all, of course, in the US, but also across much of the OECD as a whole—not least in such once peripheral economies as Spain and Ireland, where construction has been the linchpin of recent growth. In the major Eurozone economies, on the other hand, where mortgages have never been so central to financial markets, such effects have been subdued. One moment of truth will come for EMU if and when there is any abrupt, as distinct from gradual, decline in the American housing market. Relatively immune to mortgage fevers during the boom, how far would the Eurozone be sheltered from a transatlantic recession?

The role of Germany in the new Europe remains no less ambiguous. Absorption of the DDR has restored the country to its standing at the beginning of the twentieth century as the strategically central land of the continent, the most populous nation and the largest economy. But the longer-term consequences of reunification have still to unfold. Internationally, the Berlin Republic has unquestionably become more assertive, shedding a range of post-war inhibitions. In the past decade the Luftwaffe has returned to the Balkans, *Einsatztruppen* are fighting in West Asia, the Deutsche Marine patrols in the Eastern Mediterranean. But these have been subcontracted enterprises, in NATO or UN operations governed by the United States, not independent initiatives. Diplomatic postures have been more significant than military. Under Schröder, close ties were developed with Russia, in an entente that became the most distinctive feature of his foreign policy. But this was not a second Rapallo Pact, at the expense of western neighbours. Under Chirac and Berlusconi, France and

Italy courted Putin scarcely less, but with fewer economic trumps in hand. In Europe itself, the Red-Green government in Berlin, for all its well-advertised generational lack of complexes, never rocked the boat in the way its Christian-Democrat predecessor in Bonn had done. Since 1991, in fact, there has been no action to compare with Kohl's unilateral recognition of Slovenia, precipitating the disintegration of Yugoslavia. Merkel has moved successfully to circumvent the will of French and Dutch voters, but was in no position to deliver this on her own. The prospects of any informal German hegemony in Europe, classically considered, seem at present remote.

Part of the reason for the relatively subdued profile of the new Germany has, of course, been the costs of re-unification itself, for which the bill to date has come to more than a trillion dollars, saddling the country for years with stagnation, high unemployment, and mounting public debt. This was a period in which France, though no greyhound itself, consistently outpaced Germany, posting faster rates of growth for a full decade, from 1994 to 2004, with over double its increase in GDP in the first five years of the new century. In 2006, substantial German recovery finally arrived, and the tables have been turned. Currently the world's leading exporter, the German economy now looks as if it might be about to exercise once again something like the European dominance it enjoyed in the days of Schmidt and the early Kohl. Then it was the tight money policies of the Bundesbank that held its neighbours by the throat. With the euro, that form of pressure has gone. What threatens to replace it is the remarkable wage repression on which German recovery has been based. Between 1998 and 2006, unit labour costs in Germany actually *fell*—in a staggering feat, real wages declined for seven straight years— while they rose some 15 per cent in France and Britain, and between 25 and 35 per cent in Spain, Italy, Portugal and Greece. With devaluation now barred, the Mediterranean countries are suffering a drastic loss of competitiveness, that augurs ill for the whole southern tier of the EU. Harsher forms of German power, pulsing through the market rather than issuing from the high command or central bank, may lie in store. It is too soon to write off a regional *Grossmacht*.

Germany has now been re-united for sixteen years. A single currency has circulated for eight years. The enlargement of the

EU is just over three years old. It would be strange if its outcomes were already clearer. In practice, of course, the expansion of the EU to the East was set in motion in 1993, and completed— for the moment—in 2007, with the accession of Romania and Bulgaria, and at one level it is plain why it should be perhaps the principal source of satisfaction in today's chorus of European self-congratulation. All nine former 'captive nations' of the Soviet bloc have been integrated without a hitch into the Union. Only the lands of a once independent Communism, in the time of Tito and Hoxha, wait to join the fold, and even there a start has been made with Slovenia. Capitalism has been restored smoothly and speedily, without vexing delays or derogations. Indeed, as the director-general of the EU Commission for Enlargement has recently observed: 'Nowadays the level of privatization and liberalization of the market is often higher in new Member States than old ones'.[9] In this newly freed zone, rates of growth have also been considerably faster than in the larger economies to the west.

No less impressive has been the virtually frictionless implantation of political systems matching liberal norms— representative democracies complete with civil rights, elected parliaments, separation of powers, alternation of governments. Under the benevolent but watchful eye of the Commission, seeing to it that criteria laid down at Copenhagen in 1993 were properly met, Eastern Europe has been shepherded into the comity of free nations. There was no backsliding. The elites of the region were in most cases only too anxious to oblige. For their populations, constitutional niceties were less important than higher standards of living, once the late-communist yoke was thrown off, although few if any citizens were indifferent to the humbler liberties of speech, occupation or travel. When the time for accession came, there was assent, but little enthusiasm. Only in two countries out of ten—Lithuania and Slovenia—did a majority of the electorate turn out to vote for it, in referenda which most of the population elsewhere ignored, no doubt in part because they regarded it as a *fait accompli* by their leaders anyway.

Still, however technocratic or top-down the mechanics of enlargement may have been, the formal unification of the two halves of Europe is a historical accomplishment of the first order.

---

9. Eneko Landabaru, 'The Need for Enlargement and the Differences from Previous Accessions', in George Vassiliou (ed.), *The Accession Story: The EU from Fifteen to Twenty-Five Countries*, Oxford 2007, p. 15.

This is not because it has restored the countries of the East to an age-long common home, from which only a malign fate—the totalitarian grip of Russia—wrested them after the Second World War, as the ideologues of Central Europe, Kundera and others, have argued. The division of the continent has deeper roots, and goes back much further, than the pact at Yalta. In a well-received book, the American historian Larry Wolff has taxed travellers and thinkers of the Enlightenment with 'The Invention of Eastern Europe' as a supercilious myth of the eighteenth century. The reality is that from the time of the Roman Empire onwards, the lands now covered by the new member-states of the Union were nearly always poorer, less literate and less urbanized than most of their counterparts to the west: prey to nomadic invasions from Asia; subjected to a second serfdom that spared neither the German lands beyond the Elbe nor even relatively advanced Bohemia; annexed by Habsburg, Romanov, Hohenzollern or Ottoman conquerors. Their fate in the Second World War and its aftermath was not an unhappy exception in their history, but—catastrophically speaking—par for the course.

It is this millennial record, of repeated humiliation and oppression, that entry into the Union offers a chance, finally, to leave behind. Who, with any sense of the history of the continent, could fail to be moved by the prospect of a cancellation in the inequality of its nations' destinies? The original design for EU expansion to the East was a joint product of German strategy under Kohl and interested local elites, seconded by assorted Anglo-American publicists. It aimed to fast-track Poland, Hungary and the Czech Republic into the Union, as the most congenial states of the region, with the staunchest records of resistance to communism and most westernized political classes, leaving less favoured societies to kick their heels in the rear. Happily, this invidious redivision of the East was avoided. Credit for preventing it must go in the first instance to France, which from the beginning advocated a 'regatta' approach, insisting on the inclusion of Romania, which made it difficult to exclude Bulgaria; to Sweden, which championed Estonia, with the same effect on Latvia and Lithuania; and to the Prodi Commission, which eventually rallied to comprehensive rather than selective enlargement. The result was a far more generous settlement than originally envisaged.

What of the upshot of expansion from the other end, for the Union itself? Thanks to the modesty of the share of Structural Funds allocated to the East, its financial cost has been significantly less than once estimated, and the balance of trade has favoured the more powerful economies of the West. This, however, is the small change of enlargement. The real takings—or bill, depending on who is looking at it—lie elsewhere. Core European capital now has a major pool of cheap labour at its disposal, conveniently located on its doorstep, not only dramatically lowering its production costs in plants to the East, but capable of exercising pressure on wages and conditions in the West. The archetypal case is Slovakia, where wages in the auto industry are one-eighth of those in Germany, and more cars per capita are shortly going to be produced—Volkswagen and Peugeot in the lead—than in any other country in the world. It is the fear of such relocation, with closure of factories at home, that has cowed so many German workers into accepting longer hours and less pay. Race-to-the-bottom pressures are not confined to wages. The ex-Communist states have pioneered flat taxes to woo investment, and now compete with one another for the lowest possible rate: Estonia started with 26 per cent, Slovakia offers 19 per cent, Romania advertises 16 per cent, and bids at 15 per cent are being mooted in Poland.

The role configured by the new East in the EU, in other words, promises to be something like that played by the new South in the American economy since the seventies: a zone of business-friendly fiscal regimes, weak or non-existent labour movements, low wages and—therefore—high investments, registering faster growth than in the older core regions of continent-wide capital. Like the US South, too, the region seems likely to fall somewhat short of the standards of political respectability expected in the rest of the Union. Already, now that they are safely inside the EU and there is no longer the same need to be on their best behaviour, the elites of the region show signs of kicking over the traces. In Poland, the reigning twins defy every norm of ideological correctness as understood in Strasbourg or Brussels. In Hungary, riot police stand on guard around a ruler who has vaunted his mendacity. In the Czech Republic, months pass without parliament being able to form a government. In Romania, the president insults the prime minister in a phone-in call to a television talk-show. But as in Kentucky or Alabama, such provincial quirks add a touch of folkloric colour to the drab metropolitan scene more than they disturb it.

All analogies have their limits. The distinctive role of the new South in the political economy of the US has depended in part on immigration attracted by the region's climate, which has given it rates of demographic growth well above the national average. Eastern Europe, which offers no comparably broad Sunbelt, is much more likely to suffer out-migration, as the recent tide of Poles arriving in Britain, and similar numbers from the Baltics and elsewhere coming to Ireland and Sweden, suggest. But labour mobility in any direction is—and, for obvious linguistic and cultural reasons, will remain— far lower in the EU than in the US. Local welfare systems, inherited from the Communist past, and not yet much dismantled, are also potential constraints on a Southern path. Nor does the East, with less than a quarter of the population of the Union, have anything like the relative weight of the South in the United States, not to speak of the political leverage of the region at federal level. For the moment, the effect of enlargement has essentially been much what the Foreign Office and the employers lobbies in Brussels always hoped it would be: the distension of the EU into a vast free-trade zone, with a newly acquired periphery of cheap labour.

The integration of the East into the Union is the major achievement to which admirers of the new Europe can legitimately point. Of course, as with the standard encomia of the record of EU as a whole, there is a certain gap between ideology and reality in the claims made for it. The Community that became a Union was never responsible for the 'fifty years of peace' conventionally ascribed to it, a piety attributing to Brussels what in any strict sense belonged to Washington. When actual wars threatened in Yugoslavia, far from preventing their outbreak, the Union if anything helped to trigger them. In not dissimilar fashion, publicists for the EU often imply that without enlargement, Eastern Europe would never have reached the safe harbour of democracy, foundering in new forms of totalitarianism or barbarism. There is more substance to this argument, since the EU has supervised stabilization of the political systems of the region, with a good deal of direct interference. But it too exaggerates dangers in the service of vanities. The EU played no role in the overthrow of the regimes installed by Stalin, and there is little sign that any of the countries in which they fell were at risk of lapsing into new dictatorships, had it not been for the saving hand of the Commission. Enlargement has been a sufficient historical annealment, and—so far—economic success, not to require claims that it has also been, counter-factually, a political deliverance. The standard hype demeans rather than elevates what has been accomplished.

*   *   *

There remains the largest question. What has been the impact of expansion to the East on the institutional framework of the EU itself? Here the glass darkens. For if enlargement has been the principal achievement of the recent period, the constitution that was supposed to renovate the Union has been its most signal failure, and the potential interactions between the two remain a matter of obscurity. The 'Convention on the Future of Europe' decided on at Laeken met in early 2002, and in mid-2003 delivered a draft European Constitution, agreed by the European Council in the summer of 2004. Delegates from candidate countries were nominally included in the Convention, but since the Convention itself amounted to little more than window-dressing for the labours of its president, Giscard d'Estaing, assisted by a British factotum, John Kerr—the two real authors of the draft—their presence was of no consequence. The future charter of Europe was written for the establishments of the West—the governments of the existing fifteen member-states who had to approve it, relegating the countries of the East to onlookers. In effect, the logic of a constituent will was inverted: instead of enlargement becoming the common basis of a new framework, the framework was erected before enlargement.

The ensuing debacle came as a brief thunderclap to the Western elites. The Constitution—more than five hundred pages long, comprising 446 articles and 36 supplementary protocols, a bureaucratic elephantiasis without precedent—increased the power of the four largest states in the Union: Germany, France, Britain and Italy; topped the inter-governmental complex in which they would have greater sway with a five-year presidency, unelected by the European Parliament, let alone the citizens of the Union; and inscribed the imperatives of a 'highly competitive' market, 'free of distortions' as a foundational principle of political law, beyond the reach of popular choice. The founders of the American republic would have rubbed their eyes in disbelief at such a ponderous and rickety construction. But so overwhelming was the consensus of the continent's media and political class behind it, that few doubted it would come into force. To the astonishment of their rulers, however, voters made short work of it. In France, where the government was unwise enough to dispatch copies of the document to every voter—Giscard complained of this folly with his handiwork—little was left of it at the end of a referendum campaign in which a spirited popular opposition, without the support of a single mainstream party, newspaper, magazine, let alone radio or television programme, routed an establishment united in endorsing it. Rarely, even in recent French history, had a *pensée* quite so *unique* been up-ended so spectacularly.

In the last days of the campaign, as polls showed increasing rejection of the Constitution among the voters, panic gripped the French media. But no local hysterics, though there were many, rivalled those across the border in Germany. 'Europe Demands Courage', admonished Günter Grass, Jürgen Habermas and a cohort of like-minded German intellectuals, in an open letter dispatched to *Le Monde*. Warning their neighbours that 'France would isolate itself fatally if it were to vote "No" ', they went on: 'The consequences of a rejection would be catastrophic', indeed 'an invitation to suicide', for 'without courage there is no survival'. In member-states new and old 'the Constitution fulfils a dream of centuries', and to vote for it was a duty not just to the living, but to the dead: 'we owe this to the millions upon millions of victims of our lunatic wars and criminal dictatorships'.[10] This from a country where no democratic consultation of the electorate was risked, and pro forma ratification of the Constitution was stage-managed in the Bundesrat to impress French voters a few days before the referendum, with Giscard as guest of honour at the podium. As for French isolation, three days later the Dutch—told, still more bluntly, that Auschwitz awaited Europe if they failed to vote yes—threw out the Constitution by an even wider margin.

Such two-fold popular repudiation of the charter for a new Europe was not in reality a bolt from the blue. The Constitution was rejected, not because it was too federalist, but because it seemed little more than an impenetrable scheme for the redistribution of oligarchic power, embodying everything most distrusted in the arrogant, opaque system the EU appeared to have become. Virtually every time—there have not been many—that voters have been allowed to express an opinion about the direction the Union was taking, they have rejected it. The Norwegians refused the EC *tout court*; the Danes declined Maastricht; the Irish, the Treaty of Nice; the Swedes, the euro. Each time, the political class promptly sent them back to the polls to correct their mistake, or waited for an occasion to reverse the verdict. The operative maxim of the EU has become Brecht's dictum: in case of setback, the government should dissolve the people and elect a new one.

Predictably, amidst the celebrations of the fiftieth anniversary of

---

10. See *Le Monde*, 20 May 2005.

the Treaty of Rome, Europe's heads of state were soon discussing how to cashier the popular will once again, and reimpose the Constitution with cosmetic alterations, without exposing it this time to the risks of a democratic decision. At the Brussels summit in June 2007, the requisite adjustment—now renamed a simple treaty—was agreed. To let Britain disavow a referendum, it was exempted from the Charter of Fundamental Rights to which all other member-states subscribed. To throw a sop to French opinion, references to unfettered competition were tucked away in a protocol, rather than appearing in the main document. To square the conscience of the Dutch, 'promotion of European values' was made a test of membership. To save the face of Poland's rulers, the demotion of their country to second-rank in the Council was deferred for a decade, leaving their successors to come to terms with it.

The principal novelty of this gathering to resuscitate what French and Dutch voters had buried was Germany's determination to ensure its primacy in the electoral structure of the Council. Polish objections to a formula doubling Germany's weight, and drastically reducing Poland's, had—for reasons that voting theory in international organizations has long made clear, as experts in such matters pointed out—every technical consideration of fairness on their side. But issues of equity were no more relevant than issues of democracy to the outcome. After blustering that demographic losses in the Second World War entitled Poland to proportionate compensation in the design of the Union, the Kaczynski twins crumpled as quickly as the country's pre-war colonels before the German blitz. Brave talk forgotten, it was all over in a phone-call. For the region where Poland accounts for nearly half the population and GDP, the episode is a lesson in the tacit hierarchy of states it has entered. The East is welcome, but should not get above itself. For these purposes at least, *Deutschland* is once again *über alles*.

Not that crumbs are unavailable. As the British, Dutch, and French rulers, so the Polish too received, with the postponement of their demotion, the fig-leaf needed to dispense them from submitting the reanimated Constitution to the opinion of their voters. It was left to Ireland's premier Ahern—along with Blair, another of the conference's recent escapees from a cloud of corruption—to exclaim, in a moment of unguarded delight: '90 per cent of it is still there!' Even loyal commentators have found it difficult to suppress all disgust at the cynicism of this latest exercise in the 'Community method'. The contrast between such realities and the placards of the touts for the new Europe could scarcely be starker. The truth is that the light of the world, role-model for humanity at large, cannot even count on the consent of its populations at home.

2

What kind of political order, then, is taking shape in Europe, fifteen years after Maastricht? The pioneers of European integration—Monnet and his fellow-spirits—envisaged the eventual creation of a federal union that would one day be the supranational equivalent of the nation-states out of which it emerged, anchored in an expanded popular sovereignty, based on universal suffrage, its executive answerable to an elected legislature, and its economy subject to requirements of social responsibility. In short, a democracy magnified to semi-continental scale (they had only Western Europe in mind). But there was always another way of looking at European unification, which saw it more as a limited pooling of powers by member-governments for certain—principally economic—ends, that did not imply any fundamental derogation of national sovereignty as traditionally understood, but rather the creation of a novel institutional framework for a specified range of transactions between them. De Gaulle famously represented one version of this outlook; Thatcher another. Between these federalist and inter-governmentalist visions of Europe, there has been a tension down to the present.

What has come into being, however, corresponds to neither. Constitutionally, the EU is a caricature of a democratic federation, since its Parliament lacks powers of initiative, contains no parties with any existence at European level, and wants even a modicum of popular credibility. Modest increments in its rights have not only failed to increase public interest in this body, but have been accompanied by a further decline in it. Participation in European elections has sunk steadily, to below 50 per cent, and the newest voters are the most indifferent of all. In the East, the regional figure in 2004 was scarcely more than 30 per cent; in Slovakia less than 17 per cent of voters cast a ballot for their delegates to Strasbourg. Such *ennui* is not irrational. The European Parliament is a Merovingian legislature. The mayor in the palace is the Council of Ministers, where real law-making decisions are taken, topped by the European Council of the heads of state, meeting every three months. Yet this complex in turn fails the opposite logic of an inter-governmental authority, since it is the Commission alone—the EU's unelected executive—that can propose the laws on which the Council and (more notionally) the Parliament deliberate. The violation of a constitutional separation of powers in this dual authority—a bureaucracy vested with a monopoly of legislative initiative—is flagrant. Alongside this hybrid executive, moreover, is an independent judiciary, the European Court, capable of rulings discomfiting any national government.

At the centre of this maze lies the obscure zone in which the rival law-making instances of the Council and the Commission interlock, more impenetrable than any other feature of the Union. The nexus of 'Coreper' committees in Brussels, where emissaries of the former confer behind closed doors with functionaries of the latter, generates the avalanche of legally binding directives that form the main output of the EU: close on 100,000 pages to date. Here is the effective point of concentration of everything summed up in the phrase—smacking, characteristically, of the counting-house rather than the forum—'democratic deficit', one ritually deplored by EU officials themselves. In fact, what the trinity of Council, Coreper and Commission figures is not just an absence of democracy—though it is certainly also that—but an attenuation of politics of any kind, as ordinarily understood. The effect of this axis is to short-circuit—above all at the critical Coreper level—national legislatures, which are continually confronted with a mass of decisions over which they lack any oversight, without affording any supranational accountability in compensation, given the shadow-play of the Parliament in Strasbourg. The farce of popular consultations that are regularly ignored is only the most dramatic expression of this oligarchic structure, which sums up the rest.

Alongside their negation of democratic principles, two further, and less familiar, features of these arrangements stand out. The vast majority of the decisions of the Council, Commission and Coreper concern domestic issues that were traditionally debated in national legislatures. But in the conclaves at Brussels, these become the object of diplomatic negotiations—that is, of the kind of treatment classically reserved for foreign or military affairs, where parliamentary controls are usually weak to non-existent, and executive discretion more or less untrammelled. Since the Renaissance, secrecy has always been the other name of diplomacy. What the core structures of the EU effectively do is to convert the open agenda of parliaments into the closed world of chancelleries. But even this is not all of it. Traditional diplomacy typically required stealth and surprise for success. But it did not preclude discord or rupture. Classically, it involved a war of manoeuvre between parties capable of breaking as well as making alliances; sudden shifts in the terrain of negotiations; alterations of means and objectives—in short, politics conducted between states, as distinct from within them, but politics nonetheless. In the disinfected universe of the EU, this all but disappears, as unanimity becomes virtually *de rigueur* on all significant occasions—any public disagreement, let alone refusal to accept a prefabricated consensus, increasingly being treated as if it were an unthinkable breach of etiquette. The deadly conformism of EU summits, smugly celebrated by theorists of 'consociational democracy' as if it were anything other than a cartel of self-protective elites, closes the coffin of even real diplomacy, covering it with wreaths of bureaucratic piety. Nothing is left to move the popular will, as democratic participation and political imagination are each snuffed out.

These structures have been some time in the making. Unreformed, they could not but be reinforced by enlargement. The distance between rulers and ruled, wide enough in a Community of nine or twelve countries, can only widen much further in a Union of twenty-seven or more, where economic and social circumstances differ so vastly that the Gini coefficient in the EU is now higher than in the US, the fabled land of inequality itself. It was always the calculation of adversaries of European federalism, successive British governments at their head, that the more extended the Community became, the less chance there was of any deepening of its institutions in a democratic direction, for the more impractical any conception of popular sovereignty in a supranational union would become. Their intentions have come to pass. Stretched to nearly 500 million citizens, the EU of today is in no position to recall the dreams of Monnet.

So what? There is no shortage of apologists prepared to explain that it is not just wrong to complain of a lack of democracy in the Union, conventionally understood, but that this is actually its greatest virtue. The standard argument, to be found in journals like *Prospect*, goes like this. The EU deals essentially with the technical and administrative issues—market competition, product specification, consumer protection and the like—posed by the aim of the Treaty of Rome to assure the free movement of goods, persons and capital within its borders. These are matters in which voters have little interest, rightly taking the view that they are best handled by appropriate experts, rather than incompetent parliamentarians. Just as the police, fire brigade or officer corps are not elected, but enjoy the widest public trust, so it is—at any rate tacitly—with the functionaries in Brussels. The democratic deficit is a myth, because matters which voters do care strongly about—preeminently taxes and social services, the real stuff of politics—continue to be decided not at Union but at national level, by traditional electoral mechanisms. So long as the separation between the two arenas and their respective types of decision is respected, and we are spared demagogic exercises in populism—putting issues the masses cannot understand, and which should never be on a ballot in the first place, to referenda—democracy remains intact, indeed enhanced. Considered soberly, all is for the best in the best of all possible Europes.

In an unreflective sense, this case might seem to appeal to a common immediate experience of the Union. If asked in what ways they have personally been affected by the EU, most of its citizens—at least those who live in the Eurozone and Schengen belt—would certainly not mention its technical directives; they would probably answer that travel has been simplified by the disappearance of border controls and the need to change currencies. Beyond such conveniences, a narrow stratum of professionals and executives, and a somewhat broader flow of migrant workers and craftsmen, have benefitted from occupational mobility across borders, though this is still quite limited, with less than 2 per cent of the population of the Union living outside their countries of origin. In some ways, more significant may be the programmes that take growing numbers of students to courses in other societies of the EU. Journeys, studies, a scattering of jobs: agreeable changes all, not vital issues. It is this expanse of mild amenities that no doubt explains the passivity of voters towards rulers who ignore their expressions of opinion. For nearly as striking as repeated popular rejection of official schemes for the Union is lack of reaction to subsequent flouting of it. The elites do not persuade the masses; but, to all appearances, they have little to fear from them.

Why then is there such persistent distrust of Brussels, if so little of what it does impinges on ordinary life, and at that quite pleasantly? Subjectively, the answer is clear. There are few citizens who are not banally alienated from the way they are governed at home—virtually every poll shows how little they believe in what their rulers say, and how powerless they feel to alter what they do. Yet these are still societies in which elections are regularly held, and governments that become too disliked can be evicted. No one doubts that democracy, in this minimal sense, obtains. At European level, however, there is all too obviously not even this vestige of accountability: the grounds for alienation are cubed. If the EU really had zero impact on what voters actually care about, of course, their distrust could be dismissed as a mere abstract prejudice. But in fact the intuition behind it is accurate. Since the Treaty of Maastricht, the Union has by no means been confined to regulatory issues of scant incidence or interest to ordinary folk. It now has a Central Bank, without even the commitment of the Federal Reserve to sustain employment, let alone its duty to report to Congress, that sets interest rates for the whole Eurozone, backed by a Stability Pact that requires national governments to meet hard budgetary targets. In other words, determination of macro-economic policy at the highest level has shifted upwards from national capitals to Frankfurt and Brussels. What this means is that just those issues that voters do indeed usually feel strongest about—jobs, taxes and social services—fall squarely under the guillotines of the Bank and the Commission. The history of the past years has shown that this is no academic matter. It was pressure from Brussels to cut public spending which led the Juppé government to introduce the fiscal package that detonated the great French strike-wave of the winter of 1995, and brought him down. It was the corset of the Stability Pact that forced Portugal—a small country unable to ignore it—into slashing social benefits and plunged the country into a steep recession in 2003. The government in Lisbon did not survive either. The notion that today's EU comprises little more than a set of innocuous technical rules, as value-neutral as traffic-lights, is an idle one.

Historically, there was from the beginning a third vision of what European integration should mean, distinct from either federalist or inter-governmentalist conceptions of the Community. Its far-sighted theorist was Hayek, who already before the Second World War had envisaged a constitutional structure raised sufficiently high above the nations composing it to exclude the danger of any popular sovereignty below impinging on it. In the nation-state, electorates were perpetually subject to *dirigiste* and redistributive temptations, encroaching on the rights of property in the name of democracy. But once heterogeneous populations were assembled in an inter-state federation, as he called it, they would not be able to re-create the united will that was prone to such ruinous interventions. Under an impartial authority, beyond the reach of political ignorance or envy, the spontaneous order of a market economy could finally unfold without interference.

By 1950, when Monnet was devising the Schuman Plan, Hayek himself was in America, and played little part in shaping discussion of integration. Later, rejecting the idea of a single currency as statist, in favour of competing private issues, he would come to the conclusion that the Community itself remained all too *dirigiste*. But in Germany, there was a school of theorists that saw the possibilities of European unity in similar terms, the Ordo-Liberals of Freiburg, whose leading thinkers were Walter Eucken, Wilhelm Röpke and Alfred Müller-Armack. Lacking Hayek's intransigent radicalism, they were close to Ludwig Erhard, the reputed architect of the post-war German miracle, and thereby had more real influence in the early days of the Common Market. But for thirty years, this was still a somewhat recessive gene in the make-up of the Community, latent but never the most salient in its development.

With the abrupt deterioration in the global economic climate in the seventies, and the general neo-liberal turn that followed in the eighties, Hayekian doctrine was rediscovered throughout the West. The leading edge of the change came in the UK and US, with the arrival of Thatcher and Reagan. Continental Europe never produced comparably radical regimes, but the ideological atmosphere shifted steadily in the same direction. The collapse of the Soviet bloc sealed the transformation of working assumptions. By the nineties, the Commission was openly committed to privatization as a principle, pressed without embarrassment on candidate countries along with other democratic niceties. Its most powerful arm had become the Competition Directorate, striking out at public sector monopolies in Western and Eastern Europe alike. In Frankfurt the Central Bank conformed perfectly with Hayek's pre-war prescriptions. What was originally the least prominent strand in the weave of European integration had become the dominant pattern. Federalism stymied, inter-governmentalism corroded, what had emerged was neither the rudiments of a European democracy controlled by its citizens, nor the formation of a European directory guided by its powers, but a vast zone of increasingly unbound market exchange, much closer to a European 'catallaxy' as Hayek had conceived it.

The mutation is by no means complete. The European Parliament is still there, as a memento of federal hopes forgone. Agricultural and regional subsidies, legacies of a cameralist past, continue to absorb most of the EU budget. But of a 'social Europe', in the sense intended by both Monnet and Delors, there is as little left as a democratic Europe. At national level, welfare regimes that distinguish the Old World from the New persist, of course. With the exception of Ireland, the share of state expenditure in GDP remains higher in Western Europe than in the United States, and the larger part of an academic industry—the 'varieties of capitalism literature'—is dedicated to showing how much more caring ours, above all the Nordic versions, are than theirs. The claim is valid enough; the self-satisfaction less so. For as the numbers of long-term jobless and pensioners have risen, the drift of the age has been away from earlier norms of provision, not beyond them. The very term 'reform' now means, virtually always, the opposite of what it denoted fifty years ago: not the creation, but a contraction, of welfare arrangements once prized by their recipients. Historically, the two chief structural advances beyond the post-war gains of social democracy—the Meidner plan for pension funds in Sweden, and the thirty-five-hour week in France—have both been rolled back. The tide is moving in the other direction.

Today's EU, with its pinched spending (just over 1 per cent of Union GDP), minuscule bureaucracy (around 16,000 officials, excluding translators), absence of independent taxation, and lack of any means of administrative enforcement, could in many ways be regarded as a *ne plus ultra* of the minimal state, beyond the most drastic imaginings of classical liberalism: less even than the dream of a nightwatchman. Its structure not only rules out a transfer, of the sort once envisaged by Delors, of social functions from national to supranational level, to counter-balance the strain these have come under from high rates of unemployment and growing numbers of pensioners. Its effect is to accentuate, rather than compensate, pressure on national systems of social provision, as so many impediments to the free movement of factors of production. As a leading authority explains: 'The neo-liberal bias of the EU, if it exists, is justified by the social-welfare bias of current national policies', which 'no responsible analyst believes can be maintained'—'European social policy exists only in the dreams of disgruntled socialists'. The salutary truth is that 'the EU is overwhelmingly about the promotion of free markets. Its primary interest group support comes from multinational firms, not least US ones'. In short: regnant in this Union is not democracy, and not welfare, but capital. 'The EU is basically about business'.[11]

3

That may be so, enthusiasts might reply, but why should it detract from the larger good that the EU represents in the world, a political community that stands alone in its respect for human rights, international law, aid to the poor of the earth, and protection of the environment? Could the Union not be described as the realization of the Enlightenment vision of the virtues of *le doux commerce*, that 'cure for the most destructive prejudices' as Montesquieu described it, pacifying relations between states in a spirit of mutual benefit and the rule of law?

In the current repertoire of tributes to Europe, it is this claim— the unique role and prestige of the EU on the world's stage—that now has pride of place. What it rests on, ubiquitously, is a contrast with the United States. America figures as the increasingly ominous, violent, swaggering Other of a humane continent of peace and progress—a society that is a law to itself, where Europe strives for a legal order binding on all. The values of the two, Habermas and many a fellow-thinker explain, have diverged: widespread gun culture, extreme economic inequality, fundamentalist religion and capital punishment, not to speak of national bravado, divide the US from the EU and foster a more regressive conception of international relations. Reversing Goethe's dictum, we have it better here.

The crystallization of these images came with the invasion of Iraq. The mass demonstrations against the war of 15 February 2003, Habermas thought, might go down in history as 'a signal for the birth of a European public'.[12] Even such an unlikely

---

11. Andrew Moravcsik, 'In Defence of the "Democratic Deficit": Reassessing Legitimacy in the European Union', *Journal of Common Market Studies*, Vol. 40, No. 4, November 2002, p. 618; *Financial Times*, 14 June 2005; 'Conservative Idealism and International Institutions', *Chicago Journal of International Law*, Vol. 1, No. 2, Autumn 2000, p. 310.
12. *The Divided West*, p. 40.

figure as Dominique Strauss-Kahn, recently installed head of
the IMF, announced that they marked the birth of a European
nation. But if this was a Declaration of Independence, was
the term 'nation' appropriate for what was being born? While
divergence with America over the Middle East could serve as a
negative definition of the emergent Europe, there was a positive
side that pointed in another conceptual direction. Enlargement
was the great new accomplishment of the Union. How should
it be theorized? In late 1991, a few months after the collapse of
the Soviet Union and a few days after the summit at Maastricht,
J.G.A. Pocock published a prophetic essay. A trenchant critic
of the EU, which he has always seen as involving a surrender
of sovereignty and identity—and with them conditions also of
democracy—to the market, though one never yet completed,
Pocock observed that Europe now faced the problem of
determining its frontiers, as 'once again an empire in the sense
of a civilized and stabilized zone which must decide whether to
extend or refuse its political power over violent and unstable
cultures along its borders'.[13]

At the time, this was not a formulation welcome in official
discourses on Europe. A decade later, the term it loosed with
irony has become a common coin of complacency. As the
countdown to Iraq proceeded, the British diplomat Robert
Cooper, special adviser on security to Blair, and later to Prodi
as head of the Commission, explained the merits of empire to
readers of *Prospect*. 'A system in which the strong protect the
weak, in which the efficient and well-governed export stability
and liberty, in which the world is open for investment and
growth—all of these seem eminently desirable'. Of course,
'in a world of human rights and bourgeois values, a new
imperialism will . . . have to be very different from the old'.
It would be a 'voluntary imperialism', of the sort admirably
displayed by the EU in the Balkans. Enlargement ahead, he
concluded, the Union was en route to the 'noble dream' of a
'cooperative empire'.[14]

Enlargement in the bag, the Polish theorist Jan Zielonka,
now at Oxford, exults in his book *Europe as Empire* that
its 'design was truly imperialist'—'power politics at its best,
even though the term "power" was never mentioned in the

---

13. 'Deconstructing Europe', p. 287.
14. 'The Next Empire', *Prospect*, October 2001.

official enlargement discourse', for this was a 'benign empire in action'.[15]

In more tough-minded style, the German strategist Herfried Münkler, holder of the chair of political theory at the Humboldt University in Berlin, has expounded the world-historical logic of empires—which stabilize adjacent power vacuums or turbulent border zones, holding barbarians or terrorists at bay—in an ambitious comparative work, *Imperien*, whose ideas were first presented as an aide-mémoire to a conference of the ambassadors called by the *Aussenamt*. While naturally loyal to the West, Münkler disavows normative considerations. Human rights messianism is a moral luxury even the American empire can ill afford. Europe, for its part, should take the measure of its emergent role as a sub-imperial system, and match its required tasks to its capabilities without excessive professions of uplifting intent.

The prefix, of course, poses the question that is the crux of the new identity Europe has awarded itself. How independent of the United States is it? The answer is cruel, as even a cursory glance at the record shows. In many ways, perhaps at no time since 1950 has it been less so. The history of enlargement, the Union's major achievement—extending the frontiers of freedom, or ascending to the rank of empire, or both at once, as the claim may be—is an index. Expansion to the East was piloted by Washington: in every case, the former Soviet satellites were incorporated into NATO, under US command, before they were admitted to the EU. Poland, Hungary and the Czech Republic had joined NATO already in 1999, five years before entry into the Union; Bulgaria and Romania in 2004, three years before entry; even Slovakia, Slovenia and the Baltics, a gratuitous month—just to rub in the symbolic point?—before entry (planning for the Baltics started in 1998). Croatia, Macedonia and Albania are next in line for the same sequence.

The expansion of NATO to former Soviet borders, casting aside undertakings given to Gorbachev at the end of the Cold War, was the work of the Clinton administration. Twelve days after the first levy of Poland, Hungary and the Czech Republic had joined the Alliance, the Balkan War was launched—the first full-scale military offensive in NATO's history. The successful blitz was an American operation, with token auxiliaries from Europe, and virtually no dissent in public opinion. These were

---

15. *Europe as Empire: The Nature of the Enlarged European Union*, Oxford 2006, pp. 54–7.

harmonious days in Euro-American relations. There was no race between the EU and NATO in the East: Brussels deferred to the priority of Washington, which encouraged and prompted the advance of Brussels. So natural has this asymmetrical symbiosis now become that the United States can openly specify what further states should join the Union. When Bush told European leaders in Ankara, at a gathering of NATO, that Turkey must be admitted into the EU, Chirac was heard to grumble that the US would not like being instructed by Europeans to welcome Mexico into the federation; but when the European Council met to decide whether to open accession negotiations with Turkey, Condoleezza Rice could telephone the assembled leaders from Washington to ensure the right outcome, without hearing any inappropriate complaints from them about sovereignty. At this level, friction between Europe and America remains minimal.

Why then has there been that sense of a general crisis in transatlantic relations, which has given rise to such an extensive literature? In the EU, media and public opinion are at one in holding the conduct of the Republican administration outside NATO to be essentially responsible. Scanting the Kyoto Protocol and the International Criminal Court, sidelining the UN, trampling on the Geneva Convention, and stampeding into the Middle East, the Bush regime has on this view exposed a darker side of the United States, one which has understandably been met with near-universal abhorrence in Europe, even if etiquette has restrained expressions of it at diplomatic level. Above all, revulsion at the war in Iraq has, more than any other single episode since 1945, led to the rift recorded in the painful title of Habermas's latest work, *The Divided West*.

In this vision, there is a sharp contrast between the Clinton and Bush presidencies, and it is the break in the continuity of American foreign policy—the jettisoning of consensual leadership for an arrogant unilateralism—that has alienated Europeans. There is no question of the intensity of this perception. But in the orchestrations of America's *Weltpolitik*, style is easily mistaken for substance. The brusque manners of the Bush administration, its impatience with the euphemisms of the 'international community', and blunt rejection of Kyoto and the ICC, offended European sensibilities from the start. Clinton's emollient gestures were more tactful, if in practice their upshot—neither Kyoto nor the ICC ever risked passage into law while he was in office—was often much the same. More fundamentally, as political operations, a straight line led from the war in the Balkans to the war in Mesopotamia. In both, a casus belli—imminent genocide, imminent nuclear weapons—was trumped up; the Security Council ignored; international law set aside; and an assault unleashed.

United over Yugoslavia, Europe split over Iraq, where the strategic risks were higher. But the extent of European opposition to the march on Baghdad was always something of an illusion. On the streets, in Italy, Spain, Germany, Britain, huge numbers of people demonstrated against the invasion. Opinion polls showed majorities against it everywhere. But once it had occurred, there was little protest against the occupation, let alone support for the resistance to it. Most European governments—Britain, Spain, Italy, the Netherlands, Denmark, Portugal in the West; all in the East—backed the invasion, and sent troops to bulk up the US forces holding the country down. Out of the fifteen member-states of the EU in 2003, just three—France, Germany and Belgium—came out against the prospect of war before the event. None condemned the attack when it was launched. But the declared opposition of Paris and Berlin to the plans of Washington and London gave popular sentiment across Europe a point of concentration, confirming and amplifying its sense of distance from power and opinion in America. The notion of an incipient Declaration of Independence by the Old World was born here.

Realities were rather different. Chirac and Schröder had a domestic interest in countering the invasion. Each judged their electorates well, and gained substantially—Schröder securing re-election—from their stance. On the other hand, American will was not to be trifled with. So each compensated in deeds for what they proclaimed in words, opposing the war in public, while colluding with it *sub rosa*. Behind closed doors in Washington, France's ambassador Jean-David Levitte—currently diplomatic adviser to Sarkozy—gave the White House a green light for the war, provided it was on the basis of the first generic UN Resolution 1441, as Cheney urged, without returning to the Security Council for the second explicit authorization to attack which Blair wanted, that would force France to veto it. In ciphers from Baghdad, German intelligence agents provided the Pentagon with targets and coordinates for the first US missiles to hit the city, in the downpour of Shock and Awe. Once the ground war began, France provided airspace for USAF missions to Iraq (passage Chirac had denied Reagan's bombing of Libya), and Germany the key transport hub for the campaign. Both countries voted for the UN resolution ratifying the US occupation of Iraq, and lost no time recognizing the client regime patched together by Washington.

As for the EU, its choice of a new president of the Commission in 2004 could not have been more symbolic: the Portuguese ruler who hosted Bush, Blair and Aznar at the Azores summit on 16 March 2003 that issued the ultimatum for the assault on Iraq. Barroso is in good company. France now has a foreign minister, Bernard Kouchner, who had no time for even the modest duplicities of his country about America's war, welcoming it as another example of the *droit d'ingérence* he had always championed. Sweden, where once a prime minister could take a sharper distance from the war in Vietnam than De Gaulle himself, has a new minister for foreign affairs to match his colleague in Paris: Carl Bildt, a founder member of the Committee for the Liberation of Iraq, along with Richard Perle, William Kristol, Newt Gingrich and others. In the UK, the local counterpart has proudly restated his support for the war, though here, no doubt, the corpses were stepped over in pursuit of preferment rather than principle. Spaniards and Italians may have withdrawn their troops from Iraq, but no European government has any policy towards a society destroyed by America that is distinct from the outlook in Washington.

For the rest, Europe remains engaged to the hilt in the war in Afghanistan, where a contemporary version of the expeditionary force dispatched to crush the Boxer Rebellion has killed more civilians this year than the guerrillas it seeks to root out. The Pentagon did not require the services of NATO for its lightning overthrow of the Taliban, though British and French jets put in a nominal appearance. Occupation of the country, which has a larger population and more forbidding terrain than Iraq, was another matter, and a NATO force of five thousand was assembled to hold the fort around Kabul, while US forces finished off Mullah Omar and Bin Laden. Five years later, Omar and Osama remain at large; the West's puppet ruler Karzai cannot move without a squad of mercenaries from DynCorp International to protect him; production of opium has increased ten-fold; the Afghan resistance has become steadily more effective; and NATO-led forces—now comprising contingents from thirty-seven nations, from Britain, Germany, France, Italy, Turkey and Poland down to such minnows as Iceland—have swollen to 35,000, alongside 25,000 US troops. Indiscriminate bombing, random shooting, and 'human rights abuses', in the polite phrase, have become commonplaces of the counter-insurgency.

In the wider Middle East, the scene is the same. Europe is joined at the hip with the US, wherever the legacies of imperial control or settler zeal are at stake. Britain and France, original suppliers of heavy water and uranium for the large Israeli nuclear arsenal, which they pretend does not exist, demand along with America that Iran abandon programmes it is allowed even by the Non-Proliferation Treaty, under menace of sanctions and war. In Lebanon, the EU and the US prop up a cabinet that would not last a day if a census were called, while German, French and Italian troops provide border guards for Israel within the country. As for Palestine, the EU showed no more hesitation than the US in plunging the population into misery, cutting off all aid when voters elected the wrong government, on the pretext that it must first recognize the Israeli state, as if Israel had ever recognized a Palestinian state, and renounce terrorism—read: any armed resistance to a military occupation that has lasted forty years without Europe lifting a finger against it. Funds now flow again, to protect a remnant valet in the West Bank.

Questionable some of this record may be, lovers of Europe might reply. But these are external issues, that can scarcely be said to affect the example Europe sets the world of respect for human rights and the rule of law within its own borders. The performance of the EU or its member-states may not be irreproachable in the Middle East, but isn't the moral leadership represented by its standards at home what really counts, internationally? So good a conscience comes too easily, for the War on Terror knows no frontiers. The crimes committed in its name have stalked freely across the continent, in the full cognizance of its rulers. Originally, the sub-contracting of torture—'rendition', or the handing over of a victim to the attentions of the secret police in client states— was, like so much else, an invention of the Clinton administration, which introduced the practice in the mid-nineties. Asked about it a decade later, the CIA official in charge of the programme, Michael Scheuer, simply said: 'I check my moral qualms at the door'.[16] As one would expect, it was Britain that collaborated with the first renditions, in the company of Croatia and Albania.

16. See Dick Marty's first report to the Council of Europe of 7 June 2006, *Alleged Secret Detentions and Unlawful Inter-state Transfers Involving Council of Europe Member States*, Strasbourg, footnote to paragraph 30.

Under the Bush administration, the programme expanded. Three weeks after 9/11, NATO declared that Article V of its charter, mandating collective defence in the event of an attack on one of its members, was activated. By then American plans for the descent on Afghanistan were well advanced, but they did not include European participation in Operation Enduring Freedom—the US high command had found the need for consultations in a joint campaign cumbersome in the Balkan War, and did not want to repeat the experience. Instead, at a meeting in Brussels on 4 October 2001, the allies were called upon for other services. The specification of these remains secret, but—as the second report to the Council of Europe by the courageous Swiss investigator Dick Marty, released in June 2007, has shown—high on the list agreed on this occasion must have been a stepped-up programme of renditions. Once Afghanistan was taken, the Bagram air base outside Kabul became both interrogation centre for the CIA and loading-bay for prisoners to Guantánamo. The traffic was soon two-way, and its pivot was Europe. In one direction, captives were transported from Afghan or Pakistani dungeons to Europe, either to be held there in secret CIA jails, or shipped onwards to Cuba. In the other direction, captives were flown from secret locations in Europe for requisite treatment in Afghanistan.

Though NATO initiated this system, the abductions it involved were not confined to members of the North Atlantic Council. Europe was eager to help America, whether or not fine print obliged it to do so. North, South, East and West: no part of the continent failed to join in. New Labour's contribution occasions no surprise: with up to 650,000 civilians dead from the Anglo-American invasion of Iraq, it would have been unreasonable for the Straws, Becketts, Milibands to lose any sleep over the torture of the living. More striking is the role of the neutrals. Under Ahern, Ireland furnished Shannon to the CIA for so many westbound flights that locals dubbed it Guantánamo Express. Social-Democratic Sweden, under its portly boss Göran Persson, now a corporate lobbyist, handed over two Egyptians seeking asylum to the CIA, who took them straight to torturers in Cairo. Under Berlusconi, Italy helped a large CIA team to kidnap another Egyptian in Milan, who was flown from the US airbase in Aviano, via Ramstein in Germany, for the same treatment in Cairo. Under Prodi, a government of Catholics and ex-Communists has sought to frustrate the judicial investigation of the kidnapping, while presiding over the expansion of Aviano. Switzerland proffered the overflight that took the victim to Ramstein, and protected the head of the CIA gang that seized him from arrest by the Italian judicial authorities. He now basks in Florida.

Further east, Poland did not transmit captives to their fate in the Middle East. It incarcerated them for treatment on the spot, in torture-chambers constructed for 'high value detainees' by the CIA at the Stare Kiejkuty intelligence base, Europe's own Bagram—facilities unknown in the time of Jaruzselski's martial law. In Romania, a military base north of Constanza performed the same services, under the superintendence of the country's current president, the staunchly pro-Western Traian Băsescu. Over in Bosnia, six Algerians were illegally seized at American behest, and flown from Tuzla—beatings in the aircraft en route—to the US base at Incirlik in Turkey, and thence to Guantánamo, where they still crouch in their cages. Down in Macedonia, scene of Blair's moving encounters with refugees from Kosovo, there was a combination of the two procedures. A German of Lebanese descent was kidnapped at the border; held, interrogated and beaten by the CIA in the country; then drugged and shipped to Kabul for more extended treatment. When it eventually became clear, after he went on hunger-strike, that his identity had been mistaken, he was flown blindfolded to a NATO-upgraded air-base in Albania, and deposited back in Germany.

There the Red-Green government had been well aware of what happened to him, one of its agents interrogating him in his oubliette in Kabul—Otto Schily, the Green minister of interior, was in the Afghan capital at the time—and accompanying his flight back to Albania. But it was no more concerned with his fate than with that of another of its residents, a Turk born in Germany, seized by the CIA in Pakistan and dispatched to the gulag in Guantánamo, where he too was interrogated by German agents. Both operations were under the control of today's Social-Democratic foreign minister, Frank-Walter Steinmeier, then in charge of the secret services, who not only covered for the torturing of the victim in Cuba, but even declined an American offer to release him. In a letter to the captive's mother, Joschka Fischer, Green foreign minister at the time, explained that the government could do nothing for him. In 'such a good land', as a leading admirer has recently described it,[17] Fischer and Steinmeier remain the most popular of politicians. The new interior minister, Wolfgang Schäuble, is more robust, publicly calling for assassination rather than rendition in dealing with deadly enemies of the state, in the Israeli manner.

Such is the record set out in Marty's two detailed reports to the Council of Europe (nothing to do with the EU), each an exemplary document of meticulous detective work and moral passion. If this Swiss prosecutor from Ticino were representative of the continent, rather than a voice crying in the wilderness, there would be reason to be proud of it. He ends his second report by expressing the hope that his work will bring home 'the legal and moral quagmire into which we have collectively sunk as a result of the US-led "war on terror". Almost six years in, we seem no closer to pulling ourselves out of this quagmire'.[18] Indeed. Not a single European government has conceded any guilt, while all continue imperturbably holding forth on human rights. We are in the world of Ibsen—Consul Bernick, Judge Brack and their like—updated for postmoderns: pillars of society, pimping for torture.

What has been delivered in these practices are not just the hooded or chained bodies, but the deliverers themselves: Europe surrendered to the United States. This rendition is the most taboo of all to mention. A rough approximation to it can be found in what remains in many ways the best account of the relationship between the two, Robert Kagan's *Paradise and Power*, whose benignly contemptuous imagery of Mars and Venus—the Old World, relieved of military duties by the New, cultivating the arts and pleasures of a borrowed peace—has predictably riled Europeans. But even Kagan grants them too much, as if they really lived according to the precepts of Kant, while Americans were obliged to act on the truths of Hobbes. If a philosophical reference were wanted, more appropriate would have been La Boétie, whose *Discours de la servitude volontaire* could furnish a motto for the Union. But these are arcana. The one contemporary text to have captured the full flavour of the transatlantic relationship is, perhaps inevitably, a satire, Régis Debray's plea for a United

---

17. Timothy Garton Ash, 'The Stasi on our Minds', *New York Review of Books*, 31 May 2007.

18. Dick Marty, *Secret Detentions and Illegal Transfers of Detainees Involving Council of Europe Member States: Second Report*, 8 June 2007, paragraph 367.

States of the West that would absorb Europe completely into the American imperium.[19]

Did it have to come to this? The paradox is that when Europe was less united, it was in many ways more independent. The leaders who ruled in the early stages of integration had all been formed in a world before the global hegemony of the United States, when the major European states were themselves imperial powers, whose foreign policies were self-determined. These were people who had lived through the disasters of the Second World War, but were not crushed by them. This was true not just of De Gaulle, but of figures like Adenauer and Mollet, of Eden and Heath, all of whom were quite prepared to ignore or defy America if their ambitions demanded it. Monnet, who did not accept their national assumptions and never clashed with the US, still shared their sense of a future in which Europeans could settle their own affairs, in another fashion. Down into the seventies, something of this spirit lived on even in Giscard and Schmidt, as Carter discovered. But with the neo-liberal turn of the eighties, and the arrival in power in the nineties of a post-war generation, it faded. The new economic doctrines cast doubt on the state as a political agent, and the new leaders had never known anything except the Pax Americana. The traditional springs of autonomy were gone.

By this time, on the other hand, the Community had doubled in size, acquired an international currency, and boasted a GDP exceeding that of the United States itself. Statistically, the conditions for an independent Europe existed as never before. But politically, they had been reversed. With the decay of federalism and the deflation of inter-governmentalism, the Union had weakened national, without creating a supranational, sovereignty, leaving rulers adrift in an ill-defined limbo between the two. With the eclipse of significant distinctions between Left and Right, other motives of an earlier independence have also waned. In the syrup of *la pensée unique*, little separates the market-friendly wisdom of one side of the Atlantic from the other, though as befits the derivative, the recipe is blander still in Europe than America, where political differences are less extinct. In such conditions,

---

19. *L'Édit de Caracalla ou plaidoyer pour les États-Unis d'Occident*, Paris 2002; extracted in Régis Debray, 'Letter from America', *New Left Review* II/19, January–February 2003.

an enthusiast can find no higher praise for the Union than to compare it to 'one of the most successful companies in global history'. Which firm confers this honour on Brussels? Why, the one in your wallet. 'The EU is already closer to Visa than it is to a state',[20] declares New Labour's infant prodigy. Europe exalted to the rank of a credit-card.

Transcendence of the nation-state, Marx believed, would be a task not for capital but for labour. A century later, as the Cold War set in, Kojève held that whichever camp accomplished it would emerge the victor from the conflict. The foundation of the European Community settled the issue for him. The West would win, and its triumph would bring history, understood as the realization of human freedom, to an end. Kojève's prediction was accurate. His extrapolation, and its irony, remain in the balance. They have certainly not been disproved: he would have smiled at the image of a chit of plastic. The emergence of the Union can be regarded as the last great world-historical achievement of the bourgeoisie, proof that its creative powers were not exhausted by the fratricide of two world wars; and what has happened to it as a strange declension from what was hoped from it. Yet the long-run outcome of integration remains unforeseeable to all parties. Even without shocks, many a zig-zag has marked its path. With them, who knows what further mutations might occur.

---

20. Leonard, *Why Europe Will Run the 21st Century*, p. 23.

3

THEORIES

2007

Larger now than the Roman Empire of two thousand years ago, more opaque than the Byzantine, the European Union continues to baffle observers and participants alike. Concepts have failed even its most prominent actors and analysts. For De Gaulle it was simply, and somewhat contemptuously, *ce machin*. For Jacques Delors, whose sympathies were the complete opposite, it still remained a kind of flying saucer—an 'unidentified political object', as he called it. For the leading constitutional authority on the EU, it is a *golem*. Such perplexities are not just quirks of terminology. They correspond to a painful reality, the enormous structural gap between the institutions of Europe and its citizens, attested by every opinion poll, steadily sinking rates of participation in Union elections, not to speak of popular understanding of its decision-making processes. This distance is in turn reproduced in the literature about the EU. Here writing falls into two widely differing categories, with only occasional crossovers between them. There is a popular literature aimed at a general audience, produced by publicists—or, less frequently, politicians—that enters into the mediasphere, becoming an element in the intellectual ether. Shifts of register within it need to be attended to in their own right.

On a far vaster scale is the professional literature about the EU, by now a veritable industry, with a perpetually expanding assembly line of journals, monographs, papers, conferences, research projects, collections, commentaries and more. No less than three hundred Jean Monnet chairs of European studies now adorn universities and institutes across the Union. Little of the huge output of this world penetrates any wider public consciousness, the bulk of it remaining as technical as the regulations and directives of Brussels themselves, sometimes more so. But if this is partly due to its subject matter, it is also a function of the discipline that dominates academic discussion of the EU, political science. Alfred Cobban's definition of this branch of learning—a device 'for avoiding that dangerous subject politics, without achieving science'—has not lost its sting fifty years later.

A more or less concurrent French and American invention— today's Sciences-Po was founded in 1872, in the wake of France's defeat in war with Prussia; the Civil War was the comparable watershed in the US—political science crystallized in the twentieth century as a distinctively American enterprise. This may have something to do with what is the most striking single feature of the scholarly literature on the EU today. Few of the leading contributions to it are written by Europeans. Virtually all the most original recent work on the Union comes, in one way or another, from America. Indeed, there is a sense in which the field was largely an American creation. Historically, few would contest that the first serious theorization of European integration was the work of an American scholar, Ernst Haas, whose study of the European Coal and Steel Community, *The Uniting of Europe,* appeared in 1958, a year after the Treaty of Rome was ratified, setting a paradigm for analysis of the Common Market that remained dominant for a quarter of a century. Haas's standpoint was, famously, neo-functionalist: that is, focussed on the ways in which the ECSC, sprung from a convergence of interest groups— businesses, parties, unions—in the original Six, had unleashed a dynamic process of integration. In that process, he argued, the interdependence of economic sectors would lead, in a slow cascade of spillovers, to a steadily more extensive pooling of sovereignty in supranational institutions.

Although Haas's intellectual framework derived entirely from the American political science of the period, his motivation was biographical. Coming from a German Jewish family that emigrated from Frankfurt for Chicago in the late thirties, when he was in his early teens, he was led—as he later explained— to study European unity by his boyhood experience of the costs of nationalism. With the re-emergence of De Gaulle as a decisive actor on the European stage in the sixties, followed by the economic turbulence of the early seventies, Haas came to the conclusion that in underestimating the continuing force of national sentiments, he had over-rated the technical automaticity of integration in Europe.[1] He ended his days writing a massive two-volume comparative study of nationalism across the globe. But his neo-functionalist paradigm, though not without its critics—Stanley Hoffmann was an early case—founded a tradition that produced works like those of Leon Lindberg and others, remaining a central reference point in the field ever since.[2]

In the eighties, Haas's legacy would be sharply attacked by Alan Milward, whose *European Rescue of the Nation-State*, argued no less famously that the European Community, far from being a supranational project weakening traditional sovereignties, was the product of a continental drive to strengthen them, moved by a post-war search for security—social and national; welfare and defence—that had nothing to do with functional spillovers between interdependent industries.[3] This was in every way an intellectual landmark: nothing was the same after it. But already in these years, the founding states of the Treaty of Rome produced no research comparable to this contribution from Britain, not itself even a member of the European Economic Community in the period under study. Nor, when Milward's later research concentrated mainly on his own country, has continental work compensated. In France, no native scholar could be found to fill the first chair in European studies at the Sciences-Po: a Belgian, Renaud Dehousse, had to be imported instead. In Germany, with its long tradition of *Rechtslehre*, distinguished constitutional theorists like Dieter

---

1. See his comments on 'the lessons taught us all by General De Gaulle' in the preface to the second edition of *The Uniting of Europe*, Stanford 1968, p. xiv: 'The original theory, implicitly if not explicitly, assumed the existence of the condition we have come to label "the end of ideology". Therefore, the conditioning impact of nationalism was defined out of existence but not empirically examined. I do not regret having done this, because an important point was made in the process: the mutability of the concept of "nation" and of the intensity of national feeling was underlined. But the point was made too strongly, because a new kind of national consciousness has since become discernible, particularly in France'.

2. Hoffmann on Haas: *The European Sisyphus*, 1995, pp. 34, 84–9, dating from 1964 and 1966 respectively. Lindberg: *The Political Dynamics of European Economic Integration*, Stanford 1963, and with Stuart Scheingold, *Europe's Would-be Polity*, Englewood Cliffs 1970.

3. For Milward's *Rescue*, published in 1992, see Chapter 1 *passim*. above. A second edition came out in 2000. His view of neo-functionalism is to be found in *The Frontier of National Sovereignty*, pp. 2–5, and in his subsequent *Politics and Economics in the History of the European Union*, London 2005, pp. 33–5, Schumpeter Lectures given in Graz, which continued to show his unrivalled mastery of the historical record, across the whole range of EU states, with a bravura linkage of Ireland and Denmark.

Grimm have made punctual interventions of note, some in debate with normative philosophers like Habermas. But no syntheses of the order of Kelsen or Schmitt have been forthcoming. In Italy, if the European University Institute in Florence has rotated many an eminence, it has been more in the style of an extra-territorial enclave than a native centre of production. In the past decade, the magnetic compass has swung back, more decisively than ever before, to the United States.

Europeans are certainly not absent from the landscape of scholarship of Europe. But they do not occupy its commanding terrain. That has become a province of Greater America—that is, of thinkers born, based or formed in the United States. Of the half dozen or so most important current theorists of European integration, there is scarcely a cis-Atlantic native or career among them. This is not simply a product of an American predominance in political science. In history, economics, sociology, philosophy, jurisprudence: wherever we look, the pattern is the same.

No attempt to understand the EU today, or where it might be going, can bypass this bloc of writing. Its popular accounts of the Union are straws in the political wind. Of more intellectual significance is what the best-qualified minds trained on the Union now have to say about it. Their reflections can be divided into two broad sets of argument, each posing the question of the nature of the EU. The first treats this as a problem of history, the second as an issue of policy. Roughly: what kind of historical phenomenon is the Union? What sort of political future could it—or should it—have? The two agendas overlap, obviously, since a judgement as to what the EU has been is likely to govern what is thought possible or desirable for it to become, and few authors restrict themselves to either. But the distinction itself is clear enough, and one can begin with the history.

I

Setting the pace has for some time been Andrew Moravcsik's *The Choice for Europe: Social Purpose and State Power from Messina to Maastricht* (1998), widely hailed as the leading synthesis since Milward. Director of the European Union Program at Princeton, where his wife Anne-Marie Slaughter is author of her own prospect for *A New World Order*, Moravcsik is currently the most prominent US authority in the field, a tireless commentator on EU affairs in the columns of *Newsweek* and the pages of *Prospect*. The theoretical background of his work lies in the notion developed by, among others, Robert Keohane at Harvard—where Moravcsik was a younger associate—of an 'international regime', understood as a set of formal or informal principles, rules and procedures determining a common horizon of expectations, and so conduct, for inter-state relations. The particular problem addressed by Keohane's major work *After Hegemony* (1984) was how high levels of cooperation could persist among the advanced capitalist states, once the paramountcy of the US that had been responsible for its post-war institutions—Bretton Woods, the IMF, GATT, NATO—passed away, as he thought it had in the early seventies.

The target of this conception was the dominant realist school of international relations theory in the USA, descended from Hans Morgenthau, which insisted on the ineliminably conflictual nature of relations between sovereign states in the world political arena. This standpoint, Keohane thought, could not make sense of the degree of pragmatic harmony between the leading states of the OECD after the collapse of Bretton Woods. Nor, however, could the alternative of neo-functionalist theory supply the answer: its stress on common ideals and economic ties was in Keohane's words 'naive about power and conflict'.[4] He proposed instead a synthesis of realism and neo-functionalism that would leave both behind, by modelling as it were the tender-minded phenomenon of international cooperation with the tough-minded tool-kits of rational choice and game theory.

A decade later, Moravcsik started to apply this line of thinking to the European Community. This was a field, however, where the balance of intellectual forces—at any rate in North America—was the opposite of that which had confronted Keohane. Here it was the neo-functionalism developed by Haas and his pupils that enjoyed most influence, an approach that stressed the specificity of European integration as a process founded on functional economic interdependencies, but driven by federalist political ideals. For the neo-functionalists, this was a combination that was gradually leading to a *sui generis* structure of supranational character, undercutting national sovereignty in a way unlike any other inter-state arrangement of the post-war epoch.

Moravcsik's manifesto of 1993, 'Preferences and Power in the European Community: A Liberal Intergovernmentalist Approach',

---

4. *After Hegemony: Cooperation and Discord in the World Economy*, Princeton 1984, p. 7.

took aim directly at this construction.[5] The right starting-point for understanding the process of integration, he asserted, was not what was specific to but what was standard in the EU. The Community had to be seen as another variant of a common pattern of international cooperation, requiring no analytical instruments to capture it beyond those already supplied by regime theory. In analyzing it, pride of place should be given neither to the role of the European Commission in Brussels, nor to the Court in Luxembourg, let alone the Parliament in Strasbourg, but rather to traditional bargaining between member-governments whose key deals set the terms—and limits—of European cooperation. The principal refinement needed to standard regime theory was simply the inclusion of the domestic politics of each state within the theory. 'Governments', Moravcsik explained, 'evaluate alternative courses of action on the basis of a utility function', shaped 'in response to shifting pressure from domestic social groups, whose preferences are aggregated through political institutions'.

The correct way to look at European integration was thus as an exemplar of 'liberal inter-governmentalism'—liberal in that it supposed private individuals and voluntary associations as the basic actors in politics, and assumed that increased traffic in goods and services across borders would spur 'reciprocal market liberalization and policy coordination'.[6] This was an approach governed by rational choice theory—essentially an extrapolation of the procedures of neo-classical economics to other domains of life—modelling the conduct of states on the behaviour of firms. 'The essence of the EC as a body for reaching major decisions remains its transaction-cost reducing function', contended Moravcsik.[7] True, this was an international regime which, unusually, involved governments in pooling and delegating elements of sovereignty. But they did so 'as a result of a cost-benefit analysis of the stream of future substantive decisions expected to follow from alternative institutional designs',[8] which led them to prefer the efficiency gains to be realized by arrangements particular to the EC. Since states make rational choices, it follows that they seldom err in their decisions. Governments bargaining for advantage with one

---

5. *Journal of Common Market Studies*, Vol. 31, No. 4, December 1993, pp. 472–523.

6. Andrew Moravcsik, 'Preferences and Power', pp. 483, 485.

7. 'Preferences and Power', p. 508.

8. 'Preferences and Power' p. 509.

another remain firmly in control of the outcomes. 'Unintended consequences and miscalculations' have at best—so Moravcsik—'played a role at the margins, as they always do in social life'.[9]

The Choice for Europe seeks to illustrate this vision by treating the history of European integration as a sequence of five 'grand bargains' between governments, to each of which Moravcsik devotes detailed attention: the Treaty of Rome in the fifties; the creation of the Common Agricultural Policy and the Luxembourg compromise in the sixties; the European Monetary System in the seventies; the Single European Act of the eighties; and the Treaty of Maastricht in the nineties. The argument is single-minded. At no point, Moravcsik maintains, was European integration driven either by geo-political calculations—France's need to contain Germany; Germany's need to recover respectability—or by federal idealism—Monnet's dreams of supranationalism; or by considerations of social welfare—as Milward had argued, showing a regrettably weak grasp of American social science.[10] Throughout, the primary motivation in the construction of today's Union has been just the commercial interests of the contracting partners. The result of their rational computations has been 'the most successful of postwar international regimes'.

This thesis is hammered home with a mass of dense documentation, most of it revolving around Franco-German relations, with admiring glances at Britain. De Gaulle is cut down to size as little more than a disingenuous lobbyist for French farmers. Macmillan, on the other hand, is hailed as a clairvoyant statesman, whose (failed) bid to get the UK into the Community was 'an extraordinary act of leadership'.[11] Indeed, from the first discussions of a common market at Messina onwards, 'British diplomacy was far-sighted, efficient and well-informed—close to the ideal rational actor'.[12] But in the overall balance-sheet of successive bargains, Moravcsik's narrative intimates, it was Germany that shaped the process of integration most. From Rome to Maastricht, it can gradually be deduced, Bonn was generally more formative than Paris. Italy's part in the story is ignored. The tale is one virtually without missteps. Governments, Moravcsik

---

9. 'Liberal Intergovernmentalism and Integration: A Rejoinder', *Journal of Common Market Studies*, Vol. 33, No. 4, December 1995, p. 626.

10. Review of Milward's *European Rescue of the Nation-State* in *Journal of Modern History*, March 1995, p. 127.

11. Andrew Moravcsik, *The Choice for Europe*, Ithaca 1998, p. 176.

12. *The Choice for Europe*, p. 131.

assures us, not only foresaw the immediate consequences of their decisions, 'they almost never misperceived the direction of future change'.[13]

The sheer bulk and self-confidence of *The Choice for Europe* has made of it, notwithstanding many an objection from historians, the central reference in a field dominated by political scientists of not dissimilar outlook. Its inadequacy to its object is, however, quite clear. For what Moravcsik's construction is *ab initio* unable to explain is why the standard objectives of inter-capitalist state cooperation, as codified in regime theory, could not have been achieved after the war in Western Europe by free-trade agreements of a conventional kind, without creation of any complex of supranational institutions or derogations of national sovereignty. Why shouldn't the EC have looked more like NAFTA? From a 'liberal intergovernmentalist' perspective, the European Commission, the Parliament and the Court of Justice enshrined in the Treaty of Rome can only appear gratuitous: unnecessary headaches down the road on which the six governments of the mid-fifties were so prudently and soberly steering.

What such a conception ignores, of course, is the critical fact that the institutional origins of the European Community were deliberately framed in dynamic, open-ended terms—that is, unlike other forms of international agreement, they were declared to be stepping-stones in view of an ultimate objective whose exact shape was left unspecified. In the famous formula which has haunted Eurosceptics ever since, the first words of the Treaty of Rome spoke of an 'ever closer union among the peoples of Europe'. It is this teleological aspiration that set European integration categorically apart from the normal world of international agreements. No stable equilibrium was aimed at by the first Coal and Steel Community, or the Common Market that followed it. On the contrary, what they set in motion was an unstable process, potentially concatenating towards a long-term end. This structure was inconceivable without the shaping role of the federalist—not inter-governmentalist—vision of Jean Monnet and his contemporaries. The history of the EC is inexplicable without the impetus to instability genetically engineered into it from the start.

What then of the rationality of the subsequent process? The rhetoric of rational choice is often empty, since any decision—no

---

13. *The Choice for Europe*, p. 491.

matter how seemingly aberrant: let us say, at the limit, Jonestown itself—can be read off from some putative preference structure. In *The Choice for Europe*, the relevant parameters of choice are specific enough: commercial gains. The question is whether the model they imply can be got to match the real world. The nervous tics of the text itself suggest the answer. For its relentless insistence that every important agreement in the history of the Community was determined above all by—mostly sectoral— economic interests is counterpointed by continual saving clauses noting evidence to the contrary, the better to dispatch it off-stage again, as so many residuals.

Such admissions-denegations are scattered throughout the book in a compulsive refrain. They recur at every juncture: the Treaty of Rome, the EMS, British entry, the SEA, Maastricht. Treaty of Rome: 'geopolitical ideas and security externalities were not entirely unimportant'. Macmillan's bid for membership: 'we cannot definitively exclude geopolitical prestige as a motivation'. German reactions to De Gaulle's veto of the bid: 'I do not rule out geopolitical motivations altogether'. Creation of EMS: 'this is not to relegate European symbolism and geopolitical arguments to complete insignificance'. The Single European Act: 'we should not exclude ideological considerations entirely'. German support for monetary union: 'domestic deliberations and cleavages prevent us from dismissing federalist ideology entirely'. French quest for Maastricht: 'we cannot dismiss the ideological explanation entirely'. Forty years of integration: 'we should not neglect geopolitical interests and ideas altogether'. Typicality of EC for relations among industrial nations in general: 'although we can reject objective geopolitical circumstances as the source of preferences, we cannot entirely dismiss the role of ideas. Yet until ideas are clearly measured [*sic*] and more precisely theorized, claims for the importance of ideology cannot be more than speculative'.[14] In no case does any serious exploration of, or reflection on, what is gestured at follow. Invariably, the factors momentarily conceded and effectively deleted are either geo-political or ideological. What their repetition indicates is simply the extent to which the evidence cannot be stretched to garb the theoretical framework. Tears and holes start to appear as soon as the fabric is pulled.

Of all these, the most gaping is Moravcsik's treatment of the role of De Gaulle in Community affairs. 'Grain, not grandeur', he

---

14. *The Choice for Europe*, pp. 90, 175, 205, 268, 403, 405, 477, 488, 496.

declares, lay behind the General's refusal to admit Britain to the EC in the sixties—essentially, nothing to do with shutting the gates against a Trojan horse from Washington, just a desire to bolster the price of French wheat. Historians have left little standing of the selective use of documents, loose quotation, and forcing of evidence employed to generate this result.[15] Beyond such flexing of the record to bend the intentions of a particular, famously obdurate actor to a preconceived schema, however, is the general premise on which *The Choice for Europe* is built: the belief that political miscalculations and unintended consequences are typically confined—as Moravcsik puts it—to 'the margins of social life'.

A less eccentric view would be that most of history is a web of unintended effects. The defining events of the past century, the two World Wars, are probably the most spectacular cases on record. Much of the inspiration for the building of the European Community, by contrast, came from the goal of avoiding their repetition in the Old World. But the edifice was entirely unprecedented, the architects never at one, the design ever more complex, the process extended far beyond the span of any government. How could it be otherwise than a minefield of misreckonings?

Among the most recent of these were the hopes invested in the SEA by Thatcher and Delors—opposite, but equally disappointed: the one furious that it paved the way towards a single currency, the other mortified that it proved a dead-end for a more social market. Or the beliefs of Kohl and Mitterrand that monetary union would quicken growth and lessen tensions between Germany and France. Once he reaches Maastricht, even Moravcsik forgets himself to the point of writing that 'it is unclear whether the economic benefits truly outweighed the costs for any single country, or whether the expectations of the various governments were fully compatible'.[16] So much for the unfailing rationality and foresight of the interested parties. As for the Stability Pact imposed by Germany to discipline laxer neighbours, it rebounded so quickly against the Federal Republic that Berlin was among the first to violate it. Such counter-finalities have punctuated integration ever since the Schuman Plan was announced in 1950.

---

15. See, in particular, Jeffrey Vanke, 'Reconstructing De Gaulle', and Marc Trachtenberg, 'De Gaulle, Moravcsik, and Europe', in *Journal of Cold War Studies*, Vol. 2, No. 3, Fall 2000, pp. 87–100 and 101–16.

16. *The Choice for Europe*, p. 470.

Blindness to these is due not just to the dogmatics of rational choice, but to the curiously apolitical cast of *The Choice for Europe*, much of which reads like a swollen theoretical side-bar to the technocratic discourse of committees and functionaries in Brussels itself. Not, of course, that Moravcsik himself is in any way unpolitical—it would difficult to suspect a more mainstream New Democrat. His manifest aversion to De Gaulle is not simply as a figure too unmistakably resistant to the postulates of his theory, but also as a ruler whose 'incoherent' foreign policy, pursuing French independence in defiance of Atlantic solidarity, was fortunately doomed to failure. But such conventional American dislike of a threat to Washington is no spur to any serious analysis of the balance of different forces in France, or any other country, at the time. In Moravcsik's optic, the domestic interests informing government policies boil down to little more than various producer lobbies, with virtually no attempt to reconstruct or even refer very much to the party systems and ideological landscapes of the period. Just how drained of politics the result becomes can be judged from— one example among many—his description of Thatcher's regime as a 'centrist coalition',[17] a notion she would have regarded as slanderous, and her opponents as risible.

The best antidote to such dehydration comes from another, younger American scholar, Craig Parsons at the University of Oregon. In a brilliantly executed study of France's part in the history of integration, *A Certain Idea of Europe*, Parsons shows how far the political realities of the French role in the building of Europe were from the utility functions of assorted economic interest groups. After the Second World War French elites, confronted with the problem of avoiding a re-run of their failures after the First, had— Parsons argues—three options: traditional realist diplomacy, pragmatic inter-state cooperation led by France and Britain, and direct Franco-German integration within a supranational community. Each was informed by a distinct set of ideas that cross-cut Right/Left attachments along the non-Communist spectrum, and set the agenda for decisions. That 'community' approaches

---

17. Andrew Moravcsik, 'Negotiating the Single European Act: National Interests and Conventional Statecraft in the European Community', *International Organization*, Vol. 45, No. 1, Winter 1991, p. 52.

prevailed over either confederal or traditional lines of action was never due to pressure in favour of them from domestic lobbies, industrial or agrarian. Underdetermined economically, it was the outcome of a 'historic battle of ideas'.[18]

But if a series of leaders—Schuman, Mollet, Giscard, eventually Mitterrand—had sufficient, if nearly always temporary, political leeway to impel integration without there being any organized demand for it, they equally never benefitted from it. Elected for other reasons, they fell from power for other reasons, in domestic contests unrelated to European issues. Indeed, every party responsible for a major advance towards European unity was punished at the polls, not thereby but thereafter: the MRP after the Coal and Steel Community (1951); the SFIO after the Treaty of Rome (1958); the UDF after the European Monetary System (1981); the PS after the SEA (1986) and again after Maastricht (1992). Yet each time the step forwards, once made, acted as an institutional constraint on subsequent leaders who had originally opposed it, but once in office were turned in favour of it—De Gaulle in 1958, Mitterrand in 1983, Chirac in 1986, Balladur in 1993, Chirac again in 1995. The 'conversion mechanism' was the accomplished fact, and the costs of trying to reverse it: not a spillover, but a ratchet effect.

While restoring quite unshakeably the driving role of political ideas in European integration, Parsons is careful not to overstate the success of federalism as its accelerator. Without the community commitment of successive French leaders, he remarks, 'today's Europe would look much like the rest of modern international politics'. But it does not fully represent them either, for although federalist directions prevailed at several crucial stages, they always had to contend with alternative—confederal or traditional—projects that slowed them down or boxed them in, making of the Union that eventually emerged a product of oscillations between the three.[19] Coolly dismissing Moravcsik's edifice as 'embedding a poorly supported argument in a largely untested theory', and eschewing all comparable hubris, A Certain Idea of Europe shows what a lucid political science immune to the fevers of rational choice can accomplish.

*   *   *

18. Craig Parsons, A Certain Idea of Europe, Ithaca 2003, p. 235.
19. A Certain Idea of Europe, pp. 27, 235.

Of entirely different inspiration is the work of John Gillingham, a historian at St Louis whose *European Integration 1950–2003* offers the first true narrative of the process of unification from the time of Schuman to that of Schröder, in a bravura performance that lights up the all too often leaden skies of the field like an aurora borealis. Resolved to 'cast aside official language'—what he calls Brussels-Volapük—'whenever possible and use standard terms and common measurements in order to demystify ideas, events and persons',[20] Gillingham has written an unfailingly vivid and pithy—at times even, as he himself notes, too racy—account of the complex story of European unification, on a grand scale. Its registers run a gamut from theoretical analysis of underlying economic processes to the dynamics of political manoeuvre or surprises of diplomatic settlements, to pungent portraits of their dramatis personae, always with a keen curiosity for ideas—both those that moved leading actors historically, and those developed afterwards to situate them. Its span, not confined to the major states, is virtually continental.

The intellectual convictions governing the narrative come from Hayek, to some extent also the Freiburg School of Ordo-liberals around Walter Eucken and Wilhelm Röpke, mentors of Ludwig Erhard. Politically, this is a tradition on the intransigent right of the spectrum, and Gillingham makes no secret, with many a colourful expression, of his hostility to anything on the left of it. But as a paradigm for understanding the history of the Community, Austrian economics has obvious advantages over the neo-classical variant on which rational choice is based, since as Gillingham remarks, it envisages market systems as inherently unstable—dynamic processes of discovery in which information is always imperfect—rather than as a set of utility functions tending towards equilibrium. Unexpected or ironic outcomes are, necessarily, no strangers to it.

What is then the historical yield of a Hayekian vision of European unity? For Gillingham, two antithetical models of integration have coexisted from the start. Negative integration is the removal of all barriers to the free movement of factors of production within the Community, entrusting the unification of economic life to the natural workings of the market, conceived in Hayek's terms as a spontaneous order. Positive integration is

---

20. *European Integration 1950–2003: Superstate or New Market Economy?*, Cambridge 2003, p. xvi.

the attempt to orchestrate a set of uniform practices into being by state intervention. For a quarter of a century after the Second World War, the dominant social arrangements at national level, combining capital controls, fixed exchange rates and extensive welfare systems, represented an 'embedded liberalism',[21] more or less throughout the West. Transposed to European level, the effect was an unstable amalgam of positive and negative integration, in which proponents of the former initially had the upper—though never a free—hand. From Monnet's design of the Coal and Steel Community in 1950 through to the first years of Hallstein's presidency of the Commission in the late fifties and early sixties, projectors of a social Europe, to be shaped in the spirit of French indicative planning and German bureaucratic legalism, held the initiative, until Hallstein over-reached himself in 1965, provoking De Gaulle to pull France out of the Council, and put an abrupt stop to further supranational schemes.

But if the empty chair crisis spelt the end of 'chiliastic Monnetism' in the EC, it was a much larger change that in due course shifted the balance of forces away from positive to negative integration. This was the 'regime change' that supervened across the advanced capitalist world after the collapse of the Bretton Woods system in the early seventies. Here the term—not a euphemism for overthrowing foreign governments, Gillingham explains, but a notion taken from the work of Douglas Forsyth and Ton Notermans, an American historian of modern Italy and a Dutch political scientist based in Norway[22]—signifies a set of system-wide policy constraints affecting all governments, no matter what their complexion. Just as the great deflation of the

---

21. Gillingham takes the term from John Ruggie, 'International regimes, transactions, and change: embedded liberalism in the post-war economic order', in Stephen Krasner (ed.), *International Regimes*, Ithaca 1983, pp. 195–231. The most notable contribution to this canonical collection of early US regime theory is the blistering attack on the whole notion of international regimes by the late Susan Strange which, in effect, concludes the volume: 'Cave, Hic Dragones', pp. 337–54. Strange not only pointed out the vacuity of the idea that American hegemony was over, but also noted the extent to which the future of Europe was—already—being more debated by US scholars than by their counterparts in Europe.

22. Douglas Forsyth and Ton Notermans, 'Macreconomic Policy Regimes and Financial Regulation in Europe, 1931–1994', in Forsyth and Notermans (eds), *Regime Changes*, Providence 1997, pp. 17–68. Here 'regimes' signifies macro-policy packages of monetary and financial regulation, held to set parameters for labour-market, industrial and social policies.

Slump years had over time imposed a new regime, governed by the goal of full employment, so the inflation that broke loose in the seventies would eventually create another one, dictated by the imperatives of monetary stability.

With this came the downfall of embedded liberalism, and a revival of the principles of a classical liberalism. Under the new regime, markets were freed from statist interference and international mobility restored to capital. Social expenditures were cut, unions weakened, and corporatist practices abandoned. This great change did not occur immediately—the seventies were a time of futile attempts to patch up corporatist arrangements— or automatically. It required powerful ideas and political will to give birth to an international consensus. Credit for these belongs to Thatcher's rule in England, inspired by the lessons of Hayek and other critics of the preceding order. By the mid-eighties, the conditions had matured for European integration finally to swing over in the right direction, with the long overdue abolition of obstructions to an unimpeded single market within the Community. The sweeping deregulation package of the SEA, drafted by an emissary from London, was 'at bottom . . . Mrs Thatcher's baby'.[23] Negative integration, the only viable kind, was at last in the saddle.

Yet its triumph, too, would be qualified. At the head of the Commission, Delors worked tirelessly against the grain of liberalization, even when apparently yielding to it, hitching Structural Funds—that is, otiose regional subsidies—to the SEA, and manoeuvring towards monetary union. It is characteristic of Gillingham's treatment of individuals that, though he judges Delors an arrant 'constructivist', incapable of understanding the virtues of a spontaneous order, whose legacy was mostly pernicious where it was not ineffectual, he has no difficulty acknowledging that he was 'an undeniably great figure', whose 'exceptional energy, political talent and ideological commitment' made him one of a kind, as Monnet had been.[24] In the end, by pressing European leaders on down the road from the SEA to Maastricht, Delors provoked the furious resistance of Thatcher, that led to her fall at home. But his own dreams of a social Europe were no more successful than hers of a truly liberal one. 'Delors's economic plans went down the drain. So, too, did Thatcher's

---

23. Gillingham, *European Integration*, p. 231.
24. *European Integration*, p. 152.

hopes that market reforms would sweep away the detritus of socialism and corporatism. Both leaders eventually parted the scene in anger, convinced the other had won'.[25]

Thus although regime change was irreversible, and has given European integration not just a new lease on life, but for the first time a life that is real and not artificial, the nineties became a time of misguided schemes and largely frustrated energies. At national level, there was welcome progress with privatization nearly everywhere. The public sector has been reduced by nearly half across the OECD, and state intervention in the economy has contracted sharply. Welfare systems have proved less tractable, but Gillingham can record significant improvements in most countries and commend star performers overall: Finland, Spain, Estonia. But at European level, there was no compelling economic rationale for the introduction of a single currency—Hayek, after all, had advocated competing private issues—and no community-wide securities market had issued from it, which to acquire real depth would in any case need general privatization of pension funds. The CAP had not been dismantled, and even the historic feat of enlargement had been marred by mean-spirited provisions ensuring that new members 'will have to buy a full-price ticket in order to see only half the show'.[26] The upshot is a continuing stand-off. Positive and negative integration still confront each other in the Union like cobra and mongoose.

What explains this unsatisfactory outcome? Retrograde opposition to liberalization from unions, public sector employees and the left is only to be expected. But however recalcitrant, these are groups bereft of ideas, without a future. Governments bear the main responsibility for not facing them down. Nearly all have indeed been agents of neo-liberalism, as their enemies charge. But the term is over-rated. Neo-liberalism has in general been less a principled conviction than a pragmatic tacking to regime change, whose practitioners have mostly been professed socialists— Thatcher's government was the exception in openly proclaiming the virtues of capitalism. Ideologically speaking, therefore, since it adopts pro-market policies with stealth rather than candour, let alone ardour, 'neoliberalism is a dull weapon', incapable of delivering a quietus to the baleful alliance of unions and transfer-

---

25. *European Integration*, p. 230.
26. *European Integration*, p. 412.

recipients who block change in the old Union.[27] The distressing fact is that since the departure of Thatcher, 'there is no serious, organized political constituency for classical liberalism anywhere in Europe today, not even on the conservative political right'.[28] But without a return to it—the concluding judgement—the Union is at risk of discord and decline.

Framed by a strong economic theory, Gillingham's book is nevertheless, in keeping with its subject, essentially a political history of European integration. For the European economies themselves, the commanding study comes from Barry Eichengreen, who teaches at Berkeley. In many ways, *The European Economy since 1945: Coordinated Capitalism and Beyond* (2007) moves in close parallel to Gillingham's work. In certain others, it reverses its signs. Eichengreen covers both Western and Eastern Europe throughout, but his periodization is identical. The economic history of the continent divides into two contrasting phases, the watershed between them lying in the early seventies. In the first phase, 'extensive growth' was achieved by making good war-time destruction of capital and diversion of manpower, and then drawing on a backlog of (principally American) technological advances and still abundant reserves of rural labour, to make up for lost time and converge towards US levels of productivity and income. In the second phase, 'intensive growth' was required, demanding riskier investments in faster and more abrupt forms of technological innovation. Eichengreen's story is of the way Europe flourished during the former, then stumbled at the latter.

What made extensive success possible, he argues, was a set of institutional arrangements comprising a mixture of cooperative trade-unions, responsible employers' associations, long-term bank credits to industry, and last but not least, governments taking active charge of the needs of growth, in some cases with elements of indicative planning. This 'coordinated capitalism' was a historically admirable model in its time. But once the limits of extensive growth were reached, it became a fetter on Europe's ability to adapt to the imperatives of intensive growth. The new conditions demanded lower taxes, less job protection, greater income disparities, higher levels of general education and R&D,

---

27. *European Integration*, pp. 150, 498.
28. *European Integration*, p. 498.

and—most important of all?—more venture capital for innovative start-ups, raised from readier-to-gamble financial markets rather than stick-in-the-mud banks. Rooted in attachments to the past, European resistance to these changes exacted a heavy price. Between 1945–1973 and 1973–2000, GDP growth per capita fell by over half.

As for the onset of the crisis that brought extensive growth to an end, though completion of industrial catch-up and running-out of rural labour also come into it, Eichengreen lays main emphasis on the breakdown of labour restraint in Europe in the late sixties and early seventies, as a new generation of workers with no memories of mass unemployment set off a wage explosion that led to a decade of inflation. But as an explanation of the deceleration of growth, this will hardly do, since without any comparable union militancy, the slow-down took hold in America as well. Elsewhere, the epochal change is attributed to the impact of discontinuous technological innovation and financial globalization. But these are never themselves causally grounded, remaining descriptions rather than historical explanations, in this much like regime change in Gillingham's account.[29]

Politically, of course, Eichengreen's study is far more generally benevolent to Europe. His intellectual sympathies, more clearly on display in *Globalizing Capital* (1996), have lain not with Hayek, but Polanyi. The Hungarian was in nearly every way the antithesis of the Austrian, and the unstated difference is plain in *The European Economy since 1945*. The embedded liberalism of the post-war settlement that Gillingham treats as at best a provisional expedient, already laden with vices to come, becomes the notably effective and imaginative—*un*spontaneous—order of a coordinated capitalism, which only earns Eichengreen's praise. His respect for what it represented persists to the end. Europe's

---

29. The same is true of Forsyth and Notermans' account of the regime changes of the thirties and seventies, as they admit: 'A more significant limitation of our argument is that it does not explain fully the timing and causes of the deflationary and inflationary nominal price movements that triggered the policy changes we explore. We do not claim to have developed a comprehensive explanation for why the containment of inflation through microeconomic instruments failed during the 1970s and 1980s. Nor have we explained why the pre-1914 gold standard did not produce deflationary pressures as severe as those that developed beginning in the late 1920's . . . We have proposed neither a comprehensive explanation for the Great Depression, nor for the long postwar economic expansion, nor for the downturn since 1973': *Regime Changes*, p. 68.

recent productivity record may not be so much worse than that of the US; if Americans earn more, Europeans are not necessarily worse off, since they enjoy more leisure and security, and are surrounded by less poverty and crime. The EU needs to adjust to intensive growth, but are not parts of it already showing the way? The Dutch and Irish, he suggests, have already got things more or less right, with neo-corporatist arrangements that combine fiscal discipline, wage moderation and hi-tech investment. Perhaps European capitalism may not have to renounce its habits of coordination after all, but merely slough off one set of them for another.

The suggestion, however, is half-hearted—more a wistful glance back than a confident look forwards. It is not just that in small countries like Holland or Ireland, external vulnerabilities have always favoured corporate solidarities not readily achievable elsewhere. Equally significant, what in each case Eichengreen singles out as the key to their success is essentially wage restraint. His general instruction to Europe for getting on board the train of intensive growth is the same. Labour must settle for less— flatter incomes, more wage dispersal, and less job security.[30] In other words, a standard neo-liberal package in just the ironically pejorative sense Gillingham gives the term.

The European Economy since 1945 ends by asking whether the EU could not adopt Anglo-Saxon-style financial markets—as it is now more or less sensibly doing—without following suit in its labour and product markets. That will depend, Eichengreen suggests, on whether further technical innovation in the next decades is incremental or radical. If it were the former, the European model would be open to reinvention; if the latter, international competition would probably force thoroughgoing Americanization. Formally, judgement is left suspended there. But substantively, there is no doubt which prospect is inscribed in the logic of the argument. Earlier, Eichengreen has already made clear that 'comprehensive' reform of the European model is required, and explained at length that enlargement of the EU provides it with an open-shop East to match the US South—obviously, to far larger potential dynamic effect than parish-pump concertation in Wassenaar or Dublin could ever furnish. So, too, he concedes that the probability is that technical innovation will continue to

---

30. Barry Eichengreen, *The European Economy Since 1945: Coordinated Capitalism and Beyond*, Princeton 2006, p. 333.

involve radical and discontinuous, rather than gentle or gradual, changes.[31] Entailed, if never stated, is only one plausible outcome: that ultimately, the Old World is likely to be compacted into the shapes of the New.

From economics to sociology is a short step in the literature on the Union—no more than a stroll across the hall at Berkeley, to the office of Neil Fligstein, the author of the most ambitious study of the social underpinnings of European integration, misleadingly titled *Euroclash*.[32] Taxing much discussion of the EU with too state-centred a focus, Fligstein sets his sights on a larger reality, 'the creation of a European society'. This is not the same object as explored by scholars like Göran Therborn or Hartmut Kaelble, tracking social changes since the war in every domain of life across the continent.[33] Fligstein's aim is to demonstrate, with a mass of carefully assembled statistical evidence, the emergence of something more specific: the sphere of social interactions created by, and tied to, European integration. What forms do these take? First and foremost, there is the market: the daily transactions of rising intra-European trade, and the increasing numbers of intra-European mergers and acquisitions, enabled—but also regulated— by the directives of Brussels, where business interests gather to press their cases and concerns, also in increasing numbers. 'These figures tell a compelling story', Fligstein writes, of how 'trading, litigating, legislating and lobbying'—the 'key indicators of European integration'—have grown over time.[34] Travel within Europe has steadily grown, to a point where by 1997 a quarter of the population of the pre-enlargement EU had been outside their native country in the past year. European-wide civic associations too—professional, scientific and non-governmental organizations—have multiplied. Culturally, two out of every three West Europeans can speak a second language; well over a million students have followed courses outside their homeland; degrees in higher education are gradually being harmonized.

---

31. *The European Economy Since 1945*, pp. 415–16.

32. *Euroclash: The EU, European Identity and the Future of Europe*, New York 2008.

33. Respectively, *European Modernity and Beyond: The Trajectory of European Societies 1945–2000*, London 1995, and *Sozialgeschichte Europas: 1945 bis zur Gegenwart*, Munich 2007.

34. Fligstein, *Euroclash*, p. 54.

But if a genuinely European society, distinct from the particular national communities that make up the EU, has crystallized, it is not shared equally by all inhabitants of the Union. Those who have materially benefitted most from integration, who interact socially most often across national borders, and who have the strongest sense of a collective European identity, form an upper-class minority, drawn from business, government, high-income professions and the academy. A larger middle class has only intermittent contact with life beyond local frontiers, while the lowest classes have little or none. Since these layers are the most exposed to the costs—however temporary—of economic integration, they are potential protesters against it. Undeniably, Europe has so far been—at any rate socially and culturally—a 'class project'. A clash of interests could therefore break out over it, in conditions of economic crisis.[35]

But though bannered in its title, the notion of a clash is purely virtual in Fligstein's book, without any presence in it. In part this is because the lower classes, lacking any sense of a supranational identity, simply do not belong to the European society that is the focus of his work, and so fall outside its framework. But more fundamentally, it is because a force is at work within that society which transcends the possibility of any conflict of interests. For the upper classes that compose it do not just consist of the wealthy, with their often selfish attachment to their own good fortune, but also of a more selfless group, motivated by ideals—the educated. These, Fligstein suggests, are 'the real moral engine of the EU'. For 'at its core, one of the reasons that educated people support the European project is because the European values they espouse are identical with the Enlightenment values that have been a hallmark of educated people for over two hundred years. Indeed, if Europe stands for anything, it is the completion of the Enlightenment project of democracy, rule of law, respect for the differences of others, and the principles of rational discourse and science'.[36] With ethical guidelines as compelling as these, why should the Union fear division over mundane questions of relative advantage? As higher education spreads, more and more young people will study abroad, and 'the best new jobs' in a shifting economy will increasingly be 'in services such as banking, real estate, and insurance', or computer programming, requiring higher

---

35. *Euroclash*, pp. vii, 6, 15–18, 139, 251, 253.
36. *Euroclash*, p. 178.

skills and paying higher salaries. Predictable sociological changes should of themselves create a more unified Europe, imbued more evenly with the values of the Enlightenment.

So glowing with enthusiasm for the forward-looking achievements of the Union is Fligstein that his work might have more aptly been entitled *Eurodash*. Again and again, he is 'amazed', as he recounts, at 'the marvellous character of what has happened'. On page after page, the epithet 'remarkable' resounds like a compulsive refrain.[37] But triumphalism of vocabulary is not matched by coherence of construction. On the one hand, no more than 'a very small number of people are deeply involved with other Europeans on a daily basis', 'only a tiny part of the population is directly involved', while 'the vast majority of Europeans still remain firmly tied to the nation'. On the other hand, those with 'deep economic and social ties with their counterparts across Europe' comprise 10 to 15 per cent of the inhabitants of the Union—that is: no less than 38 to 56 million people, or at the upper range more than the entire population of Britain or Italy, and not far short of that of France. As for those who are 'partly European', they compose another 40 to 50 per cent of the population—or getting on for 200 million.[38] The fantastical nature of these figures is the product of a switch of definitions. Whereas an emergent 'European society' is computed by intensity of actual social interactions, measured objectively, these inflated percentages are simply taken from opinion polls that asked people whether, notionally, they felt European or not. It goes without saying that the gap between the two is enormous. The reality answers to Fligstein's first description, not his second. Those deeply involved, on a daily basis, with non-nationals form a very small minority of the citizens of the EU, one that has fallen since enlargement. To speak of them as a 'society', as if they composed a self-connecting whole, is a metaphor, not a truth.

That even this minority scarcely possesses much self-awareness of its existence is suggested by the appearance of *Euroclash*

---

37. *Euroclash*, pp. vii, 10, 33, 34, 69, 123, 187, 191, 192, 244, 251.

38. Compare *Euroclash* pp. 4, 138, 14, 250. Oscillation between these emphases recurs throughout the book. For example, 'one must be circumspect about how far the process of creating a European society has gone. A very small number of people in Europe are interacting with people from other European countries on a daily basis'—followed a hundred pages later by 'the likelihood of social interaction between people who live in different countries in Europe has expanded dramatically over the past twenty-five years': pp. 29, 165.

itself. American dominance of a field of work could hardly be more graphically expressed. In a bibliography of some 260 items, there is just one book in French, one in German. Even allowing for writing in English by Europeans—overwhelmingly from the cultures closest to the United States: Germany, Scandinavia, the Netherlands—the proportion of authors originating outside the Anglosphere is about one-seventh of the total. All central references to work on the Union in the body of the text itself are to American scholars. It would be wrong to impute this to parochialism. Fligstein has made use of what findings from the continent were material to his research. But here, as elsewhere, Europeans figure as under-labourers, whose work has been employed for a synthesis exceeding them.

2

If these stand as currently the most authoritative economic and social prognoses of the Union, what do the rival historical theories of integration as a political process have to say about the present, in the wake of the rejection of the European Constitution? Moravcsik, as might be expected, allows no doubts to cloud an unfailingly sunny vista. The Union has just completed its most successful decade ever, with an enlargement to the east that has cost little and required no significant modification of its already satisfactory institutions. These continue to deliver policies which, he can inform satisfied readers of *Prospect*, are 'in nearly all cases, clean, transparent, effective and responsive to the demands of European citizens'.[39] What then of the Constitution? Little more than an unnecessary exercise in public relations, whose demise, far from representing a failure of the EU, actually demonstrates its stability and success.

But isn't there any democratic deficit in the Union? None whatever—the very question arises from a confusion. The EU deals with issues best handled by experts, of little direct concern to voters: trade barriers, rules of competition, product regulations, legal adjudication, foreign assistance. Insulation of

---

39. Andrew Moravcsik, 'The EU ain't broke', *Prospect*, March 2003, p. 38. Although it is not a major part of his case, Fligistein largely concurs with Moravcsik's arguments for dismissing concern with a democratic deficit, while allowing that he may over-estimate the stability of present arrangements: *Euroclash*, pp. 228ff, 240, 216ff.

such areas from popular decision-making is not just practicable, it is desirable. Citizens understand this: they have little respect for their parties or parliaments, but hold their armies, courts and police in high regard. Those political issues people do care about, because they are directly affected by them—essentially, tax-rates and social services—are decided at national level, as they should be, where the Union, lacking any independent fiscal base or civil administration, does not impinge. In its own sphere, however, the EU needs to be shielded from demagogic interference by referenda or other hopeless attempts at direct democratic decision-making. 'Forcing participation is likely to be counterproductive, because the popular response is condemned to be ignorant, irrelevant and ideological'.[40] In any case, the wish to democratize the Union is bound to fail, because *it runs counter to our consensual social scientific understanding of how advanced democracies actually work*'[41] (italics in original). For we should never forget that 'political learning, mobilization, deliberation and participation are extremely expensive for rational citizens'.[42] Fortunately, the masses realize this themselves, declining to pay the high costs in time and attention that interest in EU affairs would require. They would quickly turn against any effort to get them more involved: far from enhancing the legitimacy of the Union, schemes to democratize it would only render it less popular. Such features of the defunct Constitution as might be of some use can be quietly infiltrated through national parliaments without attracting undue public attention, for 'the EU's greatest tactical advantage is that is, in a word, so *boring*'.[43]

As a casuistic for chloroforming any residual trace of popular will, these avowals have the merit of candour. But if the legitimacy of the Union does not lie in some inappropriate democracy, what is its raison d'être? Moravcsik's answer—as we have seen above—is commendably straightforward: 'The EU is overwhelmingly about the promotion of free markets. Its primary interest group support comes from multinational firms, not least US ones'.[44] Or, more bluntly still: 'The EU is basically

---

40. 'What Can We Learn from the Collapse of the European Constitutional Project?', *Politische Vierteljahresschrift*, 47, 2006, Heft 2, p. 227.

41. 'What Can We Learn from the Collapse?', p. 221.

42. 'What Can We Learn from the Collapse?', p. 221.

43. 'What Can We Learn from the Collapse?', p. 238.

44. 'Conservative Idealism and International Institutions', *Chicago Journal of International Law*, Fall 2000, p. 310.

about business'.[45] So it should remain. The neo-liberal bias of the Union is '*justified*', for no responsible analyst believes current national welfare systems in Europe are sustainable.[46] Nor can or should they be rearticulated at Union level. 'Social Europe is a chimera'. In its perfect rationality, on the other hand, actually-existing Europe is the best of all international regimes.

Moravcsik's Panglossian outlook is alien to Gillingham. Far from any triumphalism, the diagnosis of the current state of the Union offered by his *Design for a New Europe* (2006) tends towards an extreme alarmism. The repudiation of the Constitution at the polls is stark evidence of a crisis in the legitimacy of the EU, and one for which there is good reason. Since the era of Delors, bureaucratic corruption, prejudice and meddling have been hallmarks of the unaccountable Commission in Brussels, where only the internal market and competition portfolios have retained integrity. The Parliament in Strasbourg remains an impotent talking-shop. For much of the time the Council has been hi-jacked by absurd French projects such as a global positioning system in outer space to rival the comprehensive American one already in existence, not to speak of rotten deals to extend the life of a moribund Common Agricultural Policy. What credibility could such a retrograde and venal contraption enjoy? The essentially simple tasks of negative integration have been perverted into a machinery of such complexity and opacity that few citizens can make head or tail of it.

Worse, in its resistance to scientific advances in agriculture, the EU has sunk into actual obscurantism. The blockade by Brussels of GM crops—Monsanto, the world's leading producer of them, is based in St Louis—represents a *ne plus ultra* of statist ignorance and incompetence. The same Canute-like attitude threatens to render the EU incapable of coping with the two greatest challenges it faces today: on the one hand, the momentous transformations under way as a new scientific revolution makes info-, nano- and bio-technology the cutting edge of industrial innovation; on the other, the entry of vast reserves of cheap labour into the world

---

45. 'Conservative Idealism and International Institutions', p. 310.

46. Andrew Moravcsik, 'In Defence of the "Democratic Deficit": Reassessing Legitimacy in the European Union', *Journal of Common Market Studies*, Vol. 40. No. 4, 2002, p. 618.

market, available for mass production of traditional goods at
much lower prices than in the past. Lagging behind US in the first,
Europe is already under pressure from China, tomorrow perhaps
India or Brazil, in the second.

Less publicly discussed, it is the former that is more critical.
Confronted with technological changes comparable to those of
the Industrial Revolution, blurring 'the very distinctions between
plants and animals, the animate and inanimate, and even life
and death', the EU has been incapable of unleashing the market
dynamism needed to compete with these.[47] What is to be done?
Gillingham's remedies are draconian. Certainly, the abolition of
the CAP and liberalization of services are essential. But beyond
such measures, whose necessity has so often been bruited without
being acted on, more radical changes are required: nothing less
than a true 'bonfire of inanities' that would wind up regional
funds, ditch the euro, downsize the Commission, flog off the
buildings in Brussels, and convert the Parliament into a small and
harmless consultative body. Ideally stretching from Ireland to
the Ukraine, a free-trade zone encumbered with no more rules or
bureaucrats than EFTA of old, such a Europe would reclaim and
extend democracy as the true final purpose of integration.

The exasperation of these proposals—half tongue in cheek?—
has something of the spirit of the more uncompromising passages
in Hayek. But in another sense, they depart from his legacy quite
sharply. Hayek's vision of 'inter-state federalism', as he called
it, was expressly designed to safeguard the free workings of the
market *from* democracy, against whose dangers he was always on
his guard, preferring to envisage a 'demarchy' dispensing with the
fetish of universal suffrage.[48] His reasoning was just that which
would take shape in the European Central Bank—that the higher
above national sovereignty regulation of the market could be
raised, the more insulated it would be from electoral pressures for
state intervention or redistribution from below. For his disciple
to turn the argument round, as if the aim of integration, rightly
conceived, were to promote democracy rather than protect us
from it, is a whimsical move. But beyond further enlargement—
Gillingham writes with special sympathy for the Ukraine, not the
most popular candidate in Brussels—it remains a gesture without
institutional specification.

---

47. John Gillingham, *Design for a New Europe*, Cambridge 2006, p. 153.
48. *Law, Legislation and Liberty*, Vol. 3, London 1979, p. 40.

Design for a New Europe abstains from any scheme that might be taxed with constructivism. What it offers is, in effect, a sweeping demolition plan—negative integration as gelignite under Commission, Parliament, Structural Funds and Monetary Union alike. The extremity of these proposals reflects the baffled note on which Gillingham's large history of European integration concludes. For what his narrative cannot explain is why the forces liberated by regime change should suddenly fade at the end of the story—true liberals vanishing, leaving behind only governments without conviction in deadlock with oppositions without a future. The balance of social forces below the surface of political events is missing.

In their prescriptive upshots, the accounts of the EU offered by Moravcsik and Gillingham are polar opposites. One would keep everything as it is. The other would level much of it to the ground. Behind such divergences lie two contrasting outlooks, each devoted to the market, but differing completely in their conceptions of public life. The first conceives politics as if it were little more than a branch of economics, subject to the same kind of calculus of utilities and predictability of outcomes. The second, by contrast, seeks to insulate economics as far as possible from politics, as a system whose spontaneous workings can only be impaired, and risk being destroyed, by government intervention of any kind. Here consequences, in any important sense, are always unintended: to benign effect in the market, to ironic or malign effect, for the most part, in the state. One of J.G.A. Pocock's most formidable essays, and his longest, is a historical reconstruction of 'the varieties of Whiggism'. The varieties of liberalism have not been less. Curiously, in the galaxy of current versions, Europe might be described as a virtual object of predilection. Among these, 'liberal inter-governmentalism' and 'classical liberalism' are by no means the last word.

3

Mentally, perhaps even more than materially, America weighs on Europe. If citizens of the EU must now look to the US for leading accounts of the community to which they belong, that is not the only way in which their past and present are being written from a transatlantic vantage-point. The most rigorous thinker to have reflected on the paradoxes of integration is an Italian, Giandomenico Majone, now retired at the EUI in Florence. Trained in Pittsburgh, he wrote his doctorate at Berkeley, and has taught at times at Harvard and Yale. More than stages of a career, however, attach him to the United States. The specialist field he commands, and the sources of his theory of Europe, are peculiarly American. The title of his first book on the subject, *Regulating Europe*, announces his angle of vision.

In Europe itself, the term 'regulation'—in so far as it had any currency at all—was long associated principally with a school of economists of Marxist derivation originating in France, who were interested in the ways in which production, credit and consumption became interconnected in distinct 'structural forms', or rules of reproduction of the system, in successive phases of capitalist development. In recent years, the word has acquired a more familiar ring in the vocabulary of a bureaucratic officialdom, without gaining much salience in public consciousness, not to speak of popular wisdom. Even in England, where regulatory bodies started to proliferate well before the rest of Europe, few have more than the vaguest notion of what functions, let alone personnel, lie behind their grey acronyms. The world of Oftel, Ofgem, Ofwat, Ofreg, remains a closed book to most citizens.

In the US, on the other hand, regulation has been a central part of the political landscape for more than a century, ever since the Interstate Commerce Act of 1887 set up a federal commission to regulate the railroads. In due course, there followed regulative agencies in one industry after another, most created during the Progressive and New Deal eras. The result has been, in Majone's words, that 'as every student of the subject knows, in America regulation is a distinct type of policy-making that has spawned a distinct theoretical and empirical literature'.[49] Majone's undertaking has been to bring this body of thought back across the water, to dramatic intellectual effect.

He begins by observing that nationalization was for long the functional equivalent of regulation in America. Wherein then lay the distinction between them? The answer is to be found in the 'significant ideological and institutional differences between the American and European approach to the political control of

---

49. 'Introduction', in Giandomenico Majone (ed.), *Deregulation or Re-regulation? Regulatory Reform in Europe and the United States*, London 1990, p. 1.

market processes. The long tradition of regulation in the United States expresses a widely held belief that the market works well under normal circumstances, and should be interfered with only in specific cases of "market failure" such as monopoly power, negative externalities or inadequate information. In Europe, popular acceptance of the market ideology is a more recent phenomenon'.[50] It would be wrong, however, to treat the contrast as simply a matter of collective beliefs. There is an objective difference, Majone goes on, between nationalization and regulation, that makes the latter inherently superior as a solution to market failures. Public ownership was supposed to serve multiple purposes: industrial development, full employment, social equity, national security. Such goals were not only often incompatible, their very diversity detracted from the pursuit of efficiency, eventually casting the idea of nationalization itself into discredit. Regulation, by contrast, has just one 'normative justification'—efficiency—and so avoids the redistributive tensions, and confusions, generated by nationalization. Whereas redistribution is a zero-sum game in which one group must lose what the other obtains, 'efficiency issues, on the other hand, may be thought of as positive-sum games where everybody can gain, provided the right solution is discovered. Hence, such issues could be settled, in principle, by unanimity'.[51]

Since, however, 'unanimity is practically impossible in a large polity', the task of improving market efficiency is best entrusted to expert regulatory agencies. The key feature of these, as they gradually evolved in the United States, came to be delegation: that is, the abandonment by the state of any attempts to direct the work of the agencies it had created to regulate the market, leaving these to the discretion of those it appointed to them. This development was consummated with the reforms of the Reagan administration, which went still further by devolving most federal expenditures to third parties of various kinds in civil society. So conceived, the logic of regulation is an increasingly complete severance of expert authority from the popular will. Majone employs the idiom of a Californian school of conservative economics, property rights theory, to express this. Regulation represents a 'partitioning of

---

50. Majone, *Deregulation or Re-Regulation?*, p. 2; see also *Regulating Europe*, London 1996, p. 10.

51. Majone, 'From the Positive to the Regulatory State', *Journal of Public Policy*, Vol. 17, No. 2, May–August 1997, p. 162.

political property rights',[52] that transfers public powers from fickle legislatures, subject to partisan majorities that can change every half-decade, to independent authorities capable of making credible long-term commitments, without interference from voters.

In Europe, realization of the advantages of this arrangement was long delayed. There, the first 'nationalizations coincided with the first worldwide depression of the capitalist economy (1873–1896) which shattered popular and elite support of the market for almost one century'.[53] By the 1980s, however, this had finally changed. It was Britain that led the way with the privatizations of the Thatcher years. The growth of regulation here, as subsequently on the continent, has in effect been the complement to the advance of privatization—that is, a set of agencies whose task is to ensure that firms do not abuse monopoly power as the state once did, or generate an excess of externalities. As this pattern spreads, the balance of functions performed by the modern state alters, shifting away from the provision of welfare or stabilization of the business-cycle towards a more indirectly regulative role. There is no reason to be shocked by this change, which accords with long-standing principles of the modern *Rechtsstaat*. 'Within the non-majoritarian model of democracy—which is just another name for constitutional democracy', Majone writes, 'reliance upon qualities such as expertise, credibility, fairness, or independence has always been considered more important than reliance upon direct political accountability'—if only 'for some limited purposes'.[54] The main task that regulatory agencies are called upon to fulfil is to rectify market failures. Their actions may have redistributive consequences, but they must not themselves pursue any redistributive ends, which require more directly political decisions by elected legislatures. The nation-state, although the balance of its activities may have altered, continues to provide for welfare, stability and defence, as well as regulation. It remains a multi-purpose creation.

---

52. See Majone, 'The Politics of Regulation and European Regulatory Institutions', in Jack Hayward and Anan Menon (eds), *Governing Europe*, Oxford 2003, pp. 300–305. The property rights school, descending from the ideas of Ronald Coase of the University of Chicago, is associated principally with the work of Harold Demsetz and Armen Alchian of UCLA in the seventies.

53. 'The Rise of the Regulatory State in Europe', *West European Politics*, No. 17, 1994, p. 81.

54. *Governing Europe*, p. 311.

The essence of the European Union, however—this was Majone's master-stroke—is to be *just* a regulative authority writ large: that is, a form of state stripped of redistributive and coercive functions, purified to maintenance tasks for the market. In practice, to be sure, *ad hoc* programmes of sectoral or regional redistribution—a lamentable Common Agricultural Policy and the like—have been tacked onto the EU. But these can be regarded as adventitious accretions that do not alter its overall character, which is unprecedented. It is a 'regulatory polity'. This conclusion might seem to anticipate more or less exactly Moravcsik's recent depictions of the EU, on which Majone's influence—he started writing earlier, and more trenchantly—is fairly clear. But his own theory of the Union is quite distinct. The EU cannot be reduced to an inter-governmental regime, and Moravcsik's attempt to model it as the outcome of least-common-denominator bargaining is little more than the crude application of a Ricardian theory of economic rent, incapable of explaining even episodes apparently most favourable to it, let alone more complex innovations like the Single European Act, where the role of the Commission as policy entrepreneur was critical.[55]

For the reason why the EU distils in a unique concentrate a more general, diffuse transformation of the modern state is that, just because it possesses no independent powers of taxation, and must make do with a tiny fraction of the revenues at the disposal of its member-states—a budget of less than 1.3 per cent of Union GDP, where public expenditures can account for up to 50 per cent of national incomes—there has been a virtually inbuilt drive within the Commission to expand its authority by the alternative route of regulation.[56] The rationale for the multiplication of technical directives from Brussels is in this sense overwhelming. For the beauty of regulation is that it requires minimal funding— just the salaries of a handful of experts—since the costs of regulation are borne, not by the regulatory authority, but by the firms or individuals subject to its rulings. Thus defenders of the EU as it exists today can point out, as they regularly do—Moravcsik is indefatigable on this point—that it employs

55. Renaud Dehousse and Giandomenico Majone, 'The Institutional Dynamics of European Integration: From the Single Act to the Maastricht Treaty', in Stephen Martin (ed.), *The Construction of Europe: Essays in Honour of Emile Noel*, DorDercht 1994, pp. 92–93; Majone, *Regulating Europe*, p. 62.

56. 'The EU could increase its competences only by developing as an almost pure type of regulatory state': Majone, 'From the Positive to the Regulatory State', p. 150.

a mere 18,000 functionaries, less than a provincial city, for a population of some 400 million. But this small cadre generates an immense web of regulations, far outnumbering laws passed by national legislatures themselves. As early as 1991, directives and regulations issued by Brussels already exceeded all pieces of legislation passed in Paris. Delors's prediction that by the end of the century 80 per cent of all economic and social legislation in the Union would be of Community origin was 'perhaps politically imprudent', but it 'did not lack solid empirical support'.[57] The EU is no mere façade.

But if the commanding function of the EU is regulatory, what then is its distinctive structure? Here Majone moves from an American to a European tool-box, drawing on an interest in the history of political thought and a gift of crisp conceptual clarity that are characteristically Italian, recalling something of Norberto Bobbio or Giovanni Sartori. *Dilemmas of European Integration* (2005) argues that the Union is not, and will not become, a federation, because it lacks a *demos* capable of either creating or supporting one. But nor is it a mere inter-governmental regime. Rather, in a classical, insufficiently remembered, sense of the term, the EU is a confederation, as Montesquieu once conceived it. What does this mean? That the underlying form of the Union is a 'mixed constitution' of the pre-modern type, formulated in antiquity by Aristotle and Polybius, and realized in mediaeval and pre-absolutist realms as a polity composed 'not of individual citizens but of corporate bodies balanced against each other and governed by mutual agreement rather than by a political sovereign'.[58] The confederal character of the EU lies in its projection of this design to inter-state level. Displaying neither separation of powers—the Commission enjoys both executive and legislative rights—nor division between government and opposition, nor significant polarity between Left and Right, the 'prime theme of the internal political process' in the EU is rather a jockeying among autonomous institutions—the Commission, the Council, the Court, the Parliament—over their respective prerogatives.

---

57. 'Understanding regulatory growth in the European Community', in David Hine and Hussein Kassim (eds), *Beyond the Market: The EU and National Social Policy*, London 1998, p. 16.

58. Majone, *Dilemmas of European Integration: The Ambiguities and Pitfalls of Integration by Stealth*, Oxford 2005, p. 46.

'Policy emerges as an epiphenomenon of this contest rather than from opposing ideological positions'.[59]

In such a system, it makes no sense to speak of a popular sovereignty that can only operate at national level, which is where electorates want to keep it—so much so that, the more powers the European Parliament acquires, the fewer people bother to vote for it. 'It follows that Europe's "democratic deficit" is, paradoxically speaking, democratically justified'.[60] What then are the benefits of the confederation? For Majone, though the Treaty of Rome showed some traces of *dirigisme*, unavoidable in that bygone era, its governing principle was the basic maxim of economic liberalism: the separation of *dominium* from *imperium*—property from rule, the market from the state. In upholding it, Majone can be nearly as radical as Gillingham, pressing for regulatory powers in the Union to be handed over to the wisdom of business and professional associations, rather than continuing to be held by a residually statist Commission—Reagan's salutary reforms across the ocean setting the challenging example. America, inspiration from the outset for Majone's regulatory theory of Europe, returns as admonition at the end. 'It would be unwise', he tells us, 'to forget that international competition takes place not only among producers of goods and services but, increasingly, among regulatory regimes as well'.[61]

The cool reduction of the EU to a modest confederal station serves a strong intellectual purpose. The elegance of Majone's construction is to link a general thesis about politics in the West to an argument about the evolution of the modern state, based on a theoretical deconstruction of its functions, that can present the Union as if it were an effectual apex of universal transformations under way. The key to this construction is the notion of 'non-majoritarian democracy', which—Majone assures us—is not only the silent constitutional basis of the EU, but the preferred model of nearly all advanced countries, apart from a few wayward exceptions like Britain. There is thus no discrepancy, but rather a natural fit between emergent national, and community, institutions. It is this that underwrites the legitimacy of the principle of regulation—not redistribution—as the wave of the future at both levels, even if constitutional theory has not quite caught up with

---

59. *Dilemmas of European Integration*, p. 50.
60. *Dilemmas of European Integration*, p. 40.
61. Majone, 'From the Positive to the Regulatory State', p. 165.

it. As over-attachment to the welfare state declines, 'independent regulatory bodies and other specialized agencies would seem to be in a better position than government departments to satisfy the new demands of the electorate'.[62] As a regulatory polity the EU, far from weakening democracy, actually enhances it by providing judicial and consumer protection for citizens against their own governments, in the form of rulings by the Court or directives from the Commission against which ministers cannot appeal.[63]

But what does the magisterially evasive term 'non-majoritarian' actually mean? Majone explains that 'non-majoritarian institutions' are 'public institutions which, by design, are not directly accountable either to voters or to elected officials'.[64] How then, on this definition, could there possibly be a non-majoritarian *democracy*? The notion would be a contradiction in terms. The work of the illicit elision, from agencies to a polity, is to lend persuasive force to the idea that regulation is ceasing to be a subsidiary or sectoral set of activities in a modern state, and instead is becoming its central function, symbolically resumptive of public life as a whole. When constrained to spell out what 'non-majoritarian democracy' means, Majone appeals to Madison: it is those forms of democracy whose overriding objective is to protect minorities from the 'tyranny of the majority' and offer a safeguard against 'factionalism'. But where are the tyrannical majorities or internecine factions to be found today? Nothing in Majone's description of political trends in Europe, where on the contrary voters are by and large content with the way things are going, and ideological divisions are at an all-time low, corresponds to them. Madison has been hi-jacked for purposes quite alien to him. The effect of the construction is to extrapolate 'market failures' as if they were a contemporary version of the menacing mob the Founders had in mind. The gap between their political fears and the 'efficiency issues' that dominate Majone's agenda is glaring.

Nor, of course, can questions of efficiency be separated from issues of redistribution, as allowing unanimous solutions mediated by experts. Aware of the difficulty, Majone seeks to turn it with the proviso that the two can be cleanly divided, as long as decisions regarding efficiency have no 'wealth effects'—

---

62. Majone, *Regulating Europe*, p. 299.
63. 'International Economic Integration, National Autonomy, Traditional Democracy: An Impossible Trinity?', EUI Working Papers, pp. 23ff.
64. Majone, *Regulating Europe*, p. 285.

that is, include compensations to those who might otherwise suffer economically from them. He offers as an illustration the way in which the EU's efficiency-promoting monetary union was accompanied by the creation of a redistributive 'Cohesion Fund'. But the example undoes the distinction. Cohesion Funds had to be added onto monetary union at Maastricht precisely because the latter was *not* unanimously thought to be beneficial in equal measure to all—as Majone himself puts it, 'the richer member states were particularly interested' in further integration, and so had to make side-payments to poorer members that had reason to doubt they would do so well out of the arrangements.[65] Nor was there much evidence of any real balance between the two, such that the net redistributive effect was likely to be neutral. In fact, Majone himself goes on to observe that the EU's regional funds are not particularly effective in redistributing income between individuals in the poorer parts of the Union, without adding that the same could be said of their effect as between not a few regions: witness the Mezzogiorno. In significant political matters, the wish to cleave efficiency from redistribution as separate issues is an ideological dream. What it serves to do is essentially to insulate the status quo. The EU makes rules; it does not change the position of the players. That is what is best about it.

Yet, although approving the general structure of the Union as he construes it, Majone shows little of Moravcsik's complacency. The failure of the European Constitution was not a bagatelle, let alone a sign of success. The draft Treaty included at least one significant feature that would have crystallized the EU's true character as a confederation, namely the right to secession; so too its provisions for common arrangements in defence and foreign policy, tasks appropriate to a confederation. The defenestration of the Constitution by voters expressed a growing popular distrust of the Union, which lacks the seal not of political legitimacy—there is no popular desire to democratize it—but of economic performance. Since, however, the central purpose of the EU is economic, its lacklustre showing in both employment and productivity growth, across an entire business cycle from 1995 to 2005, cannot but undermine its legitimacy.

Nor are the results of the two major institutional changes to the Union in this period anything to boast of. Both the single currency and enlargement were pushed through with a combination of

---

65. *Regulating Europe*, pp. 295–8.

meticulous precision in their technical requirements and calculated vagueness about their general—economic and political— implications. In each case, the 'uncertainties and ambiguities have been carefully concealed from the general public', and the upshot has so far been unimpressive or counter-productive. The advent of the euro, by the admission of even such a staunch European as Mario Monti, the long-time commissioner first for the Internal Market and then for Competition, has yet to yield much by way of results. More gravely, the—often restrictive— decisions of the European Central Bank have an all too evident impact on the economic welfare of citizens. 'For the first time, the outcomes of a European policy directly and visibly affect the general public rather than special interests or small groups of experts. Hence, much more than in the past, poor economic performance threatens the credibility of EU institutions, and erodes the narrow legitimacy basis on which the entire edifice of European integration rests'.[66]

What of enlargement? The inclusion of countries as poor as Romania and Bulgaria has converted the EU into a zone with a higher Gini-coefficient of income inequality than the arch-capitalist USA itself. This is no mere statistical effect, but a political determinant of the fate of needed reform in the Union. For it is fear of social dumping from the East that has blocked completion of the single market in services, which would have been uncontroversial when the Union was confined to the fifteen states of the West. Since services now account for 70 per cent of Union GDP and over 50 per cent of employment, this is a crippling limitation, too little advertised, of the whole process of integration. Contrary to a widespread belief, the EU is still far from a truly common market. Here lies one of the reasons for the sluggishness of growth within it.

Yet current uncertainties go deeper. They are rooted in the nature of European integration itself, which has always been an elitist project, enjoying no more than a passive consent of the population. That licence is now running out, as the huge gap between voters and parliament in even such an exemplary land of liberal outlook as the Netherlands has made clear—the Dutch referendum, naturally, striking Majone much more than

---

66. 'Is the European Constitutional Settlement Really Successful and Stable?', *Notre Europe*, October 2006, p. 5—an intervention that is a direct response to Moravcsik.

that of the French. 'Most key ideas of modern history, from popular sovereignty to the idea of the nation and the principle of nationality, were originally advanced by intellectual and political elites', Majone remarks. 'But these ideas proved their vitality by their capacity to mobilize people and push them to political action. This is not the case of European integration'. Over half a century, there has been 'a certain europeanization of intellectual, economic and political elites', but 'no "europeanization of the masses" has taken place even remotely comparable to that "nationalization of the masses" . . . which occurred in all countries of West Europe at the end of the Napoleonic wars'.[67]

The gulf between those above and those below remains irreparable. It is dictated by the way unification was originally designed, and has always proceeded. 'No realistic assessment of the EU . . . is possible without keeping constantly in mind the elitist nature of the project'—since 'the functionalist (or Monnet) approach to European integration taken in the 1950s entails a fundamental trade-off between integration and democracy. The logic of the approach is such that any time a choice between integration and democracy has to be made, the decision is, and must be, always in favour of integration'. To see this, one need only look at the Commission's monopoly of legislative initiative— 'a flagrant violation of both the constitutional principle of the separation of powers and the very idea of parliamentary democracy'.[68] So long as there is a sufficient material pay-off for this voiding of familiar constitutional norms, the masses will go along with it. But if the elites fail to deliver adequate levels of employment and job security, or increases in purchasing power, the Union could start to pitch.

In this diagnosis the tension, already visible in Gillingham's work, becomes tauter and more extreme, between what in Majone takes the form, in effect, of an apology for oligarchy and an afterthought for democracy. On the one hand, the EU is approved as a system of confederal power of distinguished intellectual lineage, rightly shielded from decision by popular majorities, where 'the growing importance of nonmajoritarian institutions' is proof that 'reliance upon qualities such as expertise, professional discretion, policy consistency, fairness, or independence of judgement is considered to be more important than reliance upon direct democratic

---

67. Majone, *Regulating Europe*, p. 7.
68. *Regulating Europe*, p. 7.

accountability'.[69] On the other hand, the Union is a regrettably hierarchical project, whose anti-democratic design was the outcome of a deliberate choice, for which Monnet bears responsibility, capable of alienating a passive citizenry as soon as GDP falters.

But is the EU a confederation in the first place? Not in any sense to be found, certainly, in *L'esprit des lois*. There Montesquieu's *république fédérative* was a union of city-states, provinces or cantons—such entities being necessarily small in size—for mutual defence against aggression from larger monarchies. He did not use the word 'confederation', and his description of a federated republic is incompatible with what the term has come to mean or the way in which it is employed by Majone, since it not only includes armed intervention from without to quell any popular rising in a constituent unit, but specifies that such units must renounce the right to treaties with other powers, since they 'give themselves up entirely, with nothing more to resign' in such a union once formed[70]—as if forces from Brussels were entitled to crush riots in Budapest, and the UK to be forbidden membership in NATO. Nor can Montesquieu, of all thinkers, be enlisted without paradox as a champion of mixed government, as opposed to the separation of powers. Though his idealized portrait of England as 'the one nation that has for the direct end of its constitution political liberty' reproduces the standard local formula of a mixed monarchy—the trinity of king, lords and commons—Montesquieu's innovation was to overlay this with a vision of the executive, legislature and judiciary as three independent powers, which never corresponded to island realities but transformed the expectations of the world.

For the credentials of a conception of mixed government as a hodgepodge of overlapping corporate bodies, Majone would have done better—as his invocation of mediaeval and pre-absolutist models implies—to go back 150 years, to Althusius as the appropriate ancestor. Where this can lead is to be seen in the work of Jan Zielonka, as noted above.[71] In his *Europe as Empire* (2006), the Union is extolled as a post-modern version of the Holy Roman Empire, superseding statist conceptions of political order for a complex realm of governance in which crude majoritarian

---

69. Majone, *Dilemmas of European Integration*, p. 37.
70. Montesquieu, *De l'esprit des lois*, Book IX, 1–3.
71. Chapter 2, pp. 68–69.

rule is becoming a thing of the past. Enlargement, seen by Majone as—at any rate so far—a shadow threatening progress towards the realization of a single market, is here greeted with Anglo-Polish elation as the *coup de grâce* to delusions of a European super-state.

Stretched to the Dnieper and the Bug, the EU according to Zielonka is now irrevocably a neo-mediaeval maze of variegated jurisdictions, whose unity will not rest on bureaucratic directives of any kind but on spontaneous market adjustments. True, the Middle Ages saw a good deal of predatory conduct—but also precocious welfare systems and the valuable doctrine of just wars. There is still much to be learnt from these. Democracy? 'Whether the evolving European governance system can still be called "democratic" is a matter of debate'.[72] In any case we are moving beyond traditional notions of rule by the people. Elections are a crude means of controlling officials. More effective can be 'policy networks' lobbying for specific decisions. Individual citizens should be able to contest these—but not, it is to be hoped, by populist referenda or unruly demonstrations. Private litigation and appeals to the ombudsman are a better path.

If Zielonka's notion of a luxuriant neo-mediaeval empire can be regarded as no more than an elaborate conceit, its upshot is still instructive—protestation after the event, not representation before it, as the future political norm. In effect, a return to petitions submitted to the prince. Majone is more realistic. The denial of democracy in the Union can be neither avoided nor stabilized. Integration has left little room for decisions from below. But once legitimacy is shifted from the will of voters to the fortune of markets, it becomes captive to their vagaries. Continuous high growth is a promise harder to keep than representative government. Maybe the will of the people cannot be circumvented so easily after all? In holding Monnet responsible for 'sacrificing democracy on the altar of integration', Majone implies an alternative was possible. But his premises preclude one. Monnet and his colleagues should not have proceeded by stealth, he explains in *Dilemmas*, but put the federal state they had in mind to the electorates of Europe. The reproach is a bluff, however, since for Majone such a prospect has never been acceptable to voters, yet the integration that has occurred—even if it has not so far acquired its true name—is just what he thinks it should be: a confederation exempt from the demands of popular sovereignty.

---

72. Jan Zielonka, *Europe as Empire: The Nature of the Enlarged European Union*, Oxford 2006, p. 117.

The charge against Monnet is a sign of unease. For viewed historically, the boot is on the other foot. Monnet's federalism envisaged just what Majone's confederalism rules out, namely the creation of a United States of Europe answerable to its population through the ballot. Hence the parliamentary structures built into the ECSC and EEC from the start, and the importance for Monnet of the European Defence Community, whose significance for the history of integration Parsons rightly stresses. That the EDC was aborted, and the European Parliament proved ineffective, have been not fulfilments but frustrations of Monnet's vision, which even now is not quite banished from the scene, as the oscillations of his critic suggest. In 2005, Majone could open *Dilemmas of European Integration* by hailing the architecture of the EU as 'the successful prototype of postmodern confederation'.[73] Two years later, surveying the wreckage of the Constitution, it had become a precarious edifice swaying on all too cramped foundations.

The location along the ideological spectrum of the four leading accounts of the Union thus far considered is clear enough. Spanning the significant differences between Moravcsik, Gillingham, Eichengreen and Majone are a set of overlapping commonalities. Hostility to any smack of federalism; minimization of the bearing of classical democratic norms; elevation of negative over positive integration; preference for voluntary over mandatory regulation; rejection of welfare barriers to market dynamism—no one analysis or prescription features all of these in equal measure, but there is a family resemblance between them. Conventionally speaking, they represent a phalanx of neo-liberal opinion, more or less pronounced or nuanced as the case may be. Where they diverge most sharply is in prognosis. Essentially agreeing on what the Union should be, they vary widely as to whether it is likely to become what it ought. Moravcsik displays a eupeptic optimism *à toute épreuve*, Majone expresses an unexpected pessimism, Eichengreen traces a prudently hedged scepticism, Gillingham gives voice to an agitated alarmism. Do such extreme discrepancies reflect on the commonalities, or do they simply mirror the normal opacity of the future?

4

At other points along the spectrum, there is less congregation of authority. Conceptions that break with the premises of the neo-

---

73. Majone, *Dilemmas of European Integration*, p. v.

liberal consensus are more dispersed and isolated, though by no means intellectually weaker. Here too, however, it is thinkers from America who make the running. The leading cases come, respectively, from philosophy, jurisprudence, and comparative politics. Larry Siedentop's *Democracy in Europe* (2000) stands out as a refreshingly idiosyncratic—that is, old-fashioned and independent-minded—vision of dangers in the Union, and remedies for them. The degree of its deviance from current conformism is suggested by the indignant response of Moravcsik, scarcely able to contain his disbelief that it should pay no attention to 'mainstream contemporary analyses'.[74] In fact, what separates Siedentop from these is the distance between a classical political liberalism, inspired by Tocqueville—his title echoing *Democracy in America*—and the ruling neo-liberalism of the period, to which such an outlook can only appear out of joint.

A career at Oxford has left its mark on Siedentop—Isaiah Berlin, of whom he has some interesting criticisms, is a central reference for him—but his starting-point could not be more squarely American. Federalism is a US invention, inscribed in the Constitution of 1787. Can Europe ever hope to emulate it? Montesquieu had believed there could be no liberty in a modern state that was of any size, hence necessarily a monarchy, without an aristocracy capable of restraining royal power. By devising a constitution that preserved liberty in a vast republic, Madison proved him wrong: a federation in a commercial society could realize what intermediary bodies had secured in a feudal society, without benefit of a nobility. Tocqueville, who first understood this, saw too the distinctive configuration that sustained America's successful federalism: a common language; common habits of local self-government; an open political class composed mainly of lawyers; and shared moral beliefs, of Protestant origin. Binding the new structure together, moreover, was—unacknowledged— the ghost of Britain's imperial state, that had accustomed the colonists to a single sovereign authority, now reinvented as a federation with powers of taxation and means of coercion.

Europe, by contrast, remains divided by a multiplicity of languages and sovereignties, ancient states with distinct cultures and no experience of common rule. Nor does it possess anything that resembles either the social stratum or the credal unity that

---

74. 'Despotism in Brussels? Misreading the European Union', *Foreign Affairs*, May–June 2001, p. 117.

buoyed the young liberal republic in America. On the contrary, it still bears the scars of a destructive anti-clericalism, and a divisive class consciousness, unknown across the Atlantic— calamitous legacies of the eighteenth and nineteenth centuries, fortunately now attenuated, yet not entirely effaced. In one sense, such burdens of the past render all the more remarkable the steps towards unity achieved by Europeans since 1950. But if their outcome remains not only incomplete but unhappy, the reason lies also, and above all, in the ideological drought of the present. For Tocqueville could only contemplate with melancholy what has happened to liberalism since his day, its rich vision of human flourishing dwindled to the thin alternatives of a utilitarianism of wants or a contractualism of rights. In this reduction, any active conception of citizenship vanishes. We are left with the roles of mere consumers or litigants.

The result has been a conception of European integration dominated by an arid economism, as if the Union were solely a matter of market efficiency. Such a narrow calculus has naturally been unable to engage popular imagination, leaving a void that could be filled only by competing governmental projects. Here just one contender has had a coherent vision. Britain, still without even a written constitution, and in the grip of a political culture continuing to rely on customs rather than ideas, is in no position to propose a compelling future for the Union. Germany, though itself possessing a federal framework that could in principle offer a mock-up of arrangements for a European federation, remains disabled by guilt for its still too recent past. France alone has had the institutional apparatus and political will to impose a design on the EU, whose formative years coincided with its own post-war recovery. The result is a Union to a large extent created in its own *étatiste* image—a centralizing administrative structure, in which decisions are reached behind closed doors by power-brokers in Brussels.

In France itself, this famously elitist, rationalist model of government, descending from Louis XIV, through the Revolution and Napoleon, has time and again fomented its antithesis: anarchic rebellion in the streets, popular risings against the state. The great danger facing the European Union, as a still more remote version of the same bureaucratic style of rule, is that one day it too could provoke such mass rejection—civil disorder on a continental scale. Today's combination of economism and *étatisme* is a toxic formula for future unrest. A wide-ranging political debate is needed to prevent Europeans feeling that the EU is merely the resultant of 'inexorable market forces or the machinations of elites which have escaped from democratic control'.[75] The Union requires new foundations.

What should these be? Siedentop's answer takes him back to America. For a genuine federation, composed of active local self-government rather than a system of bureaucratic directives, Europe needs an open political class, communicating in a common language, and a shared set of beliefs, shaping a moral identity. To create the first, he recommends a small and powerful European Senate, composed of leading parliamentary figures from each country elected by, and serving concurrently in, their national legislatures. English, already widespread as the informal Latin of the continent, should become the official language of the Union, in which senators could get to know one another as intimately as their homologues on the Hill. Meanwhile, less exclusive recruitment to the legal profession—where Britain is a particularly bad offender—should gradually supply the human material of a new political class, in a European system that is anyway already highly juridified.

There remains the trickiest question of all. Where is Europe's counterpart to America's civil religion—Tocqueville's 'habits of the heart'—to come from? Faithful to US example here too, Siedentop replies that a liberal constitution for Europe would in itself be an answer, affording a moral framework in which individuals become conscious of their equality as citizens, and so acting in the fashion of a surrogate religion, as 'a source of identity and right conduct'.[76] But is a mere surrogate quite enough—don't Americans, after all, rely on the original article as well? To the scandal of Moravcsik, Siedentop does not flinch from following his argument through. Liberal constitutionalism is indeed just the latest frontier of Christianity, as the world religion that historically combined universalism and individualism, its moral equality of souls before God leading eventually to an equal liberty of citizens under the state.

For a European democracy to acquire cohesion and stability without sacrificing individualism, this link needs to be recovered. A weak-minded multiculturalism substituting for it—to which even such a liberal light as Berlin, perhaps because of his Jewish

---

75. Larry Siedentop, *Democracy in Europe*, London 2000, p. 1.
76. *Democracy in Europe*, p. 101.

background, was not altogether immune—should be rejected. The Union must assume its tolerant, but not shame-faced, underlying Christian identity. All this will take time. Siedentop ends on an Augustinian note. Europe needs something like its own version of the complex federalism that took shape in America, but not yet. To rush towards the goal in current conditions, before the Union is ready for it, could produce only the caricature of a federation, dominated by an elite without any true sympathy or understanding for federalism.

Unlike any other work of significance in its field, *Democracy in Europe* has won a European readership, with translations into most of the languages of the original Community. It owes its reception to attractive qualities that set it apart from the mass of technical literature on integration: a direct argument and engaging prose accessible to anyone. In both its sensitivity to the contrasting political cultures of the leading states of Western Europe, and its dismissal of the intellectual poverty of standard celebrations of the Union, it is a rarity in the writing on the EU, where philosophical reflection of any kind is for the most part at a discount. That said, the effect of its calque of American virtues for European users is simply to reproduce the constitutional blankness it criticizes—as if Evangelical faith and the US congressman were conceivable, let alone desirable, implants in the body politic of the Old World. No original proposals for Europe eventuate, in a case that dissolves into vagueness just where the sharpest clarity is required: at the virtually opposite meanings of federalism on the two continents, as a centripetal force in America, creating a new sovereignty, and a centrifugal one in Europe, devolving older sovereignties.

For invoking Tocqueville, Siedentop has not remembered him. The historic achievement of American federalism, in Tocqueville's eyes, was to overcome the weaknesses of the European confederations—Dutch, Swiss, German—that Montesquieu had praised. It had done so by endowing a central authority with its own taxes and troops, and the power to enact laws with direct effect on its citizens, where confederations in Europe had no independent means to enforce their will on the states that composed them. *Democracy in America* is a far more centralizing text than *Democracy in Europe*. Tocqueville's principal misgiving about the US republic, in fact, was that the federal government still lacked sufficient strength to deal with potential resistance from the states. The Founders 'gave money and soldiers to the Union, but the states kept the love and prejudices of the peoples', hence the 'absurd and destructive doctrine' that allowed Connecticut and Massachusetts to refuse to send their militias into the war with England in 1812.[77]

But Tocqueville's overall verdict was clear. In America, he explained, 'the central power acts without an intermediary upon the governed, administers them and judges them itself, as national governments do, but it acts in this way only in a restricted sphere. Evidently that is no longer a federal government, it is an incomplete national government. So one has found a form of government that is neither precisely national nor federal; but one stops there, and the new word that ought to express the new thing still does not exist'.[78] Such robust views would be an embarrassment in Brussels, where talk of an incomplete national government could only set the teeth of its functionaries on edge. By comparison, Siedentop's recipes are weak medicine.

Philosophical and legal approaches to the EU are necessarily quite distinct, but in moving from one to the other at their best, we remain in Greater America. Of Israeli origin—he describes himself as the 'quintessential wandering Jew'—the jurist Joseph Weiler, after teaching at Michigan and Harvard, now holds a chair at New York University. Since law in a virtually pure state, without any of its normal accoutrements of administration or enforcement, is the defining medium of the EU, lawyers play an enormous part in both the workings of the Union and the meanings extracted from them. So it is not altogether surprising that even a heterodox legal mind can play more of a role in its affairs than orthodox eminences in other disciplines. Weiler's services to the Union include helping to draft the European Parliament's Declaration of Human Rights and advising the Commission on the Treaty of Amsterdam.

But such insider roles have done nothing to blunt intellectual interventions of notable sharpness and verve. The iconography of literature on the EU, like so much of what lies between its covers, is typically of mortal dullness: dominated either by its dreary supermarket-sticker logo—even Gillingham's book is a victim—or such uplifting clichés—Moravcsik's—as a stream-lined clipper cresting the waves, its sails billowing with the flags

---

77. Alexis de Tocqueville, *Democracy in America,* Harvey Mansfield and Delba Winthrop (eds), Chicago 2000, pp. 157, 160.
78. *Democracy in America,* p. 149.

of the member-states. With the cover of Weiler's *The Constitution of Europe*, from which the grotesques of Ensor's savage anarchist masterpiece, *Christ's Entry into Brussels in 1889*, leer out at us, we are invited into a different world

The central chapter of the book, 'Fin-de-Siècle Europe: Do the New Clothes Have an Emperor?', sets the note. What kind of a polity is the EU? Weiler disposes of inter-governmental and confederal paradigms without ceremony, as 'wishful ideological thinking' that not only 'masks serious problems of social control and accountability' but induces 'complacency as regards the assault on democracy that the Union often represents'.[79] If the EU is not captured by either of these descriptions, it is because the Community, though historically it has often strengthened its member-states, cannot be reduced to a design of which they remain the masters, even if this was what they intended. Rather, in many ways 'the Community has become a *golem* that has ensnared its creators'.[80] The European Court of Justice is a prime example of this involuntary sorcery. Weiler offers a dazzling analysis of the changing functions and fortunes of the Court, showing the way in which it seized the initiative in establishing an ever-widening supranational jurisdiction that caught governments unawares, before eventually triggering a reaction from them that took the form of stepping up the role of the Council of Ministers and its diplomatic minions in Brussels, at the expense of the Commission. In this dialectic, developments on the legal and political planes moved in opposite directions, both of them departing from the Treaty of Rome.

Although Weiler admires the work of the Court, he warns against excessive celebration of it. Ever since it attracted greater public attention, and increased its caseloads, it has become far more cautious, no longer playing much of a dynamic role in today's Union. The Council of Ministers and its Committee of Permanent Representatives (Coreper)—the secretive hub of most deal- and decision-making in Brussels—have, on the other hand, certainly not drawn in their claws. For Weiler, the Council not only distorts a proper distribution of powers at Union level, by exercising executive control over legislative activity, but castrates parliamentary authority at national level by the volume, complexity and timing of decisions passed down to it for theoretical approval.

---

79. Joseph Weiler, *The Constitution of Europe*, Cambridge 1999, p. 269.
80. *The Constitution of Europe*, p. xi.

The European Parliament, with its huge constituencies and feeble powers, is no counterweight. Moreover, within the Council itself, ideological divisions are typically neutralized, since governments are always of different complexions, evacuating normal political conflict or debate for a technocratic consensus—a 'consociational' style of rule that is the formula for a cartel of elites.

The upshot of this institutional drift is bleak. In the beginning, the Community stood for ideals of real significance in post-war Europe: peace, prosperity and supranationalism. Today, the first two are banalities, and the third has been reduced to banknotes. 'The Europe of Maastricht no longer serves, as its grandparents the Europe of Paris and Rome, as a vehicle for the original foundational values'.[81] Already with the Single European Act, not just a technocratic programme for the free movement of factors of production was in train, but 'a highly politicized choice of ethos, ideology and political culture', enthroning the market as the measure of social value.[82] In this Europe, where politics is increasingly commodified, individuals are indeed empowered, but as consumers, not as citizens. Nor is enlargement changing this: for, as the prevailing idiom would put it, 'when a company issues new voting shares, the value of each share is reduced'.[83] Public life risks sinking into rounds of bread and circuses, without further dignity or legitimacy.

What is to be done? Weiler, no enemy of markets as such, would have them conceived in the spirit of Paine rather than Friedman, as forms of sociability as well as exchange, arenas 'for the widening of horizons, for learning about and learning to respect others and their habits'—hence in themselves a kind of community too.[84] Citizenship, however, is a political bond, and the issue posed since Maastricht is how it can be made effective simultaneously at national and at supranational level. With a sly wave to Marcuse, Weiler casts this as the problem of conjoining Eros and civilization: the nation as abiding, existential focus of romantic attachments, the Union as modern framework of an enlightened reason, each as necessary for a democratic Europe as the other.

The Constitution of Europe concludes with four concrete

---

81. *The Constitution of Europe*, p. 258.
82. *The Constitution of Europe*, p. 89.
83. *The Constitution of Europe*, p. 264.
84. *The Constitution of Europe*, p. 256.

proposals to this end. On collection of a sufficient number of signatures, citizens should be able to place legislative initiatives, in areas subject to Community law, before voters on the occasion of elections to the European Parliament, which if passed by requisite majorities would be binding on the Union and its member-states. Complementing this Legislative Ballot, a 'European Public Square' could be created in which the complete set of decision-making processes in the Community—in particular, the currently impenetrable recesses of comitology in Brussels—would be posted on the internet for the inspection of citizens, above all the younger generations for whom the Web will be like print of old. A Constitutional Council, in turn, would arbitrate issues of juridical competence, a continual bone of contention, within the Union. Finally, the EU should be able to raise a small income tax directly from its citizens to bind the two together with one of the classic ties of democratic representation.

The ideas themselves are uneven. Weiler thinks his internet scheme—Lexcalibur, as he would call it—the most important and far-reaching, whereas to a sceptical eye it looks the flakiest: as if future teenagers will be eagerly scanning the 97,000 pages of Community directives or the hydra-headed minutes of Coreper for their political caffeine. The suggestion that a Constitutional Council be modelled on the tame French version is not much of a recommendation. But the Legislative Ballot is at once a highly imaginative and perfectly feasible proposition, one that would sow panic in European establishments. The idea of a direct fiscal tie between the Union and its citizens is not quite so original, but no less relevant and radical for that. The essential point is that with proposals like these, the discursive terrain has shifted. We have left the establishment consensus that the European constitutional order inhabits the best of all possible worlds, namely that of the second-best, for any other is impossible.

On this alternative terrain, one distinguished mind has envisaged a far more sweeping reconstruction of the Union. Philippe Schmitter, originally a pupil of Haas at Berkeley, later teacher at Chicago and Stanford, first made his name as a Latin Americanist, before becoming one of the world's most inventive and wide-ranging comparatists, writing extensively on corporatism, regional integration and—perhaps in particular—the problems of transition from authoritarian to democratic regimes, in South America and

Southern Europe. Stationed at the European University Institute
in Florence at the turn of the century, he published in 2000 what
remains in many ways the most remarkable single reflection on
the EU to date, *How to Democratize the European Union . . .
and Why Bother?* Typically, although a shorter early draft exists
in Italian, this arresting work has never been translated into any
other language of the Union, testimony enough to the provincial
indifference with which it has abandoned thought of itself. As a
systematic set of proposals for political change of visionary scope
and detail, the text recalls another age, as if written by a latter-
day Condorcet. An exercise of this kind normally belongs to a
utopian style of thought, indifferent to constraints of reality. But
a more worldly temperament, in every sense, than Schmitter's
would be hard to find. The second part of his title expresses the
spirit of the other side of his intelligence, an ironic detachment
worthier of a descendant of Talleyrand. The crossing of two such
antithetical strains makes for a work unique in the literature on
the Union.

Schmitter begins by noting that the EU is neither a state nor
a nation. Although it has irrevocably crossed the threshold of
any mere inter-governmental arrangement, it displays neither the
coincidence of territorial and functional authority that defines a
state, nor the collective identity that marks a nation. Few of those
subject to its jurisdiction understand it, and with good reason.
'The EU is already the most complex polity that human agency
. . . has ever devised'.[85] It is plainly far from anything that could
be described as an accountable structure under popular control.
What would it take to democratize it? Little less than a reinvention
of three key institutions of modern democracy: citizenship,
representation and decision-making. Schmitter coolly specifies an
agenda for the transformation of each. Of the resulting sixteen,
sardonically designated 'modest proposals', it is sufficient to
indicate the following.

Citizenship? To promote a more active liberty in the Union:
direct referenda to coincide with elections to the European
Parliament, themselves to be held electronically over an entire
week, with voters having the right to determine the terms of office
of their favoured candidates. To make for the first time a reality
of universal suffrage: multiple votes for adults with children. To

---

85. Philippe Schmitter, *How to Democratize the European Union . . . and
Why Bother?*, Lanham 2000, p. 75.

foster social solidarity: denizen rights for immigrants; conversion
of the total monies now spent on the CAP and Structural Funds
into a 'Euro-stipendium' to be paid to all citizens of the Union
with an income less than a third of the European average.

Representation? To create a more effective legislature—
capping the size of the European Parliament, seating MEPs
proportionate to the logarithm of the population of each
member state, and assigning all other than symbolic work of the
assembly to commissions, as in Italy. To encourage more Union-
wide political organization: half of the EU electoral funds now
allocated to national parties in member-states to be switched to
party formations in the EP, vested with the right of nominating
half the candidates on their respective national lists.

Decision-making? To manage equitably the complexities of a
Europe with so many member-states, of vastly differing sizes—
division of the Union into three 'colleges' of states by ascending
number of citizens, votes weighted within each by logged value.
Three simultaneous presidencies of the European Council, one
from each college, nominating a president of the Commission to
be approved by a majority in each college and of the EP; decisions
in the Council of Ministers likewise to require a concurrent
majority of the weighted votes in all three colleges.

Schmitter, like Weiler, is not necessarily the best judge of which
of his own proposals are the most significant. He argues that it is
the alterations in the Union's decision-making rules he outlines that
have the greatest potential for democratizing it—changes in Euro-
citizenship and Euro-representation having less immediate pay-
offs. This seems implausible, as his 'collegiate' orders appear least
close to the tangible experience of ordinary voters, as a structure
not only of considerable technical alembication, but operational
at the remotest peak of European power. Ground-level changes in
citizenship look much more explosive and swiftly transformative.

Schmitter rightly underlines the importance of the 'symbolic
novelty' of his suggestions for these, designed to have a benign
shock effect to bring home the value-added of being a European
as well as a national citizen. To engage people, indeed, politics
must become more fun. As the American Founders, thinking it
impossible to stop the causes of factions— regarded at the time as
the worst of evils afflicting a republic—devised instead institutions
to control their effects, so if there is no hope of doing away with
today's equivalent—the trivialization of politics by the media—
the antidote can only lie, *inter alia*, in making politics more

entertaining.[86] The contrast with Moravscik's prescriptions for a popular sedative—the more boring, the better—could hardly be more pointed. Later suggestions include voter lotteries for funding of good causes, electronic balloting, and participatory budgets. But these are trimmings. The boldest and most substantial single idea in Schmitter's arsenal is certainly the proposal for a Euro-stipendium financed out of the abolition of the common agricultural and regional funds. As *bien-pensant* critics have not failed to point out, this would be bound to unleash redistributive struggles in the Union—the appalling prospect, in other words, of social conflicts that might engage the passions and interests of its citizens. In short, the worst of all possible dangers, the intrusion of politics into the antiseptic affairs of the Union.

How does Schmitter himself view the social context in which he offers his reforms? Not through the lens of the *philosophe*, but the lorgnette of the Congress of Vienna. There is, and for the foreseeable future will be, no popular demand or spontaneous pressure from below to democratize the Union. So why bother with schemes to render it more accountable? The reasons can only lie in underlying structural trends, which could eventually erode the legitimacy of the whole European enterprise. Among these are 'symptoms of morbidity'—Gramsci's phrase—in national political systems themselves: distrust of politicians, shrinkage of parties, drop in voter turnout, spread of belief in corruption, growing tax evasion. Another is decline in the permissive consensus that the process of integration once enjoyed, as Europeans have become increasingly bemused and restive at secretive decisions reached in Brussels that affect more and more aspects of their existence. National leaderships lose credibility when major policies issue from bureaucratic transactions in Brussels, without Union institutions themselves gaining transparency or authority. Such degenerative trends now risk being exacerbated by monetary union, removing macro-economic instruments from member-states, and by enlargement, giving veto powers to as little as a quarter of the population of the EU. Democratization can still be deferred. But not indefinitely.

Nor, however, can it be realized suddenly or completely. Well before the ill-fated European Convention, Schmitter had dismissed the possibility that such proceedings could succeed. Constitutions

---

86. See Philippe Schmitter and Alexander Trechsel, *The Future of Democracy in Europe: Trends, Analyses and Reforms*, Council of Europe 2004.

are born of revolutions, putsches, wars, economic collapses, not of routine peacetime conditions. The only way the European polity could—democratically—be constitutionalized would be through a Constituent Assembly with a mandate approved by a prior referendum of all European citizens. In the interim, the way forward must be a return to Monnet's method, now relying not on economic spillovers to advance integration, but on political increments of democracy to transform it in similar, gradually cascading fashion—*petits pas* once again yielding, in the end, *grands effets*.

It is appropriate that the most cogent programme for the democratization of the EU should come from an heir of neo-functionalism: the charge that Monnet's method precluded one could not be more directly refuted. But Schmitter's intellectual background includes more than Haas. His reflections end with a final, disabused twist. Where is the force that might take up his programme? One historical agent has been unequivocally strengthened by the EU, he writes. 'That is the European bourgeoisie'. Could it rise to the challenge? Alas, it is too comfortably ensconced in power as it is, with little reason to alter the status quo. 'Ideologically, its "liberal" positions have never been more dominant; practically, its "natural" opponent, the organized working class, has been weakened'. Were integration to come under threat from below, the bourgeoisie would be much more likely 'to seek retrenchment behind a phalanx of technocrats than to take the risk of opening up the process to the uncertainties of transparency, popular participation, mass party competition, citizen accountability and redistributive demands'.[87] Indeed. There is an echo here of Weber's disappointment with the German bourgeoisie of his time. But in the EU, no quest for a charismatic leader to resolve the impasse—Weber's solution— could be of avail. Perhaps after all, democratization of the European polity, like liberalization of the economy before it, will have to come like a thief in the night, overtaking all agents—elites and masses alike, if in uneven measure—before any are fully aware of what is happening.

Schmitter's construction thus at once refutes and confirms Majone's critique of the 'Monnet method'. A radical iconoclasm of democratic ends is joined, for lack of anything credible that is better, with a sceptical reversion to traditional stealth in means. Yet in these reflections, a frontier common to all the theorizations

---

87. Schmitter, *How to Democratize the European Union*, pp. 128–9.

so far considered starts to be crossed. The language of class does not belong to the discourse of Europe. Schmitter's freedom with it reflects a working background in Latin America, where the vocabulary of rule has always been more robust, and a personal culture extending well beyond the triter Anglo-Saxon verities, as far as the exotic shores of pre-war corporatism or post-war socialism. He once authored a paper describing the EC as 'a novel form of political domination'.[88] What such intimations indicate is a gap. The reigning literature on Europe spreads across disciplines: politics, economics, sociology, history, philosophy, law are all represented. Missing, however, in the recent literature is any real political economy of integration, of the kind that Milward offered of the founding years of the Community. For that, one has to move outside the bounds of liberal discourse on Europe.

Unsurprisingly, the best work on this—all too uncomfortably concrete—terrain, of class forces and social antagonisms, metamorphoses of capital and fissures of labour, alterations in contract and innovations in rent, has been done by Marxist scholars. Here what has been called the Amsterdam School, a group of mainly Dutch scholars inspired by the example of Kees van der Pijl, who pioneered the study of transnational class formations, has led the way. The result has been not only a great deal of detailed empirical research into the business metabolisms of integration, but a consideration of the wider array of forces sustaining the turn the EU has taken since the eighties. Putting Gramsci's conceptual legacy to ingenious use, this is a line of interpretation that distinguishes between 'disciplinary' and 'compensatory' forms of neo-liberal hegemony (as it were: Thatcher's and New Labour's) within the Union, and—developing a hypothesis first suggested by Milward—seeks the social base of these pendular forms in a new rentier bloc with an over-riding interest in hard money, whose complex ramifications now extend into the better-off layers of the private-sector working class itself. Parallel with this work, a

---

88. Whose 'class bias is so severe that one wonders whether EC doesn't really stand for "Executive Committee for managing the general affairs of the Bourgeoisie!" This is hardly surprising (and not even scandalous) in this epoch of renewed faith in markets and entrepreneurial virtue': see 'The European Community as an Emergent and Novel Form of Political Domination', Working Paper 1991/26, Centro de Estudios Avanzados en Ciencias Sociales, Madrid 1991, p. 26.

spirited revisionist history of both the ideological origins and the economic outcomes of integration, each contravening received opinions, is under way—it too proceeding from Marx rather than Ricardo or Polanyi. Even in this heterodox left field, it should be said, the US presence is visible. The leading collection of the Amsterdam School, *A Ruined Fortress?* (2003), is orchestrated by a chair-holder from upstate New York, Alan Cafruny; the editor and principal contributor to the revisions of *Monetary Union in Crisis*, Bernard Moss, is an American based in London.[89]

What explains the strange pattern of expatriation—it would plainly be wrong to speak of expropriation—of European studies, understood as enquiry into the past and future of the Union? American dominance of the field in part, no doubt, reflects the famously greater resources, material and intellectual, of the US university system, which assures its lead in so many other areas. There is also the longer tradition and greater prominence in the US of political science, the discipline for which European integration is the most obvious hunting-ground. More generally, an imperial culture has to monitor major developments around the world: it could be argued that contemporary China or Latin America do not differ substantially from Europe, so far as the balance of scholarship is concerned. Still, the much greater density, not to speak of ancestry, of university research in today's Union would not lead one to expect particularly similar outcomes.

Yet it is difficult to avoid the feeling that a more specific factor is also at work. The United States remains the most unchanging of all political orders, its constitution petrified apparently forever in its eighteenth-century form. In the title of a recent study, it is the 'Frozen Republic'. Europe, on the other hand, has now been the stage for a continuous political experiment for half a century,

---

89. See, respectively, Alan Cafruny and Magnus Ryder (eds), *A Ruined Fortress? Neo-Liberal Hegemony and Transformation in Europe*, Lanham 2003, in which Stephen Gill's keynote essay 'A Neo-Gramscian Approach to European Integration' is particularly striking; and Bernard Moss (ed.), *Monetary Union in Crisis: The European Union as a Neo-Liberal Construction*, Basingstoke 2005, whose leading essay, alongside Moss's own contributions, is by another American scholar, Gerald Friedman of Amherst, whose 'Has European Economic Integration Failed?', shows how limited the efficiency gains from trade across member-state borders have been, given the similarity of national factor endowments in the Union.

with no precedent and still no clear end in sight. The novelty and restlessness of this process seem to have made it a magnet of attraction for minds formed in a culture at once constitutionally saturated and paralyzed, offering an outlet for intellectual energy frustrated at home. That, at any rate, would be one reading of the situation. To this could be added the intellectual advantages often afforded, historically, by distance. In the nineteenth century, no native mind came near Tocqueville, perhaps even Bryce, as thinkers about America. Why should not America return the compliment to Europe today? That, at any rate, would be one reading of the situation.

But there is, all too plainly, a further and final strand in the tangle of reasons why Americans have captured the narratives of Europe. The drift of the Union has been towards their presuppositions. The result is something like a new ideological affinity between subject and object. Another way of putting this would be to say that Europe has, to a striking extent, become the theoretical proving-ground of contemporary liberalism. Nowhere are the varieties of that liberalism on such vivid display as in the deliberations on the Union. Even within the span of neo-liberal interpretations, the contrasts are notable. Moravcsik offers a technocratic, Gillingham a classical economic, Eichengreen a post-social, Majone a non-majoritarian version. Set apart from these, and differing again, are Siedentop's classical political, Weiler's communitarian, Schmitter's radical-democratic versions. At one extreme, democracy as understood in a traditional liberal conception is all but extinguished; at the other, all but transfigured. Keohane, Hayek, Polanyi, Montesquieu, Tocqueville, Paine are among the variegated inspirations of this array. Do they exhaust the possibilities of describing the Union? Tocqueville's words come back: 'One stops there, and the new word that ought to express the new thing still does not exist'.

II. THE CORE

FRANCE

I · 2004

France is, of all European countries, the most difficult for any foreigner to write about. Its intractability is a function, in the first instance, of the immense output on their society produced by the French themselves, on a scale undreamt of elsewhere. Seventy titles just on the electoral campaign of spring 2002. Two hundred books on Mitterrand. Three thousand on De Gaulle. Such numbers, of course, include a huge amount of dross. But they are not mere logomachy. High standards of statistical rigour, analytic intelligence, literary elegance continue to distinguish the best of French writing about France, in quantities no neighbouring land can rival.

Confronted with this mass of self-description, what can the alien gaze hope to add? The advantages of estrangement, would be the anthropological reply—Lévi-Strauss's *regard éloigné*. But in England we lack the discipline of real distance. France is all too misleadingly familiar: the repetitively stylized Other of insular history and popular imagination; the culture whose words are still most commonly taught, movies screened, classics translated; the shortest trip for the tourist, the most fashionable spot for a secondary residence. London is now closer to Paris than Edinburgh by train; there are some fifteen million visits by Britons to France every year, more than from any other country. The vicinity is lulling. Its effect is a countrywide equivalent of the snare against which every schoolchild struggling with French is warned. France itself becomes a kind of *faux ami*.

Local connoisseurs are seldom of much help in correcting the error. It is striking that the two best-known recent English historians of France, Richard Cobb and Theodore Zeldin, have taken the national penchant for the whimsical and eccentric to extremes, as if so defeated by their subject they had to fall back, in compensation, on a parodic exhibition of French images of Anglicity, as so many historiographic Major Thompsons. Less strenuous contributions—political science, cultural studies, the higher journalism—offer little antidote. Reportage itself often seems mortified: few dispatches are so regularly flat as those filed from Paris, as if it were somehow the death-bed of the correspondent's imagination. A bright obscurity covers the country, screening its pitfalls for cross-Channel commentary. What follows is unlikely to escape a share of them.

I

The current scene is as good a place to start as any, since it offers a pregnant example of the illusions of familiarity. Newspapers, journals and bookshops brim with debate over French decline. Gradually trickling to the surface in the past few years, *le déclinisme* burst into full flow with the publication last winter of *La France qui tombe*, a spirited denunciation of national default—'the sinister continuity between the fourteen years of François Mitterrand and the twelve of Jacques Chirac, united by their talent for winning elections and ruining France'—by Nicolas Baverez, an economist and historian of the Centre-Right.[1] Rebuttals, vindications, rejoinders, alternatives have proliferated. Baverez looks at first glance like a French version of a Thatcherite, a neo-liberal of more or less strict persuasion, and the whole controversy like a re-run of long-standing debates on decline in Britain. But the appearances are deceptive. The problem is not the same.

Britain's diminution since the war has been a long-drawn-out process. But its starting-point is clear: the illusions bred by victory in 1945, under a leader of 1914 vintage, followed virtually without intermission by the realities of financial dependency on Washington, austerity at home, and imperial retreat abroad. By the time consumer prosperity arrived, a decade later, the country was already lagging behind the growth of continental economies, and within a few more years found itself locked out of a European Community whose construction it had rejected. In due course

---

1. Paris 2003, p. 131. For a pained reply from the *juste milieu*, see Alain Duhamel, *Le désarroi français*, Paris 2003, p. 163ff.

the welfare state itself—a landmark when first created—was overtaken elsewhere. There was no dramatic reckoning with the past, just a gradual slide within a framework of complete political stability.

Abroad de-colonization was conducted steadily, at little cost to the home country, but owed much to luck. India was too big to put up a fight for. War in Malaya, unlike Indochina, could be won because the communist movement was based on an ethnic minority. Rhodesia, unlike Algeria, was logistically out of range. The costs to the colonized were another matter, in the bloody skein of partitions left behind: Ireland, Palestine, Pakistan, Cyprus. But British society appeared unscathed. Yet, like the welfare state with which it was often coupled as a principal achievement of the post-war order, withdrawal from empire too eventually lost its lustre, when the abscess of Ulster reopened. The decisive development of the period lay elsewhere, in the abandonment after the Suez expedition of any pretension by the British state to autonomy from the US. Henceforward the adhesion of the nation to the global hegemon—internalized as a political imperative by both parties, more deeply by Labour even than Conservatives—cushioned loss of standing in the popular imagination, while exhibiting it to the world at large. Intellectual life was not so dissimilar, vitality after the war coming largely from external sources, emigrés from Central and Eastern Europe, with few local eminences. Here too there was subsidence without much tension.

A sense of decline became acute only within the British elites when fierce distributional struggles broke out in the seventies, with the onset of stagflation. The outcome was a sharp shift of gravity in the political system, and Thatcher's mandate to redress the fall in the country's fortunes. Neo-liberal medicine, continued under New Labour, revived the spirits of capital and redrew the social landscape—Britain pioneering programmes of privatization and deregulation internationally as it had once done welfare and nationalization. A modest economic recovery was staged, amid still decaying infrastructures and increasing social polarization. With the recent slow-down in Europe, claims of a national renaissance have become more common, without acquiring widespread conviction.

Overseas, Thatcher's most famous success was regaining the puny Antarctic colony of the Falklands; Blair's, brigading the country into the American invasion of Iraq. Pride or shame in such ventures scarcely impinge on the rest of the world. Internationally, the country's cultural icon has become a football celebrity. Little alteration of political arrangements; moderate growth but still low productivity; pinched universities and crumbling railroads; the unmoved authority of Treasury, Bank and City; an underling diplomacy. The record lacks high relief. The British way of coming down in the world might itself be termed a mediocre affair.

France has been another story. Defeat and occupation left it, after Liberation, at a starting-point far below that of Britain. The Resistance had saved its honour, and Potsdam its face, but it was a survivor rather than a victor power. Economically, France was still a predominantly rural society, with a per capita income only about two-thirds of the British standard. Sociologically, the peasantry remained far its largest class: 45 per cent of the population. Politically, the Fourth Republic floundered into quicksands of governmental instability and colonial disaster. Within little more than a decade after Liberation, the army was in revolt in Algeria, and the country on the brink of civil war. The whole post-war experience appeared a spectacular failure.

In fact, the Fourth Republic had in some ways been a period of extraordinary vitality. It was in these years that the administrative structure of the French state was overhauled, and the technocratic elite that dominates the business and politics of the country today took shape. While cabinets revolved, civil servants assured a continuity of *dirigiste* policies that modernized the French economy at nearly twice the clip of growth rates in Britain. French architects—Monnet and Schuman—laid the foundations of European integration, and it was French politicians who clinched the Treaty of Rome: the birth of the European Community, just before the Fourth Republic expired, owed more to France than any other country. French literature, in the days of Sartre, Camus and de Beauvoir, enjoyed an international readership probably without equal in the post-war world, well beyond its standing between the wars.

So when De Gaulle came to power, on the back of military revolt in Algiers, the estate he inherited—apparently dilapidated—in fact offered solid bases for national recovery. He, of course, promised much more than that. France, he had famously announced, was inconceivable without *grandeur*. In his vocabulary the word had connotations that escape the vulgar claims of 'Greatness' attached to Britain; it was a more archaic and abstract ideal, which appeared even to many of his compatriots out of keeping with the age. Yet it is difficult to deny it to the man, and the reconstruction over which he presided. It is conventional to pair him with Churchill, as statues in the national pantheon. But, beyond romantic legend, there is a discrepancy between them. De Gaulle's historical achievement was much larger. Colourful as it was, Churchill's role in twentieth-century Britain proved by comparison quite limited: an inspirational leadership of his country, crucial for a year, in a war won by Soviet troops and American wealth, and a brief epilogue of nondescript office in time of peace. The image he left was huge, the mark modest. Little in post-war Britain, save lingering imperial illusions, is traceable to him.

In exile, De Gaulle's war-time leadership was more purely symbolic, and his adjustment to peace, at which he threw in a hand stronger than Churchill's, little more successful. But he was a generation younger, with an altogether more reflective and original cast of mind. When he returned to power a decade later, he had mastered the arts of politics, and proved a strange singleton of modern statecraft. In the West no other post-war leader comes near his record. The largest colonial conflict of the century—at its height, the French army in Algeria numbered 400,000, and probably as many Algerians died, in a war that uprooted nearly two million—was brought to a dexterous end, and resistance to the settlement by those who had put him in power crushed. A new Republic was founded, with institutions—above all, a strong presidential executive—designed to give the country firm political stability. High-technology modernization of the economy proceeded apace, with major infrastructural programmes and rapidly rising living standards in the towns, as growth accelerated. Large farming was shielded by the CAP, a French construction, while the countryside started to empty, and the capital regained its pristine splendour.

Most striking, of course, was the transformation of the French state's position in the world. As the Cold War continued, De Gaulle made France the only truly independent power in Europe. Without breaking with the United States, he built a nuclear deterrent that owed nothing to America, and cocked it *à tous azimuts*. Withdrawing French forces from NATO command, boycotting US operations under UN guise in the Congo, stockpiling gold to weaken the dollar, he condemned the American war in Vietnam and Israeli arrogance in the Middle East, and vetoed British entry into the Common Market: actions unthinkable in today's cowering world, as they were for Britain's rulers at the time. No country of the period was so plainly removed from any notion of decline. Equipped with a vigorous economy, an exceptionally strong state, an intrepid foreign policy, France displayed a greater élan than at any time since the Belle Epoque.

The radiance of the country was also cultural. The arrival of the Fifth Republic coincided with the full flowering of the intellectual energies that set France apart for two generations after the war. Looking back, the range of works and ideas that achieved international influence is astonishing. It could be argued that nothing quite like it had been seen for a century. Traditionally, literature had always occupied the summit on the slopes of prestige within French culture. Just below it lay philosophy, surrounded with its own nimbus, the two adjacent from the days of Rousseau and Voltaire to those of Proust and Bergson. On lower levels were scattered the *sciences humaines,* history the most prominent, geography and ethnology not far away, economics further down. Under the Fifth Republic, this time-honoured hierarchy underwent significant changes. Sartre refused a Nobel in 1964, but after him no French writer ever gained the same kind of public authority, at home or abroad. The *nouveau roman* remained a more restricted phenomenon, of limited appeal within France itself, and less overseas. Letters in the classical sense lost their commanding position within the culture at large. What took their place at the altar of literature was an exotic marriage of social and philosophical thought. It was the products of this union that gave intellectual life in the decade of De Gaulle's reign its peculiar brilliance and intensity. It was in these years that Lévi-Strauss became the world's most celebrated anthropologist; Braudel established himself as its most influential historian; Barthes became its most distinctive literary critic; Lacan started to acquire his reputation as the mage of psychoanalysis; Foucault to invent his archaeology of knowledge; Derrida to become the antinomian philosopher of the age; Bourdieu to develop the concepts that would make him its best-known sociologist. The concentrated explosion of ideas is astonishing. In just two years—1966–7—there appeared side by side *Du miel aux cendres, Les mots et les choses, Civilisation matérielle et capitalisme, Système de la mode, Écrits, Lire le Capital* and *De la grammatologie,* not to speak—from another latitude— of *La société du spectacle.* Whatever the different bearings of these and other writings, it does not seem altogether surprising that a revolutionary fever gripped society itself the following year.

The reception of this effervescence abroad varied from country to country, but no major culture in the West, not to speak of Japan, was altogether exempt from it. This owed something, of course, to the traditional *cachet* of anything Parisian, with its overtones of mode as much as of mind. But it was also certainly an effect of the novelty of the elision of genres in so much of this thinking. For if literature lost its position at the apex of French culture, the effect was not so much a banishment as a displacement. Viewed comparatively, the striking feature of the human sciences and philosophy that counted in this period was the extent to which they came to be written increasingly as virtuoso exercises of style, drawing on the resources and licences of artistic rather than academic forms. Lacan's *Écrits,* closer to Mallarmé than Freud in their syntax, or Derrida's *Glas,* with its double-columned interlacing of Genet and Hegel, represent extreme forms of this strategy. But Foucault's oracular gestures, mingling echoes of Artaud and Bossuet, Lévi-Strauss's Wagnerian constructions, Barthes's eclectic coquetries, belong to the same register.

To understand this development, one has to remember the formative role of rhetoric, seeping through the dissertation, in the upper levels of the French educational system in which all these thinkers—*khâgneux* and *normaliens* virtually to a man—were trained, as a potential hyphen between literature and philosophy. Even Bourdieu, whose work took as one of its leading targets just this rhetorical tradition, could not escape his own version of its cadences; far less such as Althusser, against whose obscurities he railed. The potential costs of a literary conception of intellectual disciplines are obvious enough: arguments freed from logic, propositions from evidence. Historians were least prone to such an import substitution of literature, but even Braudel was not immune to the loosening of controls in a too flamboyant eloquence. It is this trait of the French culture of the time that has so often polarized foreign reactions to it, in a see-saw between adulation and suspicion. Rhetoric is designed to cast a spell, and a cult easily arises among those who fall under it. But it can also repel, drawing charges of legerdemain and imposture. Balanced judgement here will never be easy. What is clear is that the hyperbolic fusion of imaginative and discursive forms of writing, with all its attendant vices, in so much of this body of work was also inseparable from everything that made it most original and radical.

The vitality of France's culture under De Gaulle was not, of course, merely a matter of these eminences. Another sign of it was possession of what was then the world's finest newspaper, *Le Monde*. Under the austere regime of Hubert Beuve-Méry, Paris enjoyed a daily whose international coverage, political independence and intellectual standards put it in a class by itself in the Western press of the period. The *New York Times,* the *Times* or *Frankfurter Allgemeine* were provincial rags by comparison. In the academic world, this was also the time when the *Annales,* still a relatively modest affair during the Fourth Republic, became the dominant force in French historiography, winning for it both a more central role within the public culture—something it had once enjoyed, but long lost—and a great arc of overseas influence. Braudel's command of the *sixième section* of the École Pratique des Hautes Études allowed him to rejuvenate the social sciences, and lay the foundations of what would become the fortress of the autonomous Maison des Sciences de l'Homme, regrouping disciplines and talents in a manner worthy of the Consulate. Last but not least, of course, was the cinema. Here, as in much else, the origins of a spectacular burst of creativity lay in the sub-cultures of the Fourth Republic. One of its features, still undiminished through the sixties, had been the number and variety of its journals of ideas, which played a much more important part in intellectual life than anywhere else in the West. Sartre's *Temps modernes,* Bataille's *Critique,* Mounier's *Esprit* were only the best known of these. It was in this milieu that Bazin's *Cahiers du cinéma* had its place, as the crucible in which the passions and convictions of the future directors of the Nouvelle Vague were formed.

Their debut on the screen coincided with the arrival of De Gaulle in power. *Les quatre cents coups* and *Les cousins* opened in 1959, *À bout de souffle* in 1960. After the war Paris had notoriously ceased to be the capital of modern painting, a position it had held for a century. But within the visual arts as a whole, it might be said that France recouped with brio in moving pictures. Or if, with equal plausibility, we regard film as the art that has taken the place of the novel as the dominant narrative form of the age, Godard might be seen as the contemporary equivalent of the great French writers of the past, producing one tour de force after another—*Le mépris, Bande à part, Une femme mariée, Pierrot le fou, Deux ou trois choses, La Chinoise, Week End* punctuating the decade as had once the latest volumes by Balzac or Proust. No other country, even Italy, came near the blaze of the French cinema in these years.

*   *   *

Today, all this has passed. The feeling is widespread that the
Fifth Republic, as it approaches its half century, presents a fallen
landscape. The economy, after crawling forward at 1.3 per cent
a year through the nineties, is today sunk in yet another trough,
with a widening deficit, rising public debt and very high levels of
unemployment. Well over 9 per cent of the labour force, itself
reduced by high rates of early retirement, is out of work. One-
quarter of French youth is jobless; two-fifths among immigrant
families. Secondary education, once the best in Europe, has been
steadily deteriorating; large numbers now emerge from it scarcely
literate. Although France still spends more on a pupil in its lycées
(for the first time outclassed, except at the very highest level,
by private schools) than on a student at its universities, France
has one of the lowlier rates of reading in the OECD. Scientific
research, measured by funding or by discovery, has plummeted:
emigration, virtually unknown in the past, now drains the
country's laboratories.

The political system, riddled with corruption, is held in
increasing public contempt. Nearly a third of the electorate—a
far larger number than voted for any single candidate—refused to
cast a ballot in the first round of the presidential elections of 2002,
in which the incumbent got less than a fifth of the vote; 40 per
cent abstained in the legislative elections. The National Assembly
is the weakest parliament in the Western world, with more than
one resemblance to the echo chambers of the First Empire. The
current ruler of the country would be in the dock for malversation
had a Constitutional Court not hastened to grant him immunity
from prosecution—a trampling of equality before the law that not
even his Italian counterpart, in what is usually imagined to be a
still more cynical political culture, has yet been able to secure.
Foreign policy is a mottled parody of Gaullism: vocal opposition
to the pretext for US war in the Middle East, followed by practical
provision of air-space and prompt wishes for victory once the
attack was under way, then eager amends for disloyalty with a
joint coup to oust another unsatisfactory ruler in the Caribbean,
and *agrément* for the puppet regime in Baghdad. At home the
prestige of public works, as late as the nineties still a touchstone
of national pride, lies in the mortuary dust and rubble of Roissy.

Economic stress and political corrosion could still, it might
be argued, leave intact what are the essential values of France,
both in its own eyes and those of the world. No other nation,
after all, has so conspicuously based its identity on culture,

understood in the broadest sense. But here too, as much as—in some ways, perhaps even more than—in matters of industry or state, the scene at large is dismal: in the eyes of many, a veritable *dégringolade*. The days of Malraux are long gone. No better symbol of current conditions could be found than the fate of his hapless descendant as court philosopher, the *salonnier* Luc Ferry, minister of education under Chirac—derisively pelted with his latest opuscule by teachers when he tried to tour schools to persuade them of the latest round of downsizing reforms, and then summarily terminated as an embarrassment to his patron.

More generally, a sense of cheapening and dumbing-down, the intertwining of intellectual with financial or political corruption, has become pervasive. Press and television, long given to the incestuous practices of *renvoyer l'ascenseur*—is there an equivalent so expressive in any other language?—have lost earlier restraints, not only in their dealing with ideas, but with business and power. The decline of *Le Monde* is emblematic. Today, the paper is a travesty of the daily created by Beuve-Méry: shrill, conformist and parochial—increasingly made in the image of its Web-site, which assails the viewer with more fatuous pop-ups and inane advertisements than an American tabloid. The disgust that many of its own readers, trapped by the absence of an alternative, feel for what it has become was revealed when a highly uneven polemic against the trio of managers who have debauched it—Alain Minc, Edwy Plenel and Jean-Marie Colombani—sold 200,000 copies in the face of legal threats against the authors, later withdrawn to avoid further discomfiture of the three in court.

La face cachée du Monde, a doorstop of six hundred pages mixing much damaging documentation with not a few inconsistencies and irrelevancies, unfolds a tale of predatory economic manoeuvres, political sycophancies and vendettas, egregious cultural back-scratching, and—last but not least—avid self-enrichment, unappetizing by any standards. 'Since *Le Monde* was founded', Beuve-Méry remarked after he retired, 'money has been waiting below, at the foot of the stairs, to gain entry to the office of the editor. It is there, patient as always, persuaded that in the end it will have the final word'.[2] The media conglomerate

---

2. Pierre Péan and Philippe Cohen, *La face cachée du Monde*, Paris 2003, p. 604.

erected by Colombani and his associates gives notice that it has taken up occupation. But, powerful a motive as greed at the top may be, the kind of journalism they represent is too pervasive to be explained simply by this. A deeper focus can be found in Serge Halimi's exposure of the interlocking complicities—across the spectrum—of establishment commentary on public affairs, in *Les nouveaux chiens de garde*.[3] What this sardonic study of mutual fawning and posturing among the talking heads and editorial sages of Parisian society shows is a system of connivance based at least as much on ideological as material investment in the market.

The world of ideas is in little better shape. Death has picked off virtually all the great names: Barthes (1980); Lacan (1981); Aron (1983); Foucault (1984); Braudel (1985); Debord (1994); Deleuze (1995); Lyotard (1998); Bourdieu (2002); Derrida (2004). Only Lévi-Strauss, now a hundred years old, survives. No French intellectual has gained a comparable international reputation since. Lack of that, of course, is no necessary measure of worth. But while individual work of distinctive value continues to be produced, the general condition of intellectual life is suggested by the bizarre prominence of Bernard-Henri Lévy, far the best known 'thinker' under sixty in the country. It would be difficult to imagine a more extraordinary reversal of national standards of taste and intelligence than the attention accorded this crass booby in France's public sphere, despite innumerable demonstrations of his inability to get a fact or an idea straight. Could such a grotesque flourish in any other major Western culture today?

If this is what lays claim to philosophy, literature is not far behind. Today's leading novelist, Michel Houellebecq—the 'Baudelaire of the supermarket' in the eyes of admirers—occupies a position not unlike that of Martin Amis in English letters, as the writer by whom readers most like to be shocked, though beyond the commonplaces of sex and violence, their forms of *épater* are asymmetrical: flamboyance of style and *bienséance* of sentiments in Amis; provocation of ideas and banality of prose in Houellebecq. The French version, coming out of science fiction, is less conventional in intellectual outlook—capable of the occasional unsettling, if never very deep, apothegm—but, as might be expected of its origins, poorer in literary imagination. In

---

3. Paris 1997. This marvellous little dissection has gone through seventeen editions since it first appeared, for a sale of some 300,000 copies. No English equivalent exists, though *The Guardian* and its consorts cry out for one.

principle, the steady drone of flat, slack sentences reproduces the demoralized world they depict, not the limits of the writer's talent. But a glance at the doggerel of Houellebecq's poetry suggests that the match between them is only too natural. That writing of this quality could command official acclaim says something about another, now more long-standing, weakness of French culture. Criticism has remarkably little place in it. The standard idea of a book review—see *La Quinzaine littéraire, Le Nouvel observateur, Le Monde des livres, Libération,* virtually *passim*—is what would elsewhere be regarded as not much above a puff. The rule has its exceptions, of course, but these tend to simple inversion, the obloquy as another ritual. No equivalent of the *TLS* or the *LRB,* of *L'Indice* or the books section of *The New Republic,* even of the dull pages of *Die Zeit,* exists: truly sustained, discriminating engagement with a work of fiction, of ideas or of history has become rare.

It was not always like this. The culture of the Fourth Republic and the early years of the Fifth, when political divisions were stronger and conflict within and between journals was livelier, involved much more genuine argument and criticism than can be found today. *Cahiers du cinéma* is a striking case in point. What is it now? Another commercial magazine in Colombani's stable, that could be mistaken on the newsstands for *Elle.* If French cinema itself has not fallen as far, this is mainly due to the continuing flow of works from its original transformers: Godard, Rohmer and Chabrol are still as active as when they began. As for its contemporary output, the one film France has successfully exported in recent years, *Amélie,* is kitsch sickly enough to make even Hollywood squirm.

2

The current French scene cannot, of course, be reduced to its least appealing expressions. No mere inventory of failings could capture the uneven realities of a society in motion; other features and forces have yet to be considered. It is also true that all inter-temporal comparisons are subject to distortion and selective illustration. In the case of France, still haunted by the assured regency of the General, perhaps more so than elsewhere. But the present unease is not a chimera, and requires explanation. What lies behind the apparent subsidence of institutions, ideas, forms, standards? An obvious first hypothesis would be that the life of

what was once the 'French exception'—that is, all those ways
in which this society and its culture escaped from the mediocre
routines of the Atlantic ecumene surrounding it—has gradually
been squeezed out of the country by two irresistible forces: the
world-wide advance of neo-liberalism, and the rise of English as a
universal language. Both have certainly struck at the foundations
of traditional conceptions of France. Historically neither Right
nor Left, however passionately divided in other ways, ever trusted
the market as an organizing principle of social order: *laissez-faire*
is a French expression that was always foreign to French reality.
Even today, so deep is suspicion of it that here, uniquely, the
contemporary term 'neo-liberal', with all its negative connotations,
has little currency, as if it were redundant: 'liberal' alone remains
enough, for a still considerable range of opinion, to indicate the
odium. The *Gleichschaltung* of Western economic arrangements
that began in the era of Thatcher and Reagan was thus bound to
bear especially painfully on a national inheritance of economic
intervention and social protection, common to the Fourth and
Fifth Republics alike.

Coinciding with the economic pressure of deregulated financial
markets, and often experienced as simply its cultural dimension,
came the victory of English as the unstoppable global medium
of business, science and intellectual exchange. For the smaller
countries of Northern Europe—Benelux and Scandinavia—this
merely confirmed a widespread bilingualism anyway. The political
and intellectual elites of the Federal Republic had always been so
deeply in thrall to the United States, as the country's saviour from
a discreditable past, that the post-war pretensions of German were
small. Italians have never imagined their language as of much
moment to anyone but themselves. France was in a completely
different situation. French had once been the common tongue of
the Enlightenment, spoken by upper classes across the continent,
sometimes even—Prussia, Russia—preferred to their own. It
remained the standard idiom of diplomacy in the nineteenth
century. It was still the principal medium of the European
bureaucracy of the Community, down to the nineties of the last
century. Long identified with the idea of French civilization—
somewhat more than just a culture—it was a language with a
sense of its own universality.

The intellectual fireworks of the *trente glorieuses,* spraying
aloft and exploding far beyond the borders of France, sustained
this notion. But the conditions that produced them depended

on the training of an immensely self-assured, spiritually—often also practically—monoglot elite, in the key Parisian lycées and École Normale that formed generation after generation of talents within an intense, hothouse world. The rise of the École Nationale d'Administration, founded only in 1945, to become the nursery of high-fliers in politics and business—Pompidou was the last *normalien* to rule the country—already tended to shift privileged education in a more technocratic direction. Then, after 1968, university and school reforms followed the pattern elsewhere: broadening access to education, without the resources necessary to maintain the standards of the narrower system.

Democratization on the cheap inevitably undermined the morale and cohesion of a national institution that had been the pride of the Third Republic. The prestige of the *instituteur* plummeted; curricula were restlessly rejigged and degraded, the average *lycéen* now getting only a wretched smattering of French classics; private schools spread to take up the slack. This is a familiar story, which could be told of virtually every Western society. Over-determining it in France were the brutal blows to cultural self-esteem from the invasion of English, through the circuits of business, entertainment and journalism. In the past two decades, the proportion of French films screened every year has dropped from a half to a third: at present 60 per cent are American. *Le Monde* now distributes the *New York Times*—suitably selected—at weekends. One of the most important props of national identity is under acute stress. In these conditions, some degree of disintegration in intellectual performance was to be expected.

But while economic and cultural pressures from the Anglosphere have imposed increasing constraints on a wide range of French traditions and institutions, political changes within French society have also been critical in bringing the country to its present low waters. Here an obvious coincidence strikes the eye. De Gaulle presided over the apogee of France's post-war revival. His rule culminated in the explosion of May–June 1968. A year later he was gone. But by then the social energies released in that crisis, racing to the verge of upheaval, had been defeated. No comparable élan has ever reappeared. Ever since, on this reading, France has been sunk in the long post-partum depression of a still-born revolution—what should have been the turning-point of its modern history which, as in 1848, failed to turn.

Seductive though such a conjecture may seem, the actual sequence of events was more complicated. Although the immediate revolutionary thrust of 1968 was broken, the energies behind it were not extinguished overnight. Politically speaking, for a time most of them flowed into more conventional channels of the Left. The early seventies saw a rapid growth in the membership of the Communist Party, the reunification of the Socialist Party, and in 1972 their agreement—seeming to bury Cold War divisions—on a Common Programme. Although Giscard narrowly won the presidency in 1974, polls indicated that the legislative elections scheduled for the autumn of 1978 would give a clear-cut victory to the Left, creating the first Socialist-Communist government since the war, on a platform repudiating capitalism and calling for sweeping nationalizations of banks and industries.

It was this prospect, unleashing something close to panic on the Right, that precipitated the real break in the intellectual and political history of post-war France. Mobilization to stop the spectre of Marxism making its entry into the Hôtel Matignon was rapid, radical and comprehensive. The noisiest shots in the campaign were fired by former *gauchiste* intellectuals, launched by the media as the Nouveaux Philosophes between 1975 and 1977, warning of the horrors of Soviet totalitarianism and its theoretical ancestry. If a straight line could be drawn from Engels to Yezhov, would the French be mad enough to let Marchais and Mitterrand extend it into their own homes? Packaged under lurid titles—*La cuisinière et le mangeur d'hommes, La barbarie à visage humain*—and patronized by the Elysée, the message enjoyed timely reinforcement from the French translation of Solzhenitsyn's *Gulag Archipelago* in 1974. Lacking much scholarly tradition of Sovietology, France had long lagged behind the US, UK or Germany in public awareness of the details of Stalin's regime: what was common knowledge elsewhere during the Cold War could come as a revelation to *le tout Paris* during détente.

For a brief period Solzhenitsyn could thus exercise, as a local admirer was to put it, the 'moral magistracy' traditionally accorded by the French to one of their own great writers[4]—a role that, of course, expired when his disobliging opinions of the West and other inconveniences came to light. But while it lasted, the effect was considerable, helping to put BHL and his fellow thinkers into orbit. In the midst of the mounting Communist scare, the PCF itself then offered a sigh of relief to its opponents by suddenly ditching its alliance with the PS, for fear of becoming a junior partner in

---

4. Pierre Grémion, 'Écrivains et intellectuels à Paris. Une esquisse', *Le Débat*, No. 103, January–February 1999, p. 75.

it, so destroying any chance of the Left winning a majority in the National Assembly. By 1981, when Mitterrand finally won the presidency, the Common Programme was a thing of the past, and the party a spent force. The Left gained the epaulettes of office after it had lost the battle of ideas.

For the uncertainties of the late seventies had galvanized into being an 'anti-totalitarian' front that would dominate intellectual life for the next two decades.[5] The Russian sage and the Nouveaux Philosophes were only the advance criers of much stronger, more durable forces set in train in those years. In 1977, Raymond Aron—who had just joined *L'Express,* to be able to intervene more actively in politics—was preparing a new journal, *Commentaire,* to defend the Fifth Republic against what appeared to be the deadly threat of a Socialist-Communist regime, coming to power on a well-nigh revolutionary programme. By the time the first number of the journal appeared, on the eve of the elections of March 1978, there had occurred the 'divine surprise' of the rupture between the PCF and the PS. Nevertheless, as he explained in a formidable opening essay, 'Incertitudes françaises', there was good reason for continuing apprehension and vigilance. The factors that had made France so unstable and prone to violent upheavals in the nineteenth century—the lack of any generally accepted principle of legitimacy; peasant acceptance of any regime that left the gains of 1789 on the land intact; the powder-keg role of Paris—all these might have passed away in the prosperous, industrialized democracy of Pompidou and Giscard. But the depth and predictable length of the economic crisis since the early seventies, when world recession had set in, was underestimated by the French, while—even with the recent fortunate division of the Left—French socialism had not yet cast off all maximalist temptations. If the PS were still to pursue PCF voters and bring Communists into government, 'France will live through years of perhaps revolutionary, perhaps despotic, turmoil'.[6]

Commentaire went on to become the anchor journal of the liberal Right, distinguished not only by its intellectual avoirdupois, but its international horizons—a function in part of its close

---

5. The best study of this phenomenon is Michael Christofferson's meticulously documented *French Intellectuals Against the Left: The Antitotalitarian Moment of the 1970s,* New York 2004, *passim.*

6. Raymond Aron, 'Incertitudes françaises', *Commentaire,* No. 1, 1978, p. 15.

connexions, under the direction of Raymond Barre's *chef de cabinet,* with functionaries, politicians and businessmen, as well as the academy. Two years later it was joined, and soon outpaced, by a partner in the liberal Centre. *Le Débat,* launched in a sleeker format by Pierre Nora under the auspices of Gallimard, had a more ambitious agenda. Nora opened the journal with a programme for intellectual reform. In the past, French culture, steeped in humanist traditions, had been dominated by an ideal of rhetoric that had led from the role of the *instituteur* to the cult of the great writer, and had permitted every kind of ideological extravagance. Now, however, the legitimacy of the intellectual lay in positive knowledge certified by the competent institutions—essentially, the university. This change could not do away with the agonistic tensions inherent in intellectual life, but it confronted intellectuals with a new set of tasks: not only to promote democracy in society at large, but to practice it within the sphere of thought itself, as a 'republic *in* letters'. The aim of the new journal would thus be to organize what was still a rarity in France, genuine debate. The ground for that had been cleared by the demise of the three major schemas for understanding history, operative since the eighteenth century. The ideologies of Restoration, of Progress, and of Revolution were now all equally dead, leaving the road at last open for the modern social sciences. *Le Débat* would stand for 'information, quality, pluralism, openness and truth', and against every kind of irresponsibility and extremism.[7]

Addressing the perennial French query, 'Que peuvent les intellectuels?', this manifesto did not touch directly on politics, beyond indicating that a 'complete democracy' was to be found in the United States, not in France. When Mitterrand took the presidency a year later, Nora struck a cautious note, stressing the personal character of his victory. Although not suspect of any tenderness towards totalitarianism, would this former ally of the Communists draw the necessary consequences of the 'great change of mentality in the past four years that has turned the image of the Soviet regime upside down', and adopt the requisite foreign policy to confront the principal enemy?[8] These were concerns shared by *Esprit,* a journal that had once been the voice of an anti-colonial and neutralist Catholic Left, but which on the

7. 'Que peuvent les intellectuels?', *Le Débat*, No. 1, March 1980, pp. 1–19; 'Continuons Le Débat', No. 21, September 1982, pp. 3–10.

8. 'Au milieu du gué', *Le Débat*, No. 14, June–July 1981, pp. 3–6.

retirement in 1976 of its post-war editor Jean-Marie Domenach had repositioned itself as a frontline fighter in the anti-totalitarian struggle. In these years, as Nora would later note, *Commentaire, Le Débat* and *Esprit* formed a common axis of what would have elsewhere been called Cold War liberalism, albeit each with its own inflexion and constituency.

Of the three, *Le Débat* was the central creation. Not simply as the house journal of Gallimard, with resources beyond those of any rival, but because it represented a real modernization of styles and themes in French intellectual life. Extremely well edited—in time Nora turned over its day-to-day running to Marcel Gauchet, a transfuge from the *Socialisme ou barbarie* wing of the far Left— the journal devoted its issues to a generally temperate exploration of three main areas of concern: history, politics and society, with frequent special numbers or features on a wide range of contemporary topics: the biological sciences, the visual arts, social security, the institutions of heritage, post-modernism and more. If it was less international in horizon than it originally set out to be, it was rarely parochial. It was never, of course, an impartial forum for objective debates, as its prospectus had suggested, but it would have been a duller affair had it been. It was, on the contrary, an urbane *machine de guerre*.

Behind its political project stood one commanding figure. Nora's brother-in-law was the historian François Furet, whose *Penser la Révolution française*—published just at the political crossroads of 1978—had in no time made him the country's most influential interpreter of the French Revolution. From a wealthy banking family, Furet had been formed in the post-war Communist Party at the height of the Cold War, when it included a group of future historians—among them Emmanuel Le Roy Ladurie, Maurice Agulhon, Jacques Ozouf—to rival its British counterpart. In France too, it was the Twentieth Party Congress in Moscow and the Hungarian Revolt that broke up this nursery of talents. Furet left the Party at some point after 1958 and while pursuing— initially fairly conventional—historical research, became a regular contributor to *France-Observateur,* the independent left weekly that was the principal organ of opposition to the Algerian War, and to De Gaulle's rule in the Fifth Republic. In 1965 he co-authored, with another brother-in-law, an illustrated history of the French Revolution designed for a general readership, which argued it had been 'blown off course' *(dérapée)* by a series of tragic accidents in 1792, destroying the liberal order at which it had originally aimed, and ushering in Jacobin dictatorship and the Terror instead.[9]

Thirteen years later, *Penser la Révolution française* was a more potent proposition—an all-out assault, invoking Solzhenitsyn and the current political conjuncture, on the catechism of Marxist interpretations of the Revolution. Furet offered instead the insights of two liberal-conservative Catholic thinkers, Tocqueville in the mid-nineteenth century and Cochin in the early twentieth, as the keys to a real understanding of the 'conceptual core' of the Revolution: not the interplay of social classes, but the dynamics of a political discourse that essentially exchanged the abstractions of popular will for those of absolutist power, and in doing so generated the terrifying force of the new kind of sociability at work in the revolutionary clubs of the period. Delivered with great polemical verve, this verdict led, logically enough, to a pointed taking of distance from the *Annales* school—its facile notion of *mentalités* 'often a mere Gallic substitute for Marxism and psychoanalysis'— as no less incapable of grappling with the upheaval of 1789 and what followed. Needed was rather an 'intellectualist history that constructs its data explicitly from conceptually posed questions'.[10]

Furet's major application of this credo, which appeared in 1988, was a large political history of France from Turgot to Gambetta, conceived as the playing-out over a century of the explosive dialectic of principles released by the attack on the Ancien Régime.[11] Whereas in his earlier writing he had maintained that with Napoleon's coup d'état in 1798, 'the Revolution is over', he now extended its life-span to the final fading away of monarchism as an active force under the Third Republic, in 1879. Only then were republic and nation finally reconciled, and the original goals of 1789 realized in a stable parliamentary order. The tormented path from starting-point to terminus, threading its way through the commotions of 1815, 1830, 1848, 1851 and 1871, was to be traced as a working-out of the tensions and contradictions of the first historical experiment in creating a democracy.

---

9. Francois Furet and Denis Richet, *La Révolution*, 2 vols., Paris 1965–6; *The French Revolution*, London 1970.

10. *L'Atelier de l'histoire*, Paris 1982, pp. 24–5, 29; *In the Workshop of History*, Chicago 1984, pp. 16, 20.

11. *La Révolution: de Turgot à Jules Ferry 1770–1880*, Paris 1988; *Revolutionary France 1770–1880*, Oxford 1992.

The motor of Furet's history is essentially a genealogy of
ideas. But he was not an intellectual historian in the sense
that Pocock or Skinner have given the term. Although he was
capable of acute insights into thinkers who interested him,
there is scarcely any detailed textual scrutiny of a given body of
writing in his work, and no attention to languages of discourse
in the Cambridge tradition. Ideas are treated rather as stylized
forces, each of them embodied in particular individuals,
around whom a narrative of high political conflicts is woven.
Furet was also fascinated by ceremonials as the public
symbolization of ideas, and *La France révolutionnaire 1770
–1880* is studded with set-piece descriptions of them, from
the coronation of Napoleon to the funeral of Thiers. At the
other pole of his imagination were personalities, and here he
had an outstanding gift for mordant characterization. Out of
this trio of elements—ideas: rituals: persons—Furet produced
an unfailingly elegant, incisive story of the making of modern
France, largely cleansed of its social or economic dimensions,
and all but completely insulated from its imperial record
abroad, which issued into an utterly focussed contemporary
political conclusion. He was not a great historian, of the
calibre of Bloch or Braudel. But he was an exceptional force in
French public life in ways they were not.

For his historical work was part of a larger enterprise. No
modern historian has been so intensely political. There was a
virtually seamless unity between his work on the past and his
interventions in the present, where he was an institutional and
ideological organizer without equal. He owed that role to his
person, a mixture of the dashing and the reserved. There was—a
foreign colleague once observed—a hint of Jean Gabin in his
taciturn charm. As early as 1964, he was orchestrating the merger
of a declining *France Observateur* with a more right-wing stable
of journalists from *L'Express,* and picking the necessary editor to
ensure that the periodical to be created out of the fusion would
have the correct politics. As Jean Daniel, who still presides over
Le Nouvel Observateur—for four decades the unfailing voice of
Centre-Left proprieties—recollected twenty-five years later: 'I will
not forget the pact we made; the choice in favour of his controversial
theses on the Revolution and on Marxism which he proposed to
me; and the surprise on his face at finding me an accomplice already
so primed and determined to be at his side. I want to record the
debt I owe him, and his family of thought, for the real intellectual

security they gave me'.[12] This disarming confession, from one of
the most powerful journalists in the land—Daniel even adds, in all
innocence: 'One day we all found ourselves, without knowing it,
running behind Augustin Cochin because Furet was pushing us in
the back'—could have been echoed by many another kingpin of the
Parisian establishment in the years to come. The network of Furet's
connexions and placements was eventually referred to in the press
simply as 'the galaxy'.

If the *Nouvel Observateur* gave Furet a central base in the media,
his control of the École des Hautes Études en Sciences Sociales,
which he helped to create out of Braudel's old *sixième section*,
and of which he became director in 1977, put him in command of
the most strategic institution of the academy, bringing a research
elite together across disciplines in the Rockefeller-funded building
on the Boulevard Raspail, freed from the teaching burdens and
administrative tares of the French university—'like going to the
cinema without paying for a ticket', as he cheerfully put it. The
launching of *Commentaire* and *Le Débat*, in both of which he
was active from the start, supplied him with flanking positions
in the world of journals. Then, after Mitterrand's accession to
power, he helped create in 1982 the Fondation Saint-Simon, an
alliance of insider intellectuals and industrialists formed to resist
any socialist temptations in the new regime, and guide it towards
a more up-to-date understanding of market and state. Bankrolled
by big business—the boss of the Saint-Gobain conglomerate was a
moving spirit along with Furet, who acquired a seat on the board
of one of his companies—the Fondation operated as a political
think-tank, weaving ties between academics, functionaries,
politicians; organizing seminars; publishing policy papers; and
last but not least, hosting dinners every month for Schmidt, Barre,
Giscard, Chirac, Rocard, Fabius and other like-minded statesmen,
at which common ideas were thrashed out over appropriate fare.

Two years later, Furet set up—or was granted—the Institut
Raymond Aron, as a committed outpost of anti-totalitarian
reflection, of which he became president, that in due course would
be integrated into the fold of the EHESS itself. Then in 1985 he
extended his range with a transatlantic connexion, taking up a
seasonal position with the Committee on Social Thought at the
University of Chicago, where he secured financial backing from

---

12. 'Journaliste et historien', *Commentaire*, No. 84, Winter 1998–1999,
p. 917.

the Olin Foundation to pursue research on the American and French Revolutions. The Bicentennial of 1789 was looming, and Furet voiced fears that this would become an occasion for the Mitterrand regime, in which Communist ministers still sat, to organize an official consecration of the mythologies of Jacobinism and the Year II of the Republic. With his colleague Mona Ozouf, he set to work to make sure this did not happen.

On the eve of the potentially risky year, a huge—twelve-hundred-page—*Dictionnaire critique de la Révolution française* appeared, covering Events, Actors, Institutions and Ideas. Its hundred entries, written by some twenty carefully selected contributors, supplied a comprehensive rebuttal of left-wing legends and traditional misconceptions of the founding episode of modern democracy.[13] The overwhelming impact of this admirably designed and executed compendium of moderate scholarship removed any danger of neo-Jacobin festivities in 1989. The fall of communism in the East offered further, conclusive vindication of the original impulse of the Revolution, against its ensuing perversions. When the Bicentennial arrived, Furet was the unquestioned intellectual master of ceremonies, as France paid homage to the inspiring principles—duly clarified—of 1789, and turned its back at last on the atrocities of 1793–4.[14]

To dispatch the wrong past, and recover the right one, was part and parcel of the country's overdue arrival in the safe harbour of a modern democracy. In tandem with the *Dictionnaire critique*, Furet co-authored in the same year *La République du centre* for the Fondation Saint-Simon, subtitled: 'The End of the French Exception'. After the absurd nationalizations of its first phase, Mitterrand's regime had put paid to socialism by embracing the market and its financial disciplines in 1983, and then buried anti-clericalism by bowing to the demonstrations in favour of Catholic schools in 1984. In doing so, it had finally made the country a normal democratic society, purged of radical doctrines and theatrical conflicts. France had now found its equilibrium in

---

13. The best critical assessment of the Dictionary is to be found in Isser Woloch, 'On the Latent Illiberalism of the French Revolution', *American Historical Review*, December 1990, pp. 1452–70.

14. For a lively account of Furet's role in 1989, see Steven Kaplan, *Farewell, Revolution: The Historians' Feud, France, 1789–1989*, Ithaca 1995, pp. 50–143, the second part of Kaplan's survey of the Bicentennial, released two years earlier in a single French volume as *Adieu 89*.

a sober Centre.[15] So entire did liberal triumph seem that on the tenth anniversary of his journal in 1990, Nora—rejoicing that the 'leaden cape of Gaullo-Communism was now lifted from the nation'—could announce with Hegelian satisfaction: 'The spirit of *Débat* has become the spirit of the epoch'.[16]

In Britain, the early nineties saw the breakdown of Thatcher's rule and the passage to a less strident neo-liberal agenda, under the atonic stewardship of Major. In France, the trend was in the opposite direction: the dominance of a market-minded consensus reached its height in the early years of the second Mitterrand presidency. The gains of the front of opinion articulated by François Furet and his friends were there for all to see. France was finally delivered of its totalitarian temptations. The shades of the Revolution had been laid to rest. The Republic had found its feet in the safe ground of the Centre. Only one heritage of the past had yet to be thoroughly purged of its ambiguities: the Nation. This task fell to Pierre Nora. In his editorial on the tenth anniversary of *Le Débat* in 1990, Nora had hailed the 'new cultural landscape' of the country, and within another couple of years, he completed his own monumental contribution to it. Originating in a seminar at the EHESS in 1978–80—the same conjuncture as *Le Débat* itself—the first volume of *Les lieux de mémoire* came out under his direction in 1984. By the time the last set appeared in 1992, the enterprise had swollen to seven volumes and some 5,600 pages, mustering six times as many contributors as the *Dictionnaire critique de la Révolution française,* from a more ecumenical range of scholars. Its aim, Nora declared in his initial presentation of the project, was an inventory of all those realms of remembrance where French identity could be said to have symbolically crystallized.

Under this capacious heading, 127 essays—most of high quality—surveyed a bewildering pot-pourri of objects, ranging from such obvious items as the Tricolour, the Marseillaise and the Panthéon, through the forest, the generation and the firm, to conversation, the industrial age, and mediaeval lineages, not to

---

15. 'La France unie', in François Furet, Jacques Julliard and Pierre Rosanvallon, *La République du centre*, Paris 1988, pp. 13–66.

16. 'History has upheld us'. See 'Dix ans de Débat', *Le Débat*, No. 60, May–August 1990, pp. 4–5.

speak, obviously, of gastronomy, the vine and Descartes. What united them, Nora explained, was their status for his purposes: 'unlike all the objects of history, realms of memory have no referent in reality'—they are 'pure signs, that refer only to themselves'.[17] The post-modern flourish is not to be taken too seriously. For what these signs actually referred to were, variously, the Republic, the Nation or just Frenchness at large. But since these too were symbolic, the exploration of them that *Les lieux de mémoire* offered would be a history of France 'to the second degree'—one concerned not with causes, actions or events, but rather effects and traces.

That did not mean it was less ambitious than its predecessors. The *Annales* had sought a total history, in reaction to the narrowness of traditional political narratives. But since symbols united material and cultural facts, and the ultimate truth of politics could well lie in its symbolic dimension, the study of realms of memory converted politics into the register of a history paradoxically more totalizing than the Annalism it might now be replacing.[18] What had made this possible was the abandonment of visions of the future as a controlling horizon for interpretations of the past, in favour of a consensual support for institutions of the present. At a time when the French were no longer willing to die for their country, they were 'unanimous in discovering their interest and affection for it', in all the diversity of its manifold expressions. It was as if 'France was ceasing to be a history that divides us to become a culture that unites us, a property the shared title to which is treated as a family inheritance'.[19] Escape from traditional forms of nationalism, such as that regrettable pair, Gaullism and Jacobinism, far from weakening sentiments of national belonging, had strengthened them as the French entered into the healing domains of common remembrance.[20]

Les lieux de mémoire was an enormous critical and public

---

17. 'Entre Mémoire et Histoire', *Les lieux de mémoire*, I, *La République*, Paris 1984, p. xli. The English-language editions of the work do not correspond to the French, having been adapted for American readers.

18. 'Présentation', *Les lieux de mémoire*, II/I, *La Nation*, Paris 1986, pp. xix–xxi.

19. 'Comment écrire l'histoire de la France?', *Les lieux de mémoire*, III/I, *Les France*, Paris 1992, pp. 28–9.

20. Nora's reserve towards Gaullism was consistent. One of his most interesting contributions to *Les lieux de mémoire* conjoins Gaullism with Communism as, each in its own way, vehicles of a powerful illusion.

success, and in due course became the model for not a few imitations abroad. But it was always plain that it must count as one of the most patently ideological programmes in post-war historiography anywhere in the world. It was Renan, after all, who had famously defined a nation as much by what it had to forget—the slaughter of sixteenth-century Protestants and thirteenth-century Albigensians were his examples—as to remember: a caution it might have been thought all the more difficult to ignore a century later. Yet Nora could cheerfully introduce his enterprise with the words:

> Even though tolerably well thought-out—in keeping with the required typology, the state of scientific knowledge of the questions, and the competences available to deal with them—the choice of subjects contains an element of the arbitrary. Let us accept it. Such complaisance in our favourite imaginaries undeniably involves a risk of intellectual regression and a return to that Gallocentrism which contemporary historiography fortunately endeavours to transcend. We should be aware of this, and on our guard against it. But for the moment, let us forget it [sic]. And let us wish, for this handful of fresh and joyous essays—soon to be followed by armfuls more—a first innocent reading.[21]

The effect of these convenient protocols, as not a few Anglophone historians pointed out,[22] was to repress memories, not just of social divisions, but even, largely, of such inescapable symbols of the political past—their monuments literally astride the nation's capital—as Napoleon and his nephew: figures presumably no longer relevant in the 'decentralized, modern' France, at rest within the 'pacific, plural' Europe celebrated by Nora. More widely, the entire imperial history of the country, from the Napoleonic conquests through the plunder of Algeria under the July Monarchy, to the seizure of Indochina in the Second Empire, and the vast African booty of the Third Republic, becomes a *non-lieu* at the bar of these bland recollections. Both Nora and Furet had been courageous critics of the Algerian War in their youth.[23] But by the

---

21. 'Présentation', *Les lieux de mémoire*, I, p. xiii.
22. See, among others, Steven Englund, 'The Ghost of Nation Past', *Journal of Modern History*, June 1992, pp. 299–320, and David Bell, 'Paris Blues', *The New Republic*, 1 September 1997, pp. 32–6.
23. See Pierre Nora, *Les Français d'Algérie*, Paris 1961; and, for a brief glimpse, François Furet, *Un itinéraire intellectuel. L'historien-journaliste, de France-Observateur au Nouvel Observateur (1958–1997)*, Paris 1999, pp. 60–64—a selection of texts by Mona Ozouf that does not linger on his early years. The

time they came to embalm the nation thirty years later, each had eliminated virtually any reference to its external record from their retrospections. One would scarcely know, from Furet's history of the nineteenth century, that France had a colonial empire at all, let alone that his particular hero Jules Ferry was the Rhodes of the Third Republic. Nora's volumes reduce all these fateful exertions to an exhibition of tropical knick-knacks in Vincennes. What are the *lieux de mémoire* that fail to include Dienbienphu?

Wrapping up the project eight years later, Nora noted criticisms made of it, and sought to turn them by complaining that although conceived as a 'counter-commemoration', his seven volumes had been integrated into a self-indulgent heritage culture, of whose vices he had always been well aware, but which would remain pervasive as long as France had not found a firm new footing in the world.[24] This ingenious sophistry could not really conceal, after the fact, that the whole enterprise of *Les lieux de mémoire* was elegaic through and through: the antithesis of everything that Roland Barthes, no less fascinated by icons, but more concerned with a critical theory of them, had offered in *Mythologies,* deconstructing the emblems of *francité*—a coinage Nora at one point even borrows, divested of its spirit—with a biting irony remote from this erudition of patriotic appeasement, published with expressions of gratitude to the Ministry of Culture and Communications.[25] All too plainly, the underlying aim of the project, from which it never departed, was the creation of a *union sucrée* in which the divisions and discords of French society would melt away in the fond rituals of post-modern remembrance.

The intellectual limitations of an undertaking are one thing. Its political efficacy is another. The orchestral programme of which

extent of its omissions is demonstrated by Michael Christofferson in 'François Furet Between History and Journalism, 1958–1965', *French History*, Vol. 1, No. 4, 2001, pp. 421–7, who shows that Furet, writing under pseudonyms, was a prolific commentator on French politics, from a position well to the left of his later outlook, down to 1965.

24. 'L'ère de la commémoration', *Les lieux de mémoire*, III/III, Paris 1992, pp. 977–1012.

25. *Mythologies*, Paris 1957, pp. 222ff; significantly, the example Barthes used to analyze the nature of myth was an icon of imperial *francité* from *Paris-Match*, just what *Les lieux de mémoire* set out to forget.

Nora and Furet were the lead conductors in these years is best
described as the enthronement of liberalism as an all-encompassing
paradigm of French public life. In this contemporary design they
could draw on the legacy of the great French liberal thinkers of
the early nineteenth century: above all Constant, Guizot and
Tocqueville, whose works were waiting to be rediscovered and
put to active modern use.[26] This was not the least important labour
of the anti-totalitarian front of the time, and good scholarly work
resulted, in the service of constructing a perfectly legitimate
pedigree. Still, there was an ironic contrast between forebears
and descendants. Under the Restoration and the July Monarchy,
France produced a body of liberal political thought substantially
richer than England, let alone America in the same period. But as a
political force, liberalism was incomparably weaker. The mishaps
of its leading minds—the repeated contrast between noble ideas and
shabby actions—were the symptom of that discrepancy: Constant
the turncoat of the Hundred Days, Tocqueville the hangman of
the Roman Republic, two champions of liberty who connived at
successive Napoleonic tyrannies; Guizot the frigid mechanic of
exclusion and repression, chased from the country amid universal
reprobation. The discredit of such careers was one reason for the
neglect that befell their writings after their deaths. But even in
their own time, they never really caught the imagination of their
contemporaries. Classical French liberalism was a fragile bloom,
in ungrateful soil. A hundred and fifty years later, matters were
very different. The comprehensive rehabilitation of liberal themes
and attitudes that set in from the mid-1970s onwards produced
no political thinkers to compare even to Aron. But what it lacked
in original ideas, it more than made up for in organizational reach.
The phrase *la pensée unique,* coined twenty years later—though
like all such terms, involving an element of exaggeration—was
not inaccurate as a gauge of its general dominance.

The international conjuncture, of course, formed a highly
favourable environment for this turn: the global ascendancy of
Anglo-American neo-liberalism offered a formidable backdrop
to the French scene. But no other Western country saw quite so
decisive an intellectual victory. The achievement was a national
one, the fruit of a coordinated campaign waged with skill and

---

26. An intelligent example is Pierre Manent, *Histoire intellectuelle du
libéralisme. Dix leçons*, Paris 1987, which ends with this trio. It is characteristic
of much of this French discussion that Mill does not rate a mention.

determination by Furet, Nora and their allies across two decades. It combined institutional penetration and ideological construction in a single enterprise, to define the acceptable meanings of the country's past and the permissible bounds of its present. Here, as nowhere else, history and politics interlocked in an integrated vision of the nation, projected across the expanse of public space. In this respect the Communist Party Historians Group in Britain, though its members were to be no less politically active, and produced much more innovative history, were tyros beside their French contemporaries. There has rarely been such a vivid illustration of just what Gramsci meant by hegemony. He would have been fascinated by every nook and cranny of *Les lieux de mémoire*, down to its entries on street-names, a favourite subject of his, or the local notary; and he would have admired the energy and imagination with which the legacy of the Jacobins, his heroes, was liquidated—feats of a 'passive revolution' more effective than the original Restorations of the nineteenth century themselves, around which so much of his theory in the *Prison Notebooks* was built. As if on cue, indeed, Furet ended his career with an obituary of communism as the rule of capital was restored in Russia, closing the century's 'socialist parenthesis'.

By comparison with the rest of Furet's work, *Le passé d'une illusion*—flirting with the ideas of Ernst Nolte in its linkage of Bolshevism to Nazism, topics with which he had little prior acquaintance—was a pot-boiler. Appearing in 1995, it rehearsed so many Cold War themes long after the event that some wits remarked it read like the intellectual equivalent of a demand for reimbursement of the Russian loan.[27] But this in no way affected its success in France. Acclaimed as a masterpiece by the media, it was an immediate best-seller, marking the height of Furet's fame. With this sensational coping-stone in place, the arch of anti-totalitarian triumph seemed complete.

3

Nine months later, France was convulsed by the largest wave of strikes and demonstrations since 1968. The Juppé government, attempting under pressure from Brussels to push through a neo-liberal restructuring of social security arrangements, had

---

27. Denis Berger and Henri Maler, *Une certaine idée du communisme*, Paris 1996, p. 187.

provoked such popular anger that much of the country was brought to a halt. The resulting political crisis lasted for six weeks and split the intellectual class down the middle. Virtually the entire anti-totalitarian coalition endorsed Juppé's plans as a much-needed initiative to modernize what had become an archaic system of welfare privilege. Ranged against it, for the first time a consistent alternative spectrum of opinion materialized. Led by Bourdieu and others, it defended the strikers against the government.

Politically speaking, the confrontation between the palace and the street ended with the complete defeat of the regime. Juppé was forced to withdraw his reforms. Chirac jettisoned Juppé. The electors punished Chirac by giving a majority to Jospin. Intellectually, the climate was never quite the same again. A few weeks later Furet, playing tennis at his country house, fell dead on the court. He had just been elected to the Académie française, but had not yet had time to don the green and gold, grip his sword and be received among the Immortals.

But well before the end he had begun to express misgivings. Certainly, Gaullism and Communism were for all practical purposes extinct. The Socialist Party had abandoned its absurd nationalizations, and the intelligentsia had renounced its Marxist delusions. The Republic of the Centre he wished for had come into being. But the political architect of this transformation, whose rule had coincided with the ideological victories of moderate liberalism, and in part depended on them, was François Mitterrand. Furet's judgement of him was severe. A genius of means, barren of ends, Mitterrand had indeed destroyed the PCF and forced the PS to accept the logic of the firm and the market. But he had also abused the spirit of the Constitution by installing the simulacrum of a royal court in the Elysée; he presided over a regime whose 'intellectual electro-encephalogram is absolutely flat'; and he had signally failed to the rise to the world-historical occasion when Soviet Communism collapsed.[28] It was impossible to feel any warmth for a presidency so cynical and void of ideas. Barre or Rocard, admired by the Fondation Saint-Simon, would have been preferable.

Behind this disaffection, however, lay a deeper doubt about the direction that French public life was taking. Already by the late eighties, Furet had started to express reservations about

28. François Furet, 'Chronique d'une décomposition', *Le Débat*, No. 83, January–February 1995, pp. 84–97.

the discourse of human rights that was becoming ever more prominent in France, as elsewhere. Impeccably liberal though it might seem—it had, after all, been the *pièce de résistance* at the ideological banquet of the Bicentenary—the ideology of human rights did not amount to a politics. A contemporary surrogate for what had once been the ideals of socialism, it undermined the coherence of the nation as a form of collective being, and gave rise to inherently contradictory demands: the right to equality and the right to difference, proclaimed in the same breath. Its enthusiasts would do well to re-read what Marx had said about human rights.[29] The increasing cult of them was narrowing the difference between French and American political life.

Closer acquaintance with the US sharpened rather than lessened these anxieties. Furet remained a staunch champion of the great power that had always been the bastion of the Free World. But from his observation post in Chicago, much of the scenery of Clinton's America was off-putting, if not disturbing. Racial integration had paradoxically undone older black communities, and left ghettoes of a sinister misery with few equals in Europe. Sexual equality was advancing in America (as it was in Europe, if mercifully without the same absurdities), and it would change democratic societies. But it would neither transform their nature nor produce any new man, or woman. Political correctness was a kind of academic aping of class struggle. Crossed with the excesses of a careerist feminism, it had left many university departments in conditions to which only an Aristophanes or Molière could do justice. Multi-culturalism, as often as not combined with what should be its opposite, American juridification of every issue, led inevitably to a slack relativism. In the desert of political ideas under another astute but mindless president, the peculiar liberal variant of utopia it represented was spreading.[30]

Furet's final reflections were darker still. His last text, completed just before he died, surveyed France in the aftermath of the elections called by Chirac that had unexpectedly given the PS a legislative majority—in his view, an almost incredible blunder by a politician he once thought had governed well. But Jospin offered little that was different from Juppé. Right and

---

29. Furet et al., *La République du centre*, pp. 58–62.
30. 'L'utopie démocratique à l'américaine', *Le Débat*, No. 69, March–April 1992, pp. 80–91; 'L'Amérique de Clinton II', *Le Débat*, No. 94, March–April 1997, pp. 3–10.

Left were united in evading the real issues before the country: the construction of Europe; the tensions around immigration; the persistence of unemployment, which could only be reduced by cutting social spending. Under Mitterrand, French public life had become a 'depressing spectacle', amid a general decomposition of parties and ideas. Now lies and impostures were the political norm, as voters demanded ever newer doses of demagogy, without believing in them, in a country that stubbornly 'ignored the laws of the end of the century'.[31]

What were these laws? Historically, the Left had tried to separate capitalism and democracy, but they formed a single history. Democracy had triumphed since 1989, and with it capital. But its victory was now tinged with malaise, for it was accompanied by an ever vaster disengagement of its citizens from public life. It was impossible to view that withdrawal without a certain melancholy. Once communism had fallen, the absence of any alternative ideal of society was draining politics of passion, without leading to any greater belief in the justice of the status quo. Capitalism was now the sole horizon of humanity, but the more it prevailed, the more detested it became. 'This condition is too austere and contrary to the spirit of modern societies to last', Furet concluded. He ended in the spirit of Tocqueville, lucidly resigned to the probability of what he had resisted. 'It might one day be necessary', he conceded, 'to go beyond the horizon of capitalism, to go beyond the universe of the rich and poor'. For however difficult it was even to conceive of a society other than ours today, 'democracy, by virtue of its existence, creates the need for a world beyond the bourgeoisie and beyond Capital'.[32]

Inadvertently, then, the passing of an illusion had itself been the source of a disappointment. Victor of the Cold War it might be, but actually existing capitalism was an uninspiring affair. It was understandable that utopian dreams of a life without it had not vanished. In his last historical essay, Furet even forgot himself so far as to write once again of the 'revolutionary bourgeoisie' that had carried France out of the Ancien Régime, almost as if he now saw merit in the catechism he had so long denounced.[33] Two

---

31. François Furet, 'L'énigme française', Le Débat, September–October 1997, pp. 43–9.

32. François Furet, Le Passé d'une illusion, Paris 1995, p. 579; The Passing of an Illusion, Chicago 1999, p. 502.

33. 'L'idée française de la Révolution', Le Débat, No. 96, September–October 1997, pp. 28–9.

centuries later, the dénouement he wished for had come, but it lay like so much clinker in his hands. A liberal Midas was left staring at what he had wanted.

Posthumously, if there were two sources of Furet's final disarray, capitalism and the condition of his own country, it was to be the second that scattered his following. There had always been a tension within the new French liberalism between its political loyalty to America and its emotional attachments to France. Its project had envisaged an ideal union of the principles of the sister Republics of the Enlightenment. But *e pluribus unum* and 'one and indivisible' are mottoes at war with each other. For liberals, what counted for more? An atomistic individualism with no logical stopping-place, breaking the nation into so many rival micro-cultures, whose unification must become ever more formal and fragile? Or a collective identity anchored in common obligations and stern institutions, holding the nation resolutely—but perhaps also oppressively—together?

It was over this dilemma that the anti-totalitarian front fell apart. The first skirmish occurred in the early eighties, when Bernard-Henri Lévy announced that there was a generic 'French Ideology', stretching from Left to Right across the twentieth century, saturating the nation with anti-Semitism and crypto-fascism. This was too much for *Le Débat*, which demolished Lévy's blunders and enormities in two blistering pieces, one by Le Roy Ladurie and the other by Nora ('un idéologue bien de chez nous'), rebuffing attempts to discredit the Republic in the name of the Jewish question.[34] The next occasion for dispute was, predictably enough, posed by the Muslim question, with the first affair of the *foulards*, in the late eighties. Could head-scarves be worn in schools without undermining the principles of a common secular education established by the Third Republic? This time the split was more serious, pitting advocates of a tolerant multi-culturalism, American-style, against upholders of the classical republican norms of a citizen nation.

---

34. Emmanuel Le Roy Ladurie, 'En lisant *L'Idéologie française*', and Pierre Nora, 'Un idéologue bien de chez nous', *Le Débat*, No. 13, June 1981, pp. 97–109. A year earlier, Nora had written that Lévy possessed a kind of undeniable legitimacy, conferred by the genuine desire for knowledge that 100,000 readers had invested in him: *Le Débat*, No. 1, p. 9.

Eventually, simmering ill-feeling over these issues burst into the open. In 2002, Daniel Lindenberg, a historian close to *Esprit*, unloosed a violent broadside against the authoritarian integrism, hostility to human rights and contempt for multi-culturalism of so many former fellow-fighters for French liberalism—notable among them leading lights of *Le Débat* and *Commentaire*. Such tendencies represented a new *rappel à l'ordre*, the eternal slogan of reaction. Lindenberg's pamphlet, although a crude piece of work, recklessly amalgamating its various targets, not only received a warm welcome in *Le Monde* and *Libération*. It pointedly appeared in a collection edited by Furet's colleague Pierre Rosanvallon, fellow architect of the Fondation Saint-Simon and co-author of *La République du centre*, recently promoted— many eyebrows had been raised—to the Collège de France. This was the signal for virtual civil war in the liberal camp, with a standard Parisian flurry of rival open letters and manifestoes, as Gauchet and his friends hit back in *L'Express* and columns of the press closer to them. The disintegration of the comity of the late seventies was complete.[35]

By then, however, a much larger change in its position had occurred. Furet's misgivings at the upshot of modernization were a murmur against the background of more menacing sounds from the depths of the country. Among the masses, neo-liberalism *à la française* had not caught on. From 1983 onwards, when Mitterrand made the decisive turn towards the logic of financial markets, the French electorate had unfailingly rejected every government that administered this medicine to it. The pattern never varied. Under a Presidency of the Left, Fabius—the first Socialist premier to hail the new 'culture of the firm'—was turned out in 1986; Chirac, who launched the first wave of privatizations for the Right, was rejected in 1988; Bérégovoy, Socialist pillar of the *franc fort,* was ousted in 1992; Balladur, personifying an Orleanist moderation in the pursuit of economic liberty, fell at the polls in 1995. Under a Presidency of the Right, Juppé—the boldest of these technocrats,

---

35. Daniel Lindenberg, *Le rappel à l'ordre. Enquête sur les nouveaux réactionnaires*, Paris 2002; and *contra*, Alain Finkielkraut, Marcel Gauchet, Pierre Manent, Philippe Muray, Pierre-André Taguieff, Shmuel Trigano, Paul Yonnet, 'Manifeste pour une pensée libre', *L'Express*, 28 November 2002. For a dry comment on the dispute, see Serge Halimi: 'Un débat intellectuel en trompe l'oeil', *Le Monde diplomatique*, January 2003, p. 3.

who attacked social provisions more directly—was first crippled by strikes and then driven from office in 1997; Jospin—who privatized more than all his predecessors put together—thought that after five self-satisfied years of government he had broken the rule, only to be routed in the elections of 2002. Today Raffarin, after two years of dogged attempts to take up where Juppé left off, has already lost control of every regional administration in the country save Alsace, and sunk lower in the opinion polls than any prime minister in the history of the Fifth Republic. In twenty years, seven governments, lasting an average of less than three years apiece. All devoted, with minor variations, to similar policies. Not one of them re-elected.

No other country in the West has seen such a level of disaffection with its political establishment. In part, this has been a function of the constitutional structure of the Fifth Republic, whose quasi-regal presidency with its (till yesterday) seven-year terms of office, has both encouraged and neutralized continual expressions of electoral ill-humour within an otherwise all too stable framework of power. Where the Fourth Republic combined instability of cabinets with rigidity of voting blocs, the Fifth has inverted the pattern, uniting apparently immovable policies with congenitally restless electors.[36] Such restlessness has not just been a by-product of institutional over-protection. More and more plainly as the years went by, it reflected disbelief in the nostrums of neo-liberal reform that every government, Left or Right, unvaryingly proposed to its citizens.

These did not remain mere paper. Over twenty years, liberalization has changed the face of France. What it liberated was, first and foremost, financial markets. The capital value of the stock market tripled as a proportion of GNP. The number of share-holders in the population increased four times over. Two-thirds of the largest French companies are now wholly or partially privatized concerns. Foreign ownership of equity in French enterprises has risen from 10 per cent in the mid-eighties to nearly 44 per cent today—a higher figure than in the UK itself.[37] The rolling impact of these transformations will be felt for years

---

36. René Rémond, by no means a critic of the upshot, makes this argument: 'Instabilité législative, continuité politique', Le Débat, No. 110, May–August 2000, pp. 198–201.

37. Nicolas Véron, 'Les heureuses mutations de la France financière', Commentaire, No. 104, Winter 2003–4, offers a gratified balance-sheet of these changes.

to come. If they have not yet been accompanied by much run-down of the French systems of social provision, that has been due to caution more than conviction on the part of the country's rulers, aware of the dangers of provoking electoral anger, and willing to trade sops like the thirty-five-hour week for priorities like privatization. By Anglo-American standards, France remains an over-regulated and cosseted country, as the *Economist* and *Financial Times* never fail to remind their readers. But by French standards, it has made impressive strides towards more acceptable international norms.

Such progress, however, has done nothing to allay popular suspicion and dislike of Anglo-Saxon ideas about them. The nineties saw the runaway success of literature attacking the advent of a new unbridled capitalism, with one best-seller after another: Pierre Bourdieu's massive indictment of its social consequences in *La misère du monde* (1993); the novelist Viviane Forrester's impassioned tract *L'horreur économique* (1996); the weathercock Emmanuel Todd's *L'illusion économique* (1998), an onslaught against laissez-faire from an intellectual once an ardent warrior for the Free World. By the mid-nineties, the rising tide of disgust with neo-liberal doctrines was so evident among voters that Chirac himself, seeking election in 1995, made the centre-piece of his campaign denunciation of *la pensée unique* and the fractured society it had created. When—like all his predecessors—he then readopted it in office, the result was, almost overnight, the industrial tremors that shook Juppé down. Looking around amid the débris, a chronicler at *Le Débat* concluded gloomily: 'The liberal graft has not taken'.[38]

But in the divorce between official policies and popular feelings there was another element as well, more social than political. Since De Gaulle, the rulers of the Fifth Republic have become the most hermetic governing caste in the West. The degree of social power concentrated in a single, tiny institution producing an integrated political, administrative and business elite is, indeed, probably without equal anywhere in the world. The ENA accepts only 100 to 120 students a year—in all about five thousand persons since its foundation, out of a population of over fifty million. But these not only dominate the top rungs of the bureaucracy and the management of the largest companies, but furnish the core of the political class itself. Giscard, Fabius, Chirac, Rocard,

---

38. Pierre Grémion, *Le Débat*, No. 103, January–February 1999, p. 99.

Balladur, Juppé and Jospin are all *énarques;* as were eleven out of seventeen ministers in the last Socialist government; both main rivals, Strauss-Kahn and Hollande, for Jospin's succession on the Left; not to speak of Chirac's dauphin on the Right, Dominique de Villepin, recently foreign and now interior minister.

The inbreeding of this oligarchy has inevitably spawned pervasive corruption. On the one hand, the practice of *pantouflage*—high functionaries gliding noiselessly from administration to business and politics, or back again—gives many an opportunity for diversion of public, or private, funds to partisan purposes. On the other, since the main political parties lack any significant mass memberships, they have long depended on milking budgets and trafficking favours to finance their operations. The result is the morass of jobbery that has, no doubt only partially, come to light in recent years, of which Chirac's tenure as mayor of Paris has been the most flagrant example to come before the *juges d'instruction.*

But no matter how crushing the evidence, the judiciary has so far been unable to put any significant politician behind bars. Chirac secured immunity from prosecution from a tame Constitutional Court, and is currently shielding Juppé; Mitterrand's foreign minister, Roland Dumas—himself a former member of the Court—has been acquitted after a trial, and Strauss-Kahn cleared even without one. Few French citizens can have much doubt that all these figures, and many more, have broken the law for political advantage, or—in the spirit of Giscard's diamonds—personal gain. But since Left and Right are equally implicated, and close ranks against any retribution, the venality of the political class is proof against consequences within the system. There is little moralizing strain in French culture, and less vocal indignation at corruption than in Italy. But this has not signified mere indifference. What it has fed is a deepening alienation from the elite running the country, and contempt for its revolving cast of office-holders.

Electoral abstention, rising to levels well above the EU average, has been one symptom of this disenchantment, though recently Britain under New Labour has beaten all comers. Another has been more distinctively, indeed famously—or infamously— French. From the mid-eighties onwards, the Front National attracted at least a tenth of the electorate, climbing to nearly 15 per cent for Le Pen in the presidential contest at the end of the decade. At the time, the size of this vote for an openly xenophobic party, organized by veterans of the far Right, set France apart from any other European country. Widely thought to be fascist, the FN appeared a peculiar national stain, and potential threat to French democracy. What could explain such an extraordinary recidivism? In fact, the initial conditions for the FN's success were perfectly intelligible and local. No other European society had received such a large settler community from its colonial empire: a million *pieds-noirs* expelled from the Maghreb, with all the bitterness of exiles; and no other European society had received such a large influx of immigrants from the very zone once colonized: two and a half million *maghrébins*. That combination was always likely to release a political toxin.

The Front could also count, beyond its original base in the *pied-noir* communities, on pockets of nostalgia for Vichy— Tixier-Vignancour's voters in the fifties, a diminishing asset—or loyalty to the liturgy of Cardinal Lefèbvre. But the conditions of its real take-off lay elsewhere. Le Pen's electoral break-through came in 1984, a year after Mitterrand had abruptly jettisoned the social vision of the Common Programme and embraced orthodox monetarism. The neo-liberal turn of 1983 did not lead the Communist Party, which had four unimportant seats in the cabinet, to break with the government. Rather, as it would again under Jospin, it clung to the crumbs of office, regardless of the political cost of doing so, let alone considerations of principle. Its reward for adding to the follies of the Third Period those of the Popular Front—first, blind sectarianism in 1977–8, then feeble opportunism—was self-destruction, as more and more of its working-class electorate abandoned the Party. It was the gap created by the resulting compression of the political spectrum that gave the FN its chance, as it picked up increasing numbers of disgruntled voters in decaying proletarian suburbs and small towns. For many, the system of *la pensée unique* had left only this acrid alternative.

The arrogance and self-enclosure of the political class did the rest. Excluding the Front from any presence in the National Assembly by eliminating proportional representation, and shielding itself against any settlement of accounts with corruption, the establishment merely confirmed Le Pen's denunciations of it as a conspiracy of privilege, which he could deliver with an oratorical flair none of its suits could match. The more Left and Right united to treat the Front as a pariah, the more its appeal as an outsider to the system grew. Overt racism against Arab immigrants, and a somewhat more muffled anti-Semitism, took their place in its

repertoire alongside a generalized, raucous populism. The two
stresses that eventually cracked liberal hegemony apart, the
tension pitting multi-culturalism and republicanism against each
other, and the resistance of opinion to the virtues of the market,
were exactly the terrain on which it could flourish, at the most
sensitive intersection between them.

The limits of the Front as a political phenomenon were at the
same time always plain. Shunned by the Right, after initial furtive
overtures by Chirac, and over-dependent on the personality
of Le Pen, it lacked any professional cadre and never acquired
administrative experience, vegetating between polls in a resentful
sub-culture. Its brawling style at the hustings alarmed as much
as it attracted. Above all, its main calling card—the immigrant
issue—was inherently restrictive. The appeal of fascism between
the wars had rested on massive social dislocation and the
spectre of a revolutionary labour movement, a far cry from the
tidy landscape of the Fifth Republic. Immigration is a minority
phenomenon, virtually by definition, as war between the classes
was not. In consequence, xenophobic responses to it, however
ugly, have little power of political multiplication. Aron, who had
witnessed the rise of Nazism in Germany and knew what he was
talking about, understood this from the start, criticizing panicky
over-estimations of the Front. In effect, from the mid-eighties
onwards its electoral scores oscillated within a fixed range, never
dropping much below a national average of 10 per cent and never
rising above 15 per cent.

In 2000, the political system underwent its most significant
change since the time of De Gaulle. Chirac and Jospin, each
manoeuvring for advantage in the presidential elections of 2002,
colluded to alter the term of the presidency from seven to five
years, Giscard brokering the deal between them. Ostensibly, the
aim of the change was to reduce the likelihood of 'cohabitation'—
possession of the Elysée and Matignon by rival parties, which had
become increasingly frequent since 1986—and so give greater unity
and efficiency to government, too often compromised by strains
between president and prime minister. In fact, what the revision
amounted to was a massive increase in the power of the presidency,
promising a thorough-going personalization of the political
system along American lines, since it was clear that if elections
for the executive and the legislature were held in the same year, in
France's highly centralized society, a victorious president would
almost automatically always be able to create a tame majority for

himself in the National Assembly in the immediate wake of his own election—as had happened on every occasion since 1958. The result could only be to weaken a legislature already *fainéant* enough, and further accentuate that excess of executive power Furet had termed a national pathology. A referendum was held to ratify this reduction of checks and balances in the constitution. Just 25 per cent of the electorate turned out for it, of whom four-fifths voted for a change trumpeted by the establishment as a great step forward in French democracy, bringing it into line with advanced countries elsewhere.

But there was still a potential glitch. The existing electoral calendar required elections to the Assembly to be held by the end of March 2002, and the presidential election in April–May—so reversing the intended scheme of things, and risking that the vote for the legislature would determine that for the executive, rather than the other way round. Jospin, confident that he enjoyed the esteem of the electorate, rammed through an extension by three months of the life of the Assembly, to clear the way for conquest of the Elysée. Few self-interested constitutional manipulations have backfired so spectacularly.

In the spring of 2002, the campaign for the presidency starred Chirac and Jospin as leading candidates, running on platforms whose rhetoric was almost indistinguishable. When the results of the first round came in, dispersion of the vote of the *gauche plurielle*—Socialists, Communists, Greens and Left Radicals— between its constituent candidatures, all symbolic save the premier himself, knocked Jospin out of the contest with a humiliating 16.18 per cent of ballots cast, leaving Le Pen, with 195,000 votes more, to go through to the second round against Chirac, who himself got a miserable 19.88 per cent, a nadir for any incumbent president. Had the legislative elections been held first, Jospin's coalition would almost certainly have won—the combined Left vote he could have counted on, if the scores in April were an indication, was up to 10 per cent higher than that of the Right—and in its wake he would have taken the Elysée.

The most startling feature of the presidential poll, however, lay neither in the gross miscalculation of the PS, nor in the fact that Le Pen overtook Jospin. There was in fact no net increase in the combined vote of the far Right at all, compared with 1995.[39] The

---

39. Le Pen got 230,000 votes more than in 1995, and his former lieutenant Bruno

salient reality was the depth of popular antipathy to the political establishment as a whole. Far larger than the vote for any of the contestants was the number of abstentions and blank or invalid ballots—nearly 31 per cent. Another 10.4 of the electorate voted for rival Trotskyist candidates of the far Left; 4.2 for the cause of hunting, shooting and fishing. In all, nearly two out of three French voters rejected the stale menu of the consensus presented to them.

Establishment reaction was unanimous. What mattered was one apocalyptic fact. In the words of a typical pronouncement: 'At eight o'clock on April 21, a mortified France and a stupefied world registered the cataclysm: Jean-Marie Le Pen had overtaken Lionel Jospin'.[40] Everywhere hands were wrung in national shame. The media were flooded with editorials, articles, broadcasts, appeals explaining to the French that they faced the brown peril and must now rally as one to Chirac against it, if the Republic was to be saved. Youth demonstrated in the streets, the official Left rushed to the side of the president, even much of the far Left decided it was the moment of *no pasarán*, and they too must weigh in behind the candidate of the Right. Chirac—afraid he would be worsted in any argument with Le Pen, who would be sure to embarrass him by recounting past secret tractations between them—declined any television debate, and knowing the result was a foregone conclusion, scarcely bothered to campaign.

The second round duly gave him a majority of 82 per cent, worthy of a Mexican president in the hey-day of the PRI. On the Left Bank, his vote reached virtually Albanian heights. The media switched in the space of fifteen days from the hysterical to the ecstatic. The honour of France had been magnificently restored. After an incomparable demonstration of civic responsibility, the president could now set to work with a new sense of moral purpose, and the country hold its head high in the world again. Authoritative commentators observed that this was France's finest

---

Mégret, who had split away from the FN, received 670,000, making a combined increase of 900,000. But in 1995 Philippe de Villiers had won 1,440,000 votes, with comparable appeals. In 2002 his Mouvement pour la France did not enter the presidential race.

40. Jean-Jacques Chevallier, Guy Carcassonne, Olivier Duhamel, *La Ve République 1958–2002. Histoire des institutions et des régimes politiques en France*, Paris 2002, p. 488; a standard reference work in France, as its publishers describe it.

hour since 1914, when the nation had closed ranks in a sacred union against another deadly enemy.

Actually, if an analogy were needed, the unanimity of 2002 was closer in spirit to that of Bordeaux in 1940, when the National Assembly of the Third Republic voted overwhelmingly to hand power to Pétain, convinced that this was a patriotic necessity to avert catastrophe. This time, of course, tragedy repeated itself as farce, since there was not even a trace of an emergency to warrant the consecration of Chirac. In the first round of the elections, the combined poll of the Right was already 75 per cent higher that of the FN and its split-off—a difference of more than four million votes; while given the lack of any major contrast in the ideas and policies of Chirac and Jospin, it was clear that many who had voted for the latter would switch to the former without prompting in the second round anyway. There was never the faintest chance of Le Pen winning the presidency. The frantic calls from the Left to rally behind Chirac were entirely supernumerary—merely serving to ensure that it was crushed in the legislative elections in June, when as a reward for its self-abasement the Right took the National Assembly with the largest majority in the history of the Fifth Republic, and Chirac acquired a plenitude of power he had never enjoyed before. It was a *journée des dupes* to remember.

4

The wild swings of the vote in this ideological whirligig—Chirac transmogrified from a symbol of futility and corruption, trusted by less than a seventh of the electorate, into an icon of national authority and responsibility in the blink of an eye—can be taken, however, as symptoms of an underlying pattern in the country's political culture. Under the Fifth Republic, the French have increasingly resisted collective organization. Today fewer than 2 per cent of the electorate are members of any political party, by far the lowest figure in the EU. More striking still is the extraordinarily low rate of unionization. Only some 7 to 8 per cent of the work-force are members of trade-unions, well below even the United States, where the comparable figure (still falling) is 11 per cent; let alone Denmark or Sweden, where trade-unions still account for two-thirds to three-quarters of the employed population. The tiny size of industrial and political organizations speaks, undoubtedly, of deep-rooted individualist traits in French culture and society, widely remarked on by natives and foreigners alike: sturdier in many ways than their more celebrated American counterparts, because less subject to the pressures of moral conformity.

But the French aversion to conventional forms of civic association does not necessarily mean privatization. On the contrary, the paradox of this political culture is that the very low indices of permanent organization coexist with exceptional propensities for spontaneous combustion. Again and again, quite suddenly, formidable popular mobilizations can materialize out of nowhere. The great revolt of May–June 1968, still far the largest and most impressive demonstration of collective agency in post-war European history, is the emblematic modern example that no subsequent ruler of France has forgotten.

The streets have repeatedly defied and checked governments since. In 1984, Mauroy fell from office after his attempt to curb private education unleashed a massive confessional mobilization in defence of religious schools—half a million rallying in Versailles, a million pouring onto the boulevards of Paris. In 1986, protests by hundreds of thousands of students, from universities and *lycées* alike, fighting riot police in clashes that left one young demonstrator dead, forced Chirac to withdraw plans to 'modernize' higher education. His government never recovered. In 1995, Juppé's schemes to cut and reorganize social security were met with six weeks of strikes, engulfing every kind of public service, and nation-wide turbulence, ending in complete victory for the movement. Within little over a year, he too was out of power. In 1998, it was the turn of truckers, pensioners and the jobless to threaten Jospin's regime. Aware that such social tornadoes can suddenly twist towards them out of a clear sky, governments have learnt to be cautious.

Signs of this characteristic duality, the coexistence of civil atomization and popular inflammability, can be found in the deep structures of much French thought. They form one of the backgrounds to Sartre's theorization of the contrast between the dispersion of the 'series' and the welding of the 'pledged group', and the quicksilver exchanges between them, in his *Critique de la raison dialectique*. But the most distinctive effect of the problem they pose has been to produce a line of thinkers for whom the social bond is basically always created by faith rather than reason or volition. The origins of this conception go back to Rousseau's insistence—revealingly at variance with his own voluntarist construction of the general will—that a civil religion alone could found the stability of a republic. The derision into which the Cult of the Supreme Being fell after the overthrow of the Jacobins did not discredit the theme, which underwent a series of conservative metamorphoses in the nineteenth century. Tocqueville became convinced that dogmatic beliefs were the indispensable foundation of any social order, especially democracies like America, in which religion was more omnipresent than in Europe. Comte conceived the mission of positivism as the establishment of a Religion of Humanity that would anneal the social divisions tearing the world of the Industrial Revolution apart. Cournot argued that no rational construction of sovereignty was ever possible, political systems always resting in the last resort on faith or force. In some ways most radically of all, Durkheim reversed the terms of the equation with his famous notion that religion is society projected to the stars.

What all these thinkers rejected was the idea that society could ever be the outcome of a rational aggregation of the interests of individual actors. The branch of the Enlightenment that produced the utilitarian tradition in England became a dead bough in post-revolutionary France. No comparable way of looking at political life ever developed. Constant, whose assumptions came closest to it, remained a forgotten half-foreigner. In the twentieth century, the same underlying vision of the social resurfaced between the wars with a semi-surrealist tint, in the theories of the sacred proposed by Roger Caillois and Georges Bataille at the Collège de Sociologie. In the late twentieth century, this intellectual line has seen yet further avatars in the work of two of the most original thinkers of the Left, at odds with every surrounding orthodoxy. In the early eighties, Régis Debray was already advancing a theory of politics as founded on the constitutive need, yet inability, of every human collectivity to endow itself with internal continuity and identity, and in consequence its dependence on an apex of authority—by definition religious, understood in a broad sense—external to it, as a condition of its vertical integration.

In this version, set out in *Critique de la raison politique* (1981), the theory sought to explain why nationalism, with its characteristic cults of the eternity of the nation and the immortality of its martyrs, was a more powerful historical force than the socialism for which Debray had once fought in Latin America. By the time of *Dieu, un itinéraire* (2001), it had become a comparative account of changes in the ecologies, infrastructures and orthodoxies of Western monotheism, from 4000 BCE to the present, which took religion as an anthropological constant for all times: however protean its historical forms, the permanent horizon of any durable social cohesion. Far from such speculations leading to any reconciliation with the status quo, they long continued to be accompanied by political interventions held scandalous by the Parisian consensus—not least scathing comment on NATO's war on Yugoslavia, still a touchstone of *bien-pensant* sensibility in Paris as in London today. Perhaps in absolution, Debray has since compromised himself by preparing the ground for the Franco-American coup in Haiti. But the establishment can scarcely count on him.

A comparable case is France's most incisive jurist, Alain Supiot. Drawing on the work of the maverick legal philosopher Pierre Legendre, Supiot has renewed the idea that all significant belief-systems require a dogmatic foundation by focussing its beam sharply, to the discomfort of their devotees, on the two most cherished creeds of our time: the cults of the free market and of human rights.[41] Here too, the logic of the argument, in each case brilliantly executed, is ambiguous: demystifying, yet also normalizing, each as the latest illustration of a universal rule, a necessity beyond reason, of human coexistence itself. A French habit of mind is at work here. The fact that the genealogy of such claims is so distinctively national does not in itself, however, disqualify them: any general truth will have a local point of origin. But the predicament they point to is an archetypally French one. If singular agents will not associate freely to shape or alter their condition, what is the pneuma that can unexpectedly transform them, from one day to the next, into a collective force capable of shaking society to its roots?

For the guardians of the status quo, these are thoughts of the small hours, quickly dispelled in the sunlight of an exceptional morning in French history. 'Never has the country been economically so powerful nor so wealthy', Jean-Marie Colombani rhapsodized in the year 2000. 'Never has the dynamism of the country equipped it so well to become the economic locomotive of Europe'. There was better still: 'never has there been in France such a palpable "happiness in living" as at this threshold of the

---

41. For an extended statement, see his *Homo Juridicus*, London–New York 2007.

twentieth-first century'.[42] Bombast of this kind often has a nervous undercurrent. Much of the book which ends with this peroration is devoted to warning of the damage done to a healthy French self-understanding by critics like Debray or Bourdieu. In fact, the editor of *Le Monde* could have looked closer to home. The ebbing of the liberal tide in France has left a variety of unsettling objects on the beach.

Among them is the remarkable success of the daily's antithesis in the monthly that bears its name—*Le Monde diplomatique* having about as much in common with Colombani's paper as, in the opposite direction, today's *Komsomolskaya Pravda* has with the original. Under the editorship of Ignacio Ramonet and Bernard Cassen, it has been a spirited hammer of every maxim in the neo-liberal and neo-imperial repertoire, offering a critical coverage of world politics in sharp contrast with *Le Monde*'s own shrinking perimeter of attention. Enjoying a readership of some quarter of a million in France, *Le Monde diplo* has become an international institution, with over twenty print editions in local languages abroad, from Italy to Latin America, the Arab world to Korea, and a further twenty on the internet, including Russian, Japanese and Chinese: in all, an audience of one and a half million. No other contemporary French voice has this global reach.

The journal, moreover, has not only been a counter-poison to the reigning wisdom, but an organizer as well. In the wake of the Asian financial crisis of 1997, it set up ATTAC, an 'association for popular education', which today has branches throughout the EU, to stimulate debates and proposals unwelcome to the IMF and the European Commission. For any periodical, an organizational function exacts a price—typically, reluctance to shock its readers, of which the journal has not been free. Yet its animating role has been remarkable. In 2001 *Le Monde diplomatique* and ATTAC were instrumental in creating the World Social Forum in Porto Alegre, launching the 'alter-globalization' movement that would become a principal rallying-point of protesters against the neo-liberal order across the latitudes. Here, on an unfamiliar transnational stage, France resumed something of its historic place as vanguard land of the Left, acting as the ignition for radical ideas and forces beyond its borders.

A similar interlocking of national and global effects can be found elsewhere in the *gauche de la gauche* that has emerged in

---

42. *Les infortunes de la République*, Paris 2000, p. 165.

the past decade. The moustachioed figure of José Bové symbolizes another side of it. Who could be more archetypally French than this Roquefort-maker from the Larzac, foe of GM and McDonald's? Yet if alter-globalization has international heroes, the charismatic farmer who founded a Peasant Confederation at home and helped create Via Campesina at large, active from the Massif Central to Palestine and Rio Grande do Sul, is among them. Characteristically, the French media put up with him so long as they could treat him as a piece of harmless folklore. Once he had the temerity to criticize Israel, it was another matter. Overnight, he became a *bête noire,* a disreputable demagogue giving the country a bad name abroad.

The role of Pierre Bourdieu in these years belongs to the same constellation. Son of a postman in a remote village of the Béarn, in the borderlands with Spain, his trajectory bears many similarities to that of Raymond Williams, son of a railwayman in the marches of Wales, who was aware of the kinship between them. They shared steep ascents from such backgrounds to elite positions in the academy, and then feelings of acute alienation within the oblivious worlds of the *cumulard* and the high table they had reached, that made each steadily more radical after he had won an established reputation. Even the typical complaints made of their prose—in the eyes of critics, sharpened by political hostility, a laboured, reiterative heaviness—were of a likeness. For both, the central experience that set the agenda of a life's work was inequality. In Bourdieu's case, the finest pages of the *Esquisse pour une auto-analyse* he wrote just before he died are his recollections of the bruised bleakness of his schooldays in the lycée at Pau.[43]

After induction into sociology in Algeria—it is striking how many leading French intellectuals were, in one way or another, marked by time in the colony: Braudel, Camus, Althusser, Derrida, Nora—Bourdieu developed work along two major lines, study of the mechanisms of inequity in education, and of stratification in culture. These were the enquiries—*Homo academicus, La distinction, Les règles de l'art*—that made him famous. But in the last decade of his life, dismayed by what neo-liberal governments had done to the poor and the vulnerable, he turned to the fate of the losers in France, and the political and ideological systems that kept them there. *La misère du monde,*

---

43. *Esquisse pour une auto-analyse*, Paris 2004, pp. 117–27.

which appeared two years before the social explosion of late 1995, can be read as an advance documentary for it. When it came, Bourdieu took the lead in mobilizing intellectual support for the strikers, against the government and its watchdogs in the media and the academy. Soon he was to be found in the forefront of battles over illegal immigration, in defence of the *sans-papiers*, becoming the most authoritative voice of unsubdued opinion in France. *Raisons d'Agir*, the intellectual guerrilla he created to harry the consensus, specialized in flanking attacks on press and television: Halimi's *Les nouveaux chiens de garde* and Bourdieu's own *Sur la télévision* were among its grenades. He was planning an Estates-General of social movements in Europe when he died. His friend Jacques Bouveresse, France's leading semi-analytic philosopher, an attractive but very different kind of thinker, has paid him perhaps the best tribute, not only in writing well about him, but contributing *Schmock* (2001)— pointed reflections on Karl Kraus and modern journalism—to a common enterprise.

Bourdieu's intransigence was a refusal to bend within the social sciences. But a similar sensibility can be seen in the better French cinema of recent years: films like Laurent Cantet's *L'emploi du temps*, or *La vie rêvée des anges* of Eric Zoncka, that show the cruelties and waste of Colombani's *vivre heureux*. France also saw perhaps the most ambitious attempt so far to trace the overall shape of the mutations in late twentieth-century capitalism, in a work whose title deliberately recalls Weber's classic on its origins. *Le nouvel esprit du capitalisme* (1999), by Luc Boltanski and Eve Chiapello, links industrial sociology, political economy, and philosophical enquiry in a sweeping panorama of the ways in which relations between capital and labour have been reconfigured to absorb the cultural revolution of the sixties, and engender new dynamics of profit, exploitation, and emancipation from all residues of the ethic that preoccupied Weber. This critical synthesis so far lacks any Anglophone equivalent. But, not unlike Bourdieu's work, it also suggests a strange asymmetry within French culture of the past decades. For although its theoretical object is general, all its empirical data and virtually all its intellectual references are national. Such introversion has not been confined to sociology. The involution of the *Annales* tradition after Bloch and Braudel offers another striking illustration. Whereas British historians of the past thirty to forty years have distinguished themselves by the geographical range of their work, to a point where there is scarcely any European country that does not count among them a major contribution to the sense of its own past, not to speak of many outside Europe,[44] modern historians of repute in France have concentrated overwhelmingly on their own country. Le Roy Ladurie, Goubert, Roche, Furet, Chartier, Agulhon, Ariès: the list could be extended indefinitely. The days of Halévy are over.

More generally, if one looks at the social sciences, political thought or even in some respects philosophy in France, the impression left is that for long periods there has been a notable degree of closure, and ignorance of intellectual developments outside the country. Examples of the resulting lag could be multiplied: a very belated and incomplete encounter with Anglo-Saxon analytic philosophy or neo-contractualism; with the Frankfurt School or the legacy of Gramsci; with German stylistics or American New Criticism; British historical sociology or Italian political science. A country that has translated scarcely anything of Fredric Jameson or Peter Wollen, and could not even find a publisher for Eric Hobsbawm's *Age of Extremes,* might well be termed a rearguard in the international exchange of ideas.

Yet if we turn to arts and letters, the picture is reversed. French literature itself may have declined in standing. But French reception of world literature is in a league of its own. In this area, French culture has shown itself exceptionally open to the outside world, with a record of interest in foreign output no other metropolitan society can match. A glance at any of the better small bookshops in Paris is enough to register the difference. Translations of fiction or poetry from Asian, Middle Eastern, African, Latin American and East European cultures abound, to a degree unimaginable in London or New York, Rome or Berlin. The difference has structural consequences. The great majority of writers in a language outside the Atlantic core who have gained an international reputation have done so by introductory passage through the medium of French, not English : from Borges, Mishima and Gombrowicz, to Carpentier, Mahfouz, Krleža or Cortazar, up to Gao Xinjiang, the recent Chinese Nobelist.

44. To select only one, often out of several, per case: Spain—Elliott; Italy—Mack Smith; Portugal—Boxer; Germany—Carsten; Netherlands—Israel; Sweden—Roberts; Poland—Davies; Hungary—Macartney; China—Needham; Spanish America—Lynch.

The system of relations that has produced this pattern of Parisian consecration is the object of Pascale Casanova's path-breaking *La république mondiale des lettres,* the other outstanding example of an imaginative synthesis with strong critical intent in recent years. Here the national bounds of Bourdieu's work have been decisively broken, in a project that uses his concepts of symbolic capital and the cultural field to construct a model of the global inequalities of power between different national literatures, and to illuminate the gamut of strategies that writers in languages at the periphery of the system of legitimation have used to try to win a place at the centre. Nothing like this has been attempted before. The geographical range of Casanova's materials, from Madagascar to Romania, Brazil to Switzerland, Croatia to Algeria; the clarity and trenchancy of the map of unequal relations she offers; and, not least, the generosity with which the ruses and dilemmas of the disadvantaged are explored, make her book kindred to the French élan behind the World Social Forum. It might be called a literary Porto Alegre. That implies a beginning, with much fierce argument and discussion to come. But whatever the outcome of such criticisms or objections, *The World Republic of Letters*—empire more than republic, as Casanova shows—is likely to have the same sort of liberating impact at large as Said's *Orientalism,* with which it stands comparison.

The wider puzzle remains: what explains the strange contrast between a unique literary cosmopolitanism and so much intellectual parochialism in France? It is tempting to wonder whether the answer lies simply in the relative self-confidence of each sector—the continuing native vitality of French history and theory inducing indifference to foreign output, and the declining prestige of French letters prompting compensation in the role of a universal dragoman. There may be something in this, but it cannot be the whole story. For the function of Paris as world capital of modern literature—the summit of an international order of symbolic consecration—long precedes the fall in the reputation of French authors themselves, dating back at least to the time of Strindberg and Joyce, as Casanova demonstrates.

Moreover, there is a parallel art that contradicts such an explanation completely. French hospitality to the furthest corners of the earth has been incomparable in the cinema too. On any day, about five times as many foreign films, past or present, are screened in Paris as in any other city on earth. Much of what is now termed 'world cinema'—Iranian, Taiwanese, Senegalese—

owes its visibility to French consecration and funding. Had directors like Kiarostami, Hou Hsiao-Hsien or Sembène depended on reception in the Anglo-American world, few outside their native lands would ever have glimpsed them. Yet this openness to the alien camera has been there all along. The brio of the New Wave was born from enthusiasms for Hollywood musicals and gangster movies, Italian neo-realism and German expressionism, that gave it much of the vocabulary to reinvent French cinema. A national energy and an international sensibility were inseparable from the start.

Such contrasts are a reminder that no society of any size ever moves simply in step with itself, in a uniform direction. There are always cross-currents and enclaves, deviances or doublings-back from what appears to be the main path. In culture as in politics, contradiction and irrelation are the rule. They do not disable general judgements, but they complicate them. It is not meaningless to speak of a French decline since the mid-seventies. But the current sense of the term, that of Nicolas Baverez and others, which has given rise to *le déclinisme*, is to be avoided. It is too narrowly focussed on economic and social performance, understood as a test of competition. Post-war history has shown how easily relative positions in these can shift. Verdicts based on them are usually superficial.

Decline in the sense that matters has been something else. For some twenty years after the end of the *trente glorieuses,* the mood of the French elites was not unlike a democratic version of the outlook of the early forties: a widespread feeling that the country had been infected with subversive doctrines it needed to purge, that healthier strands in the nation's past needed to be reclaimed, and—above all—that the forms of a necessary modernity were to be found in the Great Power of the hour, and that it was urgent either to adapt or adopt them for domestic reconstruction. The American model, more benign than the German, lasted longer. But eventually, even some of those addicted to it began to have doubts. At the end of this road, might there not wait a sheer banalization of France? From the mid-nineties onwards, a reaction started to set in.

It is still far from clear how deep that goes, or what its outcome will be. The drive to clamp a standard neo-liberal straitjacket onto economy and society has slowed, but not slackened—Maastricht alone ensuring that. What could not be achieved frontally may arrive more gradually, by erosion of social protections rather than assault on them; perhaps the more typical route in any case. A creeping normalization, of the kind the current low-profile government led by Raffarin is pursuing, risks less than a galloping one of the sort admirers look to from Nicolas Sarkozy, the latest d'Artagnan of the right, and in French conditions may prove more effective. It will not be the Socialist Party, in office for sixteen out of the past twenty-four years, that halts it. Its cultural monuments, the shoddy eye-sores of Mitterrand's *grands travaux* and vulgarity of Jack Lang's star-shows, rightly detested by conservative opinion, were the epitome of everything signified by the progress of banalization.

Outside the country, attitudes of passionate francophilia that were still quite common between the wars, have virtually disappeared. Like most of its neighbours, or perhaps more so, France arouses mixed feelings today. Admiration and irritation are often expressed in equal measure. But were the country to become just another denizen of the cage of Atlantic conformities, a great hole would be left in the world. The vanishing of all that it has represented culturally and politically, in its pyrotechnic difference, would be a loss of a magnitude still difficult to grasp. How close such a prospect is, remains hard to fathom. Smith's dry rejoinder to Sinclair comes to mind: there is a great deal of ruin in a nation. The hidden stratifications and intricacies of the country, the periodic turbulence beneath the pacified surface of a consumer society, sporadic impulses—gathering or residual?— to careen fearlessly to the left of the left, past impatience with democratic boredom, are so many reasons to think the game is not quite over yet. After pointing out all the reasons why France was no longer subject to the revolutionary fault-lines of the nineteenth and early twentieth centuries, and had at last achieved a political order that enjoyed stability and legitimacy, Raymond Aron nevertheless ended his great editorial of 1978 with a warning. 'Ce peuple, apparemment tranquille, est encore dangereux'. Let us hope so.

II · 2009

'I agree', wrote Pierre Nora in response to the survey above, 'with the general diagnostic of languor and creative anaemia in France of recent years, except that I live what he calls the French *dégringolade* in a more painful than mocking way, and conceal the word "disaster" which comes to mind under the more presentable term "metamorphosis"'.[45] However, he went on, to sketch a decay was one thing, to explain it another. There, disagreement must be complete. For two reasons: in point of method, to focus on just a political and cultural parabola was too narrow, not say idealist; and as to framework, developments in the hexagon could not be understood without reference to more general transformations in Europe, and the world at large. A 'brutal and mysterious levelling of cultural production' was undeniable in his home country.[46] But in substance, matters were no better elsewhere. They were only more visible in France, for a series of reasons historically specific to it.

Four of these, in Nora's view, stood out. First was the unusually close political connexion between a centralizing state and the linguistic, educational and cultural institutions of the country, which had long made of the humanities a touchstone in the formation of politicians, writers, intellectuals and scientists alike, whose gradual abandonment had dealt a fatal blow to all four sectors of activity. Second came the collapse, at the end of the totalitarian era, of the myths of revolution and nation, nourished by Communism and Gaullism. Third was the reversal of the very mechanisms of modernization that had given post-war France its élan, into so many brakes on further development: as witnesses, the crisis of its welfare state, the frictions in its constitution, the troubles of its cultural institutions—universities, publishers, theatre, cinema. Finally, there was the mutation in the very form of the nation-state, affecting virtually all countries, and unsettling their sense of themselves, which France could not but register with

---

45. 'La pensée réchauffée', in *La pensée tiède*, Paris 2005, p. 101; as often happens in translation, a misleading title for the reflections above, since the principal ideas at issue were not tepid, nor were they only at issue, without reference to political life.

46. 'La pensée réchauffée', p. 111.

especial sharpness, as the oldest nation-state on the continent, whose traditional forms of identity—centralist, statist, imperial, military, peasant, Christian, secular, universalist—had lasted longest and were struck simultaneously.[47]

Much of this can be conceded. The peculiar intimacy of the links between state and culture, and the centrality of classical forms of rhetorical training to them, form part of the case developed above. The general disturbances of national identity, and France as an illustration of them, are discussed elsewhere,[48] emphasis falling on this occasion simply on the pressures of the macro-economic regime change in the Atlantic world since the eighties, and the rise of English as a planetary lingua franca in the same period. That said, Nora's broader complaint is perfectly justified: no analysis essentially restricted to political and cultural developments could hope to be fully satisfactory—in any detail, the social is missing. But if we are to explain why the scene today is so different from that of the late fifties or sixties, most of the answer must lie at this level. There, Nora's proposition is readily acceptable, if we invert its terms. Attention should probably go, first of all, to the ways in which Gaullist modernization destroyed the social bases of the very exceptionality to which it gave such remarkable (if contradictory) expression. It was only because the much deeper changes it entrained—disappearance of the peasantry, reconfiguration of the working class, multiplication of urban middle strata, rise of new kinds of capital—were working themselves out, that the ideological successes of a new French liberalism became possible in the late seventies.

Such a presumption is, of course, only algebraic. The actual inter-relations between transformations of social structure and changes in cultural or political life remain to be teased out, and could well prove more complicated and unpredictable than initially supposed. The fates of Communism and Gaullism, invoked by Nora, are a case in point. Across the decade from the May Revolt to the break-up of the Union of the Left, the descent of the PCF into a kind of senile dementia was certainly one of the conditions of the ease of the neo-liberal turn under Mitterrand, ending in the party's virtual extinction. But the distinctive character of French Communism remains something of an unresolved mystery

---

47. 'La pensée réchauffée', pp. 112–4.

48. 'Fernand Braudel and National Identity', *A Zone of Engagement*, London 1992, pp. 251–78.

to this day. What explains its peculiarly numbskull insensibility? Historically, unlike its English counterpart after the mid-nineteenth century, the French working class was never radically alienated from the world of ideas and culture; nor, from the time of the Third Republic, was education typically viewed with distrust as an emblem of privilege. Why then did the party that came to represent it after the war prove so ideologically crass? The corset of Stalinism is no answer, as a glance at the contrast in cultural outlook with the PCI makes plain. It is sometimes forgotten that the opportunities of French were far greater than those of Italian Communism, since it was not politically isolated in the seventies, nor excluded from office in the eighties. Yet it listened to no voice in society outside its own wooden head. On the Left, the upshot was all too predictable: a deaf communism generating a blind anti-communism, the one as vacant as the other. The underlying social logic of this impasse has yet to be unravelled.

Gaullism might seem a more straightforward case, its life-span in principle unlikely to extend much beyond that of the hero who embodied it. But its fate, too, leaves questions to which neither his mortality nor any general waning of the nation-state offers an answer. Abroad, after all, what has the French political class gained by abandoning the diplomatic and strategic independence the General bequeathed it, and returning to the Atlantic fold? At home, the constitution of the Fifth Republic was certainly an instrument designed for his suzerain person, that might well have been regarded as counter-productive once he passed, as Nora rightly implies it became. But far from reducing its presidentialism, the same class has colluded to render it yet more extreme—not a brake on, but an accelerator of, the assorted dysfunctions of the Republic. The fates of welfare or education, also figuring among these, tell another story, of once coherent systems lamed by expansion beyond the constituencies for which they were designed, eventually becoming mechanisms of exclusion, or mock-inclusion, for lack of the resources their ostensible democratization required, amid one of the most unequal distributions of income in Europe. The past thirty-five years have certainly seen profound socio-economic changes in France, and a cortège of maladies has accumulated with them. But even when we have taken their full measure, the unalterable fact remains the complete incapacity of the governing class to respond to them. Nora's reflections treat mainly of the cultural plane, but it is the political that poses the sharpest questions.

I

There, in yet another of the violent oscillations in the needle of public sentiment that have been a hallmark of the late Fifth Republic, Chirac's second presidency was as unanimously decried at exit as it had been acclaimed at entry. Once again, electoral docility had not stilled popular disaffection. In the spring of 2005, the entire political establishment received its most stinging rebuff in thirty years, when an attempt to force through the oligarchic charter for a European Constitution was overwhelmingly rejected in the referendum that Chirac, in another of his tactical miscalculations, had called to ratify it. The opposition that undid the charter, making reasoned use of the internet to expose official propaganda, came from below, ATTAC taking the lead. The fury and disbelief of the mainstream media and domesticated intelligentsia, after an unprecedented barrage in support of the Constitution, knew no bounds: only xenophobia could account for the result. What in fact the defenestration of the Constitution showed was how vulnerable the pretensions of the two major parties backing it—Gaullists who no longer had much to do with Gaullism, Socialists even less with socialism—had become to the novelty of democratic argument escaping media control. The debacle was such that Raffarin had to go. To replace him, Chirac picked a long-time intimate, the career diplomat De Villepin, as premier.

Five months later, two young immigrants—aged fifteen and seventeen, families from Mauretania and Tunisia—were electrocuted fleeing police harassment outside Paris. Riots erupted around cities across the country. The antithesis of everything evoked by the term 'suburb' in English, the *banlieues* that exploded are typically high-rise slums concentrating populations of Maghrebin and African origin, bleak zones of racial dereliction and repression, where youth unemployment—not confined to immigrants—is double the national average. Targeting the most visible symbols of the consumer society from which they were excluded, night after night the insurgents torched cars in a pyre of social anger, amid violent clashes with the police. By the time the uprising had been brought under control, three weeks later, some nine thousand vehicles had gone up in flames, in the most spectacular repudiation of the ruling order since May 1968. Scarcely had the last charred saloon been cleared from the streets than the country's universities and lycées rose in a massive wave of protest at government measures to make it easier for employers to hire and fire youth on temporary basis, the so-called *contrat première embauche*. Strikes, demonstrations, occupations, this time with trade-union support, cascaded into a movement of such magnitude, lasting for upwards of two months, that Chirac had to withdraw the plan, sealing the fate of De Villepin, whom he had hoped might succeed him.

Shocks like these had, in the past, all but invariably presaged a change of guard at the Elysée, allowing the Socialist Party to look forward to victory at the polls the following year, without— as had become traditional—having to offer more than token changes of policy. But this was to count without the fluidity that Chirac's decline had released within the ranks of the Right. There an alternative capable of a sharper demarcation from him than anything the PS could offer was waiting. Once another of Chirac's protegés, Sarkozy had betrayed him for Balladur in 1996, and only grudgingly been readmitted to office as minister of the interior in 2002. In this post, he rapidly built a reputation for toughness on crime and immigration, tightening rules on residence in France and promising to sandblast youthful rabble from the *banlieues*. Buoyed by popularity in the polls, by 2004 Sarkozy had taken control of the ruling party's machine as its new president, a powerful base from which to assert his independence of the Elysée, and dissociate himself from the discredit into which Chirac's reign was falling. The final fiasco of the CPE, from which he had been careful to take his distance, assured him the uncontested candidacy of the Centre-Right in 2007.

Against him, the PS ran Ségolène Royal, a hitherto second-rank figure, companion of the party's general secretary, picked by its membership as the least shop-worn candidate it could offer. Weightless and inexperienced, it soon became clear she enjoyed little confidence among her colleagues and was no match for Sarkozy. Footling attempts to show she was as tough on crime and as proud a patriot only underlined her lack of any independent programme; the choice of Bernard-Henri Lévy as confidante, her want of any judgement.[49] After a vapid and disorganized campaign, she was routed at the polls, Sarkozy coasting to victory by two million votes. In this outcome, however—less disastrous for the PS, after all, than Jospin's debacle five years earlier— neither Royal's weaknesses as a candidate, nor the traditional

---

49. *Ce grand cadavre à la renverse*, Paris 2007, pp. 9–16, 157–60, for the latter's breathless account of how he was first wooed by his old friend Sarkozy, and then rallied to the 'courage and solitude' of Royal.

pallor of the Socialist alternative, were the critical factor. That lay in Sarkozy's reconfiguration of the electorates of the Right.

There, his record at the Ministry of the Interior, and unabashed appeals at the hustings to the country's need for greater security, in its streets and on its borders, cut the ground from under much of Le Pen's constituency. In the first round of the election, he took up to a million votes from the Front National, concentrated in its petty-bourgeois—as opposed to working-class—base: Le Pen's score among small shopkeepers, craftsmen and employers was more than halved, while Sarkozy's virtually doubled by comparison with Chirac in 2002. To this social stratum, he added a massive demographic sweep among pensioners, in the second round garnering nearly two-thirds of the vote of the elderly.[50] Fear—of immigrants and the unruly young—was the principal cement of this bloc. But it was by no means the only emotion to which Sarkozy owed his victory. By 2007 the sensation of a creeping national decline, topic of many an earlier publication, had become far more widespread, as Chirac's regime was seen to disintegrate. As a notorious thorn in the side of the Elysée, Sarkozy was in much better position to capitalize on this than Royal, who had never taken any distance from her patron Mitterrand or from Jospin. He now did so with éclat. Promising a clean break with accumulated inertias, he assured voters that France could be revived by reforms based on the values of hard work, merit and honest competition—liberating labour markets, lowering taxes on inheritance, giving autonomy to universities, fostering national identity. With this prospectus, he captured a large majority of the age-group between twenty-five and thirty-four, attracted to him not by fears, but hopes of freer and more prosperous careers.

The combination of appeals to security and identity on one side, and to mobility and opportunity on the other, which gave him his convincing victory, made Sarkozy an object of acute detestation and alarm in the opposite camp. There, lurid depictions of him as the offspring of a wedding between Le Pen and Thatcher, if not actually a crypto-fascist, circulated freely. Such images were not without effect, rallying not only the youngest cohort of voters to Royal, but the constituencies of the far Left, many of whose electors plumped for her *ab initio*, and all of whose candidates clung to her skirts in the second. One phalanx of intellectuals

---

50. For an overall analysis of the vote, see Emmanuel Todd, *Àprès la démocratie*, Paris 2008, pp. 136–40.

declared that 'never had a candidate of the right so symbolized social regression', while another warned that Royal's defeat would mean nothing less than 'grave dangers to fundamental liberties'.[51] Such overwrought lamentations, not unlike the hysterics of 2002 at the imaginary threat of Le Pen capturing the presidency, served only to disarm the opposition before the actual character of the regime with which it was confronted, once this was in place.

For Sarkozy's first move, far from speeding to the right, was to welcome as many lights of the Centre–Left into his administration as he could find, starting with the Socialist paladin of human rights, Bernard Kouchner, promptly appointed foreign minister; Jospin's deputy chief of staff Jean-Pierre Jouyet, given the portfolio on Europe; Royal's one-time chief economic adviser, Éric Besson, installed as secretary of state in the Matignon. This should scarcely have come as a surprise: during the campaign itself, Sarkozy had not hesitated to invoke Jaurès and Blum as inspirations for the country, not to speak of the young Communist resistance hero Guy Môquet, soon afterwards, as a model for its youth. Such ecumenical overtures were not confined to matters of ideology. Gender and race were no less liberally accommodated. Half of the new cabinet was composed of women, and three members of the full government were of Maghrebin or African origin, one a stalwart of SOS Racisme itself.

If the instrumental character of such appointments, designed both to demoralize the PS and to provide the administration with cover for the sharper end of its policies, was plain enough, their condition of possibility lay in the actual programme on which the government was embarked. For, as it soon proved, both hopes—in the euphoric visions of the business press—and fears—in the agitated imagination of the left—of the new presidency were exaggerated. Sarkozy did not retreat from his campaign commitments, but these were never as radical as his more ardent admirers supposed, or his own rhetoric implied. The most divisive of them, a handsome present to the rich of tax cuts and abolition of inheritance tax, was prudently slipped through before the immediate glow of his victory had faded. Thereafter, taking care to avoid any set-piece confrontations, the government's measures were generally introduced after at least an appearance, and often substance, of

---

51. Both before the first round: see 'Avant qu'il ne soit trop tard', *Nouvel Observateur*, 1 March 2007; and 'Appel de 200 intellectuels pour Ségolène Royal', *Libération*, 18 April 2007.

negotiation. Unions, weak enough in France anyway, were cajoled with talks into acceptance of limitation of strikes in public services, abolition of special pensions on the railways in exchange for higher final wages, and voluntary circumvention of the thirty-five-hour week. Universities have been granted autonomy, allowing them to raise money from private sources and compete in attracting talent, but selection of students has not been introduced, and an increase in public funding of higher education has been promised. The retail sector has been liberalized, without greatly threatening small shopkeepers. Immigration laws have been stiffened, but as elsewhere in Europe, mostly to symbolic effect.

As a prescription for the reinvigoration of French society, the dose of neo-liberalism has so far been quite modest. Apart from anything else, the state itself has not been put on much of a diet. Having promised voters he would increase their purchasing power, Sarkozy was in no position to tighten fiscal discipline. Within a year of his coming to power, growth had slowed, the budget had sunk deeper into the red, and inflation had doubled. Failure to raise taxes or cut public spending was, in the eyes of Anglo-Saxon commentators otherwise well disposed towards him, bad enough. Worse was Sarkozy's lack of respect for the principles of a free market, where politically inconvenient. Not scrupling to denounce firms for outsourcing jobs, he has promoted national champions in industry, brokering state-led mergers in energy and armaments in defiance of admonitions from Brussels, and repeatedly attacked the European Central Bank for undermining growth by restricting the supply of money. Soon after his inauguration, indeed, he could be heard—to the dismay of Le Monde, which had hoped this odious expression was a thing of the past—criticizing la pensée unique itself.

To date, in short, Sarkozy's approach to the task of bringing France up to scratch, as understood by a modern liberalism, has—not in style, but substance—been closer to that of a Raffarin than a Thatcher, even though as a ruler he enjoys far more power than the first, or even the second. Reforms, though relatively consistent, have not been radical.[52] What explains the apparent paradox? In part, the very personalization of power that his presidency has introduced. For the first time in the history of the Fifth Republic, the executive is concentrated entirely in one

---

52. The most lucid analysis of the limitations of Sarkozy's agenda is offered by Roland Hureaux: 'Nicolas Sarkozy peut-il réussir?', Le Débat, No. 146, September–October 2007, pp. 102–10.

omnipresent ruler—Sarkozy acting not just as the head of state, at a certain distance from day-to-day administration, as envisaged by the Constitution and respected by his predecessors, but as the visible manager of every detail of government. Jospin's ill-starred tampering with electoral tenures and calendars had made this collapse of any separation between presidential authority and partisan responsibility possible. But it required the full blast of Sarkozy's temperament to make it a daily reality. From the start, the hazards of such activism were clear: the Elysée would no longer be a shelter if anything went wrong.

To this political change was now added a cultural turn. By the new century, traditional barriers between public and private life in France were breaking down, with the spread of pulp journalism along Anglo-Saxon lines. Revelling in the new celebrity culture, Sarkozy went out of his way, both before and after his election, to play the super-star of a *Vanity Fair* world— blazoning a glamorous marriage and sporting every modish accessory for the attention of photographers and reporters. When, after well-advertised affairs, his wife finally abandoned him amid media pandemonium, he wasted no time acquiring a successor of even more doubtful taste: nude modelling, husky singing, kitsch romancing. This was overstepping the mark. Much of Sarkozy's own conservative base was affronted by such '*pipolisation*', and his ratings fell like lead, from close to 70 to 37 per cent, faster than those of any ruler since the late fifties. The speed of this fall in public esteem could not but cool any too hasty reformist zeal.

Beyond such circumstantial setbacks, however, there are more structural reasons why Sarkozy's sweeping powers have not led to any comparable transformation of the social landscape. While real enough measured by the Gaullist past, French decline was not, economically speaking, of the same order as the British when Thatcher came to power—productivity was higher, profitability greater, the currency more stable, public services superior. At elite level, lesser ills called for milder remedies. At popular level, more drastic solutions ran the risk of explosive reactions. If more limited in scale than the strikes of 1995, the turbulence of 2006–7 remained a warning. *Manchestertum* pure and simple was never an option. No regime in France could abandon all pretence of paternalism. The hallmark of Sarkozy's rule has rather been an ideological and practical eclecticism, veering rapidly in whichever direction the preservation of its project of semi-liberalization has pointed. Where, sociologically speaking, opposition lacks critical mass, attack on it can be truculent, as in the case of the country's research establishment. Where resistance threatens to become contagious—national demonstrations over falling household incomes—there is a switch to placation. The edginess of every government in recent memory has not disappeared. Contemplating the Greek riots of late 2008, Sarkozy told a deputy from his party: 'The French adore me with Carla in a carriage, but at the same time they guillotined a king. It is a land of regicides. Over a symbolic measure, they can turn the country upside down. Look at what happened in Greece'.[53] In the glare of Athenian fires, impending reform of lycées was quickly put on hold.

In foreign affairs, on the other hand, such domestic constraints cease to hold. The politics of the Fourth Republic were marked by deep conflicts over the external policies of the governments of the day, as the Cold War descended, colonial insurgencies multiplied, and European integration began. This was the epoch of Indochina, the Ridgeway riots, the European Defence Community, Algeria—issues capable of dividing voters, splitting parliaments, toppling governments. With the Fifth Republic, that came to an end. The change was due to the success of De Gaulle in disengaging France from North Africa, dominating the direction of the European Community, and where necessary defying the will of the United States. These were achievements that united virtually the whole nation, from Right to Left, behind them. What is striking since, however, is the ease with which his successors have gradually abandoned his legacy, without significant electoral incidence or popular reaction. Pompidou promptly admitted Britain to the Community; Giscard pushed for monetary union; Mitterrand signed up for the American war in the Gulf; Chirac for the war in the Balkans. At no point was Gaullism ever openly repudiated, and each presidency could claim its share of continuity with the first: maintenance of the Franco-German axis, not unfriendly relations with the Soviet Union, advancement of Romania, opposition to the attack on Iraq. The drift, away from a classically independent foreign policy as De Gaulle had conceived it, was always incremental, leaving margins for local reinflection or reversal.

---

53. Remark to a UMP deputy, reported in *Le Monde*, 13 December 2008.

Sarkozy has broken more cleanly with the diplomatic traditions once upheld by Couve or Jobert. Proclaiming unrestricted admiration for the United States from the start, and promising a full return of France to military integration in NATO, under American command, he has aligned Paris with Washington on every major political issue of the War on Terror. Alone among European nations, France has increased its contingent in Afghanistan. Where his predecessor accepted the prospect of an Iranian nuclear capability without undue alarm, Sarkozy has not hesitated to threaten Iran with an aerial attack from the West if it should show any such temerity. Within a few days of a meeting between Bush and Sarkozy at Camp David, the French foreign minister was speeding to Baghdad with warm wishes for the work of liberation in Iraq. A fulsome state visit to Israel, replete with reference to biblical entitlements, passed without a word on the fate of the Palestinians, and the EU has for the first time been pushed into a formal embrace of Tel Aviv as a privileged partner for mutual consultations with Brussels.

The new French Atlanticism does not spell mere passive submission to the will of the United States. Within the European Union, on the contrary, Sarkozy has been active in pursuit of a clear-cut goal: to strengthen it as a more compact and powerful ally of America. Naturally, this implies no federalism. The aim is tighter inter-governmental direction of the EU, by a select company of its major states, optimally at French initiative. To this end, Sarkozy worked with Merkel to design a way of circumventing the defeat of the European Constitution by French voters. Reproducing every key feature of the original, the Lisbon Treaty was duly passed through parliament without the inconvenience of a popular vote. Although the Treaty was signed during a German presidency, the driving force behind it was France, as the leading country where the Constitution had stumbled. So too, when Irish voters rejected the Treaty, the *Aussenamt* was furious, but it was Sarkozy who led the campaign to pressure Dublin to hold a second vote on it before New Labour might be turned out of office, and the project risk a final quietus from a Conservative government in London.

If successful, as must be probable, the skills in political sleight-of-hand displayed in this institutional engineering are likely to leave a more durable mark on Europe than the merely theatrical gestures of the French presidency of the Union in 2008—creation of yet another symbolic pan-Mediterranean organization; mediation in a conflict over South Ossetia, more or less bound to end in much the same way without it; pledges of less pollution, and more coordination in handling immigrants. Behind such image-building, however, lies a coherent purpose: not simply shepherding the disparate states of the EU into the habit of common ventures, verbal or material as the occasion may be, but convincing them these require firm leadership by the big-hitters of the Union. The potential tensions in this conception of Europe lie, obviously enough, in future relations with Berlin. Sarkozy's repeated attacks on the restrictive monetary regime of the European Central Bank have faded as the ECB has been forced by events to loosen it, moderating what might otherwise have become an acute source of friction between the two countries. But in wooing Britain—treated as France's natural military partner—so persistently, Sarkozy has inevitably weakened the Franco-German axis of old. Whether common economic pressures of recession bring the three countries closer together, or fault-lines between them more into the open, remains to be seen. Viewed structurally, problems of coordination are inherently greater between three parties than two. But for the moment, the complement of Sarkozy's sharp swerve towards America has been his energetic act as pace-setter for a Europe projected as second-in-command on the global stage. Here too, as domestically, French sensibilities that might be ruffled by one side of his rule are salved by another, as the stock of the nation appears to rise, along with that of its leader, in the Union.

2

The new political dispensation, even if it lasts only five years, rather than—more than possible, as things stand—ten, cannot but reconfigure the intellectual field in France, though in just what ways it is too early to say. The connexions between power and thought, traditionally closer than in any other Western country, are likely, however, to remain so.[54] They form, indeed, the guiding theme of the most substantial current consideration of the 'future of French intellectuals', the subtitle of *Les fils maudits de la République* by Gérard Noiriel, not only France's leading

---

54. For a sardonic report on the extent of politicians' consultation of intellectuals, if not necessarily acceptance of their advice, see Jade Lindgard, 'La grande "chasse aux idées", ou comment les politiques en consomment un maximum, sans toujours s'en servir', in Stéphane Beaud et al., *La France invisible*, Paris 2006, pp. 473–84, covering Sarkozy, Fabius, Bayrou and Royal.

authority on immigration, but a social historian of wide-ranging horizon. Since the era of the Dreyfus Affair, his argument runs, the country's intellectuals can be divided into three types, defined by the relation between knowledge and politics each represents. 'Revolutionary' intellectuals, from Péguy to Nizan or Sartre, sought to reincarnate the figure of the Enlightenment *philosophe*, 'complete' thinkers, uniting political, scholarly and publicistic roles, long after the modern division of social and intellectual labour had barred this fusion. With the collapse of Marxism and the absence of any prospect of revolution after 1968, this non-university species became effectively extinct, leaving only a scattering of 'radical' intellectuals—philosophers, like their predecessors, but now ensconced in the academy—of more modest ambitions, and marginal standing.

The 'governmental' intellectual, by contrast, was typically a historian, in command of key academic positions and intimate connexions with officialdom. In a line from Seignobos to Furet, such figures were counsellors to power, of moderate reformist or conservative persuasion. They had excelled at the weaving of networks of influence, aiming at—and not infrequently achieving—a general hegemony of a conformist stripe. The 'specific' intellectual, on the other hand, was to be found above all in sociology, from Durkheim or Simiand to Bourdieu. This type had learnt the lesson that science means specialization, and renounced pretensions to either political subversion, or moral magistracy, of the state. Commitment to the more sober duties of empirical research and accurate scholarship did not, however, mean seclusion in an ivory tower. Specific intellectuals sought, on the contrary, to put their knowledge at the service of their fellow citizens, sharing in a democratic spirit the fruits of their labours with society at large, as Durkheim had enjoined them to do.[55]

The core of Noiriel's book, which appeared in 2005, is made up of a detailed dissection of the anti-totalitarian nexus around *Le Débat*, as the great contemporary example of moderate historians in hegemonic action. Treatment of the governmental intellectual, in fact, is twice as long as that of the other two, which flank this centrepiece. Noiriel's portrait of this type, highly critical, ends with its discredit in 1995. Since the revolutionary intellectual is now a bygone figure, the specific intellectual is left as the single

---

55. *Les enfants maudits de la République. L'avenir des intellectuels en France*, Paris 2005, pp. 203–12.

commendable ideal today. The taxonomy, with its many local demonstrations of interest, is delivered with clarity and dignity. But it is a straitjacket into which much untidy reality cannot be fitted. The counter-revolutionary intellectual, no mean figure in the past, disappears from sight; even latter-day epigones, rarely attached to universities yet scarcely without influence in the public sphere, have no place in Noiriel's schema. Nor is governmental always a literal description of the posture of all those so classified; pertinent enough for Lavisse or Seignobos, it is perhaps less so for Furet, who was often more scornful than respectful of successive rulers of the country, his hegemonic capacity depending as much on a position to the side, or above, as within the councils of the day.

The principal weakness of Noiriel's inventory lies, however, in its idealization of the figure it recommends. It was Foucault, as he notes, who invented the slogan of the 'specific intellectual', promoting it as a salutary alternative to the part played in the past by Sartre, with whom Foucault sought to settle accounts. But anything less like examples of sober empirical scholarship than the Nietzschean sightings of *Les mots et les choses*, or its author's fulsome endorsement of the Nouveaux Philosophes, let alone panurgic metaphysics of power, could hardly be imagined. Foucault's own career, indeed, crested on the very wave of media-driven publicity—the emergent universe of journalistic fashions and corruptions that became so powerful in the course of the seventies—that is a particular target of Noiriel's dislike, and cause for his insistence on its contrast with that of scientific research.[56] If the coiner of the term himself so often embodied its negation as a generic publicist, there is good reason to doubt its cogency.

Nor did Bourdieu, temperamentally Foucault's opposite—shunning rather than seeking the glare of klieg lights—but equally a critic of the pretensions of philosophical or literary intellectuals, if in his case in the name of the modern rigour of the social sciences, live up to it: in his last years, as Noiriel admits, coming to occupy a position in French life not unlike that of Sartre. Durkheim, the patron saint of the line, is scarcely better as an advertisement for the specific intellectual, openly explaining that his 'science of morality'—unlike 'subversive or revolutionary theories' that

---

56. Elsewhere, Noiriel himself—attractively capable of self-correction— has noted how little Foucault's hunger for publicity and wild generalizations corresponded to the figure he recommended: *Penser avec, penser contre. Itinéraire d'un historien*, Paris 2003, p. 246.

were not scientific—taught a 'wisely conservative outlook': one dedicated from the outset to combating Marxism, and culminating at the end in the most banal chauvinism.[57] More generally, to identify specific intellectuals with the social sciences, as distinct from philosophy or history, is a needless *apologia pro domo sua*, that they belie. As if ultimately aware that the category is broken-backed, the conclusion of *Les fils maudits de la République* suddenly strikes another note, declaring all intellectuals, whatever their styles, basically progressive and appealing to them to unite against discrimination throughout the world. Bourdieu too was led on occasion to speak, no more convincingly, in the manner of Benda, of an intellectual 'corporatism of the universal'. An analytic of division cannot be made to yield an ethic of unanimism.[58]

Another way of looking at Noiriel's inventory of roles is to consider how far the current scene offers telling illustrations of it. Here the obvious place to start is the governmental type whose profile in the period from the mid-seventies to mid-nineties he etches so vividly. For if the high tide of a belated Cold War liberalism had passed by the end of the century, sequels and mutants continue to occupy much of the landscape. Whatever the blows it received as the conjuncture turned, no paradigm as powerful and pervasive as the vision articulated by Furet could disappear overnight. The most significant trajectory has been that of the thinker who could be regarded as his principal heir, Pierre Rosanvallon.

---

57. *De la division du travail social*, Paris 1893, p. v. By 1915, he was telling his compatriots that an 'aggressive temper, bellicose will, contempt for international law and human rights, systematic inhumanity, institutionalized cruelties' were among the 'multiple manifestations of the German soul' (sic). Aganst the 'morbid mentality' and 'social pathology' of the 'monster' across the Rhine was ranged the legitimate confidence of France that behind it stood the superior force of the 'nature of things'. '*L'Allemagne au-dessus de tout*'. *La mentalité allemande et la guerre*, Paris 1915, pp. 3, 46–7. Seignobos was a fellow-member of the committee publishing this rubbish. 'Intellectuels spécifiques et intellectuels de gouvernment, même combat!', Noiriel is obliged to note, after complaining that Nizan—whose scathing description of Durkheim's efforts to give 'official morality the appearance of science' has lost none of its point—had linked the two men: *Les fils maudits de la Republique*, pp. 223–5; for Nizan on Durkheim, see *Les chiens de garde*, Paris 1932, pp. 189–92.

58. For apposite comment on this part of *Les enfants maudits*, and assessment of the strengths and weaknesses of the book as a whole, see Serge Halimi's review, 'Une arrière-garde de l'ordre social', *Le Monde Diplomatique*, September 2005.

Originally on the staff of the Catholic trade-union federation, the CFDT, where he wrote the speeches of its leader Edmond Maire, articulating its ideology of *autogestion* and a 'Second Left', by the early eighties he was a rising star in Furet's constellation, becoming the secretary of the Fondation Saint-Simon. His first work as a historian belonged to the general recovery at the time of France's post-revolutionary liberalism. *Le moment Guizot* (1985) set out to rehabilitate the intellectual, if not political, reputation of the leading statesman of the July Monarchy as a vital stimulus for thinking about contemporary democracy. Three years later, he co-authored with Furet and Jacques Julliard the satisfied balance-sheet of *La République du centre*, celebrating the end of the French exception, even if—this was his contribution—not all, certainly, was yet entirely well with the political system, which needed to be more creatively connected to society at large.[59] So far there was not a great deal to distinguish him from other younger lights of the galaxy.

In the nineties, however, he embarked on a large-scale enterprise aiming to excavate the origins and tensions, first of universal suffrage (*Le sacre du citoyen*, 1992), then of democratic representation (*Le peuple introuvable*, 1998), and finally of popular sovereignty (*La démocratie inachevée*, 2000), since the Revolution. Across this broad canvas, he modified Furet's legacy in two ways. The bane of modern French history had not been just the deep-rooted traditions left by the Jacobin voluntarism of the First Republic itself, but also those inherited from the elitist rationalism of the Restoration and the July Monarchy. The result had long been to condemn France to oscillations between an illiberal democracy and an undemocratic liberalism. This impasse had been surmounted not with the top-down arrival of the Third Republic, as Furet had believed, but only when there developed from below, some two decades later, institutions of a new social pluralism—trade-unions, professional associations, political parties—together with a new kind of juridical and social thought. It was that silent revolution of the 1890s, amplified and stabilized by the 1920s, which had finally put France on the *terra firma* of a true liberal democracy.[60]

---

59. Not more representation, but deliberation was needed in France: 'Malaise dans le représentation', *La République du centre*, Paris 1988, p. 180.

60. Pierre Rosanvallon, See *Le peuple introuvable*, pp. 105–276, announcing the birth of a 'new collective sensibility'. *La démocratie inachevée* takes up the

Dangers, of course, still surrounded it—the general temptations of totalitarianism or corporatism in the twentieth century, not to speak of the specifically national affliction of a lingering revolutionary monism. Even today, not all was well. By the time Rosanvallon reached his second volume, the Juppé government had been routed on the streets, after a battle in which he had championed its neo-liberal reforms—a defeat he would describe five years later, in a sour retrospect for Le Débat, as the triumph of an addled refusal of modernity that was the contemporary opium of the people.[61] The trilogy, therefore, could not end on quite the same note as that struck by La République du centre. Far from France having finally reached a mature—if still far from perfect—political equipoise, it was actually in the eighties, Rosanvallon explained, that a 'balanced democracy' had started to crumble, producing an unfamiliar disarray, that so far from being comforted by the fall of communism, was even in part attributable to it, as the energizing contrast of democratic to totalitarian systems fell away. The popular will seemed to many increasingly evanescent, with less and less purchase on government. The idea of a sovereign people, however, was not to be abandoned. It had rather to be redefined more realistically, shorn of the metaphysics that had too long attended it, if the French were to enter, as they must, 'an ordinary age of politics'.[62]

With this ringing agenda, Rosanvallon was received into the Collège de France. There he has sought to emulate the mode of Furet in creating an extensive network of influence across intellectual and political establishments alike. Organizationally, early years in the backrooms of a trade-union bureaucracy and later experience as major-domo at the Fondation Saint-Simon well equipped him to do so. Within no time, close relations with big business acquired at the Fondation had yielded funding for a new 'intellectual workshop' to succeed it, the Republic of Ideas, and an arrangement with a leading publisher for a series of books under the same title, followed in due course by a Web-site for broader divulgation of sympathetic notions. Scarcely had the series been

---

theme, with 'the silent revolution of the mandate' (pp. 255ff). The overlapping themes of the trilogy relieve Rosanvallon of the burdens of any too exacting chronology, allowing for considerable flexibility of periodization. Treatment of the half century between 1930 and 1980 is very cursory, and Vichy is ignored altogether.

61. 'L'esprit de 1995', Le Débat, No. 111, September 2000, pp. 118–20.
62. Pierre Rosanvallon, La démocratie inachevée, p. 397. Italics in original.

launched than it sent up a Very light signalling its patron's break with associates of the recent past. Hard on the heels of more predictable contributions—its immediate predecessor was *Kaboul-Sarajevo*, from Michael Ignatieff—came Daniel Lindenberg's philippic against the distrust of multi-culturalism from a new breed of reactionaries, which had all too often found expression in *Le Débat*. With this, Rosanvallon, who had no doubt chafed for some time at playing second fiddle in the liberal orchestra, made it clear that he was henceforward going to be the composer.

His next project was a second triptych, on the scale of the first, devoted to the transformations of popular sovereignty in the new century, but conceived in a more resolutely constructive spirit. Rawls and Habermas, he explained, had undeniably done much to renovate political thought. Yet their approaches to it had remained too normative, ignoring the complexity of actual democratic experience as it evolved over time, which had been far from linear. What was needed now was rather a philosophical history of the political, closer in inspiration to Foucault, but focussed on the problems of democracy rather than of power.[63] Prominent among these was the gap between procedural legitimacy, conferred by elections, and substantive political trust, increasingly withheld from governments, however correctly voted into office. The tension between the two, however, was no recent phenomenon, but went back a long way, generating a set of institutional forms counter-balancing electoral rule. In the first volume of his new trilogy, *La contre-démocratie* (2006), Rosanvallon offered an inventory of 'systems of organized distrust', complementing rather than cancelling the verdict of the ballot-box: mechanisms of oversight (from muckrakers to the internet), of veto (from ephors to strikes) and of judgement (from attainders to juries). In the second, *La légitimité démocratique* (2008) he turned to the ways in which legitimacy itself was no longer delivered just by a majority at the polls, but had undergone a 'revolution' with the growth of institutions based on other principles: impartiality (quangos, central banks), reflexivity (constitutional courts, social sciences), proximity (*bains de foule*, television). In a third volume, still to come, the nation as a form of political community awaits a more complex reinvention, in similar style.

---

63. 'Towards a Philosophical History of the Political', in Dario Castiglione and Iain Hampsher-Monk, *The History of Political Thought in National Context*, Cambridge 2002, pp. 201–2.

Contemporary democracy, properly understood, was thus a richer affair than the thin models of it proposed by Schumpeter or Popper, as a mere choice between competing elites for office. It was to be conceived, not in a spirit of minimalism, but one of positively minded realism. Naturally, it remained imperfect, and liable to one perversion in particular—the pathology of populism, in which certain forms of 'counter-democracy' threaten to swallow up democracy itself.[64] But if vigilance was required against this danger, the balance-sheet of recent developments was far less negative than conventional expressions of disillusionment with the fate of representative government would have it. The truly 'remarkable phenomenon' of the period was neither a decline in political engagement nor a rise in the sway of deregulated markets. It was the growth of a self-organizing civil society, expanding an 'indirect democracy' around and beyond electoral systems.[65] Admittedly, this gain had gone together with a loss in salience of the political sphere, more narrowly conceived. But here lay the task of the social sciences, to help repoliticize democracy by endowing it with a more sophisticated understanding of its own destiny. In so doing, a 'philosophical history of the political' could unite knowledge and action in a single undertaking. Aron and Sartre had embodied, each with intellectual grandeur, the opposite temptations of their generation: an icy reason and a blind commitment, equally impotent. 'The author of these lines', Rosanvallon concluded, 'has sought to escape that impasse by formulating a theory of democracy no longer divorced from action to bring it to life'.[66]

This gesture, at once of succession and supersession, indicates the place in the nation's culture to which Rosanvallon aspires; beyond it, allusions to Rawls and Habermas, the appropriate international standing. Of these hopes, the second rests on an enterprise at least comparable in intention. There can be little doubt that Rosanvallon's accounting of democracy, past and present, is empirically richer than theorizations of an original position or communicative reason. But that advantage is more limited than it might seem, and comes at a price. For, in keeping with its inspiration, in the philosophical history of the political there is more philosophy than history. Foucault's versions of the past, Vincent Descombes once remarked, characteristically had

---

64. Pierre Rosanvallon, *La contre-démocratie*, Paris 2006, pp. 269–78.
65. Rosanvallon, *La démocratie inachevée*, p. 393.
66. *La contre-démocratie*, Paris 2006, p. 322

the form of 'once upon a time'[67]; parables for present instruction, rather than true studies of *res gestae*, they assembled evidence to illustrate philosophemes conceived independently of it. Rosanvallon's trilogies are of the same nature. They display an impressive diligence and erudition, but these rarely yield a true narrative, unfolding instead an eclectic catalogue of dicta and data mustered to serve the intellectual purpose to hand.

More transparently than in the cases of Rawls or Habermas, that purpose is apologetic. Where they outline a normative order in principle embedded in the existing institutions and understandings of Western society, yet in practice often regrettably distorted by them, Rosanvallon moves in the opposite direction, seeking to show that it is a misunderstanding of our actually existing democracy to suppose that it fails to live up to the values of popular sovereignty, which it fulfils in subtler and richer ways than usually imagined. The function of the argument is one of ideological compensation. Rather than lamenting the decay of electoral systems as vehicles of the democratic will, we should be celebrating the emergence of non-electoral forms of accountability and the common good. The bewildering array of surrogates brigaded to this end borders at times on the comic: not only constitutional courts, street processions or auditing commissions, but central banks, ratings agencies and 'political conversations', of which we are solemnly told there are fifteen million every day in Britain.[68] All such are gages of democratic health, though it must be wondered whether, after recent performances, Moody's or the SEC will survive the next edition. But the objective of the exercise is clear: as Rosanvallon puts it, 'a certain desacralization of electoral life' and 'multiplication of functional authorities' are essential for that complex sovereignty in which for the first time 'democracy can be wholly and completely liberal'.[69]

The core of this extended argument for 'the importance of not being elected' is, of course, a variant of theories of the regulative state in the Anglo-Saxon world, developed with exemplary clarity by Giandomenico Majone. But where Majone and others have focussed their attention on the European Union, as the purest case of a regulative polity without unnecessary electoral pretensions,

---

67. *Le même et l'autre. Quarante-cinq ans de philosophie française (1933–1978)*, Paris 1979, p. 139.

68. Pierre Rosanvallon, *La légitimité démocratique*, Paris 2008, pp. 327.

69. *La démocratie inachevée*, pp. 407–8.

Rosanvallon—who has not so far made any reference to their work—has transferred the same construction downwards to the nation-state itself, on the whole regarded by them as still the domain of a traditional majoritarian democracy, based on popular verdicts at the polls. The shift, however, accounts for the deliberative, even at moments demonstrative, wrapping around the regulative core in Rosanvallon's model. For liberals of Majone's conviction, the market—properly superintended by neutral agencies—is the ultimate seat of impartial judgements that voters cannot trust themselves to deliver. But Rosanvallon is a social, rather than an economic, liberal in the strict sense. So popular forms of veto— marches, strikes, protests—find their place in the repertoire of complex sovereignty, which would otherwise seem too harshly technocratic. But that these remain at best ancillary can be seen from the risks attributed to them. In counter-democracy from below lies the perpetual danger of populism: no comparable peril is ever attested for regulative authority from above. The one is the principle of a new general will; the other, the *supplément d'âme* of a dispossession of the old.

Is the achievement of Furet repeatable? Rosanvallon is not a negligible successor. Like his mentor, he offers a sweepingly didactic vision of the national past, culminating in pointed conclusions for the present; combines positions of power in the academy, prominence in the media, patronage in publishing; enjoys close connexions with the worlds of business and politics; has gathered round him a levy of younger associates and pupils— now adding to this portfolio, outreach on the internet. Still missing, though no doubt the next step, is ascent to America, for which the assiduity in his latest work of footnote references to every cranny of its social sciences can be read as an extended *captatio benevolentiae*. But though in all these respects the public profiles of the two historians as organizers and thinkers are so similar, Rosanvallon's impact has so far remained much more limited. In part, this has had to do with differences of personality and style. Furet possessed an elusive charisma which his stolid successor could scarcely hope to reproduce. His writing, too, had a verve and mordancy lacking in Rosanvallon's well-turned, somewhat priestly, prose—a contrast perhaps in part attributable to background, training in the PCF offering considerably more *tranchant* than formation in the CFDT, with its touch of unction.

But the more significant reasons for the drop in influence lie in the conjuncture, and the relation of each project to its moment. Furet was writing at the height of the restoration of the late seventies and eighties, when neo-liberalism was carrying all before it, and could concentrate his polemical gifts on demolition of the myths of the Revolution, Jacobin or Bolshevik. Rosanvallon operates in a far less favourable situation. Not only has the liberalism they stood for taken something of a battering in France, but in these lowering times a more awkward task has fallen to him: not so much attacking the old as embellishing the new, with a constructive interpretation of the changes that have supervened, as a work in progress towards a still more—'wholly and completely'—liberal future. The result is a disabling quotient of euphemism, giving his output a pervasive air of blandness that has inevitably limited its appeal. The social dimension of this liberalism—the sense in which Rosanvallon claims ground to the left of the republican commitments of Le Débat—has not offset this handicap.[70] If anything it has merely exposed him to the misfortunes of French Socialism at large, reducing him to the status of a local Giddens rather the loftier international models to which he aspires. Successive plunges into political waters have led only to a series of déboires: humiliation with Juppé in 1995, debacle over the European Constitution in 2006—he was beside himself at this victory of populism—and rebuff with Royal in 2007. The République des Idées remains active, even if a leading member of its network has already defected to Sarkozy, and Rosanvallon in reserve as counsellor to a future prince, should the PS recover. But, at any rate for the moment, what is striking is the gap between intention and effect.

---

70. Inviting comparison with Rosanvallon is the tetralogy under way from Marcel Gauchet, L'Avènement de la démocratie, whose first volumes, La révolution moderne and La crise du libéralisme, appeared in 2007. The parallels between the two projects, as offering at once a genealogy, pathology and redemptive apology of liberalism, are very close. The main difference is that Gauchet, who starts his story much earlier, around 1500, pitches it at a more general and philosophical level—'an extreme stylization of the analysis'—and pivots it on the emergence of the West from religious belief, and the crises this gradual exit has provoked. Otherwise, the intention—'to de-banalize liberal democracy'—and even the periodization are virtually the same. Gauchet, however, dwells more on the strains that accompanied the arrival of liberal democracy after 1880, when imperialism puts in an appearance as an 'infantile disorder of globalization', and on the perils of totalitarianism that interrupted its progress after 1918. Today, as in Rosanvallon, the troubles afflicting liberal democracy must be seen as a 'crisis of growth', leading —for Gauchet, in a somewhat longer run—to its constructive recomposition.

3

What of French Socialism itself? The peculiarity of the PS, within the gamut of its sister parties in Western Europe, has long lain in a dual external determination setting it apart from even the Mediterranean counterparts closest to it. Like the Spanish, Portuguese and Italian parties of the eighties, it is an organization whose leaders come from the ranks of a sleek-suited technocracy and state administration; cadres and core electors, from white-collar employees in the public sector; finances from businesses close to it; and media backing from *bon ton* press and periodicals. Like them, it lacks any trade-union base, and has virtually no proletarian roots.[71] Like them, too, it was a recent re-make, producing a political form little continuous with the past. But its genesis was otherwise quite different, not the transformation of an existing organization, but the creation of a new one out of a merger of several older organizations—a more difficult enterprise, whose condition was, in effect, an external federator. As architect of the PS, without whom it might not have come into being, and would certainly never have come to power when it did, Mitterrand belonged to no socialist tradition. Once president of the Republic, he controlled the party from afar, playing off its different components against one another, without ever becoming fully identified with it. The consequence, after his departure, was that French Socialism was left with a now entrenched factional structure, without its master-builder. The contrast with the disciplinary organizations of González, Craxi or Soares is marked. The PS has always been a much less unitary structure.

The second difference has lain in the ideological field surrounding the party. Initially outgunned in voters and members by Marchais, Mitterrand famously outmanoeuvred the PCF, reducing it first to impotence, and eventually to near-extinction. But to do so, he had to avoid moving too openly into a more capitalist universe of political discourse. For though French Communism was visibly shrinking, down to the end of his first tenure it continued to weigh in the force-field of national memory and ideology. Even after

---

71. By 1998, just 5 per cent of its members were workers; no more than 13 per cent were even employees. In the first years of the new century, its total effectives were actually fewer in number than those of a now politically insignificant Communist Party: Henri Rey, *La gauche et les classes populaires*, Paris 2004, pp. 47, 49, 52.

1989, as events were soon to show, popular insurgencies drawing inspiration from the country's revolutionary traditions could not be altogether discounted. So however neo-liberal the policies of his regime, Mitterrand was careful not to cross the line of political decorum that required the PS be more—or other—than a mere local version of social democracy. His successors, possessed of less authority in the party and more evidence of continuing radical attachments in the population, have hesitated to come out of the ideological closet ever since, even as they have drifted steadily further to the right.

The result has been to accentuate the acrimony of personal rivalries without political differences, in a structure paralyzed by its inability to close the gap between its pretensions and its practices. In this stasis has gathered a deepening sink of corruption, as successive notables have been caught with their hand in a till of one kind or another—Dumas, Strauss-Kahn, Dray, Kouchner, all naturally unscathed by the law, with no doubt more to come. With Sarkozy, finally, have come desertions, and with them demoralization. Currently riven between two equally tarnished mediocrities, Aubry and Royal, with many another predator waiting in the wings, the PS is a party without any stable principles or identity.[72] After years of looking wistfully, if furtively, at Blairism in Britain, it has missed that bus, gone to the wrecking-yard in its country of origin. Like the former Communists in Italy, many of its leaders now hope to skip the awkward staging-post of social democracy, long shunned, for a direct route to social liberalism. There is no sign the public is impressed. Effectively, the party is adrift, relying on its inherited status as the default alternative to Centre-Right rule, whenever that should falter, *sans plus*.

That this might not be enough, even in the event of a steep drop in support for Sarkozy, is already becoming conceivable. To the left of the PS, the forces that led popular opposition to victory over the European Constitution in 2005 did not fare well in its aftermath. Far from capitalizing on this spectacular success, they

---

72. For a portrait of the 'moral economy of cynicism' and rival careerisms from top to bottom of the latter-day PS, all the more devastating for being not unsympathetic to its subject, see Rémi Lefebvre and Frédéric Sawicki, *La société des socialistes*, Paris 2006. In this Hobbesian world 'where militant is wolf to militant', in the words of one of its members, a former leader—Pierre Mauroy, no less—can remark that 'if the disgusted leave, only the disgusting will remain': pp. 201, 214.

dispersed and lost momentum, unable to agree on any common programme of action, or electoral lists. ATTAC, key to the organization of much of the battle against the EU charter, divided into antagonistic camps soon afterwards, and went into decline. *Le Monde diplomatique*, weakened by both the failure of the long teachers' strike of 2003, demoralizing one of its traditional readerships, and tensions over the perennial apple of republican discord, the issue of the veil, lost a third of its circulation. In April 2007, the combined tally of all candidates of the far Left dropped 40 per cent below its level in 2002, while total voter turnout rose 10 per cent. The press could hardly contain its satisfaction. At *Le Monde* Colombani congratulated his fellow-citizens for flocking to the polls and sensibly dividing their votes between the two leading candidates, each impressive in their way, in an exemplary display of civic responsibility.

The idyll did not last long. Within a month Colombani had been unceremoniously ousted by journalists at *Le Monde*, which had been steadily losing money, followed in due course, with still less dignity, by Minc—both men promptly enlisted for counsel by Sarkozy. Plenel had been dropped overboard well before. This turmoil, reflecting the economic crisis of the mainstream press, was not in itself a signal for any departure from the paper's general conformism, but spoke of the disorientation under the new presidency of what had once been a compact organ of the Centre-Left establishment. Popular humours proved no more stable. The fall in Sarkozy's own ratings, steep enough, could be regarded as par for the course at the Elysée since the nineties. Newer was not only the complete lack of any corresponding gain by the PS, but the re-emergence of a revolutionary phoenix to its left. Of the range of Trotskyist candidates standing in 2007, one only had more or less held onto previous ground, the young postman Olivier Besancenot, representing the Ligue Communiste Révolutionnaire. But that was at a mere 4 per cent of the vote, three times that of the PCF, but still reassuringly minimal.

By the autumn of 2008, however, disgust with the PS had become so widespread that Besancenot, an appealingly fresh face even to the media, suddenly soared past all possible Socialist leaders in the polls, becoming France's leading alternative to Sarkozy in popular opinion. On the strength of this—personal and still, of course, virtual—showing, the Ligue decided to dissolve itself, and give birth to a New Anti-Capitalist Party, broader and more unsectarian in character. What its fortunes will be remains to be seen. Two years into the new presidency, the social and intellectual setting is not entirely unfavourable for it. France is the only major country in Europe where high school and university students have mobilized *en masse*, year after year, against governments of the day, creating a sub-culture of libertarian and solidaristic impulse likely to mark a generation. It is among this youth that the ideas of the most radical sector of the intelligentsia, once again often coming from philosophy, have gained ground, as the standing of Alain Badiou or Jacques Rancière attest. The new party might well prove marginal or ephemeral. Dependence on an individual shooting-star is one obvious danger. Another lies simply in the electoral system of the Fifth Republic, which in abolishing proportional representation was designed from the outset to cripple the PCF, and continues to corner any potential challenge to the system, by forcing adherence to whatever nominal alternative to the Centre-Right survives the first round—indeed, as 2002 showed, when Besancenot called on voters to rally to Chirac, in the last resort adherence to the Centre-Right itself, *um schlechteres zu vermeiden*. Since the New Anti-Capitalist Party has declared that it rejects on principle any alliance with the PS of the kind that destroyed the PCF, it could only escape the logic of the lesser evil lying ahead if it actually overtook the Socialists in the first round.

Notionally, that is not completely impossible. Two months into 2009, Besancenot was considered the best opponent of Sarkozy by the French, well ahead of all other possible candidates, and topping preferences for Aubry and Royal combined. Such ratings, however, come and go. What seems clear is that the dual voltage of France's deep political culture, with its characteristically sudden switches from conformity to insurgency and back again, is not yet over. Less clear is which of these poles a deepening economic crisis will favour, or whether it might—as respectable opinion would wish—bring to an end, at last, their alternation.

GERMANY

1 · 1998

On a perfect autumn evening, Helmut Kohl closed his election campaign in the cathedral square of Mainz, capital of the Rhine-Palatinate, where he began his political career. As night fell, the towers of the great sandstone church glowed a dusky red above the Baroque marketplace illuminated below, packed with supporters and onlookers. Making his way to the front of this picturesque scene, the 'Chancellor of Unity' delivered a confident address to the crowd of Christian Democratic loyalists, brushing aside barracking from pockets of far left youth on the edges of the square. Security was not tight. On a screen beside the podium the huge pear-shaped face of the statesman, with its heavy bonhomous jaw and sharp feral eyes, was projected into the darkness. From surrounding cafés, bystanders watched the scene with the low-key curiosity of spectators at a possible farewell.

Forty-eight hours later Kohl's helicopter alighted on the grounds of his residence in Bonn, an almost domestic sight as it came in across the Rhine low over the heads of strollers and cyclists along the river path—a quieter Sunday afternoon could not be imagined. Although the polls had not yet quite closed, by then he would have known he had lost the election. An hour later, the first projections on television—in Germany, with nearly perfect proportional representation, they are highly accurate—were being received with relief and delight in the headquarters of Social Democracy. But it would be difficult to speak of elation. Party workers remain proletarian in ways that have largely disappeared in Britain—victory hailed not just with beer and sausages, but hampers overflowing with cigarette packets; a certain stolidity could be expected. But the oddly subdued atmosphere reflected national reactions as a whole. There was none of the jubilation surrounding Blair's arrival in Downing Street, however forced much of that may have been.

In part, the election campaign itself was responsible for the absence of excitement. Avoiding any sharp challenges or radical commitments, Gerhard Schröder promised no more than a reformist modicum, under the slogan 'We don't want to change everything, just improve many things'. In point of fact, the SPD's platform involved more reversal of Kohl's tax measures than New Labour of Major's economic policies. But the general tone of its appeal to the electorate—ceremoniously respectful of Kohl's stature as a European statesman—was a good deal less combative than the campaign mounted by Millbank in 1996. In the minds of party managers, the prospect of a Grand Coalition with the CDU was never far away, setting limits to any too divisive rhetoric. Expecting—often, according to opinion polls, wanting—such an outcome, voters were not stirred.

But in the noticeably low-key reactions to the result of the election, a more pervasive state of mind could be detected too. Living in Germany over the previous year, one was often struck by the resistance of so many Germans to registering the scale of the changes about to overtake their country. Politically, every opinion poll made it clear long in advance that, whatever the exact election result, the next chancellor was going to be a Social Democrat—bringing a change of government after a longer spell of unbroken conservative rule than in any other West European society. Geographically, the capital of the country was about to shift back to Berlin—an upheaval of much greater significance, with no recent parallel in any other European country. Economically, the national currency was scheduled to disappear with the arrival of European monetary union: a transformation with a quite special charge in Germany, where the D-mark long served as a surrogate for more traditional forms of national identity. The sudden interlocking of three such basic alterations would make a formidable agenda for any society. Yet the prevailing mood could have been described as a state of denial.

Against this background, the gap between the reception and the result of the September election becomes more understandable. But viewed objectively, it is still striking enough. Recalling the popular enthusiasm that greeted Willy Brandt's victory in 1972, which put the SPD in office for a decade, many observers commented on the lack of any comparable electricity in the air this time. The paradox is that the electoral upheaval in 1998 was greater. There are two ways of looking at this. One is to compare the relative performance of the two major parties. Between 1949 and 1994, the combination of the CDU and Bavaria's Christian Social Union outpolled the SPD by an overall average of some 7 per cent—a structural predominance of the Right far greater than in Britain, let alone France. Even at the height of its success in 1972, the SPD could secure a margin over the CDU/CSU of no more than 0.9 per cent. In 1998, for the first time ever, the SPD was well ahead of its rival—scoring 5.7 per cent more than the CDU/CSU, a historic reversal.

But there is another and more significant measure of the scale of the change, that puts this success into proportion. In 1972 the SPD won 45.8 per cent of the electorate. In 1998 it got just 40.9 per cent—well below its level even in 1980. There was no simple triumph of Social Democracy, old or new, here. The larger reality lay elsewhere. Overshadowing the performance of the SPD itself was the total score for the Left. With the Greens taking 6.7 per cent and the post-communist Party of Democratic Socialism (PDS) 5.1 per cent, for the first time in German history the Left as a whole won a clear-cut absolute majority of the country—52.7 per cent, a figure it has never reached in Britain.

What was the pattern of this victory? In West Germany after the war, religion was always the most reliable index of the regional strengths of Right and Left. Christian Democracy was inter-confessional, but invariably predominated in the Catholic south—Bavaria, Baden-Württemberg, Rhine-Palatinate; whereas Social Democracy always did better in the Protestant north and centre—Lower Saxony, the Ruhr, Hessen. The exceptions were Schleswig-Holstein in the far north, where the large refugee population from the east initially tipped the balance towards the CDU, and the Saar in the far south, with its iron and coal the most working-class of all *Länder*, which later swung to the SPD. The correlation was always somewhat asymmetrical, since a majority of practising—as opposed to passive—Protestants voted Christian Democrat, so that SPD dominance in Lutheran Germany was never as secure as CDU in Catholic, and over time the link between religion and partisan preference has weakened.

But in 1998 the confessional gradient in the West German electorate was as striking as it had ever been. The SPD's highest scores came in the three northern-most *Länder* (higher still in its traditional bastions in the city-states of Hamburg and Bremen)—

all above 45 per cent; followed some way down by a middle belt of Hessen and the Rhine-Palatinate at 41 per cent; ending in the far south with Bavaria and Baden-Württemberg, the two firmest strongholds of Christian Democracy, at around 35 per cent. The Saar was once again the exception, with the highest SPD vote in the country, over 52 per cent. Nation-wide, the CDU/CSU took 46 per cent of the Catholic and 36 per cent of the Protestant vote— the SPD, vice-versa, 46 per cent of the Protestant and 32 per cent of the Catholic. It was among non-believers that the SPD piled up a crushing margin over its rival—41 to 21 per cent.[1]

Class, of course, has been the other great determinant of German voting patterns. In the West, Christian Democracy this time lost more working-class votes than Social Democracy gained—the SPD increasing its share by only a percentage point. Schröder's appeal, pitched expressly to 'the New Middle', proved most effective with white-collar employees, where the SPD gained 6 per cent nation-wide, and pulled over significant numbers of the self-employed, some of them former Green supporters. There was little gender variance in the vote, with the exception of young women under twenty-four, who went for the SPD much more strongly than their male counterparts.

The truly dramatic change, however, came in the East. Traditionally, this was uniformly Protestant terrain, with large working-class concentrations in Berlin, Leipzig, Chemnitz, Dresden, Merseburg—enlarged by DDR industrialization after the war. It had long been reckoned natural SPD territory, in the event of reunification. The CDU's complete command of the democratic *Anschluss* of 1990 ensured the exact opposite. Promising 'blooming landscapes' to the Eastern compatriots he had released from bondage, Kohl won a landslide in the former Communist *Länder* in 1990 and the critical margin for victory in the much closer national race of 1994. Four years later, disillusionment was complete, and popular anger at the collapse of employment in the East scythed the CDU vote, which fell to little more than a quarter of the total—a drop twice as steep as in the West. For the first time the SPD became the leading party in the region, if still with a much lower vote than in the West (35.6 to 42.4 per cent). Post-Communist success made the difference. The PDS took over 20 per cent in the East: more than two million votes.

In the electoral geography of Germany, these results are likely

---

1. For breakdowns of the vote, see 'Wahlsonderheft', *Der Spiegel*, 29 September 1998.

to prove the real landmark. In the East the balance of forces has swung far away from that in the West, and will probably stay there. The contrast between the two nations can be seen from the total vote for the Left (SPD, Greens, PDS) in each: 60.3 per cent in the East against 50.6 in the West. Here was the pivot on which the precise parliamentary arithmetic of Schröder's government finally turned. It was the twelve 'excess' mandates—beyond its proportional quota—the SPD won in the East that gave the Red–Green bloc its majority in the Bundestag. If the CDU had held its losses in the East to their level in the West, there would have been a Grand Coalition instead.

On view, then, is potentially the emergence of a long-run sociological majority for the Left in Germany, as the East reverts to what might be called a historical 'default position', where the SPD and PDS regularly dominate. The religious landscape could be critical here. The one durable legacy of the DDR was Jacobin: within two generations, it achieved an astonishing de-Christianization of the population. Today 80 per cent of East German youth have no confessional affiliation whatever—the comparable figure is 10 per cent in West Germany—and no more than 7 per cent of Easterners are church-goers of any kind.[2] Lutheranism has given way to an irreligion still more inhospitable than the Evangelical Church to any hegemony by a Christian Democratic Right.

I

What kind of government has come out of this drastic shake-up? It is conventional to compare Schröder with Blair. One genuine point in common is the way both were effectively picked as candidates by the media before they were chosen by their party—comparison with Blair, in Schröder's case, being part of the anointing process itself. Telegenic looks, rhetoric of modernization, pursuit of the New Middle, the inspirational call of 'time for a change': other parallels are ready to hand. But in some ways they are misleading. This has partly to do with the political figure himself, and more largely with his party. Where Blair—private schooling, stint at Oxbridge, lucrative practice at the bar—is a typical product of

---

2. Baptisms had dropped from 77 per cent in 1950 to 17 per cent by 1989: Hartmut Kaelble, Jürgen Kocka and Hartmut Zwahr (eds), *Sozialgeschichte der DDR*, Stuttgart 1994, p. 272.

a privileged middle-class background, Schröder—whose father was killed on the Russian front—comes from the broken debris of post-war German society. His mother was a charwoman; first job behind the counter in an ironmonger's shop; degree eventually obtained at night school. He became a leader of the Jusos, the SPD's youth organization, in the early seventies, when it was a rebellious arena well to the left of the party, and took active part in mass demonstrations of the time. In the eighties, though no firebrand, he helped topple Helmut Schmidt, and as late as 1994 was blocked by party elders as too unreliable to run for chancellor. The aura of moderate pragmatism is quite recent. But there is no lack of charm: rugged good looks, attractive thick voice, mischievous smile.

The larger difference, however, is institutional. The SPD is not in thrall to its chancellor. The party remains a very different animal from New Labour. Twice the size, with 700,000 individual members, sociologically its sub-culture remains noticeably more working class. The atmosphere of an SPD rally in any big industrial town is closer to Labour meetings of the sixties or seventies than to anything in today's Britain. The contrast is rooted not so much in any lag of modernization of the SPD—whose Bad Godesberg programme turned to the middle class long before Labour—as in the greater strength of German manufacturing, whose world-class performance has shielded workers in the West from the extremes of de-industrialization that have broken up so much of the traditional identity of the British working class. Trade-unions weathered the eighties better, and enjoy stronger relations with the party.

But a still more important difference between the two organizations lies in the regional distribution of power in the SPD. Germany's federal structure means that political careers are made first and foremost in the *Länder*, whose rulers always offer a repertoire of possible candidates for chancellor. By winning four successive federal elections, Kohl achieved a remarkable concentration of power in the CDU, but even he could not stop bitter enemies in the party from becoming important regional figures, like Biedenkopf ('King Kurt') in Saxony. The SPD has never allowed the same personalization of authority as the CDU in a single leader. When it has been in power, the pattern has always has been a diarchy—Brandt and Wehner, or Schmidt and Brandt—with the chancellor flanked by a party chairman exercising major independent power, not to speak of the SPD regional prime ministers.

Schröder, catapulted within six months of winning a provincial election in Hanover to leadership of the country, is entitled to the gratitude of his party for its victory. But he has no deep following within it; indeed was widely distrusted, the party's attitude recalling the pithy maxim of one of Claud Cockburn's characters: 'charm and dependability—so rarely go together'. The favourite of members and apparatus alike remains Oskar Lafontaine, whose skill, charisma and discipline galvanized the SPD machine in the years of Kohl's decline. Another post-war orphan from a poor family, educated by Jesuits in the Saar, Lafontaine became the brightest of 'Brandt's grandchildren', the generation of SPD politicians who came to prominence in the eighties. Chairman of the SPD, and minister of finance, he is the first Western politician of aggressively Keynesian outlook in twenty-five years.

The direction of the government, of course, will not be set just by the SPD leadership. The rules of any German coalition give significant leverage to the lesser partner. The Greens did not do particularly well in the September election, losing about a hundred thousand votes after a lack-lustre campaign, distinguished mainly by sectarian attacks on the PDS. The party, always somewhat erratic, has lost direction in recent years, as some of its less attractive features have taken their toll—what might be called the bohemian version of the *Spiessbürger* smugness of the Bonn Republic, especially evident in attitudes to the East, where the party is virtually non-existent. On some fiscal and social issues, the exclusively middle-class base of the party, not insensible to neo-liberal themes, can put it to the right of the SPD. Nevertheless, on balance the weight of the Greens should tilt the government in less conventional directions than Social Democracy left to its own devices would take.

The figure of Joschka Fischer, the new foreign minister, indicates why. Son of another victim of the war, a labourer expelled from Bohemia in 1946, he is an expressive survivor of the student radicalism of the late sixties. In those years, he led one of the most daring 'spontaneist' groups in Frankfurt, Revolutionary Struggle, fellow spirits of the better-known *Lotta Continua* in Italy. With his comrades, he took a job on the assembly line in an Opel factory to rouse the working class to revolt. When GM flushed them out, Fischer turned to the squatters' movement in Frankfurt, organizing a mobile strike-force—the *Putzgruppe*— to block police actions against housing occupations, matching where need be violence with violence. Eventually a demonstration against the death of Ulrike Meinhof in 1976 got out of hand, and a policeman was nearly killed. Fischer was arrested on suspicion of responsibility, but released for lack of evidence.[3]

Changing his mind about the legitimacy of civil violence after some years driving a cab and dabbling in philosophy, he joined the Greens and quickly rose to the top as their most flexible and articulate leader. Unencumbered with doctrine, he was soon minister for the environment in a Red–Green coalition in Hessen, winning the admiration of the press for hard-headed ambition and political realism, though the portfolio itself bored him. As a deputy in the Bundestag, he specialized in the tart put-down, cutting through official bombast. His new job as chief of German diplomacy has a certain piquancy—the diplomatic hypocrisies of 'the international community' have not been his natural idiom. But he is a learner. Under Fischer's guidance, the Greens have welcomed the expansion of NATO to Russia's borders, impervious to criticism from the left of the SPD.

This career can be seen as a cameo of a wider parabola. Fischer is the first prominent politician in Western Europe who in origin is a chemically pure product of 1968. The revolt of that year left deeper and more durable traces in German society than anywhere else. The mass movements were more spectacular in France and Italy, but they did not have the same cultural staying-power. Three features set the German upheaval apart. Morally, here alone the awakening of '68 was also a first attempt to settle accounts with the national past, as a generation started to discover and confront the record of its parents in the Nazi years, in what became a watershed in the history of the country. Intellectually, the revolt drew on a much richer complex of indigenous ideas than its counterparts elsewhere. The students who triggered the movement not only read Marx with the ease and lack of distance we might Smith or Mill—studying any classic in one's own language is a very different experience from scrutinizing celebrated texts from another—but were surrounded by the legacy of Benjamin, the presence of Horkheimer and Adorno, the interventions of Marcuse, the debut of Habermas. Where in other lands there was a rediscovery of long-forgotten texts and traditions, here

3. For this incident, airbrushed out of other accounts of Fischer in these years, see Christian Schmidt, '*Wir sind die Wahnsinnigen . . .*', Munich 1998, pp. 89–94.

there was a living continuity. The Frankfurt School occupied a unique position within the generally conservative culture of the Federal Republic—paradoxically, there was no collective body of social and philosophical work remotely rivalling it in power or influence. Naturally, its conceptual after-images persisted long past the street battles.

Finally, there was a peculiar strain in the national culture at large, that sustained and relayed the moment of the late sixties and the early seventies into the Green movement a decade later. This was, of course, the long and chatoyant tradition of German Romanticism—interpreted broadly, from *Werther* to Wenders, the most enduring single strand in the sensibility of the country's intelligentsia. The combination of sheer imaginative energy and theoretical ambition that stamped the *Frühromantik*—the ambience of the Schlegels, Novalis, Jean Paul, Tieck, Schleiermacher; Hölderlin and Kleist off-stage—made it an explosive force far beyond the sentimental reach of the Lake Poets or the vaticinations of Hugo: a star-burst that could never be repeated or forgotten, as its consequences worked their way through successive agitated generations. In a great variety of different registers, two motifs remained constant in that descent: an acute sense of the mystery of the natural world, and of the high calling of youth. Inevitably, the political issue of this tradition was dimorphous. Its contribution to movements of the Right—figures like Friedrich Schlegel or Adam Müller were, after all, ultras in their day—is well known. But its influence on the Left was critical too. Benjamin, whose *One-Way Street* emits the first flashes of ecological warning in the Marxist tradition, came out of the turn-of-the-century *Jugendbewegung*. When Adorno later engaged in his famous dispute with him, it is no accident he should have appealed *inter alia* to two exquisite passages of Jean Paul.[4]

The Greens are populist heirs to this tradition. The revolutionary ferment of '68, however utopian, was on such a scale that when it ebbed, it left behind a dense fenland of counter-cultural enclaves in West Germany—a sympathetic, if no longer especially strenuous, milieu whose characteristic bookshops and cafés can be found in even the most unlikely settings. Here the environmental concerns of the eighties found a natural habitat.

---

4. Letter of 10 November 1938: Theodor Adorno, Walter Benjamin, *Briefwechsel 1928–1940*, Frankfurt 1994, pp. 373–4. The passages came from Jean Paul's *Herbst-Blumine* of 1820.

Ecology was from the start, and in principle remains, the leitmotif of Green politics.[5] But the Greens also appealed to a wider band of intellectual opinion, not necessarily enamoured of their positive programmes, but accepting them as at least negatively preferable to social democratic stuffiness. There is no way of knowing in advance what power will do to this movement. All that is clear is that Germany is the one country where the question of what has ultimately become of the experience of '68 is going to be put to a direct test.

The immediate agenda of the Red–Green government, although it has provoked outcries from business lobbies and establishment journalists, is inoffensive enough. The package is more radical than New Labour's, but not decisively so. Fiscal policy will be somewhat more redistributive; a reduction in social wage costs will be financed by a novel energy tax; more corporatist arrangements are envisaged for job-creation, in the shape of an 'Alliance for Work' supposedly uniting all social partners. Changing Germany's laws of citizenship, notoriously based on the principle of *jus sanguinis*, to facilitate naturalization of the country's four million immigrants, is a much more significant reform. This is an unambiguous act of emancipation, of direct human consequence. Labour's tortuous constitutional manoeuvres are scarcely an equivalent. But if Schröder's programme seems less conservative than Blair's, this is also a function of its context. Kohl was no Thatcher: the centre of political gravity never shifted so far to the right in Germany.

2

The move of the capital to Berlin will be a much more dramatic change than any act of the coalition. No feature of the post-war Federal Republic defined it more sharply than the location of the government in Bonn. Over time the population became strongly attached to this arrangement. But it always had two sides to it. On the one hand, the absence of a major political capital prevented any territorial concentration of economic or political power, allowing the Federal Republic to revert to what had been the natural order of Germany for centuries—the coexistence of a large number of regional centres of roughly comparable size, the

---

5. For the early days of the party, see Werner Hülsberg, *The German Greens: A Social and Political Profile*, London 1988, pp. 64–139.

pattern of the Enlightenment. The happy results of this dispersion of vitality and influence between Munich, Frankfurt, Hamburg, Stuttgart, Cologne and other cities are evident to any visitor from over-centralized societies like England or France, and keenly felt by the citizens themselves.

On the other hand, there had to be a capital somewhere, and here the choice of Bonn was peculiarly deadening. Adenauer was determined to prevent Frankfurt—the obvious choice, for reasons of both geography and history—from becoming provisional capital after the war, because he feared it would tend to have a Socialist majority, and anyway riff-raff might take to the streets. Bonn was picked as an urban zero, a small Catholic university town where no mob would ever gather, a stone's throw from Adenauer's base in Cologne.[6] The intention was to isolate politics in a bureaucratic capsule from the influence of any popular life. It succeeded all too well. The real virtues of the Federal Republic became identified with its artificial capital. This was always a confusion. Regional variety and autonomy did not require sterilization of public argument. Federalism was not dependent on this parliamentary parking-lot; it was diminished by it.

At the beginning, not even Adenauer dared suggest that Bonn was anything but an interim location. The Constitution of 1949 laid it down that as soon as Germany was reunified, Berlin would become the nation's capital once again. But since unity appeared a remote horizon, gradually more and more vested interests became encrusted in the status quo. When the Wall finally came down, Bonn became the theatre of an astonishing spectacle. Far from the Constitution being automatically respected, a massive campaign was mounted in the West to keep Bonn as capital of the unified country. As the assembled parliamentarians prepared to vote on the issue, the town for the first time became a caricature of what it was set up to avoid: a cauldron of self-interested passions as shop-keepers, waiters, cab-drivers, not to speak of burly local MPs, refused service to, abused or threatened any deputy who had declared in favour of Berlin. When the vote came, it spoke volumes for the egoism of the Western political class. Kohl and Schäuble, the architects of absorption of the East, spoke for

---

6. For the political and financial operation required to secure the decision for Bonn, see Henning Köhler, *Adenauer: Eine politische Biographie*, Frankfurt 1994, pp. 495–509, which makes it fairly clear that it included bribes to purchase the votes of various deputies.

Berlin. Brandt, in the most courageous speech of his career, rightly compared the prospect of remaining in Bonn to the notion of a French government clinging to Vichy in 1945.[7] But the majority on both their benches was shamelessly ready to break the promise of the Constitution. The SPD actually voted to stay in Bonn by the wider margin (126 to 110; CDU/CSU 164 to 154). The hostility of the Catholic south to a transfer of the capital to the Protestant north was predictable enough. But, strikingly, more rapacious even than Bavaria in its resistance to a move was the over-weight province of North-Rhine Westphalia, clinging to Bonn as a honey-pot of local prebends. Honour was saved only by the Liberals and PDS, whose decisive majority in favour (70 to 27) created the final narrow margin (338 to 320) for Berlin.

This was a moment of truth, casting a sharp retrospective light on the Bonn Republic. Left to their own devices, the Western deputies would never have moved back to Berlin—they voted by a thumping majority to stay in Bonn (291 to 214). The implied prospect for the East would have been a modern equivalent of Victorian rule of Ireland from London. But if such colonial administration from afar was averted, what will take its place in the new capital remains to be seen. No European city has accreted so many misleading legends as Berlin. To resist them is easier, however, than to capture the elusive realities now taking shape behind them. Most people—not just foreigners, but Germans themselves—associate Berlin with Prussian military tradition, Bismarck's autocracy, Nazi violence and megalomania. In fact, Frederick II preferred his complex in Potsdam. Bismarck disliked Berlin so much that, after unification, he wanted to make Kassel—a Protestant version of Bonn—the capital of the country. Not a single Nazi leader of any prominence came from Berlin. Hitler loved Munich and relaxed at the other end of the country in Berchtesgaden. Berlin was not a natural setting for reaction. In 1848 it saw the sharpest fighting at the barricades of any city in Germany. By the turn of the century, it was the most industrialized capital in Europe, with a working-class population to match. In 1918 it led the November Revolution, and in 1919 was the scene

---

7. Brandt's intervention can be found in Helmut Herles (ed.), *Die Haupstadt-Debatte. Der Stenographische Bericht des Bundestages*, Bonn 1991, pp. 36–40. The collection edited by Alois Rummel, *Bonn: Sinnbild der deutscher Demokratie*, Bonn 1990, gives some idea of the prior campaign to keep the capital on the Rhine.

of the Spartakusaufstand. In the Weimar period, it was a Social Democratic and Communist stronghold.

The Third Reich and the Cold War cut off these traditions. After the fall of Hitler, the occupation and division of Berlin masked the question of what, if any, underlying continuities might have survived. The 1998 elections offer a startling answer. The Left won every single district. The map of the city is just one colour, in two shades: bright Social Democratic red in the west and south-east, deep post-Communist red in the centre and north-east. Compare Paris, long a permanent fief of the Right; Rome, where Fini's ex-fascists are the largest party; or even London, where Ken Livingstone will never sweep Finchley or Kensington. Bismarck's nightmare has come true. Berlin is going to be the most left-wing capital in Europe.

The electoral profile of a city is, of course, only one index of its character. What kind of a metropolis is the future Berlin otherwise likely to become? A true *Hauptstadt* is a synthesis of three functions—the focus of a country's political life, as seat of government; a nexus of wider economic activities; and a magnet of emergent cultural forms. The fundamental question is whether these will, in fact, intersect in Berlin.[8] The city remains the largest city in Germany, with a population over twice that of its nearest rival: 3.4 million inhabitants dispersed across some 550 square miles, a quarter of it woods and lakes. During the Cold War, both parts received preferential treatment as showcases of their respective regimes. Subsidies were, of course, far higher in the West, where everything from factories to art-shows was lavishly funded in the battle against Communism; but the East got more investment than the rest of the DDR too.

In the nineties, the prospect of Berlin becoming once again the capital of a united Germany was widely expected to set off an anticipatory boom, as building contracts for ministries and corporate headquarters multiplied, real estate prices rose, employment grew and immigrants poured in. Ironically, however, Berlin has suffered a sharp economic decline since unity. Even after the formal decision to move from Bonn, resistance delayed the transfer of government by nearly a decade. Meanwhile, after Berlin became a 'normal' *Land* with the end of the Cold War,

---

8. For succinct comparative reflections, see Gerhard Brunn, 'Europäische Hauptstädte im Vergleich', in Werner Süss (ed.), *Hauptstadt Berlin*, Vol. 1, Berlin 1995, pp. 193–213.

tax-payers in the West saw no reason to continue its privileges, and once subsidies were cut, industries left—while in the East, unification triggered a general industrial collapse, engulfing Berlin as much as anywhere else.

The results are stark. Since 1989 the population has fallen, with an exodus to the surrounding countryside; 200,000 industrial jobs have been destroyed; growth is currently negative; bankruptcies are twice the national average; and unemployment is running at nearly 20 per cent. A few international companies have set up their local HQs in Berlin, but virtually no major German corporation has made the move. Incredibly, with less than a year to go before the arrival of the whole paraphernalia of government in the city, housing prices have actually been dropping. Set beside the sleek affluence of Munich, Hamburg or Frankfurt, the future capital is going to remain a poor relation.

In this setting, what is likely to be the impact of the slow descent of federal political power, like some cumbersome dirigible, into the middle of the city? No issue has attracted more polemic in Berlin than the design of the new *Regierungsviertel*—the complex of governmental buildings that are bound to become insignia of the capital in the collective imaginary. Every month there are public debates on different aspects of the reconstruction of the city, held in the Council of State building where Honecker once presided over the DDR. To participate in one is a memorable experience: experts and pundits at loggerheads, audiences dividing passionately, and—unmatched for choleric lack of inhibition— the master builder of the city, urban planner Hans Stimmann, white-maned and red-brick in complexion, yelling at the top of his voice in a style few would associate with a municipal authority, let alone a German one.[9] But the stakes are high. For here not only the shape of the future but the place of the past, not only relations between the public and the private, but tensions between East and West, are at issue.

The original plans for a unified Berlin envisaged building a completely new government district in the centre, with a

---

9. By formation an industrial architect, politically once a member of the '68 generation, now a stalwart of the SPD, Stimmann has stood in general for a 'critical reconstruction' of pre-divided Berlin, preserving a relatively low sky-line, while yielding to claims of a more contemporary ambition, under the rubric of a 'European city', where war and division had left wastelands: Hans Stimmann (ed.), *Babylon, Berlin etc.: Das Vokabular der Europäischen Stadt*, Basel 1995, pp. 9–10.

contemporary architecture worthy of the élan of Schinkel, integrating the torn halves of the city. This vision was soon abandoned, ostensibly on grounds of cost. In reality, it was ditched out of a mixture of continuing resentment at the prospect of a move from Bonn in the Western *Länder*, indifference to the fate of the East of the city in West Berlin itself (which, with twice the population, calls the shots in local government), and rejection of any risk of magnificence in a German capital. The result has been two-fold. The new government 'axis'—its line truncated where it would have extended to the East—is now restricted to the West.[10] Here the florid Wilhelmine shell of the Reichstag has been fitted out with an oversize transparent dome and high-tech interior by Foster—inverting the gesture of the narrow Baroque façade stripped onto the Khruschevian girth of the *Staatsratgebäude* across the border.

Official pieties would have it that the Reichstag has been restored in honour of its valiant defence of democratic values in the past. In reality, of course, it was here that German democracy tamely voted Hitler into power, electing him chancellor of its own parliamentary will. The real reason for the resuscitation of the building is that the ruin was a symbolic property of the West, rather than the East, in the Cold War. It would have been better to start afresh. Axel Schultes's new executive office, where Schröder will take up residence next year—a light, elegant structure— shows what might have been done. Between the two will lie low-slung parliamentary facilities, pleasing enough, but now purged of the open concourse where it was once envisaged citizens could mingle and contend within the arcades of power. To the north, just across the Spree, the graceful curve of the Lehrte railway station— which may prove the most beautiful of the new public buildings— will dominate. To the south, the commercial centre run up by Daimler-Benz and Sony on the site of the old Potsdamer Platz, frittering away the combined talents of Piano, Isozaki, Rogers, Jahn and Moneo, will no doubt end up as a blowzy shopping-mall—sealed off from its surroundings as if planted in a suburb— like every other a tomb of conviviality.

In the East, on the other hand, there are no major new federal projects. The worst relics of the DDR, tinted fun-vault and

---

10. Michael Wise's *Capital Dilemma*, Princeton 1998, offers a fine, historically informed, overview of both the construction of the new government district in the West, and the preservation of the Nazi ministries in the East.

bulbous TV-tower, have been left in place at the end of a still inarticulate Unter den Linden. The private sector has developed the area around the Friedrichstrasse, with offices, shops and restaurants—Nouvel, Johnson, Rossi—that offer somewhat more life, though it is still quite thin. The principal contribution of the state is going to be the conspicuous refurbishment of two Nazi landmarks, Schacht's Reichsbank and Goering's Air Ministry, as the Foreign Office and Finance Ministry of the Berlin Republic. Any idea of new creations—well within the purse of the authorities—banished, Fischer and Lafontaine can now dispatch affairs where Hitler once inspected. Setting aside excuses of cost, which may have had some validity for keeping such buildings under the DDR but have lost any today, the official rationale for reoccupying these hideous structures is that it is even a sort of atonement to do so—since they may serve as a daily reminder of the enormities of the past, which it would be wrong to level. A widespread rhetoric—the same argument is used for preserving the direst eyesores left by the Second Reich or the DDR—insists that they are 'historical documents' upon which the German people must learn to meditate.

The chance of a generously unitary political capital in Berlin has thus been refused, in favour of a reduced precinct in the West and the updating of sinister mausolea in the East. This bureaucratic option is defended on two grounds. Firstly, that any attempt to build an integrated government district might be seen as a dangerous hubris or arrogant over-statement by the German nation within Europe; and secondly, that Germans need constant remembrance of the darkness of their own past. Evident is an ideological will to fix civic memory on images stamped by guilt or nostalgia—the element of guilt mostly coming from the West, the element of nostalgia (for the Palace of the Republic, etc.) from the East. The result is a kind of an antiquarian masochism—a clinging to what is aesthetically ugly, often *because* it was also morally and politically ugly, in the name of truth to history.

Such mortification betrays a deep intellectual confusion. For public buildings are not documents, but monuments. A historical document is a text that can be studied, in an archive or library, when a researcher needs to consult it—otherwise it does not impose itself on anyone. An urban monument, by contrast, is an unavoidable daily sight imposed on all who pass by or use it. You cannot put a public building away in a file. Such structures must be judged in the first place on aesthetic grounds. The political or ideological functions they may, or may not, have served can change over time, but are never decisive for political reality, which has its own arena and dynamic, built not out of bricks but social relations. Italian Fascism was capable in its day of pleasing or striking buildings, which have continued to be used, indeed enjoyed: no one has ever thought of blowing up the railway station in Florence. Nazi edifices like the Reichsbank or Luftwaffe HQ should have been demolished not so much because of their associations, but because they are brutal and forbidding as architecture.

The idea that Germans need such buildings as perpetual hair-shirts, to earn the trust of their neighbours, is not just a misconception. For Europeans do not on the whole fear the ghosts of Bismarck, Hitler or Honecker: neither Wilhelmine Imperialism, nor Nazism, nor Stalinism, are serious threats today. A constant preoccupation with them can easily become a screen for more pressing issues, as in Freudian terms an obsession with imaginary dangers typically functions as a displacement—that is, repression—of quite other, real problems. So it is that Europe has some reason for misgivings about a reunited Germany. But its rational fears relate to contemporary institutions: not the legacies of Ludendorff or Speer, but the overweening reach of the Bundesbank, as the most powerful institution in the country, over the lives and jobs of millions of Europeans—a hegemony now entrenched in the design and personnel of the European Central Bank. It is the fanatical cult of sound money, the insistence on arbitrary and anti-social criteria for convergence in the Treaty of Maastricht, the relentless pressure for a 'Stability Pact' after it, which a self-critical German public should have been concerned about. But, with few exceptions—Helmut Schmidt the most eloquent—here national complacency has been virtually boundless. Hans Tietmeyer and Otmar Issing have exercised their enormous, continent-wide power from the most inconspicuous and modest of buildings in Frankfurt. What nicer symbol of German good conscience?

A better relationship between aesthetics and politics would reverse these morbid terms. There should have been no inhibition in Berlin about erecting the finest—the most delicate or the most magnificent—buildings that any contemporary architect can design: the more, and the more integrated, the better. That would have been not just a contribution to a real annealing of the city, but a gift to European unity as well. When we go to Paris, or to Rome, or to Barcelona—cities built with a generous sense of

splendour—we do not think of them as exclusively French, or
Italian, or Catalan possessions. They are sources of a common
delight. It is in that confident spirit, for which sensuous beauty—
not sheer utility, and still less self-flagellating memory—is the
highest urban value, that the rest of Europe must hope Berlin can
still in some measure be rebuilt.

As for 'historical documents', for those who want them, there
is a perfect solution. Lying underground—like an archive, where
only the interested need go—are Hitler's bunker and the far larger
subterranean lair built for his government, just south of Unter
den Linden, which the Russians lacked the technology to destroy.
Officially, the authorities have not yet admitted the existence
of these potent remnants of the Third Reich. Why not restore
these for reflective viewing? The question embarrasses the loyal
functionaries of the *Denkmalschutz*, who off the record reply: it
would be wrong to erase them and it would be wrong to restore
them—it is best they remain hidden, abandoned to the natural
processes of time. Overground, meanwhile, pedestrians can suffer
the Air Ministry. Amid such confusions the one true resolution of
the problems of historical memory, in their gravest sense, stands
out: Daniel Libeskind's—all but literally—fulgurating museum
of Jewish history, a zinc-clad masterpiece in which the past is
represented with awesome power in its rightful place.

If the economic prospects of Berlin remain precarious, and its
political function guarantees only that MPs and civil servants will
reside there, what of its cultural role? In many ways, this is the
decisive question for the future of the city, since not only does
political life quicken if there is a real cultural tissue around it,
but the level of economic activity is likely to depend critically on
the specific weight of the communications industry in the capital.
Everyone remembers the extraordinary cultural vitality of Berlin
in Weimar days. Could something of that return? During the Cold
War, both parts of the city maintained, heavily subsidized for
reasons of prestige, complexes of great distinction in the worlds
of theatre and music. DDR writers tended to be concentrated in
East Berlin, with fewer counterparts across the Wall. An extensive
bohemia—the 'alternative scene': the term *Szene* is used much
more freely and indiscriminately in German than English—
flourished in the West, where there was exemption from national
service, and by the end there was even a modest pendant to it in

the East. The end of the Cold War hit all this hard. The virtual collapse of the Berliner Ensemble suggests the general trend. Music survived much better than drama; Berlin offers perhaps still the best repertoire of any big European city. No doubt theatre will recover too. The nineties have been a strange time in limbo for Berlin, no longer the spoilt child of inter-bloc rivalry and not yet the capital of a reunited country. The real question, however, is whether the arrival of government will eventually attract those elements of a metropolitan culture the city lacked even at its heyday as the front-line of the Cold War.

In the Bonn Republic, Cologne and Düsseldorf became the centre of the art world; Munich got the film industry; television was based in Mainz and Cologne; the most influential newspaper and publishing houses were in Frankfurt; the leading weeklies came out of Hamburg; the two major media empires—Holtzbrinck and Bertelsmann—have their headquarters in Stuttgart and the miniscule company town of Gütersloh. In the Weimar period, by contrast, most of this range of activities was concentrated in Berlin, with the art galleries of Cassirer, the UEFA film studios in Babelsberg, the Ullstein and Mosse publishing empires.[11] Today, there are signs that younger artists are coming back to the city, but the Rhenish grip on the art market remains unshaken. Modernization of the traditional complex in Babelsberg— technically in Potsdam—where DEFA made its name under the DDR, probably ensures that the cinema will become an important industry again. Nor is it difficult to imagine Berlin becoming once more the literary capital of the nation: already the German novelist most recently admired abroad, detective-story writer Bernhard Schlink, teaches constitutional law at the Free University; the most gifted literary critic of the younger generation, Michael Maar, has just moved to the city; the leading intellectual journal in the country, *Merkur*, has relocated to Berlin, even if its animating iconoclast and aesthetician, Karl-Heinz Bohrer, edits it—a nice European touch—long-distance from Paris.

But the *pièces de resistance* of today's culture industry are missing: television, press, publishing. Not a single TV station of moment operates in Berlin. The big West German publishing houses—many of them originally from Berlin—have not budged from Frankfurt, Hamburg or Munich, at most setting up secondary

---

11. For images of the position of Berlin at the time, see Peter Gay, *Weimar Culture*, New York 1968, pp. 127–36.

offices in the city. Bertelsmann and Holtzbrinck have bought up the two leading dailies, *Tagesspiegel* and *Berliner Zeitung*, with respective readerships in the West and East, and are battling it out with heavy investment in a circulation war. But neither paper has any national weight, or approaches the *Frankfurter Allgemeine* or the *Süddeutsche Zeitung* in resources or quality. If matters continue as they are, the paradoxical prospect is of a major capital city without any newspaper of authority. The tabloid monopoly of Springer's *Bild-Zeitung* remains—in the circumstances, perhaps fortunately—in Hamburg. It is hard to imagine this constellation persisting once the federal government and diplomatic corps are truly back in the centre of Berlin. But for the moment the signs are not encouraging.

This is the view from above, where money shapes a culture. What of the impulses below? In the twentieth century, the creativity of a metropolis has nearly always been linked with its capacity to attract immigrants. Here Berlin should in principle enjoy a privileged position. It is often thought, not least by Germans themselves, that the city already harbours the highest concentration of foreigners in the Federal Republic. This is an illusion. In fact, the proportion is lower than in any major city of the West: 12 per cent, as against 21 in Munich, 24 in Stuttgart, 28 in Frankfurt—a graphic reflection of relative employment opportunities.[12] Much the largest immigrant community in Germany is, of course, the Turks. Their lack of political or cultural integration into German society, by comparison with immigrant groups in Britain or France, is usually—and not without substantial reason—attributed to the Federal Republic's iniquitous citizenship laws, based essentially on blood-line. But it is also true that Germany's lack of a colonial past has contributed to the difficulties: there was no empire to equip new entrants with the elements of a common language, which certainly facilitated integration of arrivals from the Caribbean or Maghreb. If anything, the boot of an imperial past was on the other foot—Ottoman domains far exceeding Hohenzollern. In France, Turkish immigrants have proved the most closed of all immigrant groups, with lower rates of exogamy—the surest mechanism of assimilation—than any other. Predictably, their contribution to the diversification of German culture at any level, from letters to sport, has so far been very limited. The change of

---

12. Statistisches Bundesamt (ed.), *Datenreport 1997: Zahlen und Fakten über die Bundesrepublik Deutschland*, Mannheim 1998.

laws and official climate promised by the new government may start to change this.

But beyond its Turkish enclaves, what Berlin can in particular expect are major waves of immigrants from Poland, Russia and the Baltic region—its traditional hinterlands. The building-trades are already largely Polish. The Russian community—artists, gangsters, students, merchants, claimants of Jewish origin— is rising daily: an impressive spectacle of social mixture at any Orthodox service. It is now common to hear Russian spoken all over Germany, but this startling change is due to the exodus of *Volksdeutsche* from Kazakhstan. The catchment in Berlin comes more largely from classical streams. Out of all this, a metropolis that is cosmopolitan in a stronger sense than anything Germany has known hitherto is likely to emerge.

Logically, the counter-cultural Left has sought to make the most of the newcomers, as a glance at the pages of the *Tageszeitung*, Berlin's counterpart to *Libération* in Paris or *Il Manifesto* in Rome (naturally no equivalent in England), makes clear. The *taz* has the least national audience of this trio of dailies that are offspring of '68, but thanks to the value of the building it owns, is financially the most secure.[13] Theoretically, it should benefit from a large student population—the city has three major universities—that showed its mettle last winter in prolonged demonstrations against its deteriorating conditions of study, blocking the Brandenburger Tor at all hours. In practice, the German university system is now so institutionally waterlogged that it offers little impetus to any wider culture. Here the legacy of '68 has been at its most equivocal, failing to abolish the archaism of too many features of German academic life, while superadding dubiously populist ones to them. The result has been an intellectual stalemate, identified with a generation of placeholders, that has triggered powerful reactions elsewhere.

By the eighties, talent had passed to the right—typically out of the campus and into the world of *belles lettres* and critical journalism. Bohrer pioneered this turn when he was editor of the literary pages of the *FAZ*. Here was where younger spirits could make stylish sorties against received social-liberal wisdom, and

---

13. For its origins in the late seventies, see Sabine Von Dirke, '*All Power to the Imagination': The West German Counterculture from the Student Movement to the Greens*, Lincoln 1997, pp. 120–42.

test unconventional ideas without too much worthy inhibition. Today the liveliest publicists are still to be found in this—by German standards—somewhat rakehell atmosphere rather than in the stodgier pages of *Die Zeit*. So it is with the newer generations at large. The enormous international prestige of Habermas is misleading. Thirty-year-olds, even of impeccably progressive outlook, can often be heard expressing more admiration for the brio of Jünger or Schmitt. Social Democracy has come to power without much depth of direct support in intellectual opinion. At this level, the trend—first with the radicalization to the left of the sixties, then with the opposite swing of recent years—has gone against it. If by the end the Kohl regime had few sympathizers, Schröder cannot count on any prior groundswell in his favour.

3

In Berlin, the ingredients of a classic modern capital lie scattered or incomplete. Perhaps they will never become a coherent whole, of the kind we know or remember elsewhere, and the city will offer instead only the image of a post-modern dyslexia. Many Germans hope so. For the new government, however, more is at stake than simply the fate of the city. The larger meaning of the move to Berlin was always to bring East Germany back into the centre of national life, as an equal part of the country. Potentially, the transfer of supreme political power into the midst of the former DDR should have far-reaching compensatory effects— psychological and practical—for its population. But the inordinate delay over the move, and the Western bias in its implementation, have weakened expectations. In many ways, despite massive federal investment, the gulf between the two parts of Germany remains as deep as ever. Western largesse and contempt have gone together. In 1990 no attempt was made to write a Constitution in common for a united Germany, as the *Grundgesetz* had laid down should be done. The DDR was simply annexed, and Western codes imposed down to the smallest regulations. Felicity and prosperity for all were promised in exchange. Ten years later, unemployment is officially running at 18 per cent, but more tough-minded economists reckon the real rate is closer to 40 per cent. Two-thirds of the Eastern population tell pollsters they do not feel full citizens in their own country.

Ideally, what the 'new *Bundesländer*' needed after unification was an indigenous political movement capable of expressing the common experience of a humiliated people, and forging a powerful regional identity out of it—something like an Eastern equivalent of the CSU, the hugely successful party that has ruled Bavaria without interruption since the fifties, while never ceasing to be an important player in federal politics. In East Germany, of course, the sociological lay of the land would have situated such a regional party on the left, rather than right, end of the spectrum. But such a movement was never in the cards, because of the divisions within Eastern society itself. Some of these were inter-provincial. Saxons, Thuringians, Brandenburgers, Pomeranians each had their own pre-Communist histories, and none any liking for East Berlin, whose privileges under the DDR were as much resented as those of West Berlin in the Federal Republic.

But more deeply, the Eastern population was split by the Communist experience itself, between those who suffered and those who subsisted. By the standards of Yezhov or Ceaus,escu, or even Gottwald, the DDR was a mild regime—the execution count was low, and the labour camp absent. But it was also a staggeringly invasive one, whose systems of surveillance and delation honeycombed society to a degree never reached, if only for reasons of technology, even in the Russia of the thirties.[14] Levels of repression and fear were quite sufficient to create a large permanently embittered minority of the population, and leave unhappy memories in many more. At the same time, the regime assured a secure and orderly existence for those who did not step out of line; decent unpolitical lives could be led; there was little material misery, even some scope for a residual idealism. Post-Communist attitudes are thus polarized sharply, between a vengeful minority on one side, a majority with more mixed feelings about its experience of the two systems, and a minority on the other side attached to much of what it recalls of the old order and hostile to what it has encountered in the new.

Only the last has found stable political expression. The PDS, as successor organization to the SED that ran East Germany, was often dismissed in the early years after unification as simply the party of 'Ostalgie'—a crypto-Stalinist throw-back to the DDR, dependent on the ageing functionaries and accomplices of a police state. In fact,

---

14. By the late eighties, the functionaries of the Ministry of State Security numbered 100,000 and informants some 250,000: David Childs and Richard Popplewell, *The Stasi: The East German Intelligence and Security Service*, London 1996, pp. 82, 86.

more than any other post-Communist party in Eastern Europe, the
PDS has evolved into a lively radical movement of the Left. Much of
the credit for this transformation is due to its leader Gregor Gysi, the
only Jewish politician of note—not by accident from the East—in
today's Germany, whose quick wits, imaginative flair and irreverent
sense of fun reverse every stereotype, to the point of making most
Western parliamentarians look like heavy apparatchiks. Together
with a handful of colleagues—Chairman Lothar Bisky, a former
scientist, is the most important—he rejuvenated the ranks of the
party and widened its support. At first confined mainly to the north
of the old DDR, and very reliant on SED veterans, this year it scored
over 20 per cent evenly throughout East Germany, with its strongest
vote coming from younger, well-educated women, who now often
provide its personable representatives in *Länder* institutions. The
appeal of the PDS reaches to an even newer generation: enthusiastic
teenage campaigners thronged headquarters on election night.
Numerically, with over ninety thousand members, this is much the
largest party in East Germany. The bureaucratic weight of the past
is still visible in the internal structures of the PDS, especially as
it tries to gain a foot-hold in the unfamiliar ground of the West
German Left, but it is diminishing.

The SPD, by comparison, will not only be governing the whole
country from the new capital, but with 35 per cent of the vote in the
East is now the leading electoral force in all the new *Länder*. Yet
organizationally, with no more than 27,000 members in the whole
zone, it remains a shadow of the PDS. In the first years after the war,
the SPD under Kurt Schumacher stood firmly against the division of
Germany, with far more feeling for national unity than the CDU.
But during the long decades of the Cold War it over-adapted to the
Bonn Republic, to the point where in 1989–90 the party leadership—
Lafontaine was then its candidate for chancellor—completely
misjudged the dynamic of unification, proving incapable of either
welcoming or canalizing it into a better institutional form. The
perception that it was basically reluctant to accept national unity
handed electoral victory to Kohl. Few voices were raised against
the folly of this course, whose deeper origins have been trenchantly
criticized by party freethinker Tilman Fichter.[15]

The SPD now has a historic chance to start again. Breaking
Cold War taboos, Lafontaine lost no time after the election in

---

15. *Die SPD und die Nation. Vier sozialdemokratische Generationen zwischen
nationaler Selbstbestimmung und Zweistaatlichkeit*, Frankfurt 1993, pp. 167ff.

authorizing the formation of the first SPD–PDS governing coalition, in Mecklenburg-Vorpommern—a Red–Deep-Red alliance that is a potential majority across most of the East. Both parties stand to gain from cooperation: the PDS becoming a normal political partner, the SPD connecting with local realities from which it has been isolated. Social democracy will need to be in much closer touch with ways of life and feeling in the East, if popular disappointments are to be avoided, that might otherwise be explosive. The distinguished oral historian Lutz Niethammer, who now teaches in Jena, believes that beneath the surface calm of the first post-Communist student generation, there is often a suppressed rage at the way in which the whole world of their childhood, with which their most intimate memories are bound up, is now dismissed as worthless by the official version of the past. Meanwhile, widespread youth unemployment and urban dislocation are so much kindling in the streets outside.

Here, in ominously concentrated form, is the general problem on which the fate of the new government will turn. Germany now has over four million registered unemployed. This is not a society like Britain, where rule by the radical Right long inured public opinion to the permanence of large-scale unemployment. Massive joblessness is still perceived on all sides as a scandal. The SPD's promise to tackle it is likely to make or break the incoming regime. How does it plan to address the issue? Its stance is two-headed. Schröder's answer is the nebulous 'Alliance for Work'—a neo-corporatist entente between government, firms and unions to improve supply-side conditions for investment, combining lower payroll taxes with wage restraint and a more flexible labour market. The Federation of German Industries, under the hawkish leadership of Hans-Olaf Henkel, has already expressed its hostility to the higher energy taxes that are the price-tag on this scheme. Lafontaine, on the other hand, has gone for demand-side measures: lowering of personal taxation, and reduction of interest rates. Here the contrast with Britain could not be more pointed. Where Brown's first act was to transfer control over monetary policy to the Bank of England, Lafontaine's opening move was to attack the Bundesbank publicly for persisting with a deflationary course in defiance of government objectives. There has been a predictable outcry at this break with German convention.

*   *   *

But success or failure in bringing down unemployment will not be decided within Germany alone. The arrival of the single European currency will change all parameters. This last, and most momentous, of all the changes now underway in Germany tacitly divides the government too. Prior to his nomination as SPD candidate for chancellor, Schröder did little to hide a sceptical reserve towards any sacrifice of the D-mark to the euro. Once adopted by his party, he altered his tone; his outlook perhaps somewhat less. In the spring of 1998 the Willy Brandt Haus, the svelte new headquarters of the SPD in Berlin, hosted a debate between Schröder and Habermas.[16] If in many ways an impressive occasion, it was also a disconcerting one. Habermas spoke eloquently of the need for common social and economic policies in the European Union, as the limitations of any national framework became ever more apparent, ending with a direct challenge to the SPD: 'Have you any offensive strategy for Europe at all?' In reply, Schröder held forth fluently on the *Bundnis für Arbeit*, the compatibility between competitive performance and social justice, the importance of a modern culture, but said scarcely a word about Europe. A few months earlier, asked his view of measures to create jobs by introducing a thirty-five-hour week in France and Italy, he replied simply: 'Good news. Our German firms will beat theirs all the more easily'.

Lafontaine always struck a different note, telling audiences long before the election that effective responses to unemployment and inequality would inevitably require coordinated European action, beyond the limits of Maastricht. Within days of taking office, he had criticized the European Central Bank for its attachment to high interest rates, proposed a target zone of the euro against the dollar, and called for a political counterweight to the ECB in the macro-economic affairs of the Union. Such ideas represent a complete reversal of the historic role of Germany in the EU. It was at German insistence that the ECB was given absolute power—without a trace of popular accountability—to determine the money supply, and therewith rates of growth and employment, in Europe; that draconian convergence criteria were made the condition of entry into the single currency; that a deflationary Stability Pact was imposed on national budgets even after entry.

---

16. For this exchange, see Julian Nida-Rümelin and Wolfgang Thierse (eds), *Jürgen Habermas und Gerhard Schröder über die 'Einbeziehung des Anderen'*, Essen 1998.

This is the framing order Europe was used to, and had come to accept.

Germany's entry into monetary union is thus unlikely to be smooth, for either itself or Europe. The new government is already under attack from the media, put out by Schröder's disappointment to date of business expectations. The size of its electoral victory is no guarantee of a secure life. The most stable of all political orders in post-war Europe has entered a period of unpredictable turbulence, like some vast placid river gradually starting to churn and tumble towards the rapids. Of only one thing can we be sure. Germany will not be a dull place. 'That great and ambiguous country', as Eric Hobsbawm once called it, is going to occupy centre stage over the next years.[17] What kind of future it will come to represent remains hidden, not least to the Germans themselves. The phrase that lingers in the mind is a form of the interrogative peculiar to this culture. All European languages have a colloquial expression appending a negative query at the end of an affirmative statement—isn't it?; *n'est-ce pas?*; *no es?* German, although it has an equivalent, *nicht wahr?*, goes further. Here teenagers round off their sentences with a single, more radically indeterminate word, seductive and unsettling. *Oder?*

---

17. 'Confronting Defeat: the German Communist Party', *New Left Review* I/61, May–June 1970, p. 92.

II · 2009

A decade after Helmut Kohl's fall from power—two since the Berlin Wall came down—in what directions, and how swiftly or sluggishly has the broadened German river flowed? The country has undergone enormous structural changes since the fall of the Wall. Polity, economy, culture and society have been subject to acute, often contradictory pressures. It is barely a decade since the federal capital was relocated, three hundred miles to the east; less than that since the D-mark disappeared and Germany assumed its dominant position within the Eurozone. Politically, a new post-unification landscape began to emerge only with the elections of 1998, when fatigue with Kohl's sixteen-year reign, broken promises in the East, and, above all, slow growth and stubbornly high rates of unemployment ushered in a Red–Green coalition. No attempt to track Germany's current direction can avoid consideration of these fundamental shifts.

In 1998 Gerhard Schröder's most prominent single pledge had been to halve the number of jobless within his term of office. How was this to be done? Oskar Lafontaine, newly installed as finance minister, had no doubts: reanimation of the German economy depended on scrapping the deflationary Stability Pact that Bonn had imposed as a price for monetary union, and boosting domestic consumption with counter-cyclical policies along Keynesian lines. After a few months of frustration, he was overboard.[18] Schröder, relieved to be shot of a rival, opted for orthodoxy: balancing the budget came first. Lafontaine's successor, Hans Eichel, became a byword for wooden, if far from successful, devotion to the task of consolidating public finances. Tax cuts, when they came, were for capital not labour, assisting corporations and banks rather than consumers. Growth did not pick up. When the SPD–Green government faced the voters again in 2002, its economic record was in effect a washout. Schröder had boasted he would reduce unemployment to 5 per cent. As the coalition went to the polls, it was just under 10 per cent. A scattering of modest social reforms, the most significant a long-

---

18. The immediate background to Lafontaine's exit lay in a violent, national and international, press campaign against him: Joachim Hoell, *Oskar Lafontaine: Eine Biographie*, Braunschweig 2004, pp. 197–205.

overdue liberalization of the rules for naturalization, had done little to offset this failure.

Externally, on the other hand, the coalition enjoyed a less constrained field of operations. Within a year of coming to power, it had committed Germany to the Balkan War, dispatching the Luftwaffe to fly once again over Yugoslavia. Presented as a vital humanitarian mission to prevent another Holocaust on European soil, German participation in Operation Allied Force was greeted with all but unanimous domestic applause: by Centre–Right opinion as robust proof of the recovered national self-confidence of the country as a military power, by Centre–Left as an inspiring example of international conscience and philanthropy. In the media, the decisive conversion of the Greens to military action was the occasion for particular satisfaction. Two years later, the Bundeswehr had left Europe behind to play its part in the occupation of Afghanistan; a suitable regime for that country was fixed up between interested parties in Bonn, and a German general was soon in command of allied forces in Kabul. This expedition too met with general approval, if—a remoter venture—less active enthusiasm among voters. Germany was becoming a normal force for the good, as responsible as any other power in the democratic West.

In public standing, this transformation stood Red–Green rule in good stead. It made Fischer, its most profuse spokesman, the most popular politician in the land. But this was a position foreign ministers in the *Bundesrepublik*, usually representing smaller parties, had long enjoyed, as pastors of the nation's conscience— not merely the interminable Hans-Dietrich Genscher, but even the imperceptible Klaus Kinkel possessing the same esteem in their time. Nor, of course, did loyalty to NATO distinguish government from opposition. Prestige in performance abroad is rarely a substitute for prosperity at home, as figures on a larger scale—Bush Senior or Gorbachev—discovered. Heading into the elections in 2002, the SPD–Green coalition was far behind the CDU/CSU in the polls. The Christian Democrats had been seriously damaged by revelations of Kohl's long-standing corruption—the party was extremely lucky these emerged after he had ceased to be ruler, rather than while in office.[19] But the solidarity of a political class, few of whose houses were not also built of glass, ensured that, as elsewhere in the West, the incriminated was never prosecuted, let alone punished;

---

19. For financial and political details of Kohl's malfeasance, see Edgar Wolfrum, *Die geglückte Demokratie*, Stuttgart 2006, pp. 477–8.

the waters rapidly closed over the episode without much benefit to the Social Democrats. With the economy still floundering, the opposition looked primed for victory.

In the summer of 2002, however, the countdown to the invasion of Iraq, signalled well in advance, altered the atmosphere. Regime change in Baghdad, however welcome a prospect in itself, clearly involved bigger risks than in Belgrade or Kabul, making public opinion in Germany much jumpier. Sensing popular apprehension, and fortified by the reserve of France, Schröder announced that Berlin would not join an attack on Iraq even—Habermas was scandalized—if the UN were to authorize one. Fischer, devoted to the previous American administration, was reduced to muttering assent in the wings, while Christian Democracy was caught thoroughly off-balance—unable to back Washington openly, yet unwilling to fall into line behind the chancellor. Schröder's advantage was complete: this time, German pride could sport colours of peace rather than war, and to boot, the opposition could not share them. It only remained for the biblical intervention of a flood in the East, when the Oder burst its banks, permitting a well-televised display of hands-on energy and compassion, to put him over the top. When the votes were counted in October, the SPD had a margin of six thousand votes over the CDU/CSU, and the coalition was back in power with a majority of three seats in the Bundestag.[20]

Once banked electorally, public opposition to the attack on Baghdad could recede, and discreet practical support be extended to the American war effort, German agents providing undercover identification of targets for Shock and Awe. In Europe, the occupation—as distinct from invasion—of Iraq was anyway soon accepted as an accomplished fact, losing political salience. But Schröder was careful to maintain the entente with Chirac he had formed during the run-up to the war, gratifying the Elysée both economically and politically, by conceding an extension of the Common Agricultural Policy and continued French parity with Germany in the weighting arrangements of the Treaty of Nice. Close alignment with France had been, of course, traditional German

---

20. While traditional contrasts in former West Germany between an SPD north and a CDU/CSU south were accentuated, the principal novelty of the vote was its gender distribution, women for the first time favouring the SPD over the CDU/CSU by virtually the same margin—some 4 per cent—as men preferred Christian to Social Democrats. For the data, see Dieter Roth, 'A Last Minute Success of the Red-Green Coalition', *German Politics and Society*, Vol. 21, No. 1, Spring 2003, pp. 49–50.

policy since the days of Adenauer. For Schröder, however, it now afforded cover for overtures to Russia that were precluded when the USSR still existed, and might otherwise have been suspect of a second Rapallo. Warmly supported by German business, enjoying lucrative contracts in Russia, Schröder's friendship with Putin—'a flawless democrat', in the chancellor's words—met with a cool reception in the media. Geopolitically, the growth of ties between Berlin and Moscow was the most significant novelty of Schröder's tenure. But politically, it counted for little at home.

There, as his second term began, the economic problems that had originally elected him remained apparently intact. Aware how narrowly he had escaped punishment for failing to deal with them, and goaded by criticisms in the press, Schröder now decided to bite the neo-liberal bullet, as authorized opinion had long urged him to.[21] In the autumn of 2003, the Red–Green coalition passed a package of measures, dubbed Agenda 2010, to break the much-decried *Reformstau*—blockage of needed improvements—in the Federal Republic. It comprised the standard recipes of the period: cutting the dole, raising the age of retirement, outsourcing health-insurance, reducing subsidies, abolishing craft requirements, extending shopping hours. German Social Democracy had finally steeled itself to the social retrenchment and deregulation of the labour market from which Christian Democracy, in its long years in power, had flinched. Editors and executives, even if mostly wishing the Agenda had been tougher, were full of praise.

The SPD had, in fact, passed a more concentrated and comprehensive bout of neo-liberal legislation than New Labour, a much-invoked model, was ever to do. But the political landscape in which Agenda 2010 was introduced was not that of Britain under Blair. On the one hand, there was no Thatcherism in Germany for Social Democracy to inherit—it had been forced to do the same originating job for capital itself, rather than simply extending it further in the same direction. On the other, the German working-

---

21. The standard view, expressed as an incontrovertible—foreign and domestic—consensus, could be found in the *Economist*: 'Most analysts readily agree on what is wrong with the German economy. First and foremost, the labour market is far too sticky. Second, taxes and social-security contributions are too high and profits too low. Third, and not unconnected, social security payments, pensions and health-care arrangements are too generous. And fourth, there is far too much red tape'. See 'A Survey of Germany', 7 December 2002, p. 10.

class and its organizations remained substantially stronger than in Britain. If trade-union density was comparable—less than a third of the work-force in either case, falling more sharply in Britain—the Confederation of German Trade Unions (DGB) commanded significantly greater bargaining power, through traditional corporatist institutions of wage negotiation and co-determination, than the TUC; while the SPD itself, with over double the membership of New Labour, was far less hollowed-out as a party. The result was twofold: the neo-liberal thrust of Agenda 2010, coming not from the radical right but a hang-dog centre, was inevitably much weaker than that of Thatcher's regime, while the resistance to it within a still—relatively—uncastrated labour movement was much stronger than among Blair's following.

Predictably enough, the neo-liberal turn, conducted without zest and received without enthusiasm, misfired. For all its fanfare in the media, Agenda 2010 had minimal effect on the economy: even the most benevolent estimates could not attribute more than 0.2 per cent of additional GDP growth to it.[22] But its effect on the political scene was another matter. The final dose of the package, 'Hartz IV', cutting unemployment benefits—and named after the human-relations chief of Volkswagen, a long-time intimate of Schröder in Lower Saxony, who designed it—was too bitter for the unions to swallow with good grace. Growing unrest in the base of the SPD, and limited breakaways from it in the Ruhr and elsewhere in the West, ensued. In the *Länder*, the party lost one election after another. As evidence of its unpopularity mounted, discontent with Schröder grew. Finally, in the spring of 2005, the SPD was routed even in its traditional stronghold of North Rhine–Westphalia, the most populous state in the federation, where its boss had been promoted to the ministry responsible for framing Agenda 2010. Fearing to repeat the fate of Helmut Schmidt in 1981, repudiated by his own party for drifting too far to the right, Schröder decided on a pre-emptive strike, calling elections a year early, before he could be challenged.

To do so, he had to circumvent the Constitution, which forbade dissolution of parliament at the will of the chancellor, by staging a fake vote of confidence from which his deputies were instructed to abstain, to ensure his own defeat. This transparent violation of the *Grundgesetz* received approval from the highest court in the land, in a graphic illustration of the limits of Germany's

---

22. *The Economist*, 22 December 2007.

post-war legalism: since the leaders of both the SPD and the CDU, each for their own reasons, wanted to break the law, the judges accommodated them. Merkel, now heading the CDU/CSU ticket, could not wait to cash its lead—20 points ahead—in the opinion polls; Schröder could be sure the SPD had no choice but to rally to him. The contest that followed was fiercer than any since the attempt to bring down Brandt in 1972. By now the media, the *Frankfurter Allgemeine*, *Welt* and *Spiegel* leading the pack, were in full cry after Schröder, rounding on him for empty opportunism, and clamouring for a sharp break with the paralytic corporatism of the past. Egged on by the press, where she was hailed as the Thatcher the country needed, Merkel ran a stridently neo-liberal campaign, promising a society based on individual effort and flat taxes, without mollycoddling. Schröder, seeing his chance, counter-attacked with brio, ridiculing her fiscal proposals and denouncing the new CDU as a threat to social solidarity.[23] So effective was his onslaught that by polling day Merkel's huge initial advantage had evaporated. When votes were counted, the CDU/CSU was ahead of the SPD by a mere 1 per cent, with four seats more in the Bundestag, and no parliamentary majority even with its ally the FDP. Schröder had to step down, but to govern Merkel had to form a Grand Coalition with his party.

I

Few greeted this outcome with much expectation. At best, it was generally held, if the two main parties had to share the onus of necessary but unpopular measures, rather than being able to blame each other for them, liberal reforms had somewhat more chance of reaching the statute-book. At worst, conflicts between them could lead to still direr immobilism. In fact, however, beneath the political surface of polls and parties, deep structural changes had

23. For Schröder's sense of the priorities of a statesman, see the self-portrait in his mistitled *Entscheidungen*, Hamburg 2006: 'For me an electoral campaign is the most interesting time in the life of a politician. I have taken part in countless campaigns, spoken in hundreds of town squares, shaken thousands of hands, given innumerable autographs. Certainly doing and shaping politics, reaching decisions, is the central task of a politician, his duty so to speak. But for me the elixir is the electoral campaign, the direct encounter with voters, the competition and struggle for votes, the exchange of argument. Technocrats can make decisions too, journalists can also be know-alls; but politicians alone can and should conduct electoral campaigns': p. 496.

been underway, altering the parameters of rule. The unification of Germany had transformed the country, in two equally paradoxical ways. The long stagnation of the German economy, the central social fact of the years since 1989, is normally attributed in large measure, and not without reason, to the enormous costs of absorbing the former DDR—about $1.3 trillion at the latest count, requiring massive exceptional taxation, diversion of investment from productive innovation to infrastructural and environmental reconstruction, and escalating public debt. Notoriously, Germany's lapse from grace was so drastic that the country which had originally gone out of its way to clamp the Stability Pact, forbidding any country to run a deficit of over 3 per cent of GDP, like a fiscal Iron Virgin into Europe's Monetary Union, became itself the worst recidivist from it, violating the Pact's provisions six times in defiance of the Commission.

But in what seemed such a heavy burden to German capital also lay the conditions of its reinvigoration. For unification decisively weakened labour. When West German trade-unions attempted to extend their organizations to the East, and uphold nation-wide wage rates comparable to those in the West, they encountered industries that were crumbling so fast, and workers so beaten by surrounding unemployment, that failure was more or less foreordained. But once the East could not be integrated into the traditional corporatist arrangements of *Modell Deutschland*, these inevitably came under increasing strain in the West too. Cheaper labour in the former DDR was soon overtaken by still lower wage costs in Eastern Europe, as the prospect and then reality of EU enlargement drew a growing volume of German investment into Slovakia, Hungary, the Czech Republic, Poland and elsewhere. Beyond these, in turn, lay outsourcing of plants to Asia, Latin America, the Middle East, driving the original wedge of unification yet further into the domestic economy, prising loose the labour market.

The result was a steep decline, not just in the numerical strength of German trade-unions—membership of the DGB dropping from 11 million in 1991 to 7.7 million in 2003—but in their ability to resist unrelenting pressures from German capital. Real wages fell for seven successive years, giving German firms an ever sharper competitive edge in high-end international markets. By 2004, Germany was once more—as it had been in the seventies—the world's leading exporter of manufactures. Such success was built, not on an outstanding performance in productivity—US gains were significantly greater in the same period—but on wage repression, as workers were forced to accept longer hours and less pay under threat of outsourcing, and domestic consumption remained flat. But with a swelling export surplus, investment increased; and once the business cycle kicked up, growth at last accelerated in 2006, just as Merkel settled into office. By early 2008, unemployment had dropped by nearly two million. The serum of deregulation, injected from the East, seemed finally to have worked.

Yet, in a second and reverse paradox, the unification which transformed the economic constitution of the country, releasing a less inhibited, more ruthless capitalism, has shifted its political landscape in the opposite direction. For the vast sums poured into the East, though they modernized the fixtures and fittings of society—communications, buildings, services, amenities—failed to create any commensurate industrial prosperity or sense of collective dignity and equality within the Federal Republic. The DDR was shabby, authoritarian, archaic by the standards of Bonn. But in the shadow of the state, all were employed and still relatively equal. With annexation by the West, and rapid demolition of the larger part of its industrial park, carpetbaggers arrived and jobs disappeared. In the rest of the ex-Soviet empire, the immediate sequels to Communism were often harsher, as countries that were poorer to start with fell into their own patterns of dislocation and recession. But, not squeezed into the same instant compression-chamber of competition, they had more breathing space for adjustment and reconversion; it was not long before their rates of growth were higher and rates of unemployment lower than those of the *neue Bundesländer*. This superior performance had not just economic, but sociological roots. In Poland, Slovakia, and Hungary, the restoration of capitalism was accomplished by local political elites—typically a combination of ex-dissidents and former party functionaries on the make—who made sure its fruits went principally to them. However popular or unpopular they might be at any point in the electoral cycle, they were an integral part of the local society.

In East Germany, no comparable stratum emerged. There, top political, economic and cultural positions in the new *Länder* were rapidly dominated—indeed, often virtually monopolized—by an influx of Westerners. Thus although unification would raise overall living standards in the East, as even the jobless received

Western-style benefits, capitalism was widely experienced as a colonization rather than self-promotion, let alone emancipation. Even where it brought material benefits, it was not appropriated as a native dynamic, but remained inflicted, a force still felt as substantially alien.[24] Had all boats risen in the same tide, as Kohl promised, this effect would certainly have been less. But the painful sense of a cashiered past—a life-world irretrievably devalued—was not just a subjective reaction to the consequences of unification. It had an objective reflexion in the demographic disaster that overtook the East in these years, as the old lingered, the young left, and the middle-aged were shelved. A population of 16 million in 1989 had collapsed to 12.5 million by 2008, and was set to fall further—perhaps much further—with the exodus of young women to the West. Between 1993 and 2008, no less than two-thirds of eighteen- to twenty-nine-year-olds born in the East had abandoned it.[25] In the DDR, a leading writer from the region has remarked, buildings rotted, but they contained people, who had work; now the buildings are brightly refurbished, and the people are dead or gone. A quarter of the housing stock is empty, and many a smaller centre of habitation, particularly in the north, risks becoming a ghost-town.

In these conditions, the one party to defend a certain memory and express a regional identity could scarcely fail to flourish. When Kohl fell, the PDS had a fifth of the vote in the East. When Schröder fell, it had a quarter, and was the second-largest party in the region, a whisker ahead of the CDU and not far short of the SPD. Such growth was not uninterrupted, nor without setbacks: a drop in its vote in 2002, loss of office in Mecklenburg-Vorpommern, a sharp rebuff for its acceptance of social retrenchment in Berlin in 2006. Nor was the evolution of the party itself any linear progress. Its two most prominent leaders, Gysi and Bisky, withdrew for

24. By 2003–4, the number of those who identified themselves with the East still far outnumbered those who did so with Germany as a whole: Katja Neller, 'Getrennt vereint? Ost-West Identitäten, Stereotypen und Fremdheitsgefühle nach 15 Jahren deutscher Einheit', in Jürgen Falter et al., *Sind wir ein Volk? Ost-und Westdeutschland im Vergleich*, Munich 2006, pp. 23–5. For some comparative observations on the outcome of unification in the ex-DDR, see Claus Offe, *Varieties of Transition. The East European and East German Experience*, Cambridge, MA 1997, pp. 148–58.

25. See *International Herald Tribune*, 9 November 2007. Demographically, Germany as a whole has one of the lowest rates of reproduction in the world. In the 2009 federal elections, voters over the age of fifty will be as large a bloc as all other age-groups combined.

a period, after failing to convince it that German troops needed to be available for military missions dispatched by the Security Council. Its members remained extremely advanced in years: three-quarters of them pensioners, more than half over seventy. In a sense, such severe limitations made the resilience of the PDS all the more remarkable.

What transformed a regional into a national force was the neo-liberal turn of the Schröder government. There were demonstrations all over Germany against Hartz IV, but the PDS mobilized the largest in its Eastern bastions, some hundred thousand strong. In the West, the groupings based in the unions that broke away from the SPD formed a list that ran, without great success, in the next *Land* polls, and wary discussion of some kind of cooperation between the two forces followed. It was Schröder's decision to call a snap election in 2005 that galvanized what might otherwise have been a protracted and inconclusive process. Running on a common platform as simply *Die Linke*—'the Left'—their combination took 8.7 per cent of the national vote, ahead of the Greens and not far short of the FDP, netting fifty-four seats in the Bundestag.[26] The catalyst for this success was Oskar Lafontaine, returning to the political scene as the leader of the Western wing of Die Linke. Hated for quitting Schröder's government even before its turn to the right, and feared for his tactical and rhetorical skills, Lafontaine was henceforward the *bête noire* of the SPD—a traitor who still undeservedly enjoyed national recognition, and could now encroach on its electoral base. So, in effect, it proved. In one *Land* election after another in the West, where the PDS had never been able to gain a foothold, Die Linke easily cleared the threshold for entry into the Assembly—Bremen, Hamburg, Lower Saxony, Hessen—with a varied array of local candidates. More ominously still, national opinion polls gave Die Linke between 10 and 13 per cent of the electorate, making it potentially Germany's third-largest party.

Behind the rise of Die Linke has also lain the long-term decline of the two dominant parties of the Bonn Republic. In the mid-seventies

26. For the emergence of Die Linke, see Dan Hough, Michael Koss and Jonathan Olsen, *The Left Party in Contemporary German Politics*, Basingstoke 2007, pp. 134–53, a study also covering the evolution of the PDS under the Red–Green coalition.

the CDU/CSU and SPD commanded 90 per cent of the electorate. By 2005, their share had sunk to 70 per cent. Remorselessly, secularization and tertiarization have shrunk what were once the core electorates of each. Church-going Catholics, 46 per cent of the CDU/CSU vote in 1969, had plummeted to 12 per cent in 2005; unionized manual workers from 25 per cent of the SPD vote to just 9 per cent. Their memberships too have fallen steeply: the SPD from over 940,000 in 1990 to just under 530,000 in 2008; the CDU from some 750,000 to a fraction over 530,000—the first time it has surpassed its rival; the CSU, which has held up best, from 186,000 to 166,000.[27] After the war, under an electoral system that distributes seats in the Bundestag proportionately to the votes of any party with at least 5 per cent of the ballots cast, the formation of a government had usually required the participation of the FDP, which held the balance between the two blocs. With the emergence of the Greens in the seventies, this three-party system gradually became a four-way contest, making a government without the FDP possible for the first time in 1998, the Red–Green coalition.

The consolidation of Die Linke, were it to hold, would transform this political calculus, making it mathematically more difficult for any two-party combination to achieve the requisite majority in parliament, other than a Grand Coalition between Christian and Social Democracy along current lines. This has long been the normal formula in Austria, and might eventually become so, *faute de mieux*, in Germany. But the political traditions of the two countries are not the same. The institutionalized carve-up of positions in state and economy between Catholics and Socialists in the *Proporz* system, a reaction-formation arising from the experience of civil war in the Austria of the thirties, has never had a counterpart in the Federal Republic. Here grand coalitions, anyway liable to be destabilized by the cycle of competitive *Länder* elections, have always been regarded by both parties as abnormal makeshifts that encourage extremism on their flanks, to be wound up as soon as possible. In the sixties, it was the CDU that lost ground in the Grand Coalition, to the advantage of the SPD. Today it is the other way around,

---

27. See, respectively, David Conradt, 'The Tipping Point: The 2005 Election and the De-Consolidation of the German Party System?', *German Politics and Society*, Vol. 24, No. 1, Spring 2006, p. 13; Hermann Schmitt and Andreas Wust, 'The Extraordinary Bundestag Election of 2005', *German Politics and Society*, Vol. 24, No. 1, Spring 2006, p. 34. For the statistics, see Table 1 in Oskar Niedermeyer, 'Parteimitglieder in Deutschland: Version 2008', *Arbeitshefte aus dem Otto-Stammer-Zentrum*, 13, Berlin 2008.

Merkel and her colleagues benefitting at the expense of a seemingly
rudderless Social Democracy, as Schröder's departure left a divided
party, tacking clumsily away from the centre to counter the rise of
Die Linke, to the ire of its neo-liberal wing, without much to show
for it electorally. With its ratings currently around a quarter of the
electorate, depths never reached before in post-war history, the SPD
faces the prospect of a structural crisis. For what unification has
delivered is, in effect, a new political system.

In the Berlin Republic, the combined forces of the SPD, Greens
and Left have to date commanded a sociological majority that
was never available to Social Democracy during the Bonn years:
some 53 per cent in 1998, 51 per cent in 2002 and 2005, as against
successively 41 per cent, 46 per cent and 45 per cent for the CDU,
CSU and FDP. But this structural alteration of the underlying balance
of forces in the country so far remains ideologically debarred from
expression at federal level. The PDS and now Die Linke have been
treated as beyond the pale of respectable partnership in national
government, considered tainted by descent from Communism. In
1998 and 2002, the SPD and the Greens did not need the PDS for
a majority in the Bundestag. But in 2005, Schröder ceased to be
chancellor only because of the taboo against forming a government
with the support of the Left. Had the SPD and Greens been willing
to do so, the three parties together would have enjoyed a robust
parliamentary majority of forty. Since this combination remained
unthinkable, the SPD was forced into the arms of the CDU/CSU as
a junior partner, unsurprisingly to its detriment.

The record of the Grand Coalition has for the most part been an
uninspired tale of wrangling over low-level social-liberal reforms
as the economic upswing of 2006–7 reduced unemployment and
absorbed the deficit with increased tax revenues, before the country
plunged into deep recession in late 2008. Merkel, presiding over
a recovery that owed little to her tenure, and a depression no less
beyond her control, has benefitted from both, with ratings that
far outstrip those of any potential SPD candidate for her post in
2009. But this popularity, probably as passing as any other, owes
more to a carefully cultivated manner of unpretentious womanly
Sachlichkeit, the staging of foreign policy spectacles—G-8,
Eurosummit—and the current fear of instability, than to any special
reputation for domestic efficacy. In opposition Merkel occupied
positions on the tough right of the political spectrum, supporting
the invasion of Iraq and attacking welfare dependence. In power,
though more anti-communist than Schröder, and cooler to Russia,

she has otherwise cleaved to the centre, leaving little to distinguish her incumbency from his. *Fortwursteln* remains the tacit motto.[28]

Trapped into a debilitating cohabitation, its poll numbers steadily sinking, as matters stand the SPD risks a crushing defeat in 2009. Attempts to stop the spread of Die Linke with a few social gestures—a call for a federal minimum wage, restoration of commuter subsidies—have made little impression on the electorate. In desperation, the party's hapless chairman Kurt Beck—the fourth in five years—called for amendments to Hartz IV, as the heaviest albatross round its neck, before being ousted by the still strong SPD right, which has installed Schröder's long-term factotum, Frank-Walter Steinmeier, now foreign minister, as its candidate for chancellor. Beyond such floundering, younger office-holders have started to contemplate the unthinkable, coming to terms with the Left. The statistical logic of a Red–Green–Dark Red coalition, long theoretically plain, risks becoming more and more a practical torment for German Social Democracy. In Berlin, Klaus Wowereit has held the capital for the SPD in a compact with the PDS-Linke for seven years, without even Green support. But for political purposes, Berlin counts as part of the East, and its big-city profile anyway separates it from the rest of the country—Wowereit belonging to the phenomenon of the good-time mayor of the metropolis, strong on shows and happenings, somewhat less so on budgets or utilities, that has produced Livingstone in London, Delanoë in Paris, Veltroni in Rome. Its electoral arithmetic is too atypical to offer any wider paradigm. More significant has been the debacle of the SPD in Hesse, where the local party leader Andrea Ypsilanti, after sternly promising not to make any deal with the Left, attempted to form a Red–Green government dependent for a hair-breadth majority on the support of Die Linke. With this, a step would have been taken whose implications escape no one. Once the taboo was broken in a Western *Land*, it could be replicated at federal level.

---

28. For a lucid analysis of the systemic obstacles to the taking of radical measures by any German government to date, and a pessimistic forecast for the Grand Coalition, see Wolfgang Merkel, 'Durchregieren? Reformblockaden und Reformchancen in Deutschland', in Jürgen Kocka (ed.), *Zukunftsfähigkeit Deutschlands*, Berlin 2006, pp. 27–45.

Between that cup and the lip, however, there remains a considerable distance. In part this is because, for the draught of an alternative coalition to be drunk—bitter enough, for the apparat of the party—the Greens have to be willing too. But their days of counter-cultural insurgency are long over. Once ensconced in office in the Berlin Republic, they shifted further to the right than the SPD under Schröder, embracing market-friendly and NATO-proud policies that would have been anathema in the seventies. The party has become an increasingly tame prop of the establishment, its ranks filled with politically correct yuppies competing with the FDP as a softer-edged version of German liberalism. Fischer's own evolution, from bovver boy of the *Putz* faction of Revolutionary Struggle in Frankfurt to golden boy of Madeleine Albright, was an exaggerated version of this development. But his prominence as the Green talisman on the hustings, and consistent flattery in the media, meant that he could take the party further into a *Kaisertreu* Atlanticism than it might otherwise have gone.[29] With his departure, the Greens have shown signs of trying to row back from the Western adventure in Afghanistan, if only on seeing how unpopular it was becoming. Structurally, however, the party has altered sufficiently to be a possible partner in power with the CDU. A Black–Green coalition is already in place in Hamburg and, niceties of energy policy aside, much of the party is in many ways now ideologically closer to Merkel than to Lafontaine. How far its voters would accept a connubium with the Centre-Right is less clear, and the principal inhibition on such a scenario.

If the Greens dislike talk of a 'left bloc', the SPD is more divided, with younger figures like the party's deputy chair, Andrea Nahles, willing to toy with the prospect of such a combination in future. But its old guard, not to speak of the eager neo-liberal modernizers, both viscerally anti-Communist, remain appalled at

---

29. In the words of a satisfied historian: 'Joschka Fischer embodies the integrative achievement of Federal Germany's successful democracy: beginning as a rebellious streetfighter, he rose through various posts to the summit of the Foreign Office, where he won respect beyond partisan frontiers. Fischer marched so long through the institutions that he became an institution himself': Wolfrum, *Die geglückte Demokratie*, p. 479. For a more astringent portrait, see Michael Schwelien, *Joschka Fischer. Eine Karriere*, Hamburg 2000. Schwelien is a writer for *Die Zeit* who spotted in advance the likely successor to Fischer in his favourite, the 'eel-smooth' Cem Özdemir, current Green chairman: pp. 62, 65–6.

GERMANY 255

the idea, and enjoy widespread intellectual support. For left-liberal historians like Hans-Ulrich Wehler and Heinrich August Winkler, the very thought of the SPD supping with the Stalinist Gysi and the renegade Lafontaine recalls nightmares of Weimar, when the party failed to see the need to abandon its Marxist illusions and forge a firm alliance with the Catholic Centre and moderate Liberals against the dangers of revolutionary extremism.[30] The press, naturally, brings its weight to bear in the same sense. In Hesse, the right of the party had no hesitation in torpedoing the prospect of a SPD government, preferring to hand power back to a Black–Yellow coalition—which won a crushing victory after Ypsilanti was ditched by her own second-in-command—rather than permit contamination by Communism. Would not the SPD in any case fatally lose the middle-ground, if it were tempted to treat with the pariah to its left? Such arguments could paralyze the sociological logic of a realignment for a long time.

What finally of Die Linke itself? Like any hybrid formation, it faces the task of welding its disparate fractions into a political force with a common identity. Prior to the fusion, its PDS component had suffered a yet steeper attrition of membership—biologically determined—than the large parties, even as it increased its electorate. The ability of the new party to appeal to a younger generation across the country will be critical to its future. Programmatically, resistance to further deregulation of markets and erosion of social protections gives it a strong negative position. With positive economic proposals, it is not better endowed than any other contingent of the European left. In principle—even in practice, as the experience of Berlin shows—its domestic stance is not so radical as to rule out collaboration of the SPD with it. The sticking-point lies elsewhere, in Die Linke's refusal to underwrite German military operations in the Western interest abroad. This is where the real dividing-line for the European political class is drawn. No force that refuses to fall in with the requirements of the Atlantic imperium—as the Greens in Germany did effusively; the PCF in France and Rifondazione Comunista in Italy morosely, to keep impotent junior ministries—can be regarded as *salonfähig*. Only acceptance of NATO expeditions, with or without the figleaf of the UN, qualifies a party as a responsible partner in government. It is here—the conflict over Gysi in the PDS can taken

---

30. For vigorous raising of this alarm, see Hans-Ulrich Wehler's intervention, 'Wird Berlin doch noch Weimar?', *Die Zeit*, 5 July 2007.

as a prodrome—that the pressure of the system on Die Linke will be most relentlessly applied.

2

If the long-run effect of unification has been to unleash an antithetical double movement within Germany, shifting the economy effectually to the right and the polity potentially to the left, the interplay between the two is bound to be mediated by the evolution of the society in which each is embedded. Here the changes have been no less pronounced, as the landscape of the Berlin Republic has become steadily more polarized. At the top, traditional restraints on the accumulation and display of wealth were cast to the winds, as capital markets were prised loose and Anglo-American norms of executive pay naturalized by German business. Schröder, slashing corporate and upper-bracket income tax, and rejecting any wealth tax, gave his own *enrichissez-vous* blessing to the process. Structurally still more important, by abolishing capital gains tax on the sale of cross-holdings, his government encouraged the dissolution of the long-term investments by banks in companies, and reciprocal stakes of firms, traditionally central to German corporatism—or in the consecrated phrase, the 'Rhenish' model of capitalism. In its place, shareholder value was increasingly set free. The first major hostile take-over, an operation hitherto unknown in Germany, came within a year of Schröder's assumption of power, when Vodafone seized Mannesmann. Hedge funds and private equity companies were soon pouring into the country, as banks and firms unloaded their cross-holdings. By 2006, foreigners had acquired an average of more than 50 per cent of the free float of German blue-chip companies—the top 30 concerns on the Dax index.[31] In the opposite direction, German capital surged abroad, its volume of acquisitions level with inward investment, as more and more manufacturing moved offshore to cheaper locations. Nearly half the total value-added of German exports is now produced outside the country.[32] The business press had every reason for its

31. 'The Coming Powers: How German Companies are Being Bound to the Interests of Foreign Investors', *Financial Times*, 1 April 2005. Lower down, the *Mittelstand* remains traditionally patriarchal, with 94 per cent of all German companies family-controlled, some of them large concerns: *Financial Times*, 9 December 2008.

32. *Financial Times*, 30 March 2007.

satisfaction at *Kapitalentflechtung*, the unravelling of an older and more restrictive *Modell Deutschland*.

In these years, conspicuous among the expressions of the change was the emergence of a new breed of American-style managers with little time for sentimental talk of trade-unions as partners or employees as stake-holders—downsizing in good years or bad, maximizing shareholder value without corporatist inhibitions, and rewarding themselves on a hitherto frowned-on scale. The emblematic figure of this transformation has been Josef Ackermann, imported from Switzerland to run the Deutsche Bank, the country's largest financial institution and currently a leading forecloser of mortgages in the US. Embroiled in a prosecution for his role in the sale of Mannesmann, but a notable success in boosting profits and cutting staff, he soon collected a salary twelve times that of his famous precursor Alfred Herrhausen, an intimate of Kohl assassinated in 1989. At €14 million a year, this is still only a fraction of the earnings of the best-paid US executives, but a sufficient alteration of scale to attract wide public comment.[33] Younger bosses in the same mould at Siemens, Daimler, Allianz and the like aspired to similar levels of remuneration. Below, the growth of long-term unemployment and the increase in jobless— often immigrant—youth have created a corresponding under-class of those beneath the official poverty-line, reckoned at about a fifth of the population. This too has aroused considerable public discussion, as a running sore—perhaps lurking danger—unknown to the Bonn Republic. Avarice at the top, abandonment at the bottom: neither comforts the self-image of a socially caring, morally cohesive democracy enshrined in the post-war consensus.

So far, the increasing inequality they promise remains moderate enough, by Anglo-American standards. Gated communities are still a rarity. Slums, where immigrants—now about one in five of the urban population—are most concentrated, may be coming into being. But ghetto riots have yet to break out. Comparatively speaking, German capitalism continues to be less starkly polarized than many of its competitors. But the trend, as elsewhere, is clear enough—between 2003 and 2007, corporate profits rose by 37 per cent, wages by 4 per cent; among the quarter of lowest-paid

---

33. Rainer Hank, 'Angekommen im Globalen Kapitalismus. Die Manager der Berliner Republik', *Merkur*, No. 689–90, September–October 2006, p. 909.

workers, real wages had actually dropped by 14 per cent since 1995.[34] Less typical is popular perception of these changes. The Bonn Republic was famous for the Americanism of its official outlook and cultural life, possessing the political establishment and intellectual class most loyal to Washington in Europe, steadfast in its 'unconditional orientation to the West', in Habermas's ardent phrase. Much of this was the reflex subservience of the defeated, as—consciously, or unconsciously—tactical and temporary as in other such cases. But there was always one striking respect in which West Germany after the war did resemble, more than any other major European society, not in self-delusion but reality, the United States. This was in the relative absence of a traditionally stratified hierarchy of social class in the country. The two national patterns were, of course, not quite alike; still less was that absence absolute. But in certain respects a family resemblance obtained all the same.

The reason lies in the fall of the Third Reich, which took down with it so great a part of the elites that had colluded with Hitler. The loss of East Prussia and Silesia, and the creation of the DDR, destroyed the bulk of the aristocratic class that had continued to loom large, not least in its domination of the armed forces, during the Weimar Republic. The industrial dynasties of the Ruhr were decapitated, Krupp, Thyssen and Stinnes never recovering their former positions. Individual survivors of these formations—a Dönhoff or Lambsdorff; a Porsche or Mohn—could make careers or rebuild businesses after the war. But collective identity and power were decisively weakened. West Germany, bourgeois enough by any measure, felt relatively classless, because in that sense topless. Even today, if one compares its elites to those of Britain, France or Italy, which survived the war more or less intact, it is much less clear how they are recruited: no public schools, no *grandes écoles*, no clerical preferment. Indeed, in that respect the *Bundesrepublik* appears more socially acephalous than the US itself, where Ivy League colleges have always provided a fast-track to Washington or Wall Street, and the Gini coefficient is anyway far higher. But if the Bonn Republic lacked any clear-cut privileged stratum above, it contained labouring masses below with a far greater sense of their past, and position in society, than their counterparts in America. The German proletariat, historically a later arrival than the British, never developed quite the same

---

34. *Financial Times*, 28 August 2008.

cultural density, as of a world set apart from the rest of society. But if its collective identity was in that sense somewhat weaker, its collective consciousness, as a potential political actor, was nearly always higher. Though both are greatly diminished today, the German working class—less pulverized by de-industrialization, in an economy where manufacturing still counts for more; less demoralized by frontal defeats in the eighties—retains a practical and moral influence in the political system which British workers have lost.

In this configuration, in which the absence of long-standing elites enjoying traditional deference is combined with the presence of a—by no means aggressive, but unignorable—labour movement, the impact of sharpening inequalities and a more visible layer of managerial and other *nouveaux riches* has been significantly more explosive than elsewhere. Virtually everywhere in the world, opinion polls show a widespread belief that inequality has been increasing over the past decades, and that it should be reduced. They also show how few believe it will be. Passive resentment rather than active protest is the keynote. Redistribution has low electoral salience, where it acquires any at all. Germany looks like being the exception. There, public feeling has swung strongly against ongoing polarization of incomes and life-chances, forcing Merkel to toss a few sops to social solidarity, under pressure from the CSU and the labour component of her own party, and leading the SPD to attack hedge funds as locusts, and back-track from Agenda 2010, even before the collapse of financial markets in 2008.[35] This was, above all, the context that enabled Die Linke to make such widespread gains, as the most egalitarian party on offer. Here not just the residual strength of labour organizations in the West provided favourable terrain. The party also benefitted from having the deepest roots of any in the East, where labour may be weak, but inequality is least accepted as the natural order of things. Its rise is all the more striking for running so clean against the trend of the period. But if Germany, before any other country in Europe, has thrown up a new force to the left of the established order, it

---

35. In the summer of 2007, nearly three-quarters of those polled thought the government was doing too little for social justice, 68 per cent wanted to see a minimum wage enacted, and 82 per cent a return to retirement at the age of sixty-five: Thomas E. Schmidt, 'Demoskopie und Antipolitik', *Merkur*, No. 709, June 2008, p. 532.

is also because the theme of 'social injustice' has become, for the moment at least, a national argument.

3

Of its nature, this is a discourse of division: some enjoy advantages that others do not, and there is no defensible reason for their fortune and our want. Elementary thoughts, but novelties in the establishment politics of the Federal Republic. There, the leitmotif has always been, and remains, consensus— the unity of all sensible citizens around a prosperous economy and a pacified state, without social conflicts or structural contradictions. No other political system in post-war Europe is so ideologically gun-shy, averse to any expression of sharp words or irreconcilable opinions, so devoted to banality and blandness. The quest for respectability after 1945, federal checks and balances, the etiquette of coalitions, all have contributed to making a distinctively German style of politics, an unmistakable code of high-minded, sententious conformism. This was not, of course, a mere ideological mannerism. It reflected the reality of a bipartisan—Christian and Social Democratic—convergence on a corporatist model of development, designed to square all interests: naturally, each according to their station, or *Mitbestimmung* writ large, as a charter for social harmony.

This consensus is now, for the first time since the late sixties, under serious pressure. From one direction, demands for social justice risk splitting the fictive unity it has cultivated. The received name for this danger, abhorrent to every self-respecting pundit and politician, is populism—incarnate in the demagogue Lafontaine. It threatens the legacy of Bonn from the left. But the same consensus was also under pressure from an opposite direction. This came from opinion attacking it in the name of liberalism, and calling for a new paradigm of politics worthy of the move to Berlin. For these critics of the status quo, the vital spirit that post-war Germany always lacked is what Anglo-American societies have long possessed: a sense of individual liberty, suspicion of the state, faith in the market, willingness to take risks—the tradition of Locke, Smith, Jefferson, Ricardo, Mill and their successors.[36] Politically, the marginality of the

36. For a pungent version of this complaint from the chief editor of *Die Zeit*, see Josef Joffe, 'Was fehlt?', *Merkur*, No. 689–90, September–October 2006.

FDP reflected the weakness of any such outlook in the Federal Republic. Even the nearest German equivalent after 1945, the Freiburg School of Ordo-liberals—Eucken, Müller-Armack, Röpke—still had, for all their positive influence on Ludwig Erhard, too limited a vision of what a free society requires, as the capture of their originally anti-statist slogan of a 'social market economy' by the clammy corporatism of later years had shown. A more radical break with inveterate national reflexes, closer to the intransigent temper of a Hayek or Popper, was required.

This line of argument, hitting the post-war settlement at an unfamiliar angle, has been a development of intellectual opinion, distant from any obvious popular mood, but resonating across a wide band of the media. How significant is it politically? German tradition, famously, tended to separate the world of culture from that of power, as a compensation or sphere superior to it. In his recent study *The Seduction of Culture in German History*, Wolf Lepenies convicts this inclination of a significant share of the blame for the country's surrender to authoritarianism, from the Second to the Third Reich, pointing in particular to the failure of so many German thinkers and writers to defend Weimar democracy, indeed their often outright hostility or contempt towards it. In the post-war period, so this case goes, such attitudes gradually waned. 'Germany's special path eventually flowed into the mainstream of parliamentary democracy, the market and the rule of the law. Playing off culture against civilization no longer made much sense. It also no longer made much sense to think of culture as a substitute for politics'. By 1949 Leo Strauss was complaining that German thinking had become indistinguishable from Western thought in general. Actually, Lepenies comments, in such assimilation lay 'one of the great political success stories of the twentieth century'.[37] The temptations and delusions of Germany as *Kulturnation* were eventually set aside for a sturdy adjustment to the everyday world of contemporary politics in Bonn.

From this perspective, there was a troublesome interlude around 1968, when students rejected the new normalcy under the influence of traditions now out of time, not necessarily of the same stamp as those uppermost between the wars, but in their way no less disdainful of markets and parliaments. However,

---

37. *The Seduction of Culture in German History*, Princeton 2006, p. 128.

such revolutionary fevers were soon over, leaving behind only a mild counter-cultural *Schwärmerei*, eventually issuing into an inoffensive Greenery. Thereafter, the intellectual climate in the Federal Republic by and large reflected the stability of the political system. No culture is ever made of one piece, and cross-currents persisted. But if Kohl's long rule, as distinct from the system over which he presided, found few admirers, the cultural 'dominant' of the period could be described as a theoretical version of the practices of government, in more left-liberal register. The two emblematic thinkers of these years might indeed be said to illustrate, each in their own way, the validity of Lepenies's diagnosis, exhibiting the reconciliation of culture and power in a pacified German democracy. They shared, appropriately enough, a common American point of departure, in Talcott Parsons's *Social System*—a work which nowhere else in Europe enjoyed such a reception.

Habermas's huge *Theory of Communicative Action*, which appeared in 1981, supplied an affirmative variation on Parsons, developing his idealist emphasis on value-integration as the basis of any modern social order into a still loftier conception of consensus, as not only the hallmark of a political democracy, but touchstone of philosophical truth. Luhmann offered a saturnine variant, radicalizing Parsons's account of differentiated sub-systems within society—economy, polity, family, etc.—into a theory of their complete autonomization as self-reproducing, self-adjusting orders, without subjective agency or structural interpenetration, functioning simply to reduce the complexity of the environments outside them. Though less palatable to polite opinion, Luhmann's tacit construction of the Bonn Republic as a matter-of-fact complex of so many mechanisms of technocratic routine disavowed any critical intent. If Habermas told his readers that things could be as they should be—and, under the protection of the *Grundgesetz*, mostly were—Luhmann's message was dryer, but no less reassuring: things were as they had to be.

On the heights of social theory, these bodies of thought commanded the terrain. In history, the other discipline of greatest public projection, the scene was much more varied, with significant conservative figures and schools continuously active. But here, too, the cutting edge of research and intervention— the 'societal' history associated with Bielefeld—was a left-liberal loyalism, critical of the Second Reich as an antechamber of the

Third, and tracing the path of a reactionary *Sonderweg* that, in
separating Germany from the West, had led to disaster. Here
political emphasis fell on the contrast between a calamitous past
and a transfigured present: the Bonn Republic as everything
that Weimar had not been—stable, consensual, faithful to the
international community. As prolific as Habermas, a close
friend from school-days, Hans-Ulrich Wehler was no less active
a presence in the public sphere, sustaining the values of the post-
war settlement with a distinctive *tranchant* of his own. Still more
pointed as instruction for the present was the work of Heinrich
Winkler on the German labour movement between the wars,
dwelling on the blindness of the SPD in failing to understand
that compromise with parties of the bourgeois centre could
alone save German democracy, as had thankfully been upheld
since the war.

The hegemony of a left-liberal culture in essential syntony with the
character of the political system—while always keeping a critical
distance from its particular incumbents—was never exclusive.
Powerful earlier bodies of writing, dating back to the inter-war
period, continued to circulate and exercise influence to other
effects, less hospitable to the status quo. The Frankfurt School had
been one of these, central in detonating the rebellion of the late
sixties. Consensus was not a value dear to it. But once the hyper-
activist turn of the revolt had passed, or was crushed, and the
legacy of Adorno and Horkheimer was put through the blender
of Habermas's philosophy of communication, little memory was
left of the critical theory for which they had stood. Dissonance
now increasingly came from the right. There could be found
the still active figures of Heidegger, Schmitt, Jünger, Gehlen, all
compromised during the Third Reich, each an intellectual legend
in his own right. Of these, Heidegger, the best known abroad,
was probably of least importance, his post-war reception greater
in France than Germany itself, where under American influence
analytic philosophy gained entry early on, and his runic ontology
had only a narrow purchase on the political or social issues of
the period, as one generically desolate vision of technological
modernity among others.

The other three, all—unlike Heidegger—masters of a terse,
vivid German prose, were of greater moment: Schmitt, the most
ruthlessly brilliant, unstable mind of his generation, for his

kaleidoscopic ability to shake sovereignty, law, war, politics into sharply new and unsettling patterns; Gehlen, for his uncanny sense of the closure of ideological and artistic forms in the 'crystallizations' of a *post-histoire*, and the probability of student and guerrilla rebellions against it; Jünger, for the arresting arc of a trajectory from lyricist of a machine civilization to seer of ecological disaster. The calendars and areas of their influence were not the same, in part depending on their personal situations. Schmitt, institutionally the most ostracized, was intellectually the most consulted, constitutional lawyers flocking to his ideas early on.[38] Gehlen, who died much younger, was stylized as a counter-weight to Adorno. Jünger, who lived longest, regained the most complete *droit de cité*, ending up with every kind of honour, indeed decorated by Mitterrand. But, though never 'residual', in Raymond Williams's sense, the intellectual world such thinkers embodied could not compete with the post-war consensus as any kind of public doctrine. It was an alternative to the dominant discourse, inescapable yet peripheral, incapable of displacing it. Hegemony remained left-liberal.

Around the mid-eighties, there were the first premonitions of a change. Habermas's last great book, *The Philosophical Discourse of Modernity*, appeared in 1985. Intellectually, it was already on the defensive—a noble rescue operation to save the idea of modernity from the descendants of Nietzsche, from Bataille to Foucault to Derrida, who were darkening it once more into an ecstatic antinomianism. If the dangers Habermas discerned were principally French, it was not long before German sub-variants materialized. Peter Sloterdijk's *Critique of Cynical Reason*, greeted respectfully by Habermas himself, had set the ball rolling two years earlier: a best-seller born of a sojourn with the guru Bhagwan Rajneesh in Poona. Over the next twenty years, a torrent of sequels poured out, zig-zagging across every possible terrain of frisson or fashion, from psychotherapy to the ozone layer, religion to genetic engineering, and catapulting Sloterdijk to the status of talk-show host and popular celebrity—a Teutonic

---

38. Schmitt's juridical influence is documented in Dirk van Laak, *Gespräche in der Sicherheit des Schweigens. Carl Schmitt in der politischen Geistesgeschichte der frühen Bundesrepublik*, Berlin 1993; and his wider intellectual impact in Jan-Werner Müller, *A Dangerous Mind: Carl Schmitt in Post-War European Thought*, New Haven 2003 pp. 76ff, which as its title indicates, extends beyond the German field itself.

version, more erudite and bear-like, of Bernard-Henri Lévy. The sway of communicative reason could hardly survive this triumph of public relations. Habermas's pupils Albrecht Wellmer and Axel Honneth have continued to produce honourable work, on occasion more radical in tenor than that of their mentor, of late increasingly preoccupied with religion. But the philosophical props of the peace of Bonn have gone.

In the historical field, the story was different. There the mid-eighties saw a more direct assault on left-liberal heights, which was successfully repulsed, but marked a shift of acceptable opinion all the same. The *Historikerstreit* of 1986 was set off by Ernst Nolte's argument that Nazi atrocities were a reaction to prior Bolshevik crimes, and should not be treated as either unique, or as absolute definitions of the German past. But it soon involved a wider group of conservative historians, making less extreme claims, but in the eyes of their critics—Wehler and Habermas among them—nonetheless not only palliating the criminality of the Third Reich, but undermining the necessary centrality of the Judeocide to the identity of post-war Germany, as memory and responsibility.[39] National rehabilitation was not to be had in this fashion. There could be no question who won this dispute. Soon afterwards, however, the tables were turned, when in their zeal to preclude any revival of national sentiment the leading lights of left-liberalism—Winkler, Wehler, Habermas—expressed their reserve or opposition to reunification of the country, even as it was plainly about to become a reality. However justified were their objections to the form it took, there was no concealing the fact that this was a transformation of Germany they had never conceived or wished for, as their antagonists had. Here too the dominant had dissolved.[40]

---

39. Habermas: 'Eine Art Schadensabwicklung', in Piper Verlag, '*Historikerstreit*', Munich 1987; Wehler: *Entsorgung der deutschen Vergangenheit?*, Munich 1988.

40. Within a year of the *Historikerstreit*, there had appeared sociologist Claus Leggewie's knockabout tour through what he took to be the emergent forms of a new conservatism, *Der Geist steht rechts. Ausflüge in die Denkfabriken der Wende*, Berlin 1987. In this constellation, the most significant figure was Armin Mohler, secretary to Jünger and friend of Schmitt, famous as the author of *Die konservative Revolution in Deutschland, 1918–1932. Grundriss ihrer Weltanschauungen*, which had appeared in 1950, on whom see pp. 187–211.

4

In the gradual change of intellectual atmosphere, one catalyst stands out. Since the war, Germany's leading journal of ideas has been *Merkur*, which can claim a record of continuous distinction arguably without equal in Europe. Its remarkable founding editor, Hans Paeschke, gave it an interdisciplinary span—from the arts through philosophy and sociology to the hard sciences— of exceptional breadth, canvassed with consistent elegance and concision. But what made it unique was the creed of its editor. Inspired by Wieland's encyclopaedism, Paeschke gave the ecumenical range of his Enlightenment model a more agonistic twist, combining the capacity for *Gegenwirkung* that Goethe had praised in Wieland—who had published Burke and Wollstonecraft alike—with a *Polarisierung* of his own, as twin mottos for the journal. These remained the constants in *Merkur*'s changeable liberalism—first conservative, then national, then left, as Paeschke later described its phases: an editorial practice welcoming opposites, and setting them in play against each other. 'The more liberal, the richer in tensions.'[41] At one time or another Broch, Arendt, Curtius, Adorno, Heidegger, Brecht, Gehlen, Löwith, Weizsäcker, Voegelin, Borkenau, Bloch, Schmitt, Habermas, Weinrich, Benn all appeared in its pages. Uninterested in the *Wirtschaftswunder*, hostile to the Cold War, regarding Adenauer's Germany as a 'pseudomorphosis', Paeschke maintained good relations with writers in the East, and when the political scene changed in the sixties, was sympathetic to both the student revolt and the turn to an *Ostpolitik*. Averse to any kind of *Syntheselei*, he conceived the journal socratically, as a dialectical enterprise, in keeping with the dictum *Der Geist ist ein Wühler*.[42] Spirit is not a reconciler, but a trouble-maker.

Paeschke retired in the late seventies, and in 1984 the succession passed to Karl-Heinz Bohrer, pre-eminently equipped for the role of *Wühler*. A student of German Romanticism, and theorist of Jünger's early work, Bohrer made his début in *Merkur* in 1968, with a defence of the student revolt against liberal

---

41. 'Kann keine Trauer sein', *Merkur*, No. 367, December 1978, p. 1180: Paeschke took the title of this beautiful farewell to the journal he had edited from Gottfried Benn's last poem, written a few weeks before his death, published in *Merkur*.

42. 'Vorbemerkung', in *Merkur: Gesamtregister für die Jahrgänge I–XXXII, 1947–1978*, Stuttgart 1986, p. x. The phrase comes from Burckhardt.

attacks in the mainstream press, praising it as the expression, at its best, of an eclectic anarchism.[43] Not the Frankfurt School, he argued, but the French Surrealism that Benjamin had admired and Adorno dismissed, was the appropriate inspiration for rebellion against the detestable *juste milieu* of the Bonn system.[44] These were the sentiments of a writer who was soon making a name for himself as editor of the literary section of the country's leading conservative newspaper, the *Frankfurter Allgemeine Zeitung*, before falling out with his superiors and being packed off as correspondent to London. A decade later, he returned to the charge in *Merkur* with a bravura survey of the fate of the movements of 1968—compared with those of 1848 and 1870–1—as uprising and counter-culture, covering politics, theatre, film, art, theory and music, and marking 1974 as the end of a revolutionary epoch in which Blake's tiger had stalked the streets. A mere restoration of 'old-bourgeois cultural piety' was no longer possible, but the new culture had by now lost its magnetism: only an artist like Beuys retained an anarchic force of subversion.[45] Bohrer's own deepest allegiances were to 'suddenness' as the dangerous moment, without past or future, in which true aesthetic experience ruptures the continuity of existence, and so, potentially, the social fabric. Captured by Nietzsche, Kierkegaard, Hofmannsthal, and Jünger—in their own ways Woolf or Joyce, too—the sudden found its political expression in the decisionism of Schmitt.[46] The central figure in this pantheon, combining more than any other its aesthetic and political moments—epiphany and act—remained Jünger, the subject of Bohrer's *Ästhetik des Schreckens*, the work that won him a chair in modern German literary history at Bielefeld.

On taking charge of *Merkur* soon afterwards, Bohrer opened his editorship in spectacular fashion, with a merciless satire on the petty-bourgeois philistinism, provincialism and consumerism of Bonn politics and culture, complete with a ruinous portrait of Kohl as the personification of a mindless gluttony.[47] This was a state,

---

43. 'Die Missverstandene Rebellion', *Merkur*, No. 238, January 1968.

44. 'Surrealismus und Terror', *Merkur*, No. 258, October 1969.

45. 'Die ausverkauften Ideen', *Merkur*, No. 365, October 1978.

46. 'Der gefährliche Augenblick', *Merkur*, No. 358, March 1978; themes developed in *Plötzlichkeit: zum Augenblick des ästhetischen Scheins*, Frankfurt 1981, of which there is an English translation, *Suddenness: on the Moment of Aesthetic Appearance*, New York 1994.

47. 'Die Ästhetik des Staates', *Merkur*, No. 423, January 1984. For a striking

wanting all aesthetic form, that could only be described in the spirit of the early Brecht, or Baudelaire on Belgium. A three-part pasquinade on the German political class followed, depicting both the new-found CDU–FDP coalition and the SPD opposition to it with blistering derision.[48] Time did not soften these judgements. At the turn of the nineties, Bohrer unleashed another ferocious fusillade against German provincialism, in a six-part series covering government, literature, television, advertising, press, songs, stars, movies, cityscapes, and culminating in special scorn for delusions that the enthusiasm of his compatriots for Europe was anything other than a tourist form of the same parochialism. From the 'pastoral boredom' of Die Zeit and the FAZ, to the 'fussy sentimentalism' of Grass or Walser, to the grotesqueries of Kohl as 'Giant of the Caucasus', and Genscher as his Sancho Panza, little escaped Bohrer's scathing report. At best, the Frankfurt of the sixties had not been quite so dreary as Düsseldorf or Munich, and Fassbinder was a bright spot.[49]

The polemical élan of such broadsides was never just destructive. From the beginning, Bohrer had a normative ideal in mind. Germany was in need of a creative aesthetics of the state. It was the absence of one that produced the dismal landscape scanned in his first editorial, and its many sequels. To those who taxed him with that 'aestheticization of politics' which Benjamin had identified as peculiar to fascism, he replied that in fact every democratic state that respected itself had its own aesthetic, expressed in its capital city, public buildings, ceremonies, spaces, forms of rule and rhetoric—contemporary America, England, France or Italy supplied the evidence, to which a special issue of Merkur was devoted.[50] It was in these that the identity of the nation acquired tangible legitimacy, and shape: a state without its own distinctive symbolic forms, in which politics was reduced to mere social assistance, was hardly worth the name. It was time for Germany to put the stunted half-life of the Bonn Republic behind it.

---

analysis of Bohrer's style of attack in this and later texts, see Gustav Seibt, 'Vom Bürgerkönigtum,' in Deutsche Erhebungen, Springe 2008, pp. 142–54.

48. 'Die Unschuld an die Macht', Merkur, No. 425, March 1984; Merkur, No. 427, May 1984; Merkur, No. 431, January 1985.

49. 'Provinzialismus', Merkur, No. 501, December 1990; Merkur, No. 504, March 1991; Merkur, No. 505, April 1991; Merkur, No. 507, June 1991; Merkur, No. 509, August 1991; Merkur, No. 510, November 1991.

50. 'Ästhetik und Politik sowie einige damit zusammanhängende Fragen', Merkur 451–2, September–October 1986.

When the Berlin Wall came down five years later, but reunification was still quite uncertain, and resisted by the liberal left in the West, Bohrer was thus well positioned to publish, in the *Frankfurter Allgemeine*, perhaps the most powerful single essay of the time in favour of German unity, 'Why We Are Not a Nation— and Why We Should Become One'.[51] His leading adversary was Habermas, treated with the respect Bohrer had always shown him. The contribution to *Merkur* immediately following his famous 'Aesthetics of the State' had, indeed, been an article by Habermas on the peace demonstrations against the stationing of Pershing missiles, and when the *Historikerstreit* came two years later, Bohrer had not hesitated to side with him. But Habermas's resistance to unification, worthy though his notion of a disembodied constitutional patriotism might be as an abstract ideal, was a delusion. Behind it lay a 'negative chiliasm', in which the Judeocide stood as the unconditional event of the German past, barring the country from any recovery of a traditional national identity, with its own psychic and cultural forms. 'Did our specifically "irrational" tradition of Romanticism have to be so thoroughly destroyed by the bulldozers of a new sociology?', he asked pointedly.

With reunification and the transfer of the capital to Berlin came possibilities of another kind of Germany, for which Bohrer had polemicized. For with them faded the intellectual nimbus of the old order. But if the arrival of the Berlin Republic marked the passage to a new situation, it was not one which Bohrer viewed in any spirit of complacent vindication. When *Merkur* took stock of the country in late 2006 with a book-length special issue, 'On the Physiognomy of the Berlin Republic', under the rubric *Ein neues Deutschland?*—a virtuoso composition, containing essays on everything from ideology to politics, journalism to architecture, slums to managers, patriots to professors, legitimacy to diplomacy—Bohrer's editorial, 'The Aesthetics of the State Revisited', made clear how little he had relented.[52] Germany was now a sovereign nation once more; it had

---

51. *Frankfurter Allgemeine Zeitung*, 13 January 1990; for an English version of this text, see *New German Critique*, Winter 1991, No 52. Its translator, Stephen Brockmann, would later describe Bohrer's arguments as 'a foundational discourse for the triumphal conservatism that emerged on the German right in the wake of reunification'. For this judgement, see his *Literature and German Reunification*, Cambridge 1999, p. 57.

52. 'Die Ästhetik des Staates revisited', *Merkur*, No. 689–90, September–October 2006. The title of the special number alludes, of course, ironically to the official daily of the former DDR.

a proper capital; and globalization ruled out any retreat into the self-abasing niche of the past. These were welcome changes. But in many respects the lowering heritage of the Bonn era lived on. In Berlin itself, the new government quarter was for the most part a vacuous desolation, inviting mass tourism, redeemed only by the restoration of the Reichstag—even that banalized by fashionable bric-a-brac and political correctness, not to speak of the droning addresses delivered within it.[53] Alone in its dignity was the ensemble of Prussian classicism, at length recovered, extending east from the Brandenburg Gate to the Gendarmenmarkt. Nor had Berlin's return to the position of a national capital had any transformative effect on other German cities, or even aroused their interest: if anything, each had become more regional, the country more centrifugal, than ever. The feel-good patriotism of the World Cup of 2006, with its sea of fresh-faced flag-waving youth, as vapid as it was vulgar, was the obverse of the lack of any serious statecraft at the helm of the republic, of which Merkel was only the latest dispiriting, institutionally determined, incarnation. Missing in this order was any will to style. The expressive deficit of the Bonn Republic had not been overcome.

True independence of mind, Bohrer would subsequently remark, was to be found in those thinkers—Montaigne, Schlegel, Nietzsche—who replaced *Sinnfragen* with *Formfragen*,[54] a substitution that could be taken as the motto of his own work. But *Sinn* and *Form* are not so easily separated. Bohrer's critique of the deficiencies of the German state, both before and after the move to Berlin, could by its own logic never remain a purely formal matter, of aesthetics alone. From the beginning, his editorial interventions in *Merkur* had a substantive edge. A state that respected itself enough to develop a symbolic form was one that knew how to assert itself, where required, in the field of relations between states. From his post in London, Bohrer had admired British resolve in the Falklands War, and he thereafter consistently backed Western military interventions, in the Balkans and the Middle East. The deficit of the German state was thus not just a matter of buildings or speeches, it was also one of arms. Bohrer was a scathing critic of Kohl's failure to join in Operation Desert Storm; advocated the

---

53. For a mocking tour of the fixtures and fittings of the new Bundestag, and of the government district at large, see Gustav Seibt's deadly squib, 'Post aus Ozeanien', *Merkur*, No. 689–90.

54. 'Was heisst unabhängig denken?', *Merkur*, No. 699, July 2007, p. 574.

dispatch of German ground troops to Yugoslavia; and handed
Schröder a white feather over Iraq. With such belligerence has
gone a shift of cultural reference. Paeschke subtitled *Merkur* 'A
German Journal of European Thought', and kept his word—
Gide, Eliot, Montale, Ortega, Russell appearing alongside his
native eminences. Few German intellectuals of his generation
were as well equipped to maintain this tradition as Bohrer, whose
contempt for the provincialism of Bonn and all it stood for was
rooted in personal experience. Steeped in Anglo-French culture,
after working in London, he later lived much of the time in Paris.

But by the turn of the century, a change had come over the journal
under him. The presence of Europe faded. Contributors, topics
and arguments were now more and more insistently American.
Bohrer had never been an enthusiast for the EU, his view of it
close to a British scepticism—he liked to invoke the *Spectator*—
he had long admired. Intellectual sources in the United States,
however, were something new. The combination of a hawkish
Aussenpolitik and multiplying signatures from the Heritage
Foundation or Cato Institute can give the impression that a
German version of US-style neo-conservatism has of late taken
shape in *Merkur*. Bohrer rejects any such classification. If he is to
be labelled at all, it should be as a 'neo-liberal' in the spirit, not of
the IMF, but of Richard Rorty, at once patriot and ironist. That
he cannot, in fact, be aligned with either kind of transatlantic
import is clear not only from his more accurate self-description
elsewhere as an 'anti-authoritarian, subjectivist liberal', but from
the occasion that produced it, an essay on the fortieth anniversary
of the student revolt in Germany.

'Eight Scenes from Sixty-Eight'—clipped reminiscences of
that year: so many strobe-lit flashes of Dutschke and Krahl,
Enzensberger and Adorno, Habermas and Meinhof—is sometimes
acerbic, but for the most part unabashedly lyrical in its memories
of the intellectual and sensual awakening of that year: 'Who has
not known those days and nights of psychological, and literal,
masquerade and identity-switching, does not know what makes
life exciting, to vary Talleyrand's phrase'.[55] Reitz's *Zweite Heimat*
offered an unforgettable re-creation of them. The worst that could
be said of '68-ers was that they destroyed what was left of symbolic

---

55. 'Acht Szenen Achtundsechzig', *Merkur*, No. 708, May 2008, p. 419.

form in Germany. The best, that they were never *Spiesser*. If they left a residue of fanaticism, today that had perhaps become most conspicuous in root-and-branch denunciations of '68 by former participants in it. Bohrer had little time for such renegades. He was not Daniel Bell: the antinomian held no fears for him.

5

Looking back on Paeschke's command at *Merkur*, Bohrer once remarked of it that though Schlegel's *Athenaeum* was a much more original journal than Wieland's *Teutsche Merkur*, it was the latter—which lasted so much longer—that marked its epoch; regularity and consistency requiring that eccentricity be curbed, if authority was to be gained. This was a lesson Paeschke had learnt. He himself, however, came out of the Romantic, not the Enlightenment tradition, and took some time to see it, before attempting to conjugate them.[56] As Bohrer's tenure moved towards its appointed end, the results of that effort were visible. In intention, at any rate, authority has increasingly materialized, in the shape of contributors from just those organs of opinion Bohrer had once castigated as the voices of a pious *ennui*: editors and columnists from *Die Zeit*, *Die Welt*, the *FAZ*, coming thick and fast in the pages of the journal. Here a genuinely neo-liberal front, excoriating the lame compromises of the Schröder–Merkel years, is on the attack, aggressively seeking to replace one 'paradigm' with another. Flanking it, if at a slight angle, is the journal's theorist of geopolitics, Herfried Münkler, author of an ambitious body of writing on war and empire,[57] whose recent essays in *Merkur* offer the most systematic prospectus for returning Germany, in the new century, to the theatre of *Weltpolitik*.

The logic of the inter-state system of today, Münkler suggests, may best be illustrated by an Athenian fable to be found in Aristotle. In an assembly of beasts, the hares demanded equal rights for all animals. The lions replied, but where are your claws and teeth? Whereupon the proposal was rejected, and the hares

---

56. 'Hans Paeschke und der Merkur. Erinnerung und Gegenwart', *Merkur*, No. 510–11, September–October 1991.

57. For a penetrating critique of his major recent work, *Imperien*, which came out in 2005, see Benno Teschke, 'Empires by Analogy', *New Left Review* II/40, July–August 2006.

withdrew to the back rows again. Moral: for equal rights to obtain, there must be a reasonable equality of powers. In their reaction to the American lion's attack on Iraq, countries like France and Germany protested like so many hares, earning only leonine contempt. Even united, Europe could not itself become a lion overnight, and should realize this. But what it could, and should, become is a continental fox in alliance with the lion, complementing—in Machiavelli's formula—the force of the one with the cunning of the other; or in contemporary jargon American hard power with European soft power. The loyalty of the fox to the lion must be beyond question, and each must overcome current resentment against the other—the lion feeling betrayed, the fox humiliated, by what has happened in the Middle East. But once good relations are restored, the fox has a special role to play in the cooperation between them, as a beast more alert than the lion to another, increasingly prominent species in the animal kingdom—rats, now multiplying, and spreading the plague of terror. Such rodents do not belong to the diet of lions; but foxes, which have their own—lesser, but still sharp—teeth and claws, can devour them, and can halt their proliferation. That zoological duty will require of Europe, however, that it develop a will to fashion a world politics of its own—*eine eigener weltpolitische Gestaltungswille*. The necessary self-assertion of Europe demands nothing less.[58]

What of Germany? In contrast to the Second Reich and the Weimar Republic, both deeply insecure, and the rabid attempt to over-compensate such insecurity in the Third Reich, the Berlin Republic exhibits a new and warranted self-confidence. Post-war Germany long sought to buy its way back into international respectability, simply with its cheque-book. Kohl, helping to defray the costs of the Gulf War without participating in it, was the last episode in that inglorious process. Since his departure, the Federal Republic has finally assumed its responsibilities, as a self-confident 'medium power' within the European Union: dispatching its armed forces to the Balkans, to Afghanistan and to Congo, not in any selfish pursuit of its own interests, but for the common good, to protect others. Such is the appropriate role for a medium power, which must rely more on prestige and reputation than repression for its position in the world, and has naturally

---

58. Münkler, 'Der Selbstbehauptung Europas. Fabelhafte Überlegungen', *Merkur*, No. 649, May 2003.

sought a permanent seat in the Security Council commensurate with its contribution to the operations of the UN.[59]

Yet Germany, politically integrated into the EU and militarily into NATO, still relies too much on its economic weight for its role as a sovereign state in the world. It needs to diversify its portfolio of power, above all by recovering the ideological and cultural attraction it formerly possessed, becoming once again the *Kulturnation und Wissenschaftslandschaft* of old. The attraction of the new Berlin as an international city, comparable to its radiance in Weimar days, will help. But soft power alone will not be enough. All Europe, and Germany within it, confronts resistance to the existing world order of capitalism, not from a China or India that are now sub-centres of it, but from the periphery of the system. There, terrorism remains the principal challenge to the post-heroic societies of the West, of which Germany is the deepest example. It would be naive to think it could be defeated by mere economic aid or moral exhortation.[60]

Propositions such as these, adjusting Prussian modes of thought to contemporary conditions, aim at making policy. Münkler, no figure of the right, but a frequenter of the SPD, is listened to within today's Wilhelmstrasse, which has organized ambassadorial conclaves to discuss his ideas. German diplomats, he writes with satisfaction, are readier to play on the different keyboards of power he recommends than, so far, are politicians. Here is probably the closest interface between the review and the state to be found in *Merkur*. The influence of a journal of ideas is never easy to measure. Bohrer's enterprise has certainly played a critical role in dethroning the comfortable left-liberalism of the post-war intellectual establishment. But its destructive capacity has not—or not yet—been equalled by an ability to construct a comparable new consensus. The kind of hegemony that a journal like *Le Débat* for a period achieved in France has been beyond it. In part, this has been a question of form: the essays in *Merkur*, closer to a still vigorous German tradition of *belles lettres*, remain less 'modern' than the more empirical, better documented, contributions to the French review. But it has also been a function of Bohrer's own distinctive handling of his office. In the tension

---

59. 'Die selbstbewusste Mittelmacht. Aussenpolitik im souveränen Staat', *Merkur*, No. 689–90, September–October 2006.

60. 'Heroische und postheroische Gesellschaften', *Merkur*, No. 700, August–September 2007.

between Schlegel and Wieland, although he would respect the goal of authority, his own higher value has always been idiosyncrasy—that is, originality, of which the strange cocktail of themes and positions he developed out of Romantic and Surrealist materials in his own texts, effervescent and potent enough by any measure, was the presiding example. Editorially, even in its late neo-liberal moods, *Merkur* always comprised contrary opinions, in the spirit of Paeschke's *Gegenwirkung*. But the underlying impulse was polarizing, not in his but in the avant-garde sense, inaugurated by the *Athenaeum*. To Bohrer's credit, conventional authority was forfeited with it.

In this case, however, the distance between trenchancy and influence can be taken as the index of a wider disconnexion, between the political and cultural life of the Berlin Republic at large. Under the dispensation of Bonn, notwithstanding obvious contrasts between them, there was a basic accord between the two. In that sense, Lepenies's thesis that in post-war Germany culture by and large ceased to be at odds with politics, as both became in the approved sense democratic, is sound. Habermas's notion of a 'constitutional patriotism' peculiar to the Federal Republic can be read as a tacit celebration of that harmony. Since 1990, on the other hand, the two have drifted apart. When, midway through the eighties, Claus Leggewie published his polemic *Der Geist steht rechts*, he was premature. Twenty years later, that such a shift had occurred was plain. Intellectual energy had passed to the right, no longer just a *fronde*, but a significant consensus in the media—a climate of opinion. The political class, however, was still tethered to its familiar habitat. Neither Red–Green nor Black–Red coalitions had much altered the *juste milieu* of Bonn descent. The equilibrium of the West German system of old, however, was broken. A series of torsions had twisted its components apart. The economic sphere has been displaced to the right. The political sphere has not yet drifted far from the centre. The social sphere has moved subterraneously to the left. The intellectual sphere has gravitated in the opposite direction.

What the eventual outcome of these different tectonic shifts might be remains beyond prediction. The crash of the global economy, wrecking German export orders, has forced the country into a downward spiral as the coalition in Berlin enters its final year, amid mounting tension between its partners. If the CDU maintains the large lead it currently enjoys over the SPD in the opinion polls, and the FDP holds up sufficiently, a Black–Yellow government could emerge that, till yesterday, would have had a freer hand to deregulate the social market economy more radically, according to neo-liberal prescriptions. The slump will put these on hold. But since the FDP's identity depends on an assertive anti-statism, a drift back to older forms of corporatism, beyond emergency measures, would not be easy. If, on the other hand, electoral dislike of growing inequality and social insecurity combines with widespread fear of any kind of instability, the vote could tilt back to the dead-point of another Grand Coalition. Changes in intellectual climate must affect the working-through of either formula, though the extent of their incidence could be another matter. A few years ago, the international soccer championship was promoted with billboards across the country proclaiming 'Germany—the Land of Ideas'. Where there is sport, infantilism is rarely far away. The country's traditions of thought have, fortunately, not yet sunk to the *reductio ad abiectum* of an advertising slogan for football. But that their specific weight in society has declined is certain.

Viewed comparatively, indeed, German culture in the past third of a century has been distinguished as a matrix less of ideas than of images. In that respect, one might say that it exchanged roles with France, philosophy migrating west across the Rhine, while painting, photography, cinema travelled east. It is in the visual arts that German culture has been most productive, often pre-eminent. In their different ways: Beuys, Richter, Trockel, Kiefer; the Bechers, Struth, Gursky, Ruff; Fassbinder, Syberberg, Reitz— no other European society of the period has had quite this palette. More of it, too, has touched on the history of the country and its transformations than anywhere else, and more explosively. The cinema, as one might expect, has been the most direct site of this. Fassbinder's *Marriage of Maria Braun,* with the immolation of its heroine as the bellowing commentary on the World Cup final of 1954 reaches a crescendo, closes with a pallid, reversed-out image of Helmut Schmidt filling the screen, as the grey death's-head of the *Wirtschaftswunde*r. Reitz's *Heimat* trilogy, the first part of which was released in 1984, just as Kohl was consolidating his power, ends in the prosperous, united Germany of the new century with the destruction by financial predators of the family firm of one brother, the crash of the plane of another into the cliffs above the Rhine, the suicide of a Yugoslav orphan in the river below, the burial of a fabled trove of paintings by an earthquake: settings and intimations of a modern Ring Cycle. Its final image is of the youngest female survivor, looking out into the darkness, her features slowly resembling, as the camera closes in, the mask of a haunted animal. Art has its premonitions, though they are not always right.

6

ITALY

I · 2002

Italy has long occupied a peculiar position within the concert of Europe. By wealth and population it belongs alongside France, Britain and Germany as one of the four leading states of the Union. But it has never played a comparable role in the affairs of the continent, and has rarely been regarded as a diplomatic partner or rival of much significance. Its image lacks any association with power. Historically, that has no doubt been one of the reasons why Italy has long been the favourite country of foreigners. Germans, French and English alike have repeatedly expressed a warmth of affection for it they have rarely felt for one another, even if the objects of their admiration have differed. Few of their comments are without some contemporary ring. Escaping from the pruderies of Weimar to Rome, Goethe found it 'morally salutary to be living in the midst of a sensual people'.[1] In Italy, Byron decided that 'there is, in fact, no law or government at all; and it is wonderful how well things go on without them'.[2] Stendhal, who knew the country better, felt at times that 'music alone is alive in Italy, and all that is to be made in this beautiful land is *love*; the other enjoyments of the soul are spoilt; one dies poisoned of melancholy as a citizen'. Yet Italians were also, paradoxically, masters of another practice: 'Never, outside Italy, could one guess at the art called *politics* (way of making others do what is agreeable to us, when force or money is not to hand). Without patience, without absence of anger, no one can be called a politician. Napoleon was

---

1. 1 November 1786, *Italienische Reise*, Leipzig 1913, Vol. 1, p. 126.
2. 2 January 1821, Byron's *Letters and Journals*, Vol. 8, Cambridge, MA 1978, p. 55.

truly small in this respect, he had enough Italian blood in his veins to be subtle, but was incapable of using it'.[3] The list of such fond dicta could be extended indefinitely.

In diametric contrast stands the characteristic tone of native commentary on Italy. Most languages have some self-critical locution, usually a word-play or neologism, to indicate typical national defects. Germans can cite Hegel's contemptuous description of local identity politics: *Deutschdumm*; the French deplore the vauntings of *franchouillardise*; Peruvians term a hopeless mess *una peruanada*; Brazilians occasionally mock a *brasileirice*. England seems to have lacked such self-ironic reflexes: 'Englishry'—the gift of Tom Nairn, a Scot—is without currency in its land of reference. Italy lies at the opposite pole. In no other nation is the vocabulary of self-derision so multiple and so frequent in use. *Italietta* for the trifling levity of the country; *italico*—once favoured by Fascist bombast—now synonymous with vain posturing and underhand cynicism; bitterest of all, *italiota* as the badge of an invincible cretinism. It is true that these are terms of public parlance rather than of popular speech. But the lack of self-esteem they express is widespread. The good opinion of others remains foreign to the Italians themselves.

In recent years, this traditional self-disaffection has acquired an insistent political catchword. Starting in the late eighties, and rising to a crescendo in the nineties, the cry has gone up that Italy must, at last, become 'a normal country'. Such was the title of the manifesto produced in 1995 by the leader of the former Italian Communist Party.[4] But the phrase was a leitmotif of speeches and articles across the spectrum, and remains an obsessive refrain in the media to this day. Its message is that Italy must become like other countries of the West. Normality here, as always, implies more than just a standard that is typical. What is not typical may be exceptional, and so better than it; but what is not 'normal' is infallibly worse than it—abnormal or subnormal. The call for Italy to become a normal country expresses a longing to resemble others which are superior to it.

---

3. 17 November 1816, 7 January 1817: *Voyages en Italie*, Paris 1973, pp. 9, 423.

4. Massimo D'Alema, *Un paese normale. La sinistra e il futuro dell'Italia*, Milan 1995. Heading the list of the criteria of normalcy: 'a market economy open to competition', p. 63.

The full list of the anomalies that set Italy apart vary from one account to another, but all highlight three features. For forty years of continuous Christian-Democratic hegemony, there was no real alternation of government. Under this regime, political corruption acquired colossal proportions. Intertwined with it, organized crime became a power in the land as the operations of the Mafia extended from Sicily to Rome and the north. Other national shortcomings are often noted: administrative inefficiency, lack of respect for the law, want of patriotism. But in the widespread conviction that the condition of Italy is abnormal, immovable government, pervasive corruption and militarized crime have had pride of place. For a careful and balanced account of them, there is no finer study than Paul Ginsborg's *Italy and Its Discontents*, the work of an English historian in Florence, originally published in Italian, the latest monument to critical admiration of the country by a foreign scholar.[5]

Long-standing occupation of office, of course, has not been peculiar to Italy. Swedish Social Democracy was in office for over forty years, Red–Black coalitions in Austria for nearly as long; the government of Switzerland is virtually unchangeable. Far from suffering grave ills, these societies are usually regarded as among the best administered in Europe. Japanese political corruption long exceeded Italian; while French and German have not come so far behind. The Mafia is truly *sui generis* in Sicily, but in a less ethnographic sense has its counterparts throughout most of Eastern Europe and, famously, Russia. Northern Ireland, the Basque lands and Corsica are reminders that in Western Europe itself more than one regional periphery is haunted by endemic violence. Many distinctions would have to be made, in each respect, for real analytic comparison. But it can still be argued that it is less any one of its maladies that has marked Italy out as abnormal, than a fatal combination of them to be found nowhere else.

In any case, if an *idée fixe* takes hold in a society, it is unlikely to have appeared from nowhere. In Italy, fascination with foreign models—the desire to emulate a more advanced world—was from the start bred by the belated unification of the country, and ensuing weakness of the national state. Piedmontese attachment

---

5. Originally published in Italian as *L'Italia del tempo presente: Famiglia, società civile, Stato 1980–1996*, Turin 1998, the English edition covers developments up to end of the first Centre-Left government in 2001. See especially chapters 5 and 6.

to the French prefectural system, imposed down the peninsula regardless of regional identities, was an early example; somewhat later, Crispi's admiration for Germany as an imperial power another. In that sense, the anxious looking abroad for institutions to imitate, so pronounced in recent years, has deep historical roots: it is the re-emergence of a recurrent theme. Contemporary versions, moreover, are reinforced by the unhappy experience of the one period when Italy did not follow any external model, but in originating Fascism pioneered a major political innovation that spread to other states. To many since then, Italian native invention has seemed damned: better to revert to the safety of imitation. By the 1980s the way in which Christian Democracy came to be imagined by its opponents mapped it onto the disastrous alternative pattern of national singularity. It was the *Balena Bianca*, a monstrous sport of nature, akin to Melville's murderous denizen of the sea.[6] According to legend, it was the final harpooning of this beast that ushered in the Second Republic.

I

For such is the usual way Italians label the political order today. In this version, the First Republic that emerged at the end of the Second World War collapsed, amid dramatic convulsions, in the early nineties. Out of its demise there has emerged a more modern configuration, still incomplete, but already a critical improvement on its predecessor. It is the full accomplishment of this Second Republic, for which there remains some way to go, that would at last render Italy a normal country. So runs the official interpretation, widely shared on all sides, of the past decade. Here too, of course, a foreign paradigm is in the background. The passage from the First to Second Republic in Italy is conceived by analogy with the transition from the Fourth to Fifth Republic in France. There were, after all, striking similarities between the regimes created after 1945 in both countries: rapid economic growth, strong ideological polarization, large mass parties, constant changes of cabinet with little or no change of political direction, increasing discredit of the governing class, inability to control violent crises in the Mediterranean periphery.

In each case, there was a supervening international context for the fall of the old Republic: the end of European colonialism in the case of France, and the end of the Cold War in the case of Italy.

---

6. White was the symbolic colour of the DC.

Umberto Bossi's Lega Lombarda, merging in 1991 with other parties to form the Lega Nord, the battering-ram that weakened the struts of the traditional party system in Italy, even had its petty-bourgeois precursor in the movement of Pierre Poujade, whose emergence hastened the final crisis of the Fourth Republic. In all these respects, a French reference could seem to make much sense in the Italian situation of the early nineties, legitimating hopes of a cathartic purge of the accumulated ills of the old order, and reconstruction of the state on a sounder basis. The task of the hour was to emulate the historic achievement of De Gaulle in founding a stable Fifth Republic to the north. But who was to figure as the Italian equivalent in such a repro-scenario?

In April 1992 the ruling coalition—dominated since the eighties by Giulio Andreotti, the perennial 'Beelzebub' of Christian Democracy, and Bettino Craxi, the taurine boss of the Socialists—was once again returned to power at the polls. Bossi's movement, a recent entrant into the party system, had made startling advances in the north, but not enough to affect the national outcome.[7] It seemed business as usual. But a month later, magistrates in Milan issued the first official warnings to leading figures in both dominant parties that they were under investigation for corruption. At virtually the same moment, the motorcade of Giovanni Falcone, the prosecutor who had become a symbol of determination to root out the Mafia in Sicily, was blown up in an ambush outside Palermo. Hit by these two thunderbolts, the old order suddenly disintegrated. Over the next months, the Milanese magistrates unleashed a blizzard of further investigations against the political class and its business partners, now dubbed by the press *Tangentopoli*—Bribesville. Within little more than a year, Craxi had fled to Tunisia and Andreotti was charged as an accomplice of the Mafia. By the autumn of 1993, more than half the members of the Senate and Chamber of Deputies had been served notices that they were under suspicion for corruption—taken by public opinion as tantamount to guilt—and a referendum had abrogated the system of proportional representation that had elected them. In this whirlwind, the traditional rulers of Italy were swept away. By the spring of 1994 the Christian Democratic and

7. The ecology of the early League is laid out in Ilvo Diamante, *La Lega. Geografia, storia e sociologia di un nuovo soggetto politico*, Rome 1993, pp. 19–42. In 1992, the party took 8.65 per cent of the vote and won fifty-five seats in the Chamber of Deputies.

Socialist parties had vanished. Lesser allies were consumed along with them.

From the wreckage, only one major party emerged unscathed. The logical candidate for the role of renovator appeared to be the descendants of Italian Communism, recently refashioned as the Party of the Democratic Left (PDS). Like Gaullism in France, Communism in Italy had been excluded from the stabilization of the post-1945 regime, forming an opposition in waiting, with a mass following, undiscredited by the degeneration of the system. Like De Gaulle in 1958, the PDS in 1992–3 was not responsible for the fall of the old order, and just as he had used the colonels' revolt in Algiers, which he did not inspire, to come to power in Paris, so the PDS sought to utilize the magistrates' assault on Tangentopoli, with which it had no connexion, to force open the doors of office in Rome, barred to it since 1947. In constructing the Fifth Republic, De Gaulle drew in a heteroclite range of allies— Antoine Pinay, Guy Mollet and other strange bedfellows formed part of his first coalition, helping him to push through his new constitution, before he discarded them. So too the PDS teamed up with a variegated array of outsiders and opportunists—the self-important notable Segni, from Christian Democracy; the Radical maverick Pannella; the still Fascist leader Fini—to push through the referendum of 1993, undermining the proportional electoral system on which the First Republic had been based.[8]

Here, however, the analogy breaks down. Once installed in Paris, De Gaulle was firmly in charge of the reorganization of the French political system, controlling all the initiatives, taking up and casting off assorted camp-followers, as he set about reconstructing the state. The PDS, on the other hand, jumped on the makeshift bandwagon of a referendum that had been launched by Segni, lending it mass mobilizing capacity, but not political direction. The contrast points to a larger difference. Notwithstanding the parallels between them, the heirs of Italian Communism were in a far weaker position than De Gaulle. Permanently excluded from government in Rome at much the same time as the General withdrew to Colombey-les-Deux-Églises, the PCI never kept, however, the same intransigent distance from the political system

---

8. For his own account, see Mario Segni, *La rivoluzione interrotta*, Milan 1994, whose general tone is: 'The referendum of 18 April carried Italy from the First to the Second Republic. That evening, I confess, I felt truly proud'— sentiments shared by virtually all organs of established opinion at the time.

of the First Republic as he had from the Fourth. By the eighties, the PCI had long become a semi-insider at regional level in Italy, embedded in various provincial coalitions, and a tacit partner of the DC at the national level, where most legislation was passed with its assent.[9] So it too was in some degree implicated in the typical practices of *sottogoverno*—commissions on public works contracts, subsidies to affiliated organizations, residences for party notables—that marked the old order. When the crisis broke, it was risky for the PDS to pose too aggressively as a champion of clean government.

A larger difficulty lay in the overall evolution of the PCI since the war. The party had received from Antonio Gramsci, whose *Prison Notebooks* were first published in 1948, a great intellectual inheritance. Out of it, with whatever elements of tactical selection or suppression, the PCI created a mass political culture without counterpart on the European Left. In Italy no other party had a comparable patrimony—the originality of Gramsci's ideas was not only widely accepted at home, but from the sixties onwards increasingly recognized abroad. Here, then, was one purely Italian tradition that was undeniably vital and uncompromised. But the PCI in the age of Togliatti was not just a sprig of native growth. It was a component of a disciplined international movement, commanded by the USSR. After the war, its strategy was for its own reasons—if in line with Moscow's wishes anyway—consistently moderate, and over time the party became increasingly independent of the calculations of Soviet diplomacy. But in internal structure it remained a Stalinist organization, still externally associated with Russia. Wrong-footed by radical student and worker upsurges in the late sixties, completely at variance with its parliamentary outlook, it reacted by purging the liveliest dissidents in its own ranks—the gifted Manifesto group—and gradually vesting its hopes in a deal with Christian Democracy to run the country jointly.

But the Soviet connexion was not severed. Typically, the PCI's most right-wing leader, the formidable Giorgio Amendola, who openly urged his party to become an Italian edition of British

---

9. For the extent of this collaboration, estimated at times to cover up to 90 per cent of laws passed, see Frederic Spotts and Theodor Wieser, *Italy: A Difficult Democracy*, Cambridge 1986, pp. 113–15. Reversing the standard description of the political system of the period, Alessandro Pizzorno and others would later describe it as a *conventio ad includendum*.

Labour, was also the most firmly attached to it, regularly spending his holidays in Bulgaria. When the Christian Democrats rejected the 'Historic Compromise' offered by the Communists, preferring the Socialists as more pliable partners, the leadership of the PCI detached itself more openly from Moscow. But by the eighties, it was very late, and after years of caution the only way it could think of doing so was to swing to the opposite pole of Washington—its last real leader, Enrico Berlinguer, declaring that the party now felt safer under the protection of NATO. Its well-wishers in the media applauded warmly, but it did not gain greater electoral credibility. When the Berlin Wall came down in 1989, a new leadership hastily jettisoned the party's name, and soon began to repudiate most of its past. Conducted without much intelligence or dignity, the operation was of little benefit.[10] De Gaulle, who had been the foremost French imperialist of the forties, emerged unscathed from the collapse of France's colonial empire in the sixties, deftly negotiating Algerian independence in the higher interests of the nation. The re-labelled PDS, abandoning its heritage for a lukewarm ideological pottage, no longer seemed to represent any distinctive Italian tradition, and was not respected by the electors for its sacrifice. In the elections of 1992, on the eve of the national crisis, its vote sank to a record low—16.5 per cent, or less than half its score fifteen years earlier.

Still, by the end of 1993, the political landscape had been scythed so clean of rivals or opponents that the party seemed on the brink of power, if only by elimination of alternatives. A coalition built around the PDS had just elected the mayors of Rome, Naples, Venice, Trieste, Palermo. New electoral rules it had helped to design, in which most parliamentary seats would be decided on a first-past-the-post system, were in place. The Left looked poised for its first victory since the war. Instead came a thief in the night. In the last week of January 1994, Silvio Berlusconi, proprietor of Italy's largest media empire, announced that he would lead a Pole of Liberty to save the country from the clutches of the PDS-led cartel. Within days, he had launched a political movement, named after the chant of national football fans—'Forza Italia!'—and

---

10. For measured, but bitter reflections on the way the turn was conducted, see Alberto Asor Rosa, *La sinistra alla prova. Considerazioni sul ventennio 1976–1996*, Turin 1996, pp. 124–42. Even within the leadership of the subsequent PDS, there was considerable unhappiness at its abruptness: see Giuseppe Chiarante, *Da Togliatti a D'Alema. La tradizione dei comunisti italiani e le origini del PDS*, Rome-Bari 1996, pp. 210–16.

organized by the executives of his holding company Fininvest,[11] and had forged alliances with Bossi's Lega in the north and Fini's Alleanza Nazionale in the south, to form a common front against the danger of a Red government. Two months later the Pole of Liberty swept to power with a clear majority. The Italian Left had been swiftly and completely outflanked in the competition to be the standard-bearer of a Second Republic by a coalition of the Right.

Amidst the rhetoric on all sides of the need for a new political start, there was some ironic logic to this outcome. The victorious triumvirate of Berlusconi, Bossi and Fini were fresh forces on the Italian political scene, in a way that the PDS and its associates, most of them fixtures of the First Republic, were not. Economically, Berlusconi owed his economic fortune to favours received from the old order. Genealogically, Fini came out of the Fascist tradition loyal to the Republic of Salò. But as major political actors, they were unknown quantities and could project an aura of novelty more easily. As for Bossi, he was the great, genuine interloper of the late eighties and early nineties. Berlusconi's feat in uniting these disparate forces, virtually overnight, was remarkable. Bossi's Lega, based on local manufacturers and shopkeepers in the smaller towns of the north, was raucously hostile to Roman bureaucracy and southern clientelism—the electoral strongholds of Fini's Alleanza. The former standing for radical devolution and deregulation, the latter for social protection and statist centralization, each detested the other.

Forza Italia, the first party in the world to be mounted as if it were a company, would have been impossible without Berlusconi's personal wealth and control of television air-time. But the key to its political success lay in his ability to mediate these two natural enemies into flanking allies, at opposite ends of the peninsula where they did not compete with each other. The Left lost because it showed no comparable capacity for aggregation. The coalition of the Right took some 43 per cent of the vote; the Left 34 per cent; what remained of a Catholic Centre—closer in outlook to the latter than the former—16 per cent.[12] Under proportional

---

11. The best study of the way in which the party was constructed is Emanuela Poli's carefully documented *Forza Italia: Strutture, leadership e radicamento territoriale*, Bologna 2001.

12. For detailed analysis of the results, see Stefano Bartolini e Roberto D'Alimonte (eds) *Maggioritario, ma non troppo. Le elezioni politiche del 1994*, Bologna 1995, especially Luca Ricolfi, 'Il voto proporzionale: il nuovo spazio italiano', pp. 273–315.

representation, there would have been a Centre-Left government. But, under a first-past-the-post system, tempered only with a residual element of PR, the lack of an electoral bloc between Left and Centre ensured defeat for both. The PDS had been hoist by the petard of its support for Segni's referendum.

2

Robbed of victory at the last minute, the Left took defeat hard. How could the Italian people have voted for such a dubious figure as Berlusconi? Dismay was not confined to the PDS and its penumbra. It was shared by wide sectors of the Italian establishment: the industrialists Agnelli at the head of Fiat, and De Benedetti of Olivetti—each with influential mouthpieces in the press, *La Stampa* and *La Repubblica*; Scalfaro, the president of the Republic; technocrats in the central bank; many magistrates and most intellectuals; enlightened Catholic opinion. Abroad the *Financial Times* and *Economist* made their disapproval of Berlusconi known early on, and have not relented to this day. The Left thus had a broad sounding-board when, after the initial shock of its setback in March 1994, it started to launch bitter attacks on the legitimacy of Italy's new prime minister. Two fundamental, inter-related charges could be laid against him. Berlusconi's control of the bulk of private television, not to speak of his press and publishing outlets, was incompatible with high public office—leading not only to obvious conflicts of economic interest, but violating a political separation of powers essential to any democracy. Moreover, there was good reason to suspect that he had amassed the extraordinary wealth that allowed him to build up his media empire by every kind of corruption. His propaganda to the contrary, the country's new ruler embodied the worst of the old order: a combination of impropriety and illegality that would be a standing danger to any free society. Roughly speaking, this continues to be the prevailing foreign view of Berlusconi.

Of its factual validity, there can be little question. The son of a minor bank official, Berlusconi made his first fortune as a suburban developer in Milan, before moving into commercial television in the mid-seventies. The city was the political base of Craxi, the strongman of the PSI, who was determined to break the Christian Democrats' priority of power and prebends at the top levels of the Italian state. The DC had long relied on extensive corruption to finance its machine, but its political force rested on its mass base as a Catholic party, linked to the Church. The PSI, lacking any comparable roots in society, was forced to resort much more comprehensively to extortion to make up for its popular deficit—and by increasing competition for the spoils, sharply upped the stakes of corruption. Under Craxi, a generation of political streetfighters had clawed their way to control of the party, liquidating all its old leaders and traditions—where their opposite numbers in the PCI rose by obedience and conformity within a bureaucracy that put a premium on caution, evasion and anonymity. Adept at adroit manoeuvres and rapid tactical turns, the PSI grouping often showed a capacity for political initiative that left a lamely defensive PCI standing. But it was a machine that required constant financial lubrication. By the time Craxi achieved his goal of becoming premier, the speculative boom of the mid-eighties was fostering a climate of ostentatious consumption, in which earlier restraints on the political class were anyway dissolving. The PSI now set the tone for government, the DC following suit. In 1987 the 'super-bribe' dished out between the ruling parties for the creation of the petrochemical complex Enimont came to $100 million alone.[13]

Berlusconi's career tracked this structural change in the last decades of the First Republic. His first real-estate deals depended on planning permission from the PSI-dominated city council of Milan. When he moved into television, he already enjoyed a close friendship with Craxi, who in due course became godfather to one of his children and witness at his second wedding. As the PSI moved towards joint power with the DC in the political system, so Berlusconi's television empire grew. When Craxi became prime minister in 1983, Berlusconi already controlled—in defiance of the Constitutional Court—two nation-wide channels. Finally provoked into action by his acquisition of a third, praetors blacked out all three stations one night in October 1984. Craxi immediately issued a decree allowing them to return to the air, and when Parliament declared it unconstitutional, rammed through a law temporarily confirming it. Six years later, legislation specifically tailored to ratify Berlusconi's control of 80 per cent of the country's commercial television—the so-called Legge Mammi—was forced on Parliament by Andreotti, under PSI pressure, at the

---

13. Gianni Barbacetto, Peter Gomez, Marco Travaglio, *Mani pulite, la vera storia. Da Mario Chiesa a Silvio Berlusconi*, Rome 2002, supply a full account: pp. 153–68.

cost of a vote of confidence that split his own party.[14] Obviously, it was unlikely such extraordinary state favours were granted to a single businessman without any considerations in exchange.

Eventually Berlusconi's empire came to include not only his television stations and hugely profitable advertising agency, but some of Italy's most prestigious publishing houses, its most popular retail chain, and the country's most successful football club. But from the start there was another side to Berlusconi, closer in self-image to Reagan than Murdoch. As a young man, he had been a crooner on Adriatic cruise-ships, warbling into the microphone with Fedele Confalonieri—later his tough chief executive in Fininvest—tinkling on a white piano at his side. He wanted not just to accumulate companies and dominate markets, but to charm and impress audiences as well. Vain of his looks— there is an almost naive touch of the bounder, in the sleek face and over-large smile—Berlusconi has always sought glamour and popularity, attributes more of the stage than the board-room. The trade-mark of his conversation is the *barzelletta*—the kind of 'funny story' of which Reagan was a tireless fund, somewhat more off-colour. Such vulgarity is not the least of the reasons why Berlusconi is so detested by many Italians. But this is the culture of his television stations, with their high ratings, and was no handicap when he entered the political arena. The educated might grit their teeth as he became premier, but large numbers of voters were attuned to this style.

In office, however, Berlusconi's lack of any previous political experience soon told. Rather than displaying any resolute autocratic drive, he was curiously hesitant and indecisive, quickly backing down when his first initiatives—attempts at an amnesty for Tangentopoli offences, and scaling back of pensions—ran into strong opposition. But his tenure was in any case short-lived. In the months leading up to the election, the Milan magistrates had started public investigations against a whole series of leading Italian industrialists—among others, the bosses of Fiat, Olivetti and Ferruzzi—but had not yet reached Berlusconi. Once he was prime minister, however, they went into top gear. The Milan pool of magistrates, the posse of Mani Pulite, the 'Clean Hands' that had cracked open Tangentopoli, was not a neutral or apolitical force. Italian prosecutors and judges—it is a peculiarity of the

---

14. For this episode, see Giuseppe Fiori, *Il venditore. Storia di Silvio Berlusconi e della Fininvest*, Milan 1995, pp. 174–86.

system that there is no career division between them—are a highly politicized body, in which tacit party affiliations and overt professional factions are taken for granted. The Milan pool was no exception. It was by no means ideologically homogeneous (one prominent member was close to the PDS, another to Fini's AN[15]) but it was united in hostility to the venality of the First Republic. The dismay felt by the Left at the way Berlusconi had usurped the promise of a cleaner democracy was one thing. The anger of the prosecutors in Milan was a more serious matter. In late November a phone call from the head of the Milan pool tipped off Scalfaro, president of the Republic, that an *avviso di garanzia* was about to be issued against the prime minister on suspicion of corruption. Berlusconi was just preparing to leave for Naples, where he was due to preside over a World Ministerial Conference on Organized Transnational Crime. The next day, the humiliating notice was served on him in full session in Naples.

Amid the uproar that followed, a second trap was sprung. Since its defeat in the spring, the PDS had acquired a new leader. In his early forties, Massimo D'Alema was cast more in the mould of the PSI's Young Guard under Craxi, skilled in the arts of ambush and volte-face, than of his slow-moving forebears in the PCI. Behind the scenes he had been working on Bossi, feeding his jealousy of Berlusconi, who had upstaged his revolt against the old order, and the class dislike of the rough-neck for the magnate. By December D'Alema had achieved his aim. The Lega, which held a third of the seats in the ruling coalition, suddenly announced it was pulling out of the government. Berlusconi had lost his majority and was forced to resign. The first government of the Second Republic had lasted just nine months—below the average even for the First.

According to the doctrine that all major parties now swore by, political transparency required the calling of new elections. Since 1992 no vice of the First Republic had been more unanimously decried than the practice of constantly shifting alliances in Parliament to form new cabinets, without resort to the consent of the voters. In the Second Republic, so this doctrine went, voters who cast their ballots for a ticket could be assured that their intentions would not be turned upside down by opportunist switches of allegiance in the Chamber of Deputies. Bossi owed most of his parliamentary delegation to voters who had chosen the Pole of Liberty rather than the Lega, in constituencies where

---

15. Gerardo D'Ambrosio and Piercamillo Davigo, respectively.

Forza Italia had stood down for his party. When Bossi abruptly switched sides, Berlusconi thus had reason to feel betrayed, and to demand fresh elections to determine where the democratic will lay. Dissolution of the Chamber was the prerogative of the president, whose constitutional role was supposed to be *supra partes*. Scalfaro, however, fearing Berlusconi might be returned to office if voters were allowed to express their feelings too soon, spatchcocked together another cabinet under the banker Lamberto Dini. His more than willing collaborator was D'Alema, who—in keeping with the habits of the First Republic, and entirely contrary to the professed principles of the Second—orchestrated Centre-Left support for the government, in order to gain time and prepare conditions for a more favourable electoral result down the line. Bossi's truculently xenophobic party, the PDS leader explained, was really 'a rib of the Left'.[16] In due course Dini himself—another defector from Berlusconi's team—was transmuted into a pillar of the Centre-Left coalition.

In this paradoxical outcome of the first test of the new order lies a clue to the genetic code of Italian political culture. Critical to it is a notion that has no corresponding term in other European languages: *spregiudicato*. Literally, this just means 'unprejudiced'—a term of praise in Italy, as it is elsewhere. Such was the original eighteenth-century meaning of the word, when it had a strong Enlightenment connotation, which it preserves to this day. The first entry in any Italian dictionary defines it as: 'independence of mind, freedom from partiality or preconception'. In the course of the nineteenth century, however, the word came to acquire a second meaning, which the same dictionaries render as: 'lack of scruples, want of restraint, effrontery'. Today—this is the crucial point—the two meanings have virtually fused. For other Europeans, the 'unprejudiced' and the 'unscrupulous' are moral opposites. But for the Italians *spregiudicatezza* signifies, indivisibly, both admirable open-mindedness and regrettable ruthlessness. In theory, context indicates which applies. In practice, common usage erodes the distinction between them. The connotation of *spregiudicato* is now generally laudatory, even when its referent is the second rather than the first. The tacit, everyday force of the term becomes: aren't scruples merely prejudices? An occasional hint along these

---

16. *Una costola della sinistra*: phrase pronounced on 12 February 1995.

lines can be found in the libertine literature of pre-Revolutionary France, when characters were described as *sans préjugés*, signifying lack of sexual inhibition. In contemporary Italy, however, the elision is systematic and its principal employment has become the field of power.

Understood in this sense, *spregiudicatezza* appears a common denominator of the most variegated figures and forces of the Italian scene. It does not abolish the political differences between them, as if they were indistinguishable in cynicism, but rather bathes them in a general ether, in which the technicolour contrasts of moral battle, as perceived elsewhere, give way to a spectrum of glinting half-tones—*moiré* surfaces that continually alter according to the angle from which they are viewed. Examples could be multiplied at will: the eminent theorist of democracy, universally respected as a personification of ethical principle, with no qualms about tanks bombarding the Russian parliament; the incorruptible judge, nemesis of subversion, offering kind words for the youth gangs of the Republic of Salò when his party needs them; the rising politician, declaring Mussolini the greatest statesman of the twentieth century at one moment, certified as a guardian of the constitution by a Resistance veteran at the next; the fearless prosecutor, utmost foe of bribery, in receipt of limousine and free loan from business friends. The prevalence of double standards does not mean that the standards themselves are always the same; ideological and political contrasts are as real and robust as anywhere else. Nor does a ubiquitous pragmatism preclude genuine outbreaks of moralism. No national culture is ever entirely coherent, and it would be a mistake to dismiss the intensity of civic indignation at Tangentopoli, which formed the exceptional backdrop to these years. But coexisting with popular disgust at official venality, and underlying it as a bedrock default position, was the traditional lack of prejudice of the Italian public at large: what could be an apter description of voter indifference to Berlusconi's flagrant reputation from the start?

The Dini government brought further vivid illustration of the same sensibility. Most of its members were handpicked by Scalfaro, whose presidential role in the crisis was hailed by the Left as setting a high example of responsibility and probity for the Second Republic. In fact Scalfaro was a not untypical Christian Democrat of the old order, who had adorned some of the governments most execrated by the advocates of system change. In those days, he was noted for an incident in which, once sitting in a restaurant, he had risen to his feet and slapped an unknown woman at the next table, for a frock he judged too *decolleté*. For four years, however, he had served in the shadows as Craxi's minister of the interior. Amidst the cascade of scandals that tumbled out in 1992–3, functionaries of SISDE—the secret service that is the Italian equivalent of MI5—reported that they had been in the practice of passing a monthly envelope stuffed with 100 million lire, no questions asked, to successive heads of the Ministry. Four ministers were named. The Roman prosecutors opened investigations into two of them, Antonio Gava and Vincenzo Scotti, both already politically dead in the water, and cleared the third, Nicola Mancino, by coincidence the current incumbent.

The fourth was Scalfaro, now president. Not only did the prosecutors refuse to consider any evidence against him, but they charged the witnesses with 'subversion' for their deposition— in the memorable formula of Chief Prosecutor Vittorio Mele, 'independently of whether what they say is true or not'. Not an eyebrow was raised on the Left. A commission of enquiry into the whole affair, chaired by a Sicilian judge, in due course declared Scalfaro blameless. When the Dini government was formed, this judge—Filippo Mancuso—was handsomely rewarded with the Ministry of Justice. Soon, however, frictions arose over his handling of the magistrates in Milan, widely judged vexatious. Scalfaro was now also put out by his conduct, and the Centre-Left moved a no-confidence vote against him in Parliament. When the day came for the motion in the Senate—the debate was televised—the gravel-voiced Mancuso mounted the tribune, and announced to a stunned nation that he had altered his report on the SISDE slush-funds at the instigation of Scalfaro, acting through his palace familiar Gifuni. Uproar followed. The Centre-Left, beside itself with indignation at this aspersion, voted Mancuso out of office and into oblivion.[17] A president who had spared the country a dangerous ordeal at the polls was above suspicion: only the prejudiced could associate him with malversation.

In the short-run, such acrobatics were not misjudged. Scalfaro's delaying tactics had given the Centre-Left a respite, and D'Alema

---

17. For this sequence, see 'Soldi SISDE. Su Scalfaro vince Mele', *Corriere della Sera*, 12 November 1993; Riccardi Scarpa, *Scalfaro*, Rome 1999, pp. 71–7; Barbacetto et al, *Mani pulite*, pp. 105–6, 393–5.

made good use of it. When elections were held in the spring of 1996, the PDS had found a credible candidate to put up against Berlusconi in the person of Romano Prodi—an economist of Catholic background generally respected for his management of the state holding company IRI—and had cemented a broad *Ulivo* (Olive Tree) coalition behind him. Berlusconi, on the other hand, had been unable to repair his alliance with the Lega, which fought the election alone. Total votes cast showed an actual increase in support for the Centre-Right, but since it was now divided and the Centre-Left united, the result was a narrow parliamentary majority for an Olive Tree government.[18] Prodi was installed as premier, with a PDS vice-premier. The promise of the winning coalition was a coherent modernization of Italian public life, eliminating national anomalies and bringing the country fully up to Western standards. Now, surely, the hour of the Second Republic had struck.

3

Confronting the victors lay a complex agenda. The collapse of the First Republic had been triggered by corruption and criminality. But behind these long-standing ills, two other pressures had played a critical background role. The first was the Treaty of Maastricht, signed in 1992, setting out the 'convergence criteria' for entry into European monetary union. These required a drastic compression of Italy's public debt and budgetary deficit, which for years had been running at levels far above those of the other major EU economies. Abroad it was widely doubted whether Italy was capable of such belt-tightening. The second urgency came from northern regionalism. The revolt of the Lega threatened to undermine the unity of the country, if no federal solution was forthcoming. Besides these supra- and sub-national forcing-houses of change, there was the unfinished work left by the national crisis of 1992–3 itself. By mid-decade the militarist turn of the Mafia in Sicily had been crushed, and excesses of political corruption curbed. But no stable legal order had been established: justice remained a word, not a system. Deficiencies of taxation, administration

---

18. For the results, see Paolo Natale, 'Mutamento e stabilità nel voto degli italiani', in Roberto d'Alimonte and Stefano Bartolino (eds), *Maggibritario per caso*, Bologna 1997, pp. 208ff.

and education were widely advertised. Last but not least, the new electoral system had proved unsatisfactory to nearly everyone. Neither fish nor fowl, instead of reducing the number of parties in Parliament, as intended, it had multiplied them. To strengthen the executive, many argued, it would be necessary to rewrite the Constitution.

In this forest of tasks, Prodi was in no doubt which had priority. By training and temperament, his principal concerns were economic. As premier, his over-riding objective was to ensure Italy's compliance with the Maastricht criteria for entry into the single currency in 1998. Normalcy, in this version, was conceived as full integration—without any of the surreptitious derogations and defaults of the past—into a liberalized European economy. That meant tight budgetary discipline to control inflation, reduce the deficit and moderate the volume of public debt. In short, an orthodox macro-economic framework, mitigated where possible— Prodi was committed to this—by traditional social concerns.

In its pursuit of this goal, the Centre-Left government was consistent and effective. To the uneasy surprise of German bankers, the Maastricht targets were met on schedule, Italy entered monetary union, and has enjoyed lower interest payments on its public debt ever since. This strenuous effort was accompanied, not by any sweeping tax reform—Italy is still a country where the state extracts proportionately more from workers than from restaurateurs or lawyers—but at least more effective, and somewhat less inequitable, fiscal catchment. The cost of convergence was steep: the slowest growth of any major industrial society in the nineties, and virtually no reduction in very high levels of youth and regional unemployment—over 20 per cent in the south. Still, there is no question that entry into European monetary union was the major achievement of the Ulivo experience. It was also, however, the one most continuous with the directives of the past. Maastricht was signed, indeed partly shaped, by Andreotti, and the most drastic fiscal squeeze to implement the Treaty was the work of Giuliano Amato, a lieutenant of Craxi in the last days of the First Republic. In this sense Prodi acted as competent executor of a legacy handed down by the DC and PSI of old, on which financial and industrial elites had always been united.

But, of course, monetary integration was not the main plank of the modernization promised by the slogan of the Second

Republic. That was to be constitutional, electoral and administrative reform, to give Italy the kind of honest and efficient government its neighbours enjoyed. Here it was not Prodi, but D'Alema and the PDS who were to the forefront from the start. In early 1997 D'Alema pushed through the creation of a bicameral Commission to revise the constitution, with himself as chairman. Since constitutional changes required a two-thirds majority in Parliament, hence some kind of deal with the opposition, the effect of the *Bicamerale* was to give him a public arena for tractations with Berlusconi and Fini, inevitably at Prodi's expense as head of government. In the Commission D'Alema, with the aim of drawing them into a pact to marginalize smaller parties in the political system, under a stronger—if necessary, semi-presidential—executive, went out of his way to express respect for both leaders, hitherto objects of the fiercest obloquy on the Left. Soon all three were exchanging mutual compliments, as prospective partners in the task of bringing responsibility and clarity of government to Italy. The effect was to confer a quite new level of political legitimation on Berlusconi.

At this many ordinary members of the PDS itself, not to speak of other supporters of the Ulivo government, had to swallow hard. The charges that had helped bring Berlusconi down three years earlier had been by the standards of Tangentopoli relatively small beer: pay-offs to the Guardia di Finanza, tax police not above suspicion of their own shake-downs. By now Berlusconi had been convicted in the lower courts both on this count and a further charge of falsifying company accounts, and the Milan pool was widening its trawl through his labyrinth of holding companies. For lay opinion, the various cases against him still seemed somewhat technical. But in early 1996, bugs planted under the ashtrays of a bar led to the arrest of a leading Roman judge, Renato Squillante—the name means 'trilling'— and two colleagues, on charges of delivering a favourable verdict to the tune of 678 billion lire, in a bankruptcy suit brought by the Rovelli family, in exchange for bribes of more than 60 billion lire.[19]

The trail that led to them had started from a pretty blonde antique-dealer in Milan, Stefania Ariosto, an intimate of Berlusconi's milieu.

---

19. For coverage of the ensuing labyrinth, Barbacetto et al, *Mani Pulite*, pp. 419–74.

When he went into politics, Berlusconi took with him his two most prominent legal advisers, Vittorio Dotti and Cesare Previti. One was from Milan and the other from Rome, and they hated each other. Ariosto had been the mistress of Dotti, and possibly of Previti too. Questioned by the pool in Milan, she reported seeing Previti hand over large sums in cash to Squillante on a festive boat-trip along the Tiber, and on other occasions. In due course Swiss bank accounts confirmed a pattern of transfers between Previti, two colleagues and the Roman judges that matched exactly the bribe with which they were charged. Further investigations indicated that Berlusconi himself had paid nearly half a million dollars to Squillante, through Previti, for a favourable ruling in his take-over battle for the SME food and catering conglomerate. The nature of these allegations—the systematic purchase of senior judges, in the capital itself—exceeded any previous scandals in the downfall of the First Republic, most of them concerned with corruption in the executive, not at the heart of the judiciary itself.

Such was the background that Italians, reading in their newspapers the cordial debates in the Bicamerale, were invited to forget. In exchange for a constitutional deal, Berlusconi wanted curbs on the magistrates, which D'Alema was ready to consider. But the complicated manoeuvres of the PDS in the Bicamerale eventually foundered on the hostility of the Lega—which saw that it would be cut out of the deal—and the calculations of Berlusconi's shrewder advisers, content with the degree of absolution he had already gained, and disinclined to let D'Alema claim laurels as the architect of a new constitutional settlement. In the summer of 1998, after many a draft scheme had been swapped back and forth, the opposition abruptly announced no dice.

This was a serious blow to the PDS, but a few months later D'Alema recouped. From the start, the government had depended on the support in Parliament of one force that did not belong to the coalition, the fraction of the PCI that had rejected the terms of its mutation in 1989, and as *Rifondazione Comunista* (RC) had since taking root as a party to the left of the PDS. That autumn, when Prodi's budget made too few concessions to keep Rifondazione in line, D'Alema took the opportunity to topple him. This was done with a silken touch—just enough informal dangling of hopes to Rifondazione for a more left-wing government under himself, while he lingered far from the scene in South America, and fortuitous failure to ensure that every available deputy in the coalition was present for the motion of confidence when he got back. Prodi fell one vote short in the Chamber, and was not deceived. D'Alema had shown himself master of the skill Stendhal rightly saw as peculiarly Italian: the art of politics as a virtuoso exercise of subjective will and intelligence, without—an effect of the long absence of national unity—any corresponding sense of the state as an objective structure of power and obligation. This is the combination already visible in Machiavelli, whose inverse could be found in the imperial culture of Spain, which cut off his dreams. After a decent interval of days, the identity of the new prime minister was no surprise.

There was a cost to this elegant operation. When Prodi's resentment threatened to become dangerous, it was deftly neutralized by exporting him to Brussels as president of the EU Commission, where he was soon out of his depth. But a spectacle of intrigue and division, recalling only too vividly the mores of the First Republic, had been given to the public, damaging the credibility of the Ulivo as a renovating force. Still, for the PDS the parliamentary coup was a necessary step towards Italian normalcy in a sense that was, in its view, more important. The heirs of the PCI were the centrepiece of the ruling coalition—in fact, the only substantial party organization in it—and freely referred to as the 'principal share-holder' in the government. Yet an anachronistic prejudice still prevented them from converting effective into symbolic power, as would have occurred in any other European country, so they argued. Determined to break this taboo, D'Alema installed himself in the Palazzo Chigi.

What were the fruits of this closing of the gap between the *pays réel* and the *pays légal* in the Centre-Left? The top priority of the PDS had all along been to change the electoral system. Constitutional reform, much bruited, was always a means to this rather than an end in its own right—a bargaining chip in negotiations with the Right, which had initially wanted a strong presidential system. But the former Communists were not alone in feeling that a drastic electoral reform, abolishing the hated 'Mattarellum', or hybrid system concocted in the throes of crisis five years earlier, was the key to founding a stable Second Republic.[20] Virtually the entire press clamoured for one, while Segni and Pannella— the authors of the original referendum abrogating proportional

---

20. Named after its author, the DC deputy Sergio Mattarella. For its emergence, see Paolo Pombeni, 'La rappresentanza politica' in Raffaele Romanelli, *Storia dello Stato italiano dall'Unità a oggi*, Rome 1995, pp. 120–24.

representation—were agitating for a second referendum to finish the job. Different foreign models, most of them Anglo-American in inspiration, were advocated by the interested parties. Far the most trenchant and lucid intervention in these debates came from Giovanni Sartori, the world's leading authority on comparative electoral systems, occupying a chair at Columbia and columns in the *Corriere della Sera*, who in a series of coruscating polemics championed the French model of a directly elected presidency and two-round majority voting.[21]

The PDS was not enamoured of a French-style presidency, fearing that its personalization of power would give an advantage to Berlusconi or Fini. But it urgently wanted the *double tour*. In fact, this had been its over-riding strategic priority from the start. The reason was always clear. Under the existing rules, the party was stuck at around 20 per cent of the electorate—the largest party in the mosaic of the Centre-Left, but still a smallish one by European standards. Unable to advance further in straightforward electoral competition, it needed a restriction of the range of voter choice to eliminate its rivals to the left, and potentially somewhat to the right of it. Above all, the PDS wanted to clear the decks of any challenge from Rifondazione, as a force capable of attracting disaffected voters from its own ranks, and subjecting a Centre-Left government to unwelcome pressure from without. This was an objective, however, that had to remain tacit. Sartori, more candidly and consistently, argued that the *double tour* was vital to wipe out both the Lega and Rifondazione, as twin menaces to the emergence of a stable, non-ideological order in which all policies converged towards the liberal centre.

A huge amount of energy was invested by D'Alema and his party in trying, by one means or another, to force this change through, in the hope that Berlusconi would find it to his advantage too. But, though tempted for a time, Berlusconi soon realized that a much quicker and surer route back to power lay in renewing his alliance with Bossi, who was implacably hostile to the *double tour*. The eventual result of five years of unremitting, and increasingly

---

21. See *Come sbagliare le riforme*, Bologna 1996, and *Una occasione mancata?*, Rome–Bari 1998. Denouncing the 'Italian cunning' that had 'proportionalized' the first-past-the-post component of the Mattarellum, Sartori did not want a pure French system, fearing that if only two candidates were allowed into the second round of voting, in Italian conditions this would lead to extreme parties on the flanks of each of these cutting deals in the first round to retain their leverage, while eliminating options in the centre, for which at least three candidates were needed: *Come sbagliare*, pp. 71, 51.

desperate, efforts by the PDS to change the rules of the political game was little short of farce. After strenuous demands for the *double tour*, when D'Alema fell from office in the spring of 2000 with only a year to go before new elections, the PDS suddenly backed the Segni–Pannella referendum for a complete first-past-the-post system (which it had always hitherto rejected) and when that failed, unsuccessfully converted to a full proportional system along German lines (anathema to it for a decade) purely as a means of staving off looming defeat in the upcoming polls. A more futile and ignominious pilgrimage of opportunism would be difficult to imagine. As for the ledger of constitutional reform, it remains bare.

Far more pressing, in reality, was the need for reform of Italian justice, with its mixture of a Fascist-derived legal code, arbitrary emergency powers, and chaotic procedural and carceral conditions. Here, indeed, has long been a panorama without equivalent elsewhere in Western Europe. There is no *habeas corpus* in Italy, where anyone can be clapped into jail without charges for over three years, under the system of *custodia cautelare*—'preventive detention'—that is responsible for locking up more than half the country's prison population. Not only can witnesses be guaranteed immunity from prosecution, under the rules of *pentitismo*, but they can be paid for suitable testimony by the state, without even having to appear in court, or any record being visible of what they receive for their evidence—perhaps from the manila envelopes that, according to SISDE operatives, were pocketed every month by Scalfaro and his peers. In the magistracy, as noted, there is no separation of careers, and little of functions, between prosecutors and judges: in Italian parlance, those who lay charges are simply identified with those who are supposed to weigh the evidence for them, as *giudici*. In the prisons themselves, some fifty thousand inmates are jammed into cells built for half that number. The trial system has three stages, whose average length runs for ten years, and the backlog of cases in the courts is now more than three million.[22] In this jungle, inefficiency mitigates brutality, yet also compounds it.

Such was the system suddenly mobilized by crusading magistrates against political corruption in the north and the Mafia

---

22. See, *inter alia*, Matt Frei, *Getting the Boot: Italy's Unfinished Revolution*, New York 1995, p. 73.

in the south. The personal courage and energy with which the pools in Milan and Palermo threw themselves at these evils had no precedent in the recent history of Italian administration. In Sicily, investigators risked their lives daily. But they too were the products of a culture that discounted scruples. *Custodia cautelare* was used as an instrument of intimidation. Illegal leaks of impending notices of investigation were regularly employed to bring down targeted office-holders. Tainted evidence was mustered without qualms—in the case against Andreotti, a key witness for the state was a thug who inconveniently committed another murder while on the public payroll for his deposition. Any idea of separating the careers of prosecutor and judge was attacked with ferocity. The rationalization of these practices was always the same. Italy was in a state of emergency; justice could not afford to be over-nice about individual rights. But, of course, they were not just responses to an emergency, but also perpetuated it. A widespread contempt for law is not to be cured by bending its principles. 'We will turn Italy inside out like a sock',[23] Piercamillo Davigo, the clearest mind of the Milan pool, is said to have declared, as if the country were a discardable item from the laundry basket.

At the height of the prestige of Mani Pulite in the first half of the nineties, when its star prosecutor Antonio Di Pietro topped all media ratings, few doubts were voiced about the work of the magistrates on the Left. D'Alema himself was never caught up in this uncritical acclaim. But here too, short-term tactical calculations over-rode any coherent set of principles. For the most part, conscious of the popularity of the magistrates, the PDS sought to capitalize on their role. D'Alema eventually recruited Di Pietro as a senator in a safe PDS seat in 1997, even while upholding Berlusconi's credentials as a national leader, regardless of the legal charges against him. Whatever private misgivings may have been felt in the upper reaches of the party, there was no public criticism of the worst features of Italian justice—preventive detention, mercenary testimony, fusion of prosecutors and judges. The field was thus left open for the Right to make a self-interested case for more defensible alternatives, with a cynicism that only discredited them. In this field of force, no structural reforms of any moment were possible.[24] At

---

23. *Rivoltare l'Italia come un calzino*: Davigo would later claim that it was not he who had used the phrase, but Giuliano Ferrara, at that time minister of justice.

24. For a balanced assessment of the Italian judicial system, see David Nelken,

the end of five years of Ulivo government, the magistrates had over-reached themselves in pursuit of Andreotti on too gothic charges of which he was acquitted, yet failed to clinch far more plausible accusations against Berlusconi. Meanwhile Italy was treated to the tragic spectacle of the head of the Milan pool applauding Adriano Sofri's imprisonment, on the evidence of a *pentitismo* that the Left defending him could never bring itself to disavow.[25] Conditions in the prison system remained as disastrous as ever.

Elsewhere the Centre-Left's performance was more respectable, if nowhere very striking. Administrative regulations were to some extent simplified—no minor matter for the citizen, in a country with over fifty thousand laws where Germany has about five thousand—and fiscal resources devolved to the regions. There was a limited reform of the university system, where traditionally three-quarters of students never complete their degree; but without more funding, substantial progress remains unlikely. On the other hand, the chance of improving the quality of the Italian media was thrown away, when the PDS, in its pursuit of a deal with the heads of Mediaset in the Bicamerale, chose to reject the term-limits independently set by the constitutional court on Berlusconi's television franchise. In foreign policy, D'Alema made the country the run-way for NATO bombing of Yugoslavia, a step further than Christian Democracy ever went in bending to the will of the United States, and in general the Centre-Left showed less independence of Washington—in the Middle East as well as the Balkans—than the regimes of Andreotti or Craxi had done before them.

Little in this record was calculated to inspire enthusiasm among the electors of the Ulivo coalition, let alone those who had voted against it. In the spring of 2000, regional elections handed the Centre-Left a heavy defeat. With a national reckoning only a year away, D'Alema could see the writing on the wall and quickly stepped down, to avoid being tarred with impending defeat. The most astute Italian politician of his cohort, he once tersely

---

'A legal revolution? The judges and *Tangentopoli*' in Stephen Gundle and Simon Parker (eds), *The New Italian Republic: From the fall of the Berlin Wall to Berlusconi*, London 1996, pp. 191–205.

25. On 14 October 1997, Francesco Saverio Borrelli expressed his 'complete agreement' with the verdicts condemning Sofri. For these, see Carlo Ginzburg, *The Judge and the Historian: Marginal Notes on a Late-Twentieth-Century Miscarriage of Justice*, London 2002.

remarked after meeting Blair: '*manca di spessore*', 'A bit thin'. But if he noticed the beam—the disc-jockey's vacant smirk—in the eye of the other, he could not see the mote in his own. His culture was no doubt somewhat more solid, but it was not enough. Excess of tactical guile, shortage of ideal reflection: the eventual upshot was a self-destructive reduction, to standard neo-liberal clichés of even the poor remains of 'European social democracy', to which the PDS nominally aspired. The party would have done better to remain loyal to Prodi, who was respected by the public, and accept the rules on which he was elected. Voters had looked to the Ulivo for steady government, which D'Alema's ambitions had undermined. As it was, the experience of the Centre-Left came full circle, when its final premier became the initial re-tread of the decade, Craxi's former counsellor Amato.[26] Understandably, it did not care to present him as its candidate to fight the Centre-Right a year later.

4

In these conditions, Berlusconi's victory in May 2001—with Bossi securing his flank once more in the north, and Fini in the south—was a foregone conclusion. The actual shift in votes, as in the previous election, was small. The Centre-Right, which already had a majority of voter preferences in 1996, this time converted it into a parliamentary landslide. Berlusconi had retained his following among housewives, conservative Catholics, small entrepreneurs, the elderly and the thirty-year olds. But now the renamed 'House of Liberties' got more votes than the Centre-Left from the bulk of the working class in the private sector, as well. The key to the scale of its victory lay in the damning verdict of the electorate on the record of the Centre-Left in power—large numbers of those who actually voted for the Ulivo confessing they had more confidence in the capacity of the Centre-Right to solve the various problems facing the country.[27] In the two epicentres of the crisis of the First Republic, Lombardy and Sicily, Berlusconi scored the cleanest sweeps of all.

---

26. In reality, more than just an advisor, Amato was the 'key organizer' of successive governments under Craxi, who was not much interested in the detail of policies: see David Hine, *Governing Italy*, Oxford 1993, pp. 206, 209.

27. ITANES, *Perché ha vinto il centro-destra*, Bologna 2001, pp. 19, 30, 37, 52, 62–5, 162–3.

Retrospectively, the Centre-Left is now faced with the bill for its manoeuvres to abort Berlusconi's administration in 1994. Then his parliamentary majority was far smaller; his political experience shorter; his financial empire weaker; his legitimacy more fragile. Thinking to gain time for itself by keeping him out of power, the Centre-Left merely allowed him to become better prepared for exercising it. For this time, Berlusconi's position is much stronger. Forza Italia is no longer a shell, but an effective party, capable of playing something closer to the role of Christian Democracy of old. Fininvest has recovered from its difficulties. His allies are unlikely soon to challenge him. His opponents have conceded his status as a national leader. In these conditions, fears can be heard that Italian democracy is at risk, should Berlusconi and his unsavoury outriders succeed in consolidating their grip on the country. Could Italy be staring at the prospect of a creeping authoritarianism, once again organized around the cult of a charismatic leader, but this time based on an unprecedented control of the media—now public as well as private television—rather than squads and castor-oil?

Two structural realities tell against the idea. Fascism rose to power as a response to the threat of mass insurgency against the established order from below—the danger that the 'revolution against capital' Gramsci had hailed in Russia mght spread to Italy. Today there is no such ferment in the lower depths. The working class is atomized, there are no factory councils, the PCI has vanished, radical impulses among students and youth have waned. Capitalism in Italy, as elsewhere, has never looked safer. Historically, the second condition of Fascist success was nationalist self-assertion, the promise of an expansionist state capable of attacking neighbours and seizing territory by military force. That too has passed. The days of the autarkic state are gone. Italy is closely enmeshed in the European Union, its economy, military and diplomacy all subject to supranational controls that leave little leeway for independent policy of any kind. The ideological and legal framework of the EU rules out any break with a standard liberal-democratic regime. There is neither need, nor chance, of Berlusconi becoming an updated version of Mussolini.

Programmatically, in fact, not a great deal separated Centre-Right from Centre-Left in the electoral contest last year. The familiar agenda of governments throughout the Atlantic world— privatization of remaining state assets, deregulation of the labour market, scaling back of public pensions, lowering of tax rates—

belongs to the repertoire of both. How far the House of Liberties in practice moves beyond its predecessor remains to be seen. Private education and health care will be given a longer leash. Berlusconi has also promised tougher measures against immigrants, whose fate—this is the one terrain on which a knuckle-duster Right has space in Europe—will certainly get worse. But in general socio-economic direction, far from representing any radical form of reaction, Berlusconi's regime is already suspect of being too moderate—that is, insufficiently committed to the market—in the judgement of the business press, distrustful of his pledges to launch a major programme of public works and steer investment to create a million and a half new jobs. In the EU, the new government has been less automatically compliant with establishment opinion than its predecessor, earning furrowed brows in Brussels and laments from the opposition in Rome that it is jeopardizing Italy's reputation abroad. But its self-assertion has so far been essentially gestural, amounting to little more than dropping the dreary functionary from the WTO first imposed on it as foreign minister, and quarrelling over the location of a branch office of the EU's alimentary bureaucracy. On issues of any real significance, there is unlikely to be any serious departure from today's official European consensus.

All this might suggest that the upshot of Berlusconi's government will be as unexceptional as that of its closest ally in Europe, the Centre-Right in Spain. Aznar's party, after all, is the direct descendant of a fascist regime that lasted twice as long as the Italian, and killed many more of its citizens; yet today it is a veritable model of political propriety, indeed a favourite interlocutor of emissaries of the Third Way from London. What is to stop Forza Italia from emulating the Partido Popular, and becoming yet another indistinguishably respectable member of the comity of democratic parties? Not much, it would seem. Yet there remains a fly in the ointment. Since taking office, one objective alone has been pursued with real energy by Berlusconi: to change the laws that still might bring him to book in the courts. The speed and determination with which his government has acted here—ramming through measures designed to make evidence against him found in Switzerland unavailable for adjudication in Italy, and attempting to set the Ariosto case back to zero, so as to defer a verdict till after the statute of limitations—is a measure of its fear that he could still be struck a mortal blow by the magistrates. Manipulating accounts and evading taxes may attract little censure in Italy. A conviction for corrupting judges on a grand scale would be more difficult to shrug off. Given the record of Italian justice to date, few would bet on one. But a surprise cannot be excluded.

Should that come, it would be a test of what has happened to the political culture of the country in the past decade. Ideological demobilization, long called for by proponents of 'normal' Italy, has been among the fruits of the Centre-Left experience. About a quarter of the electorate now abstains from expressing any preference at the polls. But if the US is taken as a model of normalcy, only half the population should vote anyway—the surest sign of popular contentment with society as it is. Gramsci thought Italy was the land of 'passive revolution'. Maybe this will prove the right sort of oxymoron for the birth of the Second Republic. Its arrival has not yielded a new constitution; rationalized the party system; modernized justice; or overhauled the bureaucracy, in any of the ways its advocates hoped it would. But—so they could equally contend—corruption has dropped from its intolerable peak in the eighties back to the manageable levels of the fifties and sixties; the Mafia has retreated, after defeat on the battlefield, to more traditional and inconspicuous forms of activity; at least Parliament is now divided along conventional lines between government and opposition; no deep disagreements set the policies of the principal parties apart; public life is increasingly drained of passion. Isn't this just the passive renovation the country needs?

Judged against these standards, the First Republic, however decomposed it became towards the end, appears in a better light. At its height it included a genuine pluralism of political opinion and expression, lively participation in mass organizations and civic life, an intricate system of informal negotiations, a robust high culture, and the most impressive series of social movements that any European country of that period could boast.[28] Intellectual conflict and moral tension produced leaders of another stature. In that respect, as well as others, there has been a miniaturization

---

28. The calmest and best retrospect of the political system created by the First Republic has been offered by Mauro Calise, *Dopo la partitocrazia*, Turin 1994. He noted that 'the Italian parliament was the only assembly among Atlantic democracies to resist the general decline of the legislature to the profit of the executive in the past half century', and foresaw much of degradation of political life under the Second Republic: pp. 60ff.

since. Italy needs honest administration, decent public services and accountable government, not to speak of jobs for its unemployed, which the old order failed to provide. But to create these, destruction of what it did achieve was not required.

Even today, not every trace of this better past has disappeared. Impulses of rebellion against the worst aspects of the new order persist. In the autumn of 1994, the trade-union movement was still capable of the largest mobilization in the post-war history of the country, putting a million people into the squares of Rome to block Berlusconi's first attempt at pension reform. In May 2001, the vacuous rituals of the G-7 were finally shattered by multitudes of young protesters in the streets of Genoa. In Italy alone there was a march of some 300,000—from Perugia to Assisi—against the war in Afghanistan. Where French Communists and German Greens have been painlessly annexed as fig leaves or sandwich-boards of the status quo, Rifondazione has remained resistant to either sectarian closure or absorption. Of the three European dailies born out of the radical movements of '68, *Libération* in Paris and *Tageszeitung* in Berlin are demoralized parodies of their original purpose; *Il Manifesto*, flanked by its monthly, is unswayed. To date the two leading contenders for a vision of globalization from the Left both come from Italy, via America: *Empire* and *Chaos and Governance in the Modern World System*—originators, Antonio Negri and Giovanni Arrighi.[29]

The hope of the Second Republic has been to root all this out. But to standardize a society at the expense of its past always risks being a violence in vain. Where, after all, does the idea of 'normalization' come from? The term was coined by Brezhnev for the Warsaw Pact invasion of Czechoslovakia in 1968, designed to force it back into conformity with the Soviet bloc. We know how that ended. Contemporary efforts to normalize Italy have sought to reshape the country in the image either of the United States, or of the Europe now moving towards it. The pressures behind this process are incomparably greater. But its results may not be quite what its proponents had in mind. Rather than lagging, it might be wondered whether Italy could be leading the march towards a common future. In the world of Enron and Elf, Mandelson and Strauss-Kahn, Hinduja and Gates, what could finally be more logical than Berlusconi? Perhaps, like others before them, the travellers to normality have arrived without noticing it.

---

29. Respectively, 2000 and 1999.

II · 2008

Today the Second Republic, as it has come be called, is fifteen years old, equivalent to the span of time stretching from Liberation to the arrival of the Centre-Left in the First Republic. An era has elapsed. What is there to show for it? For its promoters, commanding an overwhelming consensus in not only the media but public opinion in the early nineties, Italy required a comprehensive political reconstruction, to give the country government worthy of a contemporary Western society. Probity, stability, bi-polarity were the watchwords. Public life was to be cleansed of the corruptions of the old order. Cabinets were not to fall every few months. Alternation of two moderate parties—or at worst, coalitions—in office, one inclining to the right and the other to the left, would be the norm. Once the political system was overhauled along these lines, the reforms needed to modernize Italian society, bringing it up to standards taken for granted elsewhere in the Atlantic community, could at long last be enacted.

By the turn of the century, the balance-sheet of the new Republic was, for its champions, a mixed one—frustrating in many ways, but not definitively disappointing. On the positive side, the political landscape had been transformed, with the extinction of all the parties that had populated the First Republic, and the distribution of their successors into two competing blocs see-sawing in office. A great economic change had followed with Italy's entry into the Eurozone, barring henceforward the country's traditional primrose path of devaluation, inflation and mounting public debt. On the negative side, two developments were disturbing. The first, decried across the board by polite opinion, was the failure of the electoral reform of 1993 to purge the political system of lesser parties, of more radical persuasion, on the flanks of the competing coalitions now ranged against each other, and capable of extracting concessions from these in return for their support. The work of the new Republic would not be complete until such blackmail—the term invariably used—was eliminated.

The second cause for concern was, in the nature of things, less universally pressed. But the prominence of Berlusconi, as the most spectacular newcomer on the political scene, aroused anxieties that were not confined to those most averse to him. Not only was he deeply implicated in the corruption of the last phase of the First

Republic, but as a media magnate turned politician he embodied a conflict of interests felt to be intolerable in other democracies, controlling at once a private empire and public power, each at the service of the other. Fears were repeatedly expressed that here could be the makings of an authoritarian system of rule distinct from, but genetically related to, the nation's previous experience of plebiscitary power. Still, in the opening years of the Second Republic, these remained more notional than actual, since between 1994 and 2001 Berlusconi was only in office for seven months.

When, in the spring of 2001, he finally won a full term of office, warnings were widespread on the left of the danger not only of a semi-dictatorial development, but of a harsh regime of social reaction, an Italian version of the radical right. The reality, however, proved otherwise. The social and economic record of the Berlusconi government was anodyne. There was no significant attack on the welfare state. Social expenditure was not cut, pensions were raised, and employment increased.[30] Measures to loosen the labour market and up the legal retirement age remained gingerly, and tax cuts less significant than in Social Democratic Germany. Privatizations, abundant under the Centre-Left coalition of 1996 to 2001, when Italy held the European record for selling off public assets, were minimal. The main advantage of the regime for the rich lay in the amnesties it granted for the illegal stacking of wealth abroad, and flouting of building controls at home. Ostensibly tougher legislation on immigration was passed, but to little practical effect. Externally, Berlusconi joined Blair and Aznar in sending troops to Iraq, a contribution to the American occupation that the Centre-Left did not oppose. A package of constitutional reforms giving a more federal shape to the state, with greater powers for the regions—the top priority for the Northern League,

---

30. For an overall judgment of the record, in these respects, of Berlusconi's coalition in power, see Luca Ricolfi, *Dossier Italia. A che punto è il 'Contratto con gli italiani'*, Bologna 2005, pp. 101–40, and *Tempo Scaduto. Il 'Contratto con gli italiani' alla prova dei fatti*, Bologna 2006, pp. 103–17. On premises otherwise completely uncritical of the political and ideological universe of the Italian establishment—no questions asked of foreign policy or justice—Ricolfi's writing on economic and social issues has consistently shown an independence of mind rare in either academic or journalistic output of recent years: at once perfectly loyal to what might be called *la pensée unique à l'italienne* (roughly, 'modernization' at all costs), yet in its conclusions discomforting equally to Centre-Right and Centre-Left. The epigraph to *Tempo scaduto* comes from Pasolini: 'The intellectual courage to tell the truth and the practice of politics are two things irreconcilable in Italy'.

headed by Umberto Bossi—was pushed through Parliament, but came to nothing in a subsequent referendum. No great drive or application was displayed by Berlusconi in any of this.

The principal energies of his government lay, starkly, elsewhere. Berlusconi's over-riding concern was to protect himself from prosecution, amid the thicket of cases pending against him for different kinds of corruption. At top speed, three successive laws were rammed through Parliament: to block evidence of illegal transactions abroad, to decriminalize falsification of accounts, and to enable defendants in a trial to change their judges by shifting the case to another jurisdiction. When the first and third of these were voided as unconstitutional by the courts, Berlusconi reacted with a fourth, more drastic law, designed to sweep the board clean of any possibility of charges against him, by granting him immunity from prosecution as premier, along with the president, the speakers of the two Chambers, and the head of the Constitutional Court, as four fig-leaves. Amid widespread uproar, this too was challenged by magistrates in Milan, where the major trials in which he was implicated were underway, and was ruled unconstitutional six months later. But the barrage of *ad personam* laws, patently the government's most urgent agenda, had immediate, if not yet definitive, effect. No sooner was Berlusconi in office than he was absolved by an appeals court of bribing judges to acquire the Mondadori publishing conglomerate—not for want of evidence, but for 'extenuating circumstances', defined in a memorable précis of Italian justice as 'the prominence of the defendant's current social and individual position, judged by the court to be decisive'.[31] Before formal immunity against prosecution was struck down, it had closed another leading case against Berlusconi, and when it was reopened, a new court delivered the requisite judgement, absolving him.

After protecting his person came protecting his empire. By law Mediaset was due to relinquish one of its TV channels in 2003. Legislation was rushed through to allow it not only to retain the channel, but to enjoy a massive indirect subsidy for its entry into digital television. Since Berlusconi now commanded not only his own private stations, but controlled state broadcasting as well, his dominance of the visual media came close to saturation. But it failed to deliver any stable sway over public opinion. By 2005,

---

31. Alexander Stille, *The Sack of Rome*, New York 2007, pp. 273–4.

when he was forced to reshuffle his cabinet, the popularity of the government had plummeted. In part, this was due to the unseemly spectacle of the *ad personam* laws, denounced not only in the streets but by most of the press. But more fundamentally, it was a reaction to the economic stagnation of the country, where average incomes had grown at a mere 1 per cent a year since 2001, the lowest figure anywhere in the EU.

Watching its ratings drop precipitously in the polls, the ruling coalition abruptly altered the electoral system, abandoning its predominantly first-past-the-post component for a return to proportional representation, but with a heavily disproportionate premium—55 per cent of seats in the Chamber of Deputies—for the coalition winning most votes, and a threshold of 4 per cent for any party running on its own. Designed to weaken the opposition by exploiting its division into a larger number of parties than the bloc in power, the new rules played their part in the outcome of the general election held in April 2006.[32] Contrary to expectations, the Centre-Left won only by a whisker—25,000 votes out of 38 million cast for the Chamber, while actually scoring less than the Centre-Right for the Senate. On a difference of less than 0.1 per cent of the popular vote, the premium handed it a majority of no less than sixty-seven seats in the Chamber, but in the Senate it could count on a precarious majority of two, only because of the anomaly—newly introduced—of overseas constituencies. Having believed in a comfortable victory, the Centre-Left went into shock at the result, which came as a psychological defeat. Prodi, now back from Brussels, was once again premier. But this time, he presided over a government mathematically, and morally, much weaker than before.

Not only did Centre-Left rule now hang by a thread, but it lacked any organizing purpose. In the nineties, Prodi had possessed one central goal, Italy's entry into the European monetary union, whose pursuit gave his tenure a political focus. His new administration—which unlike its predecessor, now included Rifondazione Comunista, widely regarded as a formation of the extreme left, as an integral part of its coalition, rather than as

---

32. Antonio Floridia, 'Gulliver unbound. Possible electoral reforms and the 2008 election: Towards an end to "fragmented bipolarity"?', *Modern Italy*, August 2008, pp. 318–19.

an external support for it—had no equivalent coherence. At the Finance Ministry, Tommaso Padoa-Schioppa, one of the original architects of the European single currency, gave priority to reducing the public debt, which had crept back up a few points under Berlusconi, and cracking down on tax evasion, to some (although officially exaggerated) effect. A scattering of minor measures of liberalization, designed to make life easier for consumers of chemists, taxis and the like, was soon dissipated. Gestures, but no more, were made towards a thirty-five-hour week, as a placebo to keep Rifondazione quiet while the Centre-Left pursued a foreign policy of undeviating Atlanticism. Prodi's government reinforced the Italian contingent in Afghanistan; withdrew troops from Iraq very gradually, according to Berlusconi's own plan for doing so; approved an expansion of the American air force base at Vicenza that had been a launching-pad for the Balkan War; dispatched forces to Lebanon as a *glacis* for Israel; and retroactively covered kidnapping and rendition by the CIA from Italian soil.

None of this did anything for the popularity of Prodi or his ministers. Increased fiscal pressure angered the traditional tax-evading constituencies of the Right. The lack of any significant social reforms disappointed voters of the Left. Most disastrously, no attempt was made either to deal with Berlusconi's conflict of interests, or to introduce better standards of justice. Instead a sweeping amnesty was declared—in theory to clear hopelessly over-crowded prisons, but in practice releasing not only common felons, but every kind of notable convicted of corruption. This *indulto*, proclaimed by the notorious Clemente Mastella (the shadiest politician in the coalition, a former Christian Democrat from Campania who had been made minister of justice to keep his tiny party in its ranks), provoked widespread outrage. By 2007, with Prodi's own standing in free fall, the leadership of the DS— the 'Democratic Left' into which the bulk of Italian Communism had evolved—decided that its mutation into a Democratic Party pure and simple, dropping any association with the Left and absorbing assorted Catholic and ex-Radical politicians grouped in the so-called 'Daisy' component of the coalition, could allow it to escape the sinking repute of the government, and elbow Prodi aside in public view. Massimo D'Alema, foreign minister in the government, was too damaged by his role in the final debacle of previous Prodi administration to be a credible candidate to head the new formation, whose leadership fell to his long-time rival Walter Veltroni, the DS mayor of Rome, as a fresher choice.

Privately, the two men despise one another—D'Alema regarding Veltroni as a fool, Veltroni D'Alema as a knave. But outwardly, together with a motley crew of devotees and transfuges, they joined forces to give birth to a new centrist party, to be cleansed of all connexion with a compromised past. By the autumn of 2007, Veltroni was more or less openly positioning himself as the alternative to Prodi, who theoretically still had three more years in office to run—in effect, repeating an operation mounted at Prodi's expense by D'Alema in late 1998.

This time, however, the ambitions were greater and talents lesser. Veltroni's aim was not to replace Prodi at the head of the existing coalition, but to bank on early elections to bring him to power as chief of a party that would rival Berlusconi's in novelty, breadth and popular support. But his limitations had long been apparent. Vaguely resembling a pudgier, bug-eyed variant of Woody Allen, Veltroni—an enthusiast for filmic dross and football, delighted to lend his voice to a Disney cartoon; author of opuscules like 'Thirty-Eight Declarations of Love to the Most Beautiful Game in the World'—had the advantage of an image of greater sincerity than D'Alema, as more spontaneously conformist, but possessed little of his sharpness of mind.[33] In November 2007, the Centre-Right bloc was in danger of falling apart, when Berlusconi—frustrated by failures to topple the Prodi government in Parliament—suddenly folded Forza Italia into a new organization, Popolo della Libertà, demanding that his allies, other than the Lega, join it as the single national party of freedom. Both Gianfranco Fini and Pier Ferdinando Casini, leaders of the former Fascist (AN) and Catholic (UDC) components of his coalition, rebelled. Instead of capitalizing on their disaffection, and splitting the Centre-Right, Veltroni eagerly offered himself to Berlusconi as a responsible partner in the task of simplifying Italian politics into two great parties of moderate opinion.[34] What this meant was clear to all: once again, as in the mid-nineties, the attempt to strike a deal for a new electoral system designed to wipe out small parties, leaving the newly constructed PD and PdL in sole command of the political field. In the ranks of the

---

33. For a fulsome portrait, rushed out for electoral purposes, see Marco Damilano, Mariagrazia Gerina and Fabio Martini, *Veltroni. Il Piccolo Principe*, Milan 2007.

34. Pino Corrias offers a crisp account in his introduction to Peter Gomez, Marco Lillo and Marco Travaglio, *Il bavaglio*, Milan 2008, pp. 25–9.

opposition, this danger promptly brought Fini to heel, returning him to allegiance to Berlusconi, and reviving the compact of the Centre-Right. In the ruling coalition, its effect was an even deadlier boomerang.

While negotiations between Veltroni and Berlusconi were proceeding in Rome, a long-gathering crisis was about to explode in the south. In late December 2007, rubbish collectors stopped work in and around Naples, where all dumps were full, leaving huge piles of rotting garbage accumulating in streets and neighbourhoods. Waste disposal in the region had long been a lucrative racket controlled by the Camorra, shipping toxic refuse from the industrial north into illegal dumps in Campania. There, both the region and the city of Naples had been fiefs of the Centre-Left for over a decade—the governor (and former mayor) ex-PCI, the mayor ex-DC. Under this pair, Antonio Bassolino and Rosa Russo Jervolino—the first by far the more important—there had been much boasting of the outstanding work performed in the restoration of Naples to its original beauties, and the advent of clean, progressive administration in Campania. In reality, notwithstanding municipal embellishments, corruption and gangsterism had flourished unchecked, without the Prodi government paying any attention to what was going on in its bailiwick.[35] In January, the citizens of Naples finally rose up in furious protests against the mounds of putrescence visited on them. The damage to Centre-Left rule was immeasurable.

Two months later, its downfall combined, with peculiar local aptness, the outcomes of the tactical and moral blindness of the coalition. Within days of the outbreak of the garbage crisis in Naples, the wife of the minister of justice, Sandra Mastella, president of the Regional Assembly of Campania for the Centre-Left, was put under house arrest, charged with attempting to corrupt a local hospital trust for the benefit of her party, the UDEUR. Her husband resigned his ministry in protest, and was promptly reappointed by Prodi. But his loyalty already weakened by failure to respect collegial *omertà* in Naples, Mastella could see the writing was on the wall for his party anyway, if Veltroni's deal with Berlusconi went through. To block it, he switched sides, and his two senators in the upper chamber brought the government

---

35. For a detailed analysis, see Felia and Percy Allum, 'Revisiting Naples: Clientelism and Organized Crime', *Journal of Modern Italian Studies*, Vol. 13, No. 3, 2008, pp. 340–65.

down. In a riotous scene, the Centre-Right benches exploded with jubilation, corks popping and champagne spraying along the red velvet seats of the hemicycle in the Palazzo Madama.

Paying the bill for his miscalculations, Veltroni now had to fight an election at short notice, without having had the time to establish his party, or himself, as the beacon of civilized dialogue in a too faction-ridden society, on which he had counted. Rejecting any understanding with the three smaller parties to the left of it, the PD entered the lists alone, to underline its mission to give Italy a modern government, uncompromised by any participation of extremists—making an exception, at the last moment, only for Italy of Values, the small party owing allegiance to the most pugnacious of the Clean Hands magistrates, Antonio Di Pietro. Berlusconi, on the other hand, having integrated Fini's forces into his new party, had no compunction in moving into battle with allies—above all, the Lega in the north, but also the minor regionalist Movement for Autonomy in the south. The campaign itself was universally judged the dullest of the Second Republic, Centre-Left and Centre-Right offering virtually identical socio-economic platforms, until at the last minute Berlusconi promised to lower property taxes. Otherwise, the two sides differed only in their respective rhetorics of morality (how to protect the family) and security (how to suppress crime).[36] So far did Veltroni go out of his way to shun any aspersions on Berlusconi that he avoided even mentioning him by name, instead speaking throughout respectfully just of 'my adversary'. His audiences were not roused.

The magnitude of the ensuing disaster exceeded all expectations. The Centre-Right crushed the Centre-Left by a margin of 9.3 per cent, or some 3.5 million votes, giving it an overall majority of nearly a hundred in the Chamber and forty in the Senate. Gains within the victorious bloc were made, however, not by the newly minted PdL (into which Forza Italia and AN had merged), which actually ended up with a hundred thousand votes less than the two had secured in 2006. The great winner was the Lega, whose vote jumped by 1.5 million, accounting for virtually all the total increase in the score of the Centre-Right. The PD, presenting itself as the party of the progressive Centre to which all well-disposed Italians

---

36. See especially Nicolò Conti, 'The Italian political parties and the programmatic platforms: How alternative?', *Modern Italy*, November 2008, pp. 451–64; Marco Brunazzo and Mark Gilbert, 'The Right Sweeps the Board', *Journal of Modern Italian Studies*, Vol. 13, No. 3, 2008, p. 423.

could now rally, proved a complete flop. With just over 33 per cent of the vote, it mustered scarcely more votes—on one reckoning, actually less—than its component parts in 2006. Indeed, even this score was only reached by the *voto utile* of about a fifth of the former voters of the parties of the Left proper, which this time had combined into a Rainbow alliance, and been wiped out when it fell below the 4 per cent threshold, with a net loss of nearly 2.5 million votes. Overall, the value-added of the Democratic Party, created to reshape the whole political landscape by attracting voters away from the Centre-Right, turned out to be zero.[37]

I

The shock of the election of 2008 has been compared to that of 1948, when Christian Democrats—this was before opinion polls, so there was little advance warning—triumphed so decisively over Communists and Socialists that they held power continuously for another forty-four years. If no such durable hegemony is in sight for today's Centre-Right, the condition of the Centre-Left, indeed the Italian Left as a whole, is in most respects—morale, organization, ideas, mass support—much worse than that of the PCI or PSI of sixty years ago: it would be more appropriate to speak of a Caporetto of the Left. Central to the debacle has been its displacement by the Lega among the northern working class. The ability of parties of the Right to win workers away from traditional allegiances on the Left has become a widespread, if not unbroken, pattern. First achieved by Thatcher in Britain, then by Reagan and Bush in America, and most recently by Sarkozy in France, only Germany among the major Western societies has so far resisted it. The Lega could, from this point of view, be regarded simply as the Italian instance of a general trend. But a number of features make it a more striking, special case.

The first, and most fundamental, is that it is not a party of the establishment, but an insurgent movement. There is nothing conservative about the Lega, whose raison d'être is not order, but revolt. Its forte is raucous, hell-raising protest. Typically, movements of protest are short-winded—they come and go. The Lega, however, has not just become a durable feature of the

---

37. For this, see Luca Ricolfi, *Perché siamo antipatici? La sinistra e il complesso dei migliori prima e dopo le elezioni del 2008*, Milan 2008, p. 199; for overall figures, Brunazzo and Gilbert, 'The Right Sweeps the Board'.

national landscape. It is now the oldest political party in Italy, indeed the only one that can look back on thirty years of activity. This is not an accident of the random workings of the break to the Second Republic. It reflects the second peculiarity of the Lega, its dynamism as a mass organization, possessing cadres and militants that make it, in the words of Roberto Maroni, perhaps Bossi's closest colleague, 'the last Leninist party in Italy'.[38] Over much of the north, it now functions somewhat as the PCI once did, as rueful Communist veterans often observe, with big gains in one formerly Red industrial stronghold after another: the Fiat works in Mirafiori, the big petro-chemical plants in Porto Marghera, the famous proletarian suburb of Sesto San Giovanni outside Milan, setting in the fifties of Visconti's *Rocco and His Brothers*. This is not say that it has become a party based on labour. While it has captured much of the working-class vote across the north, the Lega's core strength lies, as it has always done, among the small manufacturers, shopkeepers, and self-employed in what were once White fortresses of the DC—Catholic provinces of the north-east, now increasingly secularized, where hatred of taxes and interference by the central state runs especially strong. Here resentment of fiscal transfers to the south, perceived as a swamp of parasitic ne'er-do-wells, powered the take-off of the League in the late eighties. Immigration from the Balkans, Africa and Asia, which has quadrupled over the last decade, is now the more acute phobia, laced with racism and prejudice against Islam. The shift of emphasis has, as might be expected, been a contributory factor in the spread of the League's influence into the northern working-class, more exposed to competition in the labour market than to sales taxes.

The truculence of the League's style has been perhaps an even more important source of its popular success. Defiance of the sickly euphuism of conventional political discourse, as cultivated in Rome, confirms the League's identity as an outsider to the system, close to the blunt language of ordinary people. The party's leaders relish breaking taboos, in every direction. Its political incorrectness is not confined to xenophobia. In matters of foreign policy, it has repeatedly flouted the official consensus— opposing the Gulf War, the Balkan War and the Lisbon Treaty, and advocating tariffs to block cheap imports from China,

---

38. Adalberto Signore and Alessandro Trocino, *Razza Padana*, Milan 2008, pp. 5–7.

without inhibition.[39] Breaking verbal crockery, however, is one thing; effecting policy another. Since its period in the desert between 1996 and 2001, the League has never rebelled against the orthodox decisions of the Centre-Right governments to which it has belonged, its rhetorical provocations typically operating as symbolic compensation for practical accommodation. But it is not a dependency of Berlusconi. The boot is rather on the other foot—without the League, Berlusconi could never have won the elections in which he has prevailed, least of all in 2008. The broker of the alliance between the two, Giulio Tremonti, now again minister of finance, is not by accident both the author of a critique of unfettered globalization sharper than anything Veltroni's Democrats have dared to venture, and after Berlusconi himself, the most powerful figure in the present government.[40]

If the League has been the principal nemesis of that part—the majority—of the PCI which made a pilgrimage from communism to social liberalism without so much as a stop-over at social democracy, the fate of the minority that sought to refound a democratic communism has been largely self-inflicted. Instead of keeping clear of Prodi's coalition in the elections of 2006, as it had done to good effect a decade earlier—when a pact of mutual desistance had allowed it to enter Parliament as an independent force in rough proportion to its electoral strength, and lend external, but not unconditional, support to the ensuing Centre-Left government—Rifondazione Comunista signed up as a full member. Its leader, Fausto Bertinotti, was rewarded with the post of speaker of the Chamber, nominally the third personage of the Italian State, and replete with official perquisites of every kind and automatic access to the media. This empty honour went, as hoped, to his head, ensuring that the RC became a docile appendage in the ruling coalition, unable to secure any substantive concessions from it, and inevitably sharing in the disrepute into which it fell. In keeping with this performance, the party voted war credits for Afghanistan not long after Bertinotti had explained that the great mistake of the Left in the twentieth century had been to believe that violence

---

39. *Razza Padana*, pp. 339–43, 349, 322–6.

40. Tremonti, a former associate of Craxi in the PSI, comes from Sondrio in the far north of Lombardy, deep Lega country. His *La speranza e la paura*, denouncing 'marketism, a degenerate version of liberalism', warning of the neo-colonial ambitions of China, and calling for a European industrial policy, appeared in 2008: pp. 19, 27–9, 109.

could ever be an instrument of progressive change—only its complete renunciation for an 'absolute pacifism' was now politically acceptable. Predictably, the combination of co-option and abjuration was suicidal. Facing the polls in a last-minute cartel with Greens and the remnant of the PDS that could not abide the dropping of even a nominal reference to the left in the PD, Rifondazione was annihilated. Voters in their millions abandoned a party that had scuttled its own identity.

The scale of his victory has given Berlusconi the leeway to pursue a tougher socio-economic agenda than before, of the kind long urged on him by mainstream critics and commentators inside and outside Italy. Where this would hit opposition constituencies, his coalition is ready to act: draconian cuts in higher education, and compression of teaching staff in elementary schools, promptly enacted, strike at a relatively easy target of Centre-Left support, where institutional vices are widely acknowledged. Where its own electoral base is concerned, rigour is unlikely to be any more applied than in the past. The world recession would in any case not encourage an intrepid neo-liberalism, even were it contemplated. The immediate focus of the government has lain elsewhere. Back in power, Berlusconi could return to the unfinished business of putting himself above the law. Within a hundred days of the election, Parliament had rushed through another bill for his immunity from prosecution, re-drafted by his lawyers to sidestep the grounds on which the Constitutional Court had voided the previous one. This too has already been challenged in the courts; beyond them, a campaign to abrogate it by referendum is in waiting. The political life of the country once again turns on the personal fortune, in all senses, of its billionaire ruler.

Today Berlusconi is incontestably the icon of the Second Republic. His dominance symbolizes everything it has come to stand for. Few secrets remain about the way in which he acquired his riches, and how he has used them to gain and preserve his power.[41] The larger question is what, sociologically, made this

---

41. See David Lane, *Berlusconi's Shadow*, London 2004; Paul Ginsborg, *Silvio Berlusconi*, London 2005; Alexander Stille, *The Sack of Rome*, London 2006; Giuseppe Fiori, *Il Venditore*, Milan 1995. For critical reflections on Stille's account of Berlusconi, arguing that it is over-generalized, see Donald Sassoon, 'Povera Italia', *Journal of Modern Italian Studies*, Vol. 12, No. 3, 2007, pp. 339–46.

career possible. An obvious answer would point to the unbroken sway of Christian Democracy in the First Republic, and see him essentially as its heir. The element of truth in such a reading is clear from the underlying electoral balance in the Second Republic. Proportionally, in all five elections since 1994, the total Centre-Right vote, excluding the League, has exceeded the total Centre-Left vote, excluding Rifondazione Comunista, by a margin varying between 5 and 10 per cent.[42] Italy, in other words, has always been, and remains, at bottom an extremely conservative country. The reasons, it is widely argued, are not hard to find. Fewer people move away from their areas of birth, more adult children live with their parents, average firms are much smaller, and the number of self-employed is far higher, than in any other Western society. Such are the cells of reaction out of which a body politic congenitally averse to risk or change has been composed. The sway of the Church, as the only institution at once national and universal, and the fear of a large home-grown Communism, clinched the hegemony of Christian Democracy over it, and even if each has declined, their residues live on in Berlusconi's following.

The deduction is too linear, however. Berlusconi has certainly never stinted appeals to Christianity and family values, or warnings of the persistent menace of Communism, and Forza Italia plainly inherited the bastions of DC clientelism in the south—most notoriously in Sicily. But the filigrane of Catholic continuity in his success is quite tenuous. It is not only that the White zones of the north-east have gone to the Lega, but practising Catholics—the quarter of the population that now attends mass with some regularity—have been the most volatile segment of the electorate, many in the early years of the Second Republic voting not only for the Lega but also for the PDS.[43] Nor is there a clear-cut connexion between small businesses or the self-employed and political reaction. The Red belt of central Italy—Tuscany, Umbria, Emilia-Romagna and the Marche— where the PCI was always strongest, and which the PD still holds today, is rife with both: family enterprises, flourishing micro-firms, independent artisans and shopkeepers, as well as

---

42. For the figures, see Ilvo Diamanti and Elisa Lello, 'The Casa delle Libertà. A House of Cards?', *Modern Italy*, May 2005, pp. 14–16.

43. Ilvo Diamanti and Luigi Ceccarini, 'Catholics and Politics after the Christian Democrats: The Influential Minority', *Journal of Modern Italian Studies*, Vol. 12, No. 1, pp. 49–50.

the region's cooperatives—a world not of large factories or assembly-lines, but of small property.

Berlusconi's real lineage is more pointed. Fundamentally, he is the heir of Craxi and the mutation he represented in the Italian politics of the eighties, rather than of the DC.[44] The descent is literal, not just analogical. The two men were close contemporaries, both products of Milan, their careers continuously intertwined from the time that Craxi became leader of the Socialist Party in 1976, and Berlusconi created his first major television station two years later, funded with lavish loans from banks controlled by the PSI. The relationship could hardly have been more intimate, at once functional and personal. Craxi created the favours from the state that allowed Berlusconi to build his media empire: Berlusconi funded Craxi's machine with the profits from it, and boosted his image with his newscasts. A frequent guest at Berlusconi's palatial villa in Arcore, where he was liberally supplied with soubrettes and haute cuisine, Craxi was godfather to Berlusconi's first child by the actress Veronica Lario in 1984, before he married her, and best man at the wedding when he did marry her, in 1990. On becoming premier in 1983, he rescued Berlusconi's national television networks, which were broadcasting in defiance of a Supreme Court ruling, from being shut down, and in 1990 helped ensure Berlusconi's permanent grip on them, with a law for which he received a deposit of $12 million to his account in a foreign bank. At the pinnacle of his power, Craxi cut a new figure on the post-war Italian scene—tough, decisive, cultivating publicity, in complete command of his own party, and a ruthless negotiator with others.

Three years later, with the revelations of Tangentopoli exposing the scale of his corruption, Craxi had become the most execrated public figure in the land. But he was not finished. His own career in ruins, he passed his vision of politics directly to Berlusconi, urging him to take the electoral plunge in a meeting in Milan in April 1993. According to an eye-witness,

> Craxi paced the room like a hunted animal as he talked. 'We must find a label, a new name, a symbol that can unite the voters who used to vote for the old five-party coalition', Craxi told Berlusconi. 'You have people all over the Italian peninsula, you can reach that part of

---

44. For the pedigree viewed in electoral terms, see Michael Shin and John Agnew's careful ecology, *Berlusconi's Italy: Mapping Contemporary Italian Politics*, Philadelphia 2008, pp. 78, 134.

the electorate that is disoriented, confused, but also determined not to be governed by the Communists, and save what can be saved'. Then Craxi sat down and began drawing a series of concentric circles on a piece of paper. 'This is an electoral college. It will have about 110,000 people in it, about 80,000 to 85,000 with the right to vote. Of these only about 60,000 to 65,000 will actually vote. With the weapon you have with your television stations, by hammering away with propaganda in favour of this or that candidate, all you need is to bring together 25,000 to 30,000 people in order to have a high probability of reversing the projections. It will happen because of the surprise factor, because of the TV factor and because of the desire of many non-Communist voters not to be governed by the Communists'. Craxi then got up to go. After showing him out, Berlusconi said, 'Good, I now know what to do'.[45]

Though by the end of its time the DC had, under pressure of competition, descended to the same levels of venality as the PSI, between Craxi's model of politics and Christian Democracy there was historically a significant difference. The DC not only possessed the reflected aura of a time-honoured faith, but a deep-rooted social base that Craxi's brittle machine never acquired; and it had always resisted one-man leadership, remaining an intricate network of counter-balancing factions, immune to the cult of the strongman. Down to the end, however many billions of lire its bagmen were collecting from contractors and businessmen, less went into the personal pockets of its leaders, whose life-style was never as showy as that of Craxi and his colleagues. Scarcely one of its top figures came from Lombardy. Culturally, they belonged to another world.

Berlusconi, catapulted to the political stage as Craxi fled into exile, thus embodies perhaps the deepest irony in the post-war history of any Western society. The First Republic collapsed amid public outrage at the exposure of stratospheric levels of political corruption, only to give birth to a Second Republic dominated by a yet more flamboyant monument of illegality and corruption than the statecraft of the First had ever produced— Craxi's own misdeeds dwarfed by comparison. Nor was the new venality confined to the ruler and his entourage. Beneath them, corruption has continued to flourish undiminished. A few months after the Centre-Left governor of Campania—Antonio Bassolino, formerly of the PCI—was indicted for fraud and malversation,

---

45. Marco Travaglio, *Montanelli e il Cavaliere*, Milan 2004, pp. 59–60, in Stille's translation.

the governor of Abruzzo, another stalwart of the Centre-Left—Ottavio del Turco, formerly of the PSI—was arrested, after a private-health tycoon confessed to having paid him six million euros in cash as protection money. Berlusconi is the capstone of a system that extends well beyond him. But, as a political actor, credit for the inversion of what was imagined would be the curing of the ills of the First Republic by the Second belongs in the first place to him. Italy has no more native tradition than *trasformismo*—the transformation of a political force by osmosis into its opposite, as classically practised by Depretis in the late nineteenth century, absorbing the the Right into the official Left, and Giolitti in the early twentieth, co-opting labour reformism to the benefit of Liberalism. The case of the Second Republic has been *trasformismo* on a grander scale: not a party, or a class, but an entire order converted into what it was intended to end.

Where the state has led, society has followed. The years since 1993 have, in one area of life after another, been the most calamitous since the fall of Fascism. Of late, they have produced probably the two most scalding inventories of avarice, injustice, dereliction and failure in any European country since the war. The work of a pair of crusading journalists for *Corriere della Sera*, Gian Antonio Stella and Sergio Rizzo, *La Casta* (2007) and *La Deriva* (2008), have been best-sellers—the first running through twenty-three editions in six months—and they deserve to be. What do they reveal? To begin with, the greed of the political class running the country. In the Assembly, deputies have raised their salaries virtually six-fold in real terms since 1948, with the result that in the European Parliament an Italian deputy gets some 150,000 euros a year, about double what a German or British member receives, and four times a Spaniard. In Rome, the Chamber of Deputies, Senate and prime minister occupy altogether at least forty-six buildings.[46]

The Quirinale, where the president of the Republic—currently Giorgio Napolitano, till yesterday a prominent Communist, as impervious as his predecessors—resides, puts at his disposal over nine hundred servitors of one kind or another, at last count. Cost of the presidential establishment, which has tripled since 1986? Twice that of the Elysée, four times that of Buckingham Palace, eight

---

46. Sergio Rizzo and Gian Antonio Stella, *La Casta. Cosí i politici italiani sono divenuti intoccabili*, Milan 2007, pp. 13, 46.

times that of the German president. Takings of its inmates? In 1993 Gaetano Gifuni, the Father Joseph of the Palace, at the centre of then President Scalfaro's operations to protect himself from justice, received 557,000 euros at current values for his services—well above the salary of an American president.[47] Transport? In 2007, Italy had no fewer than 574,215 *autos blus*—official limousines—for a governing class of 180,000 elected representatives; France, 65,000. Security? Berlusconi set an example: eighty-one bodyguards, at public expense. By some reckonings, expenditure on political representation in Italy, all found, is equivalent to that of France, Germany, Britain and Spain combined.[48]

Beneath this crust of privilege, one in four Italians lives in poverty. Spending on education, falling in the budget since 1990, accounts for a mere 4.6 per cent of GDP (Denmark: 8.4 per cent). Only half of the population has any kind of post-compulsory schooling, nearly twenty points below the European average. No more than a fifth of twenty-year-olds enter higher education, and three-fifths of those drop out. The number of hospital beds per inhabitant has dwindled by a third under the new Republic, and is now about half that in Germany or France. In the courts, criminal justice takes an average of four years to reach a final verdict, time that is taken into account in the statute of limitations, voiding up to a fifth of cases. In civil suits, the average time for a bankruptcy hearing to be completed is eight years and eight months. In late 2007 two septuagenarian pensioners, trying to bring a case against the Social Security Institute, were told they could get an audience in 2020. As for equality before the law, an Albanian immigrant charged with trying to steal a cow in his homeland spent more days in an Italian prison than one of the mega-crooks of the food industry, Sergio Cragnotti, who destroyed the savings of thousands of his fellow citizens. Politicians were treated still better than tycoons: Berlusconi's right-hand man Cesare Previti, convicted of corrupting judges after hearings that lasted for nine years, and sentenced to six years imprisonment, spent all of five days in jail before being released to perform community service.[49]

---

47. *La Casta*, pp. 53–60.
48. *Le Monde*, 31 May 2007.
49. Sergio Rizzo and Gian Antonio Stella, *La Deriva. Perché l'Italia rischia il naufragio*, Milan 2008, pp. v, 128–9, 134, 140, 148, 185, 218; *Il Manifesto*, 8 December 2007.

The material infrastructures of the country are in no better shape than its public institutions. Harbours: the seven major ports of Italy, put together, handle less container traffic than Rotterdam. Motorways: half the mileage in Spain. High-speed trains: less than a third of the tracks in France. Overall rail network: thirteen kilometres longer than in 1920. Airlines: Alitalia—23 long-range passenger jets to 134 for Lufthansa. All contributing to the dismal economic record of the last decade, when GDP has grown at the slowest pace anywhere in the EU, and labour productivity has barely improved: just 1 per cent between 2001 and 2006. Per capita income—still increasing at a modest 2 per cent a year between 1980 and 1995—has been virtually stationary since 2000. The gap in living standards between north and south has widened. Criminal organizations are active in more than four hundred communes of the Mezzogiorno, inhabited by some thirteen million Italians, where one in three local businessmen report widespread rackets. Labour force participation is the lowest in Western Europe, and that of women rock-bottom: thirty points below Denmark, twenty points below the US, ten points below the Czech Republic. Nor does exclusion from production mean high levels of reproduction, where the net rate is negative—0.6 or just 1.3 births per woman, projecting a fall in the population from 58 to 47 million by mid-century. Already the elderly above the age of sixty outnumber the young between eighteen and twenty-four by nearly three to one. The average voter is now forty-seven.[50]

Redeeming this desolation has, to all intents and purposes, been just one improvement, in job creation. Unemployment, which stood at 12 per cent in the mid-nineties, has dropped to 6 per cent today. But most of this work—half of all the new posts in 2006—involves short-term contracts, and much of it is precarious employment in the informal economy.[51] No counteracting dynamism has resulted. In the formula of the Neapolitan sociologist Enrico Pugliese, Italy has gone from growth without jobs in the last years of the First Republic to jobs without growth under the Second, blocking productivity gains. The predominance of small to medium firms—some 4.5

---

50. *La Deriva*, pp. vi, xvii–xviii, 24, 27, 60, 66, 72, 79–80; *Financial Times*, 13 May 2005; *Economist*, 26 November 2005.

51. *Sole 24 Ore*, 21 November 2007.

million, or a quarter of the total number in the whole of the pre-enlargement EU—has cramped expenditure on research, tethering exports to traditional lines of strength in apparel, shoes and the like, where competition from low-cost Asian producers is now most intense. High-tech exports are half the European average, and foreign investment is famously low, deterred not only by fear of extortion and maladminstration, but also by the still close defences of Italian big business, whose holding companies and banks are typically controlled by shareholder pacts between a few powerful interlocking insiders.[52]

In the past, this model flourished with a flexible exchange rate, adjusting to external challenges with competitive devaluations, and tolerating relatively high rates of domestic inflation and deficitary finance. With Italy's entry into European monetary union, the Second Republic put an end to it. Budgets were retrenched to meet the Maastricht criteria, inflation was curbed, and depreciation of the currency ceased to be possible. But no alternative model materialized. The macro-economic regime had changed, but the structure of production did not. The result was to worsen the conditions for recovery. Growth was not liberated, but asphyxiated. Export shares have fallen, and the public debt, third largest in the world, has remained stubbornly above 100 per cent of GDP, mocking the provisions of Maastricht. When the Second Republic started, Italy still enjoyed the second highest GDP per capita of the big EU states, measured in purchasing power parity, after Germany—a standard of living in real terms above that of France or Britain. Today it has fallen below an EU average now weighed down by the relative poverty of the East European states, and is close to being overtaken by Greece.[53]

2

Within this panorama of national decay, one area of ruins has a poignancy all its own. The Italian Left was once the largest and most impressive popular movement for social change in Western Europe. Comprising two mass parties, each with their own history and culture, and both committed not to ameliorating but

---

52. *Economist*, 26 November 2005; *Financial Times*, 28 March 2007.
53. *Economist*, 19 April 2008.

to overcoming capitalism, the post-war alliance between the PSI
and PCI did not survive the boom of the fifties. In 1963 Nenni
took the Socialists for the first time into government as junior
partners of the Christian Democrats, on a path that would in
time lead to Craxi, leaving Italian Communism in unchallenged
command of opposition to the DC regime in place since
1948. From the beginning, the PCI was organizationally and
ideologically the stronger of the two, with a wider mass base—
over two million members by the mid-fifties, extending from
peasants in the south through artisans and teachers in the centre
to industrial workers in the north. It also had a richer intellectual
heritage, in Gramsci's newly published *Prison Notebooks*, whose
significance was immediately recognized well beyond the party.
At its height, the PCI could draw on an extraordinary range of
social and moral energies, combining both deeper popular roots
and broader intellectual influence than any other force in the
country.

Confined by the Cold War to forty years of national
opposition, the party entrenched itself in local and later regional
administrations, and the parliamentary commissions through
which Italian legislation must pass, becoming entwined with
the ruling order at many secondary levels. But its underlying
strategy remained more or less stable throughout. After 1948,
the spoils of the Liberation were divided. Power fell to the DC;
culture to the PCI. Christian Democracy controlled the levers
of the state, Communism attracted the talents of civil society.
The PCI's ability to polarize Italian intellectual life around itself,
not only in a broad arc of scholars, writers, thinkers, artists—it
is enough to recall that, among many others, Pavese, Calvino,
Pasolini, Visconti, Pontecorvo, Nono were all at one time or
another members or sympathizers of the party—but a general
climate of progressive opinion, was without parallel elsewhere
in Europe. Owed in part to the sociology of its leadership,
which, unlike that of the French, German, British or Spanish
Communist parties, was for the most part highly educated, and
in part to a relatively tolerant and flexible handling of the 'battle
of ideas', its dominion in this sphere was the really distinctive
asset of Italian Communism. But it came at a two-fold price to
which the party remained persistently blind.

For the extent of the PCI's influence across the world of
thought and art was also a function of the degree to which it
assimilated and reproduced the dominant strain in a pre-existent

Italian culture of long standing.[54] This was the idealism which had found its most powerful, though by no means unique, modern expression in the philosophy of Benedetto Croce, a figure who over the years had acquired an almost Goethe-like position in the intellectual life of the country. It was Croce's historicist system, its prestige underwritten by the attention given it in prison by Gramsci, that became naturalized as the circumambient ether of a great deal of the post-war Italian culture over which the PCI, directly or indirectly, presided.[55] But behind it lay much older traditions that accorded pre-eminence to the realm of ideas, conceived as will or understanding, in politics. Between the fall of the Roman Empire and the completion of the Risorgimento, Italy never knew a peninsular state or aristocracy, and most of the time was subject to an array of conflicting foreign powers. The result, for long stretches, was to create an overwhelming sense of the gap between past glory and present misery among its educated elites. From Dante onwards, there developed a tradition of intellectuals with an acute sense of their calling to recover and transmit the high culture of classical antiquity, and imbued with the conviction that the country could be put to rights only by the impress of revivifying ideas, of which only they could be the artificers, on fallen realities.[56] Culture was not a sphere distinct from power: it was to be the passport to it.

In good measure, Italian Communism inherited this habit of mind. The novel form it gave to a national predisposition was drawn from, if not faithful to, Gramsci. In this version, 'hegemony' was a cultural and moral ascendancy to be won consensually within civil society, as the real foundation of social existence, that would eventually assure peaceful possession of the state, a more external and superficial expression of collective life. The commanding position the party had won in the intellectual arena thus showed it was on track to ultimate political victory. This was not what Gramsci, a revolutionary of the Third International who had never thought capital could be broken without force of arms—however important the need to win the widest popular

---

54. For some general remarks, see Christopher Duggan, *Force of Destiny*, London 2007, pp. xvii–xx.

55. For this background, see Remo Bodei, *I noi diviso: Ethos e idee dell'Italia repubblicana,* Turin 1998, pp. 16–19, 63–9, 113.

56. The most penetrating account of this syndrome is to be found in Ernesto Galli della Loggia's fundamental work, *L'Identità italiana*, Bologna 1998, pp. 31–42, 116–21.

consent for the overthrow of the ruling order—had believed. But it fitted the idealist cast of the culture at large like a glove. Within the intellectual sphere itself, moreover, the PCI reproduced the humanist bias of the traditional elites, for whom philosophy, history and literature had always been the fields of choice. Missing from the party's portfolio were the more modern disciplines of economics and sociology, and the methods they had attempted to borrow, for better or worse, from the natural sciences. Formidable though its positions looked at the heights of a hallowed cultural hierarchy, it was weaker lower down, with serious consequences for it in due course.

For when the two great changes that would alter the ecology of the PCI in post-war Italy hit the party, it was quite unprepared for either. The first was the arrival of a fully commercialized mass culture, of a kind still unimaginable in the world of Togliatti, let alone of Gramsci. Even in its heyday, there had been certain obvious limits to the influence of the PCI, and more generally of the Italian Left, in the cultural scene, since the Church occupied such a large space in popular belief and imagination. Below the level of the universities, publishers, studios or journals in which the *mouvance* of the party was so widespread, and quite distinct from the strongholds of a liberal bourgeois establishment in the press, an undergrowth of conformist magazines or shows tailored to the middle- or low-brow tastes of DC voters had always flourished. From its vantage-points in the elite culture, the PCI could view this universe with tolerant condescension, as expressions of an unenlightened if salient legacy of the clerical past whose importance Gramsci had long stressed. The party was not threatened by it.

The inrush of a completely secular, Americanized mass culture was another matter. Caught unprepared, the party's apparatus— and the intelligentsia that had formed around it—were knocked sideways. Although critical engagement with pulp was not lacking in Italy—Umberto Eco was a pioneer[57]—the PCI failed to connect. No creative dialectic, capable of resisting the blows of the new by transforming relations between the high and low, materialized. The case of the cinema, where Italy had above all excelled after

---

57. His first collection on these themes, *Apocalittici e integrati*, dates from 1964.

the war, can be taken as emblematic. There was no relay of the generation of great directors—Rossellini, Visconti, Antonioni— who had made their debut in the forties and early fifties, and whose last important works cluster in the early sixties: no combustible crossing of avant-garde with popular forms to compare with Godard in France or Fassbinder in Germany; later, only the weak brew of Nanni Moretti.[58] The result was a gap so large between educated and popular sensibilities that the country was left more or less defenceless against the cultural counter-revolution of Berlusconi's television empire, saturating the popular imaginary with a tidal wave of the crassest idiocies and fantasies—schlock so wretched the very term would be too kind for them. Unable to confront or turn the change, for a decade the PCI sought to resist it. The party's last real leader, Berlinguer, personified austere contempt for the self-indulgence and infantilism of the new universe of cultural and material consumption; after he had gone, the step from unbending refusal to gushing capitulation was a short one—Veltroni coming to resemble a beaming picture-card out of the schoolboy albums he made his name distributing with copies of *Unità*, when he became its editor.

If the PCI's idealism disabled it from grasping the material drives of the market and media which transformed leisure in Italy, the same lack of economic or sociological antennae blinded it to no less decisive changes in the workplace. Already by the turn of the sixties, it was showing less attention to these than the levy of young radicals who would go on to produce the peculiarly Italian phenomenon of *operaismo*, one of the most eruptive and strangest intellectual adventures of the European Left of the period. Unlike the PCI, the post-war PSI had possessed at least one major figure, Rodolfo Morandi, whose Marxism was of a less idealist cast, focussed on the structures of Italian industry, on which he was the author of famous study. In the next generation, he found a gifted successor in Raniero Panzieri, a PSI militant who, having shifted to Turin, started to investigate the condition of factory workers in the Fiat plants, gathering round his enterprise a group of younger intellectuals, many

---

58. Not that the Italian cinema produced no directors of the first order after the post-war generation. In the eighties and nineties, Gianni Amelio would develop out of the contrasting legacies of Antonioni and Visconti one of the finest bodies of film in Europe; but in a classical tradition, distant equally from avant-garde and popular forms. For Amelio's distinctive achievement, see Silvana Silvestri, 'A Skein of Reversals', *New Left Review* II/10, July–August 2001.

(Antonio Negri among them) but not all coming originally from
Socialist youth organizations.[59] Over the next decade, *operaismo*
took shape as a protean force, throwing up a succession of
seminal, if short-lived journals—*Quaderni rossi*, *Classe operaia*,
Gatto selvaggio, *Contropiano*—exploring the metamorphoses
of labour and industrial capital in contemporary Italy. The PCI
had nothing comparable to show, and paid scant attention to
this ebullition, even though at this stage the most influential of
the new theorists was a youngster from its own ranks in Rome,
Mario Tronti. This was a milieu whose culture was essentially
foreign to the party, indeed declaratively hostile to Gramsci,
taxed with spiritualism and populism.

The impact of *operaismo* came not just from the enquiries or
ideas of its thinkers, but their connexion with the upsurge of new
contingents of the working class, composed of young immigrants
from the south, rebelling against low wages and oppressive
conditions in northern factories—not to speak of Communist-
led unions, disconcerted by spontaneous outbreaks of militancy
and unexpected forms of struggle. To have anticipated this
turbulence gave *operaismo* a powerful intellectual headwind.
But it also fixated it on the moment of its insight, leading to
a romanticization of proletarian revolt as a more or less
continuous flow of lava from the factory floor. By the mid-
seventies, aware that Italian industry was changing once again,
and workshop militancy was in decline, Negri and others would
fall back on the figure of 'social labour' in general—virtually
anyone employed, or unemployed, wherever, by capital—as the
bearer of immanent revolution. The abstraction of this notion
was a sign of desperation, and the apocalyptic politics that
accompanied it took eventually took *operaismo* into the dead-
end of the *autonomia* of the late seventies. The PCI, however,
after missing the mutation of the sixties, had not learnt from it,
and offered nothing better by way of an industrial sociology. So
it was that when the Italian economy underwent critical further
changes in the eighties, with the rise of small export firms and a

59. The post-war culture of the Left had never been a monopoly of the PCI.
The Socialist tradition long retained a good many independent-minded figures
of stature, among them the poet and critic Franco Fortini, the theatre director
Giorgio Strehler, the philologist Sebastiano Timpanaro, not to speak of Lelio
Basso, a PSI leader of greater intellectual distinction than any PCI counterpart.
Later, of course, Norberto Bobbio, originally of the Partito d'Azione, would join
the PSI with bad timing, just as Craxi was taking it in hand.

black economy—the 'second Italian miracle', as it was hopefully
referred to at the time—the party was unprepared again. This
time the blow to its standing as the political representative of the
collective labourer proved fatal. Twenty years later, just as the
triumph of Forza Italia would dramatize its failure to react and
intervene in time to the massification of popular culture, so the
victories of the Lega would reveal its inability to respond in time
to the fragmentation of post-modern labour.

These were deficits of a *mentalité* with deeper sources than the
party's Marxism, a classical sense of intellectual values that
for all its limitations was in its own fashion rarely less than
honourable, often admirable. There was another and more
damaging side to the same idealism, however, that was specific
to Italian Communism, and for which it bore conscious political
responsibility. This was a strategic reflex that never really altered
from the Liberation onwards, and whose after-twitches continue
today. When Togliatti returned from Moscow to Salerno in the
spring of 1944, he made it clear to his party that there could be
no attempt at making a socialist revolution in Italy on the heels
of the expulsion of the Wehrmacht, already foreseeable. The
Resistance in the north, in which the PCI was playing a leading
role, could supplement but not substitute the Anglo-American
armies in the south as the main force to drive the Germans out
of the country, and it was the Allied High Command that would
call the shots once peace was restored. After twenty years of
repression and exile, the task of the PCI was to build a mass
party and play a central role in the an elected Assembly to put
Italy on a new democratic basis.

   This was a realistic reading of the balance of forces on the
peninsula, and of the determination of Washington and London
not to permit any assault on capital in the wake of German
defeat. A post-war insurrection was not on the agenda. Togliatti,
however, went much further than this. In Italy, the monarchy
which had helped install, and then comfortably cohabitated with
Fascism, had ousted Mussolini in the summer of 1943, fearful of
going down with him after the Allies landed in Sicily. After a brief
interval, the king fled with Badoglio, the conqueror of Ethiopia,
to the south, where the Allies put them atop an unaltered regional
administration, while in the north the Germans set up Mussolini
at the head of a puppet regime in Salò. When the war came to an

end, Italy was thus not treated like Germany, as a defeated power, but as a chastened 'co-belligerent'. Once Allied troops were gone, a coalition government, comprising the left-liberal Partito d'Azione, Socialists, Communists and Christian Democrats, was faced with the legacy of Fascism, and the monarchy that had collaborated with it. The Christian Democrats, aware that its potential voters remained loyal to the monarchy, and that its natural supports in the state apparatus had been the routine instruments of Fascism, were resolved to prevent anything comparable to German de-Nazification. But they were in a minority in the cabinet, where the secular Left held more posts.

At this juncture the PCI, instead of putting the DC on the defensive by pressing for an uncompromising purge of the state—cleaning out all senior collaborationist officials in the bureaucracy, judiciary, army and police—invited it to head the government, and lifted scarcely a finger to dismantle the traditional apparatus of Mussolini's rule. Far from isolating Christian Democracy, Togilatti manoeuvred to put its leader De Gasperi at the head of the government, and then joined with the DC—to the indignation of the Socialists—in confirming the Lateran Pact that Mussolini had sealed with the Vatican. The prefects, judges and policemen who had served the Duce were left virtually untouched. As late as 1960, sixty-two out of sixty-four prefects had been minions of Fascism, and all 135 of the country's police chiefs. As for judges and officers, the unreconstructed courts acquitted the torturers of the regime and convicted the partisans who had fought against them, retrospectively declaring combatants of the Fascist Republic of Salò legitimate belligerents, and those of the Resistance illegitimate—the latter hence liable to summary execution after 1943, without penal sanctions for the former after 1945.[60] These enormities were a direct consequence of the actions of the PCI. It was Togliatti himself who, as minister of justice, promulgated in June 1946 the amnesty that enabled them. A year later, the party was rewarded with an unceremonious ejection from the government by De Gasperi, who no longer had need of it.

The post-war history of Italy was thus to be entirely unlike that of Germany. There, where there had been no popular Resistance,

---

60. For all this, and more, see Claudio Pavone, *Alle origini della Repubblica*, Milan 1995, pp. 132–40.

Nazism was destroyed by both the extremity of military defeat, and the uprooting of the subsequent Allied occupations. In the Federal Republic, Fascism could never raise its head again. In Italy, by contrast, the Resistance bequeathed an ideology of—patriotic—anti-fascism, whose ubiquitous official rhetoric, in which the PCI took the lead, covered the actual continuities of Fascism, both as an inherited apparatus of laws and officials, and as an openly proclaimed creed and movement. Reconstituted as the MSI, the Fascist party was soon sitting in Parliament again, and eventually received into the establishment under its leader Giorgio Almirante. This figure, exalting Mussolini's anti-Semitic laws, had told his compatriots in 1938 that 'racism is the vastest and bravest recognition of itself that Italy has ever attempted', and in 1944, after Mussolini had been air-lifted north by the Germans, that if they did not enlist as fighters for the Republic of Salò they would be shot in the back. When Almirante died in the eighties, Togliatti's widow was among the mourners at the funeral. Today Fini, his appointed heir, is speaker of the Chamber of Deputies, and probable successor to Berlusconi as prime minister.

Beyond the obvious reproaches to this trajectory, what is most damning in the PCI's part in it was its self-destructive futility. When it had a chance to weaken Christian Democracy by sinking the sword of an intransigent anti-fascism into its flanks, to cut it away from the reactionary constituencies that had sustained Mussolini's regime, it did just the opposite. Helping the DC to establish itself as the dominant force in the country by passing a lenifying sponge across collaboration with the regime, it simply consolidated the conservative bloc under clerical command that would shut it out of power till its dying day. In this debacle, the party's conduct was without international excuse. If revolution was ruled out in post-war Italy, by 1946 the Allies had essentially left the country, and were in no position to halt a lustration of Fascism. Togliatti's naiveté in being so completely outmanouevred by De Gasperi had little to do with external influences. It was rooted in a strategic conception he had derived from Gramsci, interpreted through the gauze of Croce and his forebears. The pursuit of political power, Gramsci had written, required two kinds of strategy, whose terms he took from military theory, a war of position and a war of movement—trench or siege warfare, versus mobile assault. The Russian Revolution had exemplified the second; a revolution in the West would, for a considerable period, require the former, before eventually passing over to the latter.[61] Just as it had diluted Gramsci's notion of hegemony simply to its consensual moment, fixing it essentially in civil society, so under Togliatti the PCI reduced his conception of political strategy to a war of position only, the slow acquisition of influence in civil society, as if no war of movement—the ambush, sudden charge, rapidly wheeling attack, catching class enemies or the state by surprise—were any longer needed in the West. In 1946–7, De Gasperi and his colleagues did not make the same mistake.

By 1948 the popular élan of Liberation was broken. After electoral defeat amid the onset of the Cold War, it was twenty years before another wave of political insurgency crested in Italy. When it came, the generational rebellion of the late sixties, embracing both students and young workers, went deeper and lasted longer than anywhere else in Europe. Under Togliatti's successor Longo, somewhat more of a fighter and less of a diplomat, the PCI did not react as negatively to the youth revolt as the PCF in France. But nor did it respond creatively, failing either to connect with a culture of the streets in which high and low—the classics of the Marxist and Bolshevik past, the graffiti of the spray-can present— did for a time interact dynamically, or to renew its increasingly stationary stock of strategic concepts. When critical opposition to its inertia emerged within the party in the shape of the Manifesto group, that numbered the best minds of its post-war levy, the PCI leadership lost no time in expelling it.

The excommunication came after the Soviet invasion of Czechoslovakia, which the Manifesto condemned without reservation. Here, alongside the native idealism of its formation, lay the second reason for the continuing strategic paralysis of Italian Communism. However flexible in other respects, the PCI remained Stalinist in both its internal structures, and its external ties to the Soviet state. Despairing of one-party rule by a torpid Christian Democracy, liberal well-wishers of the party—of which there were to be many over the years—would time and again express their admiration for the PCI's sensible domestic moderation, yet exasperation that it should compromise

---

61. For a more detailed analysis of Gramsci's texts, and uses subsequently made of it, see 'The Antinomies of Antonio Gramsci', *New Left Review*, I/100, November 1976–February 1977, pp. 5–78.

its otherwise excellent record by its links to the USSR, and the organizational norms that followed from it. In reality, the two were structurally inter-related. From Salerno onwards, the party's moderation was a compensation for its relations with Moscow, not a contradiction of them. Just because it could always be taxed with a suspect kinship to the land of the October Revolution, it had to over-prove its innocence of any wish to emulate that all too famous model of change. The burden of an imputed guilt and the quest for an exonerating respectability went hand in hand.

Incapable of assuming or developing the revolts of the late sixties and early seventies, the PCI turned instead once again towards Christian Democracy, in the wistful hope that the DC had changed its ways and would now be prepared to collaborate with it in governing the country—Catholicism and Communism uniting in a 'Historic Compromise' to defend Italian democracy against the dangers of subversion and the temptations of consumerism. Proposing this pact in 1973 soon after he became the new leader of the party, Berlinguer invoked the example of Chile, where Allende had just been overthrown, as a warning of the civil war that risked breaking out, were the Left—Communists and Socialists combined—ever to try to rule the country on the basis of a mere arithmetical majority of the electorate. Few arguments could have been more obviously specious. There was not the faintest prospect of civil war in Italy, where even such outbreaks of violence as had occurred—the bomb planted by right-wing terrorists in the Piazza Fontana of Milan in 1969 was the worst case—had little incidence on the political life of the country as a whole. But once the PCI had moved to embrace the DC, the revolutionary groups to the left of it that had sprung out of the youth rebellion foresaw the emergence of a monolithic parliamentary establishment, government without opposition, and shifted towards direct action against it. The first lethal attacks by the Red Brigades began the following year.

But the political system was in no danger. The elections of 1976, in which the PCI did well, were perfectly tranquil. In their wake, the DC graciously accepted Communist support for governments of so-called 'National Solidarity' under Andreotti, without altering its policies or conceding any ministries to the PCI. Repressive legislation, gratuitously curbing civil liberties, was stepped up. Two years later, the Red Brigades seized the DC's most influential leader, Aldo Moro, in Rome, demanding the release of its prisoners in exchange for freeing him. In fifty-five days of captivity, fearing he would be abandoned by his own party, Moro wrote increasingly bitter letters to his colleagues, posing a clear threat to Andreotti were he to be at large. In this crisis, once again the PCI showed neither humanity nor common sense, denouncing any negotiations to secure Moro's release more vehemently than the DC leadership itself, which was understandably torn.

Moro was duly left to his fate. Had he been allowed to live, his return would certainly have split Christian Democracy and probably ended the career of Andreotti. The price of saving him was negligible—the Red Brigades, a tiny group that in any objective sense was never a significant threat to Italian democracy, could hardly have been strengthened by the release of a few of its members who would have been under continuous police surveillance the moment they walked out of jail. The notion that the prestige of the state could not survive such a surrender, or that thousands of new terrorists would have sprung up in its wake, was little more than interested hysteria. The Socialists realized this, and argued for negotiations. *Plus royalistes que le roi*, the Communists, in their anxiety to prove that they were the firmest of all bulwarks of the state, sacrificed a life and saved their nemesis in vain. The DC showed no gratitude. Once he had used them, Andreotti—a greater master of timing than De Gasperi himself—reduced them. When elections came in 1979, the PCI lost a million and a half votes, and was out in the cold again. The Historic Compromise had yielded it nothing, other than the disillusionment of its voters and a weakening of its base. When in the following year Berlinguer called for solidarity with Fiat workers, threatened with mass dismissals, his appeal fell on deaf ears. The last big industrial action in which the party would ever be involved was rapidly crushed.

Four years ago, reflecting bitterly on his country's politics, Giovanni Sartori remarked that Gramsci had been right to distinguish between a war of position and a war of manoeuvre. Great leaders—Churchill or De Gaulle—were such because of their instinct for wars of manoeuvre. In Italy, politicians knew only wars of position. He himself had always thought the title of Ortega's famous book *España invertebrada* would be still more apt for Italy, where the Counter-Reformation had created deep habits of conformism, and continual foreign invasions and conquests had made of the Italians specialists in survival by bending low.

Lacking any elites of mettle, this was a nation without a bone in its body.[62] Sartori was not talking at random. His addressees were the political class he described. By this time, the PCI was gone, Berlusconi was in power and his central objectives were clear: to protect himself and his empire from the law. The *ad personam* measures to secure both, pushed through Parliament, landed on the desk of the president. The Italian presidency is not a purely honorific post. The Quirinale not only nominates the premier, who must be ratified by Parliament, but can withhold approval of ministers, and refuse to sign legislation. In 2003 the incumbent was the former central banker Carlo Azeglio Ciampi, an ornament of the Centre-Left who had headed the final government of the First Republic, served as finance minister under Prodi, and is today a senator for the Democratic Party.

Imperturbably, Ciampi signed exceptional legislation not only to consolidate Berlusconi's grip on television, but to guarantee him permanent immunity from prosecution—an immunity of which Ciampi himself, as president, was also a beneficiary, as he appended his signature to it. Outside the Quirinale, anguished candle-lit appeals in the street begged him not to. But the heirs of Communism raised no objection. Indeed it had been from the ranks of the Centre-Left itself that the first draft of the bill for immunity had come. If there was hand-wringing in the press over the law, the president—constitutionally supposed to be *super partes*, and treated with all due reverence—was not put in question. Only one significant national voice was raised, not plaintively, but scathingly, against Ciampi. It came from Sartori, as a conservative liberal, who publicly asked Ciampi whether he even existed, contemptuously dubbing him a rabbit for his cowardice.

These days, it is a former Communist—Giorgio Napolitano, leader of the most right-wing faction in the PCI after the passing of Amendola—who sits in the Quirinale. By this time the first immunity law had been struck down by the Constitutional Court. But when it was given a new wrapping—after the fashion of Lisbon, one might say—and the substance of the same bill was voted through again by Berlusconi's majority in Parliament, the head of the post-Communist delegation in the Senate, far from

---

62. Giovanni Sartori, *Mala Tempora*, Rome–Bari 2004, pp. vii, 124: *un paese desossato*. Sartori's historical allusions were, of course, a considerable simplification. Apart from anything else, the Risorgimento and Resistance may have been the work of minorities, but they were hardly exercises in submission.

opposing it, explained that the Democratic Party had no objection in principle, though perhaps it should come into force only in the next legislature. Napolitano had no time for such *points d'honneur*, signing the bill into law on the day he received it. Once again, the only voices to denounce this ignominy were liberal or apolitical, Sartori and a handful of free spirits—immediately reproved by the press not only of Democratic, but Rifondazione obedience, for wanting in respect for the head of state. Such is the *sinistra invertebrata* of Italy today.

Powerful historical forces—the end of the Soviet experience; the contraction, or disintegration, of the traditional working-class; the weakening of the welfare state; the expansion of the videosphere; the decline of parties—have borne hard on the Left everywhere in Europe, leaving none in particularly good shape. The fall of Italian Communism is in that sense part of a wider story, which lies beyond censure. Yet nowhere else has such an imposing heritage been so completely squandered. The party that was outwitted by De Gasperi and Andreotti, failing to purge fascism or split clericalism, was still an expanding mass force of remarkable vitality, whatever its strategic innocence. Its descendants have colluded with Berlusconi, with no shadow of an excuse: fully aware of who he was and what they were doing. There is now an abundant literature of exposure on Berlusconi, both within Italy and without, including at least three first-class studies in English. But it is striking how limp-wristed much of this becomes when it touches on the role of the Centre-Left in helping him clean his slate and entrench his power. The complicity of its presidents in successive bids to put him—and themselves—above the law is no anomaly, but part of a consistent pattern that has seen the heirs of Italian Communism allow him to retain and expand his media empire, in defiance of what was once the law; not lift a finger to deal with his conflicts of interest; spring his right-hand man, and not a few other millionaire criminals, from jail; and repeatedly seek to cut electoral deals with him, at the expense of any democratic principle, to benefit themselves. At the end of all this, they have come away not only as empty-handed as their predecessors, but terminally emptier of mind and conscience.

3

What, for its part, has happened to the great cathedral of left-wing culture in Italy? It had started to crumble long before, its

foundations undermined with the one-time citadel of the mass
party itself. As in Germany, the shift to the right came first in the
field of history, with a revaluation of the country's dictatorship
between the wars. The first volume of Renzo De Felice's biography
of Mussolini, covering his years up to the end of the First World
War, was published in 1965. But it was not until the fourth,
covering the period from the Great Depression to the invasion
of Ethiopia, appeared in 1974—followed a year later by a book-
length interview with the American neo-conservative Michael
Ledeen, subsequently prominent in the Iran-Contra affair—that
this huge enterprise had a major impact in the public sphere,
for the first time attracting a barrage of criticism on the left as a
rehabilitation of Fascism.[63] By the time his fifth volume came out,
in the early eighties, De Felice had become an accepted authority,
enjoying ready access to the media—he would increasingly appear
on television—and meeting decreasing domestic challenge. Soon
he was calling for the end of anti-fascism as an official ideology in
Italy, and by the mid-nineties was explaining that the role of the
Resistance in what was actually a civil war in the north, in which
loyalties to the Republic of Salò had been underestimated, needed
to be demystified.[64] His eighth and last volume, incomplete at his
death, came out in 1997. In total, De Felice devoted 6,500 pages to
the life of Mussolini, over three times the length of Ian Kershaw's
biography of Hitler, and proportionately longer even than Martin
Gilbert's authorized life of Churchill: the largest single monument
to any leader of the twentieth century.

The scale of the work, poorly written and often arbitrarily
constructed, was never matched by its quality. Its strengths lay in
De Felice's indefatigable archival research, and his insistence on a
few unexceptionable truths, principally that the militants of Fascism
as a movement had come in the main from the lower middle class,
that Fascism as a system attracted support from businessmen,
bureaucrats, and higher social classes generally, and that at its height
the regime commanded a wide popular consensus. These findings,
none of them particularly original, sat in incoherent company with

---

63. Renzo De Felice, *Intervista sul fascismo, a cura di Michael Ledeen*, Rome-
Bari 1975. Without the war, Mussolini's regime would no doubt have evolved in
much the same positive direction as Franco's: pp. 60–2.

64. In heading the Republic of Salò, Mussolini was neither moved by a desire
for vengeance, nor political ambition, nor a wish to redeem Fascism by reverting
to its radical origins, but by 'a patriotic motive: a true "sacrifice" on the altar of
the defence of Italy': *Rosso e nero*, Milan 1995, pp. 114–5.

claims that Fascism was an offspring of the Enlightenment, that it had nothing to do with Nazism, that its collapse saw the death of the nation, and not least, with a hopelessly indulgent, oversized portrait of Mussolini himself as a great—if flawed—realistic statesman. Intellectually speaking, De Felice had little of the conceptual equipment or breadth of interest of Ernst Nolte, whose first book had preceded him. But his impact was much greater, not only by reason of the sheer weight of his scholarship, or even of the fact—fundamental though this obviously was—that in Germany fascism had been discredited much more absolutely than in Italy, but also because by the end of his career there was so little life left in the official post-war culture he had set out to oppose. Significantly, the most radical demolitions of his edifice came from Mack Smith in England, rather than any Italian historian.[65]

But if there was no real counterpart to the *Historikerstreit* in Italy, where De Felice could feel he had achieved most of his goals, there was also a less clear-cut shift of intellectual energies at large to the right than in Germany. De Felice's principal successor, Emilio Gentile, has devoted himself to amplifying the familiar theme that the mass politics of the twentieth century were secularized versions of supernatural faith, dividing these into malign brands—communism, nazism, nationalism—comprising fanatical 'political' religions, and more acceptable forms—notably, American patriotism—that constitute 'civil' religions: totalitarianism versus democracy in sacred dress. This is a construction that has won more of a following in the Anglosphere than in Italy itself. The same, paradoxically, might be said of the last fruits of *operaismo* on the left. There, the sober spirit of the *enquête ouvrière* had passed away with the premature death of Panzieri in the mid-sixties, and at the impulsion of Tronti and the young—then equally incendiary—literary critic Asor Rosa, its outlook underwent two drastic twists.

From Tronti came the conviction that the working class, far from having to endure successive economic transformations at the hands of capital, was their demiurge, imposing on employers and the state the structural changes of each phase of accumulation. Not in the impersonal economic requirements of profitability from above, but in the driving pressure of class struggles from

---

65. See, for his final judgement of the whole work, 'Mussolini: Reservations about Renzo De Felice's biography', *Modern Italy*, Vol. 5, No. 2, 2000, pp. 193–210.

below, lay the secret of development. From Asor Rosa came the argument that 'committed literature' was a populist delusion, for the working class could never hope to benefit from the arts or letters of a modern world in which culture as such was, by definition, irremediably bourgeois. No crude philistinism, or simple-minded Tolstoyanism, followed. Rather, it was only the high modernism of Mann or Proust, Kafka or Svevo, and the radical avant-garde, up to but not beyond Brecht, that mattered as literature—but as so many testimonies, of incomparable formal invention, to the inner contradictions of bourgeois existence, not as a legacy of any use to the world of labour. The gulf between the two could not be bridged by even the best revolutionary intentions of a Mayakovsky: it was constitutive.

> To make good literature, socialism has not been essential. To make the revolution, writers will not be essential. The class struggle takes a different path. It has other voices to express itself, make itself understood. And poetry cannot be behind it. For poetry, when it is great, speaks a language in which *things*—the hard things of struggle and daily existence—have already assumed the exclusive value of a symbol, of a gigantic metaphor of the world: and the price, often tragic, of its greatness is that what it says escapes from practice, never to return to it.[66]

When this was written, its target was the official line of the PCI, and behind it Gramsci, who had believed that the communist movement was the legitimate heir of the highest European culture, from the Renaissance, Reformation and Enlightenment onwards, and that among the problems it needed to solve in Italy was the absence of a national-popular literature. But as the upheavals of the late sixties unfolded, first Tronti and then Asor Rosa decided it made more sense to work within the PCI, where the organized working class was after all to be found, than outside it. In taking this step, Tronti transposed his vision of the primacy of struggles in the factory to the activities of the party in society, radicalizing it into a theory of the autonomy of politics as such from production. Younger than Asor Rosa or Tronti, and the most intellectually ambitious of the trio, Massimo Cacciari completed what they had started, not merely separating culture and economy from revolutionary politics, but proposing a systematic dissociation of all the spheres of modern

---

66. 'Letteratura e Rivoluzione', *Contropiano*, No 1, 1968, pp. 235–6.

life and thought from one another as so many technical domains, each untranslatable into any other. In common was only their crisis, equally visible in turn-of-the-century physics, neo-classical economics, canonical epistemology, liberal politics, not to speak of the division of labour, the operations of the market, the organization of the state. 'Negative thought' alone had been capable of grasping the depth of this crisis—Schopenhauer, Nietzsche, Wittgenstein, Heidegger.[67] What Hegel had joined, they refused: dialectical synthesis of any kind.

Operaismo had always been anti-historicist, as it was anti-humanist. In Cacciari's *Krisis* (1976), it now found inspiration in a line of nihilist thinkers, of whom Nietzsche was initially the most important for his account of the will to power, whose contemporary incarnation could only be the PCI. But there was to be no irrationalism. What the 'culture of crisis' called for were new orders and forms of rationality, specific to each practice. So in guiding the party towards its objectives, Weber and Schmitt—not Gramsci—were the indicated counsellors, each a specialist of politics as cold, lucid technique. Intellectually speaking, a more thoroughgoing rejection of the Marxism enshrined in the PCI, steeped in a Hegelian spirit of synthesis, would be difficult to imagine. But politically, the Nietzschean turn of *operaismo* proved perfectly compatible with the official line of the party in the early seventies. For what could the will to power in Italy at the time mean? Clearly, Tronti argued, it was the PCI's vocation to rule the country as the architect of an alliance between organized labour and big capital to modernize economy and society, not unlike the New Deal in America, which he had always admired—a pact of wages and profits against the parasitism of rents.

The PCI, for its part, which had always been tolerant of theoretical differences so long as they did not threaten political disturbance, accommodated the advocates of negative thought without difficulty—by this time it was no longer capable of engaging critically with such exotic outcrops anyway. Sensible of the prestige these were coming to enjoy, in due course it assured them honours in the political sphere whose autonomy they had

---

67. Ideas in part first developed in 'Sulla genesi del pensiero negativo', *Contropiano*, No. 2, 1968, pp. 131–200, at a time when Cacciari was still writing prolifically in the same journal on factory struggles in Italy, student revolts in France, guerrilla warfare in Latin America, Soviet debates on planning.

upheld. Cacciari became a deputy for the PCI, before going on to make a career as mayor of Venice, where he now sits; Tronti and Asor Rosa were eventually made senators. Inevitably, the price of such integration into a party that so conspicuously failed on the terrain of power they had appointed for it was the fade-out of *operaismo* as a coherent paradigm. Twenty years later, the PCI now only a memory, Asor Rosa would compose a melancholy balance-sheet of the Italian Left, to which he and Tronti remained in their own fashion faithful, while Cacciari today is an ornament of the right of the Democratic Party, combining—not unfittingly for an admirer of Wittgenstein—mysticism and technicism in a politics otherwise much like that of New Labour.[68] In those who came after, the intellectual legacy of negative thought was little more than an arid cult of specialization, and concomitant depoliticization.

At the crossroads of the late sixties, Negri went in the opposite direction, prospecting not a compact for modernity between capital and organized labour under the aegis of the PCI, but an escalation of conflicts between unorganized—or unemployed—labour and the state, towards armed struggle and civil war. After the crushing of the *autonomia* he had theorized, and his arrest by a Communist magistrate on trumped-up charges of master-minding the death of Moro, exile in France produced a steady stream of publications, the most notable on Spinoza. Here was prepared the metamorphosis of the non–factory worker of the late-twentieth-century *autonomia operaia* into the seventeenth-century figure of the 'multitude' in *Empire*, co-written with Michael Hardt, and appearing in the United States well before it saw print in Italy. Since the book's fame, Negri's international impact has been larger than his national influence, though a younger following exists. The same holds true of Giorgio Agamben, a late-comer

---

68. 'A virile acceptance of the administered world', as Cristina Corradi dryly describes the end-point of Cacciari's itinerary in her *Storia dei marxismi italiani*, Rome 2005, p. 231; for an earlier, and less temperate, critique, see Costanzo Preve, *La teoria in pezzi: La dissoluzione del paradigma operaista in Italia (1976–1983)*, Bari 1984, pp. 69–72. Politically speaking, the contrast with Asor Rosa and Tronti is marked, as the successive retrospects of the latter make plain. See Asor Rosa, *La Sinistra alla prova. Considerazioni sul ventennio 1976–1996*, Turin 1996, and Tronti, 'Noi operaisti', in Giuseppe Trotta and Fabio Milana (eds), *L'operaismo degli anni sessanta. Da 'Quaderni rossi' a 'Classe operaia'*, Rome 2008. One of the traits that linked the group in the sixties, as Tronti notes in his much more personal recollections, was a 'passionate love-affair with the turn-of the-century culture of *Mitteleuropa*'.

to the constellation, sharing many reference-points—Heidegger, Benjamin, Schmitt—with Cacciari, but with a political inflexion poles apart.

Viewed comparatively, the similarities of *operaismo* to strands in the *gauchisme* that flowered in France in the decade from the mid-sixties to the mid-seventies are striking—all the more so, for the lack of any direct contact between them. It seems to have been an objective concordance that took thinkers around *Socialisme ou barbarie* along much the same path as those around *Contropiano*, from a radical workerism to an anti-foundational subjectivism—although in the later Negri or Agamben, with their debts to Deleuze or Foucault, French and Italian currents flowed directly into each other. The contrasting outcome of the two experiences is largely to be explained by differences of national situation. In France, the PCF offered no temptations, and the revolt of May–June '68 was as brief as it was spectacular. In Italy, where the popular rebellion lasted much longer, Communism was less closed, and the thinkers were significantly younger, the afterlife of *operaismo* remains greater, if confined to the margins.

Retrieval of fascism on the right, eclipse of workerism on the left, have relocated the space of the centre, in which secular and clerical versions of the *juste milieu* have traditionally coexisted. There, paradoxically, the break-up of Christian Democracy, ending the rule of an overtly Catholic political party, rather than diminishing the role of religion in public life, has redistributed it more widely than ever before across the political spectrum, as DC voters have not only often divided evenly between Centre-Right and Centre-Left, but proved the most volatile single sector of the electorate, making them a 'swing factor' all the more eagerly prized by the contending blocs. In pursuit of them, former leaders of the PCI, not to speak of ex-Radicals, have fallen over each other to explain their private religious sensibility, attendance at mass from an early age, hidden spiritual vocation, and other requisites for a post-secular politics. In effect, what the Church has lost with the passing of a mass party of strict obedience, it has gained with the diffusion of a more pervasive, if lower-temperature, influence in society as a whole. With this has gone a descent into levels of superstition not seen in many years, the fruit of Wojtiła's occupancy of the papal throne, when more beatifications were pronounced (798) and saints made (280) than in the previous five centuries in the history of the Church,[69] the number of miracles necessary for sanctification was halved, and the grotesque cult of Padre Pio—a Capuchin divinely visited by stigmata in 1918, author of any number of supernatural feats—took off, to a point where the mainstream press can in all seriousness debate the veracity of his triumphs over mere laws of science.

A secular culture capable of this degree of complaisance to belief is unlikely to be more combative towards power. Under the Second Republic, opinion in the central organs of Italian print culture has rarely deviated from the standard doxa of the period. Most of its output during this time was indistinguishable from what could be found in the neo-tabloid papers of Spain, France, Germany, England or elsewhere—no self-respecting commentator failing to call for reforms to cure society's ills, for which the remedy was always the need for more competition in services and education, more freedom for the market in production and consumption, and a more disciplined and streamlined state, variations turning only on the sweeteners to be offered those on the receiving end of the necessary adjustments. Conformity of this kind has been so universal that it would have been unreasonable to have expected Italian columnists and journalists to show more independence of mind. The attitude of the press towards the law is another matter. At the forefront—after the magistrates had launched their attack on its corruption—of the hue and cry against the political class of the First Republic, it has proved remarkably submissive since Berlusconi established himself as a centrepiece of the new order, limiting itself for the most part to pro forma criticisms, without a hint of the *guerre à l'outrance* that could really have damaged him or driven him from the scene.

For that, its fire would have had to be directed not just against Berlusconi himself, but also the judges who regularly acquitted him, the statute of limitations that voided charges against him, the presidencies that assured him immunity, and the Centre-Left parties that made him into an accepted, indeed valued, interlocutor. Nothing could have been further from the general tenor of the press in these years, where complaints of malpractice are regularly tinged with fear and servility. The feebleness of this record is highlighted by the rare exceptions to it. Of these, one above all stands out, the reporter Marco Travaglio, whose implacable

---

69. See Tobias Jones, *The Dark Heart of Italy*, London 2003, p. 173.

indictments not just of the criminalities of Berlusconi or Previti, but of the entire system of connivances that has protected them, not least those of the press itself, have few parallels in the tame world of European journalism in these years. Not unexpectedly, Travaglio, whose books have sold in the hundreds of thousands, is a figure of the liberal right, expressing himself with a ferocity and freedom of tone all but unknown on the left.[70]

In Europe—this is not true, at least in the same way, of America—the world of the media as a rule reflects more than it creates the condition of a culture, whose quality ultimately depends much more on the state of its universities. In Italy, notoriously, these have remained archaic and under-funded, many departments sumps of bureaucratic intrigue and baronial patronage. The result has been a steady loss of the country's best minds to positions abroad. Virtually every discipline has been affected, as the roster of leading scholars either based or working for long stretches in the United States shows: Luca Cavalli-Sforza in genetics, Giovanni Sartori in political science, Franco Modigliani in economics, Carlo Ginzburg in history, Giovanni Arrighi in sociology, Franco Moretti in literature, to whom younger names might be added. Not a diaspora in a strong sense, since nearly all have maintained their links to Italy, most still participating in one way or another in its intellectual life, their absence has nevertheless obviously weakened the culture that produced them.

Whether any comparable levies are likely to arise out of the circumstances of recent years remains to be seen. On the face of it, the chances would seem slim. But it would be a mistake to underestimate the depth of the reserves on which the country can draw. A glance at Spain, whose modernization is now often held up by self-critical Italians as a model of what they have missed,[71] is a reminder of them. Although its economic growth has been

---

70. For a profile, see Claudio Sabelli Foretti (intervista), *Marco Travaglio. Il rompiballi*, Rome 2008. Among his books: with Elio Veltri, *L'odore dei soldi. Origini e misteri delle fortune di Silvio Berlusconi*, Rome 2001; with Gianni Barbacetto and Peter Gomez, *Mane pulite: La vera storia, Da Mario Chiesa a Silvio Berlusconi*, Rome 2002, and *Mani sporche: Così destra e sinistra si sono mangiate la II Repubblica*, Milan 2008; with Peter Gomez and Marco Lillo, *Il bavaglio*, Milan 2008. For a devastating taxonomy of Italian journalism, see Travaglio's *La scomparsa dei fatti*, Milan 2006.

71. The most extended and original example of this comparison is Michele Salvati's 'Spagna e Italia. Un confronto', in Victor Pérez-Diaz, *La lezione spagnola. Società civile, politica e legalità*, Bologna 2003, pp. 1–82.

higher, transport systems are faster, political institutions are more functional, organized crime is less widespread, and regional development more even—all real gains over Italy—Spain remains by comparison a provincial culture, with a much thinner and more derivative intellectual life, whose relative backwardness is only underlined by the modernities surrounding it. For all the disrepair of the country, the Italian contribution to contemporary letters is of different order. No country in Europe, indeed, has recently produced a monument of global scholarship to equal the five volumes on the international history and morphology of the novel edited by Moretti, and published by Einaudi—an enterprise of peculiarly Italian magnificence, of whose scale the Anglophone reader gets only a glimpse in the hand-me-down version, parsimonious in sympathy and spirit, issued by Princeton. Nor is it difficult to find examples of a continuing Italian capacity to shake received paradigms abroad. Ginzburg's manifesto 'Clues', not to speak of his essay reconstructing Dumézil, attempted by no French historian, would be one case; the distinguished classicist Luciano Canfora's recent book on democracy, censored by its outraged publisher in Germany, would be another; the political scientist Danilo Zolo's demolition of 'international justice', cherished in Britain and the Netherlands, a third. Such traditions do not die easily.

4

What, beyond the existing cross-party establishment, of political opposition? From the mid-sixties onwards, Italian Communism had another strand, neither official nor *operaista*, that proved more authentically Gramscian than anything its leadership could offer, or ultimately tolerate. Expelled in 1969, the Manifesto group around Lucio Magri, Rossana Rossanda and Luciana Castellina went on create the newspaper of that name that continues to this day, the one genuinely radical daily in Europe. Over the years, it was this current that produced far the most coherent and incisive strategic analysis of the problems facing the left, and the country—descent from Hegel, not surprisingly, supplying better equipment for the task than fascination with Heidegger. Today its legacy is in the balance, its three leading figures composing memorials of their experience, each of which will be significant. The first to appear, Rossanda's crisply elegant *Ragazza del secolo scorso*, has been a national bestseller. But in

2005 their journal was closed, and the daily is now, amid the credit crunch, at risk of disappearing. *MicroMega*, the thick bi-monthly edited by the philosopher Paolo Flores d'Arcais, is in no such danger, as part of the publishing empire whose showpieces are the Roman daily *La repubblica* and the weekly news-magazine *L'espresso*. Under the Second Republic, Flores has made of his journal the organizer of the most uncompromising and effective front of hostility to Berlusconi in Italy, playing a political role unique in the EU for an intellectual publication of this kind. A year after the victory of the Centre-Right in 2001, it was from here that a wave of impressive mass protests against Berlusconi was launched, outside and against the passivity of the Centre-Left.

In these, two other figures played a central part. One was Nanni Moretti, the country's most popular actor/film director, whose cinema had for over a decade tracked in critical, if often winsome, fashion the dissolution of the PCI and its fall-out. The other was the historian Paul Ginsborg, author of the two most commanding histories of post-war Italy, an Englishman teaching at Florence, distinguished not only as a scholar but now as a citizen in his adoptive country. In the second of his histories, covering the period from 1980 to 1998, published in English as *Italy and Its Discontents* (and in this edition going up to 2001), Ginsborg had put forward the hypothesis that, for all the evidence of egoism and greed of its yuppy stratum—the *ceti rampanti* that flourished under Craxi—there existed alongside it in the Italian middle class a sector of more thoughtful, civic-minded professionals and public employees—*ceti medi riflessivi*—who were capable of altruistic actions, and formed a potential source of renewal for Italian democracy. The proposal met with some scepticism when he developed it.[72] But in 2002 it came true. For it was the layer he had identified that essentially provided the troops for the demonstrations against Berlusconi of that year.

Therein, however, also lay their limitation. The distinctive form they took—demonstrators holding hands round public buildings, intended to symbolize the peaceful, defensive spirit of the movement—was quickly dubbed *girotondi* in the press, or 'ring-a-ring-o'-roses'. The result was to give it too easily the air

---

72. Among others, from myself: see 'Italy in the Present Tense: A Roundtable Discussion with Paul Ginsborg', *Modern Italy*, Vol. 5, No. 2, 2000, pp. 180ff.

of a children's game. The Centre-Left parties, not only disliking the reproach to themselves, but fearing political competition, did little to conceal their hostility. The *girotondini* did not respond in kind. Resolved to avoid any tempestuous actions of the kind that had met the G-7 in Genoa and vainly hoping for an alliance with trade-union leaders in hock to the Centre-Left, the movement was inhibited from mounting any tougher offensive against the government, let alone its accomplices in the opposition, and eventually undone by its *bon enfant* self-image, could not sustain itself.

When, to the fury of Veltroni, *MicroMega* courageously called for another mass demonstration against Berlusconi's return to power in the Piazza Navona last summer, the underlying contradictions of the *girotondini* burst into the open, Moretti and half the platform dissociating themselves from the more radical speakers, who this time did not spare Napolitano, the PD or the Rifondazione. Just as the impenetrable circumlocutions of the latter-day First Republic produced in reaction the calculated crudities of the Lega, so on this occasion the prissiness of much of the rhetoric of the *girotondi*, more given to pleading than savaging, detonated its opposite, a flamboyant coarseness of image and idiom—Berlusconi's bedroom boasts virtually inviting it—from comedians famous for detesting the political class, to the acute embarrassment of the better-behaved in the square—but apparently not, judging by opinion polls, most of even the Centre-Left electorate itself.[73] Politically speaking, the episode could be read as a micro-version of the polarization of the seventies, anxious propitiations from above once again provoking angry explosions from below.

In the autumn, such tensions dissolved in the torrent of student protests against the cuts in educational funding, and compression of schooling, voted through by the Centre-Right, and—a more limited—union mobilization against the government's economic response to global recession. The concessions gained are of less significance than the scale of the movements themselves. But a pattern of tactical retreats by Berlusconi and temporary surges of popular insurgency against him is not new. How it might alter as economic conditions worsen remains to be seen. Putting behind

---

73. For the flavour of this event, see the full set of speeches and reactions in the special issue of *Micromega*, entitled *Il regime non passerà! Piazza Navona, 8 luglio 2008*.

it the dangerous tools of the carpenter and the farmer, the Italian Left has adopted one symbol after another from the vegetable kingdom, or thin air—the rose, the oak, the olive, the daisy, the rainbow. Without some glint of metallurgy, it seems unlikely to make much headway.

III. THE EASTERN QUESTION

7

CYPRUS

2007

Enlargement, widely regarded as the greatest single achievement of the European Union since the end of the Cold War, and occasion for more or less unqualified self-congratulation, has left one inconspicuous thorn, amid the bouquets it regularly hands itself, in the palm of Brussels. The furthest east of all the EU's new acquisitions, even if the most prosperous and democratic, has been a tribulation to its establishment, that neither fits the uplifting narrative of deliverance of the captive nations from communism, nor furthers the strategic aims of Union diplomacy, indeed impedes them. Cyprus is, in truth, an anomaly in the new Europe. Not, however, for reasons Brussels cares to dwell upon. For this is a member-state of the EU a large part of which is under long-standing occupation by a foreign army. Behind tanks and artillery, a population of settlers has been planted relatively more numerous than those on the West Bank, without a flicker of protest from the Council or Commission. From its territory are further subtracted—not leased, but held in eminent domain—military enclaves three times the size of Guantánamo, under the control of a fellow-member of the EU, the United Kingdom.

I

The origins of this situation date back over a century, to the era of High Victorian imperialism. In 1878 the island was acquired by Britain from the Ottoman Empire, as a side-payment for Turkish recovery of three Armenian provinces, ceded to Russia, and restored thanks to Disraeli at the Conference of Berlin. Coveted as a naval platform for British power in the Middle East, the new colony had from antiquity been Greek in population and culture, with a Turkish minority introduced after Ottoman conquest in the sixteenth century. But in the nineteenth century, distant four hundred miles from Greece, it remained relatively unaffected by the national awakening that produced, first, Greek independence itself, then successive risings against Ottoman rule in Crete and its union with Greece before the First World War. In Cyprus, unrest did not materialize for another half century. Eventually, in 1931 desire for an equivalent *Enosis* boiled over in a spontaneous island-wide rebellion against British rule that left Government House in flames, and required the descent of bombers, cruisers and marines to quell.[1] Thereafter, Britain's response to this outbreak of feeling was unique in the annals of the empire: a colonial regime that ruled by decree until the day the flag was formally hauled down in Nicosia.

It was not until the post-war period, however, that a national movement really crystallized as an organized force on the island, in a strange mixture of times: post-dated in emergence, pre-dated in form. Pan-Hellenism was in many ways, as Tom Nairn pointed out long ago, '*the* original European model of successful nationalist mobilization', producing in the Greek Wars of independence the first victorious movement of national liberation after the Congress of Vienna. Yet, he went on, 'the very priority of Greek nationalism . . . imposed a certain characteristic penalty on it', conferring on Pan-Hellenic ideology increasingly 'anachronistic and out-dated' features by the twentieth century. But it was still quite powerful enough to capture the expression of popular revolt on the island after the Second World War. Once they awoke politically, the mass of the population 'found the fully-fledged, hypnotic dream of Greek nationalism already there, beckoning to them. It was inevitable that they should answer that call to the heirs of Byzantium, rather than attempt to cultivate a patriotism of their own'.[2]

1. For a lively description of these events, see Robert Holland, *Britain and the Revolt in Cyprus 1954–1959*, Oxford 1998, pp. 1–5. This outstanding work is perhaps the best single study in the historiography of decolonization. In the inter-war period, 'more than half the island's administrators came from West Africa, usually have begun their careers as cadets in Nigeria': George Horton Kelling, *Countdown to Rebellion: British Policy in Cyprus 1939–1955*, New York–London 1990, p. 12.

2. Tom Nairn, 'Cyprus and the Theory of Nationalism', in Peter Worsley (ed.), *Small States in the Modern World: The Conditions of Survival*, Nicosia 1979, pp. 32–4. For more extended reflections on the trajectory of Hellenism on the island, see Michael Attalides, *Cyprus: Nationalism and International Politics*, Edinburgh 1979, *passim*.

Union, not independence, was the natural goal of this self-determination.

Such Hellenism was not, however, an archaic import, out of season in a society that had moved beyond its conditions of origin. Its appeal was irresistible also because it found so powerful a sounding-board in an indigenous institution that was much older than romantic nineteenth-century nationalism. The Orthodox Church in Cyprus was without equivalent on any other Greek island. Autocephalous since the fifth century, its archbishop was equal in rank to the patriarchs of Constantinople, Alexandria or Antioch, and under the Ottomans had always been the acknowledged head of the Greek community. Since the British had made no attempt to offer education on the island—to the end, they ensured it had no university—the school system remained under the control of the Church. Clerical leadership of the national movement, with its inevitable freight of religious conservatism in moral and political life, was thus all but guaranteed in advance.

Not that the hegemony of the Church was complete. From the twenties onwards a strong local Communist movement developed, that was regarded by London as much more dangerous. Mindful of overwhelming majority aspirations, AKEL—as the Cypriot CP was now called—too campaigned for union with Greece when the war came to an end.[3] In 1945, it had every reason to do so, since the Communist resistance in Greece had been by far the leading force in the struggle against the Nazi occupation, in a strong position to take power once the country was cleared of it. To avert this danger, military intervention by Britain—on a scale exceeding later Soviet actions in Hungary—installed a conservative regime, complete with the discredited Greek monarchy. The result was a bitter civil war, in which the Left was crushed only after Britain and America, playing the role of Italy and Germany in Spain, weighed into the conflict to ensure the victory of the Right.

So long as the outcome in Greece was in the balance, AKEL could continue to support Enosis without undue strain, at least outwardly. Indeed, in November 1949—a month after the final defeat of the Democratic Army on the mainland—it fired what became the starting-pistol of national liberation in Cyprus, by calling on the United Nations to organize a referendum on

---

3. For the early history of the party, see T.W. Adams, *AKEL: The Communist Party of Cyprus*, Stanford 1971, pp. 21–45.

'the right of self-determination, which means union of Cyprus with Greece'. But this was to be its last moment in the van of the movement. In January 1950, moving swiftly to pre-empt this initiative, the Ethnarchy organized its own plebiscite, held in churches across the island, to which AKEL rallied. The result left little doubt about popular sentiment: 96 per cent of Greek Cypriots—that is, 80 per cent of the population of the island—voted for Enosis.

The Labour government in London, naturally, ignored this expression of the democratic will, its local functionaries dismissing it as 'meaningless'. But in the shepherd of the referendum, it had met with more than it reckoned. Five months later, Michael Mouskos was elected head of the Church, at the age of thirty-seven, as Archbishop Makarios III. Son of a goatherd, he had gone from a seminary in Cyprus to university in Athens and post-graduate studies in Boston, when he was suddenly recalled to the see of Kitium, and put in charge of the political hub of the Ethnarchy, where he rapidly showed his rhetorical and tactical gifts. The referendum had demonstrated a general will. Over the next four years, Makarios set about organizing it. Conservative peasant associations, right-wing trade-unions and a popular youth organization were built into a powerful mass base for the national struggle, directly under the aegis of the Church. Mobilization at home was accompanied by pressure abroad, in the first place on Athens to take up the issue of self-determination in Cyprus at the UN, but also—departing from the traditions of the Church—rallying support from Arab countries in the region.

None of this made any impression on London. For Britain, Cyprus was a Mediterranean stronghold it had not the slightest intention of relinquishing. Indeed, upgrading its strategic role as soon as British garrisons in the Canal Zone were judged insufficiently secure, the High Command in the Middle East was transferred to the island in 1953. A year later, the colonial secretary—now Conservative—told the Commons that possessions like Cyprus could never expect self-determination. Nor, since London refused to allow any legislative assembly in which the four-fifths of the population in favour of Enosis would enjoy a majority, was there a question even of self-government. The outlook at Whitehall remained: we hold what we have. If public justification were needed, Eden would provide one that was crude enough: 'No Cyprus, no certain facilities to protect our supply of oil. No oil, unemployment and hunger in Britain. It is as simple as that'.[4] Title to the island could dispense with normal sophistries: it was not arguable, a straightforward matter of *force majeure*.

Faced with an open assertion of indefinite colonial rule, pruned of even constitutional fig leaves, the national cause in Cyprus was inevitably driven to arms. These could be secured from only one source, the mainland. In Athens, a regime of the authoritarian Right was now in power, presiding over a system of vindictive discrimination and persecution that would last another thirty years. When the Church turned for support to Greece, what it found there could only be of one political complexion.[5] After four years of trying in vain to arouse international opinion to bring pressure to bear on Britain, in early 1954 Makarios met secretly with a retired colonel of the Greek army, George Grivas, to plan a guerrilla campaign to liberate the island.

Even by the standards of the Greek Right, not fastidious in its choice of men or means, Grivas was a *nervi* on the extreme wing of counter-revolution. A veteran of the disastrous Greek thrust into Anatolia after the First World War, he had sat out the German occupation during the Second World War, and then, with assistance from the departing Wehrmacht, organized death squads against the Left, before the British landed. But though it was decades since he had been on the island, he came from Cyprus and was committed to Pan-Hellenism in its most blinkered versions. Informally, he was in touch with the Greek General Staff. The Papagos government, newly admitted to NATO, was careful to keep him at arm's length, but looked the other way as he acquired weapons and logistics for a landing in Cyprus, where he arrived late in 1954.

On 1 April 1955, Grivas set off his first explosives on the island. Over the next four years, his 'National Organization of Cypriot Fighters'—EOKA—waged a guerrilla war of lethal efficacy, which London never succeeded in stamping out. By the end, Grivas had pinned down some 28,000 British troops with a force of not much more than two hundred men: a feat made possible—his own

---

4. Speech of 1 June 1956, at Norwich.
5. For a vivid description of the mechanisms of repression, not to speak of electoral intimidation and fraud, over which Karamanlis (1955–1963) presided, see Constantine Tsoucalas, *The Greek Tragedy*, London 1969, pp. 142–52.

gifts as a commander were quite limited—only by the breadth of support the national cause enjoyed among the population. Viewed comparatively, as a purely military performance, the EOKA campaign was perhaps the most successful of all anti-colonial resistances in the post-war period.

Politically, its impact was much more ambiguous. Grivas's virulent anti-communism left no room for AKEL in the armed struggle, in which EOKA repeatedly shot down its militants, even as the British proscribed the party and put its leaders into detention camps. Driven underground, AKEL was forced to the margins of the anti-colonial struggle, finding some political shelter only in extending support to Makarios, who ignored it. The main force of the Cypriot Left, which in normal circumstances would have been a central component of the national liberation movement, was thus effectively deleted from it. More was at stake in this than just the immediate fate of Cypriot Communism. With its trade-unions, AKEL was the only mass organization in the country with roots in both Greek and Turkish communities, integrating activists across ethnic lines.

With its exclusion went any chance of inter-communal solidarity against Government House. Cyprus had given birth to a singularly powerful revolt against Britain, combining guerrillas in the mountains and demonstrations in the streets. Led by a pistoleer and a prelate, there was in its mélange of clericalism and militarism a certain resemblance to Irish nationalism, the only other case where the Empire held a European, rather than Asian or African, people in its grip. In pedigree, Hellenism was older than Fenianism, and its goal differed: union, not separation. But this was another epoch, and in substance the constellation of forces in Cyprus was more modern. Makarios, the uncontested political leader of the struggle for self-determination, belonged to the era of Bandung, where he mingled with such as Nehru, U Thant, Ho Chi Minh, rather than De Valera or the Concordat. Reversing the relations between fighters and preachers in Ireland, his church was the less, not the more, regressive factor in the coalition against England—a difference that as time went on would widen. For its part, however ruthlessly effective it was as a clandestine organization, EOKA could not compete with AKEL above ground. The existence of a mass Left that was undislodgeable also set Cyprus apart from Irish experience.

To bring the island to heel, London dispatched no less a figure than the chief of the Imperial General Staff, Field Marshal Sir

John Harding. Within a month of his arrival in 1955, he told the
cabinet with brutal candour that if self-determination was ruled
out, 'a regime of military government must be established and
the country run indefinitely as a police state'.[6] He was as good
as his word. The standard repertoire of repression was applied.
Makarios was deported. Demonstrations were banned, schools
closed, trade-unions outlawed. Communists were locked up,
EOKA suspects hanged. Curfews, raids, beatings, executions were
the background against which, a year later, Cyprus supplied the
air-deck for the Suez expedition. As one kind of national resistance
was being hunted in cellars and hills, another was attacked round
the clock from bases a few miles away, British and French aircraft
taking off and landing at the rate of one a minute, dropping
bombs and paratroops on Egypt.[7] Failure to repossess the Canal
had no immediate impact on London's determination to hold on
to Cyprus. But with the departure of Eden, British policies began
to assume more definitive shape.

From the beginning, colonial rule had used the Turkish minority
as a mild counterweight to the Greek majority, without giving
it any particular advantages or paying overmuch attention to it.
But once demands for Enosis could no longer be ignored, London
began to fix its attention on the uses to which the community
could be put. It was not large, less than a fifth of the population,
but nor was it negligible. Poorer and less educated than the Greek
majority, it was also less active. But forty miles across the water
lay Turkey itself, not only much larger than Greece, but more
unimpeachably conservative, without even a defeated Left in
prison or exile. No sooner was the referendum of 1950 on Enosis
under way—at the very outset of the troubles in Cyprus—than
the British ambassador in Ankara advised the Labour regime in
London: 'The Turkish card is a tricky one, but useful in the pass
to which we have come'.[8] It would be played, with steadily less
scruple or limit, to the end.

Initially, Ankara was slow to respond to British solicitations
that it make itself felt on the future of Cyprus. 'Even when the
British did start to press the Cyprus button with the Turks,
the effect was not at first to trigger the instantaneous reactions

---

6. Holland, *Britain and the Revolt in Cyprus*, p. 91.

7. For details, see Brendan O'Malley and Ian Craig, *The Cyprus Conspiracy*,
London 1999, pp. 41–3.

8. Holland, *Britain and the Revolt in Cyprus*, p. 43.

that were hoped for: "curiously vacillating" and "curiously equivocal" were remarks typical of the puzzlement felt on this score in London', records the leading scholar of the subject, Robert Holland: 'It remains . . . a notable fact that it was the British who . . . had to screw the Turks up to a pitch of excitement about Cyprus, not the other way round'.[9] When the requisite excitement eventually came, London did not flinch from the forms it took. Within a month of EOKA's appearance in Cyprus, Eden was already minuting that any offer made to tamp down local unrest must have the prior approval of Turkey, which—as the Colonial Office would put it—had to be given 'a fair crack of the whip'.[10]

When the whip was cracked, it came steel-tipped. 'A few riots in Ankara would do us nicely', had noted an official in the Foreign Office.[11] In September 1955, as Cyprus was being discussed in a three-power conference in London, the Turkish secret police planted a bomb at the house where Kemal was born in Salonica. At the signal of this 'Greek provocation', mobs swarmed through Istanbul looting Greek businesses, burning Orthodox churches, and attacking Greek residents. Although no one in official circles in London doubted that the pogrom was unleashed by the Menderes government, Macmillan—in charge of the talks—pointedly did not complain.

Internal developments lent a hand to this external lever. Ready enough to kill Communists, Grivas had given EOKA strict instructions not to attack Turks, whom he had no wish to antagonize, but to target Greek collaborators with the British, above all in the police. Under EOKA pressure, their number rapidly dwindled. To replace them, Harding recruited Turks, and added a Police Mobile Reserve, dipping for the purpose into the lumpen element in the Turkish community, let loose for savagery when the occasion required. In due course, as Holland notes, the whole security machine came to depend, for anything less than large military sweeps, on Turkish auxiliaries. The result was to create a gulf between the two communities of a kind that had never existed before. It widened still further when Ankara, now fully engaged in remote control of the minority, riposted to EOKA by setting up its own armed organization on the island, the TNT—

---

9. *Britain and the Revolt in Cyprus*, p 43.

10. *Britain and the Revolt in Cyprus*, p. 52.

11. *Britain and the Revolt in Cyprus*, p. 69.

soon killing leftists on its own side—to which the British turned a blind eye.

After Suez, London started to edge towards another way of playing its chosen card, in a larger game. Hints began to be dropped that some kind of partition of Cyprus might be a solution. The Turkish premier Menderes, who had already been promised that Turkey could station troops on the island if Britain were ever forced to concede self-determination, snapped up the suggestion, telling the colonial secretary that 'we have done this sort of thing before— you will see it is not as bad as all that':[12] words to make any Greek with a memory of 1922–3 tremble. Harding disliked the idea, regarding it as underhand, and even within the Foreign Office a fear was eventually expressed that this might arouse 'unhappy memories of the Sudetenland'. Nor were US officials at all pleased when the scheme was intimated to Washington, where it was condemned as a 'forcible vivisection' of the island. If the objective in London was to keep control of Cyprus by splitting it in two under British suzerainty, the American fear was that this would arouse such anger in Greece that it risked toppling a loyal regime, handing power to the subversive forces still lurking in the country. In Britain, such concerns counted for less. Our man in Ankara, urging the need to 'cut the Gordian knot and reach a decision now for partition', had greater weight.[13]

In the event, it was Turkey that took the first practical steps. In June 1958, repeating the operation in Salonica, its intelligence agents set off an explosion in the Turkish Information Office in Nicosia. Once again, a fabricated outrage—no one was actually hurt—was the signal for orchestrated mob violence against Greeks. Security forces stood by as houses were set on fire and people were killed, in the first major communal clashes since the Emergency was declared. The upshot, clearly planned in advance, was the eviction of Greeks from Turkish areas in Nicosia and other cities, and the seizure of municipal facilities, to create self-contained Turkish enclaves: piecemeal partition, on the ground.[14]

---

12. Menderes to Lennox-Boyd, 16 December 1956: *Britain and the Revolt in Cyprus*, p. 166.

13. *Britain and the Revolt in Cyprus*, pp. 241, 194.

14. For this episode, decisive in all that followed, see Diana Weston Markides, *Cyprus 1957–1963, From Colonial Conflict to Constitutional Crisis: The Key Role of the Municipal Issue*, Minneapolis 2001, pp. 21–4ff, 159–60.

Its organizers could be sure of British complaisance. The day before the rampage—Harding was now out of it—the new governor, Labour's future Lord Caradon, had assured its leaders that the Turkish community would enjoy 'a specially favoured and specially protected state' under future British arrangements. A few months later, the colonial secretary was publicly referring to Cyprus as 'an off-shore Turkish island'.[15]

Seeing which way the wind was blowing, and fearing that Greece would buckle under British pressure, Makarios—still in exile—confronted the Greek premier Karamanlis in Athens. Implementation of the Anglo-Turkish plan for Cyprus, he pointed out, could be blocked simply by a Greek threat to withdraw from NATO if it went ahead. Karamanlis, whose historical *raison d'etre* was sentry duty in the Cold War—Costa-Gavras's film *Z* gives a good idea of the atmosphere under his regime—refused out of hand even to consider the idea.[16] Hellenism was essentially for public consumption, to keep domestic opinion quiet: for the regime, it was anti-communism that counted, and if there was a conflict between them, Enosis would be ditched without compunction. Makarios drew the necessary conclusion. Three days later, without giving any warning to the Greek regime, which was caught flat-footed, he came out publicly for the independence of Cyprus.

For the British, this had always been the worst of all conceivable scenarios. Grivas could be respected, as a staunchly right-wing foe who one day might even make—so Julian Amery thought—a good dictator of Greece. But Makarios, the origin of all their troubles, was anathema to London. Handing the island over to him would be the ultimate defeat. For the Americans, on the other hand, still worried at the possible impact of a too blatant division of Cyprus on a Greek political scene where popular feelings on the issue ran high, independence had for some time been viewed as one way out of a potentially dangerous conflict between allies. But it would have to be tightly controlled. When the UN met to debate Cyprus three months later, the US ensured that a Greek resolution calling for self-determination of the island was once again scuppered—this time thanks to a resolution moved at its behest by the dictatorship in Iran—and that instead direct talks

---

15. Holland, *Britain and the Revolt in Cyprus*, pp. 251, 288.
16. For a graphic account of this exchange, see Stephen G. Xydis, *Cyprus: The Reluctant Republic*, The Hague–Paris 1973, pp. 238–41.

would be held between Turkey and Greece, to hammer out a deal between them. In short order, Karamanlis and Menderes reached one at a hotel in Zurich.

2

The outcome was predictable. Turkey was not just the bigger military power, and on the closest terms with the colonial proprietor of the island. More fundamentally, whatever might be said of the Turkish state—no small subject, certainly—it was the completely independent creation of Kemalism, a nationalist movement that owed nothing to any outside power. The post-war Greek state, by contrast, started out life as a British protectorate and continued as an American dependency, culturally and politically incapable of crossing the will of its progenitors. Greek Cypriots were often to charge its political class with betrayal, but the spinelessness of so many of its ministers and diplomats was structural: there was no inner core of autonomy to betray. Menderes had no difficulty imposing terms on an interlocutor who retreated to his bedroom as details of the agreement were fastened down.

To avoid Enosis, Cyprus would be given a neutered independence: a Constitution stationing troops from Ankara and Athens on its soil, a foreign head of the Supreme Court, a Turkish vice-president with powers to veto all legislation, separate voting blocs for Greeks and Turks in a House of Representatives and municipal administrations, 30 per cent of the civil service, and 40 per cent of any armed force, composed of Turks, plus a requirement that all taxes be approved by a vote of Turks as well as Greeks.[17] Rounding off this package was a secret annexe, in the form of a 'gentleman's agreement'— here American supervisors, hovering nearby, made themselves felt—committing the future Republic of Cyprus in advance to join NATO and to ban AKEL. Last and most important of all, a Treaty of Guarantee between Britain, Turkey and Greece would allow any of these powers to intervene in the island, if it held there had been a breach of the settlement under it—in effect, a variant of the Platt amendment that authorized the United States to intervene in Cuba when it so decided after 1901.

It only remained for the British, who kept out of Zurich, to name their price for putting the seal of the proprietor on a transaction

---

17. There is a good critical analysis of the Constitution in Polyvios Polyviou, *Cyprus: Conflict and Negotiation*, London 1980, pp. 16–25.

so satisfactory to them. What London required were sovereign military enclaves on Cyprus—little 'Gibraltars', as Macmillan put it. There was less euphemism on the ground. 'We should open our mouths wide', wrote the key official in Nicosia.[18] The area gulped down was forty times the size of Gibraltar, and when the final Treaty of Guarantee establishing the new state and its constitution was signed, more pages were devoted to British bases in Cyprus than to all its other provisions combined—a juridical unicum.

Presented with a diktat which Karamanlis told him was unnegotiable, Makarios had to submit, taking office in 1960 as president of the new Republic. Independence had been granted, but as Holland writes: 'In Cyprus "freedom" as most people understood it had not been won; self-determination, however partisanly defined, was not applied'.[19] Far from ending the griefs of Cyprus under colonial rule, what the Treaty guaranteed was worse suffering to come. The Constitution of Zurich, designed to serve diplomatic imperatives rather than practical needs, let alone principles of equity, rapidly proved unworkable. Separate municipal administrations raised explosive issues of how to demarcate them, which even the British had not wanted to touch. Lack of progress in drawing their boundaries prompted Turkish veto of the budget, threatening more general paralysis. No agreement could be reached on forming an inter-communal army, leaving the field to the formation of irregulars on both sides.

By the end of 1963 the authors of Zurich were removed from the scene. Two years earlier Menderes had been hanged, among other things for instigating the pogrom of 1955. That summer, Karamanlis fell amid uproar over the murder of the Left MP Lambrakis by his police. Makarios, who had accepted their arrangements under duress, never regarding these as permanent, now moved to revise them. In late November he sent a set of proposals to his Turkish vice-president, Kutchuk, intended to create a more conventional democracy in Cyprus, with a unified administration and majority rule. Three weeks later, amid high tension, communal fighting broke out in Nicosia. This time it was not planned by either side, but after initial random incidents, Greeks inflicted more casualties than Turks, before a cease-fire

---

18. Holland, *Britain and the Revolt in Cyprus*, pp. 303, 306.
19. *Britain and the Revolt in Cyprus*, p. 336.

was effected. All Turkish representatives in the state withdrew from their posts, and Turkish inhabitants increasingly regrouped in consolidated enclaves with strong lines of defence. British troops policed a truce in Nicosia, but clashes persisted through February, the balance of attacks lying on the Greek side. By March a UN force had arrived to secure each community from further violence.

Makarios left no memoirs, and it is unlikely archives will shed much light on his thinking in this or later phases of his career. What is clear is that he had two courses open to him after the diktat of Zurich. He could escape from it either by continuing to pursue the goal for which he and the overwhelming majority of his compatriots had struggled, union with Greece; or by building a truly independent state in Cyprus, neither beholden to the Guarantor powers nor crippled by the impediments they had bequeathed. Once Makarios became president, he left both open. Cyprus did not join NATO, as stipulated in the gentleman's agreement, nor was AKEL banned—provisions which would have followed automatically had Cyprus been united with Greece, but which he was able to block on taking office. As head of state, his first trip abroad was to Nasser in Egypt, followed by attendance at the Non-Aligned Conference hosted by Tito, and a visit to Nehru in India. In this role he had the profile of a Third World leader, at the antipodes of the pickled Cold War politics of Restoration Greece.

At the same time, he appointed a cabinet dominated by stalwarts of EOKA, and made it clear to his electors—he had won a two-thirds majority of votes in the Greek community— that Cyprus remained entitled to the self-determination, of a free choice of union with the motherland, that had been so flagrantly denied it. Enosis might be deferred, but it was not renounced. Makarios was a charismatic leader, of great dignity and subtlety, and often spellbinding eloquence. But he could not ignore the sentiments of those from whom he drew his authority, who knew they had been cheated of their wishes, and saw no reason why they should give them up on foreign instructions. In moving to revise the mock Constitution, he was acting as they wanted him to. But in doing so, he miscalculated Turkish reactions in a way common to the Greek community. Knowing only too well that it was Britain that had manipulated Turkish fears and solicited Ankara's intervention in the first place, Greeks found it difficult to see that, however artificial the origin, the outcome was the intractable reality of a community that felt itself both entitled as of right to a disproportionate share of power on the island, and continually living on its nerves as if under imminent siege.

Prudentially, Makarios should have gone out of his way to try to win over Turkish opinion after independence, by generous economic and cultural measures in favour of it.[20] Yet it must be doubted if even these would have been of much avail. The cold fact was that Zurich had inflated the Turkish position in the state far beyond what a minority of its size could in normal circumstances have claimed. No matter what sweeteners Makarios might have offered, any constitutional alterations were, virtually by definition, bound to reduce this, and so long as the Turkish community had Ankara at its back, there was no chance of their acceptance. Tension over such changes was in any case over-determined by two further features of the situation for which Makarios bore his share of responsibility.

So long as Enosis was a goal to which the Greek population was attached, and to which he himself remained half or more committed, there was little incentive for the Turks to regard the independence of Cyprus as any basis for positive loyalty to a common state, as opposed to a mere negative shield against what would be worse. At the same time, the failure to agree on a small Cypriot army, as technically envisaged at Zurich—the Turks insisted it be ethnically separated, the Greeks that it be integrated— put Makarios, as head of state, at the mercy of guns he could not control. Grivas had been obliged to return to Greece, under the terms of the 1960 settlement. But EOKA, which had driven the British out, could hardly be denied positions in the government, and Grivas's lieutenants now commanded ministries, from which they could cover or direct irregulars formed in its image. Having no wish to multiply his adversaries in an independence struggle, Grivas himself had forbidden attacks on Turks. But as the British came to depend more and more, Black-and-Tan-style, on Turkish auxiliaries for repression, these inevitably came into the line of fire. After the British had gone, the same calculus of restraint no longer applied for EOKA. The obstacles were now irregulars on the other side, the Turkish militias fostered from Ankara. Out of this combustible material came the clashes of December 1963, Greek aggression predominating, which Makarios failed to prevent, and failed to punish.

---

20. This point is well made by Robert Stephens, *Cyprus: A Place of Arms*, London 1966, p. 173.

On the surface, Makarios could seem to have emerged from the breakdown of the Zurich arrangements in a stronger position. The UN force had brought a precarious peace. Turkey's threats to invade Cyprus were quashed by a brusque telephone call from Johnson. American schemes for 'double Enosis', dividing the island into portions to be allocated to Greece and Turkey, got nowhere.[21] In late 1965, the UN General Assembly formally called on all states to 'respect the sovereignty, unity, independence and territorial integrity of Cyprus'—the high point of Makarios's efforts to secure the international position of the Republic, free from interference by outside powers. Embarrassed to vote openly against the resolution, as too brazen an indication of their intentions, Britain and America made their displeasure clear by abstaining, along with their numerous clientele. Taken at face value—formally, the resolution obtains to this day—it was a diplomatic triumph for Makarios.

Other developments were less propitious. As ethnic clashes were subsiding in early 1964, the British furthered the concentration of the Turkish population in fortified enclaves, by sabotaging the reintegration of refugees into mixed villages. Relaying them, Americans were henceforward deeply engaged in imperial meddling on the island. Already, during colonial rule, the US had secured from Britain a series of intelligence facilities in Cyprus—tracking stations and the like—for Middle Eastern surveillance, that went unmentioned in the Treaty of Guarantee. By the early sixties, a Labour regime was back in power in London, and the British bases and listening-posts were for most practical purposes at the disposal of the overlord, as they remain today. The strategic value of Cyprus, less as an 'unsinkable aircraft carrier', in an earlier phrase, than as an all-purpose U-2, shot up after Washington placed Jupiter missiles in Turkey and Moscow retaliated by dispatching R-12s to Cuba, bringing on the Missile Crisis.

In this setting, it was vital to have a reliable *locum* in Cyprus. Visiting Washington, Makarios was told by Kennedy that he

---

21. These would later become the great 'lost opportunity' for a settlement in Cyprus, in the retrospect of the Greek Right, nostalgic for the days of absolute coincidence with Washington. See Evanthis Hatzivassiliou, *Greece and the Cold War: Frontline State 1952–1967*, London 2006, pp. 181–3, a comprehensive apologia for the Karamanlis regime, deprecating such ineffectual departures from its legacy as were made by Papandreou.

should form his own party, on the right, to check the alarming popularity of AKEL, and should desist from unnecessarily correct relations with the USSR. After the archbishop politely declined, saying he did not want to divide his flock, he became a marked man. Politically, in fact, he had little choice. At home he needed tacit Communist support to counter-balance the zealots of Pan-Hellenism; abroad he needed the diplomatic support of the Soviet bloc in the UN to counter Anglo-American attempts to reimpose schemes for partition, cleared with Turkey. Johnson had blocked a Turkish invasion, but Makarios was under no illusion that this was out of any mercy for Cyprus: Washington's concern was still about the political impact of a landing on Greece, wanting no hostilities between two NATO allies. So far as Makarios himself was concerned, in American eyes he was little better than 'Castro in a cassock'. In due course George Ball, the proconsul dispatched to sort out the situation, would remark, 'That son of a bitch will have to be killed before anything happens in Cyprus'.[22]

In the summer of 1964, the State Department told Athens in no uncertain terms that it must deal with Makarios. There, the premier was now George Papandreou, patriarch of the other dynasty with which Greece continues to be afflicted to this day, who had set British troops on his countrymen in 1944. Hastening to agree that Cyprus must be brought under NATO control if it was not to be 'transformed into another Cuba', he sent Grivas back to Cyprus, with the *placet* of Washington and London, as the man best able to replace Makarios.[23] There, Grivas took charge of the National Guard that had been created in the spring, expanding it with forces brought from the mainland, and openly announcing 'There is only one army in Cyprus—the Greek army'.[24] Quite willing to accept double Enosis, so long as the portion acceding to Turkey was small, his immediate aim was to undermine Makarios's authority by building a force loyal to himself, capable of dominating the larger part that would accede to Greece.

In April 1967, the weak government that had succeeded Papandreou was overthrown by a military junta, installing a full-blown dictatorship of the Right in Greece. AKEL, fearing what might be coming, readied plans to go underground. Grivas, predictably

---

22. Laurence Stern, *The Wrong Horse*, New York 1977, p. 84.
23. O'Malley and Craig, *The Cyprus Conspiracy*, p. 112.
24. Stanley Mayes, *Makarios: A Biography*, London 1981, p. 184.

emboldened, launched an all-out assault on two strategically placed Turkish villages. At this, Turkey mobilized to invade Cyprus, where ten thousand Greek troops were now stationed. With war seemingly imminent between two NATO allies, the US persuaded the junta to back down, and agree to the withdrawal of all Greek forces from the island. Once they were gone, and Grivas with them, communal tensions dropped, and Makarios could reassert his authority. Re-elected president with a landslide majority, he lifted road-blocks around Turkish enclaves, and started inter-communal talks with a view to a domestic settlement. A modest economic boom took off.

In this new situation, the ambiguity of Makarios's political identity—champion of union or symbol of independence—was of necessity resolved. Merging Cyprus into Greece under the junta was unthinkable. Enosis was tacitly dropped, and Cypriot linkage with Third and Second World countries strengthened. But popularity at home and prestige abroad could not offset the increasing difficulty of his underlying position. Had it been possible to abjure Enosis when colonial rule ended, and propose genuine independence as an unconditional goal to both communities, Turkish opinion might have been affected. By now, animosities had hardened: the Turkish community was entrenched in defensive enclaves and more tightly policed by Ankara than ever. But if such independence was too late on the Turkish side, it was too early for a still powerful minority on the Greek side, which denounced Makarios for betraying Enosis, and now had formidable backing in Athens. For the colonels, Makarios was not only a traitor to Hellenism, but a stalking-horse for communism. Turkey had always viewed him with cold hostility. Once the colonels were in power, it was Greece that became a deadlier threat.[25]

In March 1970, as the presidential helicopter took off from the Archbishopric, bearing Makarios to service in a monastery in the mountains, it came under fire from automatics on a roof of the nearby Pancyprian Gymnasium, where he had once gone to school. The machine was riddled with bullets, missing Makarios, but hitting the pilot, who miraculously brought it down without a crash-landing.[26] The failure of this first attempt

---

25. For this period, see the penetrating account in Attalides, *Cyprus: Nationalism and International Politics*, pp. 104–37, still much the most thoughtful analysis of the tensions in Cypriot Hellenism.

26. Mayes supplies a compelling narrative of this period: *Makarios: A Biography*, pp. 202–41.

on his life was followed by a broader range of operations against him. The next year Grivas returned secretly to Cyprus. Soon, all three Metropolitan bishops were calling on Makarios to resign. By 1973, EOKA-B—Grivas's new organization—was setting off bombs across the island, attacking police stations, and preparing snipers to pick off Makarios. In the autumn, another attempt was made to kill him, by mining his route. Hellenism, historically thwarted of a more natural outcome, was starting to destroy itself.

This was Grivas's last campaign. In January 1974 he died underground, and control of actions against Makarios passed back directly to the junta in Athens, now under still more violent leadership. The paroxysm came quickly. In early July, Makarios addressed a public letter to the junta's nominal president, detailing its successive plots against him. In it, he denounced the regime in Athens as a dictatorship that was fomenting civil war in Cyprus, and demanded the withdrawal of its officers from the National Guard, as a threat to the elected government. Two weeks later, tanks of the National Guard attacked the presidential palace, where—the scene could not have been more suggestive of the gulf between the forces in play—Makarios was receiving some Greek schoolchildren from Cairo. Bombardment began as a little girl was reciting a speech to him. Guards held off the assault long enough for Makarios to escape down a gully at the back of the building, before it went up in flames. On reaching a UN contingent in Paphos, he was airlifted to the British base in Akrotiri and out of the country to Malta.

Resistance to the coup was crushed within a few days. So completely controlled was it from Athens that the junta had not even prepared a local collaborator to front it, fetching about vainly among different candidates after the event, before eventually resorting to Nikos Sampson, a swaggering gunslinger from EOKA-B with a reputation for reckless brutality dating back to the colonial period. Hastily put together, his regime concentrated on rounding up leftists and loyalists to Makarios in the Greek community, leaving the Turks, who had every reason to fear him, strictly alone. But the coup was undoubtedly a breach of the Treaty of Guarantee, and within forty-eight hours the Turkish premier Ecevit was at the door of Downing Street, flanked by ministers and generals, demanding that Britain join Turkey in taking immediate action to reverse it.

The meeting that ensued settled the fate of the island. It was a talk among social democrats, Wilson, Callaghan and Ecevit, fellow-members of the Socialist International. Although Britain had not only a core of well-equipped troops, but overwhelming air-power on the island—fighter-bombers capable of shattering forces far more formidable than Sampson and his minders—Wilson and Callaghan refused to lift a finger. The next day, Turkey readied a naval landing. Britain, which could have removed Sampson without difficulty, singly or jointly, had warships off the coast, and could have deterred a unilateral Turkish invasion with equal ease. Again, London did nothing.

3

The result was the catastrophe that shapes Cyprus to this day. In complete command of the skies, Turkish forces seized a bridgehead at Kyrenia, and dropped paratroops further inland. Within three days, the junta had collapsed in Greece and Sampson had quit. After a few weeks' cease-fire, during which Turkey made clear it had no interest in the Treaty whose violation had been the technical grounds for its invasion, but wanted partition forthwith, its generals unleashed an all-out blitz—tanks, jets, artillery, and warships—on the now restored legal government of Cyprus. In less than seventy-two hours, Turkey seized two-fifths of the island, including its most fertile region, up to a pre-determined 'Attila Line' running from Morphou Bay to Famagusta. With occupation came ethnic cleansing. Some 180,000 Cypriots—a third of the Greek community—were expelled from their homes, driven across the Line to the south. About 4,000 lost their lives, another 12,000 were wounded: equivalent to over 300,000 dead and 1,000,000 wounded in Britain. Proportionately as many Turkish Cypriots died too, in reprisals. In due course, some 50,000 made their way in the opposite direction, partly in fear, but principally under pressure from the Turkish regime installed in the north, which needed demographic reinforcements and wanted complete separation of the two communities. Nicosia became a Mediterranean Berlin, divided by barbed wire and barricades, for the duration.

The brutality of Turkey's descent on Cyprus, stark enough, was no surprise. On previous occasions, as well as this one, Ankara had repeatedly given advance warning of its intentions. Political responsibility for the disaster lay with those who, rather than preventing, allowed or encouraged it. Primary blame is often put on the United States. There, by the summer of 1974, Nixon was so paralyzed by Watergate—he was driven from office between the first and second Turkish assaults—that American policy was determined by Kissinger alone. Much ink has been spilled over the question of whether the CIA colluded with the junta's impending coup in Nicosia, and if so, whether its advance knowledge of the putsch was shared with the State Department. What is not in doubt is Kissinger's view of Makarios, who had paid a lengthy state visit to Moscow in 1971, had imported Czech arms for use against EOKA-B, and under whom Cyprus was one of only four non-Communist countries trading with North Vietnam. Kissinger wanted him out of the way, and with Sampson in place in Nicosia, blocked any condemnation of the coup in the Security Council. Once Ankara had delivered its ultimatum in London, he then connived at the Turkish invasion, coordinating its advance directly with Ankara.

But though America's role in the dismemberment of Cyprus is clear-cut, it is Britain that bears the overwhelming responsibility for it. Wilson and Callaghan, typically, would later attempt to shift the blame to Kissinger, pleading that the UK could do nothing without the US. Then as now, crawling to Washington was certainly an instinctive reflex in Labour—had Heath survived as prime minister, such an excuse would have been unlikely. The reality is that Britain had both the means and the obligation to stop the Turkish assault on Cyprus. After first ensuring Turkish hostility to the Greek majority, it had imposed a Treaty of Guarantee on the island, depriving it of true independence, for its own selfish ends, the retention of large military enclaves at its sovereign disposal. Now, when called upon to abide by the Treaty, it crossed its arms and gave free passage to the modern Attila, claiming that it—a nuclear power—was helpless to do otherwise.

Two years later, a Commons Select Committee would conclude: 'Britain had a legal right to intervene, she had a moral obligation to intervene, she had the military capacity to intervene. She did not intervene for reasons which the Government refuses to give'.[27] The refusal has since, even by its critics, been too conveniently laid at the American door. In an immediate subjective sense, the trail there is direct enough—Callaghan, in reminiscent mood, would say Kissinger had a 'charm and warmth I could not resist'.[28]

27. Christopher Hitchens, *Cyprus*, London 1984, p. 136.
28. O'Malley and Craig, *The Cyprus Conspiracy*, p. 225.

But much longer, more objective continuities were of greater significance. Labour, which had started the disasters of Cyprus by denying it any decolonization after 1945, had now completed them, abandoning it to trucidation. London was quite prepared to yield Cyprus to Greece in 1915, in exchange for Greek entry into the war on its side. Had it done so, all subsequent suffering might have been avoided. It is enough to compare the fate of Rhodes, still closer to Turkey and with a comparable Turkish minority, which in 1945 peacefully reverted to Greece, because it was an Italian not a British colony. In the modern history of the Empire, the peculiar malignity of the British record in Cyprus stands apart.

As for Greece, the performance of its rulers, from the hotel in Zurich to the rubble in Nicosia, was irredeemable. Nor was it finished with the fall of the junta. The generals who brought the junta's rule to an end turned, predictably, to Karamanlis to restore the order to which they were jointly attached. On resuming power, his first act was to scuttle Cyprus once again, refusing it any assistance as the Turkish army launched its blitzkrieg. As in 1959, so in 1974, the only effective weapon would have been a threat to expel American bases and pull out of NATO if the US did not make the call to Ankara that Johnson had shown it could do, with immediate results. Naturally, concerned with his patrons rather than the people of Cyprus, Karamanlis did nothing of the kind. Nor did the second Papandreou, who succeeded him in the eighties, prove capable of better, other than bluster.

In what was now the Greek remnant of Cyprus, Sampson had handed over to Glafkos Clerides, head of the House of Representatives and next in line to Makarios. A figure of the Right, Clerides sought to retain power in his own hands by moving in the direction Kissinger and Karamanlis wanted—manoeuvring to keep Makarios from returning to Cyprus, and abandoning the principle of a unitary republic in pursuit of a deal based on a geographical federation with his tougher Turkish opposite number, Rauf Denktash. But the best efforts of Washington and Athens could not sustain him against the passionate loyalty of ordinary Greek Cypriots to Makarios, who returned at the end of the year to an overwhelming popular reception. When elections were held, Clerides—his party embraced diehards from EOKA-B—was routed by an alliance of the Left and loyalists to Makarios.

But though his presidency was as intact as ever, his room for initiative was limited. Tired and dispirited, under unrelenting external pressure, in 1977 Makarios accepted the idea of a bicommunal federal Republic, if with a strong central government enjoying majority consent, in the hope that the Carter administration might induce Turkey to yield some of its gains. Within a few months he was dead. Carter, far from trying to extract concessions from Turkey, laboured might and main to lift the congressional embargo on arms to it, passed out of public anger—there was no equivalent in Britain—at the invasion of Cyprus. Proud of his success in this aim, Carter would list it as one of the major foreign policy achievements of a presidency devoted to the service of human rights.

4

So matters rested, with the passing of the only European leader at Bandung, a last, anomalous survivor of the age of Sukarno and Zhou Enlai. Thirty years later, what has changed? Cyprus remains cut in two, still sliced along the Attila Line. In that sense, nothing. In other respects, much has altered. In the territory left them—58 per cent of the island—Greek Cypriots built, with the courage and energy that can come from disaster, a flourishing advanced economy. What was still an overwhelmingly agricultural society in the sixties was transformed into one in which modern services comprise over 70 per cent of GDP, as high a proportion as anywhere in Europe. Per capita income in this Cyprus—the Republic whose international recognition at the UN was won by Makarios—is equal to that of Greece, and well above that of Portugal, without benefit of handouts from the EU. Long-term unemployment is lower than anywhere else in Europe save Sweden. Tertiary education is more widespread than in Germany, corruption less than in Spain or Italy. Unionization of the labour force is higher than in Finland or Denmark, inequality lower than in Ireland.[29] Governments alternate, parties are represented fairly, elections are free of taint. By OECD standards, prosperous, egalitarian and democratic, this Republic has been a remarkable success.

The remaining 37 per cent of the island remains under occupation by the Turkish army.[30] There, Ankara set up a Turkish

---

29. For the above comparisons, see Economist Intelligence Unit, *Cyprus: Country Profile 2008*, p. 25; *European Community Statistics on Income and Living Conditions*, January 2008; EIRonline, *Trade Union Membership 1993–2003*.

30. A residual 5 per cent is covered by the UN buffer zone and British bases.

Republic of Northern Cyprus in 1983, ostensibly an independent state, in practice a regime that is an offshoot of the mainland. Local parties and politicians compete for office, and their interests and identities do not always coincide with those dominant at any given time in Turkey. But such autonomy is severely limited, since the local state, which provides the bulk of employment, depends entirely on subsidies from Ankara to cover its costs, and the police are under the direct control of the Turkish army. Development has come mostly from construction, the supply of cheap degrees from over-the-counter colleges, and tourism, catering principally to mainlanders. Average incomes are less than half those on the Greek side of the island. Poverty and crime remain widespread.

Not all of this is indigenous. Having taken two-fifths of the island, inhabited—after invasion and regroupment—by less than a fifth of the population, Turkey had a huge stock of empty houses and farms on its hands, from which their owners had been expelled. To fill them, it shipped in settlers from the mainland. What proportion of the population these now represent is a matter of dispute, in part because they have since been supplemented by temporary workers, often seasonal, and students from the mainland. Official Turkish figures suggest that no more than 25 to 30 per cent out of a total of some 260,000 persons come from the mainland; Greek estimates put the number—there were just under 120,000 Turks on the island in 1974—at over 50 per cent, given that there has also been substantial emigration. Only scrutiny of birth certificates can resolve the issue. What is not in doubt, however, is that the Turkish army maintains 35,000 soldiers in the zone it has occupied since 1974, a much higher ratio of troops to territory than Israel has ever deployed to protect its settlers in the West Bank.

If the military division of the island has remained static for thirty years, its diplomatic setting has been transformed. In 1990 Cyprus applied for membership in the European Community. Although its application was accepted three years later in principle, in practice no action was taken on it. In Brussels, the prize was enlargement to Eastern Europe, on which all energies were focussed. Cyprus was viewed as at best a distraction, at worst a troubling liability. Turkey, which had applied to join in 1987, and whose suit had been stalled, was bound to be angered at the prospect of Cyprus achieving membership before itself. For Council and Commission alike, Cyprus was the least welcome of candidates for admission to the Union. Good relations with Ankara were of much greater moment.

There matters stood until Greece, at last helping rather than harming its compatriots, in late 1994 blocked the customs union which Brussels was offering Turkey, to keep it sweet while its application to join the EU remained on hold. By this time, the second Papandreou was nominally back in office, but in advanced stages of personal and political decay. In the all too brief interval between his quietus and a dreary reversion to dynastic government in Athens—where today indistinguishably conformist offspring of the two ruling families alternate once again—there was momentarily room for some exercise of independence in European councils. The foreign minister of the time, Theodore Pangalos, greatly disliked in Brussels for his refusals to truckle, made it clear that the Greek veto would not be lifted until Cyprus was given a date for the start of negotiations for its accession. In March 1995, a reluctant France, presiding over an EU summit at Cannes, brokered the necessary deal: Cyprus was assured an accession process by 1998, and Turkey was granted its customs union.[31]

Amid the fanfare over expansion into Eastern Europe, these events were not conspicuous. But their potential for inconvenience did not escape notice in one capital. No sooner had Britain's ambassador to the UN retired at the end of the year, than he was asked by the Foreign Office to become the United Kingdom's special representative on Cyprus. Sir David—now Lord—Hannay, who began his career in Iran and Afghanistan, was Britain's foremost European diplomat, with some thirty years of involvement in EU affairs behind him. His summons came from Jeremy Greenstock, soon to become famous for his services to Blair as ambassador to the UN and special representative in Iraq. The appointment made clear the importance of the mission. 'The enlargement of the European Union', writes Hannay in his memoir *Cyprus: The Search for a Solution*, explaining his brief, 'was a major objective of British foreign policy and must in no way be delayed or damaged by developments over Cyprus', not least since Britain was 'the European country most favourable to Turkey's European aspirations'.[32]

---

31. For this turning-point, which at the time left both Turkey and Greece dissatisfied, see Christopher Brewin, *The European Union and Cyprus*, Huntingdon 2000, pp. 21–30.

32. *Cyprus: The Search for a Solution*, London–New York 2005, pp. 50, 85.

Still more favourable was the United States. From the early nineties onwards, the EU was looking over its shoulder at Washington, which made it clear that, once Eastern Europe was in the bag, the strategic priority was Turkey. As the deadline for negotiations on Cypriot accession came closer, the Clinton administration sprang into action, with pressure on European governments to admit Turkey that even Hannay found 'heavy-handed'. But manners aside, Britain and the US were at one on the need to ensure that there be no entry of Cyprus into the EU without a settlement of the island palatable to Turkey beforehand, to forestall any complications in Ankara's own bid for membership. The simplest solution would have been to block Cypriot membership until Turkey received satisfaction, but this was ruled out by a Greek threat to veto enlargement to the East as a whole if Cyprus was not included. That left only one course open: to fix Cyprus itself. In the summer of 1999, the UK and US got a resolution through the G-8 that pointedly ignored the legal government of the Republic of Cyprus, calling on the UN to superintend talks between Greeks and Turks in the island with a view to a settlement.

This was then rubber-stamped by the Security Council, formally putting Kofi Annan in charge of the process. Naturally—he owed his appointment to Washington—Annan was, as Hannay puts it, 'aware of the need for the UN to cooperate as closely as possible with the US and the UK in the forthcoming negotiations'.[33] In practice, of course, this meant his normal role as a dummy for Anglo-American ventriloquists. Recording the moment, Hannay never bothers to explain by what right the UK and US arrogated to themselves the position of arbiters of the fate of Cyprus; it went without saying. A UN special representative, in the shape of a dim Peruvian functionary, was chosen to front the operation, but it was Hannay and Tom Weston, special coordinator of the State Department on Cyprus, who called the shots. So closely did the trio work together that Hannay would boast that a cigarette paper could not have been slipped between their positions. In command was, inevitably, Hannay himself, by a long way the most senior, self-confident and experienced of the three. Successive 'Annan Plans' for Cyprus which materialized over the next four years were essentially his work, details supplied by an obscure scrivener from the crannies of Swiss diplomacy, Didier Pfirter.

---

33. *Cyprus: The Search for a Solution*, p. 105.

The first of these Plans was produced punctually a few days before the EU summit in Copenhagen in December 2002, at which the Council was due to consider the upshot of negotiations with Cyprus. The pious fiction of the secretary-general was maintained, but he had little reason to stir from New York. For its author—after Annan had 'set out the prize to be achieved . . . in terms almost identical to my CNN Turk interview'[34]—was on the spot, conferring with Blair as the various heads of state gathered in the Danish capital. The Anglo-American campaign to secure Turkish membership had acquired new urgency with the victory of the AKP at the polls in November, bringing to power the first government in Ankara for some time with which Washington and London felt completely at home, and whose leaders Tayyip Erdoğan and Abdullah Gül arrived in Copenhagen to press their suit. The UN Plan—'Annan I'—was adjusted at the last minute to give them further satisfaction, and—as 'Annan II'—presented to Clerides, now president of Cyprus. It was vital, in the eyes of its architects, to get the Plan agreed by both Greek and Turkish Cypriots before the Council took any decision on Cypriot entry into the EU. Clerides indicated, with a nod and a wink, that he was ready to sign. But to Hannay's consternation, Denktash—controlling the Turkish Cypriot delegation from afar—refused to have anything to do with it. Amid the ensuing disarray, the EU leaders had to make the best of a bad job. Cyprus was accepted into the Union, effective from the spring of 2004, and Turkey—provided it met EU norms for human rights—was promised negotiations on its candidature, effective from the winter of 2004.

The AKP proclaimed this pledge a historic achievement for Turkey, with some reason. Its success in securing a date for starting negotiations towards accession, in good part due to heavy pressure from the Bush administration, strengthened its hand at home. But it was still new to power, and in failing to bring Denktash to heel in time, had been unable to forestall the prospect of Cypriot membership in the EU without arrangements on the island agreeable to it signed and sealed in advance. Worse still, once Cyprus was inside the EU, it would have a power of veto over Turkey's own entry.

Yet Turkey was, after all, suing for acceptance of its candidacy at Copenhagen, after a long period in which it had been rebuffed. Questions of political experience aside, Erdoğan was not in that

---

34. *Cyprus: The Search for a Solution*, p. 175.

strong a position there. The more pertinent question is why the European powers, having rallied to the American case for Turkish entry, permitted such a risky inversion of the schedule for Cyprus—giving membership a green light before a settlement was reached that was supposed to be a condition of it. The answer is that the EU leaders believed, correctly, that once a Turkish government applied itself, it would have little difficulty in getting Turkish Cypriots to accept what it had decided upon. Once that was achieved, they assumed that the concurrence of the Greeks—already available at Copenhagen—could be counted on. There were still fifteen months to go before Cyprus entered, and time enough to tie down the settlement that had been missed on that occasion.

This calculation, however, assumed that they would still have the same interlocutor. Western establishments had become used to the comfortable presence of Clerides, who had been president of Cyprus for a decade, a fixture of the Right with no thought of upsetting any geo-political apple-cart of the Atlantic Alliance. Unfortunately, within two months of his gracious performance at Copenhagen, elections were due in Cyprus. In February 2003, standing for yet another term at the age of eighty-three, he was trounced by Tassos Papadopoulos, Makarios's youngest minister at independence and closest colleague in his final years, who enjoyed the support of AKEL and the Cypriot Left. His presidency was unlikely to be so pliable.

Undeterred, Hannay and his collaborators piled on the pressure. After a meeting between Annan, Weston, De Soto, and himself in New York, at which 'not surprisingly, since we had all been working closely together for over three years, there was effectively a consensus over our analysis of the situation and our prescriptions for action',[35] Annan in person was dispatched to Nicosia, with a third version of the Plan to be put to a referendum in the two parts of the island, and a summons for Papadopoulos and Denktash to agree to it a week later in the Hague. But this was now March 2003. The AKP government was not only embroiled in arguments over the impending war in Iraq—on 1 March the Turkish parliament defied Erdoğan and Gül by rejecting US demands for passage of American troops for the invasion—but in the throes of getting Erdoğan, hitherto technically debarred from becoming a deputy,

---

35. *Cyprus: The Search for a Solution*, p. 206. Álvaro de Soto was the Peruvian functionary from the UN.

into Parliament and making him premier. Amid these distractions, Ankara failed a second time to curb Denktash, who blocked the Plan once again. In frustration, Hannay threw up his hands and quit. The UN shut down its office in Cyprus.

But once the AKP regime had consolidated its hold in Ankara, and come to an understanding with the army—in October it secured a vote for Turkish troops to help out the American occupation in Iraq—it was in a position to enforce its will in northern Cyprus, where Denktash's autocratic rule had by now anyway made many restless. Signals of Ankara's displeasure were enough to swing local elections against him in December 2003, letting the main opposition party into government. The AKP had made Turkish entry into the EU its top priority, and having sorted this out, wasted no time. In January, a common position on Cyprus was hammered out with the Turkish military on the National Security Council, and the next day Erdoğan travelled to Davos to brief Annan, then flew on to meet Bush in Washington. The effect of their conversation was immediate. Annan was summoned to the White House, and twenty-four hours later had issued an invitation to the two sides in Cyprus plus the Guarantor Powers to join him for talks in New York.

There, he explained that to cut through previous difficulties, if there were once again no agreement, the UN Plan should be put directly to the voters of each community, regardless of the views of the authorities on either side. This time, the secretary-general's script had been written in America, and US diplomats brought full pressure to bear on Papadopoulos and Denktash, to force them to accept the prospect of such a diktat. The following month, talks entered their final phase at another Swiss resort, Bürgenstock in Interlaken, where the Greek delegation was headed by the younger Karamanlis—nephew of the statesman of Zurich—who had just become premier in Athens. Once again, American emissaries hovered discreetly in the background, this time as members of the British delegation (the US was not a Guarantor Power), while the foreground was dominated by the Turkish premier. A fourth edition of the UN Plan was adjusted to meet Turkish demands, and a final, non-negotiable version— 'Annan V'—was announced on the last day of March. A jubilant Erdoğan told his people that it was the greatest victory of Turkish diplomacy since the Treaty of Lausanne in 1923, sealing Kemal's military triumph over Greece.

Time was now short. The fateful day when Cyprus was due

to become a member of the EU was just a month away. The referendum extorted in New York was called for 24 April, a week beforehand, and copies of Annan V—a tombstone of more than nine thousand pages—were hastily prepared, final touches coming only in the last forty-eight hours before the vote. The approval of Turkish Cypriots was a foregone conclusion: they were not going to turn down a second Lausanne. But on 7 April, in a sombre address on television, Papadopoulos advised Greek Cypriots against the Plan.[36] Since Clerides's party had declared for it, the critical judgement appeared to be AKEL's. The combined weight of Washington, London and Brussels was brought to bear on the party, and the Greek electorate at large, to accept the Plan. From the State Department, Powell himself telephoned the leader of AKEL, Dimitris Christofias, to secure a favourable opinion. In New York, two days before the referendum, the US and UK moved a resolution in the Security Council endorsing the Plan, to impress on voters that they should not trifle with the will of the international community. To much astonishment (indeed outrage—Hannay found it 'disgraceful'), Russia used its veto for the first time since the end of the Cold War. Twenty-four hours later, AKEL came out against the Plan. When votes were counted, the results said everything: 65 per cent of Turkish Cypriots accepted it, 73 per cent of Greek Cypriots rejected it. What political scientist, without needing to know anything about the Plan, could for an instant doubt whom it favoured?

5

Hannay was not wrong in remarking—he was in a position to do so—that, for all the jungle of technical modifications that developed across its five versions, the essence of the 'Annan' Plan remained unaltered throughout. It contained three fundamental elements. The first prescribed the state that would come into being, if it were accepted. The Republic of Cyprus, as internationally recognized for forty years—repeatedly so by the UN itself—would be abolished, along with its flag, anthem, and name. In its stead, a wholly new entity would created, under another name, composed of two constituent states, one Greek and the other Turkish, each vested with all powers in

---

36. For the text of his speech, see James Ker-Lindsay, *EU Accession and UN Peacemaking in Cyprus*, Basingstoke 2005, pp. 194–202.

its territory, save those—principally concerned with external affairs and common finance—reserved for a federal level. There a Senate would be divided 50:50 between Greeks and Turks, and a Chamber of Deputies elected on a proportionate basis, with a guaranteed 25 per cent for Turks. There would be no president, but an executive Council, composed of four Greeks and two Turks, elected by a 'special majority' requiring two-fifths of each half of the Senate to approve the list. In case of deadlock, a Supreme Court composed of three Greeks, three Turks and three foreigners would assume executive and legislative functions. The Central Bank would likewise have an equal number of Greek and Turkish directors, with a casting vote by a foreigner.

The second element of the Plan covered territory, property, and residence. The Greek state would comprise just over 70 per cent, the Turkish state just under 30 per cent, of the land surface of Cyprus; the Greek state just under 50 per cent, the Turkish state just over 50 per cent, of its coast-line. Restitution of property seized would be limited to a maximum of a third of its area or value, whichever was lower, the rest to be compensated by long-term bonds issued by the federal government, at tax-payer cost, and would carry no right of return. Of those expelled from their homes, the maximum number allowed to recover residence, over a period of some twenty years, would be held below a fifth of the population of each zone, while just under 100,000 Turkish settlers and incomers would become permanent residents and citizens in the north.

The third element of the Plan covered force and international law. The Treaty of Guarantee, giving three outside powers rights of intervention in Cyprus, would continue to operate— 'open-ended and undiluted', as Hannay records with satisfaction—after the abolition of the state it was supposed to guarantee. The new state would have no armed forces, but Turkey would maintain six thousand troops on the island for another eight years, and after a further interval, the military contingent accorded it at Zurich, permanently. Britain's bases, somewhat reduced in size, would remain intact, as sovereign possessions of the UK. The future Cypriot state would drop all claims in the European Court of Human Rights,[37] and last

---

37. In 1995, the European Court of Human Rights awarded £468,000 in damages against Turkey to Tina Loizidou, a Greek Cypriot, who lost her property in Kyrenia to the occupation. After much resistance, Ankara was eventually obliged to pay up. For the Hannay plan, it was essential to stop any further

but not least, bind itself in advance to vote for Turkish entry into the EU.

The enormity of these arrangements to 'solve the Cyprus problem, once and for all', as Annan hailed them, speak for themselves. At their core lies a ratification of ethnic cleansing, of a scale and thoroughness that has been the envy of settler politics in Israel, where Avigdor Lieberman—leader of the far right Yisrael Beiteinu—publicly calls for a 'Cypriot solution' on the West Bank, a demand regarded as so extreme that it is disavowed by all his coalition partners. Not only does the Plan absolve Turkey from any reparations for decades of occupation and plunder, imposing their cost instead on those who suffered them. It is further in breach of the Geneva Conventions, which forbid an occupying power to introduce settlers into conquered territory. Far from compelling their withdrawal, the Plan entrenches their presence: 'no one will be forced to leave', in Pfirter's words.[38] So little did legal norms matter in the conception of the Plan, that care was taken to remove its provisions from the jurisdiction of the European Court of Human Rights and European Court of Justice in advance.

No less contemptuous of the principles of any existent democracy, the Plan accorded a minority of some 18 to 25 per cent of the population, for all practical purposes, 50 per cent of decision-making power in the state. To see how grotesque such a proposal was, it is enough to ask how Turkey would react if it were told that its Kurdish minority—also around 18 per cent—must be granted half of all seats in its Grand National Assembly, sweeping rights to block action in its executive, not to speak of exclusve jurisdiction over some 30 per cent of its land area. What UN or EU emissary, or apologist for the Hannay plan among the multitude in the Western media, would dare travel to Ankara

---

reparations of this kind being ordered by European courts—an estimate of the total potential compensation owing on losses in the north runs to $16 billion dollars. See William Mallinson, *Cyprus: A Modern History*, London–New York 2005, p. 145; Mallinson notes that this sum is about the same as the latest IMF loan to Turkey. For other cases before European courts, see Van Coufoudakis, *Cyprus: A Contemporary Problem in Historical Perspective*, Minneapolis 2006, pp. 90–92.

38. See Claire Palley, *An International Relations Debacle: The UN Secretary-General's Mission of Good Offices in Cyprus 1999–2004*, Oxford 2005, p. 70, the leading legal study of the UN plans, which contains a detailed comparative chart of their variations, across thirty-five pages: pp. 277–314.

with such a scheme in his brief-case? Ethnic minorities need protection—Turkish Kurds, by any measure, considerably more than Turkish Cyriots—but to make of this a flagrant political disproportion is to invite hostility, rather to restrain it.

Nor were the official ratios of ethnic power to be all. Planted across the tundra of the Plan's many other inequities, foreigners were imposed at strategic points—Supreme Court, Central Bank, Property Board—in what was supposed to be an independent country. Topping everything off, armed force was to be reserved to external powers: Turkish military remaining on site, British bases trampolines for Iraq. No other member of the European Union bears any resemblance to what would have been this cracked, shrunken husk of an independent state. Greek Cypriots overwhelmingly rejected it, not because they were misinformed by Papadopoulos, or obeyed directives from Christofias—opinion polls showed their massive opposition to the Plan before either spoke against it. They did so because they had so little to gain—a sliver of territory, and crumbs of a doubtful restitution of property—and so much to lose from it: a reasonably well-integrated, well-regarded state, without deep divisions or deadlocks, in which they could take an understandable pride. Why give this up for a constitutional mare's nest, whose function was essentially to rehouse the 'Turkish Republic of Northern Cyprus', condemned as illegal by the UN itself, as an equal partner in a structure jerry-built to accommodate it? Cut to foreign specifications, the Constitution of Zurich had proved unworkable enough, leading only to communal strife and breakdown. The Constitution of Bürgenstock, far more complicated and still more inequitable, was a recipe for yet greater rancour and paralysis.

There was, however, a logic to this. The rationale for the entire scheme, like that of its predecessor in 1960, lay outside Cyprus itself, the interests of whose communities were never more than ancillary in its calculus. The fundamental drive behind the Plan, in all its versions, was the fear that if Cyprus, as constituted, were admitted to the EU without being taken apart and retrofitted beforehand, it could veto the entry of Turkey into the Union until it relinquished its grip—soldiers and settlers—on the island. The bottom line of Hannay's calculations was thus always what would be acceptable to Ankara, helping it to seek membership of the EU without provoking public opinion or the 'deep state' in Turkey. The AKP government, viewed not inaccurately as the ideal partner for the West, could point to domestic resistance, threatening the grand common goal of its entrance into Europe, every time it wanted to secure a concession in the Cypriot side-show, and its interlocutors would fall over themselves to oblige it.

As in 1960 and in 1974, it is pointless to blame Turkey for the process that led to 2004, in this case less of a success for it anyway. On each occasion, it acted according to classical precepts of *raison d'état*, without undue sanctimony, after being invited to do so. The authors of the latest attempt on Cyprus lie elsewhere. Behind the bland official prose, Hannay's memoir has the involuntary merit of making it plain that Britain was at the end of the story, as it had been at the beginning, the prime mover in efforts to fix a cape of lead over the island. In that sense, Hannay was a lineal successor to Harding, Caradon and Callaghan, in the record of callous disregard for the fate of Cyprus as a society. Britain, of course, did not act alone. Historically, in all three crises when the future of the island was at stake, the US abetted the UK, without ever quite playing the leading role, until the last moment.

In the final episode, however, a new actor stepped on stage, the European Union. If the British set the ball rolling towards another Zurich in 1996, and the Americans followed in 1997, it was not until the end of 2002, with the arrival of the AKP in power, that the EU establishment in general rallied to the Anglo-American determination that Turkey must—for economic, ideological and strategic reasons alike—be admitted in short order to the Union. Though scattered misgivings persisted, by 2003 Brussels, in the persons of Romano Prodi as president of the Commission and Günter Verheugen, commissioner for enlargement, was fully behind London and Washington. Hannay, whose knowledge of the workings of the Commission was unrivalled, had taken care to square Verheugen well before this, securing his assurance that the EU's *acquis communautaire*—the body of rules with which candidate countries must comply, including freedoms of residence and investment certain to be a sticking-point north of the Attila Line—would not stand in the way of a settlement that annulled them in Cyprus.

Verheugen made no difficulty. On all subsequent occasions—in Ankara with Erdoğan on the eve of his flight to Annan and Bush in early 2004; at the end-game in Bürgenstock two months later—he was at pains to explain that the normal *acquis* would not apply. This despite the fact that, as Hannay notes appreciatively, 'he was precluded from clearing his lines in advance with member states': i.e., he ignored his mandate without consulting them.[39] Ponderous and self-important, a kind of German Widmerpool—now a figure of fun in his own country, since he was snapped cavorting in the nude with his secretary on a Lithuanian shore—Verheugen attempted to intervene directly in the Cypriot referendum with a lengthy interview on behalf of the Plan. Incensed when no television station would touch it, he was little short of apoplectic when the Plan was rejected. Such was, indeed, the general reaction in Brussels to the refusal by Greek voters to fall in with its will: an incredulous fury also expressed by virtually the entire European public sphere, *FT* and *Economist* in the lead, that has scarcely died down since.[40] Were another lesson needed in what the Union's dedication to international law and human rights is worth, its conduct over Cyprus supplies the most graphic to date.

6

Nor, of course, is it over. Having escaped from the trap set in Switzerland, Cyprus entered the EU politically intact a week after the referendum, on 1 May 2004. In the intervening years, the scene on the island has altered significantly for the better. Physical partition has diminished since the opening of check-points by Denktash in 2003, allowing travel across the Green Line between north and south. The immediate effect was a huge wave of visits—over two million in a couple of years—by Greeks to the north, often to look at their former homes, and an inflow of Turkish workers to the south, where they now make up a tenth of the labour force in the building industry. The more lasting result has been the granting of a large number of official Cypriot documents to Turks with legitimate rights on the island—by the spring of 2005, some 63,000 birth-certificates, 57,000 identity-cards and 32,000 passports—reflecting the magnet of EU membership, and economic growth well above the Union average.[41] In 2008, Cyprus became only the second member-state since enlargement, after Slovenia, to enter the Eurozone.

---

39. *Cyprus: The Search for a Solution*, pp. 134, 172.

40. For such reactions, see Ker-Lindsay, *EU Accession and UN Peacemaking in Cyprus*, p. 113, who writes in the same spirit.

41. For these figures, see Coufoudakis, *Cyprus: A Contemporary Problem in Historical Perspective*, p. 46.

Politically, the landscape shifted when AKEL withdrew from the government in 2007, after deciding that for the first time in the history of the Republic it would run its own candidate for the presidency. AKEL had always been far the strongest party in Cyprus, indeed for a long time the only real one, yet could never aspire to lead the state, given Pan-Hellenism and the Cold War. But the solidity of its anchorage in the trade-union and co-operative movements, and the prudence of its direction after the collapse of the Soviet bloc—it drew its conclusions from the *débandade* of Italian Communism—have given it a striking capacity to ride out adverse currents of the time. In exchange for backing Papadopoulos in 2003, it acquired key ministries for the first time, and by 2008 was ready to try for the presidency itself. In the first round of the vote in February, Christofias was the runner-up, knocking out Papadopoulos; in the second, with the support of Papadopoulos and his party, he knocked out Clerides's candidate, becoming the first Communist head of state in the EU.

A burly, avuncular figure, Christofias, who comes from a village near Kyrenia in the north, joined AKEL's youth league in his teens. In his twenties he studied in Moscow, where he got a doctorate in 1974, returning to Cyprus after the Turkish invasion. By 1988, at the relatively young age of forty-two, he had become leader of the party. Speaking with tranquil fluency, he stresses AKEL's long-standing criticism of both Greek and Turkish chauvinism, and commitment to good relations between the two communities, without attempting either to minimize or to equate the suffering of each—of which his family has personal experience: going north after 2003, 'my sisters were literally sick when they saw what had happened to our village'. The UN Plan, he argues, contained too many obvious concessions to Ankara to be acceptable, so for all his 'many, many meetings with Hannay and my good friend Tom Weston', when time was refused to reconsider it, he could not recommend the package to his party, and there can be no return to it now. But AKEL maintained links with the Turkish Republican Party (CTP), now the governing party in the north, throughout the years when Denktash forbade any contact between the two communities, holding several secret meetings with it abroad. Since the referendum the two parties, with their trade-union and youth organizations, have had regular sessions together, fostering AKEL's aim of 'a popular movement for rapprochement'.

As president, Christofias's first move has been to meet his opposite number in the north, Mehmet Talat, and arrange for what was once the main shopping street in Nicosia to be opened across the Green Line. The arrival of the two men at the head of their respective communities represents a strange convergence in the history of the island. For in origin the CTP was, as Christofias likes to describe it, a 'sister party' of AKEL—each a branch of the same communism when it was still an international movement. In the case of the CTP, it was fired in the eighties by the kind of radical Marxist students that provided the militants of the insurgent Turkish Left of the time, who on the mainland ended in their tens of thousands in the jails of the generals who staged the invasion of Cyprus. In the nineties, the party made its peace with the occupying army and today is more like the ex-Communist parties of Eastern Europe that have become bywords for all-purpose opportunism—Talat being closer to a Gyurcsány or Kwaśniewski than to his interlocutor, who is well aware of the difference.

Still, that there is some common history linking the two sides is new in any talks across the ethnic boundary in Cyprus. How far Talat is capable of a measure of independence from Ankara remains to be seen. The Turkish Cypriot political class is attached to its local privileges, which it would lose were Turkey to absorb the north, and would like to enjoy the advantages of being truly within the EU, rather than in a condition of semi-limbo. The local population does not get on particularly well with the wretched seasonal migrants—mostly from the area around Iskanderun, the nearest port on the mainland—who perform much of the manual labour it shuns for more profitable employment by the state.

For the economy remains dependent on huge subsidies from Ankara, bloating public employment at wages much higher than in Turkey itself. Retired policemen get pensions larger than the salaries of associate professors on the mainland; while private enterprise is represented by no less than six 'supermarket' universities doling out degrees to dud students from the mainland, or nearby regions of the Middle East or Central Asia. Against the potential advantages of integration into the EU stands the artificial character of the economy that would be exposed to the potential impact of the *acquis*. It is possible that the adjustment could be as painful as in East Germany.

Reunification would thus require not just institutional protections, but economic buffers for the Turkish minority, something an AKEL president would understand better than any other. A real settlement on the island can only come from within it, rather than being externally imposed, as invariably to date. The demilitarization of the island that AKEL has long demanded, with the exit of all foreign troops and bases—the withdrawal not just of the Turkish army, but the shutting down of the anachronism of British enclaves—is a condition of any true resolution. A constitution with meticulous safeguards against any form of discrimination, and genuinely equitable compensation for losses on all sides, is a far better guarantee of the welfare of a minority than provocative over-representation in elected bodies, or preordained gridlock in the state, neither durably sustainable. To devise a political system that meets these goals is hardly beyond the bounds of contemporary constitutional thought.

In the past, there was no possibility of even raising such principles, given the Turkish military grip on the island. Today, however, what the whole 'UN' process was designed to avert has come to pass. Cyprus possesses a veto over Turkish entry into the EU, and is in a position to force it to pull out its troops, on pain of exclusion. This enormous potential change has been the hidden stake of all the frantic diplomacy of the past years. It is true that a French refusal to admit Turkey to the EU, or a Turkish nationalist decathexis away from the EU, might deprive Cyprus of the lever now resting in its hands. But the Western interests vested in Turkish entry, and the Turkish interests—not least those of capital—vested in Western status, are so great that the balance of probability is against either. That does not mean Cyprus will ever use the power it now has. It is a small society, and immense pressures will be brought to bear to ensure that it does not. For the EU, notoriously, referenda are mere paper for shredding. Sometimes small countries defy great powers, but it has become increasingly rare. The more likely outcome remains, in one version or another, the sentence pronounced on another Greek island: 'The strong do what they can, the weak do what they must'.

TURKEY

2008

'The greatest single truth to declare itself in the wake of 1989', wrote J.G.A. Pocock two years afterwards, 'is that the frontiers of "Europe" towards the east are everywhere open and indeterminate. "Europe", it can now be seen, is not a continent—as in the ancient geographers' dream—but a subcontinent: a peninsula of the Eurasian land-mass, like India in being inhabited by a highly distinctive chain of interacting cultures, but unlike it in lacking a clearly marked geophysical frontier. Instead of Afghanistan and the Himalayas, there are vast level areas through which conventional "Europe" shades into conventional "Asia", and few would recognize the Ural mountains if they ever reached them'.[1] But, he went on, empires—of which in its fashion the Union must be accounted one—had always needed to determine the space in which they exercised their power, fixing the boundaries of fear or attraction around them.

A decade and a half later, the question has assumed a more tangible shape. After the absorption of all the former Comecon states, there remain the untidy odds and ends of the once independent communisms of Yugoslavia and Albania—the seven small states of the 'West Balkans'—yet to be integrated into the EU. A pocket still to be mopped up behind borders that already extend to the Black Sea, they will—no one doubts—enter it in due course. The great issue facing the Union lies further east, at the point where no vast steppe confounds the eye, but a long tradition has held that a narrow strip of water separates one world from another. No one has ever missed the Bosphorus. 'Every school-child knows that Asia Minor does not form part of Europe',

---

1. *The Discovery of Islands*, p. 278.

Sarkozy told voters en route to the Elysée, promising to keep it
so—a pledge to be taken in the spirit of the conjugal reunion on
offer in the same campaign. Turkey will not be dealt with in that
way. Within the EU the official consensus that it should become
a member-state in full standing has for some time now been
overwhelming. Such agreement does not exclude *arrière-pensées*
in this or that government—Germany, France and Austria have all
at different points entertained them—but against any passage of
these to action lies the formidable barrier of a unanimity of media
opinion more complete, and more committed to Turkish entry,
than that of the Council or Commission itself. There is also the
simple fact that no country that has been accepted as a candidate
for accession to the EU has ever, once negotiations with it were
opened, been rejected by it.

The expansion of the EU to the lands of the Warsaw Pact did
not require much political defence or illustration. The countries
concerned were all indisputably European, however the term was
defined, and all had famously suffered under Communism. To
bring them into the Union was not just to heal an ancient division
of the continent, anchoring them in a common liberal-democratic
capitalism, but to compensate the East for its misfortunes after
1945, relieving the West of a bad conscience at the difference
in fates between them. They would also, of course, constitute
a strategic glacis against any resurgence of Russia, and offer a
nearby pool of cheap labour, although this received less public
emphasis. The uncontentious logic here is not, on the face of it,
immediately transferable to Turkey. The country has long been a
market economy, held parliamentary elections, constituted a pillar
of NATO, and is now situated further from Russia than ever in
the past. It would look as if only the last of the motives in Eastern
Europe, the economic objective, applies—not unimportant,
certainly, but incapable of explaining the priority Turkey's entry
into the EU has acquired in Brussels.

Yet a kind of symmetry with the case for Eastern Europe can be
discerned in the principal reasons advanced for Turkish membership
in Western capitals. If the fall of the Soviet Union has removed
the menace of communism, there is now—it is widely believed—a
successor danger in Islamism. Rampant in the authoritarian
societies of the Middle East, its tentacles threaten to stretch into
immigrant communities within Western Europe itself. What
better prophylactic against it than to embrace a staunch Muslim
democracy within the EU, functioning as at once beacon of a liberal

order to a region in desperate need of a more enlightened political model, and sentinel against every kind of terrorism and extremism? This line of thought originated in the US, with its wider range of global responsibilities than the EU, and continues to be uppermost in American pressure for Turkish entry into the Union. Much as Washington set the pace for Brussels during expansion into Eastern Europe, laying down NATO lights on the runway for subsequent descent by the EU, so it championed the cause of Turkey well before Council or Commission came round to it.

But although the strategic argument, for the value of a geopolitical bulwark against the wrong kinds of Islam, is now standard in European columns and editorials, it does not occupy quite the same position as in America. In part, this is because the prospect of sharing a border with Iraq and Iran is not altogether welcome to many within the EU, however vigilant the Turkish army might prove. Americans, at a greater distance, find it easier to see the bigger picture. But such reservations are not the only reason why this theme, central though it remains, does not dominate discussion in the EU as completely as in the US. For another argument has more intimate weight. Current European ideology holds the Union to offer the highest moral and institutional order in the world, combining—with all due imperfections—economic prosperity, political liberty and social solidarity in a way no rival can match. But is there not some danger of cultural closure in the very success of this unique creation? Amidst all its achievements, might not Europe risk falling into—the very word a reproof— Eurocentrism: too homogeneous and inward-looking an identity, when the advance guard of civilized life is necessarily ever more multi-cultural?

Turkey's incorporation into the EU, so the case goes, would lay such fears to rest. The greatest single burden, for present generations, of a narrowly traditional conception of Europe is its identification with Christianity, as a historic marker of the continent. The greatest challenge to this heritage long came from Islam. What then could be a more triumphant demonstration of a modern multi-culturalism than the peaceful intertwining of the two faiths, at state level and within civil society, in a super-European system stretching, like the Roman Empire of old, to the Euphrates? That Turkey's government is for the first time professedly Muslim should not be viewed as a handicap, but as a recommendation for entry, promising just that transvaluation into a multi-cultural form of life the

Union needs for the next step in its constitutional progress. For its part, just as the new-found or restored democracies of the post-Communist East have benefitted from the steadying hand of the Commission in their journey to normalcy, so Turkish democracy will be sheltered and strengthened within the Union. If enlargement to Eastern Europe repaired a moral debt to those who lived through Communism, inclusion of Turkey can redeem the moral damage done by a complacent—or arrogant—parochialism. In such dual atonement, Europe has the capacity to become a better place.

In this self-critical mode, a historical contrast is often drawn. Christian Europe was for centuries disfigured by savage religious intolerance—every kind of persecution, inquisition, expulsion, pogrom: attempts to stamp out other communities of faith, Jewish or Muslim, not to speak of heretics within the faith itself. The Ottoman Empire, on the other hand, tolerated Christians and Jews, without repression or forcible conversion, allowing different communities to live peaceably together under Muslim rule, in a pre-modern multi-cultural harmony. Not only was this Islamic order more enlightened than its Christian counterparts, but far from being a mere external Other of Europe, for centuries it formed an integral part of the European system of powers itself. Turkey is in that sense no newcomer to Europe. Rather its entry into the Union would restore a continuity, of mixtures and contacts, from which we still have much to learn.

I

Such, roughly speaking, is the discourse of Turkish entry into the EU that can be heard in chancelleries and chat-rooms, learned journals and leading articles, on platforms and talk-shows across Europe. One of its great strengths is the absence to date of any non-xenophobic alternative. Its weakness lies in the series of *images d'Epinal* out of which much of it is woven, which obscure the actual stakes in Turkey's suit to join the Union. Certainly, any consideration of these must begin with the Ottoman Empire. For the first, and most fundamental difference between the Turkish candidature and all those from Eastern Europe is that in this case the Union is dealing with the descendant of an imperial state, for long a far greater power than any kingdom of the West. A prerequisite of grasping this descent is a realistic understanding of the originating form of that Empire.

The Osmanlı Sultanate, as it expanded into Europe between the fourteenth and sixteenth centuries, was indeed more tolerant— however anachronistic the term—than any Christian realm of the period. It is enough to compare the fate of the Muslims in Catholic Spain with that of the Orthodox in the Balkans under Ottoman rule. Christians and Jews were neither forced to convert, nor expelled, by the Sultanate, but allowed to worship as they wished, in the House of Islam. This was not toleration in a modern sense, nor specifically Ottoman, but a traditional system of Islamic rule dating to the Umayyad Caliphate of the eighth century.[2] Infidels were subject peoples, legally inferior to the ruling people. Semiotically and practically, they were separate communities. Taxed more heavily than believers, they could not bear arms, hold processions, wear certain clothes, have houses over a certain height. Muslims could take infidel wives; infidels could not marry Muslim women.

The Ottoman state that inherited this system arose in fourteenth-century Anatolia as one Turkic chieftainry competing with others, expanding to the east and south at the expense of local Muslim rivals and to the west and north at the expense of the remains of Byzantine power. For two hundred years, as its armies conquered most of Eastern Europe, the Middle East and North Africa, the Empire it built retained this bi-directionality. But there was never any doubt where its strategic centre of gravity, and primary momentum, lay. From the beginning, Osmanlı rulers drew their legitimacy from holy war—*gaza*—on the frontiers of Christendom. The subjugated regions of Europe formed the richest, most populous, and politically prized zones of the Empire, and the theatre of the overwhelming majority of its military campaigns, as successive sultans set out for the House of War to enlarge the House of Islam. The Ottoman state was founded, as its most recent historian Caroline Finkel writes, on 'the ideal of continuous war'.[3] Recognizing no peers, and respecting no pieties of peaceful coexistence, it was designed for the battlefield, without territorial fixture or definition.

---

2. See Bruce Masters, *Christians and Jews in the Ottoman Arab World*, Cambridge 2001, pp. 16–40: 'The social status of a Muslim was higher than that of a non-Muslim in much the same way that the codification of tradition as law established the social and legal superiority of men over women': p. 23.

3. *Osman's Dream: The Story of the Ottoman Empire 1300–1923*, New York 2005, p. 322. Although Mecca and Medina formed part of the Empire from the early sixteenth century onwards, no Ottoman sultan ever paid a pilgrimage to the Holy Places.

But it was also pragmatic. From the outset, ideological warfare against infidels was combined with instrumental use of them for pursuit of it. From the perspective of the Absolutist monarchies that arose in Western Europe somewhat later, each claiming dynastic authority and enforcing religious conformity within its realm, the peculiarity of the empire of Mehmed II and his successors lay in its combination of aims and means. On the one hand, the Ottomans waged unlimited holy war against Christendom. On the other hand, by the fifteenth century the state relied on a levy— the *devshirme*—of formerly Christian youths, picked from subject populations in the Balkans, themselves not obliged to become Muslims, to compose its military and administrative elite: the *kapı kulları* or the 'slaves of the sultan'.[4]

For upwards of two hundred years, the dynamism of this formidable engine of conquest, its range eventually stretching from Aden to Belgrade and the Crimea to the Rif, held Europe in awe. But by the end of the seventeenth century, after the last siege of Vienna, its momentum had run out. The 'ruling institution' of the Empire ceased to be recruited from the offspring of unbelievers, reverting to native-born Muslims, and the balance of arms gradually turned against it.[5] From the late eighteenth century onwards, when Russia inflicted successive crushing defeats on it north of the Black Sea, and revolutionary France took Egypt in a trice, the Ottoman state never won a major war again. In the nineteenth century its survival depended on the mutual jealousies of the predator powers of Europe more than any inner strength of its own: time and again, it was rescued from further amputation or destruction only by the intervention of rival foreign capitals—London, Paris, Vienna, in one memorable crisis even St Petersburg—at the expense of each other.

But though external pressures, potentially ever more ominous as the technological gap between Ottoman and European empires widened, might in principle have continued to neutralize one another long enough to allow for an effective overhaul of state and society to

---

4. The combination of ideological war against Christians and practical use of them went back to the earliest period of Osmanlı history, before the Straits were crossed or the *devshirme* developed: for an illuminating study of this pattern, see Cemal Kafadar, *Between Two Worlds: The Construction of the Ottoman State*, Berkeley 1995, *passim*.

5. The last *devshirme* was in 1703. For the way in which it declined, and was succeeded as a catchment for the elite by a 'vizier-pasha' stratum, see Donald Quataert, *The Ottoman Empire 1700–1922*, Cambridge 2000, pp. 33–4, 43, 99–100.

meet the challenge from the West—the example of the Porte's rebel
satrap in Egypt, Mehmet Ali, showed what could be done—the rise
of nationalism among the subject Christian peoples of the Balkans
undermined any diplomatic equilibrium. Greek independence,
reluctantly seconded by Britain and France from fear that Russia
would otherwise become its exclusive patron, shocked the Sultanate
into its first serious efforts at internal reform. In the Tanzimat period
(1839–76), modernization became more systematic. The palace was
sidelined by the bureaucracy. Administration was centralized; legal
equality of all subjects and security of property were proclaimed;
education and science promoted; ideas and mores imported from
the West. Under successive pro-British viziers, the Ottoman order
took its place within the European state system.

But the reformers of the time, however secular-minded, could
not transform the religious foundations of Ottoman rule. Three
inequalities were codified by tradition: between believers and
unbelievers, masters and slaves, men and women. Relations
between the sexes altered little, though by the end of the century
preference for boys had become less frequent among the elite, and
slavery was—very gradually—phased out. Politically, the crucial
relationship was the first. Ostensibly, discrimination against
unbelievers was abolished by the reforms. But disavowed in
principle, it persisted in practice, as they continued to be subject
to a poll tax, now disguised as payment for draft exclusion,
rom which Muslims were exempt.[6] The army continued to be

---

6. An arrangement that suited all parties: 'The army feared that an intake of
Christian peasants would be a burden to it and that non-Muslims would damage
morale. This was a serious point, because, as all observers of the Ottoman army
between 1850 and 1918 agree, the fighting spirit of the Ottoman troops was to
a very high degree religious. Attacks were always carried out under simultaneous
shouting of "Allah, Allah" and "Allahüekber" (God is great). It would be hard
to envisage a religiously mixed army to do the same. Most Muslims, especially
in the countryside, disliked the idea of Christians bearing arms (one observer
compares their feelings to those in the southern United States on the equality of
blacks). Most Ottoman Christians were equally unenthusiastic. By and large they
felt themselves to be subjects of the Ottoman state, not members of an Ottoman
nation. The idea of Ottoman nation-building (known at the time as the idea of
the "Unity of the Elements") always was limited to a small, mostly Muslim, elite.
The Ottoman government, finally, had the strongest incentive of all not actually
to conscript Christians. The emphasis on equality before the law in the 1856 edict
also meant that the *cizye* tax which Christians and Jews traditionally paid as a
tribute to the Islamic state in which they lived, had to go. Although the number
of Ottoman Christians went down considerably during the last century of the
Empire due to the loss of European provinces, they still represented nearly 30

reserved for believers, and all significant civilian offices in the state remained a monopoly of the faithful. Such protection of the supremacy of Islam was, however, insufficient to appease popular hostility to reforms perceived as a surrender to European pressures and fashions, incompatible with piety or the proper position of believers in the Empire.[7] Quite apart from unseemly displays of Western ways of life in the cities, unpopular rural taxes were extended to Muslims, while Christian merchants, not to speak of foreign interests, flourished under the free trade regime conceded by the reformers to the Western powers.

Neither consistently modern nor robustly traditional, the Tanzimat regimes were also fiscal failures. Tax-farming, officially disavowed, lingered on; rather than increasing, public revenues declined. Capitulations—extra-territorial privileges granted to foreigners—persisted. Foreign borrowing ballooned, before finally bursting into state bankruptcy in 1875. Two years later, Ottoman armies were once again thrashed by Russia, and in 1878—after a brief constitutional episode had fizzled—the Empire was forced to accept the independence of Serbia, Montenegro and Romania, and the autonomy of most of Bulgaria. For the next thirty years, power swung back from the bureaucracy to the palace, in the person of Sultan Abdülhamid II, who combined technological and administrative modernization—railways, post offices, warships—with religious restoration and police repression. With the loss of most of the Balkans, the population of the Empire had become over 70 per cent Muslim. To cement loyalty to his regime, the sultan refurbished the long-neglected title of caliph, broadcasting pan-Islamic appeals, and topping up the ranks of his administration with Arabs. But no amount of ideological bluster, or fabrication of tradition in the approved Victorian style, could alter the continued dependence of the Empire on a Public Debt Administration run by

---

per cent of the population in Abdülhamit's reign and close to 20 per cent on the eve of World War I. Not surprisingly, the *cizye* was the second most important source of tax revenue (after the tithe) of the state. No wonder, then, that the state actually preferred that the Christians should pay an exemption tax of their own, rather than serve. This indeed remained universal practice until 1909': Erik-Jan Zürcher, 'The Ottoman Conscription System, 1844–1914', *International Review of Social History*, Vol. 43, No. 3, 1998, p. 446.

7. Finkel cites the statesman Ahmed Cevdet Pasha's report of the widespread reaction when the Reform Edict of 1856 was proclaimed: 'Today we have lost the sacred, communal rights which our ancestors won with their blood. The Muslim community is the ruling community, but it has been deprived of its sacred rights. This is a day of grief and sorrow for the Muslim people': *Osman's Dream*, p. 459.

foreigners, and a European balance of power incapable of damping down the fires of nationalism in the Balkans.

There a broad swath of Ottoman rule still extended to the Adriatic, in which various insurgent bands—most prominently, the Macedonian secret organization IMRO—roamed the hills, and the cream of the army was stationed in garrison towns to hold what was left of Rumelia, the rich original core of the Empire, its 'Roman' part. Here opposition to the Hamidian reaction had become widespread by the turn of the century among the young of all ethnic groups, not least Turks themselves. In 1908 rumours of an impending Russo-British carve-up of the region triggered a military rising in Monastir and Salonika. The revolt spread rapidly, and within a couple of weeks had become irresistible. Abdülhamid was forced to call elections, at which the organization behind the uprising, newly revealed to the world as the Committee of Union and Progress, won a resounding majority across the Empire. The Young Turks had taken power.

2

The Revolution of 1908 was a strange, amphibious affair. In many ways it was premonitory of the upheavals in Persia and China that followed three years later, but with features that set it apart from all subsequent such risings in the twentieth century. On the one hand, it was a genuine constitutional movement, arousing popular enthusiasm right across the different nationalities of the Empire, and electing an impressively inter-ethnic Parliament on a wide suffrage: an authentic expression of the still liberal *Zeitgeist* of the period. On the other hand, it was a military coup mounted by a secret organization of junior officers and conspirators, which can claim to be the first of a long line of such episodes in the Third World in a later epoch. The two were not disjoined, since the architects of the coup, a small group of plotters, gained Empire-wide support, in the name of constitutional rule, virtually overnight—their party numbering hundreds of thousands within a year.[8] Nor, formally speaking, were the objectives of each distinct:

---

8. 'By late 1909, the number of CUP branches across the Empire had multiplied from 83 (some of them minor cells) to 360, while membership had grown roughly from 2,250 to 850,000': M. S̡ükrü Hanioḡ'lu, *A Brief History of the Late Ottoman Empire*, Princeton 2008, p. 160—now much the best treatment of the period.

in the vocabulary of the time, the 'liberty, equality, fraternity and justice' proclaimed by the first were conceived as conditions of securing the integrity of the Empire sought by the second, in a common citizenship shared by all its peoples.

But that synthesis was not—could never be—stable. The prime mover in the revolution was the core group of officers in the CUP. Their over-riding aim was the preservation of the Empire, at whatever cost. Constitutional or other niceties were functional or futile to it, as the occasion might be, as means: not as ends in themselves. But if they were not liberals, nor were they in any sense anti-colonial, in the fashion of later military patriots in the Third World, often authoritarian enough, but resolute enemies of Western imperialism—the Free Officers in Egypt, the Lodges in Argentina, the Thirty Comrades in Burma. The threats to the Ottoman Empire came, as they had long done, from European powers or their regional allies, but the Young Turks did not reject the West culturally or politically: rather, they wanted to enter the ring of its *Machtpolitik* on equal terms, as one contestant among others. For that, a transformation of the Ottoman state was required, to give it a modern mass base of the kind that had become such a strength of its rivals.

But here they faced an acute dilemma. What ideological appeal could hold the motley populations—divided by language, religion, and ethnic origin—of the Ottoman Empire together? Some unifying patriotism was essential, but the typical contemporary ingredients for one were missing. The nearest equivalent to the Ottoman order was the Habsburg Empire, but even it was considerably more compact, overwhelmingly of one basic faith, and in possession of a still respected traditional ruler. The Young Turks, in charge of lands stretching from the Yemen to the Danube, and peoples long segregated and stratified in a hierarchy of incompatible confessions, had no such advantages. What could it mean to be a citizen of this state, other than simply the contingent subject of a dynasty that the Young Turks themselves treated with scant reverence, unceremoniously ousting Abdülhamid within a year of taking power? The new regime could not escape an underlying legitimacy deficit. An awareness of the fragility of its ideological position was visible from the start. For the Young Turks retained the discredited monarchy against which they had rebelled, installing a feeble cousin of Abdülhamid as a figurehead successor in the Sultanate, and even trooping out, in farcical piety, behind the bier of Abdülhamid when the old brute, a King Bomba of the Bosphorus, finally expired.

Such shreds of a faded continuity were naturally not enough to clothe the new collective emperor. The CUP needed the full dress of a modern nationalism. But how was this to be defined? A two-track solution was the answer. For public consumption, it proclaimed a 'civic' nationalism, open to any citizen of the state, no matter what their creed or descent—a doctrine with broad appeal, greeted with a tremendous initial outburst of hope and energy among even the hitherto most disaffected groups in the Empire, including Armenians. In secret conclave, on the other hand, it prepared for a more confessional or ethnic nationalism, restricted to Muslims or Turks.[9] This was a duality that in its way reflected the peculiar structure of the CUP itself. As a party, it had won a large parliamentary majority in the first free elections the Empire had known, and with a brief intermission in 1912–13, directed the policies of the state. But its leadership shunned the front of the stage, taking neither cabinet posts nor top military commands, leaving these to an older generation of soldiers and bureaucrats. Behind a façade of constitutional propriety and deference to seniority, however, actual power was wielded by the party's Central Committee, a group of fifty zealots controlling a political organization in origin modelled on the Macedonian and Armenian undergrounds. The term 'Young Turks' was not a misnomer. When it took over, the key leaders of the CUP were in their late twenties or thirties. Numerically, army captains and majors predominated, but civilians also figured at the highest level. The trio who eventually occupied the limelight would be Enver and Cemal, from the officer corps, and Talat, a former functionary in the post office. Behind them, publicly less visible, but hidden drivers of the organization, were two military doctors, Selânikli Nazim and Bahaettin Şakir. All five top leaders came from the 'European' sector of the Empire: the

---

9. For this duality, see Hugh Poulton, *Top Hat, Grey Wolf and Crescent: Turkish Nationalism and the Turkish Republic*, New York 1997, p. 80. As early as 1910, Talat had told the Central Committee of the CUP in a secret speech: 'You are aware that by the terms of the Constitution, equality of Muslims and infidels was affirmed by you. One and all know and feel this is an unrealizable ideal. The Shariat, our whole past history and the sentiments of hundreds of thousands of Muslims and even the sentiments of the infidels themselves, who stubbornly resist every effort to Ottomanize them, present an impenetrable barrier to the establishment of real equality . . . There can therefore be no question of real equality until we have succeeded in Ottomanizing the Empire'.

coxcomb Enver from a wealthy family in Istanbul, the mastiff Talat and the clinical Şakir from today's Bulgaria, Nazim from Salonika, the slightly older Cemal from Mytilene.

The CUP was soon put to the test of defending the Empire it had been set up to renew. In 1911 Italy seized Libya, the last Ottoman province in North Africa, Enver vainly attempting to organize desert resistance. A year later, Serbia, Montenegro, Greece and Bulgaria combined to launch a joint attack on the Ottoman armies in the Balkans, which within a matter of weeks had all but swept them out of Europe. The CUP, which had been briefly dislodged from power in the summer of 1912, escaped the odium of this massive defeat, and when its enemies fell out with each other, was able to regain at least the province of Edirne. But the scale of the imperial catastrophe was traumatic. Rumelia had long been the most advanced region of the Empire, the prime recruiting-ground of Ottoman elites from the time of the *devshirme* to the Young Turks themselves, who kept their Central Committee in Salonika, not Istanbul, down to 1912. Its final loss, not even at the hands of a great power, reducing Ottoman domains in Europe to a mere foothold, and expelling some 400,000 Turks from their homes, was the greatest disaster and humiliation in the history of the Empire.

The effect on the CUP was twofold. The Empire was now 85 per cent Muslim, lowering any incentive for political appeals to the remaining quotient of unbelievers, and increasing the attraction of playing the card of Islam to rally support for its regime. But though the leaders of the Committee, determined to keep hold of the Arab provinces, made ample use of this, they had before them the bitter lesson taught by the Albanians, who had seized the opportunity offered by the Balkan wars to gain their independence—a defection by fellow-Muslims that suggested a common religion might not be enough to prevent a further disintegration of the state they had inherited. The result was to tilt the ideological axis of the CUP, especially its inner circle, in an increasingly ethnic—Turkish, as distinct from Muslim—direction. The shift involved no cost in outlook: virtually to a man, the Young Turks were positivists whose view of matters sacred was thoroughly instrumental.[10]

---

10. For the intellectual influences on them, see Zürcher, 'Ottoman Sources of Kemalist Thought', which points to French sources—Laffitte, Le Bon,

Nor were they disposed to accept a diminished station for the Empire. Expulsion from Rumelia did not inspire a defensive posture, but an active will to avenge defeats in the Balkans, and recoup imperial losses. 'Our anger is strengthening: revenge, revenge, revenge; there is no other word', Enver wrote to his wife.[11] The lesson the CUP drew from 1912 was that Ottoman power could be upheld only by alliance with at least one of Europe's Great Powers, which had stood aside as it was rolled up. The Young Turks had no particular preference as to which, trying in turn Britain, Austria, Russia and France, only to be rebuffed by each, before finally succeeding with Germany on 2 August 1914, two days before the outbreak of the First World War.[12] By now the CUP occupied the foreground: Enver was minister of war, Talat of the interior, Cemal of the navy. The treaty as such did not commit the Empire to declare war on the Entente, and the Young Turks thought to profit from it without much risk. They banked on Germany routing France in short order, whereupon Ottoman armies could join up safely with the Central Powers to knock out Russia, and garner the fruits of victory—regaining a suitable belt of Thrace, the Aegean islands, Cyprus, Libya, all of Arabia, territory ceded to Russia in the Caucasus, and lands stretching to Azerbaijan and Turkestan beyond.

But when France did not collapse in the West, while Germany pressed for rapid Ottoman entry into the war to weaken Russia in the East, much of the cabinet got cold feet. It was only after weeks of disagreement and indecision that Enver, the most bellicose

---

Durkheim—and Hanioğlu, 'Blueprints for a Future Society', which emphasizes German vulgar materialism—Ludwig Büchner, Haeckel—and social Darwinism: both in Elisabeth Özdalga (ed.), *Late Ottoman Society: The Intellectual Legacy*, London 1995, pp. 14–27 and 29–93.

11. Taner Akçam, *A Shameful Act: The Armenian Genocide and the Question of Turkish Responsibility*, New York 2006, p. 115, which cites a speech by Enver in which he declared: 'How could a person forget the plains, the meadows, watered with the blood of our forefathers; abandon those places where Turkish raiders had hidden their steeds for a full four hundred years, with our mosques, our tombs, our dervish retreats, our bridges and our castles, to leave them to our slaves, to be driven out of Rumelia into Anatolia; this was beyond a person's endurance. I am prepared to gladly sacrifice the remaining years of my life to take revenge on the Bulgarians, the Greeks and the Montenegrins'.

12. For the diplomatic drama, see Hanioğlu, *The Late Ottoman Empire*, p. 175; Ulrich Trumpener, *Germany and the Ottoman Empire 1914–1918*, Princeton 1968, pp. 12–20; and David Fromkin, *A Peace to End All Peace: Creating the Modern Middle East 1914–1922*, London 1989, pp. 54–76, which argues that Enver tricked the Germans into the alliance, who then tricked him over the way hostilities against Russia were eventually staged.

member of the junta now in control, succeeded in bouncing the government into war in late October 1914, with an unprovoked naval bombardment of Russian coastal positions in the Black Sea.[13] However, the Ottoman navy, even manned by German crews, was in no position to effect landings in the Ukraine. Where then was Young Turk mettle to be displayed? Symbolic forces were eventually sent north to buff out Austro-German lines in Galicia, and half-hearted expeditions dispatched, at the prompting of Berlin, against British lines in Egypt. But these were sideshows. The crack troops of the army, led by Enver in person, were flung across the Russian border in the Caucasus. There, waiting to be recovered, lay the three provinces of Batum, Ardahan and Kars subtracted from the Empire at the Conference of Berlin in 1878. In the snow-bound depths of the winter of January 1915, few returned. The Ottoman attack was shattered more completely than any comparable offensive in the Great War—fewer than one out of seven survived the campaign. As they straggled back, frostbitten and demoralized, their rearguard was left exposed.

In Istanbul, the CUP reacted swiftly. This was no ordinary retreat into the kind of rear where another battle of the Marne might be fought. The whole swathe of territory extending across both sides of the frontier was home to Armenians. What place could they have in the conflict that had now been unleashed? Historically the oldest inhabitants of the region, indeed of Anatolia at large, they were Christians whose church—dating from the third century—could claim priority over that of Rome itself. But by the nineteenth century, unlike Serbs, Bulgars, Greeks or Albanians, they comprised no compact national majority anywhere in their lands of habitation. In 1914, about a quarter were subjects of the Russian, three-quarters of the Ottoman Empire. Under the tsars, they enjoyed no political rights, but as fellow Christians were not persecuted for their religion, and could rise within the imperial administration. Under the sultans, they had been excluded from the *devshirme* from the start, but could operate as merchants and acquire land, if not offices; and in the course of the nineteenth century they generated a significant intellectual stratum—the first Ottoman novels were written by Armenians.

Inevitably, like their Balkan counterparts and inspired by them,

---

13. The best portrait of Enver in these years remains Charles Haley, 'The Desperate Ottoman: Enver Paşa and the German Empire', *Middle Eastern Studies*, No. 1, January 1994, pp. 1–51, and No. 2, April 1994, pp. 224–51.

this intelligentsia developed a nationalist movement. But it was set apart from them in two ways: it was dispersed across a wide and discontinuous expanse of territory, throughout which it was a minority, and it was divided between two rival empires, one of which posed as its protector, while the other figured as its persecutor. Most Armenians—about 75 per cent—were peasants in the three easternmost Ottoman provinces, where they numbered perhaps a quarter of the population. But there were also significant concentrations in Cilicia, bordering on today's Syria, and vigorous communities in Istanbul and other big cities. State suspicion of a minority with links across a contested border, latent popular hostility to unbelievers, and economic jealousy of alien commercial wealth made for a combustible atmosphere around their presence in Anatolia. Abdülhamid's personal animus ensured they would suffer under his rule, which saw repeated pogroms against them. In 1894–6, anywhere between 80,000 and 200,000 died in massacres at the hands of special Kurdish regiments he had created for ethnic repressions in the east.[14] The ensuing international outcry, leading eventually to the theoretical appointment—it came to nothing—of foreign inspectors to ensure Armenian safety in the worst-affected zones, confirmed belief in the disloyalty of the community.

The CUP's immediate fear, as it viewed the rout of its armies in the Caucasus, was that the local Armenian population might rally to the enemy. On 25 February, it ordered that all Armenian conscripts in its forces be disarmed. The telegrams went out on the day that Anglo-French forces began to bombard the Dardanelles, threatening Istanbul itself. Towards the end of March, amid great tension in the capital, the Central Committee—Talat was the prime mover—voted that the entire Armenian population in Anatolia should be deported to the deserts of Syria, to secure the Ottoman rear. The operation was to be carried out by the Teşkilât-ı Mahsusa, the 'Special Organization' created for secret tasks by the party in 1913, now some thirty thousand strong under the command of Bahaettin Şakir.[15]

*   *   *

14. For different estimates, see Akçam, A Shameful Act, p. 42.

15. For the origins of the Special Organization, see Philip Stoddard, The Ottoman Government and the Arabs, 1911 to 1918: A Preliminary Study of the Teşkilât-ı Mahsusa, Princeton dissertation, 1963, pp. 46–62.

Ethnic cleansing on a massive scale was no novelty in the region. Wholesale expulsion of communities from their homes, typically as refugees from conquering armies, was a fate hundreds of thousands of Turks and Circassians had suffered as Russia consolidated its grip in the northern Caucasus in the 1860s, and Balkan nations won their independence from Ottoman rule in the next half century.[16] Anatolia was full of such *mujahir*, with bitter memories of their treatment by Christians. Widespread slaughter was no stranger to the region either: the Armenian massacres of the 1890s had many precedents, on all sides, in the history of the 'Eastern Question' as elsewhere. Nor was forcible relocation on grounds of security confined to one side in the First World War itself: in Russia, at least half a million Jews were rounded up and deported from Poland and the Pale by the tsarist regime.[17]

The enterprise on which the CUP embarked in the spring of 1915 was, however, new. For ostensible deportation, brutal enough in itself, was to be the cover for extermination—systematic, state-organized murder of an entire community. The killings began in March, still somewhat haphazardly, as Russian forces began to penetrate into Anatolia. On 20 April, in a climate of increasing fear, there was an Armenian uprising in the city of Van. Five days later, Anglo-French forces staged full-scale landings in the Dardanelles, and contingency plans were laid for transferring the government to the interior, should the capital fall to the Entente. In this emergency, the CUP wasted no time. By early June, centrally directed and coordinated destruction of the Armenian population was in full swing. As the leading comparative authority on modern ethnic cleansing, Michael Mann, writes: 'The escalation from the first incidents to genocide occurred within three months, a much more rapid escalation than Hitler's later attack on the Jews'.[18] Şakir—probably more than any other conspirator, the original designer of the CUP—toured the target zones, shadowy and deadly, supervising the slaughter.

---

16. For these waves of ethnic cleansing, see Benjamin Lieberman's balanced and sobering *Terrible Fate: Ethnic Cleansing in the Making of Modern Europe*, Chicago 2006, pp. 3–52.

17. Lieberman, *Terrible Fate*, pp. 87–91, who comments that in this case, paradoxically, perhaps two-fifths of those deported ended up in Russian cities—though not St Petersburg or Moscow—from which they had hitherto been banned.

18. The *Dark Side of Democracy: Explaining Ethnic Cleansing*, Cambridge 2005, p. 152.

Without even pretexts of security, Armenians in western Anatolia were wiped out hundreds of miles from the front, as eradication caught up with them too.

No reliable figures exist for the number of those who died, or the different ways—with or without bullet or knife; on the spot or marched to death—in which they perished. Mann, who thinks a reasonable guess is 1.2 to 1.4 million, reckons that 'perhaps two-thirds of the Armenians died'—'the most successful modern murderous ethnic cleansing achieved in the 20th century', exceeding in its proportions the Shoah.[19] A catastrophe of this order could not be hidden. Germans, present in Anatolia as Ottoman allies in many—consular, military, pastoral and other—capacities, witnessed it and reported home, most in horror or anguish, at what was going on. Confronted by the American ambassador, Talat scarcely bothered even to deny it. For its part the Entente, unlike the Allies who kept silent at the Judeocide in the Second World War, denounced the extermination without delay, issuing a solemn declaration on 24 May 1915, that promised to punish as criminals those who had organized it.

Victory in the Dardanelles saved the CUP regime. But this was the only real success, a defensive one, in its war effort. Elsewhere, in Arabia, in Palestine, in Iraq, on the Black Sea, the armies of a still basically agricultural society were beaten by its more industrialized adversaries, with great civilian suffering and huge military casualties, exceeded as a proportion of the population only by Serbia. With the collapse of Bulgaria, the Ottoman lifeline to the Central Powers, at the end of September 1918, the writing was on the wall for the CUP. Talat, passing back through Sofia on a trip to Berlin, saw the game was up, and within a fortnight had resigned as grand vizier. A new cabinet, under ostensibly less compromised leaders, was formed two weeks later, and on 31 October the Porte signed an armistice with the Entente, four days before Austria on 3 November and two weeks before Germany on 11 November. It looked as if dominoes were falling in a row, from weakest to strongest.

---

19. *The Dark Side of Democracy*, p. 140. In January 2009, a document in Talat's papers, passed by his widow to the journalist Murat Bardakçi, an apologist for her husband, recorded a drop in the Armenian population of the Empire from 1, 256,000 in 1914 to 284,157 in 1916. See 'Nearly a Million Genocide Victims, Covered in a Cloak of Amnesia', *New York Times*, 9 March 2009.

3

The impression was misleading. In Vienna, the Habsburg monarchy disintegrated overnight. In Berlin, soldiers' and workers' councils sprang up as the last Hohenzollern fled into exile. In Sofia, Stamboliski's Peasant Party, which had staged a rising even before the end of the war, came to power. In each case defeat was incontestable, the old order was utterly discredited by it, and revolutionary forces emerged amid its ruins. In Istanbul there was no such scenario. The Ottoman Empire had entered the war with a gratuitous decision unlike that of any other power, and its exit was unlike that of any other too. For the CUP leaders did not accept that they were beaten. Their hand-over of the cabinet was a *reculer pour mieux sauter*. In the fortnight between their resignation from the government and the signature of an armistice, they prepared for resistance against an impending occupation, and a second round in the struggle to assert Turkish might. Enver invoked the Balkan disasters of 1912–13, when redemption had been snatched with his recovery of Edirne, as inspiration for the future.[20] Talat set up a para-military underground, Karakol, headed by close associates—including Enver's uncle—and equipped with arms caches and funds from the Special Organization, which was itself hastily dissolved, and the Unionist Party renamed. Archives were removed and incriminating files methodically destroyed.[21]

After surrender had been signed on the island of Lemnos on 31 October, but before Allied forces had entered the Straits, the CUP leaders made their final move. Dispositions were now complete, and there was no panic. During the night of 1–2 November, eight top leaders of the regime secretly boarded a German torpedo-boat, the former *Schastlivyi* captured from the Russians, which sped them to Sebastopol.[22] There Germany, still at war with the Entente, controlled the Ukraine. The party included Enver, Talat,

---

20. See Eric Zürcher, *Turkey: A Modern History*, London 2004, p. 135; Nur Belge Criss, *Istanbul under Allied Occupation 1919–1923*, Leiden 1999, p. 4. Eric Zürcher, *The Unionist Factor*, Leiden 1984, p. 84.

21. The fullest account is in Zürcher, *The Unionist Factor*, pp. 68–105.

22. For a graphic description by the naval officer in command, Lieutenant-Captain Hermann Baltzer, see *Orientrundschau*, November 1933, pp. 121–3; corroboration in the diary of of Vice-Admiral Albert Hopman, in Winfried Baumgart (ed.), *Von Brest-Litovsk zur Deutschen Novemberrevolution*, Göttingen 1971, p. 634.

Şakir, Nazım and Cemal.[23] From the Crimea, Enver made in the direction of the Caucasus, while the rest of the party were taken by stages in disguise to Berlin, which they reached in January 1919. There they were granted protection under Ebert, the new Social Democratic president of the Republic. Unionism was not Nazism, but if an analogy were wanted, it was as if in 1945 Hitler, Himmler, Kaltenbrunner, Goebbels and Goering, after laying careful preparations for Werewolf actions in Germany, had coolly escaped together to Finland, to continue the struggle.

Ten days later, the Allies entered Istanbul. At the war's end, the Habsburg Empire had spontaneously disintegrated; the Hohenzollern gave way to a republic that had to yield up Alsace-Lorraine and suffer occupation of the Rhineland, but no real loss of German territorial integrity. The Ottoman Empire was another matter, its fate far more completely at the mercy of the victors. In late 1918, four powers—Britain, France, Italy and Greece—shared the spoils, the first two dividing its Arab provinces between them, the latter competing for gains in south-west Anatolia. It would be another two years before any formal agreement was reached between them on how the Empire was finally to be dismembered. Meanwhile, they exercised joint supervision in Istanbul, initially quite loose, over an apparently accommodating cabinet under a new sultan, known for disliking the CUP.

Yet though the post-war misery of a defeated society was much worse than in Germany or Austria, its resources for resisting any potentially Carthaginian peace were greater. In the capital, Karakol was soon funnelling a flow of agents and arms into the interior, where plans had already been laid to move the centre of power during the war, and there was little foreign presence to monitor what was going on. Crucially, moreover, the October Revolution, by removing Russia from the ranks of the Allies, not only ensured that eastern Anatolia remained beyond the range of any occupation. It left the Ottoman Ninth Army, which Enver had sent to seize the Caucasus, once the Treaty of Brest-Litovsk cleared the path for it to advance all the way to Baku, intact in the region under its Unionist commander.

In the spring of 1919, another Unionist officer stepped on stage. Kemal, who also came from Rumelia, was an early member of the CUP who had risen to prominence in the defence of the

---

23. They were accompanied by Bedri, police chief in Istanbul, Cemal Azmi, governor of Trebizond, and Rusuhi, another medical doctor.

Dardanelles, before spending the rest of the war in Syria with Cemal. Uneasy relations with Enver had excluded him from the inner core of the party, absolving him from involvement with its Special Organization. Returning from Damascus in pursuit of a ministry in the post-war cabinet, he was offered instead a military inspectorate in the east. The proposal probably came out of discussions with Karakol, with whom he made contact on getting back. Once arrived on the Black Sea coast, Kemal moved inland and began immediately to coordinate political and military resistance—at first covert, soon overt—to Allied controls over Turkey. In what would in time become the War of Independence, he was assisted by four favourable factors.

The first was simply the degree of preparation for resistance left behind by the CUP leaders, which included not only extensive arms dumps and intelligence agents underground, but also a country-wide network of Societies for the Rights of National Defence as a quasi political party above ground; plus—more by fortune than forethought—a fully equipped regular army, out of Allied reach. The second was the solidarity extended by Russia, where Lenin's regime, facing multiple Entente interventions to overthrow it in the Civil War, supported Turkish resistance to the common enemy with arms and funds. The third lay in divisions of the Entente itself. Britain was the principal power in Istanbul. But it was unwilling to match its political weight with military force, preferring to rely on Greece as its regional proxy. But the Greek card—this was the fourth essential element in the situation—was a particularly weak one for the victors to play.

Not only was Greece resented as an inferior rival by Italy, and suspected as a British pawn by France. In Turkish eyes a jackal scavenging behind great powers, who were worthy adversaries of the Empire, it had made virtually no contribution to the defeat of Ottoman arms, and yet was awarded the largest occupied zones, where substantial numbers of Greeks had already been expelled by the Special Organization before the war, and ethnic tensions ran high. On top of all this, Greece was a small, internally divided state, of scant significance as a military power. A better target for a campaign of national liberation would have been difficult to imagine. Four days before Kemal arrived on the Black Sea, Greek troops landed in Smyrna and took over the surrounding region, igniting anger across the country, and creating perfect conditions for an enterprise that still looked risky to many Turks.

Within a year, Kemal had set up a National Assembly in Ankara, in open defiance of the government in Istanbul, and assembled forces capable of checking Greek advances, which had occupied more and more of western Anatolia. Another Greek push was blocked, after initial gains, in the autumn of 1921, and a year later the aggressor, still stationed on the same lines, was routed. Within ten days, Kemal's army entered Smyrna and burnt it to the ground, driving the remaining Greek population into the sea in the most spectacular of the savageries committed on both sides.[24] In Britain, the debacle of his protégé brought the rule of Lloyd George to an end. Philhellene to the last, when he threatened to take the country to war over Turkish successes in October 1922, he was ousted by a revolt in the Carlton Club.

The following summer Curzon, abandoning earlier Entente schemes for a partition of Anatolia, accepted the basic modern borders of Turkey and the end of all extra-territorial rights for foreigners within it, signing with his French, Italian and Greek counterparts the Treaty of Lausanne that formally ended hostilities with the Ottoman state. Juridically, the main novelty of the Treaty was the mutual ethnic cleansing proposed by the Norwegian philanthropist Fridtjof Nansen, who was awarded, the first in a long line of such recipients, the Nobel Peace Prize for his brainwave.[25] The 'population exchange' between Turkey and Greece reflected the relative positions of victor and vanquished, driving 900,000 Greeks and 400,000 Turks from their homes in opposite directions.

Hailed as liberator of his country, Kemal was now master of the political scene. He had risen to power in large measure on the back of the parallel state Unionism had left behind when the *Schastlivyi* slipped its moorings, and for a time had more the status of *primus inter pares* among survivors of the CUP regime than of

---

24. For a description of the conflagration, see Andrew Mango, *Atatürk*, London 1999, pp. 345–7.

25. 'If Nansen's support for a compulsory exchange of minorities across the Aegean posed any moral problems, the Nobel Prize committee were untroubled by them. Nor were any qualms expressed by the western powers who had given Nansen a mandate and encouraged him to use it creatively': Bruce Clark, *Twice a Stranger: How Mass Expulsion forged Modern Greece and Turkey*, London 2006, p. 95, who notes 'the delight in the Turkish camp when Nansen grasped the nettle first'.

an uncontested chief. As late as the summer of 1921, Enver had hovered across the border on the Black Sea coast, waiting to re-enter the fray and take over leadership from Kemal, should he fail to stem the Greek advance. Military victory made Kemal immune to such a threat, which Talat in Berlin anyway thought ill-advised, instructing his followers to stick with the new leader. But the CUP also represented another kind of danger, as a potential albatross round the legitimacy of his rule. For under the Allied occupation, trials of the key officials responsible for the Armenian genocide had been held by the government in Istanbul, and all eight of the top leaders who had sailed to Sebastopol were condemned to death *in absentia*.

The Weimar regime, fearing they might implicate Germany if extradited, had given them cover. In Berlin, they had developed their own ambitious schemes for the recovery of Turkish power, criss-crossing Europe and Asia—Talat to Holland, Sweden, Italy; Cemal to Switzerland, Georgia; Şakir and Enver to Russia; others to Persia and Afghanistan—with differing plans for a come-back.[26] Had they remained at large, they would have been an acute embarrassment to Kemal's regime, as reminders of what linked them, forcing it to take a public position it wished at all costs to avoid. By a stroke of irony, Kemal was spared this problem by the Central Committee of the Armenian Revolutionary Party, the Dashnaks. Deciding at a meeting in Erevan to execute justice on its own account, the party dispatched operatives to carry out the verdicts of Istanbul. In March 1921, Talat was felled by a revolver a few yards from his residence in the Uhlandstrasse, just off the Kurfürstendamm, in the centre of Berlin; in April 1922, Şakir and Cemal Azmi were shot a few doors down in the same street; in July, Cemal was assassinated in Tbilisi; in August, beyond the reach of Dashnak vengeance, Enver was tracked—supposedly by an Armenian Chekist—and killed fighting the Bolsheviks in

---

26. The activities of the CUP exiles, and their relations with Kemal, have yet to be carefully studied. The best treatment to date focusses on Enver's quests for Soviet assistance, and attempts to raise the banner of Islam in Central Asia, with some documentation of the role of others in Europe: Yamauchi Masayuki, *The Green Crescent under the Red Star: Enver Pasha in Soviet Russia 1919–1922,* Tokyo 1991. For the diplomatic hospitality they enjoyed in Berlin, see the memoirs of Wipert von Blücher, *Deutschlands Weg nach Rapallo,* Wiesbaden 1951, pp. 130–7. Talat's sojourn is recounted admiringly in Ingeborg Böer, Ruth Herkötter and Petra Kappert (eds), *Türken in Berlin 1871–1945,* Berlin 2002, pp. 195–201.

Tajikstan.[27] No clean sweep could have been more timely for the new order in Ankara. With the CUP chiefs out of the way, Kemal could proceed to build a Turkey in his image, unencumbered by too notorious memories of the past.

4

Three months after Enver was buried, the Ottomans finally followed the Habsburgs, Romanovs and Hohenzollerns, when the Sultanate which the CUP had so carefully preserved was abolished. A year later, after tightly controlled elections had been held, Kemal was proclaimed president of a Turkish Republic. The symbolic break with centuries of a dynastic aura to which Unionism had clung was sharp enough, but by then small surprise. No such predictable logic marked what ensued. In the spring of 1924, Kemal scrapped the Caliphate, a religious institution still revered across the Muslim world—there was a wave of protest as far away as India—and was soon closing down shrines and suppressing dervishes, banning the fez, changing the calendar, substituting civil law for the sharia, and replacing Arabic with Latin script. The scale and speed of this assault on religious tradition and household custom, embracing faith, time, dress, family, language, remain unique in the Umma to this day. No one could have guessed at such radicalism in advance, comparable only to the anti-clerical rigours of Plutarco Calles in Mexico in the same years. Its visionary drive separated Kemal from his predecessors with éclat.

But systematic though it was, the transformation that now gripped Turkey was a strange one: a cultural revolution without a social revolution, something historically very rare, indeed that might look a priori impossible.[28] The structure of society, the rules of property, the pattern of class relations, remained unaltered. The CUP had repressed any strikes or labour

---

27. For a sensational account, see Jacques Derogy, *Opération Némésis: Les vengeurs arméniens*, Paris 1986, pp. 135–48, 239–61, 275–8, 296–301. Bedri, by training a lawyer, was dispatched on a mission to Kabul, where after helping to draft constitutional and criminal codes for Amanullah's regime, he died of consumption in 1924: Sebastian Beck, 'Das Afghanische Strafgesetzbuch vom Jahre 1924 mit dem Zusatz vom Jahre 1925', *Die Welt des Islams*, August 1928, p. 72.

28. Carter Findley rightly underlines this rarity, in his imaginative study *The Turks in World History*, Oxford 2005, p. 204.

organization from the start. Kemal followed suit: Communists were killed or jailed, however good diplomatic relations with Moscow were. But if there was no anti-capitalist impulse in Kemalism, nor was there was any significant anti-feudal dimension to it either. Ottoman rule, centred on an office-holding state, had never required or permitted a powerful landowning class in the countryside, least of all in Anatolia, where peasant holdings had traditionally prevailed—the only real exception being areas of the Kurdish south-east controlled by tribal chiefs. The scope for agrarian reform was thus anyway much more limited than in Russia, or even parts of the Balkans, and no attempt at it was made.

Yet the social landscape hit by the cultural revolution was at the same time the opposite of a stable traditional order, in one crucial respect. If no class struggles lay behind the dynamics of Kemalism, ethnic upheavals on a gigantic scale had reshaped Anatolian society. The influx of Turks and Circassians, refugees from Russian or Balkan wars, the extirpation of the Armenians, the expulsion of the Greeks, had produced a vast *brassage* of populations and properties in a still backward agricultural economy. It was in this shattered setting that a cultural revolution from above could be imposed without violent reaction from below. The extent of deracination, moral and material, at the conclusion of wars that had continued virtually without interruption for over a decade—twice as long as in Europe—permitted a *Kulturkampf* that might otherwise have provoked an unmanageable explosion. But by the same token the revolution acquired no active popular impetus: Kemalism remained a vertical affair.

Though it broke, sharply and abruptly, with Ottoman culture in one fundamental respect—by abolishing its script, at a stroke it cut off new generations from all written connexion with the past—in this distance from the masses Kemalism not only inherited an Ottoman tradition, but accentuated it. All pre-modern ruling groups spoke idioms differing in one way or another, if only in accent or vocabulary, from those they ruled. But the Ottoman elite, for long composed not even principally of Turks, was peculiarly detached from its subjects, as a corps of state servants bonded by command of a sophisticated language that was a mixture of Persian, Arabic and Turkish, with many foreign loan words, incomprehensible to the ruled. If administrative Ottoman was less elaborate than its literary forms, and Turkish remained in household use, there was nevertheless a huge gulf between high and low cultures in the Empire, fixed linguistically.[29]

Kemalism set out to do away with this, by creating a modern Turkish that would no longer be the despised patois of Ottoman times, but a language spoken alike by all citizens of the new Republic. But if it sought to close the gap between rulers and ruled where it had been widest in the past, at the same time it opened up a gap which had never before existed to the same extent, leaving the overall distance between them as great as ever. Language reform might unify; religious reform was bound to divide. The faith of the Ottoman elites had little in common with the forms of popular piety—variegated cults and folk beliefs looked down on by the educated. But at least there was a shared commitment to Islam. This tie was sundered by Kemal. Once the state started to target shrines and brotherhoods, preachers and prayer-meetings, it was hitting at traditional objects of reverence and attachment, and the masses resisted it. At this level, the cultural revolution misfired. Rejected by the rural and small-town majority of the country, Kemalist secularism was, on the other hand, adopted with aggressive zeal in the cities by modernized descendants of the Ottoman elite—bureaucrats, officers, professionals. In this urban stratum, secularism became over time, as it remains today, something like an ersatz religion in its own right, in its blinkered intensity. But the rigidity of this secularism is a peculiarly brittle one. Not just because it is intellectually thin, or divorced from popular feeling, but more profoundly because of a structural bad faith that has always been inseparable from it.

There is no reason to suppose that Kemal himself was anything other than a robust atheist, of more or less French Third Republic stamp, throughout his life. In that sense, he is entitled to be remembered as a Turkish Émile Combes, scourge of monkish mystification and superstition. But in his rise to power, he could no more dispense with Islam than Talat or Enver had done. 'God's help and protection are with us in the sacred struggle which we have entered upon for our fatherland', he declared in 1920.[30] The struggle for independence was a holy war, which he led as *Gazi*, the Warrior for the Faith of original Ottoman expansion, a title he held onto down to the mid-thirties. 'God is one, and great is

---

29. For the three strata of Ottoman usage, see Şerif Mardin, *Religion, Society and Modernity in Turkey*, Syracuse 2006, pp. 320–4.

30. Poulton, *Top Hat, Grey Wolf and Crescent*, p. 91.

his glory!', he announced without a blush, in a sermon to the faithful delivered in a mosque in 1923.[31] When the Constitution of the Turkish Republic was framed in the following year, Islam was declared the state religion. The spirit in which Kemal made use of Muslim piety in these years was that of Napoleon enthroning himself with the blessing of the pope. But as exercises in cynicism they moved in opposite directions: Napoleon rising to power as a revolutionary, and manipulating religion to stabilize it, Kemal manipulating religion to make a revolution and turning on it once his power was stabilized. After 1926 little more was heard of the deity.

5

Tactical and transient, the new regime's use of Islam, when no longer required, was easily reversed. But at a deeper level, a much tighter knot tied it to the very religion it proceeded on the surface to mortify. For even when at apparent fever pitch, Turkish secularism has never been truly secular. This is in part because, as often noted, Kemalism did not so much separate religion from the state as subordinate it to the state, creating 'directorates' that took over the ownership of all mosques, appointment of imams, administration of pious foundations—in effect, turning the faith into a branch of the bureaucracy. A much more profound reason, however, is that religion was never detached from the *nation*, becoming instead an unspoken definition of it. It was this, however, that allowed Kemalism to become more than just a cult of the elites, leaving a durable imprint on the masses themselves. For if at village level secularism failed to take, nationalism sank deep popular roots. It is possible—such is the argument of Carter Findlay in his *Turks in World History*—that in doing so it drew on a long Turkish cultural tradition, born in Central Asia and predating conversion to Islam, that figured a sacralization of the state, which has vested its modern signifier—*devlet*—with an aura of unusual potency. However that may be, the ambiguity of Kemalism was to construct an ideological code in two registers. One was secular and appealed to the elite. The other was crypto-religious and accessible to the masses. Common to both was the integrity of the nation, as supreme political value.

As Christians, Greeks and Armenians were excluded from the

---

31. Mango, *Atatürk*, p. 374.

outset. In the first elections to the National Assembly in 1919, only Muslims were entitled to vote, and when populations were 'exchanged' in 1923, even Greek communities in Cilicia whose language was Turkish, so thoroughly were they assimilated, were expelled on grounds that they nevertheless were infidels—their ethnicity defined not by culture, but by religion. Such excisions from the nation went virtually without saying. But there remained another large community within the country, most of whose members spoke little Turkish, that could not be so dispatched, because it was Muslim. In ethnically cleansed Anatolia, Kurds made up perhaps a quarter of the population. They had played a central role in the Armenian genocide, Kurdish detachments supplying shock troops for the extermination, and fought alongside Turks in the War of Independence. What was to be their place in the new state?

While the struggle for independence was in the balance, Kemal promised them respect for their identity, and autonomy in the regions where they predominated. 'There are Turks and Kurds', Kemal declared in 1919, 'the nation is not one element. There are various bonded Muslim elements. Every Muslim element which makes this entity are citizens'.[32] But once victory was assured, Kurdish areas were stocked with Turkish officials, Kurdish place-names were changed and the Kurdish language banned from courts and schools. Then, with the abolition of the Caliphate in 1924, Kemal did away with the common symbol of Islam to which he himself had appealed five years earlier, when he had vowed that 'Turks and Kurds will continue to live together as brothers around the institution of the *khilafa*'.[33] The act detonated a major Kurdish revolt under a tribal religious leader, Sheikh Sait, in early 1925. A full half of the Turkish army, over fifty thousand troops, was mobilized to crush the rebellion. On some reckonings, more of them died in its suppression than in the War of Independence.[34]

In the south-east, repression was followed by deportations, executions and systematic Turkification. In the country as a whole, it was the signal for the imposition of a dictatorship, with a Law for the Maintenance of Order that closed down opposition parties and press for the rest of the decade. In 1937, in the face

---

32. See David McDowall, *A Modern History of the Kurds*, London 2004, p. 188.
33. *A Modern History of the Kurds*, p. 187.
34. Finkel, *Osman's Dream*, p. 550.

of a still more drastic programme of Turkification, Alevi Kurds rose in the Dersim region, and were put down yet more ruthlessly, with more modern weapons of destruction—bombers, gas, heavy artillery. Officially, by now the Kurds had ceased to exist. After 1925 Kemal never uttered the word 'Kurd' in public again. The nation was composed of one homogeneous people, and it alone, the Turks—a fiction that was to last another three generations.

But if Kurds were no different from Turks, whatever their language, customs or sense of themselves, what defined the indivisible identity of the two? Tacitly, it could only be what Kemalism could no longer admit, but with which it could never dispense— religion. There were still tiny Christian and Jewish communities in the country, preserved essentially in Istanbul and its environs, and in due course, these would be subjected to treatment that made it clear how fundamental the division between believers and unbelievers continued to be in the Kemalist state. But though Islam delimited the nation, it now did so in a purely negative way—it was the covert identity that was left, after every positive determination had been subtracted, in the name of homogeneity. The result has been that Turkish secularism has always depended on what it repressed.

The repression, of course, had to be compensated. Once religion could no longer function publicly as common denominator of the nation, the state required a substitute as ideological cement. Kemal attempted to resolve the problem by generating a legendary essence of race and culture shared by all in the Turkish Republic. The materials to hand for this construction posed their own difficulties. The first Turkish tribes had arrived in Anatolia in the eleventh century, recent newcomers compared with Greeks or Armenians, who had preceded them by more than a millennium, not to speak of Kurds, often identified with the Medes of antiquity. As the most casual glance at phenotypes in Turkey today suggests, centuries of genetic mixing followed. A purely Turkish culture was an equally doubtful quantity. The Ottoman elite had produced literary and visual riches of which any society could be proud, but this was a cosmopolitan culture, which was not only distinct from, but contemptuous of, anything too specifically Turkish—the very term 'Turk' signifying a rustic churl well into the nineteenth century. Reform of the script now rendered most of this heritage inaccessible anyway.

Undaunted by these limitations, Kemalism fashioned for instruction the most extravagant mythology of any inter-war nationalism. By the mid-thirties, the state was propagating an ideology in which the Turks, of whom Hittites and Phoenicians in the Mediterranean were a branch, had spread civilization from Central Asia to the world, from China to Brazil; and as the drivers of universal history, spoke a language that was the origin of all other tongues, which were derived from the Sun-Language of the first Turks.[35] Such ethnic megalomania reflected the extent of the underlying insecurity and artificiality of the official enterprise: the less there was to be confident of, the more fanfare had to be made out of it.

Observing Kemalist cultural policies first-hand in 1936–7, Erich Auerbach wrote from Istanbul to Walter Benjamin: 'the process is going fantastically and spookily fast: already there is hardly anyone who knows Arabic or Persian, and even Turkish texts of the past century will quickly become incomprehensible'. Combining 'a renunciation of all existing Islamic cultural tradition, a fastening onto a fantasy "ur-Turkey", technical modernization in the European sense in order to strike at the hated and envied Europe with its own weapons', it offered 'nationalism in the superlative with the simultaneous destruction of the historic national character'.[36]

Seventy years later, a Turkish intellectual would reflect on the deeper logic of this process. In an essay of unsurpassed power, one of the great texts in the world's literature on nationalism, the sociologist Çağlar Keyder has described the desperate retroactive peopling of Anatolia with ur-Turks in the shape of Hittites and Trojans as a compensation mechanism for its emptying by ethnic cleansing at the origins of the regime. The repression of that memory created a complicity of silence between rulers and ruled, but no popular bond of the kind that a genuine anti-imperialist struggle would have generated—the War of Independence remaining a small-scale affair, compared with the traumatic mass experience of the First World War. Abstract in its imagination of space, hypomanic in its projection of time, the official ideology assumed a peculiarly 'preceptorial' character, with all that the word implies. 'The choice of the particular founding myth

---

35. For particulars, see Poulton, *Top Hat, Grey Wolf and Crescent*, pp. 104–14.

36. Letters of 12 December 1936 and 3 January 1937, published in *Zeitschrift für Germanistik*, December 1988, pp. 691–2.

referring national heritage to an obviously invented history, the deterritorialization of "motherland", and the studious avoidance and repression of a shared recent experience, rendered Turkish nationalism exceptionally arid'.[37]

Such nationalism was a new formation, but the experience that it repressed tied it, intimately, to that out of which it had grown. The continuities between Kemalism and Unionism, plain enough in treatment of the Kurds under the Republic, were starker still in other ways. For extermination of the Armenians did not cease in 1916. Determined to prevent the emergence of an Armenian state in the area awarded it—costlessly, on paper— by Wilson in 1920, Kemal's government in Ankara ordered an attack on the Armenian Republic that had been set up on the Russian side of the border in the Caucasus, where most of those who had escaped the killings of 1915–16 had fled. In a secret telegram its foreign minister instructed Kazim Karabekir, the commander charged with the invasion, to 'deceive the Armenians and fool the Europeans', in carrying out the express instruction: 'It is indispensable that Armenia be politically and physically annihilated'.[38] Soviet historians estimate 200,000 Armenians were slaughtered in the space of five months, before the Red Army intervened.

This was still, in its own fashion, in time of war. Once peace came, what was the attitude of the Turkish Republic to the original genocide? To interested foreigners, Kemal would deplore, usually off the record, the killings as work of a tiny handful of scoundrels. To its domestic audience, the regime went out of its way to honour the perpetrators, dead or alive. Two of the most prominent killers hanged in 1920 for their atrocities by the tribunals in Istanbul were proclaimed 'national martyrs' by the Kemalist Assembly, and in 1926 the families of Talat, Enver, Şakir, and Cemal were officially granted pensions, properties and lands seized from the Armenians, in recognition of services to the country. Such decisions were not mere sentimental gestures. Kemal's regime was packed, from top to bottom, with participants in the murders of 1915–16. At one time or another his ministers of foreign affairs and of the interior;

---

37. 'A History and Geography of Turkish Nationalism', in Faruk Birtek and Thalia Dragonas (eds), *Citizenship and Nation-State in Greece and Turkey*, London 2005, p. 14.
38. See Vahakn Dadrian, *The History of the Armenian Genocide*, New York 2003, pp. 358, 371. The signatory of this cable, Ahmet Muhtar Mullaoğlu, became the Turkish Republic's first ambassador to Washington in 1927.

of finance, education and defence; and of public works, were all veterans of the genocide; while a minister of justice, suitably enough, had been defence lawyer at the Istanbul trials.[39] It was as if Adenauer's cabinets had been composed of well-known chiefs of the SS and the Sicherheitsdienst.

What of Kemal himself? In Gallipoli till the end of 1915, he was posted to Diyarbakir in the south-east in the spring of 1916, after the region had been emptied of Armenians. He certainly knew of the genocide—someone in his position could hardly have been unaware of it—but played no part in it. How he would have acted had he been in the zone at the time is impossible to guess. After the event, it is clear that he regarded it as an accomplished fact that had become a condition of the new Turkey. In this he was like most of his countrymen, for the elimination of the Armenians in Anatolia, who were at least a tenth of the population, unlike that of the Jews in Germany, who were little more than 1 per cent, was of material benefit to large numbers of ordinary citizens, who acquired lands and wealth from those who had been wiped out, as from Greeks who had been expelled, another tenth of the population. Kemal himself was among the recipients of this vast largesse, receiving *gratis* villas abandoned by Greek owners in Bursa and Trabzon, and the mansion on the hill of Çankaya that became his official residence as head of state in Ankara. Originally the estate of an Armenian family, there the presidential palace of the Republic stands today, it too planted on booty from the genocide.

Yet between taking part in a crime, and gaining from one, there is a difference. Kemal was one of history's most striking examples of 'moral luck', that philosophical oxymoron out of which Bernard Williams made a Delphic grace. By accident of military appointments, his hands were clean of the worst that was committed in his time, making him a natural candidate for leadership of the national movement after the war. Personally,

---

39. For these individuals, and the general pattern, see Akçam, *A Shameful Act*, pp. 362–4. Zürcher, pointing out that the Kemalist elite as a whole had the same regional and occupational background as the CUP—'both groups of leaders came from an almost identical pool sociologically', goes on: 'Here we touch on a very sensitive issue in the historiography of modern Turkey', and lists further prominent figures of the inter-war regime: 'one would like to know more about these people's activities during World War I'. See 'How Europeans Adopted Anatolia and Created Turkey', *European Review*, Vol. 13, No. 3, July 2005, p. 386.

he was brave, intelligent and far-sighted. Successful as a military commander, he was formidable as the builder of a state. Bold or prudent as the occasion required, he showed an unswerving realism in the acquisition and exercise of power. Yet he was also moved by genuine ideals of a better life for his people, conceived as entry into a civilized modernity, modelled on the most advanced societies of the day. Whatever became of these ideals in practice, he never turned on them.

Ends were one thing, means another. Kemal's regime was a one-party dictatorship, centred on a personality cult of heroic proportions. Equestrian statues of Kemal were being erected as early as 1926, long before monuments to Stalin could be put up in Russia. The speech he gave in 1927 that became the official creed of the nation dwarfed any address by Khrushchev or Castro. Extolling his own achievements, it went on for thirty-six hours, delivered over six days, eventually composing a tome of six hundred pages: a record in the annals of autocracy. Hardened in war, he held life cheap, and without hesitation meted out death to those who stood in his way. Kurds fell by the tens of thousands; though, once forcibly classified as Turks, they were not extirpated. Communists were murdered or jailed, the country's greatest poet, Nâzım Hikmet, spending most of his life in prison or exile. Kemal was capable of sparing old associates. But Unionists who resisted him were executed, trials were rigged, the press was muzzled. The regime was not invasive, by modern standards, but repression was routine.

It is conventional, and reasonable, to compare Kemal's rule with the other Mediterranean dictatorships of his day. In that wan light, its relative merits are plain. On the one hand, unlike Salazar, Franco or Metaxas, Kemal was not a traditional conservative, enforcing reactionary moral codes in league with the Church, an enemy of progress as the time understood it. He was a resolute modernizer, who had not come to power as a defender of landlords or bankers. For him, the state was everything, family and religion nothing, beyond discardable backstops. At the same time, unlike Mussolini, who was a modernist too—one from whom he took the penal code under which Turkey still suffers— he was not an expansionist, hoping to build another empire in the region. Recovery of so much more territory than had seemed likely in 1918 was sufficient achievement in itself, even if Turkish borders could still be improved: one of his last acts was to engineer the annexation of Alexandretta, with the collusion of a weak government in Paris. But the imperial bombast of a New Rome was precluded: he was a seasoned soldier, not an adventurer, and the fate of Enver was too deeply burnt into him. Nor, of course, did Kemal stage mass rallies, bombard the nation with speeches on radio, go in for spectacular processions or parades. There was no attempt at popular mobilization—in this, Turkey was closer to Portugal or Greece than Italy. None was needed, because there was so little class conflict to contain or suppress.

But just because his regime could dispense with a mass basis, Kemal was capable of reforms that Mussolini could never contemplate. In 1934 Turkish women were given equal voting rights, a change that did not come in Italy or France till 1945, in Greece the mid-fifties, in Portugal the mid-seventies. Yet here too the limits of his cultural revolution showed: 90 per cent of Turkish women were still illiterate when he died. The country had not been transformed into the modern society of which he had dreamt. It remained poor, agrarian, stifled rather than emancipated in the grip of the Father of the Turks, as he styled himself in the last years of his life.

By the end Kemal probably knew, at some level, that he had failed. There can be no certainty about his last years, because so much about his life remains a closely guarded secret of state. Only surmises are possible. What is clear is that he had never liked the administrative routines of rule, and from the late twenties delegated day-to-day affairs of government to a mediocre subordinate, Ismet later called Inönü, who looked after these as premier, freeing Kemal to devote himself to his plans, pleasures and fancies in the salons of Çankaya or the cabarets of the Ankara or Pera Palace Hotels. There he summoned colleagues and cronies for sessions of all-night gambling or rousting, increasingly detached from daylight realities. In these flickering conclaves, Kemal shared a predilection with Stalin and Mao— all three, at the end, nocturnal rulers, as if tyranny requires the secrecy of the dark, and reversal of the order of hours, to bind its instruments to it. Nor did similarities stop there. If Kemal's style of detachment from government resembled Mao's—in his case too, it was a distance that did not preclude tight attention to big political operations: the crushing of Dersim or the Anschluss in Alexandretta—the fantastic theories of language that occupied his mind had their counterpart in the linguistic pronouncements of Stalin's decline. All three, as they withdrew from the day, ended by suspecting those who had to live by it.

But in the taxonomy of dictators, Kemal stands apart in one unusual respect. When Politburo members assembled at Stalin's villa, liquor was poured throughout the night; but the general secretary himself was careful to keep control of his consumption, the better to force his entourage to lose theirs, with the chance of revealing themselves in their cups. Kemal's sessions were more genuine revelry. He had always been a heavy drinker, holding it well in debonair officer fashion. But in his final years, *raki* took its toll of him. Normally, absolute power is an intoxicant so much stronger than all others that alcohol, not infrequently shunned altogether, is at most only a tiny chaser. But in Kemal, perhaps because some scepticism in him—an underlying boredom with government—kept him from a full addiction to power, continual drinking became alcoholism.

Once pleasures of the will yielded to pleasures of the flesh, women were the other obvious consolation, of which Kemal did not stint himself. But they were no shield against his solitude; he was at ease only with men. In habits a soldier formed by a career in the barracks, he would have liked to move with grace in mixed society, that symbol of Western civility ever since *Lettres persanes*, but was too crude for it. A brief marriage to the Western-educated daughter of a wealthy merchant lasted little more than a year. Thereafter, random connexions and incidents followed, sometimes involving foreigners. A reputation for increasingly reckless behaviour developed. Adoptive daughters, guarded—a less up-to-date touch—by a black eunuch, multiplied. Towards the end, photographs of Kemal have something of the glazed look of a worn *roué*: a general incongruously reduced to a ravaged lounge lizard, terminal blankness nearby. Stricken with cirrhosis, he died in late 1938, at the age of fifty-seven.

A ruler who took to drink in despair at the ultimate sterility of his rule: that, at any rate, is one conjecture, to be heard among critical spirits in Turkey today. Another, not necessarily contradictory of it, would recall Hegel's description of the autocrats of Rome:

> In the person of the Emperor isolated subjectivity has gained a perfectly unlimited realization. Spirit has renounced its proper nature, inasmuch as Limitation of being and of volition has been constituted an unlimited absolute existence ... Individual subjectivity, thus entirely emancipated from control, has no inward life, no prospective nor retrospective emotions, no repentance, nor hope, nor fear—not

even thought; for all these involve fixed conditions and aims, while here every condition is purely contingent. The springs of action are no more than desire, lust, passion, fancy—in short, caprice absolutely unfettered. It finds so little limitation in the will of others, that the relation of will to will may be called that of absolute sovereignty to absolute slavery.[40]

The picture is highly coloured, and no modern ruler has ever quite fitted it, if only because ideology has typically become inseparable from tyranny, where on the whole legitimacy sufficed in classical times. But in its portrait of a kind of accidie of power, it hints at what might, on another reading, have been the inner dusk of Kemal's dictatorship.

6

His successor, whom he had wanted to discard at the end, was another figure altogether. Inönü, another CUP officer, had served under Kemal in 1916, collaborated with Karakol in the War Ministry in 1919–20, and held a senior command in the independence struggle. He was dour, pious and conservative, in appearance and outlook not unlike a less plump Turkish version of Franco. With war in Europe on the horizon by 1938, his regime sought an understanding with Germany, but was rebuffed by Berlin, at that point angling for the favour of Arab states apprehensive of Turkish revanchism. To insure itself against Italian expansion, and the potential implications for Turkey of the Nazi–Soviet Pact, Ankara then signed a defence treaty with Britain and France in the Mediterranean, shortly after the outbreak of war. When Italy attacked France in 1940, however, Inönü's government reneged on its obligations, and within a year had signed a non-aggression pact with Germany. Three days later, when Hitler invaded Russia, the Turkish leadership was 'carried away with joy'.[41]

Enver's brother Nuri, still alive, was dispatched posthaste to Berlin to discuss the prospect of arousing Turkic peoples in the USSR to rally to the Nazis, and a pair of Turkish generals, Emir Hüsnü Erkilet and Ali Fuad Erden, were soon touring the front-lines of the Wehrmacht in Russia. After briefings from Von Rundstedt in the field, they were flown to Rastenberg to meet

40. *The Philosophy of History*, New York 1956, p. 315–6.
41. Henry and Robin Adams, *Rebel Patriot: A Biography of Franz Von Papen*, Santa Barbara 1987, p. 375.

the Führer in person. 'Hitler', General Erkilet reported, brimming with enthusiasm,

> received us with an indescribable modesty and simplicity at his headquarters where he commands military operations and dispatches. It is a huge room. The long table in the middle and the walls were covered with maps that showed respective positions at the battle zones. Despite that, they did not hide or cover these maps, a clear sign of trust and respect towards us. I expressed my gratitude for the invitation. Then he half-turned towards the map. At the same time, he was looking into our eyes as if he was searching for something. His dark eyes and forelock were sweeter, livelier and more attractive than in photographs. His southern accent, his formal, perfect German, his distinctive, powerful voice, his sturdy look, are full of character.

Telling the Turks that they were the first foreigners, other than allies, to be ushered into the Wolfsschanze, and promising them the complete destruction of Russia, 'the Führer also emphasized that "this war is a continuation of the old one, and those who suffered losses at the end of the last war, would receive compensation for them in this one"'.[42] Thanking him profusely for 'these very important and valuable words', Erkilet and Fuad hastened back to convey them to the National Chief, as Inönü liked to style himself.

Their mission was not taken lightly in Moscow. Within a week, Stalin issued a statement personally denouncing Erkilet's exchange with Hitler, and soon afterwards embarked on a high-risk operation to try and cut off the prospect of joint compensations for 1918. Determined to stop the Turkish army linking arms with the Wehrmacht in the Caucasus, he sent the top NKVD operative Leonid Eitingon—responsible for the killing of Trotsky two years earlier—to Ankara to assassinate the German ambassador, Von Papen, in the hope of provoking Hitler into a punitive attack on Turkey.[43] The attempt was bungled, and its

---

42. H. E. Erkilet, *Şark Cephesinde Gördüklerim*, Istanbul 1943, pp. 218–23. Invitations for the Turkish military to inspect British positions in Iraq and Iran were declined: Lothar Krecker, *Deutschland and die Türkei im zweiten Weltkrieg*, Frankfurt 1964, p. 198.

43. For this episode, see Frank Weber, *The Evasive Neutral: Germany, Britain, and the Quest for a Turkish Alliance in the Second World War*, Columbia and London 1979, pp. 126–36, much the best study of Turkish diplomacy in these years. Fulsome appreciation of Ankara's course during the war can be found in Edward Weisband, *Turkish Foreign Policy 1943–1945*, Princeton 1973, and Selim Deringil, *Turkish Foreign Policy during the Second World War: An 'Active' Neutrality*, Cambridge 2004, who remarks guilelessly at the outset: 'A study of

origin quickly discovered. But Moscow had every reason for its
misgivings. In August 1942, the Turkish premier Saraçoğlu told
Von Papen that as a Turk he 'passionately desired the obliteration
of Russia'. Indeed, it was his view that 'the problem of Russia
can only be solved by Germany on condition that at least half the
Russians living in Russia are annihilated'.[44] As late as the summer
of 1943, another Turkish military mission was touring not only
the Eastern front but the West wall of Nazi defences in France,
before flying once more to an audience in the Wolfsschanze. The
war had revived Unionist ambitions: at one time or another,
Turkey manoeuvred to regain western Thrace, the Dodecanese,
Syria, the region of Mosul, and protectoral rights over Albania.

Nor was alignment with the New Order confined to policy
abroad. In June 1941, all non-Muslim males of draft age—Jewish,
Greek or residual Armenian—were packed off to labour camps in
the interior. In November 1942, as the battle for Stalingrad raged,
a 'wealth tax' was inflicted on Jews and Christians, who had to pay
up to ten times the rate for Muslims, amid a barrage of anti-Semitic
and anti-infidel attacks in the press—Turkish officials themselves
becoming liable to investigation for Jewish origins. Those who
could not or would not meet the demands of local boards were
deported to punishment camps in the mountains. The effect was to
destroy the larger part of non-Muslim businesses in Istanbul.

The operation, unabashedly targeting ethno-religious minorities,
was in the lineal tradition, passed down from Unionism to
Kemalism, of Turkish integral nationalism. A decade earlier Inönü
had declared: 'Only the Turkish nation is entitled to claim ethnic
and national rights in this country. No other element has any such
rights'. His minister of justice dotted the i's and crossed the t's:
'The Turk must be the only lord, the only master of this country.
Those who are not of pure Turkish origin can have only one right
in this country, the right to be servants and slaves'.[45] New in the
campaign of 1942–3 was only the extent of its anti-Semitism,
and the fact that the Inönü regime—hard pressed economically
by the costs of a greatly increased military budget—levied any

Turkish foreign policy should ideally be based on the archives. But unfortunately
this is not possible as the main Turkish archival material is closed to private
research' (p. 7), without asking himself why this might be.

44. *Documents Secrets du Ministère des Affaires Etrangères d'Allemagne*,
Paris 1946, p. 89, translated from the Soviet publication of German archives
captured in Berlin in 1945.

45. Poulton, *Top Hat, Grey Wolf and Crescent*, p. 120.

part of its exactions on Muslims at all. Jewish converts to Islam were not included among the faithful for these purposes. Such was the climate in which Hitler returned the compliment by sending Talat's remains back to Turkey, in a ceremonial train bedecked with swastikas, to be buried with full honours in Istanbul, by the Martyrs' Monument on Liberty Hill, where patriots can proceed to this day.[46]

Once, however, the tide started to turn in Russia, and Germany looked as if it might be defeated, Ankara readjusted its stance. While continuing to supply the Third Reich with the chromite on which the Nazi war machine depended, Turkey now also entertained overtures from Britain and America. But resisting Anglo-American pressures to come down on the Allied side, Inönü made it clear that his lodestar remained anti-communism. The USSR was the main enemy, and Turkey expressly opposed any British or American strategy that risked altering Germany's position as a bastion against it, hoping London and Washington would make a separate peace with Berlin, for future joint action against Moscow. Dismayed at the prospect of unconditional surrender, Inönü only issued a token declaration of war on Germany after the Allies made it a condition of getting a seat at the United Nations, a week before the deadline they had set for doing so expired, in late February 1945. No Turkish shot was fired in the fight against fascism.

Peace left the regime in a precarious position. Internally, it was now thoroughly detested by the majority of the population, which

---

46. For coverage, see *Cumhuriyet*, 25 February 1943. The British ambassador Knatchbull-Hugessen informed the Foreign Office: 'I learn that the original proposal regarding Talat's remains came from M. Saraçoğlu, a faithful henchman of the President'. See Robert Olson, 'The Remains of Talat: A Dialectic Between Republic and Empire', *Die Welt des Islams*, No. 26, 1986, p. 54. The German diplomat and fixer Ernst Jäckh, claiming that Kemal once told him 'he stood on the shoulders of our common Young Turk friend and statesman', described the scene in Istanbul: 'In the funeral procession from the "Hill of Liberty" to Talaat's reburial on Turkish soil, personal representatives of the Cabinet and a great popular crowd joined the troops, paying full military honours. It had been my privilege to make the funeral oration, at the time of his death in 1921. Now the address was delivered by our mutual friend, the doyen of political publicists, Hussein Djahid Yalcin, who, weeping over the grave, personified the historic evolution from the Young Turkish period to Ataturk's era'. See *Der goldene Pflug: Lebensernte eines Weltbürgers*, Stuttgart 1954, p. 125, 231–3, and *The Rising Crescent*, New York 1944, p. 95.

had suffered from a steep fall in living standards as prices soared, taxes increased and forced labour was extorted in the service of its military build-up. Inflation had affected all classes, sparing not even bureaucrats, and the wealth tax had made even the well-off jumpy. Externally, the regime had been compromised by its affair with Nazism—which post-war Soviet diplomacy was quick to point out—and its refusal to contribute to Allied victory even after it had become certain.

Aware of his unpopularity, in early 1945 Inönü attempted to redress it with a belated redistribution of land, only to provoke a revolt in the ranks of the ruling party, without gaining credibility in the countryside. Something more was needed. Six months later, he announced that there would be free elections. Turkey, for twenty years a dictatorship, would now become a democracy. Inönü's move was designed to kill two birds with one stone. Abroad, it would restore his regime to legitimacy, as a respectable partner of the West, taking its place in the comity of free nations led by the United States, and entitled to the benefits of that status. At home, it could neutralize discontent by offering an outlet for opposition without jeopardizing the stability of his rule. For he had no intention of permitting a true contest.

In 1946, a flagrantly crooked election returned the ruling Republican People's Party with a huge majority over a Democratic Party led by the defectors who had broken with it over the agrarian bill. The fraud was so scandalous that, domestically, rather than repairing the reputation of the regime, it damaged it yet further. Internationally, however, it did the trick. Turkey was duly proclaimed a pillar of the West, the Truman Doctrine picking it out for economic and military assistance to withstand the Soviet threat, and Marshall Plan aid began to pour in. Economic recovery was rapid, Turkey posting high rates of growth over the next four years.

These laurels, however, did not appease the Turkish masses. Inönü, after first appointing the leading pro-fascist politician in his party—responsible for the worst repression under Kemal—as premier, then attempted to steal the more liberal clothes of the Democrats, with concessions to the market and to religion. It was of no avail. When elections were held in 1950, it was impossible to rig them as before, and by now—so Inönü imagined—unnecessary: the combination of his own prestige and relief from war-time rigours would carry the day for the RPP anyway. He was stunned when voters rejected his regime by a wide margin, putting the Democrats into power with a parliamentary majority, honestly gained, as large as the dishonest one he had engineered for himself four years earlier. The dictatorship Kemal had installed was over.

7

In a famous essay, one of the most acute self-critical reflections to emerge out of any of the youthful revolts of the sixties, Murat Belge—a writer unrivalled in his intelligence of the political sensibility of his generation—told his contemporaries on the Turkish Left, as yet another military intervention came thudding down over more than a decade of ardent hopes, that they had misunderstood their own country, in a quite fundamental way. They had thought it a Third World society among others, ready for liberation by guerrilla uprisings in the towns or in the mountains. The paradox they had failed to grasp was that although the Turkey of the time was indeed 'a relatively backward country economically . . . and socially'—with a per capita income like that of Algeria and Mexico, and adult literacy at a mere 60 per cent—it was 'relatively *advanced* politically', having known 'a two-party system in which opposing leaders have changed office a number of times after a popular mandate, something which has never happened in Japan for example'.[47] In short, Turkey was unusual in being a poor and ill-educated society that had yet remained a democracy as generally understood, if with violent intermissions—Belge was writing in the aftermath of the military putsch of 1980.

A quarter of a century later, his diagnosis still holds. Since the end of the Kemalist order *stricto sensu* in 1950, Turkey has on the whole been a land of regular elections, of competing parties and uncertain outcomes, and alternating governments. This is a much longer record than Spain, Portugal or Greece—even, as to alternation, Italy—can boast of. What accounts for it? Historians point to earlier moments of constitutional debate or parliamentary contest, from late Ottoman times to mid-period Kemalism. But, however respectable in memory, such episodes were too fragile and fleeting to have been much of a foundation for the stability of a modern Turkish democracy now approaching its seventh decade. An alternative approach is more conjunctural, emphasizing the tactical reasons why Inönü made his feint towards democracy in

---

47. 'The Tragedy of the Turkish Left', *New Left Review* I/26, March–April 1981, p. 85; published under the pseudonynm 'Ahmet Samim'.

1946, and the miscalculations that ensued from it in 1950. But that leaves unanswered the question why thereafter democracy became so entrenched that even serial military interventions could not shake its acceptance as the political norm in Turkey. A more structural explanation is needed.

During the Second World War, Inönü had steered his country in much the way Franco had done Spain, tempering passive affinity and assistance to the Nazi regime with a prudent *attentisme*, allowing for better relations with the West once it looked as if Germany would be defeated. But after the war the situation of the two dictatorships, though equally anti-communist, differed. Spain was at the other end of Europe from the USSR, while Turkey was geo-politically a front-line state in the Cold War, with a long history of hostilities with Russia to boot. So there was both a more pressing interest in Washington, and a more pressing need in Ankara, for a close understanding between the two than there was in the case of Madrid, and hence for a better ideological and institutional alignment of Turkey with the West.

That in itself, however, would not have been enough to bring democracy to Turkey. American tolerance, even welcome, of authoritarian regimes in the Free World, so long as they were staunch military and political supports of Washington, would be a constant feature of the Cold War. Within a decade, after all, Franco too was hosting US bases. What really set Turkey apart from Spain was something deeper. The Spanish dictatorship was the product of a bitter civil war, pitting class against class, social revolution against counter-revolution, which the Nationalist crusade had needed German and Italian help to win. There were still a few guerrillas in the mountains resisting the regime in 1945. After the war democratization was an unthinkable option for Franco: it would have risked a political volcano erupting again, in which neither army, property nor church would have been secure.

Thirty years later, his regime had accomplished its historical task. Economic development had transformed Spanish society, radical mass politics had been extinguished, and democracy was no longer hazardous for capital. So completely had the dictatorship done its work that a toothless Bourbon socialism was incapable even of restoring the republic it had overthrown. In this Spanish laboratory lay a wider parabola of the future, which the Latin American dictators of the seventies—Pinochet is the exemplary case—would repeat, architects of a political order in which electors, grateful for civic liberties finally restored, could be trusted henceforward not to tamper with the social order. Today the Spanish template has become the general formula of freedom: no longer making the world safe for democracy, but democracy safe for this world.

Turkey could become a democracy so much earlier than Spain, a more advanced society—let alone other countries as economically and socially backward as it in 1950—because there was no comparably explosive class conflict to be contained, nor radical politics to be crushed. Most peasants owned land; workers were few; intellectuals marginal; a Left hardly figured. The lines of fissure in society, at that stage still concreted over, were ethnic more than class in nature. In these conditions, there was small risk of any upsets from below. The elites could settle accounts between themselves without fear of letting loose forces they could not control. That degree of security would not last. In due course there would be both social and ethnic turbulence, as popular unrest made itself felt; when it did so, the state would react violently.

But, sociologically speaking, the basic parameters set by the first election of 1950 have remained in place to this day. Turkish democracy has been broken at intervals, but never for long, because it is anchored in a Centre-Right majority that has remained, in one form after another, unbroken. Across four historical cycles, an underlying stability has distinguished Turkish political life. From 1950 to 1960 the country was ruled by Adnan Menderes as premier, at the head of a Democratic Party whose vote, 58 per cent of the electorate at its height, was never less than 47 per cent; still giving it four-fifths of the seats in the National Assembly, and control of the presidency, at the end of its life-span.

The birth of the party marked the moment at which the Turkish elite split, with the growth of a bourgeoisie less dependent on the state than in the pre-war period, no longer willing to accept bureaucratic direction of the economy, and eager for the spoils of political power. Its leaders were all former members of the Kemalist establishment, typically with stakes in the private sector: Menderes was a wealthy cotton planter, Bayar—president after 1950—a leading banker. But its followers were, overwhelmingly, the peasant masses who formed a majority of the nation. The recipe of its rule was a paradox rare in the Third World: a liberal populism, combining commitment to the market and an appeal to tradition in equal measure.[48] In its deployment of each, rhetoric outran reality without quite losing touch with it. On coming to power, Menderes's first key move—he did not even consult Parliament—was to dispatch troops to Korea, earning high marks in Washington and the rewards of entry into NATO and a spate of dollars for Turkish services. His regime used American assistance to supply cheap credit and assure high prices to farmers, building roads to expand cultivation, importing machinery to modernize cash-crop production, and relaxing controls on industry. In the slipstream of the post-war boom in the West, growth accelerated and per capita incomes jumped in the countryside.

This alone would have been enough to secure the popularity of the Democratic government. But Menderes played not just to the pocket, but to the sensibility of his rural constituency. Sensing his isolation after the war, Inönü had already started to edge away from Kemal's policies towards religion. The Democrats were a good deal less inhibited: new mosques shot up, religious schools multiplied, instruction in Islam became standard in state education, calls to prayer were to be heard in Arabic again, brotherhoods were legalized and opponents denounced as infidels. The equation of Turkish with Muslim identity, for long a tacit substratum of Kemalism, acquired bolder expression. This was enough to antagonize sectors of the elite committed to official versions of secularism, but it did not signify any break with the legacy of the late Ottoman or early Republican state. Menderes, indeed, went further than Inönü had ever done in erecting Kemal into an untouchable symbol of the nation, putting him in a mausoleum in Ankara and making any injury to his memory a crime punishable with severe penalties at law.

More gravely, the integral nationalism of the inter-war period was given a new impetus, when Menderes—solicited by Britain—took up the cause of the Turkish minority in Cyprus, reclaiming rights of intervention in the island relinquished at Lausanne. In 1955, as a three-power conference on its future was meeting in London, his regime unleashed a savage pogrom against the Greek community in Istanbul. Formally exempted from the population transfers of 1923, this had dwindled rapidly under state pressure in the following years, but still numbered over 100,000 in the mid-thirties, and remained a prosperous and lively part of the city's

---

48. For the classic analysis of this configuration, see Çağlar Keyder's fundamental work, *State and Class in Turkey*, London 1987, pp. 122–5.

life. In a single night, gangs organized by the government smashed and burnt its churches, schools, shops, businesses, hospitals, beating and raping as they went. Menderes and Bayar, lurking in the suburb of Florya, boarded a train for Ankara as flames lit up the night sky.[49] It was Turkey's *Kristallnacht*. Continuities with the past were not merely ideological, but even individual. In 1913 Bayar had been an operative of the CUP's Special Organization, responsible for ethnic cleansing of Greeks from the Smyrna region, before the First World War had even begun. Within a few years, only a handful of Greeks were left in Istanbul.

This time, however, there was shock in the press and public opinion, and unease even in establishment quarters at Menderes's methods. In 1957 he cruised to a third electoral victory, but with external debt, the public deficit and inflation now running high, his economic performance had lost its shine, and he turned to increasingly tough repressive measures, targeting the press and parliamentary opposition, to maintain his position. Over-confident, brutal and not very bright, he eventually set up a committee to investigate his opponents, and imposed censorship on its proceedings. He had consolidated his power by taking Turkey into the Korean War. A decade later, inspired by students in Korea who had just overthrown Syngman Rhee, whom the war had been fought to defend, students in Ankara took to the streets against his move towards a dictatorship. The universities in Ankara and Istanbul were shut down, to no avail, amid successive nights of rioting. After a month of disturbances, detachments of the army finally intervened.[50] Early one morning Menderes, his cabinet and deputies were arrested, and a committee of some forty officers took over the government.

The coup of 1960 was not the work of the Turkish high command, but of conspirators of lesser rank, who had been planning to oust Menderes for some time. Some had radical social ideas, others were authoritarian nationalists. But few had any clear programme beyond dissolution of the Democratic Party, and retribution for

---

49. Speros Vryonis Jr, *The Mechanism of Catastrophe: The Turkish Pogrom of September 6–7, 1955 and the Destruction of the Greek Community in Istanbul*, New York 2005, provides the fullest account of these events: for the role of Menderes and Bayar, see pp. 91–8.

50. For a vivid description, see William Weiker, *The Turkish Revolution 1960–1961*, Westport 1980, pp. 14–20.

its leaders, who were tried on a variety of charges, among them responsibility for the pogrom of 1955, for which Menderes was executed, though Bayar spared. In the army itself, a large number of conservative officers were purged, but the high command soon reasserted itself, crushing attempts to take matters further. In a temporarily fluid situation, in which the military were not united, a new Constitution was produced by jurists from the universities, and ratified by referendum. Designed to prevent the abuses of power that had marked Menderes's rule, it created a Constitutional Court and second chamber, introduced proportional representation, strengthened the judiciary, guaranteed civil liberties, and academic and press freedoms. It also, however, created a National Security Council dominated by the military, which acquired wide-ranging powers.

With these institutions in place, the second cycle of post-war Turkish politics was set in motion. As soon as elections were held, it became clear that the voting bloc put together by the Democrats, though at first distributed across a number of successor formations, still commanded a comfortable majority of the country. By 1965, it was consolidated behind the Justice Party led by Süleyman Demirel, which alone took 53 per cent of the vote. Thirty years later, Demirel would still be at large, in the presidential palace. A hydraulic engineer with American connexions—Eisenhower Fellowship; consultant for Morrison-Knudsen—who had been picked for bureaucratic office by Menderes, Demirel was no improvement in personality or principles on his patron. But the fate of his predecessor made him more cautious, and the Constitution of 1961, though he would tamper with it, limited his ability to reproduce the same style of rule.

In power, Demirel like Menderes benefitted from fast growth, distributed favours in the countryside, made resonant appeals to village piety, and whipped up a virulent anti-communism. But there were two differences. The populism of the Justice Party was no longer liberal. The sixties were a period of development economics throughout most of the world, and the authors of the 1960 coup, vaguely influenced by Nasserism, were no exception to the rule, seeking a strong *dirigiste* state. Demirel inherited a turn towards standard import-substituting industrialization, and for electoral purposes made the most of it. The second change was more fundamental. However burning the resentment of his cadres at the army for dethroning the Democrats, and however close to the secularist bone his religious histrionics might come, at any sign of unrest in the barracks Demirel quickly deferred to the military.

This in itself, however, was not enough to secure a dominance of the political scene otherwise comparable to that of Menderes. The Republican People's Party, trounced three times in the fifties, posed little challenge. When Inönü finally shuffled off the stage in the early seventies, the party was taken over by Bülent Ecevit, who briefly attempted to make it a Centre-Left alternative, before collapsing into the arms of the military as figurehead of the Turkish invasion of Cyprus in 1974, and ending up as an empty fossil of plaintive chauvinism. The mechanics of coalition-building in a Parliament which no longer delivered the first-past-the-post landslides of old made him premier three times, but the Kemalist bloc he inherited never came near to winning an electoral majority of the electorate,[51] sinking to a mere 20 per cent of the vote by the time he finally exited the scene.

The danger to Demirel lay elsewhere. The new Constitution had allowed a Workers' Party to run candidates for the first time. It never got more than 5 per cent of the vote, posing no threat to the stability of the system. But if the Turkish working class was still too small and intimidated for any mass electoral politics, the Turkish universities were rapidly becoming hotbeds of radicalism. Situated, uniquely, at the intersection between First, Second and Third Worlds—Europe to the west, the USSR to the north, the Mashreq to the south and east—Turkish students were galvanized by ideas and influences from all three: campus rebellions, communist traditions, guerrilla imaginations, each with what appeared to be their own relevance to the injustices and cruelties of the society around them, in which the majority of the population was still rural and nearly half were illiterate. Out of this heady mixture came the kaleidoscope of revolutionary groups whose obituary Belge was to write a decade later. In the late sixties, as Demirel persecuted left opinion of any sort, it was not long before some took to arms, in scattered acts of violence.

In themselves these too were little more than pinpricks, without significant impact on the political control of the Justice Party. But they lent energy and opportunity to movements of a much more threatening character on its other flank. In 1969, the ultra-

---

51. At its height, in the Mafeking atmosphere after the invasion of Cyprus, the Republican's People's Party got just over 41 per cent of the vote, the combined forces of Demirel, Türkes and Erbakan just under 52 per cent.

nationalist Nationalist Action Party (MHP) was created by
Alparslan Türkes, a colonel who as a young officer during the
Second World War had been an ardent pro-Nazi, and was one of
the key movers of the coup in 1960. Adopting fascist methods,
it swiftly built up paramilitary squads—the Grey Wolves—far
stronger than anything the Left could muster, and boasted a
constituency twice its size. Nor was this all. As Demirel tacked
towards the military, while the elasticity of the political system
expanded, a less accommodating Islamism emerged to outflank
him. In 1970 the National Order Party was launched by Necmettin
Erbakan, like Demirel an engineer, but at a higher level—he
had held a university chair—and with more genuine claims to
piety, as a member of a Sufi order of Naqshbandi. Running on a
more radically Muslim ticket than the Justice Party could afford
to do, and attacking its subservience to American capital, his
organization—re-dubbed the National Salvation Party—took 12
per cent in its first test at the polls.

The turbulence caused by these unruly outsiders was too much
for the Kemalist establishment, and in 1971 the army intervened
again. This time—as invariably henceforward—it was the high
command that struck, with an ultimatum ousting Demirel for
failure to maintain order, and imposing a technocratic government
of the Right. Under martial law, trade-unionists, intellectuals and
deputies of the Left were rounded up and tortured, and the liberal
provisions of the constitution cancelled.[52] Two years later, the
political scene was judged sufficiently purged of subversion for
elections to be held again, and for the rest of the seventies Demirel
and Ecevit see-sawed in coalition governments in which either
Türkes or Erbakan, or both, held casting votes, and populated the
ministries under their control.

At the time, the Grey Wolves looked the more formidable of
the newcomers to the system, rapidly capturing key positions of
the police and intelligence apparatuses of the state, from which
terror could be orchestrated with paramilitary gangs outside it.
Few terms have been as much abused as 'fascism', but there is
little question that the MHP of these years met the bill. Therein,
however, lay its limitation. Classically, fascism—in Germany
as in Italy or Spain—was a response to the threat of a mass
revolutionary movement that the possessing classes feared they

---

52. For a trenchant account, see Feroz Ahmed, *Turkey: The Quest for Identity*,
Oxford 2003, pp. 134–7.

could not contain within the established constitutional order. Where such a movement was missing, though clubs and squads might be useful for local intimidation, the risks of entrusting supreme power to any extra-legal dynamism of the right, welling up from below, were generally too high for traditional rulers. In Turkey a protean revolutionary force had emerged, attracting not just firebrands in the universities, but recruits from the religious and ethnic minorities, local support from groups of workers, even sympathizers in the educated middle class. But though it was capable of ascendancy in particular neighbourhoods or municipalities, it was never a mass phenomenon. A student-based movement, however dedicated its militants, was no match for a heavily armed state, let alone a conservative electoral majority.

Much of the traditional fabric of Turkish society was meanwhile coming apart, as migration from the countryside threw up squatter settlements in the towns, still not far removed in ways of life and outlook from the villages left behind—ruralization of the cities outrunning urbanization of the newcomers, in the famous formula of Şerif Mardin, dean of Turkish sociologists[53]—but without the same communal bonds. Though from the turn of the seventies the post-war boom was over, industrialization by import substitution was artificially prolonged by remittances from Turkish workers abroad and a ballooning foreign debt. By the end of the decade this model was exhausted: Demirel's brand of populism ended in larger deficits, higher inflation, wider black markets and lower growth than Menderes's had done. Deteriorating economic conditions were compounded by increasing civil violence, as the far Right stepped up its campaign against the Left, and a medley of revolutionary groups hit back. Worst affected were Alevis— communities suspect of a heterodoxy worse than Shiism—who became victims of the latest pogrom against a minority, the Grey Wolves acting as the Special Organization of the day.

The tipping point, however, came from another direction. In September 1980, an Islamist rally in Konya, resounding to calls for restoration of the sharia, refused to sing the national anthem, in open defiance of Kemalist prescriptions. Within a week, the army struck, closing the country's borders and seizing power in the small hours. Under a National Security Council headed by the chief of staff, Parliament was dissolved and every major

---

53. *Religion, Society and Modernity in Turkey*, pp. 217–9.

politician put behind bars. Parties were shut down; deputies, mayors and local councils dismissed. A year later, martial law would be declared in Poland, to a universal outcry in the West—a torrent of denunciations in editorials, articles, books, meetings, demonstrations. The military take-over in Turkey met with scarcely a murmur. Yet the rule of Jaruzelski was mild compared with that of Kenan Evren, commander of the Turkish Gladio. No less than 178,000 were arrested, 64,000 were jailed, 30,000 stripped of their citizenship, 450 died under torture, 50 were executed, others disappeared.[54] Europe's good conscience took it in its stride.

Mass repression was not the gateway to a dictatorship in Turkey, but to a democratic catharsis of the kind that would become familiar in Latin America. Evren and his colleagues had no compunction about the wholesale use of torture, but equally they understood the importance of constitutions. A new charter was written, concentrating power in the executive, introducing a 10 per cent threshold for representation in the legislature, and eliminating excessive civil liberties, especially those which had permitted irresponsible strikes or calumnies in the press. A referendum in which any discussion of the document was forbidden duly ratified it, installing Evren as president. In 1983 elections were held under the improved rules, and parliamentary government returned. The way was now paved for a third cycle of Centre-Right politics.

The new premier was Turgut Özal, like Demirel—to whom he owed his rise—a provincial engineer with a background in the US, whose initial move from bureaucratic and managerial positions into a political career had been made via the National Salvation Party, of which his brother was a leading light. A year before the coup, Demirel had put him in charge of the stabilization plan on which the IMF insisted as a condition of bailing Turkey out of its financial crisis—a standard deflationary package that had run into stiff trade-union opposition. When the military seized power, they retained his services, and once popular resistance was crushed, Özal's hands were no longer tied. He could now implement the

---

54. Compare Ece Temelkuran, 'Headscarf and Flag', *New Left Review* II/51, May–June 2008, p. 83, with Mehmet Ali Birand, *The Generals' Coup in Turkey: An Inside Story of 12 September 1980*, London 1987, p. 212.

reductions in public spending, hikes in interest rates, scrapping of price controls and cuts in real wages that international confidence required. A financial scandal in his team, forcing him to resign in 1982, saved him from continuing association with the junta when elections were held the following year. Creating his own Motherland Party, with the tacit backing of all three of the now banned formations of the previous Right—populist, fascist and islamist—he carried off an easy victory with 45 per cent of the vote, giving him an absolute majority in Parliament.

Squat and unprepossessing in appearance, crude in manner, Özal always had a touch of a Turkish Mr Toad about him. But he was a more considerable figure than Demirel or Menderes, with a quick, sharp mind and a coherent vision of the country's future. Coming to power at the turn of the eighties, the hour of Thatcher and Reagan, he was a local equivalent in neo-liberal resolve. The import substitution model, with its web of administered prices, over-valued exchange rates, bureaucratic licenses and subsidized public sector—all that Kemalist statism had thought to develop over the years—started to be dismantled, to give free rein to market forces. There were limits: privatization of state enterprises was more talked about than done. But overall, economic liberalization was pushed through, with highly satisfactory results for Turkish capital. Exports trebled in value. New enterprises sprang up, profits rose, and wages declined. Amid accelerating growth, and a general climate of *enrichissez-vous*, a contemporary consumerism arrived for the middle class.[55]

Simultaneously, Özal exploited religion to consolidate his position more openly than any of his predecessors. He could do this because the junta had itself abandoned military traditions of secularism, in the interests of combating subversion. 'Laicism does not mean atheism', Evren told the nation.[56] In 1982 confessional instruction was made obligatory in state schools, and from then on what had always been tacit in official ideology, the identification of nation with religion, became explicit with the diffusion of 'the Turkish-Islamic synthesis' as textbook doctrine. Özal, though an arch-pragmatist, was himself a member of

---

55. For overviews, see Çağlar Keyder, 'The Turkish Bell Jar', *New Left Review* II/28 July–August 2004, pp. 67ff; Zürcher, *Turkey: A Modern History*, pp. 306–12.

56. See the fine essay by Osman Taştan, 'Religion and Religious Minorities', in Debbie Lovatt (ed.), *Turkey Since 1970: Politics, Economics and Society*, New York 2001, p. 151.

the mystical Naqshbandi order—he liked to compare them to the Mormons, as examples of the affinity between piety and money—and used state control of religion to promote it as never before. Under him, the budget of the Directorate of Religious Affairs increased sixteen-fold: five million copies of the Koran were printed at public expense, half a million pilgrims ushered to Mecca, seventy thousand mosques kept up for the faithful.[57] The devout, the dynamic and the epicurean all had reason to be grateful to him.

In the spring of 1987, Özal capped his project to modernize the country by applying for Turkish entry into the European Community, the candidature that is still pending twenty years later. In the autumn he was re-elected premier, and in 1989 took over the presidency when Evren retired. From this peak, it was downhill. Economically, a trade deficit and overvalued currency combined with electorally driven public spending to send inflation back to pre-coup levels, triggering a wave of strikes and choppy business conditions. Corruption, rife during the boom, now lapped the presidential family itself. Politically, having gambled that he could keep the old guard of politicians out of play with a referendum banning their re-entry into the arena, which he then lost, Özal was faced with the rancour of a reanimated Demirel. Increasingly abrupt and autocratic in style, he made Turkey into a launching-pad for American strikes against Iraq in the Gulf War, in defiance of public opinion and against the advice of the general staff, and got no economic or strategic reward for doing so. Instead, Turkey was now confronted with an autonomous Kurdish zone on its south-eastern borders, under American protection.

Each cycle of the three cycles of Centre-Right rule had seen a steady weakening of one of the pillars of Kemalism as a historical structure—its compression of religion to a default identity, restricting its expressions to the private sphere. Now it was not just secularism, as officially defined, but also statism, as an economic outlook, that was eroded. Özal had gone furthest in both directions, confessional and liberal. But the deeper foundations

---

57. Huri Türsan, *Democratisation in Turkey: The Role of Political Parties*, Brussels 2004, p. 228; David Shankland, *Islam and Society in Turkey*, Huntingdon 1999, p. 30.

of the Kemalist order lay untouched. Integral nationalism has remained *de rigueur* for every government since 1945, with its invariable toll of victims. After the Greeks in the fifties and the Alevis in the seventies, now it was the turn, once again, of the Kurds. The radicalization of the late sixties had not left them unaffected, but so long as there was a legal Workers' Party, or a lively set of illegal movements in the universities, Kurdish aspirations flowed into a more general stream of activism. Once the coup of 1980 had decapitated this Left, however, the political reawakening of a new generation of Kurds had to find its own ways to emancipation.

On seizing power, Evren's junta had declared martial law in the south-east, and rapidly made any use of the Kurdish language—even in private—a criminal offence. Absolute denial of any cultural or political expressions of a collective Kurdish identity covered the whole of Turkey. But in the south-east, social and economic relations were also explosive: the proportion of landless peasants was high,[58] and the power of large landowners, long complicit with the state, was great. In this setting, one of the Kurdish groups formed in Ankara just before the coup found the natural conditions for a guerrilla war. The PKK, initially sporting Marxist–Leninist colours, but in actuality—as time would show—thoroughly pragmatic, launched its first operations across the Syrian and Iraqi borders in the spring of 1984.

This time the Turkish state, facing a much more disciplined and modern enemy, with external bases, could not crush the movement in a few months, as it had done the risings of 1925 and 1937. A prolonged war ensued, in which the PKK responded to military terror with pitiless ferocities of its own. It was fifteen years before the army and air force finally brought the Kurdish insurgency to an end, in 1999. By then, Ankara had mobilized more than a quarter of a million troops and police—twice the size of the American army of occupation in Iraq—at an annual cost of $6 billion. According to official figures, at least 30,000 died, and 380,000 were expelled from their homes. Actual victims were more numerous. In the words of a leading authority, 'unofficial estimates put the number of internal refugees at three million'.[59] The method of deportations was old, the destination new, as

---

58. 45 per cent of peasants in Diyarbakir, 47 per cent in Urfa, were without land: Ahmed, *Turkey: The Quest for Identity*, p. 163.

59. William Hale, *Turkey, the US and Iraq*, London 2007, p. 70.

the army burnt and razed villages to concentrate the population under its control, in a Turkish version of the strategic hamlets in Vietnam—invigilated slums in the regional cities.

This was the other face of Özal's rule. In his last years, he started to speak of his own half-Kurdish origins—he came from Malatya in the east—and to loosen the most draconian laws against the use of Kurdish as a language. But on his sudden death in 1993, Demirel grabbed the presidency, and torture and repression intensified. The rest of the nineties saw a succession of weak, corrupt coalitions, that reproduced the trajectory of the seventies, presiding over a disintegration of the political system and economic model of the preceding decade, as if the hegemony of the Centre-Right was fated to repeat the same parabola every generation. Once more public debt soared, inflation took off, interest rates rocketed. This time deep recession and high unemployment completed the debacle.

In the last year of the century a moribund Ecevit returned to office, boasting of his capture of the PKK leader Abdullah Öcalan—a figure out of Dostoevsky, abducted by Mossad and the CIA in Africa and delivered in a truss to Ankara, where he was soon profusely expressing his love for Turkey. By now public finances were in ruins, the price of necessities out of control. The final economic crisis was triggered by an undignified dispute between the president, now a former judge, and the premier, livid to be taxed with the corruption of his ministers. Dudgeon at the helm of the state led to panic on the stock market, and collapse of the currency.[60] Meltdown was avoided only by an emergency IMF loan, extended for the same reason as to Yeltsin's Russia— the country was too important an American interest to risk a domestic upheaval, should it founder. The fall of the government a few months later brought the aftermath of the Özal years to a close.

8

Elections in the autumn of 2002 saw a complete transformation of the political scene. A party that had not even existed eighteen months before swept the board. The AKP—Justice and Development Party—running on a moderate Muslim platform,

---

60. For the scale of the economic crisis, and its social impact, see Zülküf Aydın, *The Political Economy of Turkey*, London 2005, pp. 123–5.

won two-thirds of the seats in the National Assembly, forming a government with the largest majority since the time of Menderes. Its victory was widely hailed, at home and abroad, as the dawn of a new era for Turkey. Not only would the country now be assured stable government, after years of squabbling coalition cabinets, but—still more vital—there was the prospect of a long overdue reconciliation of religion and democracy in Turkey. For the central plank of the AKP's electoral campaign was a pledge to bring Turkey into the European Union, as a country made capable of meeting the EU's long-standing criteria for membership, above all the political *sine qua non* of the rule of law and respect for human rights. Within a month of their victory, AKP leaders had secured a diplomatic triumph at the Copenhagen summit of the EU, which gave Turkey a firm date, only two years away, for starting negotiations for its accession to the Union, provided that it had enacted sufficient political reforms in the interim. At home the general change of mood, from despair to euphoria, was dramatic. Not since 1950 had such a fresh start, inspiring so much hope, been witnessed.

The novelty of AKP rule, widely acclaimed in the West, is not an illusion. But between the standard image, to be found in every *bien-pensant* editorial, opinion column and reportage in Europe, let alone America—not to speak of official pronouncements from Brussels—and the reality of what is new about it, the distance is considerable. The party is an heir, not a founder, of its fortune. When the ban on pre-1980 politicians was lifted in 1987, the landscape of the late seventies re-emerged. Özal and Demirel disputed the mainstream Centre-Right vote, traditionally hegemonic, but weakened in the seventies by the rise of fascist and Islamist parties on its far flank. These now duly reappeared, but with a difference. Türkes had dropped much of his earlier ideological baggage, his party now touting a synthesis of religion and nation in the style of a more generic Turkish chauvinism, with somewhat greater—though still quite limited—electoral success as time went on.

Erbakan, on the other hand, became a major force. The popular constituency for Islamism was much larger, and he proved a formidable shaper of it. By 1994 he had created far the best grass-roots organization of any party, based on local religious networks, powered by modern communications and data systems. In that year, his—renamed—Welfare Party showed its mettle by capturing Istanbul, Ankara and a string of other cities in municipal

elections.[61] Town halls had never been of much importance in
the past, but the new Welfare mayors and their councillors, by
delivering services and charitable works to communities that
had never previously known such attention, made them into
strongholds of popular Islamism.

Behind this success lay longer-term changes in society. Outside the
state education system, religious schools had been multiplying since
the fifties. In the market, the media were moving steadily downscale,
the tabloid press and commercial television propagating a mass
culture that was, as everywhere, sensationalist and consumerist,
but with a local twist. By dissolving the distinctions on which the
Kemalist compression of Islam had depended, between private
life—and fantasy—and admissible public ideals or aspirations, it
favoured the penetration of religion into the political sphere. The
post-Ottoman elites could afford to look down on a popular culture
saturated with folk religion so long as the political system excluded
the masses from any real say in the government of the country. But
as Turkish society became more democratized, their sensibilities
and beliefs were bound to find increasing expression in the electoral
arena. The Muslim vote had existed for nearly fifty years. By the
mid-nineties it was much less inhibited.

On the heels of its municipal triumphs, the Welfare Party
got a fifth of the national vote in 1995, making it the largest
party in a fragmented Assembly, and soon afterwards Erbakan
became premier in a precarious coalition government. Unable
to pursue the party's agenda at home, he attempted to strike a
more independent line abroad, speaking of Muslim solidarity
and visiting Iran and Libya, but was rapidly called to order by
the foreign policy establishment, and within a year ousted under
military pressure. Six months later the Constitutional Court
proscribed the Welfare Party for violating secularism. In advance
of the ban, Erbakan formed the Virtue Party as its reincarnation.
In the summer of 2001, that in turn was banned, whereupon—
never short of inspiring names—he formed the Felicity Party to
replace it.

This time, however, he could not carry his troops with him.
A new generation of activists had come to the conclusion that
Erbakan's erratic style of leadership—veering wildly between

---

61. For these successes, see Nihal İncioğlu, 'Local Elections and Electoral
Behavior', in Sabri Sayari and Yilmaz Esmer, *Politics, Parties and Elections in
Turkey*, Boulder 2002, pp. 83–9.

firebrand radicalism and unseemly opportunism—was a liability for their cause. More importantly, the repeated crack-downs on the kind of Islamism he represented had convinced them that to come to power it was essential to drop his anti-capitalist and anti-Western rhetoric, and present a more moderate, less explicitly confessional face to the electorate, one that would not affront the Kemalist establishment so openly. These cadres had already challenged Erbakan for control of the Virtue Party, and in 2001 were ready to break away from him completely. Three weeks after the creation of the Felicity Party, the AKP was launched under the leadership of Tayyip Erdoğan. Mayor of Istanbul from 1994 to 1998, he had been briefly jailed for an inflammatory verse and was still ineligible to run for Parliament, but few doubted the practicality of his ambitions. His proven skills as orator and organizer assured his domination of the new party.

The spectacular scale of the AKP's victory in 2002, catapulting it into power, was an effect of the electoral system rather than of any overwhelming support at the polls. The party got no more than 34 per cent of the vote, far below the scores achieved by Menderes, Demirel or Özal at their height. This was transmuted into 67 per cent of seats in the Assembly by the number of other parties that fell below the 10 per cent bar—only the still-extant Kemalist RPP clearing it, with 19 per cent. The result was more a verdict on the kind of democracy the Constitution of 1980 had installed in Turkey than a tidal vote of confidence in the AKP: a combined total of no less than half the electorate was disenfranchised by the threshold for representation in Parliament.

Yet the party's disproportionate control of the legislature also corresponded to a new reality. Unlike any of its predecessors, it faced no credible opposition. All the parties associated with the debacle of the later nineties had been wiped out, other than a hastily resuscitated RPP, without any positive programme or identity, surviving on fears that a neo-Islamism was about to take over the country. A new cycle of Centre-Right dominance had begun, not discontinuous with the past, but modifying it in one crucial respect. From the start, though it mustered less numerical support than its forerunners at a comparable stage of the cycle, the AKP enjoyed an ideological hegemony over the whole political scene that none of them had ever possessed. By a process of elimination, it was left in all but sole command of the stage.

This structural change was accompanied by an alteration in the character of the ruling party itself. Since its roots in the Islamism that arose outside the establishment after 1980 were plain, and its turn towards a more moderate stance in coming to power was no less clear, the AKP has been widely described by admirers in the West as a hopeful Muslim equivalent of Christian Democracy. High praise in Europe, the compliment has not been well received by the AKP, which prefers the term 'conservative democracy', as less likely to provoke Kemalist reflexes.[62] But the comparison is mostly misleading in any case. There is no Church for the AKP to lean on, no welfare systems to preside over, no trade-unions in its tow. Nor does the party show any sign of the internal democracy or factional energies that were always features of post-war German or Italian Christian Democracy.

Still, there are two respects in which the AKP could be said to correspond, *mutatis mutandis*, to them. If its electoral base, like theirs, includes the peasantry, which still comprises 30 per cent of the population in Turkey, it draws more heavily on a teeming under-class of urban slum-dwellers, which scarcely existed in post-war Europe. But the dynamic core of the party comes from a stratum of newly enriched Anatolian entrepreneurs, completely modern in their approach to running a profitable business, and devoutly traditional in their attachment to religious beliefs and customs. This layer, as distinct from the big conglomerates in Istanbul as local notables in the Veneto or Mittelstand in Swabia were from Fiat or the Deutsche Bank, is the new component of the Centre-Right bloc commanded by the AKP. Its similarity to the provincial motors of the CDU, or DC of old, is unmistakeable.

So too is the centrality of Europe—the Community then; the Union now—as ideological cement for the party. In Turkey, however, this has been much more important, politically speaking, for Erdoğan and his colleagues than it was in Germany or Italy for Adenauer or De Gasperi. Entry into the EU has, indeed, to date been the magical formula of the AKP's hegemony. For the mass of the population, many with relatives among the two million Turks in Germany, a Europe within which they can travel freely represents hope of better-paid jobs than can be found, if at all,

---

62. See Erdoğan's address to the American Enterprise Institute, 'Conservative Democracy and the Globalization of Freedom', in M. Hakan Yavuz, *The Emergence of a New Turkey: Democracy and the AK Party*, Salt Lake City 2006, pp. 333–40.

at home. For big business, membership in the EU offers access to deeper capital markets; for medium entrepreneurs, lower interest rates; for both, a more stable macro-economic environment. For the professional classes, commitment to Europe is the gauge that Islamist temptations will not prevail within the AKP. For the liberal intelligentsia, the EU will be the safeguard against any return to military rule. For the military, it will realize the long-standing Kemalist dream of joining the West in full dress. In short, Europe is a promised land towards which the most antithetical forces within Turkey can gaze, for the most variegated reasons. In making its cause their own, the AKP leaders have come to dominate the political chequerboard more completely than any force since the Kemalism of the early Republic.

To make good its claim to be leading Turkey into Europe, the AKP took a series of steps in the first two years of its rule to meet norms professed by the Union. A reduction in the powers of the National Security Council, underway before it came to office, and of the role of the military in it, was in its own interest, as well as that of the population at large. Of more immediate significance for ordinary citizens, the State Security Courts that were a prime instrument of repression were closed down. The state of emergency in the south-east, dating back to 1987, was lifted, and the death penalty abolished. In 2004, Kurdish MPs jailed for using their own language in Parliament were finally released. Warmly applauded in the media, this package of reforms secured the AKP its European legitimacy.

The larger part of the new government's popularity came, however, from the rapid economic recovery over which it presided. The AKP inherited an IMF stabilization programme as a condition of the large loan Turkey received from the Fund in late 2001, which set the parameters for its stewardship of the economy. The ideology of the Welfare Party from which it emerged was not only anti-Western, but often in rhetoric anti-capitalist. The European turn of the AKP purged it of any taint of the first. Still more demonstratively, it put all memories of the second behind it, adopting a neo-liberal regimen with the fervour of a convert. Fiscal discipline became the watchword, privatization the grail. The *Financial Times* was soon hailing the AKP's 'passion for selling state assets'.[63] With a primary budget surplus of 6 per cent, and real interest rates at 15 per cent, subduing inflation to single

---

63. 'Investing in Turkey', *Financial Times* Special Report, 18 July 2007, p. 1.

figures, business confidence was restored, investment picked up, and growth rebounded. From 2002 to 2007, the Turkish economy grew at an average rate of some 7 per cent a year. Drawn by the boom, and fuelling it, foreign capital poured into the country, snapping up 70 per cent of the Istanbul stock market.

As elsewhere, the end of high inflation relieved the condition of the poor, as the price of necessities stabilized. Jobs, too, were created by the boom, even if these do not show up in official statistics, where the rate of unemployment—over 10 per cent—appears unaffected. But jobless growth in the formal sector has been accompanied by increased employment in the informal sector, above all casual labour in the construction industry. Objectively, such material gains remain rather modest: real wages have been flat, and—given demographic growth—the number of paupers has actually increased. Ideologically, however, they have been enough, so one acute observer argues, for the AKP to make neo-liberalism for the first time something like the common sense of the poor.[64]

But how deep does popular belief that the market always knows best ultimately run? Fiscal discipline has meant cutting social spending on services or subsidies, making it difficult for the AKP to repeat at national level the kind of municipal philanthropy on which its leaders thrived in the nineties, when the Welfare Party could deliver public benefits of one kind or another directly to its constituents. The Turkish state collects only about 18 per cent of GDP in taxes—even by today's standards, a tribute to the egoism of the rich—so there is anyway little government money to go around, after bond-holders have been paid off.[65] To hold the mass of its voters in the cities, the AKP needs to offer something more than the bread—it is not yet quite a stone—of neo-liberalism. Lack of social redistribution requires cultural or political compensations. There were also the party's cadres to be considered: a mere diet of IMF prescriptions was bound to leave them hungry.

The pitfalls of too conformist an adherence to directives from abroad were illustrated early on, when the AKP leadership attempted to force a vote through Parliament inviting American

64. Cihan Tuğal, 'NATO's Islamists: Hegemony and Americanization in Turkey', *New Left Review* II/44, March–April 2007, p. 22. This essay is the outstanding analysis to date of the AKP's rise and role in power.

65. According to the recent revision of Turkish national accounts: see Economist Intelligence Unit, *Report on Turkey*, April 2008, p. 15.

troops across Turkey to attack Iraq, in March 2003. A third of its deputies rebelled, and the motion was defeated, to great popular delight. At this stage, Erdoğan was still outside Parliament, having yet to get round the previous ban on him. Possibly harbouring a residual sense of rivalry with him, his second-in-command, Abdullah Gül, acting as premier, may not have pulled out all the stops for compliance with the US on his behalf.[66] Two months later, Erdoğan had entered Parliament and taken charge. Once premier, he rammed through a vote to dispatch Turkish troops themselves to take part in the occupation of Iraq. By this time it was too late, and the offer was rejected by the client authorities in Baghdad, nervous of Kurdish reactions. But Erdoğan's ability to impose such a course was an indication of the position he has come to occupy in the AKP's firmament.

In his person, in fact, lies a good deal of the symbolic compensation enjoyed by the mass of the party's electorate for any material hardships. Post-modern political cultures, ever more tied to the spectacle, have spawned a series of leaders out of the entertainment industry. Erdoğan belongs in this respect with Reagan and Berlusconi: after an actor and a crooner, what could be more popular than a striker? Product of a working-class family and religious schools in Istanbul, Erdoğan started out life as a professional footballer, before moving up through the ranks of the Welfare Party to become mayor of the city at the age of forty. Along the way, he found time to burnish his private-sector credentials, amassing a tidy fortune as a local businessman. Neither humble origins nor recent wealth are new for leaders of the Centre-Right in Turkey. What distinguishes Erdoğan from his predecessors is that unlike Menderes, Demirel or Özal, his route to power has not been through bureaucratic preferment from above, but grass-roots organization from below. For the first time, Turkey is ruled by a professional politician, in the full sense of the term.

On the platform, Erdoğan is a figure of pregnant native charisma. Tall and powerfully built, his hooded eyes and long upper lip accentuated by a brush moustache, he embodies three of the most prized values of Turkish popular culture. Piety—legend has it that he always prayed before bounding onto the pitch; machismo—famously tough in word and deed, with subordinates and enemies alike; and the common touch—manners and

---

66. For a sharp light on this episode, see Saban Kardaş, 'Turkey and the Iraqi Crisis', in Yavuz (ed.), *The Emergence of a New Turkey*, pp. 314–26.

vocabulary of the street-stalls rather than the salon. If no trace
of democracy is left in the AKP, whose congresses now rival
United Russia in acclamations of its leader, that is not necessarily
a black mark in a tradition that respects authoritarianism as a
sign of strength. The weaknesses in Erdoğan's public image lie
elsewhere. Choleric and umbrageous, he is vulnerable to ridicule
in the press, suing journalists by the dozen for unfavourable
coverage of himself or his family, which has done well out of
the AKP's years in power. A son's gala wedding adorned by
Berlusconi, a daughter's nuptials glad-handed by Musharraf,
have been capable of shutting down half of Istanbul for their
festivities. A son-in-law's company has been handed control of
the second-largest media concern in the country. At the outset,
the AKP enjoyed a reputation for probity. Now its leader risks
acquiring some of the traits of a tabloid celebrity, with all the
attendant ambiguities. But the personality cult of Erdoğan
remains a trump card of the party, as that of Menderes, no less
vain and autocratic, was before him. Simply, the audience has
moved from the countryside to the cities.

9

When elections came again in 2007, the ranks of the AKP had
been purged of all those who had rebelled against the war in Iraq,
relics of a superseded past. Now a homogeneous party of order,
riding five years of growth, a magnetic leader in charge, it took
47 per cent of the vote. This was a much more decisive victory
than in 2002, distributed more evenly across the country, and was
treated in the West as a consecration without precedent. In some
ways, however, it was less than might have been expected. The
AKP's score was six points lower than that of Demirel in 1965,
and eleven points below that of Menderes in 1955. On the other
hand, the ex-fascist MHP, flying crypto-confessional colours too,
won 14 per cent of the vote, making for a combined vote for the
Right of 61 per cent, arguably a high tide of another kind. Indeed,
although—because of the vagaries of the electoral threshold—the
AKP's share of seats actually fell, despite the increase in its vote
by more than a third, the MHP's success handed the two parties,
taken together, three-quarters of the National Assembly: more
than enough to alter the Constitution.

In its second term of office, the AKP has altered course. By
2007 entry into the EU was still a strategic goal, but no longer the

same open-sesame for the party. For once the Anglo-American plan to wind up the Republic of Cyprus had failed in 2004, it was faced with the awkward possibility of having to end Turkish military presence on the island, if it was itself to gain entry into the EU—a price at which the whole political establishment in Ankara has traditionally balked. So, after its initial burst of liberal reforms, the party decelerated, with few further measures of real significance to protect civil rights or dismantle the apparatuses of repression, testing the patience even of Brussels, where officialdom has long been determined to look on the bright side. By 2006 even the Commission's annual report on Turkey, typically a treasury of bureaucratic euphemisms, was here and there starting to strike a faintly regretful note.

Soon afterwards, in early 2007, Hrant Dink, an Armenian–Turkish journalist repeatedly prosecuted for the crime of 'denigrating Turkishness'—he spoke of the Armenian genocide—was assassinated in Istanbul. Mass demonstrations protested his murder. A year later, the extent of the AKP's response was to modify the charge in the penal code under which Dink had been prosecuted with a grand alteration, from 'denigrating Turkishness' to 'denigrating the Turkish nation'. Twenty-four hours after that change had been made, on May Day 2008, its police launched an all-out assault on workers attempting to commemorate the 1977 killing of trade-unionists in Taksim Square, after the AKP had banned the demonstration. Clubs, tear-gas, water cannon and rubber bullets left thirty-eight injured. Over five hundred were arrested. As Erdoğan explained: 'When the feet try to govern the head, it becomes doomsday'.

Shedding liberal ballast, once Europe moved down the agenda, has meant at the same stroke pandering to national phobias. In its first term, the AKP made a number of concessions to Kurdish culture and feeling—allowing a few hours of regional broadcasting in Kurdish, some teaching of Kurdish in private schools. These involved little structural change in the situation of the Kurdish population, but combined with selective use of state patronage in Kurdish municipalities, and a more ecumenical rhetoric, were enough to treble the party's vote in the south-east in 2007, taking it to the national average. Since then, however, the government has tacked heavily towards the traditional military approach to the region. Soon after its failure to get the scheme it wanted in Cyprus, it was confronted in the summer of 2004 with a revival of PKK guerrilla actions. On a much smaller scale than in the past, and more or less disavowed by Öcalan,[67] these now had the advantage of a more secure hinterland in the de facto autonomy of Iraqi Kurdistan, after the American march to Baghdad.

In time-honoured fashion, the Turkish high command responded by stepping up repression, throwing more tanks and gendarmes into the south-east, and pressing for cross-border attacks into northern Iraq. Mobilization of state and para-state agencies to crush the guerrillas was accompanied by a hurricane of nationalist hysteria in civil society, fed by fears of the long-term example of Kurdish autonomy in Iraq, resentments that for the first time in a century the country was having to give an account of itself to opinion in Europe, and the miseries of provincial life for unemployed youth, a prime recruiting-ground of the MHP. In this storm, Erdoğan and his colleagues took the same course as Demirel, accommodating the military—Turkish jets and troops were soon attacking across the frontier into Iraq—and upping chauvinist rhetoric. By the winter of 2007, Turkish cities were draped from one end to the other with national flags hanging out of windows or balconies; youngsters were replacing photographs of themselves with the crescent on a red field in Facebook; night after night, television news was reduced to solemn images of Erdoğan and Gül, at the head of a phalanx of army commanders, presiding at the funeral of soldiers killed in the south-east, mothers sobbing over their coffins, intercut with troops high-stepping through Diyarbakir to stentorian chants of 'One Flag, One Nation, One Language, One State'. A comparable intensity of integral nationalism has not been seen in Europe since the thirties.

The AKP's embrace of this jingoism involves no renunciation of its own objectives. If nation continues to trump religion as the master discourse of society, without contradicting it, the party has much to gain and little to lose by doing so. Tactically, its adjustment has an obvious logic. The economic outlook for Turkey is worsening. The trade deficit is huge, the influx of foreign funds covering it is mostly hot money that could exit at the first sign of trouble, inflation is in double digits again. Should the boom evaporate,

---

67. For Öcalan's performances from prison, sometimes thought to be inspired by his captors, see Michael Gunter, *The Kurds Ascending*, New York 2008, pp. 63–86.

showing muscle on the security front is a well-tried electoral alternative. Strategically, so this calculation goes, giving the military all it wants in the battle against terrorism can enable the party to work towards its own goals on other terrain. These have been two-fold: to bend society into a more consistently observant mould, and to capture the branches of the state that have resisted this. The priority given to these underlying aims, at the expense of liberal reforms, can be seen from the AKP's determination to control the presidency, by installing Gül in the post. The move raised military and bureaucratic hackles, put down with the easy electoral victory of 2007. Its political significance lay in the party's refusal to nominate any independent personality with democratic credentials, which would have yielded it political gains of another kind, in which it was not interested. Its attempt to plant a pious incompetent as governor of the Central Bank failed, but indicates its general line of action—colonization of the state by trusted minions, which has been proceeding apace at lower levels. Operating in parallel, the movement led by the exile mystagogue Fethullah Gülen—preaching an Islam impeccably pro-business, pro-modern, pro-American—has created an Opus Dei–like empire, not just controlling newspapers, television stations and hundreds of schools, but now permeating all ranks of the police.[68]

Bids to bend civil society to the will of the ruling party have followed a similar pattern. Rather than making any effort to rescind the mass of punitive articles in a penal code still modelled on that of Italian Fascism, Erdoğan tried to pass a law criminalizing adultery—three years in jail for straying from the marriage bed, desisting only when it became clear that this was too much for even his warmest admirers in Europe. The battle-front has now shifted to female head-gear. After failing to secure a ruling from the European Court of Human Rights that the Turkish ban on headscarves in public buildings, including universities, was a violation of basic rights, the AKP–MHP bloc passed two constitutional amendments abolishing it last February. The Constitutional Court has since struck these down, and the ruling party now faces formal charges of attempting to subvert the secular basis of the state. If upheld, these would lead to its

---

68. There is now a considerable literature on Gülen, on whose ideas see Berrin Koyuncu Lorasdağı, 'Globalization, Modernization, and Democratization in Turkey: The Fethullah Gülen Movement', in E. Fuat Keyman, *Remaking Turkey*, Lanham 2007, pp. 153–75.

closure and the exclusion of Erdoğan, Gül and other leaders from all political activity for five years.

The issue of scarves, trivial enough in itself, offers a perfect illustration of the warped dialectic between state and religion in the Turkey bequeathed by Kemal. Denial of the right of young women to wear on campus what they want is an obvious discrimination against the devout, excluding them from public higher education. Licensing the headscarf, as any secular girl from a provincial background will tell you, prompts fears of the reverse: brutal social pressure to wear it, on pain of ostracism or worse. The AKP is in no position to dispel such fears, since its record in office and the style of its leadership have been so persistently arrogant and bullying. Likewise, contemporary Kemalism is in no position to claim that the state must be kept inviolate from any expression of religion, since it maintains at public expense a vast directorate propagating just one faith, Islam, while curtailing the activity of all others. The successive waves of political pietism that have surged up since the fifties, of which the AKP is only the latest, are the logical revenge on its own duplicity. A genuine secularism would have cut the cord between state and religion cleanly and completely, creating a space for the everyday rejection of all supernatural beliefs. How far it has failed to do so can be judged from the verdict of one of the most sympathetic analysts of Turkish faith and society, not to speak of the statesmanship of Erdoğan himself: 'There is not the slightest doubt that it is now dangerous for a man or woman to deny openly belief in God'.[69] The army itself, supposed bastion of secularism, regularly describes those who have fallen in its counter-insurgency operations as 'martyrs'. Nation and religion remain as structurally interdependent in latter-day Kemalism as they were when the *Gazi* first established the state.

But because that interdependence could never be openly acknowledged, a tension was created within the Turkish political system, between an elite claiming to be secular and movements claiming to be faithful, each side accusing the other of want of tolerance, that has yet to abate. The AKP has not broken, but reproduced, this deadlock. Before taking office, Erdoğan famously told his followers that democracy was like a tram: we will take it to our destination, and then get off.[70] The remark has sometimes

---

69. Shankland, *Islam and Society in Turkey*, p. 170.

70. For this celebrated remark, of which there are many versions, see Ersin Kalaycıoğlu, *Turkish Dynamics: Bridge Across Troubled Lands*, Basingstoke 2005, p. 165.

been interpreted as a revelation of the hidden intentions of the AKP to use a parliamentary majority to install a fundamentalist tyranny. But its meaning can be taken as something more banal. Power, not principle, is what matters. Erdoğan is no doubt as devout an individual as Blair or Bush, with whom he got on well, but there is little reason to think that he would risk the fruits of office for the extremities of his faith, any more than would they. An instrumental attitude to democracy is not the same as either hostility or commitment to it. Elections have served the AKP well: why abandon them? Religious integrism would bar entry to Europe: why risk it?

The temptations, and pitfalls, for the party lie elsewhere. On the one hand, the AKP is under pressure from its constituency— above all the dedicated core of its militants—to show results in the long-standing struggle of the believers for more public recognition of their faith and its outward symbols. Its credibility depends on being able to deliver these. On the other hand, the unprecedented weakness of any opposition to it within the political system has given its leaders a giddy sense that they enjoy a new freedom of action. The military and the bureaucracy, certainly, remain a potential threat: but would the army dare to stage a coup again, now that Turkey is on the threshold of the Union, and all Europe is watching? The outcome of the current crisis, pitting the Court against the Assembly, will show how well the AKP has judged the new balance of forces in Turkey. A triumphant appeal to the electors, sweeping away the Constitution of 1980, is one possibility. The hubris that took Menderes to his end is another. What is clear is that the latest cycle of Centre-Right rule in Turkey is approaching a critical moment, at which its precursors stumbled.

10

Whatever the immediate outcome of the conflict between them, the latest versions of Islamism and Kemalism derive from the same founding moment as their predecessors, even as each seeks sublimation into Europe. So too do the principal potential obstacles to Turkish entry into the EU. In Turkey, these are generally held to be European racism and Islamophobia, or the prospect of the country's future weight in the European Council as its largest member. Perhaps equally relevant, if less often mentioned, is the calculation that if Turkey is admitted, it will be difficult to refuse entry to Ukraine—not quite as large, but more democratic, with a higher per capita income; a country which Romano Prodi once explained had as much chance of joining the EU as New Zealand. Such resistances are not to be minimized. But the more intractable difficulties lie within the country itself. Three of these command the rest. They have a common origin in the integral nationalism that issued, without rupture or remorse, from the last years of an Empire based on conquest.

The first, and in theory most pointed, obstacle to entry is Turkey's continued military occupation, and maintenance of a political dependency, in Cyprus. Refusal to recognize a member-state of the European Union, while demanding entry into it, requires a diplomatic sang-froid that only a former imperial power could allow itself. However eager Brussels is to welcome Ankara, the legal *monstrum* of Turkey's position in Cyprus lies still unresolved between it and accession. The second obstacle to ready incorporation in Europe is the domestic situation of the country's minorities. These are not small communities. Kurds number anywhere between nine and thirteen million, Alevis ten to twelve million, of whom perhaps two to three million are Kurds. In other words, up to a third of the population suffers systematic discrimination for its ethnicity or religion. The cruelties visited by the state on the Kurds are well advertised, but the position accorded by society to Alevis—often viewed as atheists by the Sunni majority—is even lower. Neither group forms a compact mass, subject to uniform ill-treatment. There are now more Kurds in the big cities than in the south-east, many of whom no longer speak Kurdish, and are intermarried with Turks,[71] while Alevis, concentrated only in a single mountain enclave, are otherwise dispersed throughout the land. But that neither comes near the equality of rights and respect which the Copenhagen criteria of the EU nominally enjoin is all too obvious.

Finally, there is the Armenian genocide, its authors honoured in streets and schools across the country, whose names celebrate the murderers. Talat: a boulevard in Ankara, four avenues in Istanbul, a highway in Edirne, three municipal districts, four primary schools. Enver: three avenues in Istanbul, two in Izmir,

---

71. Were repressions to be lifted, of course, Kurdish identity could well be reactivated among even the assimilated: see the level-headed discussion in Henri Barkey and Graham Fuller, *Turkey's Kurdish Question*, Lanham 1998, p. 83. Demographically the mainly Kurdish provinces in the south-east have a much higher reproduction rate than the rest of the country: McDowall, *A Modern History of the Kurds*, p. 450.

three in occupied Cyprus, primary schools in Izmir, Mugla, Elazig. Cemal Azmi, responsible for the deaths of thousands in Trabzon: a primary school in that city. Resit Bey, the butcher of Diyarbakir: a boulevard in Ankara. Mehmet Kemal, hanged for his atrocities: thoroughfares in Istanbul and Izmir, statues in Adana and Izmir, National Hero Memorial gravestone in Istanbul. As if in Germany squares, streets, and kindergarten were called after Himmler, Heydrich, Eichmann, without anyone raising an eyebrow. Books extolling Talat, Enver and Şakir roll off the presses, in greater numbers than ever.[72] Nor is all this merely a legacy of a Kemalist past. The Islamists have continued the same tradition into the present. If Talat's catafalque was borne by armoured train from the Third Reich for burial with full honours by Inönü in 1943, it was Demirel who brought Enver's remains back from Tajikstan in 1996, and reburied them in person at a state ceremony in Istanbul. Beside him, as the cask was lowered into the ground, stood the West's favourite Muslim moderate: Abdullah Gül, now AKP president of Turkey.

An integral nationalism that never flinched in exterminating Armenians, expelling Greeks, deporting Kurds and torturing dissident Turks, and which still enjoys wide electoral support, is not a force to be taken lightly. The Turkish Left, consistently among its victims, has shown most courage in confronting it. Politically speaking, the 'generation of '78' was cut down by the military coup of 1980—years of imprisonment, exile or death killing off any chance of a revival of popular attraction or activism on the same scale. But when the worst of the repression lifted, it was this levy that produced a critical culture without equal in any European country of the same period: monographs, novels, films, journals, publishing houses that have given Istanbul in many respects a livelier radical milieu than contemporary London, Paris or Berlin. This is the setting out of which Orhan Pamuk—not exempt from friendly criticism in it—along with other leading Turkish writers, comes.

---

72. For the current wave of laudatory writing on Talat, see Hülya Adak, 'Identifying the "Internal Tumors" of World War I; *Talat Paşa'nin Hatıraları* [Talat Paşa's Memoirs], or the Travels of a Unionist Apologia into "History"', in Andreas Bähr, Peter Burschel, Gabriele Jancke (eds), *Raüme des Selbst: Selbstzeugnisforschung transkulturell*, Cologne 2007, pp. 167–8. Şakir's leading eulogist is Hikmet Cicek: *Dr Bahaettin Şakir. Ittihat Terakki'den Teskilati Mahsusa'ya bir Turk Jakobeni*, Istanbul 2004.

If there is a blind spot in the outlook of this intellectual Left, it is Cyprus, about which few know much and most say less, an attitude not unlike that of British counterparts towards Northern Ireland. But on the other two most explosive issues of the time, its record has been exemplary. Defence of the Kurds has for decades been at the centre of its imagination, producing one leading writer or director—often themselves Kurds—after another, from Yas,ar Kemal, Mehmed Uzun or Yilmaz Güney (*Yol*), to such recent films as Handan Ipekçi's banned *Big Man, Little Love* (2001) and Yeşim Ustaoğlu's *Journey to the Sun* (2001). As for the fate of the Armenians, it has been the object of a historical conference in Istanbul—cancelled under political pressure at two universities, held at another—a best-selling memoir (now in English: Fethiye Çetin, *My Grandmother*), novel (Elif Shafak: *The Bastard of Istanbul*), iconoclastic reportage (Ece Temelkuran: *Deep Mountain*), and many a column in the press (Murat Belge, in *Radikal*).

But above all, the outstanding work of the historian Taner Akçam has put the realities of the Armenian genocide, and their deep deposits in the Turkish state, irreversibly on the map of modern scholarship. His path- and taboo-breaking study of it was published in Turkey in 1999.[73] A collection of key essays, *From Empire to Republic: Turkish Nationalism and the Armenian Genocide,* appeared in English in 2004, and a translation of his first book as *A Shameful Act: The Armenian Genocide and the Question of Turkish Responsibility* in 2006. Himself a prisoner, then exile, of the military repression of 1980, Akçam has been repeatedly threatened and harrassed even abroad, where Canadian and American authorities have collaborated with their Turkish counterparts to make life difficult for him. Inside Turkey, the issue of the genocide remains a danger for anyone who speaks of it, as the charges against Pamuk and the killing of Dink—both under AKP rule—make plain.

Outside Turkey, there has long been a school of historians, headed by the late Stanford Shaw, that reproduced the official mythology

---

73. *İnsan Haklari ve Ermeni Sorunu: İttihat ve Terakki'den Kurtuluş Savaşina,* published by IMGE Kitabevi in Ankara. Vahakn Dadrian, the leading Armenian-American scholar, had published the first edition of his *History of the Armenian Genocide*—it is now in its seventh—in 1995. The two are now collaborating on a joint work on the Istanbul trials.

of the Turkish state, denying that any genocide ever occurred on Ottoman soil. Bald negationism of this kind has lost academic standing. Later versions prefer to minimize or relativize, in tune with the approach of the Turkish academic establishment, rather than repress altogether the fate of the Armenians. Intellectually speaking, these can now be regarded as discredited margins of the literature, but even such treatment as is to be found in the best historians of modern Turkey working in the West offers a painful contrast with the courage of Turkish critics themselves. In the most distinguished recent authorities, evasion and euphemism are still the rule. In the terse two paragraphs granted the subject in Caroline Finkel's massive 550-page history of the Ottoman Empire, we read that 'terrible massacres took place on both sides'. As for genocide, the very word is a misfortune, which not only 'bedevil[s] any wider understanding of the history of the fate of the Ottoman Armenians'—not to speak of 'Turkish foreign relations around the world'—but 'consigns Armenia, which borders Turkey . . . to a wretched existence' (*sic*).[74]

If we turn to Sükrü Hanioğlu's limpid *Brief History of the Late Ottoman Empire*, just out, a single paragraph tells us that 'one of the most tragic events of the war was the deportation of much of the Armenian population of Anatolia', in which 'the finer details' of the government's decision that advancing Russian armies must be denied 'crucial assistance' from 'Armenian rebels' were unfortunately not observed in practice, leading to the unforeseen consequence of 'massive loss of life'.[75] Andrew Mango's acclaimed biography *Atatürk* is even more tight-lipped. There we are told that 'Eastern Anatolia is inhospitable at the best of times', and if its Armenians were 'deported', it was because they were drawn to the Russians and had risen against Ottoman rule. No doubt 'the Armenian clearances' were 'a brutal act of ethnic cleansing', but the CUP leaders had a 'simple justification: "It was them or us" '.[76] Any comment? Just a line. 'The deportations strained Ottoman communications and deprived Anatolia of almost all its craftsmen'. German railroad traffic was going to be strained too.

Even Eric-Jan Zürcher, the Dutch historian who has done more than any other scholar to bring to light the linkages between the CUP underground and Kemal after 1918, could only allow

---

74. Finkel, *Osman's Dream*, pp. 534–6.
75. *A Brief History of the Late Ottoman Empire*, p. 182.
76. Mango, *Atatürk*, p. 161.

himself, in his classic *Turkey: A Modern History*, the cautious
subjective avowal that while it 'might be hard, if not impossible'
to prove beyond doubt, 'this author at least is of the opinion
that there was a centrally controlled policy of extermination,
instigated by the CUP'. That was in 1993. A decade later, in his
revised edition of 2004, the same passage reads: 'it can no longer
be denied that the CUP instigated a centrally controlled policy
of extermination'.[77] The alteration, though its wording has gone
astray—denials continue to be heard, from chairs and columns
alike—is testimony to the impact of Akçam's work, to which
Zürcher pays generous bibliographical tribute, and expresses a
welcome shift in what a leading historian of Turkey feels can
finally be said. But it would unwise to over-estimate the change.
The reason for the pattern of evasions and contortions to be found
in so much Western scholarship on Turkey that is otherwise of a
high standard lies in the familiar fear of foreign—or expatriate—
researchers, in any society where truth is at an official discount,
that to breach national taboos will jeopardize access, contacts,
friendships, at the limit bar them from the country altogether.

Where awards or consultations are concerned, there is yet
greater cause for prudence. Zürcher's later edition marks an
advance over his earlier version where Armenians are in question.
But where Kurds are at issue, it moves in the opposite direction,
forthright statements in 1993—'Turkey will have to become a bi-
national state, with Kurdish as its second language in the media,
in education and in administration. The south-east will have
to be granted some sort of far-reaching autonomy with Kurds
governing and policing Kurds'—vanishing in 2004.[78] Since then,
Zürcher has been awarded a Medal of High Distinction by the
Turkish Ministry of Foreign Affairs, and become an adviser to
the EU Commission. Scholarship is unlikely to benefit from either
honour. Nor are political brokers often brave speakers. It would
be wrong to condemn the compromises of Western historians of
Turkey, even of such an independent spirit as Zürcher, out of
hand. The constraints they confront are real. But the pressures on
Turks themselves are much stronger. Greater safety warrants less
escapism.

---

77. Zürcher, *Turkey: A Modern History* (1993), p. 211; *Turkey, A Modern History* (2004), p. 116.
78. Compare Zürcher's 1993 edition at p. 321, and the 2004 edition at pp. 334–5.

The one signal exception in the field confirms the rule. Donald Bloxham's *Great Game of Genocide*, which came out in 2005, is the work not of an Ottomanist but of a comparative historian of extermination, with no professional connexions to Turkey. Its ill-chosen title gives little sense of the clarity and power of this work, a succinct masterpiece on the killing of the Armenians, illuminating both its national context and its international aftermaths. The treatment of the CUP's genocide by accredited historians in the West forms part of Bloxham's story, but it is the attitude of states that moves centre stage in his account. Of these, as he shows, the US has long been the most important, as the Entente power that never declared war on the Ottoman Empire in 1916–18, and whose high commissioner to Turkey from 1919 to 1927, Admiral Bristol, advocated further ethnic cleansing after it. Since America contained Greek and Armenian communities that needed to be silenced, it was there that the casuistries of later negationism were first developed in the inter-war years, before they had much currency in Europe. By the thirties Hollywood was already cancelling a movie of Franz Werfel's novel on Armenian resistance to massacres in Cilicia, after threats from the Turkish embassy that it was a calumny.

Since 1945 Turkey has, of course, acquired far more importance for the US as a strategic ally, first in the Cold War and now the War on Terror. In the past twenty years, increasing pressure from the Armenian community, now much more salient than in the twenties, and the emergence of an Armenian scholarship that has pioneered modern study of the exterminations of 1915–16 in the West, have made repression of the question more difficult. After previously unsuccessful attempts to get resolutions on it through Congress, in 2000 the House International Relations Committee voted for a bipartisan resolution condemning the Armenian genocide, carefully exempting the Turkish Republic from any responsibility for it. Ankara's response was to threaten trade reprisals, withdrawal of American military facilities in Turkey and risk of violence against Americans in Turkey—the State Department even had to issue a travel advisory—if the resolution were passed by Congress. Characteristically, Clinton intervened in person to prevent the resolution ever getting to the floor. In Ankara, Ecevit exulted that it was a demonstration of Turkish power.

In 2007 the same scenario was repeated. This time, House Speaker Nancy Pelosi—another Democratic champion of human rights—pronounced herself in favour of a resolution with 191

sponsors. But as soon as a string of party notables headed by
Madeleine Albright intervened, she heeded the pleas of the
State and Defense departments, and killed any vote on it. In the
background, Turkish threats were now combined with bribes in
an escalating drive to stop the resolution. Some \$3.2 million were
spent by Ankara on a lobbying campaign orchestrated by Richard
Gephardt, former Democratic majority leader in the House, who
had supported the resolution in 2000, when he was not yet on
the Turkish payroll.[79] Meanwhile, major Jewish organizations—
AIPAC, ADL and others—far from expressing any solidarity
with victims of another genocide, were closeted with Gül in
Washington, discussing how to deny it.[80] Ideology plays its part in
this: the uniqueness of the Nazi destruction of the Jews as a moral
patent not to be infringed. But there is also the close military and
diplomatic relationship between Israel and Turkey—IDF jets train
in Turkish air-space—that has led Tel Aviv to undertake, in the
words of a sympathetic observer, 'a concerted effort to educate
American Jewry on the strategic significance of Turkey'.[81] Not all
consciences have been stilled quite so easily. Better Jewish voices
have been raised against such collusion, but to little effect so far.

In Europe, Turkey's candidature to the EU puts a set of issues
on the agenda that is wider in Brussels than in Washington.
Here, the situation of Turks themselves, in principle of Kurds, by
extension of Cypriots, are the objects of attention, not the fate of
Armenians. In practice, the Commission's priority has been to get
Turkey into the Union at least possible cost—that is, causing as
little difficulty as it can for the AKP government, represented as a
torch-bearer of progress, held back from fully realizing EU norms
only by a retrograde judicial and military establishment. Annual
reports on the country's advance towards membership, invariably
dwelling much longer on economic than political requirements,
chalk up performances in privatization and torture in the same
imperturbable idiom—'proceeds were significant, but the

79. 'Turkey Pays for Sway in Wahington', *International Herald Tribune*, 18
October 2007. Gephardt gets \$1.2 million a year for his services.
80. 'Genocide Resolution Still Far from Certain', *Los Angeles Times*, 21
April 2007.
81. Efraim Inbar, 'The Strategic Glue in the Israeli-Turkish Alignment', in Barry
Rubin and Kemal Kirişi, *Turkey in World Politics, An Emerging Multiregional
Power*, Boulder 2001, p. 123.

agenda is not finished'; 'the Turkish legal framework includes a comprehensive set of safeguards against torture and ill-treatment. However, cases still occur'. Shortcomings are noted, but the road always leads upwards.[82]

Naturally, all potential sticking-points are excluded from these bland memorials. Cyprus? The rubric 'Regional Issues and International Obligations' does not even mention Turkey's refusal to recognize a member of the European Union it seeks to enter. Commissioner Olli Rehn, a boyish *Streber* from Finland with sights on his country's presidency, has made no secret of his indifference to ethnic cleansing on the island, telling Cypriots they 'should stop complaining against past injustice and rather work on future solutions with a pragmatic approach'—naturally, one that accepts occupation by Ankara in the wider interests of Brussels. After all, as the Commission can report with satisfaction, among other merits 'Turkey has offered to train Iraqi security forces', and demonstrated 'close alignment with EU Common Foreign and Security Policy'.[83]

Kurds? Wherever possible, avoid mention of them. In the words of an authoritative study by two leading jurists of the record of the AKP in power and the way the EU has covered it, the Union tends to use 'the term "situation in the southeast" as a euphemism for the Kurdish issue'. EU leaders have not only 'singularly failed to issue any statement' on the Kurdish question, or 'promote any democratic platform or meaningful discourse about it', but 'the glossy picture of an overall dynamic towards democratization, respect for human rights and pluralism painted by the Commission belies the reality that Turkey's attitude towards the granting of minority rights and the Kurds shows little sign of genuine change'.[84] Embarrassed by such criticisms, the Commission's latest report makes a weak attempt to meet them. Kurds and Alevis, well aware that its main concern is that they not rock the boat of accession, remain unimpressed.

Armenians? Their fate has no bearing on Turkish membership of the Union. The 'tragedy of 1915', as Rehn puts it in a now

---

82. Commission of the European Communities, *Turkey 2007 Progress Report*, Brussels 2007, pp. 14, 28.

83. *Turkey 2007 Progress Report*, pp. 74, 75.

84. 'In deciding that Turkey has fulfilled the Copenhagen criteria, the EU has manifestly failed to fulfill its responsibilities to the Kurds': Kerim Yildiz and Mark Muller, *The European Union and Turkish Accession: Human Rights and the Kurds*, London 2008, pp. 180–3.

standard euphemism, can form part of 'a comprehensive dialogue' between Ankara and Erevan, but Brussels must keep clear of it. Widely regarded inside Turkey as an honorary consul for the AKP, Rehn is perhaps exceptional even in the ranks of the current Commission for vulgar self-satisfaction and *tartufferie*. His mission statement *Europe's Next Frontiers*, replete with epigraphs from pop songs, and apothegms like 'defeatism never carries the day' or 'the vision thing is not rocket science', ends with a suitably naff conceit of his prowess on the football field: 'Don't tell the goalie, but I tend to shoot my penalty kicks to the lower left-hand corner. After all, it is goals that count—even in European integration'.[85] Such are his skills at 'democratic functionalism', we are told. Who could be surprised to learn, from the same mind, that 'the Commission's role in the accession process can be described as the friend who tells the truth'?[86]

The Barroso Commission is not, of course, either an independent, or an isolated, centre of power. It reflects the general outlook of the European political class as a whole. When the Parliament in Strasbourg, theoretically less subject to diplomatic constraints, was told by the Dutch MEP Camille Eurling, rapporteur on Turkey, that recognition of the Armenian genocide should be a condition of its accession to the Union, it was predictably the Green delegation, led by Daniel Cohn-Bendit, that sprang into action to make sure the passage was deleted, confirming the general rule that the more any political group talks about human rights, the less it will respect them. The reality is an establishment commitment to Turkish membership that brooks no cavils. Emblematic is the Independent Commission on Turkey, hailed by an admirer as a 'self-appointed group of European dignitaries'—its members included one former president, two former prime ministers, three former foreign ministers, not to speak of Lord Giddens—which 'has been a beacon of how Europe can be very fair and diligent in the pursuit of the truth, and as such has gained much praise in Europe and in Turkey'. Its findings can be imagined.

A fuller handbook is offered by the Federal Trust's volume *The EU and Turkey: A Glittering Prize or a Millstone?* No rewards for guessing the answer, but as one glowing prospectus follows another, with a decorous sprinkling of ifs and buts, more candid language occasionally breaks through. Opening the collection,

---

85. Ollie Rehn, *Europe's Next Frontiers*, Baden-Baden 2006, pp. 116–77.
86. Rehn, speech to the European Parliament, 21 May 2008.

its editor, Michael Lake—former representative of Brussels in Ankara—salutes the 'noble, even heroic' role of the Turkish Industrialists' and Businessmen's Association in propelling the historic process of reform of Turkey. With its entry into the Union, he points out, Europe will acquire a 'strategic asset of the first quality'. Closing the volume, Norman Stone deals briskly with the Armenian question. The motives of those who raise it require examination: 'Is it that hostility to Israel leads them into an effort to devalue Israel's strongest argument?' Not to put too fine a point on it, 'Why do we have to talk about such things nowadays?'[87]

Respectable opinion in Europe generally avoids such bluntness. Mainstream liberalism puts it more tactfully. In Mark Mazower's words in the *Financial Times*—variants can be found galore— 'what happened to the Armenians' should be moved 'out of the realm of politics and back into history'.[88] Let scholars dispute, and the caravan of state pass on. The difficulty with such disinterested advice, of course, is that the Turkish Republic has always treated the fate of the Armenians as an affair of state, and continues to do so. As Bloxham writes: 'Turkey has persistently lied about its past, bullied its minorities and other states in furtherance of its falsehoods, written the Armenians out of its history books'[89]—as well, of course, as spending large sums of public money to ensure that their fate stays 'out of politics' in the West, as Mazower and others would wish it.

Inevitably, such well-wishers are liable to be gingerly in their use of terms. Mazower studiously avoids reference to the G-word; Timothy Garton Ash speaks in the *Guardian* of the 'suffering of the Armenians', the circumlocution most acceptable to Ankara.[90] It is true that 'genocide' is among the most devalued terms in contemporary political language, second only perhaps to 'fascism'. But if it has been debased beyond any originating imprecision, that is due principally to the very apologists for NATO, claiming genocide in Kosovo—five thousand dead out of

---

87. Michael Lake (ed.), *The EU and Turkey: A Glittering Prize or a Millstone?*, London 2005, pp. 11, 13 (Lake); 177 (Stone). Homage to the Independent Commission comes from Hakan Altinay, p. 113.

88. 'Europe Can Learn from Turkey's Past', *Financial Times*, 12 October 2005.

89. *The Great Game of Genocide*, New York 2005, p. 228.

90. 'This Is the Moment for Europe to Dismantle Taboos, Not Erect Them', *Guardian*, 19 October 2006.

a population of a million—who are now most vehement that the term not be allowed to compromise fruitful relations with Turkey. Historically, however, as has often been pointed out, the jurist responsible for defining the notion of genocide for the post-war United Nations, Raphael Lemkin, a student at Lvov at the time of the Istanbul trials of 1919, was first prompted towards it by the killings of the Armenians by the CUP, just across the Black Sea.

Not coincidentally, another who noted their extermination was Hitler, who had a first-hand witness of it among his closest associates in Munich. The former German consul in Erzerum, Max von Scheubner-Richter, reported to his superiors in great detail on the ways they were wiped out. A virulent racist, who became manager of the early Nazi Kampfbund and the party's key liaison with big business, aristocracy and the church, he fell to a shot while holding hands with Hitler in the Beer Hall Putsch of 1923. 'Had the bullet which killed Scheubner-Richter been a foot to the right, history would have taken a different course', Ian Kershaw remarks.[91] Hitler mourned him as 'irreplaceable'. Invading Poland sixteen years later, he would famously tell his commanders— referring to the Poles, but with obvious implications for the Jews—'Who now remembers the Armenians?' The Third Reich did not need the Turkish precedent for its own genocides. But that Hitler was well aware of it, and cited its success to encourage German operations, is beyond question. Whoever has doubted the comparability of the two, it was not the Nazis themselves.

Comparison is not identity. The similarities between the two genocides were striking, far closer than in most historical parallels.[92] But they were not complete, and the differences between them are part of the reason for the enormous contrast in contemporary reaction to them. Both campaigns of extermination were launched in secrecy, under cover of war; their perpetrators were aware they were criminal, and had to be hidden. Both required special organizations of killers, controlled by political

---

91. *Hitler 1889–1936: Hubris*, London 1998, p. 211. For Scheubner-Richter, who like Rosenberg came from the Baltic, see Georg Franz-Willing, *Ursprung der Hitlerbewegung*, Oldendorf 1974, pp. 81–2, 197–8, 287–8.

92. The best discussion is by Vahakn Dadrian, 'The Comparative Aspects of the Armenian and Jewish Cases of Genocide: A Sociohistorical Perspective', in Alan Rosenbaum, *Is the Holocaust Unique? Perspectives on Comparative Genocide*, Boulder 2001, pp. 133–68.

leaderships operating informally between apparatuses of party and state. Both involved selective participation by military officers. At elite level, both combined ideologies of secular nationalism with doctrines of social Darwinism. At popular level, both drew on ancient religious hatreds, targeting groups already victim of confessional pogroms before the war. Both involved a process of escalation from local killings to systematic extermination. Both draped their actions under the guise of deportations.

The differences between them lay essentially, not in scale or intent, but in the greater instrumental rationality, and civil participation, of the Unionist compared with the Nazi genocide. Jews in Germany numbered less than 1 percent of the population, no threat to any regime. Nor was there any state that attempted to use Jewish communities in Europe for political or military ends. The Nazi destruction of the Jews was ideologically, not strategically or economically, driven. Although there was wholesale seizure of Jewish property, the proceeds were monopolized by those in power, without any large-scale benefit to the mass of the population, and the costs of extermination, when the struggle in the East was already being lost, were a dead weight on the German war effort. The Turkish destruction of the Armenians, although fuelled by ethno-religious hatred, had more traditional economic and geo-political objectives. Over ten times the relative size of the Jewish community in Germany, the Armenian minority in the late Ottoman Empire not only possessed lands and capital on another scale, but compatriots across the border, in a Russian empire that saw Armenians as potential recruits in its own schemes of expansion. When war came, fear and greed in Istanbul combined in more time-worn fashion to detonate annihilation. Both participants and beneficiaries of the cleansing in Anatolia were more numerous, and its structural consequences for society greater. One genocide was the dementia of an order that has disappeared. The other was a founding moment of a state that has endured.

But if these are real distinctions between the two catastrophes, the contrast in the way each figures in the European imaginary is so complete as all but to numb judgement. One has become the object of official and popular remembrance, on a monumental scale. The other is a whisper in the corner, which no diplomat in the Union abides. There are some presentable reasons for the difference. One genocide occurred within living memory in the centre of the continent, the other a century ago in its marchlands. The survivors of one were far more literate than of the other, and left more personal testimonies. But since the Armenian genocide was denounced by the Western powers when it occurred, as the Judeocide was not, and there were more third-party witnesses—official ones at that—of the killings as they occurred, something else is needed to explain the vastness of the discrepancy. What that is, strains no enquiry. Israel, a pivotal ally in the Middle East, requires recognition of the Judeocide, and has secured massive reparations for it. Turkey, a vital ally in the Near East, denies that genocide of the Armenians ever occurred, and insists no mention ever be made of it. The Union, and its *belles âmes*, follow suit.

This is not remote history, best left to antiquarians. The implacable refusal of the Turkish state to acknowledge the extermination of the Armenians on its territory is not anachronistic or irrational, but a contemporary defence of its own legitimacy. For the first great ethnic cleansing, which made Anatolia homogeneously Muslim, if not yet Turkish, was followed by lesser purges of the body politic, in the name of the same integral nationalism, that have continued to this day: pogroms of Greeks, 1955/1964; annexation, and expulsion of Cypriots, 1974; killing of Alevis, 1978/1993; repression of Kurds, 1925–2008. A truthful accounting has been made of none of these, and cannot be without painful cost to the inherited identity and continuity of the Turkish Republic. That is why leaders of the AKP relentlessly pursue the same negationism as their predecessors, with the same threats and yet more dollars. For all the tensions between them as traditions, Kemalism and Islamism have never been chemically separate. Erdoğan and Gül, too, are at home in the official synthesis between them, the 'Turkish nation' which, in what passes for a reform in Brussels, they have made it a crime to insult.

How, then, does Turkish membership of the Union now stand? The conventional reasons for which it is pressed within the EU are legion: militarily, a bulwark against terrorism; economically, dynamic entrepreneurs and cheap labour; politically, a model for regional neighbours; diplomatically, a bridge between civilizations; ideologically, the coming of a true multi-culturalism in Europe. In the past, what might have been set against these considerations would have been fears that such an elongation of the Union, into such remote terrain, must undermine its institutional cohesion, as a widening one step too far, compromising any chance of federal deepening. But that horse has already bolted. To reject Turkish membership on that basis would be shutting the door long after there was any point in it. The Union is becoming a vast free range for the factors of production, far from an agora of any collective will, and the addition of one more grazing ground, however large or still relatively untended, will not alter its nature.

In Turkey itself, as in Europe, the major forces working for its entry into the Union are the contemporary incarnations of the party of order: the bourse, the mosque, the barracks and the media. The consensus that stretches across businessmen and officers, preachers and politicians, lights of the press and of television, is not quite a unanimity. Here and there, surly voices of reaction can be heard. But the extent of concord is striking. What, if the term has any application, of the party of movement? It offers the one good reason, among so many crass or spurious ones, for welcoming Turkey into the Union. For the Turkish Left, politically marginal but culturally central, the EU represents hope of some release from the cults and repressions of Kemal and the Koran; for the Turkish poor, of chances of employment and elements of welfare; for Kurds and Alevis, of some rights for minorities. How far these hopes are all realistic is another matter. But they are not thereby to be denied. There is another side to the matter too. For it is here, and perhaps here alone, that notions that Europe would gain morally from the admission of Turkey to the EU cease to be multi-cultural cant. The fabric of the Union would indeed be richer for the arrival of so many vigorous, critical minds, and the manifest dignity and civility, that must strike the most casual visitor, of so many of the ordinary people of the country

It would be better if the EU lived up to some of the principles on which it congratulates itself, and were to greet the entry of a Turkey that had evacuated Cyprus, and made restitution for its occupation of it; that had granted rights to the Kurds comparable to those of the Welsh or Catalans; that had acknowledged the genocide of the Armenians. Its record makes clear how remote is any such prospect. The probability is something else: a Union stretching to Mount Ararat, in which ministers, deputies and tourists—or ministers and deputies as tourists: the Fischers, Kouchners, Cohn-Bendits enjoying their retirement—circulate comfortably by TGV between Paris or Berlin and Istanbul, blue flags with golden stars at every stop on the way, from the monument to the extermination of the Jews by the Brandenburg Gate to the monument to the exterminators of the Armenians on Liberty Hill. Former commissioner Rehn could enjoy a game of football in the adjoining park, a few metres from the

marble memorials to Talat and Enver, while bored young soldiers—
fewer of them, naturally—lounge peacefully in Kyrenia, and
terrorists continue to meet their deserts in Dersim. Turkish dreams
of a better life in Europe are to be respected. But emancipation
rarely just arrives from abroad.

IV. CONCLUSION

ANTECEDENTS

The demarcation of Europe poses one set of questions for the Union, another for the history of ideas. As a geographical expression, Europe has, of course, existed since classical antiquity. But attempts to trace later conceptions of it back to the time of Hesiod, as Denis de Rougemont famously sought to do, are artificial.[1] The unity of the Graeco-Roman world was Mediterranean, embracing both shores of the inland sea, extending east to Syria rather than north to Scandinavia. In that universe, Europe was scarcely a salient category. Nor, although historians can date the emergence of Europe to the Middle Ages, as the arena of a distinct civilization, was it a significant notion for those who lived through those centuries. Mediaeval Europe indeed displays, retrospectively, an impressive unity of religious beliefs, social practices, cultural and political institutions, replicated across all but the south-eastern quadrant of the continent. No work has demonstrated this more powerfully than Robert Bartlett's study of its expansion by proto-colonial violence, implanting common feudal hierarchies across the continent in a prefiguration of what the descendants of predatory lords, religious-military orders and crusaders would, in time to come, do to the non-European world.[2] Bartlett's title is *The Making of Europe*. But it is not to be understood in the sense of, say, Edward Thompson's *The Making of the English Working Class*. For while objectively the Europe of later ages had its birth in this period, no general subjective consciousness accompanied the process. For contemporaries, their world was Christendom.

---

1. Denis de Rougemont, *Vingt-huit siècles d'Europe*, Paris 1961. For a vibrant homage to the work and the man from today's president of the European Commission, see Barroso's address of October 2006, on the centenary of his birth.

2. Robert Bartlett, *The Making of Europe: Conquest, Colonization and Cultural Change*, London 1993, pp. 306–14.

The concept of 'Europe' did not exist for them, and to attribute it to such forebears is an anachronism.[3]

I

It was not until long afterwards, towards the end of the seventeenth century, in the coalition against Louis XIV, that the term started to acquire any general currency.[4] As late as 1713, the Treaty of Utrecht still invoked a *Respublica Christiana*, and two years later Leibniz could criticize the Abbé de Saint-Pierre, who had helped negotiate it, for his project of perpetual peace in Europe, in the name—that continued to be for him more hallowed—of Christendom.[5] It was only with the secular turn of the Enlightenment that there emerged a strong sense of Europe as such, as the designation of a unitary civilization. But when it came, it took swift and strikingly uniform hold. From the Regency to the outbreak of the French Revolution, Europe was conceived in virtually identical terms by one leading mind after another. It was Montesquieu who set the categorical note to come: 'A prince believes he will become greater through the ruin of a neighbouring state. On the contrary! The condition of Europe is such that States depend on each other. France has need of the wealth of Poland and Muscovy, as Guyenne has need of Brittany, and Brittany of Anjou. Europe is a State composed of several provinces'.[6] The formula rapidly became a trope. For Voltaire, 'Christian Europe could be regarded as a single republic divided in several states'.[7] For Vattel, modern Europe was 'a sort of republic', united for 'the preservation of order and liberty'.[8] For Robertson, 'the powers of Europe' formed 'one great political system'.[9] For Gibbon, 'Europe

3. For documentation, see Denis Hay, *The Idea of Europe*, Edinburgh 1957, who dates the first usage of the term 'European' to the Piccolomini pope, Pius II (1458–64), and the first significant substitution of 'Europe' for 'Christendom' to Commynes (*scripsit* 1488–1501): pp. 83–9.

4. H. D. Schmidt, 'The Establishment of "Europe" as a Political Expression', *The Historical Journal*, IX, 2, 1966, pp. 172–8.

5. 'Observations on the Abbé de St Pierre's 'Project for a Perpetual Peace', in Patrick Riley (ed.), *The Political Writings of Leibniz*, Cambridge 1972, pp. 180–1.

6. *Pensées*, I (1720–1734), §318, Paris 1991 (ed. Desgraves), p. 281.

7. *Le Siècle de Louis XIV* (1751), Ch. II, Paris 1937 (ed. Bourgeois), p. 10.

8. *Le Droit des gens*, III, Ch. 3, § 47, London 1958, facsimile, pp. 39–40.

9. *The History of the Reign of Charles V* (1769), Preface, New York 1833 (ed. Harper), p. v.

could be considered one great republic, whose various inhabitants have attained almost the same level of politeness and cultivation'.[10] For Burke, Europe was 'virtually one great state, having the same basis in general law, with some diversity of provincial customs and local establishments'; in it a traveller 'never felt himself quite abroad'.[11] So perceived, the unity of the continent was not an aim, but a given.

The vocabulary of the trope—a state, a republic—was political, but its meaning was essentially social. What unified Europe were common religious beliefs, public laws and customary manners—the trinity most often cited, from Voltaire to Burke. Yet, crucially, it included a political dimension, formally at odds with itself. For what also defined Europe were the virtues of division. Central to every depiction of the continent, as what most distinctively set it apart from— and above—the rest of the world, was a unique equilibrium between its constituent parts. Within its civilizational unity, the good fortune of Europe was to be divided into a set of competing yet interdependent states, each of moderate size, incapable of universal dominion. It was this balance of power that was the condition of European liberty. It was Montesquieu again who gave the first and pithiest expression to this notion: 'In Asia, strong are opposed to weak nations', he remarked, 'the one must therefore conquer and the other be conquered. In Europe, on the contrary, strong nations are opposed to strong; those who border each other have nearly the same courage. This is the grand reason for the weakness of Asia and the strength of Europe, of the liberty of Europe and the slavery of Asia'.[12] Robertson, too, judged that 'when nations are in a state similar to each other, and keep equal pace in the advances towards refinement, they are not exposed to the calamity of sudden conquests',[13] while Gibbon observed that 'the division of Europe into a number of independent states',

---

10. *The Decline and Fall of the Roman Empire* (1781), Vol. II, Ch. 38, Harmondsworth 1994 (ed. Womersley), p. 511.

11. *Letters on a Regicide Peace* (1796), I, London 1893 (ed. Keene), pp. 74–5.

12. *De l'esprit des lois* (1748), XVII, 3, *Oeuvres complètes*, II, Paris 1949 (ed. Caillois), p. 526; also XVII, 5, p. 529, dwelling on the natural geographical divisions of Europe as a bulwark of its freedoms.

13. *The History of the Reign of Charles V*, Bk. 12, p. 488. Robertson repeated Montesquieu's comparison of Europe with Asia, invoking Genghis Khan and Tamerlane sweeping everything like a torrent before them.

in which 'the balance of power will continue to fluctuate', was 'productive of the most beneficial consequences to the liberty of mankind'.[14] Voltaire was no less emphatic: 'the wise policy of the European nations to maintain among themselves, as far as possible, an equal balance of power' was a political principle 'unknown in the rest of the world'.[15] For Vattel, the political system of Europe was, more simply, inseparable from the 'famous idea of the balance of power'.[16]

That equipoise, in turn, was the condition not only of the liberties, but the arts and sciences of Europe. For here too the continent was a world apart, enjoying a commanding intellectual lead over all others. For Voltaire, it was the republic of letters, responsible for prodigious achievements of the mind, to which every country had contributed, of which Europe could be most legitimately proud.[17] But what was the spur to this cultural pre-eminence? By common agreement, it lay ultimately in the division and competition between states. As Gibbon put it: 'In all the pursuits of active and speculative life, the emulation of states and individuals is the most powerful spring of the efforts and improvements of mankind. The cities of ancient Greece were cast in the happy mixture of union and independence which is repeated on a larger scale, but in a looser form, by the nations of Europe'.[18] In the fruits of this emulation, moreover, was to be found the key to European dominion over the rest of the world. 'We cannot say that letters are a mere amusement for a number of citizens', wrote Montesquieu, 'their prosperity is so intimately linked to that of empires that it is an infallible sign or cause of it. If we cast an eye over what is now happening in the world, we will see that just as Europe dominates the other three parts of the world and prospers, while all the rest groan in servitude and misery, so Europe is in the same measure more enlightened than the other parts, which are sunk in a deep night of ignorance'.[19] If he had few illusions about what this

---

14. *The Decline and Fall of the Roman Empire* (1776), Vol. I, Ch. 3 (ed. Womersley), p. 106.
15. *Le Siècle de Louis XIV*, Ch. II, p. 11.
16. *Le Droit des gens*, III, Ch. 3, §47, p. 40.
17. *Le Siècle de Louis XIV*, Ch. XXXIV, pp. 654–64.
18. *The Decline and Fall of the Roman Empire* (1788), Vol. III, Ch. 53 (ed. Womersley), p. 421.
19. *Pensées*, §1006, pp. 379–80.

marriage of knowledge and power meant for the dominated world, others were typically more sanguine. 'The nations of Europe', Robertson remarked, are 'like one great family', since 'their acquisition of knowledge, their progress in the art of war, their political sagacity and address are nearly equal'—by contrast with the wide gap in 'character and genius which, in almost every period of history, has exalted the Europeans above the inhabitants of the other quarter of the globe, and seems to have destined the one to rule, and the other to obey'.[20]

Social similarity—political balance—intellectual emulation—cultural supremacy: such was the general syllogism of Europe, in the consensus of the Enlightenment. Although by no means always uncritical of European empire abroad—Diderot, Raynal, even Smith famously had their doubts—it was certainly contented enough with the unity of polite society at home. It was left to Rousseau, virtually alone, to strike a tarter note, deriding the cosmopolitanism of the age and its self-satisfaction: 'Say what you like, in our day there is no longer any such thing as a Frenchman, a German, Spaniard, even an Englishman. Nowadays we have only Europeans, all with the same tastes, the same passions, the same mores', he scornfully observed, 'all speaking of the public good and thinking only of themselves; all affecting moderation and wanting to be Croesus; ambitious only for luxury, passionate for gold'. So 'what do they care which master they serve, the laws of which state they obey? Provided they find money to steal and women to corrupt, they are everywhere at home'.[21] National

---

20. *The History of the Reign of Charles V*, p. 489. By contrast, for Montesquieu, 'Europe, in mastering the commerce of the three other parts of the world, has become their tyrant': *Pensées*, §568, p. 320. Robertson's sermon commemorating the Glorious Revolution dotted the i's and crossed the t's on the trope of emulation: 'All the civilized nations of Europe may be considered as forming one exclusive community. The intercourse among them is great, and every improvement in science, in arts, in commerce, in government introduced into any of them is soon known in others, and in time is adopted and imitated. Hence arises the general resemblance among all the peoples of Europe, and their great superiority over the rest of mankind'. See Richard Sher, '1688 and 1788: William Robertson on Revolution in Britain and France', in Paul Dukes and John Dunkley (eds), *Culture and Revolution*, London 1990, p. 102.

21. *Considérations sur le gouvernement de Pologne et sur sa réformation projettée* (1770–71), Ch. 3, Paris 1782, pp. 17–18. Earlier, Rousseau had been more indulgent, speaking favourably of Europe as being—unlike 'Asia or Africa, a notional collection of peoples who have only in common the name'—'a true society with its own religion, customs and even laws, from which none of the peoples who compose it can detach themselves without immediately causing

institutions were what gave character and vigour to a people, he
told the Poles, not international fashions or desires.

2

In this advice, as in much else, Rousseau was premonitory. With
the outbreak of the French Revolution, the Enlightenment image
of Europe faded from view, as social similarity collapsed under
the pressure of the Jacobin insurrection and mobilization, and
all political balance was destroyed by Napoleonic expansion.
Burke's *Letters on a Regicide Peace*—warning that France was
no ordinary community or state: 'it is with an *armed doctrine* that
we are at war'—offer a desperate register of the change. Social
revolution and national awakening put paid to the ecumene of
the one great republic. But ideal conceptions of Europe were not
extinguished. Out of the upheavals of twenty years of revolution
and war, they re-emerged in altered form to punctuate the next
century. Appropriately, it was the emblematic thinker to bridge
the worlds of the Enlightenment and of early socialism who
can be regarded as setting much of the subsequent agenda. In
October 1814, after the Bourbons were restored and before the
Hundred Days, Saint-Simon published, with the assistance of
his newly acquired disciple Augustin Thierry, a proposal for the
'reorganization of European society'. In its strange combination
of themes, his scheme prefigured nearly all future lines of
development.

Reversing the judgement of the Enlightenment, Saint-Simon
depicted the Middle Ages as the time when Europe had formed a
single, and generally peaceful, political body, united by Catholic
Christianity and its clergy. The Reformation had destroyed this
unity, unleashing the religious conflicts that had led to the Thirty
Years' War. Out of these had come the Treaty of Westphalia, which
instituted a political system based instead on the balance of power
between states. But far from benefitting the continent, once this
principle was established 'war became the habitual state of Europe',
culminating in the disastrous conflagration that had only just ended.
A century earlier, the Abbé de Saint-Pierre had conceived a project
for perpetual peace, but in accepting the residual feudalism of his
time, he had offered no more than a reciprocal guarantee between

---

troubles': 'Extrait du projet de paix perpétuelle' (1760), *Oeuvres*, III, Paris 1964,
p. 567.

tyrants for the preservation of their power. What was needed now was a system of government that extended the principles of the free constitution of England to Europe as a whole, whose first nucleus should be a joint Anglo-French parliament, setting an example to all the continent's peoples to put an end to absolutism. Once each had its own representative government—the Germans should be next in line—a European parliament would arise above them to govern the continent, every million literate citizens electing four deputies each: a scholar, a businessman, an administrator and a magistrate. There was no time to waste. Revolution still threatened, with public debt at crippling levels in England, and the recovered throne still precarious in France, where the Bourbons would do well to remember the fate of the Stuarts after their Restoration. Only with such a reorganization could Europe enjoy a peaceful and stable order. 'The golden age is not behind us, but in front of us'.[22]

In this visionary text, the three political traditions that would contest conceptions of Europe over the following century are all present in embryo.[23] Saint-Simon, who had fought in the American Revolution and made a fortune in the French Revolution, based his construction on a rejection of any return to the *ancien régimes* of Europe, and an accurate prediction of the violent overthrow of the Restoration in France. Within another decade, he would produce the first industrial version of utopian socialism. From this part of his legacy descended a sequence of revolutionary interventions and slogans for a united Europe. In the 1830s, Considérant, a disciple of Fourier, argued for a European federation based on productive labour and reciprocal recognition of rights and goods, to banish war from the continent. By the time of the Commune, when he worked with Courbet, Considérant was calling for a United

---

22. *De la réorganisation de la société europeénne*, Paris 1814, pp. 7–9, 24–26, 33–40, 47, 58–9, 63, 75–81, 97. The merits of the English constitution, Saint-Simon stressed, were also responsible for the country's prosperity, which Europe would enjoy under a similar system.

23. Compare the fate of a virtually contemporaneous scheme. In May 1814, the budding philosopher Karl Christian Krause had published *Entwurf eines europäischen Staatenbundes* in Leipzig, inspired by Kant's sketch for a perpetual peace, in the legally minded line of German idealism. Having defeated France, the victorious monarchies were urged to create—pre-eminently at German initiative—a European confederation, capital ideally in Berlin, with a view to later world government when other continents had followed this example. The text attracted no attention, falling, like the rest of Krause's writing—influential only, generations later, in Spain—into oblivion in his own country.

States of Europe on the model of the USA. Now made possible
by the progress of science and technology, it should begin with
collaboration between France and Germany.[24] In the revolutions
of 1848–9, Mazzini and Cattaneo looked to European unity as
the only safeguard against wars destructive of popular sovereignty
and nationality, Mazzini envisaging a common market, Cattaneo
a federal state.[25] Hugo added his plangent voice for a United
States of Europe, in a famous address to a peace congress in
Paris.[26] Proudhon and Bakunin followed in the 1860s—Proudhon
arguing that Europe was too big for a federation, and should
become a confederation of confederations, along Swiss lines;
Bakunin, on the eve of joining the First International, attacking
Mazzini's nationality principle as calculated to crush weaker or
more backward communities, and denouncing any bureaucratic
structure as incompatible with the insurrectionary liberty of a
United States of Europe to come.[27]

In the Second International, views divided. In 1911 Kautsky
declared that the only path to a durable peace in the world was 'the
unification of the states that belong to European civilisation into

---

24. *De la politique générale et du rôle de la France en Europe*, Paris 1840,
pp. 26–31; Jonathan Beecher, *Victor Considérant and the Rise and Fall of French
Romantic Socalism*, Berkeley—Los Angeles 2001, pp. 373–5, 402–5 ff.

25. Mazzini linked the emergence of a European literature with the rise of
political economy. Europe was 'one vast common market', and was 'marching—
by the common consent of her populations—towards a new era of union, of
more intimate association, in which, under the influence of one general thought,
the people will at last look upon one another as members of one great family', so
many 'labourers in the great workshop of nature, distributed according to their
position, their special aptitude or their vocation, but all contributing to one work,
whose fruits are to enlarge and strengthen the life of all': 'La Lega Internazionale
dei Popoli' (1847), a text originally published in English in Edinburgh. *Scritti editi
ed inediti di Giuseppe Mazzini*, Vol. 36, Imola 1922, pp. 8–10. For Cattaneo, see
the final lines of *Dell' insurrezione di Milano nel 1848 e della successiva guerra.
Memorie*, Brussels 1849, p. 306: 'In a Europe entirely free and friendly, the unity
of the barracks will give way to popular liberty; and the edifice constructed by
kings and emperors can be rebuilt on the pure American model. The principle of
nationality, provoked and enormously strengthened by the military oppression
that seeks to destroy it, will dissolve the accidental empires of Eastern Europe,
and transform them into federations of free peoples. We will have true peace,
when we have a United States of Europe'.

26. 'Discours d'ouverture du congrès de la paix' (1849), in *Oeuvres complètes:
Politique*, Paris 1985 (ed. Fizaine), pp. 299–304.

27. Proudhon: *Du principe fédératif et de la nécessité de reconstituer le parti
de la révolution*, Paris 1863, pp. 88–94; Bakunin: 'Fédéralisme, socialisme et anti-
théologisme' (1867), in *Oeuvres*, Paris 1902, pp. 14–21.

a federation with a common trade policy, a federal parliament, government and army—the establishment of a United States of Europe', a perspective Luxemburg rejected as utopian.[28] But when war broke out in 1914 the Bolsheviks themselves adopted the slogan of a republican United States of Europe in their first manifesto against it. A year later, Lenin would criticize this position, arguing that while a capitalist United States of Europe was possible as a common front of the continent's possessing classes to suppress revolution and meet the challenge of faster American rates of growth, it was wrong for Marxists to call for a socialist version. For that might imply that the revolution could not triumph in one or several countries before sweeping Europe as a whole.[29] Trotsky, by contrast, viewed the prospect of a capitalist United States of Europe as potentially a step forward that could help to create a united European working class, even if—he added a decade later—in answering to the needs of European capital to compete on more equal terms with America, reaction were to solve, not for the first time, tasks the revolution had failed to acquit. It was impossible to build socialism in a single country, as Stalin was claiming to do in the USSR, whereas Europe formed a logical field of struggle towards it.[30]

Stalin's victory in the CPSU closed down all discussion of a United States of Europe within the Third International. But not outside it. The revolutionary tradition found a final, spectacular expression during the Second World War, in the manifesto composed on the island of Ventotene by Altiero Spinelli, a member of the PCI expelled from the party for criticizing the Moscow trials, and Ernesto Rossi, a leader of *Giustizia e Libertà*, both prisoners of Mussolini since the twenties. Italy had been the classic land of radical struggle for national unity and independence, symbolized by the career of Garibaldi. The Manifesto of Ventotene drew a line under that experience. Although such nationalism had once been progressive, it had also contained the seeds of its degeneration into the imperialism that for a second time had set loose the furies

---

28. Kautsky, 'Krieg und Frieden. Betrachtungen zur Maifeier', *Die neue Zeit*, 1910–11, Bd 2, pp. 105–6; Luxemburg, 'Friedensutopien' (1911), *Gesammelte Werke*, Bd 2, Berlin 1974, pp. 499–504.

29. 'On the Slogan of a United States of Europe' (1915), *Collected Works*, Vol. 21, Moscow 1974, pp. 339–43.

30. Respectively: 'Programma Mira', *Nashe Slovo*, No. 86, 11 April 1916; 'Razoruzhenie i Soedinennye Shtaty Evropy', *Biulleten' oppozitsii*, No. 6, October 1929, pp. 9–14.

of war in Europe. Nazism had to be defeated by the Allies. But the Soviet Union, vital to victory, had become a bureaucratic despotism, while the Anglo-American powers were bent on restoration of the old order, which had brought inter-imperialist war in the first place. Once the fighting was over, therefore, the revolutionary imperative was to abolish the division of Europe into sovereign national states. Needed was a single federal union, of continental dimensions. In the struggles to come, the critical line of division was not going to be over democracy or socialism, but internationalism. The European revolution would certainly be socialist, and it would require the temporary dictatorship of a revolutionary party, as the disciplined nucleus of the new state and the democracy it would create. But it should not involve the bureaucratic statification of all property, still less of the means of public expression and organization. A free press, free trade-unions and a free judiciary, all unknown in Russia, were essential to it.[31] The manifesto, smuggled out to the mainland by Albert Hirschman's sister, is without question the most powerful vision of continental unity to emerge from the European Resistance— libertarian and jacobin motifs fused white-hot in a synthesis that is testimony to the fluidity of ideas possible before the Iron Curtain fell. Forty years later, Spinelli ended his career in full respectability, a member of the European Commission and father of the European Parliament, whose principal building in Brussels bears his name.

3

Later to emerge than this revolutionary tradition was a second filiation, closer to the best-known legacy of Saint-Simon to the nineteenth century—his conception of desirable social change as the work of scientific and industrial elites, reforming society from the summits of expert knowledge. Incorporated in his prescriptions for a European parliament, this technocratic vision passed down not only to his followers, the Saint-Simonian politicians, bankers and engineers of the Second Empire and Third Republic, but out into wider areas of reforming opinion.

---

31. 'Il Manifesto di Ventotene' (1941), in Luciano Angelino, *Le forme dell'Europa. Spinelli o della federazione*, Genoa 2003, pp. 187–201: both the social and the jacobin sections of the manifesto were drafted by Rossi, the *giellista*, rather than Spinelli, the expelled communist.

In its European applications, it was marked by a concern with detailed institutional machinery typically missing from the revolutionary line. The Franco-Prussian War and the Paris Commune were the signals for its emergence. In 1867, the League of Peace and Freedom was founded in Geneva, run for the next twenty years by Charles Lemonnier, editor of Saint-Simon's selected works and former secretary of the Crédit Mobilier, who from 1868 onwards produced a monthly journal for the League, *Les États Unis d'Europe*.[32] With Hugo as an associate and Garibaldi as its president, the League visibly descended from the republican traditions of the revolutions of 1848. But by 1872, when Lemonnier, in the wake of 'the sad and terrible year' that had just ended, published a book calling for a federal United States of Europe, a shift of emphasis was clear. A united Europe composed of republican governments required a single army, a supreme court, and a common market, and needed the consent of its citizens, expressed by universal suffrage. But it should keep completely clear of the 'social question', other than by imposing arbitration to prevent strikes, and promoting economic growth.[33]

Still more moderate, and yet more detailed, was the proposal that came five years later from the Swiss jurist Bluntschli, who after the defeat of the conservative Sonderbund in his homeland had moved to Germany, becoming a leading authority on international law. Ruling out either an American or a Swiss model, he explained that any future European union would have to respect the sovereignty of the states—carefully enumerated: eighteen in all—composing it, with major and minor powers accorded different voting

---

32. In which his first editorial took Saint-Simon's *De la réorganisation* as a founding reference: Donatella Cherubini, 'Si Vis Pacem Para Libertatem et Justitiam', in Marta Petricioli, Donatella Cherubini and Alessandra Anteghini, *Les États Unis d'Europe. Un Project Pacifiste*, Berne 2004, p. 22. The term 'pacifist' in the title and texts of this volume are to be taken in the Italian, not English sense, as meaning opposition to unjust wars, not rejection of violence as such.

33. *Les États Unis d'Europe*, Paris 1872, pp. 175–8; a work now looking back to Kant more than Saint-Simon, reproached with tactical concessions to the diplomats assembled in Vienna. Another who was driven to think of continental unity by the Franco-Prussian War was Ernest Renan, pleading with David Strauss for a European federation in 1870, a fortnight after the capitulation of Sedan: 'Lettre à M. Strauss'; *Oeuvres complètes*, Vol. I, Paris 1947, pp. 437–48. Even as late as his famous essay 'Qu'est ce qu'une nation?' of 1882, in many respects a hymn to nationalism, as properly understood, Renan could still observe that one day a European confederation would no doubt come about.

weights. The ensuing organization should have neither fiscal nor
military authority over its members, but should concentrate on
administrative and legal issues that could be resolved in common.
With this, a fully-fledged inter-governmental, as distinct from
federal, conception of European unity was for the first time set
out, and a shift towards the technicalities of constitutional law
begun.[34]

Early political science was not far behind. In 1900, the Sciences
Po organized a colloquium in Paris at which rival schemes for
European union were debated. The historian Anatole Leroy-
Beaulieu, scion of a leading establishment family, made it clear that
the slogan of a United States of Europe was counter-productive:
an American-style federation was not on the cards. The first steps
towards European unity would have to be economic—a customs
union—not political, and should start from the historic core of
European civilization, the Latin and Germanic nations of West
and Central Europe. Of the three empires surrounding these,
Russia was needed as a counterweight to Germany, and Turkey
should be admitted to avert the dangers of war over its fate. But
Britain should be kept out: it was an overseas empire, without
European solidarity, against which a confederal Europe should
be made—fear of the Anglo-Saxon powers providing a better
spur to its formation than mere democratic sentiments. Another
rapporteur, the lawyer Gustave Isambert, included Britain but
excluded Turkey on ethnic, religious and moral grounds, and
warned against dividing its member-states into two categories of
powers. Only a confederation was feasible, but it should be a strong
one, endowed with a legislature, a high court, an executive and
an army, with a capital perhaps in Strasbourg. For to entrust the
prevention of war simply to the effects of technical and economic
progress was delusive—waiting for water to erode a rock, rather
than lifting it with the lever of political will. United, a Europe of
375 million souls could lay down the law to the earth—naturally
in keeping with principles of justice and equity.[35]

---

34. 'Die Organisation des europäischen Statenvereines', *Gesammelte kleine
Schriften*, Bd 2, *Aufsätze über Politik and Völkerrecht*, Nördlingen 1881, pp.
279–312.

35. Congrès des sciences politiques de 1900, *Les États-Unis d'Europe*, Paris
1901, pp. 10, 22, 11–13, 15–18 (Leroy-Beaulieu); 144–5, 147–55 (Isambert).
Europe's colonial vocation was taken for granted by both speakers. Leroy-
Beaulieu's brother, the economist Paul, was a leading champion of French
imperial expansion in the Third Republic, close to Jules Ferry. Had Europe been

The juridical and geo-political cast of these reflections acquired further life after the First World War, when Europe's position in the world was more visibly threatened. The technocratic tradition had always been moderate in its instincts, lying more or less in the middle of the political spectrum. But in the inter-war period, its leading sequel became much more explicitly a doctrine of the centre, in both senses of the word. In the ideas, tactically variable over the years though these were, of Coudenhove-Kalergi, the Austrian count who launched the Pan-European Movement in 1923, the unity of Europe was always based on a double opposition. Ideologically, it was to be a bulwark against communism on the left, and extreme nationalism, later Nazism, on the right. Geopolitically, it would be an effective military barrier to Russia and an economic competitor of Anglo-America—later, when he adjusted his sights to include England in Europe, of the United States.[36] More self-consciously elitist than any of his predecessors, Coudenhove—whose bent was less technological than aesthetic and philosophical—sought support from the great and the good of the time: from Einstein to Rilke, Mussolini to Adenauer, Mann to Claudel, Brüning to Briand. In practice, his organization benefitted from the patronage of the clerical regimes of Seipel and Dollfuss in Austria—a country that, both stripped of its empire and denied self-determination, was the most glaring of all victims of Wilsonian diplomacy at Versailles—and from the funds of a Teutonic banking establishment—Warburg, Deutsche Bank, Melchior, Kreditanstalt—worthy of the Crédit Mobilier of old.[37]

---

united, Isambert explained, it could have stopped the United States seizing the Spanish colonies, and restrained British aggression against the Boers. Settlers, though certainly not natives, should be counted in the proportionate allocation of each nation's representatives in a European legislature. Such notes were not dissonant in this line of descent: in 1814 Saint-Simon himself had already stressed overseas settlement as one of the great missions of the Europe to come: *De la réorganisation*, p. 52.

36. *Pan-Europa*, Vienna 1924, pp. 53–8, 42–4, 157–63. Coudenhove, whose mother was Japanese, held Czech citizenship after 1918 (his estates were in Bohemia); for Hitler he was the 'world's bastard'. A good biography of him is still lacking. After the Second World War, Churchill wrote a preface to one of his autobiographies, Franz-Josef Strauss another to his advocacy of Europe as a world power.

37. For particulars, see the careful documentation in Anita Ziegerhofer-Prettenhaler, *Botschafter Europas. Richard Nikolaus Coudenhove-Kalergi und die Paneuropa-Bewegung in den zwangziger und dreissiger Jahren*, Vienna–Cologne–Weimar 2004, pp. 106–16.

Publicly, democracy was upheld by Coudenhove as a regime
of the golden mean between left and right, even if too many
democrats—bourgeois or social—were spineless defenders of it.
Earlier, he had made no secret of his liberal disdain for it as a
'lamentable interlude between two great aristocratic epochs:
the feudal aristocracy of the sword and the social aristocracy of
the spirit'.[38] In due course, once Hitler had absorbed Austria,
Coudenhove's outlook shifted away from an original anti-
parliamentarism, and he ended close to Anglo-French professions
of the connexion between liberty and collective security. But
throughout, his constitutional schemes for Europe—from a treaty
of arbitration through a customs union and a high court to a
single currency—were to be bestowed on the peoples from above.
In temperament not entirely dissimilar to Saint-Simon—another
flamboyant, semi-worldly, semi-unworldly adventurer—the
Austrian count proved in the end an appropriate descendant of the
French one: completely unpractical, yet uncannily premonitory of
what was to come.

4

Saint-Simon, however, also anticipated a third, no less significant
current of reflections on Europe. In his description of a peaceful
original unity in the Catholic faith and institutions of the Middle
Ages, and dismissal of the balance of power between states that
had been cherished by the Enlightenment as a ruinous substitute,
supposedly mitigating war while actually fomenting it, he struck
two notes that would be central to the culture of the Restoration,
and the conservative traditions that issued from it. Idealized
images of feudalism and religion, a world of graceful piety and
chivalry, as what most truly made Europe one, had already been
a leitmotif of Burke's counter-revolutionary message. But a far
more powerful, because dialectical—thereby also ambiguous—
version lay unpublished. Written three years after *Letters on a
Regicide Peace*, Novalis's *Europa* (1799) represented mediaeval
Christendom as a fabled realm of harmony, love and beauty, united
by the papacy, that had been destroyed by Luther's insurrection
against the Church, which in turn had set loose the revolution—'a
second Reformation'—in France. In its wake, Europe was now
rent by a battle between old and new worlds, that revealed the

---

38. *Adel*, Vienna 1923, p. 31.

dreadful defects of its traditional organization of states. But what if the 'primary historical goal' of the unprecedented conflict now engulfing the continent was actually to bring Europe together again? Might not war be reawakening it into a higher 'state of states', in which tradition and emancipation would be reconciled in a post-revolutionary faith to come?[39]

This volcanic text, alternatively ecstatic and ironic, was too incendiary for print in Novalis's lifetime. Goethe, when consulted, quashed its publication in the *Athenaeum*, and even when it finally saw the light of day in 1826, his fellow Romantics Tieck and Schlegel, who had suppressed it for a quarter of a century, treated it as a 'divisive' error that was better ignored—a discomfort still in a sense more perceptive than its later reception as an exalted piece of politico-religious reaction.[40] Schlegel, instrumental in censoring his friend's manifesto, moved to Paris in 1802, where he started a new journal, *Europa*—by then, a far from popular rubric—in which he began to develop a theme that would have a longer future before it than the vision of European renewal from a Christianity transformed by the French Revolution. In its first editorial, he explained that it would deal with 'the

---

39. 'Between the conflicting powers no peace can be concluded—all peace is mere illusion, mere truce. From the standpoint of cabinets, and common consciousness, no unification is conceivable. Both parties have great and urgent claims and must make them, driven by the spirit of the world and of mankind. Both are indestructible powers in the heart of man: on the one side reverence for antiquity, dependence on historical institutions, love of the monuments of ancestors and of the ancient and glorious family of the state, and joy in obedience; on the other side, the delightful sensation of freedom, unlimited expectation of tremendous provinces of activity, pleasure in things new and young, unconstrained contact with fellow members of the state, pride in human brotherhood, joy in personal rights and property of the whole, and the powerful feeling of citizenship. Let neither of these two hope to destroy the other. All conquests are meaningless here, for the innermost capital of every kingdom lies not behind earth walls and is not be taken by storm', Novalis declaimed. 'Blood will wash over Europe until the nations perceive the frightful madness that drives them round in circles', and 'a feast of love is celebrated as a festival of peace amid hot tears on smoking battlefields'. *Die Christenheit oder Europa. Ein Fragment*, Stuttgart 1966, pp. 44–6: in English, *Hymns to the Night and Other Selected Writings*, Indianapolis 1960, pp. 60–61 (translation modified).

40. For the history of the suppression and manipulation of the text, see Wm. Arctander O'Brien, *Novalis: Signs of Revolution*, Durham 1995, pp. 227–30. Schlegel, who invented the title 'Christianity or Europe' for it, tried to have the work destroyed in 1815. Burke—himself not spared Novalis's irony—would have been acutely alarmed by it. In a mystical register, its terse incandescence stands comparison perhaps only with *The Communist Manifesto*.

greatest diversity of topics', and in his first substantial essay in it, recounting his trip from Germany to Paris, he observed that while for the crowd there appeared, unquestionably, a 'European sameness', for a more discerning eye there remained significant differences between nations, and there it had to be admitted that the French had the advantage over the Germans, as closer in character and way of life to the spirit of the times. In that sense, Paris could be held the capital of the universe, and the revolution it had undertaken regarded as a welcome experiment, all the more interesting for the resistance of the material on which it was being exercised. But Northern and Southern Europe as a whole consisted of two radically different kinds of society, and their contrast was constitutive. 'What in the Orient springs from its origin with undivided force into a single form, is here divided into a manifold and unfolded with greater art. The human spirit must here decompose, dissolve its powers into infinity, and so become capable of much it would otherwise never attain'. Still, if its telluric powers—the iron force of the north and glowing embers of the south—could be harmonized, a truer Europe might yet emerge.[41] Schlegel never quite lost the nostalgia for unity of the *Frühromantik*, which in his later work would find expression in recurrent claims for the superior wisdom of the East, but the critical theme would remain diversity. In 1810, by then a sworn enemy of the revolution, he told the audience of his lectures on modern history: 'Asia, one could say, is the land of unity, in which everything unfolds in great masses, and in the simplest relations; Europe is the land of freedom, that is, of civilization [*Bildung*] through the contest of manifold individual and isolated energies ... It is precisely this rich variety, this manifoldness, that makes Europe what it is, that confers on it the distinction of being the chief seat of all human life and civilization'.[42]

By the time this was written, Schlegel had moved to Vienna, where he was rapidly integrated into the Habsburg establishment, working first for the Austrian general staff and later on schemes for a post-Napoleonic order in Germany. It was in this milieu that the second leading theme of conservative thinking about Europe, the shift away from balance-of-power principles as understood in pre-revolutionary diplomacy, took shape during the struggle

---

41. *Europa. Eine Zeitschrift* (1802–3), Darmstadt 1963 (ed. Behler), pp. 2, 28–32. *Mannigfältigkeit* is always the key term, here and in subsequent texts.

42. *Über die neuere Geschichte*, Vienna 1811, pp. 15, 11–12.

against Napoleon. Gentz, translator of Burke's *Reflections on the Revolution in France* before becoming Metternich's aide and secretary to the Congress of Vienna, can be taken as a conduit of the change. His first public interventions, in the time of the Consulate, while defending in more or less conventional terms the balance of power since Westphalia, as a system so organized that 'every weight in the political mass would find somewhere a counter-weight', had argued that more than this was required if Europe was to acquire its appropriate federal constitution. Beyond such checks and balances, positive mutuality between the powers was needed, and this must include the right to intervene in the affairs of any state that threatened the international order, as a principle of public law.[43] With the Restoration, the corollary became the axiom. The political system set in place at the Congress of Vienna, of which Metternich could regard himself as the chief guardian, if not architect, and Gentz as the theorist, was not a re-edition of the balance of power of the eighteenth century. It was a fundamentally novel one—a system not of competition, but coordination between the leading powers, to stabilize the restoration of the old order and crush any danger of revolutionary risings against it.[44] For its creators, this was no mere cartel of the

---

43. When a major state of Europe was so internally unhinged as to endanger its neighbours, they were entitled to intervene in it, not simply on grounds of political prudence, but as a matter of 'international law, properly understood': *Von dem politischen Zustande von Europa vor und nach der französischen Revolution*, Berlin 1801, Vol. 1, p. 207. The French Revolution, naturally, was just such a case. Three decades later, he continued to uphold the 'unlimited right of intervention' of any sovereign who felt their security threatened by developments in a state nearby: 'Bemerkungen über das Interventions-Recht' (March 1831), in *Schriften von Fredrich von Gentz. Eine Denkmal*, Vol. 5, Mannheim 1840 (ed. Schlesier), pp. 181–3.

44. As Gentz explained in 1818: 'The political system established in Europe since 1814 and 1815 is a phenomenon without precedent in the history of the world. In place of the principle of equilibrium, or more accurately of counterweights formed by particular alliances, the principle that has governed and too often also troubled and bloodied Europe for three centuries, there has succeeded a principle of general union, uniting all states collectively with a federative bond, under the guidance of the five principal Powers'; making of Europe 'a grand political family, united under the auspices of an areopagus of its own creation, whose members guarantee to themselves and to all parties the tranquil enjoyment of their respective rights'. See his 'Considérations sur le système politique actuellement établi en Europe', in *Dépêches inédites du Chevalier de Gentz aux hospodars de Valachie. Pour servir à l'histoire de la politique européene (1813 à 1828)*, Paris 1876, pp. 354–5.

anciens régimes, but the realization of a new kind of continental unity—the Concert of Europe. Metternich, who regarded himself as 'representing European society as a whole', could write to Wellington in 1824: 'Depuis longtemps l'Europe a pris pour moi la valeur d'une patrie'. A century later Kissinger would call him the 'Prime Minister of Europe'.[45]

In France, Guizot was no less committed to the Concert of Europe, and would become a fellow victim of the revolutions of 1848, when both rulers were toppled. But his intellectual achievement in the same cause was of another order: a historical synthesis weaving the two conservative motifs of unity and variety into a full-blown narrative of the destiny of Europe from the fall of the Roman Empire to the Restoration, in which pride of place was given to a 'prodigious diversity' as the very definition of the unity of European civilization, incomparably richer than any other. Distinctive in this vision was the—prudently— agonistic touch Guizot gave to the trope of variety that had been foregrounded by Schlegel. Europe was not just the theatre of an astonishing diversity of political systems, social structures, intellectual doctrines and aesthetic forms, but these were in 'a state of continual conflict', and this was the source of the vitality of European civilization.[46] From the collision and combination of Roman, Christian and Barbarian elements had emerged the rudiments of the mediaeval order. Out of the struggles between the nobility, the church and the commons had developed the unity of nations, annealed only by monarchy—not aristocracy, theocracy nor any republic—into the form of the modern state. Out of the Reformation, as an insurrection of the freedom of thought against the absolute spiritual power of the papacy, had come the clash between that free spirit and centralized monarchy in seventeenth-century England, the land that was a veritable concentrate of all the successive diversities of European history.

---

45. *A World Restored: Metternich, Castlereagh and the Problems of Peace 1812–1822*, Cambridge Mass. 1957, pp. 11, 321. For the depth of the change in the international system brought about by the Restoration, see Paul Schroeder's great—conservative—work, *The Transformation of European Politics 1763– 1848*, Oxford 1994, passim, and 'Did the Vienna System Rest on a Balance of Power?', in *Systems, Stability and Statecraft: Essays on the International History of Modern Europe*, New York 2004, pp. 37–57.

46. *Cours d'Histoire Moderne. Histoire générale de la civilisation en Europe depuis la chute de l'empire romain jusqu'à la révolution française*, Paris 1828, Lesson II, pp. 6–12.

Finally, out of the conflict in France between a still purer version of absolute monarchy and a yet more radical free spirit, had arisen the revolution of 1789. That, however, had been a too absolute triumph of human reason, leading to a tyranny of its own, now happily a thing of the past. For 'it is the duty, and, I believe, will be the merit of our time, to recognize that any power'—be it spiritual or temporal—'contains within it a natural vice, a principle of weakness and abuse requiring that a limit be assigned to it'.[47] Conflictivity, salutary as it was, must also be wisely contained. Its natural outcome in Europe was compromise. For if 'diverse forces are in continual conflict with one another, none can succeed in suppressing the others and taking entire possession of society'.[48] Guizot gave his lectures on the general history of European civilization in 1828, on the eve of the July Monarchy, in which he would put the principles of the *juste milieu* into practice. As a French Protestant, he had inverted the schema of Saint-Simon and the German Romantics to make of the Reformation an emancipation rather than regression, and adjusted the principles of the Restoration from the absolutist reflexes of Vienna to the constitutional maxims of Paris, detaching them from legitimism. But the unity-in-diversity of Europe was no less the work of divine providence in this Huguenot edition, still bearing the stamp of a conservatism, however liberal in intention, for which the French were not grateful.[49]

Across the Rhine, similar ideas soon found expression. Five years later, the young Leopold von Ranke, a friend of Gentz in Vienna, while maintaining that 'the complex of Christian nations in Europe should be considered as a whole, so to speak as a single state', was also telling his German readers that 'out of the clash of opposing forces, in great moments of danger—disaster, rising, rescue—the most decisive new developments are born'. It

---

47. *Cours d'Histoire Moderne*, Lesson XIV, pp. 40–41.

48. *Cours d'Histoire Moderne*, Lesson II, p. 7.

49. 'European civilization has entered, we may say, into eternal truth, by the plan of Providence; it follows the paths of God. Therein lies the rational principle of its superiority': *Cours d'Histoire Moderne*, Lesson II, pp. 11–12. For Guizot, the Crusades were 'the first European event', in which all Europe participated, 'moved by the same sentiment and acting in the same cause'. Before them, 'Europe did not exist'. They were also the gateway to greater existential diversity: 'the peoples threw themselves into the Crusades as into a new existence, wider and more varied, at once recalling the ancient freedom of the barbarians and opening the horizons of a vast future': Lesson VIII, pp. 11, 17.

was a mistake to think that the nineteenth century had done no more than shed the baleful heritage of the French Revolution: it had 'also renewed the fundamental principle of all states, that is religion and law, and given new life to the principle of each individual state'. Indeed, just as 'there would only be a disagreeable monotony if the different literatures let their individual characters be blended and melted together'—for 'the union of all must rest upon the independence of each, so that they can stimulate one another'—so it was 'the same with states and nations. Conclusive, positive predominance of any one would inflict ruin on others. A mixture of all would destroy the essence of each. Out of their separation and self-development will emerge true harmony'.[50] Ranke, watchful against contagion from the change of regime in France, and writing for a Prussian state that had yet to achieve its full place in the sun, lent a more combative note to common themes, making it clear that the principle of conflict extolled by Guizot in the European past found its classical expression in a field he had generally preferred to forget. War, as Heraclitus had noted, was the father of things. Half a century later, with the achievements of Bismarck before him, Ranke could be still more categorical: 'Historical development', he wrote in 1881, 'does not rest on the tendency towards civilization alone. It arises also from impulses of a very different kind, especially from the rivalry of nations engaged in conflict with each other for the possession of soil or for political supremacy. It is in and through this conflict, affecting as it does every domain of culture, that the great empires of history are formed'.[51]

Somewhat earlier, it was Burckhardt, once a student of Ranke, who left the most striking formulations of the passage from the differential through the conflictual to an uncompromising agonistics. From the Renaissance onwards, certainly, Europe had exhibited an 'unprecedented *variety of life*', where 'the richest formations originate, home of all contrasts, which dissolve into one unity where everything intellectual is given voice and expression. European is: the self-expression of *all* forces, in monuments, images and words, institutions and parties, down to the individual'. But in this manifold, there was nothing eirenic. Viewed with detachment, 'the life of the West *is* struggle', and

---

50. Leopold von Ranke, *Die grossen Mächte* (1833), Leipzig 1916 (ed. Meinecke), pp. 58–63.

51. *Weltgeschichte* (1881), Leipzig 1896, p. 5.

notwthstanding its 'great violence' and 'the desire to annihilate adversaries', Burckhardt held that 'history should rejoice in this profusion'. For 'a concealed supreme power here produces epochs, nations and individuals of an endlessly rich particular life'. From the 'high and distant vantage point' of a historian, the bells of Europe 'harmonize beautifully, whether or not they seem dissonant nearby: *Discordia concors*'. Only one thing was fatal to Europe: a 'crushing mechanical power', whether barbarian, absolutist or—today—the levelling pressure of the masses. But from every homogenizing danger, Europe had so far always found men to deliver it.[52]

5

Such, approximately, was the repertoire of ideas stretching from the Enlightenment to the Belle Époque and its aftermath, that could be regarded as the most direct of the 'sedimentations' conceived by the historian Krzysztof Pomian as latent connexions between successive incarnations of European unity.[53] The First World War, shattering them all in one movement, gave them new life in another, as survivors sought to draw lessons from the catastrophe, and avert any repetition of it. The inter-war period saw a flood of books, articles and schemes for a united Europe—an incomplete inventory counts some six hundred publications in different languages—in which virtually all the topics and tropes of the previous century were recapitulated, selectively or in combination, and the appearance for the first time of organizations expressly devoted to the cause.[54] Discursively, perhaps only one new theme gained salience in these years. It was difficult for Europe to regard itself any longer as paramount in the world at large. Decline, possible or actual, of the continent was now commonly discussed, as the growing wealth and power of the United States loomed over every European state, and the rapid development of the USSR and Japan was cause for alarm. Valéry's famous dictum

52. *Historische Fragmente* (notes from 1867), Stuttgart 1942 (ed. Kaegi), pp. 141–148.

53. See below, pp. 518–519.

54. See Jean-Luc Chabot's fine study of the idea of European unity in these years, *Aux origines intellectuelles de l'union européenne*, Grenoble 2005, pp. 14–16; also the good earlier account, angled more at the diplomacy involved, and covering a slightly different time-span, in Carl Pegg, *Evolution of the European Idea 1914–1932*, Chapel Hill 1983.

of 1919, 'We civilizations now know that we are mortal'—the plural quickly gave way to the singular: other 'shipwrecks were not our affair'—expressed widespread foreboding.[55] A decade later he would drily remark: 'Europe visibly aspires to be governed by a commission from America. All its politics tend in that direction'.[56] Valéry's own observations on the post-war scene, certainly striking enough—lending a pessimistic twist to the tropes both of European diversity, as now capsizing into disorder, and European superiority, as undermined by the very diffusion of its scientific advances—remained within the limits of an ironic *Kulturkritik*, without constructive issue. Other leading philosophical and literary lights of the period—Ortega, Benda, Croce—committed themselves more actively to ideals of European unity.[57]

Such eddies in the intellectual sphere were not unconnected to the political world. In 1929, official proposals for a European Union were floated through the League of Nations by France, holding public attention into 1931. The evaporation of Briand's initiative, on which he had consulted Coudenhove, owed something to the calculated vagueness of the memorandum he and his aide Alexis Léger—Saint-John Perse—presented to the governments of the time. But if it had little chance of a practical outcome anyway, this was because it essentially represented a premature attempt by France to corral Germany into a system designed to prevent its return to predominance in Europe, as the state with the largest economy and population—the reason why so many hard-boiled politicians in the Third Republic, not just the effusive Briand, but Herriot, Painlevé, even Poincaré, backed a plan that gave the appearance of being all too idealistic. But the First World

---

55. 'La Crise de l'esprit' (1919), *Oeuvres*, I, Paris 1992, p. 988: first published in English, in *The Athenaeum*—scarcely conceivable today.

56. 'Notes sur la grandeur et décadence de l'Europe' (1927), *Oeuvres*, II, p. 930: 'Not knowing how to rid ourselves of our history, we will be relieved of it by happy peoples that have none, or almost none. These happy peoples will impose their happiness on us'. Valéry explained he had first started to think along these lines in the 1890s, impressed by the victories of the United States over Spain, and Japan over China.

57. Ortega, *La Rebelión de las masas*, Madrid 1930, pp. 302–8; Benda, *Discours à la nation européenne*, Paris 1931, passim; Croce, *Storia d'Europa nel secolo decimonono*, Bari 1932, p. 358. Note the clustering of dates around the Briand Plan. Ortega was exercised by the challenge from the USSR: 'I see in the construction of Europe as a great national state the only enterprise that could thwart the victory of the "Five Year Plan" '.

War, unlike the Second, had left Germany effectively intact, and Stresemann—Briand's targeted interlocutor—had no intention of renouncing his nation's ambitions to recover the status of a great power. Britain, resistant as later to the idea of European unity as such, especially if it involved any disconnexion from America, invoked the loftier international ideals of the League of Nations to help bury the French initiative as a small-minded substitute. In Paris alone, it was not entirely forgotten. Twenty years later, when France and Germany were each sufficiently humbled by the experience of defeat and occupation to be ready for a more sober union, the Schuman Plan would make a discreet allusion to its predecessor, noting that, then as now, France had set the ball of European unity rolling.

In the short run, the triumph of Nazism in Germany put paid to any revival of such prospects.[58] In its wake, a general ferocity of intensified nationalism swept most of Eastern and Southern Europe. By 1935 Marc Bloch, commenting on a conference held under Fascist auspices in Rome three years earlier (among the participants were Rosenberg and Göring), could view current notions of Europe as little more than expressions of panic, prompted by fear of economic

---

58. In Britain alone, there was what could be regarded as a curious postscript. In the wake of Briand's failure, the millionaire heir to a Welsh industrial fortune, Baron Davies, a former secretary to Lloyd George, founded the New Commonwealth Society, acquiring no less a figure than Ernst Jäckh as its international director, the two creating in turn an institute in 1934, publishing a quarterly that five years later, in the aftershock of Munich, became the platform for a rash of schemes for 'federal union' of one kind or another. These were set off by the bestseller *Union Now*—drafted in the winter of 1933–4, but unable to find a publisher until 1939—by the American journalist Clarence Streit, which called for the 'fifteen democracies of the world'—the United States, Great Britain, the White Dominions, France, the Low Countries, the Nordic lands and Switzerland—which 'own almost half the earth, rule all its oceans, govern nearly half of mankind', to band together in an invincible federation against the Axis powers. When war broke out, the alternative of an Anglo-French union was floated in *The New Commonwealth Quarterly*, and adopted in desperation by Churchill—he had been president of the British section of the New Commonwealth Society—after the fall of Paris, in a vain attempt to get the Third Republic to fight on. Once Germany was defeated, such last-minute federalism was naturally forgotten in Britain. In America, however, the Cold War revived talk of an Atlantic union, this time against the menace of Communism, and Streit graced the cover of *Time* magazine as late as 1950. Jäckh, admirer and mourner of Talat, who had 'saved many Armenians', could congratulate himself both on his role in the German alliance with the Young Turks against Russia, anticipating America's Truman Doctrine, and on his contribution to supranational ideals in Europe: *Der goldene Pflug*, pp. 20, 219–20.

competition to the west, colonial revolt in the south, alien social forms in the east, and political discord within, which had suddenly produced such good—sincere or insincere?—Europeans.[59] Within a few years, Hitler's New Order would proclaim its own version of a united Europe, ranged under German leadership against Anglo-Saxon plutocracy to the west and Bolshevik terror to the east. Too ephemeral and instrumental to be of any deeper effect, this confiscation nevertheless left a shadow in its immediate aftermath. When Lucien Febvre gave, for the first time, a course on the history of Europe in liberated Paris during the winter of 1944–5, his conclusions were subdued. No more than a 'desperate refuge' after Versailles, the unity of Europe seemed capable of realization only by mailed force, and joy at liberation from it was now tainted with fear that the machinery of ever more murderous industrialized warfare might grind again, as the progress of scientific destruction could not be reversed. The building of a new, peaceful Europe was a herculean task—political-administrative, economic-financial and cultural-civilizational—that no mere dilute liberal pathos could manage. Yet was it even the right goal, marking a stage towards a true global fraternity, or one risking obstruction of it, and so better skipped?[60]

Two years later Federico Chabod published the first serious historical reconstruction of ideas of Europe, from the time of Queen Anne to that of Bismarck, in an introduction to a course of lectures in Rome that still remains without equal for perceptiveness.[61] But it too ended on a less than optimistic note.

---

59. 'Problemès d'Europe', *Annales d'histoire économique et sociale*, No. 35, September 1935, p. 473.

60. *L'Europe. Genèse d'une civilisation*, Paris 1999 (till then unpublished lectures notes), pp. 279, 284–9, 316, 292. Febvre drew extensively on themes both of Valéry—the ricochet from dissemination of European knowledge to the non-European world—and Bloch—Europe remaining a theatre of fear: of industrial competitors, colonial risings, communist experiments, further national conflicts: pp. 308–9.

61. 'L'Idea di Europa', based on a lecture course given in Milan in the winter of 1943–4, now in Luisa Azzolini (ed.), *Idea d'Europa e politica dell'equilibrio*, Bologna 1995, pp. 139–203. Of the extensive later literature, the two most distinguished works remain among the earliest: Heinz Gollwitzer, *Europabild und Europagedanke*, Munich 1951, covering German writing from the Enlightenment to Nietzsche, in a major work of crisp scholarship, and Carlo Curcio's vast compendium, of less analytic erudition, *Europa. Storia di un'idea*, Florence 1958, dealing with all the major cultures of the continent, and running from ancient to post-war times. French historians have tended to concentrate on the more strictly political side of ideas about Europe, starting with Pierre

Like many Italian intellectuals of his generation, Chabod had not opposed fascism in the thirties, indeed hailing Mussolini's conquest of Abyssinia,[62] but during the war he had joined the partisans in his native Val d'Aosta, and been active in the Liberation. He concluded his essay, in early 1947, with the triumph of the cult of force in the late nineteenth century, and the descent of Europe into the First World War, from which it had emerged permanently diminished. Politically, economically and culturally, it was henceforward determined or overshadowed by larger powers beyond it. At best, European intellectuals might still have something to say in a world republic of letters. In 1948, Chabod made mention of the first attempts at economic cooperation after the war, with Benelux. But there is no sign he had much confidence in the prospects of any wider European unity.[63] Further north, in the same year, the great Romanist Ernst Robert Curtius published the work on which he had been labouring for fifteen years, since the Nazi ascent to power in Germany, as an affirmation of European unity. But, as the title of his monumental *European Literature and the Latin Middle Ages* announced, this protest against every geographical or chronological 'dismemberment of Europe' retreated to one of the obscurest recesses of the past in the attempt to render it whole again—Curtius himself observing that 'no stretch of European literary history is as little known and frequented as the Latin literature of the early and high Middle Ages', as if the true unity of Europe could now only find expression in a dead language.[64]

Renouvin's *L'Idée de Fédération Européenne dans la Pensée Politique du XIXe Siècle*, Oxford 1949, and continuing—with a far wider scope—through Jean Duroselle, *L'Idée d'Europe dans l'histoire* (preface by Monnet), Paris 1965, and most recently Patrice Rolland's anthology *L'unité politique de l'Europe. Histoire d'une idée*, Brussels 2006. From Switzerland, De Rougemont's chronicle *Vingt-huit siècles d'Europe* appeared in 1961.

62. His pre-war essay 'Il Principio dell' equilibrio nella storia d'Europa' had ended with a paean to the 'amply European and human' diplomacy and 'new great mission which fascist Italy has assumed under the wise and firm leadership of the Duce', *Idea d'Europa e politica dell'equilibrio*, pp. 30–1. Curcio, a Neapolitan, had been a much more committed adherent of the regime, and was for a time purged after the war.

63. Respectively 'L'Idea di Europa', and 'Europa. Storia' in *Idea d'Europa e politica dell'equilibrio*, pp. 203, 257.

64. *Europäische Literatur und lateinisches Mittelalter*, Berne 1948, pp. 14, 21.

6

Yet within another two years Monnet had drafted the Schuman Plan, and the process of European integration that has led to today's Union was launched. What is the bearing of any of this abstruse pre-history on that process? In the early sixties, armed with a preface from Monnet himself, an authorized historian of the new Europe of *hauts fonctionnaires* had no doubt. There was nothing less than an 'abyss', wrote Jean-Baptiste Duroselle, between 'the so-called "precursors" and the Europeans of the era after 1945'. In an entirely new enterprise, his contemporaries had at last built a united Europe with the purpose of 'restoring their wealth, power and radiance to nations that had lost them'. 'What a difference', he exclaimed, from 'the Europe of universalists and cosmopolitans who denied or despised the ideal of a fatherland', the assorted 'hatchers of plans, profferers of advice, utopian system-builders' of old. He was not to imagine that the same robust scorn would in due course be poured on 'the lives and teachings of the European saints', his own practically minded heroes, by a historian committed to a still more realistic view of the role of nation-states in the creation of the Common Market.[65] Tougher minds can usually be found than those who imagine themselves tough-minded.

In reality, the ideas of Europe whose long and winding history preceded integration have continued to haunt it. Each has had its own after-life. On the left, the revolutionary tradition that took up the banner of unity earliest proved least able to hold it across the rapids of the twentieth century. There were at least two reasons for that. In this line of descent, the principal motivation of calls for a united Europe was always the prevention of war. Ideals of peace were, of course, central to virtually every shade of Europeanizing opinion, and explain why, at the beginning, the left led the field, in its sincerity and urgency: not only were the masses whose interests it sought to defend the principal victim of wars, but since the Left was always far from power, it was not exposed to temptations to launch them. But as time went on, the limitation of notions of unity springing only from the need to avoid war weakened it. This was partly because peace is of its nature not

---

65. Jean-Baptiste Duroselle, *L'Idée européenne dans l'histoire*, Paris 1965, p. 26; Alan Milward, *The European Rescue of the Nation-State*, p. 318 ff.

only a negative goal, but an abstract one, as Leibniz had pointed out, specifying no particular political or even existential order. But it was also because Europe could decreasingly be taken as a theatre potentially defining it. Peace might reign between the Powers, so long as their Concert held, but what of the rest of the world, where wars of imperial annexation or repression proceeded without interruption throughout the nineteenth century?

By the early twentieth century, the left had divided between radical and moderate wings, and Luxemburg, in her exchange with Kautsky, summed up the underlying objections of the radicals: 'The idea of European civilization is utterly foreign to the outlook of the class conscious proletariat. Not European solidarity, but *international* solidarity, embracing every region, race and people on earth, is the foundation of socialism in a Marxist sense. Every partial solidarity is not a stage towards the realization of genuine internationality, but its opposite, its enemy, an ambiguity under which lurks the cloven hoof of national antagonism. Just as we have always fought against Pan-Germanism, Pan-Slavism and Pan-Americanism as reactionary ideas, so we have nothing whatever to do with the idea of Pan-Europeanism'.[66] But as soon as the League of Nations was founded, the same reservation found expression even among moderates. Was not the League a higher instance, a more compelling ideal, than any mere European confederation? The legacy of this doubt has not gone away. In Habermas's conception of today's Union as commendably more abstract than the nation-state of old, yet still not abstract enough to represent a fully cosmopolitan value-system, and so at best a transition to a Kantian world order to be embodied in the United Nations, suitably equipped with policing powers, there is more than an echo of the same tension. In the shadow of the universal, the particular can only exist on sufferance—or, in a late corruption, as already the universal *in nuce*. The contemporary ideology that offers the Union as moral example to the world, now embedded in the self-image of its officialdom, is essentially a product of minds belonging to what was once the Left.

There was, however, another reason why this tradition faded as an active force over time. After the early utopians—the moment of Fourier and Saint-Simon—the socialist movement was little interested in political institutions. Even the federalism of Proudhon, or in more democratic-republican register Cattaneo,

---

66. *Gesammelte Schriften*, p. 503.

remained more ideational, as a principle, than articulate as a programme. The Commune was too brief an experiment to leave behind, for revolutionaries, more than the negative lesson that the existing state machines could not be appropriated, but had to be broken, if real social change was to come. For reformists, on the other hand, bourgeois parliaments were good enough, requiring little further thought, other than full extension of the suffrage. Though a united Europe remained a slogan well into the twentieth century, both wings were sterile so far as its construction was concerned. Even the Manifesto of Ventotene, remarkable in so many other ways, offered a much more developed social vision of a United States of Europe than a political structure for one.

By contrast, the technocratic line descending from Saint-Simon inherited both his attachment to institutional projections and his economic productivism. This is the combination that allows it to claim paternity rights in the eventual process of European integration, when it came. Untroubled by imperial operations overseas—indeed, not infrequently promoting continental unity at home as a way to preserve colonial supremacy abroad—it was not hampered by scruples over where the line of peace should be drawn: it was enough that Europe itself should be secured from war, and devoted to the growth of industry and the progress of science, for the well-being of all its classes. But for that, detailed administrative and legal engineering was needed, requiring all the ingenuity, if less of the fantasy, of the first modern proposal for its reorganization. The closeness of much in the institutional thinking of this tradition to the shape of the actual Community that came into existence after the Second World War is striking. In some ways, however, no less so is the extent to which it foreshadowed problems that still dog the Union. Bluntschli, who produced perhaps the most impressive single anticipation of much of the design of the EU, explained, long before Paul Kirchhof or Dieter Grimm, why there could be no federal democracy in Europe.

Federal union in America, he observed, was based on an American people bound together by a common country, language, culture, legal system and common interests. Europe, on the other hand, was composed of very different nations, divided in all these respects. There, only a confederation of states, where real political power must remain—not a sovereign parliament or an overall government—could advance the goals of a European public law, European peace, and common cultural concerns. 'The political unity of a state without a people is a contradiction in terms.

Since there is no European people, there can be no state called Europe'.[67] Nor has one arisen. But if a hybrid quasi-state were to be constructed, on these premises it could only be done from above, by those capable of joining and ruling over a popular void. The logic of such elitism is still with us. The elite does not contain as many scientists, though certainly as many bureaucrats and executives, as Saint-Simon would have wished; it is not confined to cabinets, as Bluntschli imagined it would be; nor is it adorned with many aristocrats, of birth or spirit, as hoped by Coudenhove. But of its character as a construction from on high, by—according to contemporary lights—the best and the brightest, there can be little doubt. It was Coudenhove who foresaw, and welcomed, the corollary. Writing in the twenties, he remarked that for the moment democracy was a protection against chaos. But in the Europe of the future, 'once a new, authentic nobility is constituted, democracy will disappear of itself'.[68] In that respect, today's EU would not have disappointed him.

What of the conservative tradition? Its legacies surfaced later, once regime change in the economies of the West had set in, and the Cold War was won. Then, as the EU expanded to the east, the principles of 1815–23 came into their own again: not balance, but coordination of powers, to police zones of potential turbulence and ensure ideological placidity, in the spirit of the Protocol of Troppau. Well before it was openly theorized, a modern *droit d'ingérence* was being practised by Brussels, wherever developments in the lands of former communism fell short of the expectations of a new Concert of Europe. The restoration of capitalism was naturally a very different affair from that of absolutism, its interventions more economic and political than military. But as successive actions in the Balkans would show, where force was required it would be used. The new legitimism speaks of the rule of law and human rights, not the sanctity of thrones. But geo-politically, the pedigree of even such modest operations as EUFOR and EULEX goes back to Chateaubriand's *cent mille fils de Saint Louis*.

Yet such continuities have been perhaps the less important bequest of this line to Brussels, since the principles of a Concert of Powers are no longer specifically European, but Atlantic; even, in the new century, increasingly if still imperfectly, global. Where

---

67. Bluntschli, *Gesammelte kleine Schriften*, Bd 2, pp. 293–4, 298–9.
68. Coudenhove, *Adel*, p. 36.

the greatest strength of the conservative tradition always lay was rather in its speculations on what distinguished Europe from the rest of the world. This heuristic, not programmatic, concern it paradoxically inherited from the Enlightenment. Paradoxically, since the alternative traditions, revolutionary or technocratic, were, of course, politically closer to the Enlightenment. Yet in the pursuit of the practical goal of a European unity that could no longer be assumed as a meta-political reality in the manner of the *philosophes*, they largely abandoned its intellectual agenda. In the conservative tradition, on the other hand, where constructivist slogans of a United States of Europe rarely had any standing, the question of what defined the singularity of Europe as a meaningful unit in the first place remained a central preoccupation. The result was to leave an intellectually richer deposit of ideas than either of the other traditions. The plurality of states celebrated by the Enlightenment became the diversity of forces, cultures and powers that set Europe apart from the rest of the world—the advantages of quantity transformed into virtues of quality. In the spiritual arsenal of the Union, that too lives on. But in an after-life that is less predictable.

10

PROGNOSES

I

Where then, as the first decade of the new century draws to a close, does the European Union now stand? Politically, at an interval in the theatre of constitutional reform, whose first act saw the triumphant production of a charter of rights and duties agreed by all member-states, undone in a spectacular second act by the French and Dutch electorates, imperturbably resuscitated in a third act at Lisbon, only to be spurned in a fourth by voters in Ireland. Few doubt that there will be a happy ending. But the spectacle has been instructive. The purpose of the Treaty of Lisbon was to circumvent any further possibility of popular dissent from the arrangements devised by Giscard and approved by the assembled governments in 2004, after their overwhelming rejection by voters in France and the Netherlands. This time, ratification would be reserved for parliaments, not peoples. In only one European country was a popular consultation legally unavoidable. But it could surely be discounted. Was not Ireland by tradition the greatest single beneficiary of the largesse of Brussels, and economic success-story of European integration? In Dublin, were not all three of the country's principal parties, not to speak of its trade-unions and business associations, solidly behind the treaty, under a prime minister who had played a leading role in the diplomacy around the original constitution? True, Irish voters had once before been irresponsible enough to reject a treaty, the pact approved by the council at Nice in 2000. But they had quickly been obliged to repent, and reverse themselves. They could be expected to have learnt their lesson.

In June 2008, the referendum—held back, to impress on the Irish unanimous acceptance of the treaty by their fellow Europeans, until the parliaments of eighteen other member-states had ratified it—came due. After a campaign in which the entire

Irish establishment, and assembled lights of liberal opinion, rallied behind a document which the prime minister and foreign minister alike confessed they had never read, the result was virtually the same as in France three years earlier. On a higher turnout than before, the new treaty was rejected by a margin of 53 to 46 per cent. If maverick opposition from a free-market entrepreneur, and theological reservations among the pious, contributed to the outcome, class polarization decided it—Sinn Fein's spirited attack on a gombeen bourgeoisie and all its works mobilizing those who had benefitted least from the Irish bubble. In Dublin West, where richer precincts went 70 per cent for the Treaty, poorer neghbourhoods voted 80 per cent against. The sociological divide essentially matched Dutch and French patterns.

Consternation in Brussels was no less. This time, however, it was not two of the founding Six, one of them long the most powerful member of the Community, whose electors had produced the wrong result, but one of the smallest states, peripheral in history and position, in the Union. Official fury was thus more openly and brutally expressed. The Treaty of Lisbon, moreover, was the joint creation of Berlin and Paris, an alignment not accustomed to being trifled with in matters of high concern in the EU. Steinmeier in Germany, treating Community law with the disdain of a Bethmann-Hollweg, threatened Ireland with expulsion from the Union—'exiting the integration process'—if it did not comply with the wishes of the *Aussenamt* and its partners. In France, Sarkozy announced without further ado that 'the Irish must hold a second referendum' to expunge the verdict of the first. Much of the media outcry was even more violent, leading organs of opinion in Germany, in particular, drawing the lesson that it was folly to submit any proposal for European unity to the popular will. But as matters stood there was little to be done. The Fianna Fáil regime in Dublin, after a decade in office by now deeply unpopular, was unlikely to take the risk of a second rebuff that might prove worse than the first.

Three months later, Lehman Brothers filed for bankruptcy in New York, triggering the worst financial collapse since the Great Depression. The impact on Europe of the crash in America was—*mondialisation oblige*—much quicker this time, putting paid to any notion of a decoupling of EU and US economies. By the end of 2008, Eurozone GDP had fallen more steeply even than American. Denmark, long hailed as the star performer in the labour market flexibility demanded by all right-thinking reformers, was the first to plunge into recession. Germany, the strongest economy in the Union, was soon suffering a sharper contraction of output than France or Italy, as export markets dived. Worst hit were the two countries that had posted the highest growth rates in the EU since monetary union, Spain and Ireland, in each case primed by real estate speculation. By early 2009, Spanish unemployment was over 20 per cent. The crisis struck hardest of all in Ireland, where output contracted by 8.5 per cent between the first quarters of 2008 and 2009, and the fiscal deficit soared to over 15 per cent of GDP. Though a probable death warrant for the regime in place at the next polls, in the short run the debacle of the Celtic Tiger was a diplomatic godsend to it. Amid popular panic, the government could now count on frightening voters into accepting Lisbon, however irrelevant it might be to the fate of the Irish economy.

But if the Treaty—which in June 2009 received the blessing of the German Constitutional Court, in an opinion dismissing in the same breath the claims of the European Parliament to any democratic legitimacy[1]—could now henceforward be railroaded through, under cover of the economic crisis, it bore no solutions for the crisis in the Eurozone itself. There, each national government took its own steps to deal with the emergency, with ad hoc measures to bail out banks, feed auto industries or prop up the labour market—Germany, protesting in theory, leading the way in practice. Nine months into the crisis, no coordinated strategy for dealing with it had materialized; spreads in the bond market were widening, forcing up yields in Italy, Spain, Portugal and

---

1. In an opinion written by the same judge, Udo Di Fabio, who in 2005 gratified the political establishment by tearing up the country's ban on governments fixing the time of elections at their own convenience. Of immigrant descent, Di Fabio is the Clarence Thomas of the Federal Republic, nominated to the court by the CDU, and author of the neo-conservative tract *Die Kultur der Freiheit*, lauding vigorous market competition, attacking excessive welfare dependency, and calling for a return to the values of family, religion and nation—what, updating a pre-war formula, might be called *Kinder, Firma, Kirche*, with a topping of *Volk*. The Germans had been tempted away from these and other expressions of their better nature by Hitler, who was no true German, lacking 'any drop of the decency of the Prussian servant of the state, the attachment to home and zest for life of Bavarian Catholicism, any inclination to diligence and hard work, any sense of German ways of living, of bourgeois habits and Christian traditions'. After recovering these values in the 'Golden Age' of the 1950s, Germans were now in danger of letting them crumble to a myopic hedonism, deleterious residue of the sixties: *Die Kultur der Freiheit*, Munich 2005, pp. 207, 212, 217ff—a work itself national enough in genre, what might ungenerously be called philosophical airport literature.

Greece; the Baltic economies were in free fall; the IMF was staving off bank-runs in Hungary, Romania and Bulgaria. How deep the rot has gone in the EU, and how long it might persist, has yet to be seen. What is clear is that monetary union, though it created a stable currency, has been no cure for long-standing weaknesses of the continental economies. The low interest rate regime of the European Central Bank had fuelled bubbles in Spain, Ireland and the Baltics. More generally, not merely did per capita income in the Eurozone rise more slowly between 1999 and 2008 than in the previous decade. Productivity growth actually halved. By the spring of 2009, EU unemployment was still lower than in the US, but the exposure of European banks looked significantly worse. In April, the IMF estimated that out of a total of $2.3 trillion in toxic assets poisoning the world's banking system, over half—$1.4 trillion—were held by European banks, as against $1 trillion by US banks. Write-downs in Europe were still a fraction—just a fifth—of those in America, while requirements for recapitalizing the banking system to the levels of the mid-nineties were reckoned to be nearly double.

Compared with the collapse of Wall Street in 1929, the financial crash of 2008—born of a much more explosive creation of credit—has had swifter and wider effects on the real economy across the world. Whether a comparable slump ensues is another matter, if only because all leading states of the advanced industrial world have flooded their markets with injections of public capital of one kind or another that came only haltingly and controversially in the 1930s. Just as the deregulations of the previous period were, if in differing degrees, more or less unanimous across time zones, so the bailouts of the present period have, at any rate so far, been common wisdom—whatever the doubts expressed, here and there, about their consequences in the longer term. In the blink of an eye, a *pensée unique* has become a *pénitence unique*, no less herd-like. Where in the inter-war period heterodox doctrines and iconoclastic recipes, of various sorts, were waiting in the wings, and as the Depression unfolded took central stage, today the intellectual cupboard is bare, and scarcely any alternatives have been canvassed in public debate. How long that will last is anyone's guess. What seems clear is that the crisis, if it persists, is likely to put increasing social pressure on the existing state of the EU, in which there is neither effective policy coordination nor operative national autonomy. Growing unemployment and economic distress could drive the Union in either a centrifugal or a centripetal direction: towards divergent solutions dictated by national imperatives to protect local populations, or towards deepening integration, whose most probable forms would be extension of the single market to services, harmonization of tax regimes, and creation of a common European bond market.

2

At the turn of the century, looking back at his account of the origins of the post-war Common Market, the greatest historian of European integration asked himself what might now lie in store for it, with the arrival of monetary union.[2] Milward had argued that the EEC, far from bringing any diminution of the nation-states that founded it, helped restore them to life after the catastrophes of the Second World War by delivering to their populations a material security, at once internal and external, that they had never before enjoyed. Governments answerable to voters had chosen to pool some of their prerogatives, in order to reconstruct their legitimacy by enhancing their ability to satisfy voters. Forty years later, did the same logic hold? Structurally, Milward thought, it did. Whether integration proceeded, stalled or regressed would depend, as it had always done, on its compatibility with the domestic policy choices of national governments. But in the interim, a sea-change had taken place in the way their economies were managed. Since the eighties, growth had slowed, and not only had competitive capacity declined, but social solidarity with it. Full employment and the provision of welfare—keystones of the original rehabilitation of the European nation-state—had ceased to be common priorities. The new imperatives were control of inflation, and deregulation of markets to enforce it. It was the demands of these, allied to traditional concern for the containment of Germany, that had led to a single currency and the European Central Bank at Maastricht.

Where did this leave the nation-state that was saved by the Community? 'Since all history is change, that rescue could only be temporary', for 'the process of economic development itself has eroded the political consensus which sustained both nation and supranation after the war'.[3] That did not mean the Community

---

2. Alan Milward, 'Envoi', to the second edition of *The European Rescue of the Nation-State*, London 2000, pp. 425–36.

3. 'Envoi', p. 428.

was doomed, but its destiny was now uncertain. A major
international currency managed by a central bank answerable to
no government was without precedent. It was pointless to blame
Brussels or Strasbourg for the absence of a democracy in which
the ECB might be rendered accountable. Voters would only
take the European Parliament seriously if it acquired powers of
taxation, but its lack of them—like the unelected character of the
Commission—was not any unintended flaw of the EU, but the
deliberate choice of the national governments, each democratically
elected, that had created it. 'If that however is construed as
evidence that the nation-states themselves are not truly democratic,
or that in internationalizing policies they are seeking to restrict
the force of postwar democratic pressures', Milward concluded
grimly, it was difficult to object. 'Indeed there is much to suggest
that the post-war role of more democratic political parties in
formulating the immediate post-war domestic policy choices on
which consensus depended was only a temporary phase and that
these parties, especially since 1968, have become increasingly part
of the executive'.[4] Since 1968 . . . The date, and all it implies,
says enough. Tacitly, what needed to be rescued now was not the
nation-state, but democracy within it. Or even beyond it? Forces
might emerge to propel integration further, but everything would
depend on their political nature. 'In whose interests will the brutal
power of the state continue to exist? Who will run it? And for
whom? It is the answers to these questions which will determine
the future of the European Union'.

Written as the euro came into being, these lines found their first
response six years later, in the pitched battle when the European
Constitution was submitted to a popular vote. Milward's blunt
voice, with its characteristic ironies, came from England. What of
later judgements from the core continental cultures? In France, the
country's leading authority on integration, Renaud Dehousse—a
Belgian—reacted to the result of the French referendum with
a work entitled, misleadingly, *La fin de l'Europe*. The Union,
he remarked, might be compared to the bourgeois societies
of the nineteenth century, that had replaced absolutism with
constitutions that, while they protected the liberties of the subject,
ignored women and the poor.[5] It had, in effect, yet to pass from
a censitary liberalism to a citizens' democracy. But the principles

---

4. 'Envoi', pp. 435–6.
5. Renaud Dehousse, *La fin de l'Europe*, Paris 2005, p. 71.

of such an order should be understood realistically. Neither of the opposite camps in the French referendum had grasped them. The Constitutional Treaty itself, a document opening with grotesque flourishes of diplomatic anachronism, had been touted with a rhetoric of novelty that concealed its substantial continuity with past instruments of integration, to the point that most of the fire directed against it had fastened on to an *acquis communautaire* already long embodied in the Union—imperatives of the free market, allegiance to NATO inscribed in the treaties of Nice and Amsterdam—as if these were provocative innovations, rather than on the modest though useful institutional changes it did contain. But, of course, electors had never been much informed, let alone consulted, about the *acquis*, and were anyway little interested in the intricacies of institutional machinery. They had divided into two social blocs over their perceptions of what the EU represented to them: workers, the young, the least well-off and educated, but also now a significant layer of the middle class—all those exposed to the costs and risks of the economic and social development of the past decades—against all those who stood or hoped to gain from them.

The Constitution had failed because it offered no concrete project that could have overcome this division. For legitimacy in the EU came from the output rather than the input side of its institutions—not abstract principles of accountability or subsidiarity, but the practical benefits it could deliver. This did not mean that Moravcsik's apology for the status quo, dismissing any concern with a democratic will at Union level, was valid. The French referendum had revealed a crisis of legitimacy in the EU, and one that was not unfounded, since decisions in Brussels had a real impact on national social policies, without electorates having any say in them—politicians indeed typically shifting blame to the Commission. Modernization was not a neutral process. It involved winners and losers. It could not be sealed off as a technical arena from democratic conflict. But if the Constitutional Treaty had been unable to convey any compelling project to European publics, that was because no consensus—of the kind that had informed the Community after the war—any longer existed as to the raison d'être of the Union. As objectives for Europe, neither international autonomy, nor social solidarity, nor even just a free trade zone, commanded any general agreement. But this was not set in stone. The EU will be judged by what it does, not what it is. Foreign policy ambitions should be set aside. The public goods the

Union could offer are protection of the environment and income support for the worst-off. A European social pact should not be beyond reach.

If little in Dehousse's analysis appeared to warrant this prospect, or perhaps simply proposal, its general tone remained relatively sanguine, if compared with the most conspicuous German reaction to the same conjuncture. Jürgen Habermas, who had signed one of the most intoxicated appeals to French voters to ratify the European Constitution, on pain of nothing less than regression to barbarism, dried out in the aftermath. *Ach, Europa*, which records his subsequent interventions on the EU, offers a chart of the process. The Treaty of Lisbon, though little more than a decorous Xerox of the same Constitution, met with a very different reception. For Habermas, it offered no solution to either the democratic deficit of the Union or its lack of any moral-political finality. It could only 'cement the existing chasm between political elites and citizens', without supplying any positive direction to Europe.[6] The problems the EU needed to tackle were plain. The nation-state was being drained of much of its substance, without the Union gaining powers to compensate for what it had lost. The market, no longer tamed by social rules, was increasing inequality and threatening the environment. The international scene was wanting in any united action from Europe to uphold international law and reform the UN.

The requisite solutions were clear too. The ability of citizens freely to shape the forms of their political life must be restored to them at EU level, with a harmonization of fiscal and socio-economic policies across the Union. The EU should acquire its own financial resources, and military forces capable of intervening to protect human rights around the world. For that role it needed not only a foreign minister, but a directly elected President. Time was running out to achieve these essential goals. Their urgency was so immediate that Habermas called for a Europe-wide referendum on them to coincide with the next elections to the European Parliament, due in 2009, with the requirement of a double majority—of states and of votes—for their approval. That demanded polarization. If such a referendum was not held by then, 'the future of the European Union will be settled along orthodox neo-liberal lines'.[7]

---

6. Jürgen Habermas, *Ach, Europa. Kleine politische Schriften XI*, Frankfurt 2008, p. 105.

7. *Ach, Europa*, p. 85.

The peremptory passion of these declarations has little, if any, precedent in Habermas's writing. Few of his readers could fail to be impressed by them. But if they honour him, they also lead him into contradiction. This is not just because the theorist of consensus has belatedly discovered the virtues of polarization. However much at variance this may be with the discourse ethics he has advocated for so long, it is an awakening that can only be welcomed. More embarrassing is that his call for direct popular consultation on the future of the EU cannot easily escape the charge of political occasionalism, since though long consistent in his support for a European Constitution, neither earlier nor later had Habermas shown any enthusiasm for referenda on the issues confronting Europe. Far from calling for the Germans to be allowed to vote on Maastricht, as were the French, let alone on EU enlargement, he not only contented himself with the rubber-stamping of them by the *Stimmvieh* of the Bundestag, but did so even more flagrantly when the Constititional Treaty was on the table, taking it upon himself to intervene in the French referendum without so much as a word about the absence of any popular vote in his own country. Nor were his criticisms of the Lisbon Treaty followed by any trace of support for the campaign against it in Ireland, whose referendum was merely registered—passively, after the event—as a caution to European elites.

Indeed, though now describing the role of intellectuals as an avant-garde 'early warning system', alerting society to problems over the horizon, Habermas himself showed little awareness of the extent of mass disaffection from the *arcana imperii* of Brussels until after the debacle of the Constitutional Treaty, and even in 2007 was still arguing that European populations were much more favourably disposed to integration than elites. On such grounds he urged the SPD in Germany to take up the blue and gold banner to dish the Linke—advice making clear that no domestic radicalization of outlook is in question. Once a Hegelian Marxist, he explained, he had become a Kantian pragmatist. Class society had disappeared in Europe: there was now just a society of citizens.

Why then was he pulling the emergency cord in the European caboose so vigorously? Essentially, it would seem, because of a disappointment—not in the first instance with the EU as such, but with the US. For one who had so long proclaimed a philosophical allegiance to the West, the war in Iraq, launched without the seal of the UN, had come as an affliction. If the West was to recover its balance, and reputation, it was vital that Europe be capable of acting as a genuine partner of America, and—where necessary—restraining it from ill-considered reactions to common dangers. What was needed now was a 'bi-polar community of the West', committed to reforming the United Nations in the inspiring tradition of Roosevelt, by reducing the number of regional players within it, and equipping it with effective powers of global governance, to safeguard international security and enforce respect for human rights. The two poles of that community could not, of course, be absolutely equal. For America was not only the world's sole superpower, it was 'the oldest democracy on earth, that lives on idealistic traditions and has opened itself more than any other nation, in the spirit of the eighteenth century, to universalism'.[8] But was it realistic to think it could push the necessary changes through without a loyal European partner at its side, independent of mind, but free of the slightest tremor of anti-Americanism?

Habermas's prescription for the missing 'finality' of the Union was thus much more sweeping than that of Dehousse, and its upshot virtually the opposite. Far from renouncing external ambitions, the EU should increase them, for 'foreign policy decisions, since they affect existential needs for security and deep-rooted outlooks, are always of high symbolic value for the population concerned'.[9] So long as the Union has not acquired the powers of a unitary international actor, one opportunity after another for such initiatives will go on being tragically missed. The example Habermas gives makes it clear how close the EU of his desire would cleave to the US. If only Europe could in 2007 have stationed a 'neutral force in the Middle East, for the first time since the foundation of Israel'—translated: instead of mere national contingents from France or Italy, with the German navy patrolling off the coast, a proper EU *glacis* for Tel Aviv in the zone of Lebanon invaded by the IDF. An independent foreign policy along these lines is unlikely to be much of a symbolic beacon to the European masses. In due course, with the arrival of a Democratic administration in Washington as 'idealist and universalist' as any admirer could wish, it will seem less urgent to Habermas too.

---

8. *Ach, Europa*, pp. 121–2.

9. *Ach, Europa*, p. 110. The relative weight of internal and external motives in Habermas's 'Plaidoyer für eine Politik der abgestuften Integration' can be judged from the space accorded each: about twice as much for the latter as the former.

Now that the bugbear of Bush is gone, Europe can surely relax. The lack of any EU-wide referendum is no longer likely to arouse much protest from its advocate. Whatever its limitations, Lisbon will no doubt be quietly pocketed after all.

No punctual intervention, but a panoramic synthesis, Stefano Bartolini's *Restructuring Europe* (2005) confirms Italy's claim to be the continental culture that has produced the most serious literature on the Union. Like Majone's work, the book appeared—a not insignificant fact—in English, rather than the author's native language, though unlike Majone's, Bartolini's career has been entirely Italian. In many ways, *Restructuring Europe* can regarded as the first really commanding study of the EU whose provenance is not Anglo-American. Its starting-point is calmly heterodox, a kind of historical thought-experiment. Everyone says the EU is not a state. But why not view the Union as if, rather than the opposite of the classical nation-state, it were a further development of it—how would it then look? With a tool-kit taken from Hirschman and Rokkan, Bartolini tracks back to the origins of the European state system, reconstructing the emergence of the nation-states we know today in five phases: first coercive, from feudalism to absolutism; then capitalist, with markets emerging in regions where coercion was least centralized; then national, with linguistic and cultural homogenization; then democratic, with the generalization of suffrage; and finally social-sharing, with the creation of welfare systems. The cumulative result of this long history was a fusion of war-making, commercial, national, constitutional and welfare functions within a coincidence of military, economic, cultural, political and social boundaries. In this development, the key components were the 'system-building' processes—creation of national identities, growth of political participation and arrival of social security.

Might the EU then become a sixth phase of state-formation, recapitulating on a continental scale the original five across a population of 450 million and a landmass of four million square kilometres? After 1945, integration was driven by the consequences of the Second World War, when the nation-states of Europe ceased to be self-sufficient military or economic capsules—control of security and monetary policies passing across the Atlantic. The unbearable costs of military competition and the risks of economic peripheralization had brought the Community into being, but in doing so they had broken up the coherence of the boundaries that had defined the nation-state. Maastricht could be seen as a bid to re-Europeanize monetary and security policies, but what is the balance sheet of the other dimensions of state-formation?

Bartolini's verdict is bleak. Certainly, 'centre-formation' has developed apace, amid competition between Commission, Council, Parliament, and Court of Justice, leading to expansion of competences in many a direction. But Majone's analogy of the resulting complex with the mixed constitution of mediaeval estates holds no water, since its lines of technocratic or commercial division are never clear-cut. Instead Brussels is a lair of decisional processes of staggering complexity, confounding executive and legislative functions—no less than thirty-two different procedures that 'only specialist lawyers and trained functionaries can follow'.[10] Three-quarters of the Council's decisions, approved without discussion, are pre-packaged for it in the obscure recesses of Coreper; while at a lower level, hidden from public gaze, subterranean connexions between national bureaucracies and the machinery of the Community multiply. Ninety per cent of the lobbies infesting the extended committee system in Brussels are business organizations of one kind another. Trade-union, environmental, consumer, feminist, or other 'public interest groups', by contrast, make up, all told, about 5 per cent. In real terms, the budget administered by the Commission amounted in the nineties to less than 1 per cent of Union GDP. Of this, by the end of the decade about a third was spent on Cohesion Funds, more redistributive territorially than socially. Overall, social expenditure by the EU is a miniscule one-hundredth of the total laid out by national governments. In such conditions, no 'visible or significant relevant layer of European social citizenship' exists. Monetary union, on the other hand, has created an extremely strong economic boundary for the Eurozone, patrolled by the ECB. But, so far, lacking any institutional goals other than price stability, it 'looks more like a rigid system for disciplining member states' behaviours rather than like an instrument functional to common EU interests and economic hegemony'.[11] With the beginnings of common immigration and crime control, internal security has moved into the area of Union competences, and with it some of the attributes of a coercive boundary. Last but not least,

---

10.   Stefano Bartolini, *Restructuring Europe. Centre formation, system building and political structuring between the nation-state and the European Union*, Oxford 2005, pp. 157–8.

11.   *Restructuring Europe*, pp. 284, 233, 198.

the European Court of Justice has steadily expanded the reach of its field of jurisdiction into new areas of law—most recently, and signficantly, labour law.

Set against this—still selective—accumulation of powers above, the processes that in the development of the nation-state created a complementary loyalty and identity below remain nugatory. 'Linguistic fragmentation remains an insurmountable obstacle to any mass level symbolic interaction'. The use of English is spreading, but as a global not a European standard, effacing rather than tracing any cultural boundary between the Union and the world. Political representation is scarcely more than notional, in a European Parliament whose assorted blocs are so heterogeneous that their divisions can be sublimated only because the assembly itself is so invisible and its deliberations so inconsequential domestically. European parties, so-called, neither compete for electoral rewards nor answer to any real political responsibility. They do not aggregate or channel citizens' demands in the fashion of their national counterparts, but act to dilute or suppress them. The most salient feature of their representatives is absenteeism: less than half the members of the European Parliament even bother to turn up for its resolutions, where the average attendance at votes is a mere 45 per cent.[12] Not that the EP lacks all significance, since it too has benefitted from some, partly unintended, institutional creep within the competing peak instances of the Union. But practically speaking, its main effect has been to insulate the core phenomenon of the EU as a political process, 'elite consolidation', from popular scrutiny or contestation.

This is a system that Bartolini dubs 'collusive democracy', in which elites make sure electorates cannot divide over questions to which they have no access. In such a system, issues of legitimacy—over which European elites occasionally agonize, to comic effect—never arise. For legitimacy involves, by definition, principles, for which mere performance—capable at most of securing a passive assent, something very different—can never be a substitute. The resulting order is incoherent. The nation-state, relinquishing control of its economic, legal and administrative boundaries, has attempted to retrench itself behind its cultural, social and political boundaries. But these, penetrated and eroded by the larger space

---

12. *Restructuring Europe*, p. 331. Even on the most significant votes taken by the Parliament, under the procedure of co-decision, a third of MEPs never show up.

surrounding them, are no longer what they were. Rather than
any clear demarcation or division of labour between the two
zones, of the kind imagined by Majone or Moravcsik, there is
incongruity and incompatibility. The social and political life of
its nations cannot be quarantined from the impact—infection for
some, medication for others—of the economic, bureaucratic and
judicial operations of the Union. The processes that historically
went to build the nation-state have not been recapitulated, but
unscrambled and disjoined. Critically, European integration has
seen an 'enormous expansion of socio-economic practices that
bear no or little relation to social identities and to decisional
rules'. Bartolini's conclusion affords no comfort. If acute conflicts
are not to arise in future, 'the scattered elements of identities,
interests and institutions need to be reconciled in some way into
a new coherent order'.[13] But any such way remains obscure. At
the head of the book stands an epigraph from Goethe: *Am Ende
hängen wir doch ab / Von Kreaturen, die wir machten*. The words
come from Mephistopheles; the creature is a homunculus; the
next scene Walpurgis Night.

3

What of the Union viewed in still a longer *durée*, that of European
civilization itself? Since 2001, Brussels has possessed an official
Museum of Europe, affording its citizens a historical tour of the
continent's past, culminating in the common institutions it has
acquired today. The conception inspiring it has been explained
by its academic director, the Franco-Polish historian Krzysztof
Pomian, in the pages of *Le Débat*, of which he is a co-editor,
and finds extended expression in both his *L'Europe et ses nations*
(1990) and a work co-authored with Elie Barnavi, *La révolution
européenne 1945–2007*, which appeared in 2008.[14] It can be
regarded as the nearest thing to a canonical version of Europe's
route to its present condition.

Pomian's story unfolds in three great stages. Between 1000
and 1500, Europe formed a religious, cultural and social unity
co-extensive with Latin Christianity, defined by common beliefs,

---

13. *Restructuring Europe*, pp. 410–12.

14. For Pomian's programmatic statement as director of the Museum, see
'Pour une musée de l'Europe. Visite commentée d'une exposition en projet', *Le
Débat*, No. 129, March–April 2004, pp. 89–100.

practices and institutions, replicated across the continent as far as the reach of the Roman creed. This first unification of the continent was destroyed by the Wars of Religion, which erupted with the Reformation, and lasted till the end of the seventeenth century. When these finally burnt themselves out, the arrival of the Enlightenment brought a second unification of Europe, across a more extended space, with a cosmopolitan republic of letters and a common court culture that eventually fused into a single ambience shared by all the elites of the period. This unity was in its turn undone by the explosion of the French Revolution and its Napoleonic sequel, unleashing not only popular but nationalist passions across the continent. These set in motion the fatal dynamic that would ultimately generate the Wars of Ideology of the twentieth century, when totalitarian creeds—exacerbated nationalism, fascism, bolshevism—shattered Europe in successive catastrophic conflicts. Out of these, however, emerged the third great unification of Europe: this time, no longer a by-product of other forces, as in the past, but a deliberate project—the construction of the economic and juridical Community we enjoy today. The immediate conditions of this unification lie in the defeat of fascism, the end of colonialism, the collapse of communism, the modernization of economies and life-styles. But at a deeper historical level, it would not have been possible without nostalgia for the second unification of the Enlightenment, just as the second would not have been possible without the legacy of Christianity in the first. It is the sedimentation of these successive strata in common memory that anchors European identity today.[15]

This schema has the appeal of symmetry, whatever its limitations, like that of any such proposal, as history. Since mediaeval society had no consciousness of Europe, as opposed to Christendom, and the Enlightenment sense of it was confined to a narrow layer of society, whereas the Community claims both the conscious allegiance and factual inclusion of all citizens, its tale could be summarized in Hegelian terms, as the passage of Europe, through successive ordeals, from a totality in-itself through a selectivity for-itself to a totality in-itself-for-itself. The conclusion of the triad, however, raises a difficulty. The novelty of the continent's third unification is to be a project. But a project for

---

15. Krzysztof Pomian, *L'Europe et ses nations*, Paris 1990, pp. 53–61, 91–117, 219–33; Elie Barnavi and Krzysztof Pomian, *La révolution européenne 1945–2007*, Paris 2008, pp. 261–9.

what? It is precisely the contemporary absence of one—the lack of any coherent or compelling finality—that is a refrain of even such unimpeachably well-disposed observers of the Union as Dehousse or Habermas. What motivating end—or is it ends?—the EU now serves seems to have become increasingly obscure. The building of the institutions that make up the Union was certainly a project. But, once constructed, what is the ultimate purpose of these forms? The sense of a finality lost, or gone astray in bureaucratic doldrums, is pervasive.

This was not always so. In the heroic phase of European integration, its goals were clear: to assure peace to the west of the Iron Curtain, by binding France and Germany into a common legal framework, and prosperity in the Six by creating a semi-continental market. In Milward's succinct formulation, the Community served to bring security to the population of its member-states—security in both senses, national and social, by the elimination of any risk of a third round of war between the two leading states of the region, and the provision of faster growth, higher living standards and more welfare protection. Retrospectively, it is less clear than it seemed at the time that integration was the indispensable keystone of these. The imperial order of the *pax americana*, more than any local endeavour, guaranteed the tranquillity of Western Europe. The increment to overall growth yielded by the common market was, historically speaking, quite modest, because of the similarity in output structures of the assorted national economies. The most careful recent study estimates that, taking together the creation of the Common Market, the passage of the Single European Act, and the introduction of Monetary Union, the net addition to GDP growth in the EU has been, over half a century, perhaps some 5 percent, not an overwhelming figure.[16]

Such calculations aside, however, by the eighties, neither peace nor prosperity was any longer much of a positive inspiration within

---

16. Andrea Boltho and Barry Eichengreen, 'The Economic Impact of European Integration', Discussion Paper No. 6820, Centre for Economic Policy Research, May 2008, p. 44. Based on a series of careful counterfactual controls, they conclude that the Common Market may have increased GDP by 3–4 per cent from the late fifties to the mid-seventies; that the impact of the EMS was negligible; that the Single European Act may have added around another 1 per cent; and that it is unlikely that Monetary Union has had 'more than a very small effect on the area's growth rate or even level of output': pp. 27, 29, 34, 38. These are findings of authors who, as they point out, have always been, and remain, favourable to integration.

the Community. Two generations after the war, they were taken for granted by most of its citizens, many of them aware that growth had been no less, and in some cases more, elsewhere. Victory in the Cold War made threats of invasion even more remote, and while the promise of higher living standards was once again a powerful force of attraction in the Union's enlargement to the East, citizens in the West, comprising three-quarters of its population, were no longer greatly excited by them. In the discourses of justification, official and unofficial, the emphasis shifted to solidarity, as a specially—perhaps even, in some measure, uniquely—defining value of the Union. Here European welfare systems and income distribution have been regularly contrasted with those of the United States, as more generous and less unequal.

There is little doubt that this claim has popular resonance. But though it can point to real differences between social arrangements, within a common matrix, these scarcely amount to a finality of the Union. For there is very little that is EU-specific about them. The provision of welfare remains the province of the nation-states, not of the Community, and varies widely across even Western Europe, not to speak of the continent as a whole. In fact, the range of that variation is such that there are few areas within or without the Union which do not, along one or other dimension of social security, fall within the parameters of one or other state or region of the US, which is much less unlike the mosaic of Europe than is often imagined.[17] The ideology of solidarity is much stronger in Europe than in America. The realities are closer. With predictable reforms from the incoming administration, and ongoing retrenchments by the various European governments, they are likely to become more so.

Of course, in so far as they match a single nation-state of continental dimensions against a congeries of eighteen or—depending on inclusion of the East—near thirty nation-states of widely differing sizes, histories and levels of development, socio-economic comparisons between America and Europe can be taxed with a paralogism. Brussels is not Washington: the Community neither has a central administration, nor is it a global power. But should it not become one? Is not just this the finality that would make of today's Union a coherent project? It is clear that something like this was present from the start, in the mind of Monnet himself,

---

17. See Peter Baldwin's systematic exposition, *The Narcissism of Minor Differences*, New York 2009, passim.

although it was quietly and privately expressed, and many have pressed the case more openly since. In its contemporary versions, it has typically taken two forms, geo-political and ethico-political. For the first, the Union—with a total population and economy now considerably larger those of the United States—must accept the political responsibilities of its objective status as a Great Power in the making.[18] That requires the creation of a European military apparatus and diplomacy capable of executing, and enforcing, a unitary foreign policy, in both adjacent and more far-flung regions of the world. For theorists like Cooper or Münkler the vocation of the Union, so conceived, is to become a new—this time truly benevolent—empire, not in rivalry with but autonomy from the American empire.

For a broader band of opinion, geo-political projections of this kind are neither entirely wholesome nor realistic. The proper mission of Europe on the international scene is rather ethico-political—to become something never seen in this form before, a 'normative power'. In the most radical version, offered by Habermas, the EU, in its constitutional supersession of the nation-state, is blazing humanity's trail towards world government, and needs to take on the tasks appropriate to that ultimate goal, a responsibility which the American republic—admirable though it has always been—is still, as a nation-state, less inherently inclined to fulfil. The United Nations is the universal in which Europe can sublimate, without denying, its own particularity, and seek to constitutionalize the rule of law and human rights for all peoples, by equipping the UN with the necessary machinery—Kant had overlooked this—for punishing those who violate them, whatever the outmoded attributes of national sovereignty.

Sceptical of such aims as too vaulting, the French political scientist Zaki Laïdi, on the right of the PS, proposes a moderate version. Neither a European *Realpolitik* along Cooper–Münkler lines, nor a constitutionalization of the world along Habermasian lines, is practicable, because Europeans do not see themselves as guarantors of their own security. Like the Japanese, they entrust it to the United States. But the EU can play a critical role in the world as a normative power, properly understood. For the Union itself is based on norms, through which alone its member-states

---

18. Populations: EU—470 million; US—330 million. Economies: EU—GDP $18 trillion; US—$14 trillion. See IMF, *World Economic Outlook Database*, April 2009.

have been able to pool their sovereignty without relinquishing it. In developing these norms—the Copenhagen criteria can be taken as a benchmark—the EU has become, not a model, but something more useful, a tool-box for the world, setting global standards in one area after another where the US lags behind: the environment, health care, competition. 'Regulative rather than salvational', there is no point in trying to constitutionalize such norms, since they are anyway dynamic, and evolve over time. Nor can schemes for formal equality between states abolish their real inequality. If normative power is a kind of soft power, soft power is never entirely dissociable from hard power. The EU's creation of thirteen Battle Groups with a strategic range of up to two thousand miles, and neighbourhood dispositions from Moldavia to Morocco—'a classic semi-periphery control policy'—are proof of that. But even if, inevitably, some double standards are involved, essentially the Union 'does geo-politics with norms'.[19]

Like claims for a special European solidarity, aspirations for European autonomy enjoy wide support in public opinion across the EU, at any rate west of the frontiers of the Cold War. But the ideologies expressing them are brittle, and the support is shallow. However much Europeans extol the unique virtues of the Union as a haven of political rectitude, not to speak of moral foresight, there is little sign that the rest of the world is greatly impressed. Policy-makers from Latin America, Asia, Africa or the Middle East are not knocking at the doors of the Competition Commissioner in Brussels, the National Health Service in London, or the German automobile industry for lessons in markets, waiting-lists or emissions. Lectures on human rights ring hollow from governments collaborating with torture. The collusion of the Union with military occupation and ethnic cleansing in Cyprus, and repression of genocide in Turkey, exposes its rescue missions in the Balkans and commemorations of the Shoah as something more than double standards. The autonomy of Europe, conceived as a mission of 'normativity' peculiar to it, is little more than an apologetic for post-moderns.

The less ethico-political versions have the advantage of a greater contact with reality, and smaller freight of euphemisms. Naturally,

---

19. Zaki Laïdi, *Norms over Force: The Enigma of European Power*, New York 2008, pp. 5, 8, 42–50, 120, 33, 129. The English edition is an expanded version of the French original, *La Norme sans la force. L'énigme de la puissance européenne*, Paris 2005.

they too cannot dispense with the equipage of moral rights and duties, any more than could their imperial forebears—Münkler is perfectly lucid about the continuity. But aware that the US can easily rival or outdo the EU in the rhetoric of a liberal civilization, they are less inclined to posit these as quintessentially European. Their conception of autonomy is more limited. Accepting the global imperium of America, they project a Union nested within it, patrolling its own vicinity as a sub-imperial power, in a loyal—if, where necessary, critical—solidarity with the hegemon. This is roughly the vision of the EU adopted by Sarkozy, though not yet by any other continental ruler, and implies more centralized, and on occasion mail-fisted, external operations than Brussels has hitherto been able to mount. As a geo-political prospect, it has a future. The aversion of European publics in recent years to the American role in the world—the sharp turn of French foreign policy towards Washington has not been popular at home—might seem to condemn it. But most of this has been a cultural dislike of Bush and the Republican administration for slighting European sensibilities, rather than any deeper political drift away from identification with the US. Predictably, the arrival of a Democratic administration has already generated even more star-struck enthusiasm for the new president in Europe than in America. In that sense, the conception of a Union stepping up to the plate more boldly on the international scene, without challenging the role of the manager, is likely to be perfectly acceptable. Its limitation lies only in the modest degree of autonomy that would actually be achieved. An EU unable ever to cross the will of the hegemon, on any issue the US holds important to it, is an agent diminished in advance. If this were to be the finality of the Union, it would be in miniature.

There is, however, one further conception of the kind of project that the Union could come to represent, that would connect it to some of the deepest and most persistent meditations of the past. The theme of European diversity, as the true historical signature of the continent, has its roots in Romantic thought and the Restoration. Given an agonistic twist by the end of the nineteenth century, it faded from prominence for much of the twentieth, without ever quite disappearing. But as the Cold War neared its end, it started to find potent new expression. *Penser l'Europe* (1987), by the French sociologist and all-purpose thinker Edgar Morin, was the flagship of its return. Repudiating all idealization or abstraction of Europe, Morin declared that the continent was a complex of opposites. 'We must abandon any Europe that is one, clear, distinct, harmonious, reject any notion of an original European essence or substance, drive out the idea of a European reality that would precede division and antagonism. We must, on the contrary, inscribe it in them'. The unity of Europe could be properly understood only in the light of two principles: dialogic and recursive. The first signified the presence of 'two or more different logics bound together in complex—complementary, competitive, antagonistic—fashion within a unity, in such a way that duality is preserved within it'. The second implied a 'vortex—as of air or water—in which a flux of apparently antagonistic forces become complementary', in a 'self-generating spiral, reacting back on its constituent elements to drive them and integrate them'.[20]

So at the origins of European civilization lie three radically diverse traditions, Classical, Jewish, and Christian, and between their legacies there has been permanent conflict ever since. Christianity in turn divided between Greek and Roman confessions. The Middle Ages were rent by the contest between the Empire and the Papacy, followed by the Great Schism. Bourgeois civilization undermined feudalism, the Reformation burst open the Roman Church, the Renaissance severed the links between faith and reason. Dynastic states split Europe into warring alliances, regulated by a balance of powers. Nation-states shattered the balance, bringing Europe to the apogee of its power, then plunging it into the abyss of suicidal wars, out of which a Community, still limited to production and the market, had arisen. All that had formed modern Europe had divided it, and all that divided it had formed it.

Today, Morin thought, a new awareness was emerging of 'the unparalleled cultural diversity of Europe' as its most precious patrimony, and of the need to forge a common destiny out of it. Europe's future was certainly threatened by industrial decline, demographic shrinkage, and the risks of nuclear extermination. But the most immediate menace confronting it was the totalitarian empire of the USSR. For the conflict between capitalism and socialism, in which Morin had once believed, had long been replaced by the opposition between democracy and totalitarianism. Democracy, above all, thrives on diversity and complexity, but in Europe it needed a second wind. Still, a metamorphosis of the continent had already begun, as what internationally had become little more than a province was

---

20. Edgar Morin, *Penser l'Europe*, Paris 1987, pp. 27–28.

being transformed into a 'meta-nation' capable of yet another Renaissance open to the world.[21]

In this late-twentieth-century version of Guizot's construction, traditional tensions are radicalized into a set of sharper contradictions. The Enlightenment had lauded the plurality of states in Europe. The Romantics had altered this to the value of diversity—not just number, but difference. The Restoration historians had made of diversity also contention—always controlled, however, by compromise. In Morin, Guizot's proviso is gone, replaced by the self-propelling images of the tornado or water-spout. The result is a continual slide back and forth, often in the same sentence, between variety and conflictuality, without a stopping-place in the middle or at either end. Antagonism, disorder, chaos are no less regularly invoked as positive definitions of what has made Europe than are diversity, inventiveness, complementarity, as if there were no difference between them, and no costs to be paid in equating them. European history unfolds in the benevolent medium of dialogue, and ends in the reassuring arms of democracy, two terms often taken to be all but identical in the bosom of a communicative reason. Yet in the same breath conflict does not end in a static compromise, but spirals upwards in a dynamic synthesis, generating new conflict.

But at what point, then, does such conflict becomes irreconcilable, antagonism leaving no space for productive exchange or sensible regulation—*inter arma silent leges*? Morin briefly wonders whether the critical spirit of European culture, the vital negativity that problematizes everything, might be connected with the self-destructive processes that led Europe to disaster, only to wave away the thought with bland advice: 'That cannot be decided. It must also be problematized'. Appropriately enough, the final definition of the creativity of democracy offered by *Penser l'Europe*, squaring all circles in the lively manner of the book, appeals to the very same authority that Ranke, flintier in his vision of diversity, invoked for the creativity of war: 'If democracy tends towards harmony, it is a Heraclitean harmony that integrates conflict'.[22]

Whatever else might be said of it, *Penser l'Europe*, composed with a staccato élan, can certainly be numbered among the most passionate engagements with its subject of the period. However,

---

21. *Penser l'Europe*, pp. 149, 191, 212, 199, 207, 216–17.

22. *Penser l'Europe*, p. 212; Leopold von Ranke, *Die grossen Mächte* (1833) Leipzig 1916 (ed. Meinecke), p. 58.

there is one conspicuous absence in it. In a book about the unity of Europe, Morin had very little to say about the actual Community in which he was living, about which his feelings were plainly cool. This indifference was no doubt related to the strength of his concern, as a former Communist, with the fate of Eastern Europe, at that point still with no prospect of entering the institutions of the prosperous West. But more fundamentally, it can be read as an index of the huge gap between his image of Europe and the ideal that was being increasingly preached, and practised, by the Community as the essence of the new Europe. It was not conflict—above all, not conflict—that was wanted in Brussels. The defining European value, endlessly reiterated at every meeting of the Council, not to speak of pronouncements of the Commission or speeches in the Parliament, was the exact opposite: consensus. So it has remained to this day. In official ideology, such consensus did not, of course, mean uniformity. No attendant value was more infallibly or highly praised than diversity, it too supremely European. Each member-state had its own culture and identity, and—a later discovery—within each nation every region also had its own culture and identity. All were various in their way, but all could agree on matters of common concern, as soon as discussions between them, after a healthy give-and-take, had reached their sensible conclusion.

Although *Penser l'Europe* had no time for consensus, it was noticeable that when he came to the present, Morin was remarkably vague about what kinds of salutary conflict were going to keep the vortex of Europe spiralling upwards. There was ecology, of course, and the revolt against authority and hierarchy of 1968, though this was now some twenty years in the past; and then there were the new regional identities. But his treatment of these was so perfunctory that a Eurocrat might well have felt that Morin's bluff had been called, and that in practice little separated him from the pacification of Brussels, each expounding in their own sphere the virtues of diversity. What neither anticipated were the disconcerting forms this diversity would shortly assume.

4

The blind spot was at once intellectual and political, obscuring concept and reality alike. Conceptually, although it was, and still is, often treated as comparable to them, diversity could never be a value of the same kind as liberty, equality or fraternity.

It has an intuitive appeal, encapsulated in many a popular saying—'variety is the spice of life'; 'it takes all sorts to make a world'—that is not to be discounted.[23] Yet by definition, in any stricter sense, diversity is an empty signifier, including all forms and their opposites. The Third Reich added to the diversity of European governments in the thirties; Ceausescu's regime supplied variegation in the seventies. What is different is not necessarily better or just other; it may be much worse. In current apologies, its validation typically comes from nature: what greater need could there be, for life on earth, than bio-diversity? But nature is a morally indifferent master, as thinkers from Voltaire and Sade to Nietzsche noted, whose law is the survival of the fittest. Its diversity is not juxtaposition, but inter-connected destruction, as much as creation. In this as in other cases, natural references are of no benefit to the cultural cause they are supposed to serve. All they offer is a particularly vivid illustration of the value-blankness of diversity as such, and the impossibility of separating it conceptually from antagonism.

The political myopia was a wider phenomenon. As the Cold War neared its end, immigration had not yet registered on the radar-screen of the European elites as a significant alteration of the post-war landscape. When it eventually did, however, the rhetoric of diversity was at hand to greet it. But now, as the scale of the change sank in, it took more systematic form, in the ideology of multi-culturalism. In North America, where it had originated, this was essentially a response to issues posed by language and race. In Canada, the discourse of multi-culturalism sought both to accommodate the rise of francophone nationalism in Quebec, and to neutralize it by the addition of further communities— Inuit, Amerindian, later Asian—to the roster of cultures entitled to official protection. In the United States, it developed with the growth of black resistance to discrimination and exclusion, more easily handled as the expression of an ethno-cultural identity, and of hispanophone masses, less inclined than earlier arrivals to become monoglot speakers of the state language. Each a historic land of immigration, neither society was confronting questions

---

23. There is a subtle, yet significant, distinction between the connotations of 'variety' and 'diversity'. Typically, the latter attaches to what is different but co-present, whereas the former more often implies alterations of experience over time, as in the lively imagery of folk wisdom. It was these that Fourier theorized in the figure of the Butterfly, in his taxonomy of the passions: *Oeuvres*, Vol. II, Paris 1845, pp. 145–6.

wholly new to it. Multi-culturalism emerged out of long-standing, if evolving, conditions.[24]

Transported to Europe, it was readily adaptable to establishment discourse at Union, if not always at national, level. Diversity of cultures had long been celebrated as one of the attractions of a supranational Community. All that was necessary was to extend the same appeal to differences, not between, but within its member-states, to encompass the new immigrant cultures recently introduced into them. Multi-culturalism fitted the bill perfectly: it was variety without antagonism. But though it bevelled smoothly with the official doctrine that enshrined consensus as the 'Community method', it did not with the surrounding realities of immigration. There were two principal reasons for this. To begin with, no member-state of the EU was founded on overseas immigration, as the United States and Canada always had been and remain, societies whose entire prosperity and identity were constituted, historically, by the arrival of settlers and migrants from other parts of the world, with the elimination or marginalization of earlier inhabitants. In the late nineteenth and early twentieth centuries, there were countries in Europe—France was the leading example, Germany another—that received considerable numbers of immigrants, at times proportionately as many as America. But these entered societies with centuries of continuous cultural and political history behind them, the majority coming from neighbouring lands that were relatively similar, and were assimilated without structural alteration of polity or identity, to a point where little public memory was even left of them.

Post-war immigration has been a very different matter. Not only because, Europe-wide, it has been far larger in scale. But above all, because it has not been intra- but extra-European in origin—the product, essentially, of the decolonization of Europe's overseas possessions and what was once its semi-colonial periphery. This meant, of course, that Europe was soon confronted with racial tensions not unlike those in the United States. There, however, the black population could not be regarded as immigrants and

---

24. Not that its arrival was simply continuous with previous constructions of the 'melting-pot', or failed to serve new functions. The most devastating attack on the new discourse as a cover for inequality has come from the United States, in Walter Benn Michaels's blistering critique *The Trouble with Diversity*, New York 2006. No counterpart exists in Canada, where Multiculturalism Day is now officially celebrated alongside Mother's Day, Father's Day and other such solemnities.

had never historically been regarded or treated as such. But in
Europe this, as the reception of Caribbean immigration in Britain
would show, was—very relatively speaking—the lesser flash-
point. The larger one, although the two could rarely be separated
in practice, was not race, but religion. Well over half the new
immigrants were Muslim. The ideology of multi-culturalism
underwent, accordingly, a functional mutation in Europe. With
a slide in the meaning of culture from folkways to belief-systems,
it became primarily a doctrine of the values of inter-confessional,
rather than inter-ethnic, diversity. The regression involved in
this move needs little emphasis: where the Enlightenment, not to
speak of radical and socialist movements, had looked forward to
the disappearance of supernatural beliefs, official and left-liberal
opinion now celebrated their multiplication, as if the more religion
there was, the better. Typically, of course, proponents of the
doctrine did not themselves adhere to any faith, as they celebrated
the underlying harmony of believers, themselves generally well
aware of the historic enmity, and continuing incompatibility, of
their creeds.

The effect of this twist to the tropes of diversity was, inevitably,
a massive repression of the realities of the new immigration in
Europe, where the bland pieties of multi-cultural discourse had
little connection with the harsh trends under way. By 2009, there
were estimated to be some 15 to 18 million Muslim migrants in
the richer western states of the EU, comprising a population of
375 million, with the major concentrations in France (perhaps
5.5 million) and Germany (3.6 million), followed by Britain (1.6
million), the Netherlands, Italy and Spain (1 million or so each).
Such figures are only rough reckonings, but as percentages they
are not large. With the decline of native birth rates below net
reproduction levels, however, the proportions are increasing,
principally in the big cities where the majority of the newcomers
are located. In Brussels, the capital of the EU itself, over half
the children born every year are from Muslim immigrants. In
Amsterdam, there are more practising Muslims than either
Protestants or Catholics. In London an eighth of the population is
Muslim. In the major cities of Germany, nearly half the children
under fifteen are now from immigrant families. The overall inflow
of migrants into Europe is currently some 1.7 million a year, in
the same region as legal and illegal immigration to the US. Poverty
and unemployment in these communities is nearly always above
the national average, discrimination pervasive, and endogamy

high. Nowhere does popular opinion favour the presence of the recent arrivals, and in a number of countries—France, Denmark, the Netherlands and Italy have been the most prominent to date— political parties have arisen whose appeal has been based on xenophobic opposition to it. The new diversity has not fostered harmony. It has stoked conflict.

In the rapidly increasing—scholarly and sensational—literature devoted to immigration within the Union, the most striking contribution has once again come not from Europe itself, but from the United States. Christopher Caldwell's *Reflections on the Revolution in Europe* breaks free from the prevailing morass of sanctimony and evasion surrounding the subject by the clarity of its historical analysis and sharpness of its comparative perspective. Over the past quarter of a century, Caldwell points out, America's success in integrating the most recent of its great waves of immigrants—there are now thirty-five million foreign-born citizens in the US—has rested on a set of conditions that have never obtained in Europe. A long-standing and extremely powerful machinery of ideological assimilation—'procrustean pressures on immigrants to conform'—was in place. The continent still contained a great deal of empty space. The overwhelming bulk of the newcomers came from the Catholic societies of Latin America, cultures more akin than alien to standard US patterns. They found employment in an economy that was already moving rapidly away from traditional industries to services, creating a continually expanding range of low-wage jobs, demanding few skills. They are less stigmatized by colour, or imputed criminality, than native-born blacks, avoiding mass incarceration and automatic occupation of the lowest rungs in social esteem. Even so, resistance to further arrivals, focussing on the estimated eleven million illegal immigrants in the country, has been rising.

In Europe, on the other hand, post-war immigration started as a short-run makeshift to meet labour shortages in traditional branches of industry, many soon in decline, leaving migrants in them high and dry, when they were not sent home as temporary *Gastarbeiter* anyway. Their assimilation was never a major preoccupation or programme of the state, and no social consensus was ever constructed around the need for permanent immigrant populations, which—after formal barriers went up in the seventies—continued to grow as families sought reunion and refugees asylum. With de-industrialization, high rates of unemployment in the new communities showed the economic gains from migrant labour had often been fleeting, and criminalization soon set in—the proportion of the prison population in France composed of young male immigrants approaching American levels for young male blacks. Above all, by far the largest contingent of immigrants came from the Islamic world, not only culturally distant from Europe, but set against it by a long history of mutual hostilities. However disparate by region of origin— Turks in Germany, Subcontinentals in Britain, North and sub-Saharan Africans in France—all are exposed, Caldwell insists, to contemporary forms of Muslim ideology violently inimical to the West. The net result is that by the new century, Europe has blundered unawares into an explosive political problem, that is liable to become steadily more acute as the weight of immigrants in the population rises. The persistence of its elites in minimizing it is not shared by the masses who live closest to it. Only the general economic crisis now gripping the EU is a larger issue for the peoples of the Union.[25]

Caldwell sets out to avoid, as he says, either euphemism or alarmism. In the first, he certainly succeeds. In the second, as the title of his book suggests, much less so. In this, *Reflections on the Revolution in Europe* is not unlike Robert Kagan's *Of Paradise and Power*, each offering lucid and hard-headed comparisons between America and Europe—much more compelling about both the US and the EU than conventional liberal wisdom—embedded within a global framework of uncritical neo-conservative assumptions about the world at large. In each case, the locus of aberration is the Middle East, treated as a furnace of terrorist dangers and failed states threatening the West, and casting a baleful glow onto Muslim mindscapes in Europe. The spread of radical Islam is the great danger. If *Reflections on the Revolution in Europe* conceives Salafism much as Burke once did Jacobinism—another 'armed doctrine'—this is in part because of the way religion as such figures in its argument, taken much more seriously, in a fideist American tradition, than is usual in Europe. Dismissing the *bien-pensant* cant that all major religions are basically at one with each other, Caldwell points to the long and sanguinary record of hostility between the worlds of Christianity and Islam as reason for doubting that growing Muslim populations will be easily integrated into Europe, and expecting an increase in confessional

---

25. Christopher Caldwell, *Reflections on the Revolution in Europe*, pp. 3–4, 9–10, 29–30, 127–31, 19.

tensions instead. Ancient belief-systems, on this view, matter, and the animosities between them are not arbitrary, but rooted in doctrinal incompatibility and historical experience.

Completely missing from this account, however, is not only the racist hostility and humiliation widely experienced by Muslim, and other non-European, immigrants at the hands of the rich white state and its officials—police, customs and immigration, benefits—within the Union.[26] Also lacking, no less completely, is any sense of the political basis of contemporary Arab—and by extension, wider Muslim—anger at the West. Imperialist control of the Middle East has been, and remains, perfectly secular, and it is manifestly this massive system of intrusion and domination—compounded, it is true, by the implantation of a theologically justified settler state in Israel—that, far more than differences between the Bible and the Koran, fuels hatred of the infidel. Muslim communities in the EU live under states that collaborate without shame or compunction in Western dominion over the Middle East—the British part in the invasion of Iraq, and the gratuitous installation of a French naval base in the Gulf are the only the latest examples in a long record. It would be surprising if they were quite unmoved by it.

But from this to visions of the EU as a 'giant safe-house' for terrorists is a long way.[27] The obvious reality is that for the vast majority of Muslims in Europe, religion functions as the protective shell of uprooted and vulnerable communities, rather than as a call to battle against the surrounding societies. Where collective revolt breaks out—the riots in the French *banlieues* are the classic case—it is typically among the least religiously minded of the immigrant populations, disaffected jobless youth. Between praying at the mosque and torching automobiles, there is a wide social gap. What it points to is the underlying reason why the salience of Islam is so easily exaggerated in the literature of alarmism. Immigration to Europe is driven by hopes of economic betterment—political flight is rarer—that are themselves entirely secular. If these are bruised or frustrated, religious consolation can intensify. But the

---

26. Caldwell explains that his book is about the problems immigration poses local populations, not the problems of immigrants, real though these are. But since he speculates at some length about the subjective attitudes of Muslims in Europe, it is difficult to see how their objective situations can, by his own logic, be legitimately bracketed.

27. The phrase is Walter Laqueur's: *The Last Days of Europe*, New York, 2007, p. 100; Caldwell avoids such flourishes, but the general sense is comparable.

material aim remains the same, a higher standard of living, and in the long run tends to erode the inherited faith. Consumption is a more powerful force than any confession, as Poland or Iran show. The outward signs of faith can be preserved, even paraded, as any number of ostensibly devout millionaires, of all creeds, testify; but, characteristically, the inner compulsions have gone.[28] In a post-modern society, even before their acquisition, the imagination of worldly goods has the same effect—consumerism without consumption. Where religion lives on, it is as a supplement, or sometimes reaction, to these temptations: not as the principle of an alternative social life. Islam is unlikely to be an exception, as any shopping mall in Cairo or Istanbul will intimate.

This large reservation aside, *Reflections on the Revolution in Europe* delivers one central truth. The emergence of significant immigrant communities arriving from allogenous worlds over which Europe once held sway, many raised in a faith long its principal adversary, was not willed or intended by any significant section of its population, which was never consulted. Even the employers who needed extra supplies of cheap labour typically regarded them as temporary expedients. But out of such passing calculations of advantage came lasting social changes. Whatever else mass immigration has been since the war, it was the antithesis of a project. Could it be viewed as the benign outgrowth of a spontaneous order, Hayek's catallaxy that debars any constructivist purpose? Not even that, for Hayek had drawn the line at free movement of labour across borders, as too threatening to necessary social cohesion. Viewed historically, post-war immigration was the counter-finality of the years that saw the building of the Union, a process not of integration, but of disintegration—that coming-apart of the social fabric whose effects the French sociologist of labour Robert Castel has called 'disaffiliation'.[29] Belatedly, and inadequately, official measures have sought to stitch some of the rents together again, and official ideology has tried to make of unwanted necessity a *post facto* virtue, presenting the goal of a fully multi-cultural—that is, multi-confessional—diversity as a redemptive objective of the EU to come.[30]

---

28. The classic statement of this case, yet to be either refuted or surpassed, is to be found Ernest Gellner's essay 'The Rubber Cage: Disenchantment with Disenchantment', in his *Culture, Identity, and Politics*, Cambridge 1987, pp. 152–65.

29. *Les métamorphoses de la question sociale*, Paris 1995, passim; for his motivation of the term, p. 15.

30. If the trope of diversity has supplied long-standing grounds for European

5

The Union in which this aim is proclaimed operates, its citizens are constantly instructed, by consensus. That is the 'community method', the code of supranational conduct in Europe. Such consensus is confined to those with power, as the modus operandi of a continuing elite consolidation. It has nothing to do with popular consent, which it functions to circumvent. Its elevation to a supreme value in the pantheon of the EU is, nevertheless, at striking variance with the way that successive historians, no less committed to oligarchic principles in their day, conceived the role of diversity in European development. For them, it was essentially conflictual. What had given, and gave, the continent its peculiar dynamism were its internal conflicts, unmatched by any other in their number and intensity. But if that were so, where now did such dynamism lie? Martin Malia, writing a decade later than Morin, saw the problem far more clearly. Contemporary integration, he argued, was altering the internal nature of Europe more profoundly than any development since Carolingian times. For that nature had been defined—much more than by any community of values, whether a universal Christianity, a universal reason or a universal democracy—by division and conflict, as the motors of a creative evolution. Kant had realized this disturbing paradox. For him, it was nature's law that human dispositions could be fully developed only 'by means of antagonism', or in the famous phrase, men's 'unsociable sociability'. But if Europe had now actually achieved a

---

self-congratulation, it is noticeable that less often celebrated has been what might be taken as its corollary—mixture. Ranke, as we have seen, expressly warned against it. Only the occasional *esprit fort* risked this more explosive terrain. Galiani stands out: 'Inconstancy is a physical law of all animal species. Without it, no fertility, no variety, no perfectibility. The immense variety of the nations which have peopled or intermingled in Europe, has made the perfection of our race. The Chinese have stupefied themselves only by their failure to mix with others; since the arrival of the Tartars, they have gained a lot. Here is another strange line of thought': *Correspondance inédite de l'Abbe Ferdinand Galiani*, Vol. II, Paris 1818 [1776–7], p. 272. Not that he was any triumphalist: 'Long live the Chinese! They are an ancient nation that regards us as children and scoundrels, while we think it a great thing to roam the seas and lands, bringing everywhere war, discord, our ingots, our guns, our bible and our small-pox.' Vol. I, p. 87. In later times, only Madariaga seems to have made a similar move from diversity to hybridity, remarking that perhaps the happy unity of Europe really rested on the crossing of its races, among which were to be numbered Mongols and Jews: *Bosquejo de Europa*, Mexico 1951, pp. 23–4.

permanent peace, under common laws for all, what could substitute
for such antagonisms? The ideal of European unity did not have a
mobilizing power comparable to either nationalism or socialism.
It was an affair of elites. Still, perhaps the task of creating the first
multi-national democracy in history would require a creativity no
less than that which once had brought the Europe of Christianity
or the Enlightenment into being?[31]

Prudently, Malia left unspecified the mechanisms that might
renew the creative evolution of Europe's previous history.
Nothing in his vision suggested that the new task could be
accomplished without dynamics comparable to the old—by
agreement without division, invention without antagonism. Had
he posed the question, what answers could he have ventured? For
a long line of classical thinkers, from Machiavelli to Ferguson to
Ranke, the form of conflict that most lent vigour to nations was
war.[32] After 1945, no European ever recommended it again. But
Guizot had already seen another kind of antagonism as no less
dynamic in its effects: conflict not between nations, but between
classes. Here too Machiavelli, praising strife between classes in
the Roman Republic as the secret of its greatness, had led the
way. What has been its fate in the Union? Class struggle was,
of course, the guiding principle of the revolutionary wing of
the labour movement throughout the first half of the twentieth
century. When, in the second half, the mass Communist parties
of Western Europe were first quarantined and then cancelled as
political forces, the reformist wing was left in command of the
field, in the various social-democratic parties that persist today.
Originally, they too had spoken of class, and in their own fashion
had fought, however moderately, for labour against capital.

But by the time that the regime change of the eighties set in,
both the size and cohesion of the industrial working class were

---

31. Martin Malia, 'Une nouvelle Europe?', *Commentaire*, Winter 1997/1998,
pp. 815–826.
32. For Machiavelli, the originator of the idea that conflict was a condition of
freedom and power, it was the struggles between patricians and plebs that gave
the Roman Republic both its liberty and its imperial dynamism—'Had Rome
sought to eliminate the causes of tumults, it would also have eliminated the causes
of expansion': *Opere III,* Turin 1997, (ed. Vivanti), pp. 208–17. For Ferguson,
the virtues of emulation were pre-eminently martial: 'Without the rivalship of
nations, and the practice of war, civil society itself could scarcely have found an
object, or a form': *An Essay on the History of Civil Society* (1767), Cambridge
1995 (ed. Oz-Salzberger), p. 28. For Ranke, see above, p. 494.

everywhere in decline, and the parties themselves had become electoral machines composed and controlled by upwardly mobile professionals, without roots or attachments in the world of manual labour. Intellectually, post-war social democracy was always relatively barren, borrowing what ideas it had from earlier liberal thinkers—Wicksell, Hobson, Keynes, Beveridge—but was still capable at least of a Crosland or a Meidner. But with the neo-liberal turn of the last decades of the century, full employment and welfare expansion were abandoned as practical objectives, as one social-democratic party after another adopted the reigning agendas of deregulation and privatization, compensated by a smattering of social side-payments. With this loss of their traditional raison d'être, they now face the risk of a widespread collapse of their voter support. In the European elections of mid-2009, the German brand of social-democracy got just 21 per cent of the vote, the French 16 per cent, the British 15 per cent, the Dutch 12 per cent; even in its classic Scandinavian strongholds, the Swedish version could manage no more than 24 per cent, the Danish 21 per cent. So weak has the identity of these parties become that they no longer even form a separate bloc in the European Parliament, having to dilute their grouping with 'Democrats'. So detached are they from popular opinion, that they have not been able to maintain even the degree of tactical distance from the synarchy in Brussels that parties of the Centre-Right, more aware of electoral hostility to it, have on occasion shown. The thought of any kind of conflict, let alone class struggle, is anathema to them.

The result has been to leave antagonism between immigrants and locals as the one residual principle of conflict, virtually ubiquitous in the western regions of the Union, that is impossible to ignore or repress. In effect, what has happened is that ethno-religious tensions have displaced class antagonisms. The displacement is both a substitution and a corruption of them. Workers, instead of uniting against employers or the state, turn against fellow workers; the poor revile the poor. Nor, objectively speaking, is this pure false consciousness, since in slow-growing economies, immigration can indeed, as Caldwell observes, and contrary to official rhetoric, depress the wages of the least skilled, and increase the cost of welfare rolls. The marked turn to the right of so much of the European working class over recent decades— its electoral shift towards Thatcher in England, to Le Pen and later Sarkozy in France, to the Lega Nord in Italy—has been an expression of a change in its relative position in society. It is no longer at the bottom of the social hierarchy, because immigrants occupy the rungs below it; yet at the same time it is weaker and more insecure than before, in societies where industry is no longer much honoured and inequality has been steadily rising.

Inequality within Europe; inequality between Europe and the worlds it once dominated. Immigration has deepened the first. But it is driven by the second. That inequality is far larger, and has drawn the millions from Africa, the Middle East, South Asia and Latin America who now live in the Union, in search of less hunger, danger and privation. Their arrival is an escape from these, but it is not a remedy for them. Were Europe genuinely concerned by the fate of the rest of the world, it would be spending its resources on disinterested aid to the regions where immigrants come from, not casually importing and then ejecting their labour for its own convenience. But that would indeed require a collective will capable of a true project, instead of the blind workings of the market.

Yet in a historical irony, out of these a slow change may be occurring in the contours of Europe. Pirenne argued that Europe was born as a distinct civilization when the Arab conquests split the Mediterranean, breaking the unity of the classical world into separate Christian and Muslim universes. His economic argument, based on the rupture of trade routes, has been questioned; at this level, Braudel would seek to rebind what he had undone. But few have doubted that the sweep of Islam, from Syria to Spain within a few decades, made what was no more than a geographical expression to the ancients into a cultural and political world separated from the southern shores of the inland sea. For Morin, Islam remained the external federator that not only had made Europe by enclosing Christianity within it, but against which Europe had made itself by repelling Muslim advances further north.[33] What the contemporary growth of Muslim communities within Western Europe, in contact with their homelands, suggests is the possibility of an erosion of this historic configuration. For the moment, only a distension of Europe to the Euphrates is envisaged, and the Arab world is something other, much larger and older, than the Turkish state. But Tangiers or Tunis are closer to Madrid or Paris than is Ankara, and the demographic pressures of what were once the African provinces of Rome are

---

33. *Penser l'Europe*, pp. 37ff.

greater. Europe might finally have achieved unity, only to find that its post-classical identity was beginning to dissolve, towards something closer to Antiquity.

6

Such speculations are for the long run, in which nothing can be counted out. The present landscape of the Union is another matter. Writing some four decades ago, Tom Nairn observed that ruling-class attitudes towards nationalism had varied historically: resolutely hostile in the time of the Holy Alliance, gingerly favourable in the period of Risorgimento, ruthlessly instrumental in the era of high imperialism. With the post-war epoch had come the quest for a post-national hegemony, amid a great latitude for elite manoeuvres, in the absence of any popular internationalism on the left. Should the Common Market, as it then was, be regarded as comparable—certainly not to imperialism—but to the Restoration, or to the Risorgimento? The Marxists of the time were giving it a cold shoulder. But why should it not be regarded as a development of bourgeois society like free trade, the agricultural or industrial revolution, or the nation-state, which with all their cruelties had been judged by Marx progressive, if contradictory, developments? European capitalism appeared to be evolving in a half-blind, unintentionally positive direction, but the left treated it as if 'time and contradiction had come to a stop'.[34]

The Union of today has come some way from the Common Market of the early seventies. The scene it offers is not one that inspires much warmth or confidence in its peoples. Politically, it has hardened into an oligarchic structure ever more indifferent to expressions of the popular will, even to legal appearances. The original Treaty of Rome signed by the foreign ministers of the Six consisted of blank sheets of paper, since the text had not been finalized for the solemn occasion. Diplomatic inexperience, in such a bold new enterprise? Nearly half a century later, the procedure was repeated: 'Although on 18 June 2004 the European Union's leaders had supposedly agreed their "Treaty Establishing a Constitution for Europe", not one of them could have read it, since there was still no comprehensive version of the text to which they had agreed. The complete text of the treaty,

---

34. Tom Nairn, *The Left Against Europe?*, London 1973, pp. 91–93, 145.

844 pages in typescript, would not be available until November, after they had signed it'.[35] Niceties? It hardly needs repeating that when the Constitution was rejected in the only two countries that held a referendum on it, both founder-members of the Six, it was relabelled the Lisbon Treaty, and when that was rejected in the only country to submit it to a popular judgement, its voters were told they must reverse the decision, and do so before there was any risk of voters in the larger neighbouring country, whose opposition to it was well known, being able to express their views on the matter.

The contempt for elementary principles of democracy shown by the elites of the Council and Commission and their subordinates, not to speak of an army of obedient publicists in the media, is reciprocated by the disdain of the masses for the Parliament that supposedly represents them, who ignore it in ever increasing numbers—electoral participation sinking to an all-time low of 43 per cent in 2009, down a full 20 points since the first such poll in 1979. Internationally, the same elites collude with negationism in Turkey, sanction ethnic cleansing in Cyprus, abet aggression by Israel, and subserve the occupation of Afghanistan. Socially, the EU now has a wider span of income inequality than the US, and harsher inter-ethnic relations. Economically, its performance since the crisis of the neo-liberal regime has so far been worse than that of America, and popular reactions to it more conservative.

Such, more or less, is the conjuncture in the summer of 2009. Like any other, it is subject to change, perhaps without notice. But the current drift of the Union will take more than an alteration of atmosphere to bend or reverse. European integration was conceived in the fifties on one set of premises. It has crystallized around another. Monnet, who set it in motion, imagined it as the positive creation of a supranational federation capable, not simply of freeing factors of production across unified markets, but of macro-economic intervention and social redistribution. He would not have been reassured by what has become of it. Hayek, who watched its inception with silent reserve, and never expressed much support for it—how could he be expected to abide a Common Agricultural Policy?—wanted integration as a negative prophylaxis, the demolition of barriers to free trade and estoppage of popular interference with the market. He would not

---

35. Christopher Booker and Richard North, *The Great Deception*, London 2005, p. 540.

have been satisfied by today's EU either. But of the two visions, it has evolved into a form much closer to his own.

The reasons for that evolution have lain in the general metamorphosis of capitalism as an international order since the eighties, and the extension of integration to the east twenty years later. Decisive in this process was the global deregulation of financial markets that has precipitated the present recession, even if its underlying causes go deeper, putting the neo-liberal system of the period for the first time under pressure. After the immediate shock to its prestige, however, the ideological struts of the system have so far proved resistant. In the west, public ownership as a value has remained taboo, even as public funds have been rushed on a massive scale to bail out predator banks and floundering industries. In the east, privatization continues to head the agenda. Blocking any reversion to more 'coordinated' versions of capitalism, closer in arrangements to the early years of the Community, are not only a formidable array of market and institutional interests, but the steady weakening of labour movements, and gutting of what was once their parliamentary expression in the assorted social-democracies of the continent. The latest decisions of the European Court, injected with the new rigorism of converts to liberal principles from the east, have struck down labour protections considered untouchable even in the nineties.[36]

Economically speaking, the Union remains, with its dense web of directives, and often dubious prebends, far from a perfect Hayekian order. But in its political distance from the populations over which it presides, it approaches the ideal he projected. What he did not anticipate, though it would perhaps not have surprised, and certainly not disconcerted him, is the disaffection that the regime he envisaged has aroused in the masses subject to its decisions. Yet if weaker spirits might worry about such alienation, he would have had some reason to remain unruffled. To the question whether a political order can be viable with so little popular participation, such low levels of active support, an answer could come from the United States. There, in 2008, the election of a black president was greeted as the dawn of a new epoch, galvanizing voters—above all young voters—to the polls, in a political awakening without precedent since the New Deal. In

---

36. For this development, see Alain Supiot, 'Les Europes possibles', *Esprit*, January 2009, pp. 173–4.

reality, no more than 56.8 per cent of the electorate bothered to show up for the historic decision, a mere 1.5 per cent above the turn-out that elected Bush in 2004, and well below the 60.8 per cent which put Nixon into power in 1968. Low-octane systems can run on very modest amounts of fuel.

Among the conditions of such regimes are an absence of much substantive divergence between political parties, and a widespread depoliticization of the population. Reversing historic relations, the first is now even more pronounced in the EU than in the US, where partisan antagonisms remain greater, even if rhetorical clashes typically exceed practical differences, whereas in Europe Centre-Right and Centre-Left have often become all but interchangeable, at times even indistinguishable. Such a reversal does not hold in quite the same way for the second. There, the traditional contrast between the two sides of the Atlantic has certainly dwindled. The abdication of what were once parties of the left before the advance of neo-liberalism, into whose carriers they quickly converted themselves, could hardly have failed of this effect. Once the space of political choice is narrowed so drastically, a certain decathexis of the public sphere is bound to ensue.

It is in this depoliticized setting that the issue of immigration has risen to a prominence out of all proportion with its objective place in society, becoming the *punctum dolens* of societies that rest on a social inequality and popular impotence which can never themselves be admitted to public consciousness. In the absence of any collective vision of the structures of power that hold all those without capital in their grip, let alone of how to replace them, beleaguered minorities on the margins of social existence become the focus of every kind of projection and resentment. Amid the fog-banks of a generalized insecurity, dim shapes, however wraith-like, easily acquire the lineaments of menace. Acting as incubators of xenophobia, the apparatuses of security can then provoke the kind of revolt that the intimidated majority has forgotten. Since the events of 1968, there has been no defiance of the established order to compare with them, save the riots in the *banlieues* of 2005.

Even so, the depoliticization of European publics, still relatively recent, has not become as deep as the aphasia of their counterparts in America, as a glance at the respective mediaspheres of the EU and US—television, radio, magazines, such newspapers as survive—makes clear. Below Union level, not only are the national frameworks of political life in Europe more compact and comprehensible; memories of class conflict and ideological turmoil remain less residual. Yet these have largely ceased to find expression in the party system. There the plight of the Socialist International in the leading states of the EU speaks for itself. The near-uniformity of moral and political decline in its member parties suggests the possibility that a mutation might be underway, that could leave virtually nothing of their inheritance. The pit of contempt into which New Labour has fallen, in the closing stages of the tawdriest regime in post-war British history, is an extreme case. But even without stains of office, sister parties in the core of the Union have sunk to levels of popular esteem never previously witnessed—French Socialists, German Social-Democrats and Italian Democrats struggling to retain so much as a quarter of the electorate.

Yet from the current emasculation of these parties it does not follow that all will consequently be quiet on the western front. In Britain or Spain, labour has not raised its head for nearly three decades. But in France, the strikes of 1995 brought down a government, and employers trying to close plants risk bossnapping even today. In Germany, the SPD has paid for its turn to the right with a scission in its industrial base and the emergence of a left entitled to the name. In Italy, as late as 2002 trade unions were able to mount the largest demonstration in the post-war history of the republic, in defense of pensions. In Greece, students can still hold the police at bay in pitched battles. However chloroformed legislatures or mediaspheres may be, turbulence has not yet been banished from the streets. The neo-liberal system generates reactions it cannot always control.

7

On the horizon, meanwhile, lies another kind of European order, at an angle to the semi-catallaxy within. The Union is preparing itself for the role of a deputy empire. The Treaty of Lisbon accords more substantial power to Germany within the EU, and greater formal rights to the Parliament in Strasbourg. But its principal function will be to furnish a preliminary framework for a global design, by the creation of a president of the European Council at the symbolic summit, and a vice-president of the Commission as effective foreign minister, of the Union as a whole. With these important figures in place, the EU will—so the theory goes—at last be able to punch its weight on the world stage.

Behind them, of course, the leading states of Europe will continue to manoeuvre in their own interest, and seek to fashion its policies according to their respective visions of the appropriate profile of the Union. In the past, divergences between them were often quite pronounced. But today, though points of friction between the foreign policies of the various governments persist, there is little disagreement on the overall stance that the EU should adopt in the world at large. The reason for the convergence is, of course, the new-found Atlanticism of France. There was no need to convert British, German, or Italian elites to the wisdom of hewing to the United States wherever possible. But French traditions were more refractory. In breaking with them, to position Paris firmly at the side of Washington, Sarkozy has retained of Gaullism only a formal ambition to lead the continent, voided of its content. The result, ironically, has been to enable something like the directorate of powers envisaged in the Fouchet Plan advanced by Paris in the sixties, rejected at the time by the other five member-states of the Community as potentially anti-American. The constellation today, opposite in sign, is more favourable. On all major international questions, and especially in the central theatre of the Middle East, the stars—principally London, Paris and Berlin—are now in pro-American alignment.

The outlines of a sub-imperial role to come are still emergent. But its ideologies and strategists are already in harness, and current priorities are clear. Military back-up for the United States in Afghanistan; economic sanctions and diplomatic menaces against Iran; privileged relations with Israel, and subsidies for a further Oslo; rapid deployment forces in the Horn, the Gulf and—if need be—the Balkans; more virtuous targets for reduction of carbon emissions, and regulation of financial flows, than America; comparable pressure for liberalization of services in the WTO. None of these elicits any discord, as the NATO alliance extends its 'defensive' reach to the ends of the earth.

Potentially more divisive are the geo-politics of the EU's own eastern front, with the categorical exclusion of Russia, and the prospective inclusion of Turkey, in the new Europe. Culturally and historically, this may make little sense, but politically it is perfectly consonant with the functions of a regional system within an overarching American imperium. Union dependence on Russian supplies of energy, and the need to nurture the country's recently acquired capitalism, however unpalatable the forms it may have taken, preclude more than guarded hostility to Moscow. But formally correct relations still allow for Russia to feature as a potential adversary against which Europe must fortify itself, a task anyway high on the list of concerns of its new member-states in the east. No conflict with the United States is likely here.

Turkey poses a more ticklish problem. Ever since the Clinton administration, its entry into the EU has been a top priority for Washington, as a means of anchoring a key American ally into the comity of Western nations, bolstering the military throw-weight of a loyal Europe—the Turkish army is near twice the size of that of any country now in the EU—and building a barrier against anti-imperialist dangers in the Arab world. Within the Union, the Commission in Brussels and establishment opinion in the media rallied with much further ado to Turkey's candidature, and soon every effort was being made to accelerate Ankara's passage into the EU. By 2003—the Bush administration in full cry, the Blair government in close support, Schröder and Chirac benevolent—success seemed virtually assured. But rapid closure came to grief on the rock of Cyprus, taken for granted too easily by the interested parties.

Since then, a gap has opened up between official professions and actual calculations, present and future intentions, in the capitals concerned. New Labour, of course, remains a steadfast messenger for Washington. But in France and Germany, Sarkozy and Merkel—unlike Chirac or Schröder—had to face voters for whom Turkish entry was no longer an invisible issue, and in proposing doses of neo-liberalism neither could be certain the electorate would take to, each preferred not to incur the risk of another potentially unpopular commitment. Of the two, Sarkozy went further than Merkel in appearing to set his face against Ankara. Once in office, each ruler has naturally tacked. Across Europe, elite opinion—in France and Germany no less than in other countries—remains as generally favourable to Turkish entry as popular opinion is doubtful or opposed. But in any case, the American will is not lightly crossed. In early 2009, the new US president made its priorities clear with a visit to Ankara soon after his inauguration, extolling the close ties of the two countries, and avoiding any inconvenient description of a remote past. Obama's campaign pledges swiftly buried, recognition of the Armenian genocide now has less congressional traction than under Bush.

On an issue as strategically critical as the inclusion of Turkey in the EU, Paris and Berlin, caught between masters and voters, can thus only temporize. Sarkozy, loudly repeating his opposition to Turkish entry with one side of his mouth, has made sure with the other that constitutional requirements for a referendum on it in France have been blocked, and negotiations on Turkey's accession continue as if he had never made any principled objection to it. Merkel, with a large Turkish community to consider, some of it entitled to vote, has been happy to take cover in a less exposed position behind him. These are tactics of circumstance, unlikely to affect the ultimate outcome, if only because neither ruler has an indefinite political life in front of them—Sarkozy will be gone within at most eight, and not inconceivably three years, while Merkel's hope of presiding over an unhampered Black–Yellow regime will be lucky to hold good for more than four. In the eyes of Brussels, and *a fortiori* of Washington, Turkey remains the 'glittering prize' of European expansion to come, and will not be casually relinquished. Around it, the discourse of diversity has for a good while been working overtime. What fairer trophy of multi-cultural tolerance could there be than the entry of this moderate Muslim land into the European Community? What newcomer could be better equipped, historically and actually, to share the responsibilities of a subaltern empire?

Between Russia and Turkey there remains, it is true, awkward from every respectable standpoint within the Community, the sprawling no man's land of the Ukraine. Hardly a model of constitutional stability, yet manifestly more democratic, by any standard, than Turkey; higher literacy and per capita income; less torture, no counter-insurgency, no ethnic cleansing, no genocide. Why should it be refused entry when its poorer and more repressive neighbour is ushered in? The answer is clear, but not easy to explain publicly, let alone square with the lofty professions of the Commission. The Ukrainian military is a shadow of the Turkish army; the stock market in Kiev is not a patch on that of Istanbul; the universe of Orthodoxy requires no coreligionary sepoys to check it. Last but not least, the regional hegemon is not America, in favour of a traditional client-state, but Russia, opposed to the alienation of a limb of its past. Empires can choose their terrain at will, when they are fully such. When they are no more than semi-sovereign, there are times when they must defer. So Brussels embraces Ankara and shrinks from Kiev. But Ukrainian pressure to enter the EU, which unites all parties in the country, will not go away. Somewhere in the future, a gap opening up in the eastern salient of the Union, a political Ardennes, may be in store for it.

Whether any of this will impinge on the internal politics of the Union, or unfold largely insulated from it, remains to be seen. Current European visions of a deputy empire are a replica writ large of what Britain has always represented: a special relationship with the United States, in which the junior partner plays an honourable role as help-meet and counsel, taking the initiative in its own sphere, and following its senior in theatres beyond it. In any such arrangement, the EU will certainly command more power, if without coming close to parity, than the UK ever did. In Britain, there was never any popular enthusiasm for the relationship, a matter settled between elites, but nor was there any significant dissent from it. Would a magnification of the same to a European scale be met with comparable passivity or indifference? Or, for all the current consensus among the interested capitals, might such ambitions, still in many ways embryonic, founder in advance on the centrifugal resistance of smaller member-states, unwilling to be brigaded for imperial ends by any renovated Directorate?

Neither the internal nor external direction of the Community is yet quite settled. Without clarity of means or ends, the Union seems to many adrift. Yet its apparent lack of any further coherent finality, deplored on all sides, might on one kind of reckoning be counted a saving grace, permitting the unintended consequences that have tracked integration from the start to yield further, possibly better, surprises. In principle, dynamic disequilibrium allows for that. In due course, a prolonged economic recession might reignite the engines of political conflict and ideological division that gave the continent its impetus in the past. So far, in today's Europe, there is little sign of either. But it remains unlikely that time and contradiction have come to a halt.

INDEX